The Frigid Golden Age

This book offers the first detailed analysis of how a society thrived amid the Little Ice Age, a period of climatic cooling that reached its chilliest point between the sixteenth and eighteenth centuries. The precocious economy, unusual environment, and dynamic intellectual culture of the Dutch Republic in its seventeenth-century Golden Age allowed it to prosper as neighbouring societies unravelled in the face of extremes in temperature and precipitation. By tracing the occasionally counterintuitive manifestations of climate change from global to local scales, Dagomar Degroot finds that the Little Ice Age presented not only challenges for Dutch citizens but also opportunities that they aggressively exploited in conducting commerce, waging war, and creating culture. The overall success of their republic in coping with climate change offers lessons that we would be wise to heed today, as we confront the growing crisis of global warming.

Dagomar Degroot is Assistant Professor of Environmental History at Georgetown University. He is the co-founder of the Climate History Network, an organization of more than 200 academics in the sciences and humanities.

Studies in Environment and History

Editors

Editors Emeritus

Other Books in the Series

Edmund Russell *Greyhound Nation: A Coevolutionary History of England, 1200–1900*
Timothy J. LeCain *The Matter of History: How Things Create the Past*
Ling Zhang *The River, the Plain, and the State: An Environmental Drama in Northern Song China, 1048–1128*
Abraham H. Gibson *Feral Animals in the American South: An Evolutionary History*
Peter Thorsheim *Waste into Weapons: Recycling in Britain during the Second World War*
Micah S. Muscolino *The Ecology of War in China: Henan Province, the Yellow River, and Beyond, 1938–1950*
David A. Bello *Across Forest, Steppe, and Mountain: Environment, Identity, and Empire in Qing China's Borderlands*
Kieko Matteson *Forests in Revolutionary France: Conservation, Community, and Conflict, 1669–1848*
George Colpitts *Pemmican Empire: Food, Trade, and the Last Bison Hunts in the North American Plains, 1780–1882*
John L. Brooke *Climate Change and the Course of Global History: A Rough Journey*
Emmanuel Kreike *Environmental Infrastructure in African History: Examining the Myth of Natural Resource Management*
Kenneth F. Kiple *The Caribbean Slave: A Biological History*
Alfred W. Crosby *Ecological Imperialism: The Biological Expansion of Europe, 900–1900, second edition*
Arthur F. McEvoy *The Fisherman's Problem: Ecology and Law in the California Fisheries, 1850–1980*
Robert Harms *Games against Nature: An Eco-Cultural History of the Nunu of Equatorial Africa*

Warren Dean *Brazil and the Struggle for Rubber: A Study in Environmental History*
Samuel P. Hays *Beauty, Health, and Permanence: Environmental Politics in the United States, 1955–1985*
Donald Worster *The Ends of the Earth: Perspectives on Modern Environmental History*
Michael Williams *Americans and Their Forests: A Historical Geography*
Timothy Silver *A New Face on the Countryside: Indians, Colonists, and Slaves in the South Atlantic Forests, 1500–1800*
Theodore Steinberg *Nature Incorporated: Industrialization and the Waters of New England*
J. R. McNeill *The Mountains of the Mediterranean World: An Environmental History*
Elinor G. K. Melville *A Plague of Sheep: Environmental Consequences of the Conquest of Mexico*
Richard H. Grove *Green Imperialism: Colonial Expansion, Tropical Island Edens and the Origins of Environmentalism, 1600–1860*
Mark Elvin and Tsui'jung Liu *Sediments of Time: Environment and Society in Chinese History*
Robert B. Marks *Tigers, Rice, Silk, and Silt: Environment and Economy in Late Imperial South China*
Thomas Dunlap *Nature and the English Diaspora*
Andrew Isenberg *The Destruction of the Bison: An Environmental History*
Edmund Russell *War and Nature: Fighting Humans and Insects with Chemicals from World War I to Silent Spring*
Judith Shapiro *Mao's War against Nature: Politics and the Environment in Revolutionary China*
Adam Rome *The Bulldozer in the Countryside: Suburban Sprawl and the Rise of American Environmentalism*
Nancy J. Jacobs *Environment, Power, and Injustice: A South African History*
Matthew D. Evenden *Fish versus Power: An Environmental History of the Fraser River*
Myrna I. Santiago *The Ecology of Oil: Environment, Labor, and the Mexican Revolution, 1900–1938*
Frank Uekoetter *The Green and the Brown: A History of Conservation in Nazi Germany*
James L. A. Webb, Jr. *Humanity's Burden: A Global History of Malaria*
Richard W. Judd *The Untilled Garden: Natural History and the Spirit of Conservation in America, 1740–1840*
Edmund Russell *Evolutionary History: Uniting History and Biology to Understand Life on Earth*
Alan Mikhail *Nature and Empire in Ottoman Egypt: An Environmental History*
Sam White *The Climate of Rebellion in the Early Modern Ottoman Empire*
Gregory T. Cushman *Guano and the Opening of the Pacific World: A Global Ecological History*
Donald Worster *Nature's Economy: A History of Ecological Ideas, second edition*

The Frigid Golden Age

Climate Change, the Little Ice Age, and the Dutch Republic, 1560–1720

DAGOMAR DEGROOT
Georgetown University

CAMBRIDGE
UNIVERSITY PRESS

University Printing House, Cambridge CB2 8BS, United Kingdom

One Liberty Plaza, 20th Floor, New York, NY 10006, USA

477 Williamstown Road, Port Melbourne, VIC 3207, Australia

314-321, 3rd Floor, Plot 3, Splendor Forum, Jasola District Centre, New Delhi - 110025, India

79 Anson Road, #06-04/06, Singapore 079906

Cambridge University Press is part of the University of Cambridge.

It furthers the University's mission by disseminating knowledge in the pursuit of education, learning and research at the highest international levels of excellence.

www.cambridge.org
Information on this title: www.cambridge.org/9781108410410
DOI: 10.1017/9781108297639

First published 2018
First paperback edition 2019

A catalogue record for this publication is available from the British Library

ISBN 978-1-108-41931-4 Hardback
ISBN 978-1-108-41041-0 Paperback

Dedicated to my beloved partner,
Madeleine Chartrand

Contents

Figures and Maps

FIGURES

MAPS

Acknowledgements

A long time ago, I was in a bus inching from Hamilton to Toronto at the height of rush hour in sprawling southern Ontario. As the bus crawled through traffic, I decided to pass the time by reading a then-pristine (now thoroughly tattered) copy of D. Brendan Nagle's *The Ancient World*. With the sun sinking behind the distant towers of Toronto, I came across Nagle's description of the first emergence of agriculture, then dated to around 10,000 years ago. Nagle rightly dismissed the idea that climate change was the only cause. Yet at that moment, with the sun's red light giving Toronto an apocalyptic hue, I started thinking about connecting past climate changes to human history in ways that could provide parables for our warmer future. In time, I learned to my surprise that Earth's climate suddenly cooled in the wake of the Middle Ages. I decided to draw on my Dutch heritage to explore how the precursor of the present-day Netherlands faltered in the face of this cooling.

I soon discovered that I had not exactly invented a new field. Scientists and historians, it turned out, had long implicated climate change in the downfall of ancient societies. Yet I also realized that my Dutch ancestors did not suffer so much as they thrived as Earth's climate cooled. Perhaps I could tell an original story, after all.

My journey from these exciting first speculations to the present book owes much to the brilliance, patience, and generosity of my PhD supervisor, Richard Hoffmann. I will always remember my first meeting with Richard, on a fittingly stormy day, when he painstakingly introduced me to the differences between weather, climate, and climate change. Little did I realize that these distinctions would be central to all my work on past climate change. Over the years, Richard helped me become a more exacting researcher, a more devoted teacher, and a more thoughtful person. I hope to follow his example as I prepare to supervise my own PhD students at Georgetown.

This book also reflects the tireless guidance and friendship of Petra van Dam, Colin Coates, Richard Unger, and John McNeill. Petra biked and paddled me through the landscape of the Low Countries, and steered me through the rich scholarship of the Dutch Golden Age. Colin offered unique insights and taught me to avoid what had been the bane of my writing: the dreaded passive voice. Richard asked the tough questions I needed to hear and helped me craft more tightly focused arguments. John is simply the most generous and inspiring colleague I could ask for. His suggestions have helped me craft a book that is much more accessible to a general audience than it otherwise might have been.

I am grateful for the generosity of many other colleagues across Canada, the United States, and Europe, including Milja van Tielhof, Marjolein 't Hart, Dennis Wheeler, Victor Enthoven, Emmanuel Kreike, Alan MacEachern, Karel Davids, Adriaan de Kraker, George Hambrecht, Stephen Mosley, Jürg Luterbacher, and the anonymous peer reviewers chosen by Cambridge University Press. I cherish the opportunities and good advice I received from Tom and Elizabeth Cohen, Rachel Koopmans, Ernst Hamm, and many other professors at York University, where I completed my doctorate. Amid the ups and downs of writing the dissertation, I received invaluable support from fellow graduate students Hannah Elias, Raphael Costa, Bradley Meredith, Ian Milligan, and Andrew Watson. At Georgetown, I am especially thankful for Amy Leonard, David Collins, Kathryn de Luna, Alison Games, Meredith McKittrick, Kathryn M. Olesko, John Tutino, Howard Spendelow, Gabor Agoston, Tommaso Astarita, Ananya Chakravarti, Marcia Chatelain, and Tim Newfield. All contributed to this book by giving good advice, inspiring hard work, and offering warm friendship. I am so grateful for the assistance of Suze Ziljstra, a former postdoctoral fellow (and current professor) who helped with some thorny palaeographical problems and directed me to some essential databases; Naresh Neupane, a postdoctoral fellow who improved my statistical work; and Emily Kaye, a particularly bright and hard-working undergraduate student (even by Georgetown standards!) who helped me quantify ship logbooks written during the Glorious Revolution of 1688. And of course, I am thankful for the recommendations and insights of archivists across the Netherlands and Britain.

My profound thanks to the many organizations and institutions that generously supported my research and conference activities, especially the Social Sciences and Humanities Research Council, the Ontario Student Assistance Program, the International Institute for the History and Heritage of Cultural Landscapes and Urban Environments, the Network in Canadian History and Environment, the National Science Foundation, and Georgetown University. I am grateful, too, for researchers who undertook abstract work that may not have had obvious, immediate relevance, and may not have received funding, but nevertheless made this book possible.

Of course, I owe everything to my family. My cat, Winnie, obligingly trampled my keyboard, scratched my documents, and gnawed on my books. My brother, Aldemar, and my sister, Godelinde, provided encouragement and successfully feigned interest in my scholarship. My mother-in-law, Judith Owens, helped me pitch this book to Cambridge and calmed my often-frazzled nerves. My mother, Jannie de Koning, single-handedly raised me into adulthood and gave me the confidence to believe that I could someday be a professor at a place like Georgetown. My late father, artist and author Bas Degroot, gave me the gift of insatiable curiosity about the world, its people, and its past. He taught me that good work should always serve a high purpose, and I hope this book does. My precious little daughter, Elowyn Degroot, continually motivates me to think about the future but also reminds me that there are far more important things in life than peer reviews and book drafts. Lastly, my partner and wife, Madeleine Chartrand, has been my dearest friend, closest confidante, and wisest colleague for nearly a decade. She has endured every research trip, reviewed every publication, and listened to just about every conference presentation. I dedicate this book to her with deep and everlasting gratitude.

Climate Terms

Arctic Oscillation a seesaw of atmospheric pressure between the Arctic and lower latitudes.

Atlantic Meridional Overturning Circulation (AMOC) a current that pushes warm, salty water into the Arctic and cold, less salty water down into lower latitudes.

Atlantic Multidecadal Oscillation (AMO) a 70-year oscillation between warm and cold phases in North Atlantic sea surface temperatures.

Beaufort Scale measures wind velocity on a scale from 1 to 12, where 1 is calm and 12 is a hurricane, cyclone, or typhoon.

Forcing a variable that influences Earth's climate.

Grand Solar Minimum a long period of low solar activity.

Grindelwald Fluctuation the second cold phase of the Little Ice Age, 1560 to 1628.

Intertropical Convergence Zone (ITCZ) the world-straddling belt near the equator where the southerly and northerly trade winds converge.

Little Ice Age a variable but overall cold climatic regime that affected much of the world and endured from the thirteenth to the nineteenth centuries.

Maunder Minimum the third cold phase of the Little Ice Age, 1645 to 1720.

North Atlantic Oscillation (NAO) another seesaw of atmospheric pressure consisting of a low-pressure zone near Iceland, and a high-pressure zone near the Azores.

Positive Feedback Loop a process in which a small stimulus magnifies a trend that in turn increases the stimulus.

Proxy something that responds to weather in a way that allows present-day scholars to use it in place of instrumental observations when reconstructing past climate change.

Siberian High a pressure cell over northern Asia that responds to the extent of winter snow and especially sea ice.

Trade Winds persistent winds that blow roughly from east to west towards the equator.

Weather Gage in the age of sale, the upwind position from a downwind opponent.

Note on Abbreviations, Dates, Names, and Translations

I have written Dutch names in Dutch, except where the people or institutions I describe are widely known outside the Netherlands by the English versions of their names. I have translated all Dutch quotations into twenty-first-century English, yet I have kept the spelling and grammar of early modern English quotations. Dates follow the modern Gregorian calendar, unless otherwise noted. Supplementary graphs and maps are available at: DagomarDegroot.com/Frigid.

Maps

MAP M1 The Dutch Republic (dark grey) in 1609, at the start of the Twelve Years' Truce.
All maps are by Hans van der Maarel, Red Geographics.

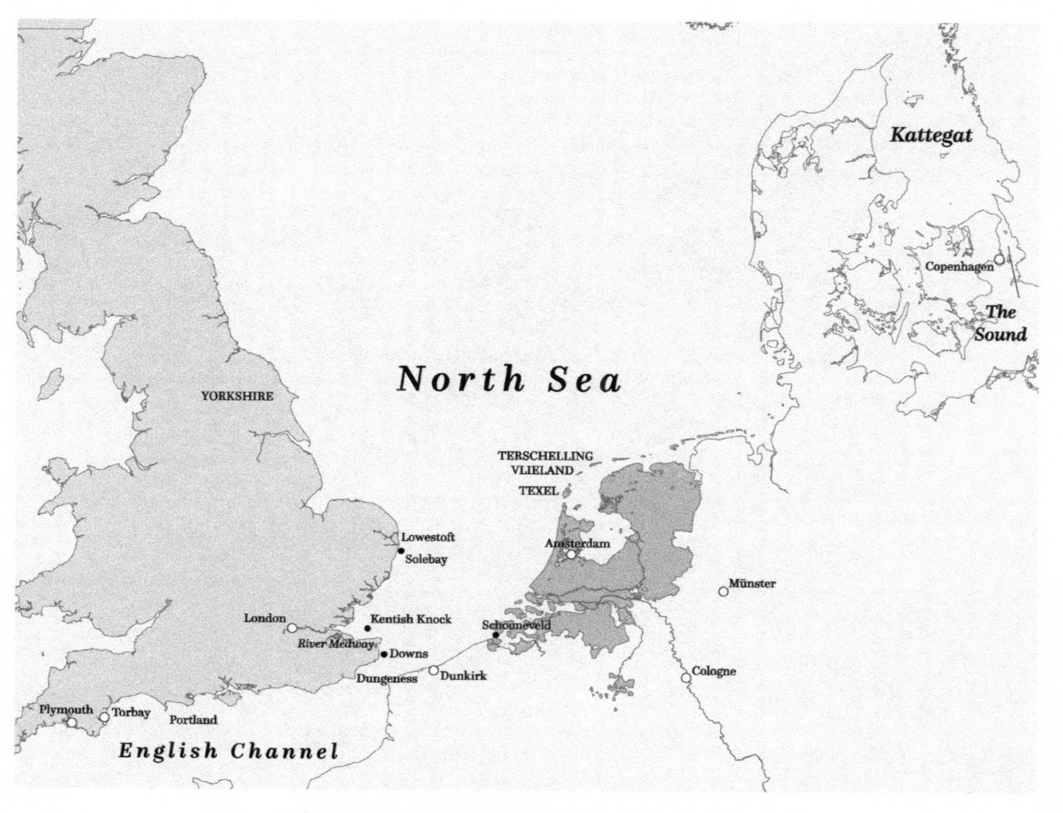

MAP M2 The North Sea region and the entrance to the Baltic Sea.

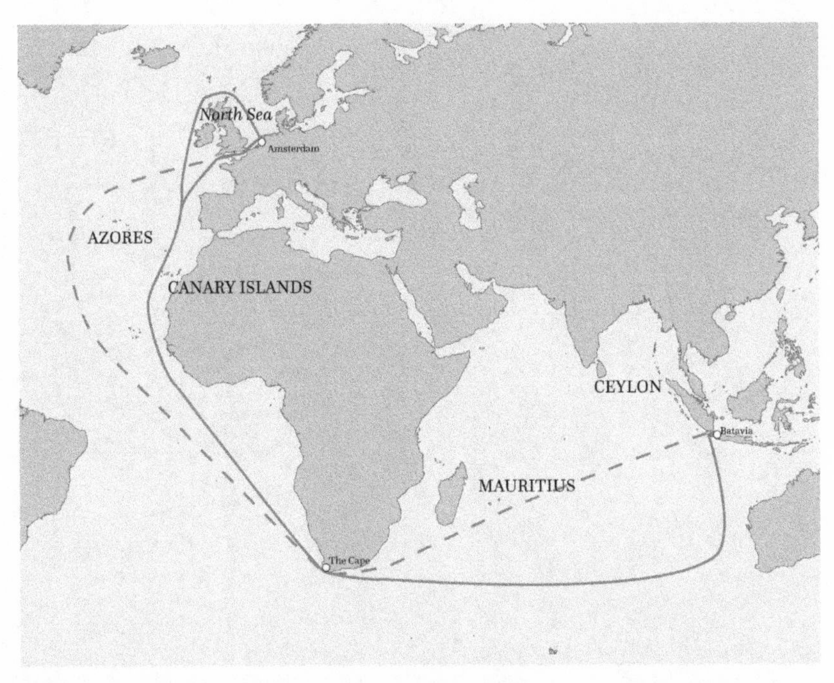

MAP M3 United East India Company routes to Asia, outbound from the Republic (solid lines, both the usual and back ways) and inbound from Asia (dashed line).

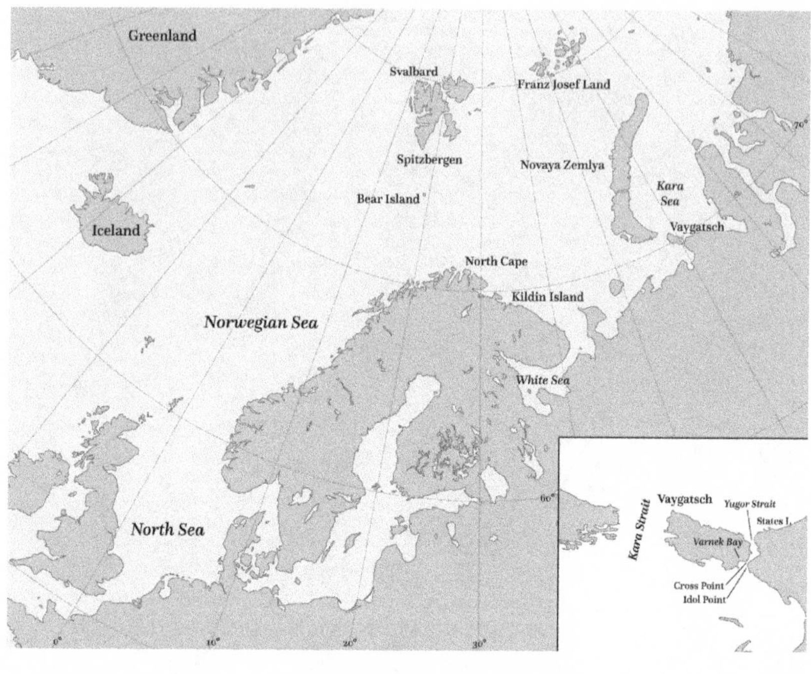

MAP M4 Top: the Arctic and Subarctic north of Europe. Inset: detail of the island Vaygatsch and the entrance to the Kara Sea. Bottom: major whaling factories on Svalbard.

INTRODUCTION

Crisis and Opportunity in a Changing Climate

The world is warming, and the pace of warming is starting to quicken. In just the time it took to research and write this book, Earth endured seven of the eight hottest years ever measured by meteorological instruments. Its average annual temperature is now roughly one degree Celsius hotter than it was midway through the twentieth century. By the end of the twenty-first century, warming may well exceed two degrees Celsius. Around the world, people are already experiencing gradual and global changes in Earth's climate through local weather events that pass quickly but have lasting consequences. Climate change is not only altering average weather but also the frequency and severity of weather extremes. Present-day warming has intensified storms, prolonged heat waves, and provoked precipitation anomalies in ways that have overwhelmed vulnerable human infrastructure and thereby exacted a fearsome toll on rich and poor societies alike. Ever more extreme weather in our warmer future could threaten the very survival of our civilization.[1]

[1] B. Kirman et al., '2013: Near-term Climate Change: Projections and Predictability'. In *Climate Change 2013: The Physical Science Basis. Contribution of Working Group I to the Fifth Assessment Report of the Intergovernmental Panel on Climate Change*, eds. T. F. Stocker et al. (Cambridge: Cambridge University Press, 2014), 981. Virginia Burkett et al., *Climate Change 2014: Impacts, Adaptation, and Vulnerability*. (IPCC WG II AR5, 2014), 13. IPCC, '2014: Summary for Policymakers'. In *Climate Change 2014: Impacts, Adaptation, and Vulnerability. Contribution of Working Group II to the Fifth Assessment Report of the Intergovernmental Panel on Climate Change*, eds. C. B. Field et al. (Cambridge: Cambridge University Press, 2014), 7. See also E. M. Fischer and R. Knutti, 'Anthropogenic Contribution to Global Occurrence of Heavy-Precipitation and High-Temperature Extremes'. *Nature Climate Change* (2015): http://dx.doi.org/10.1038/nclimate2617.

To properly appreciate and begin to address this defining crisis of our time, we must look to the past. We can gain a sense of the magnitude and causes of global warming by comparing it to the baseline of natural climatic variability, which we can only determine by reconstructing past climatic trends. We can better understand and confront the causes of warming by tracing the human histories that led us to capitalism, globalization, and industrialization. We can acquire insights into how our civilizations can adapt to human-caused warming by determining why many societies suffered, although a few thrived, when natural forces in our distant past changed Earth's climate in smaller but still significant ways.[2]

This book contributes to that third kind of 'climate history'. Midway through the thirteenth century, average annual temperatures in the Arctic and eventually around the world started falling. It was the beginning of the so-called Little Ice Age, the chilly climatic regime that is the focus of this book. Until the recent onset of global warming, the Little Ice Age may have been the most significant climatic anomaly to affect the Northern Hemisphere in at least 6,000 years.[3]

Many historians and scientists believe that the Little Ice Age endured for around six centuries, until roughly 1850. Different definitions arise, in part, from a particularly cold period between approximately 1560 and 1720 that was bookended by two frigid, decade-scale climatic regimes: the Grindelwald Fluctuation (1560–1628) and the Maunder Minimum (1645–1720). Atmospheric and oceanic circulation changed in both of these cold phases, causing patterns of precipitation and storminess to shift from region to region. Weather from season to season and year to year was also less predictable than it had been, but overall average global temperatures remained roughly one degree Celsius below the twentieth-century (c. 1900–1960) norm. In the so-called early modern centuries, from around 1450 to 1750, the lives and livelihoods of most people depended on local agriculture. Around the world, the weather of the

[2] Paul Edwards, *A Vast Machine: Computer Models, Climate Data, and the Politics of Global Warming*. (Cambridge: MIT Press, 2010), 4.

[3] For different perspectives on the term 'Little Ice Age', see Michael E. Mann, 'The Little Ice Age'. In *Encyclopedia of Global Environmental Change*, eds. Michael C. MacCracken and John S. Perry. (Chichester: John Wiley & Sons, Ltd., 2002), 504–509. John A. Matthews and Keith R. Briffa, 'The "Little Ice Age": Re-evaluation of an Evolving Concept'. *Geografiska Annaler: Series A, Physical Geography*, 87:1 (2005): 17–36. Sam White, 'The Real Little Ice Age'. *The Journal of Interdisciplinary History* 44:3 (Winter, 2014): 327–352.

Little Ice Age played a role in triggering harvest failures, commodity price shocks, famine, social unrest, and ultimately death on a vast scale.[4]

Yet a few societies prospered, and none more than the Dutch Republic, the precursor of the present-day Netherlands. Between 1590 and 1715, its coastal regions underwent an extraordinary golden age that precisely coincided with the coldest stretch of the Little Ice Age. For centuries, these regions – collectively known as the 'Low Countries' – had differed in important ways from the rest of Europe. Salt marshes and peat bogs made them mostly uninhabitable until medieval settlers in huge numbers dug up peat, drained bogs, and reared cattle that trampled what was left. The land sank in response, until it dropped below the level of the sea, and the settlers in turn built a huge web of river embankments, dikes, and drainage channels to hold back the water. They created a strange network of walled-off farmland and waterways that had few parallels anywhere else in the world.[5]

This engineered landscape was perpetually menaced by the 'water wolf': the sea that always threatened to spill over Dutch coastal defences. Yet water also helped provide the motivation and means for fantastic profits. In the fourteenth century, floods destroyed farmland across the Low Countries and prompted merchants to import from the nearby Baltic Sea. Port towns accommodated this new trade and fostered the

[4] John Brooke, *Climate Change and the Course of Global History: A Rough Journey*. (Cambridge: Cambridge University Press, 2014), 383. Shaun A. Marcott et al., 'A Reconstruction of Regional and Global Temperature for the Past 11,300 Years', *Science*, CCCIX (2013), 1198. Geoffrey Parker and Lesley M. Smith, eds., *The General Crisis of the Seventeenth Century*. (Oxford: Routledge, 2005), 7. M. J. Ingram, G. Farmer and T. M. L. Wigley, 'Past Climates and Their Impact on Man: A Review'. In *Climate and History: Studies on Past Climates and Their Impact on Man*, eds. M. J. Ingram, G. Farmer and T. M. L. Wigley. (Cambridge: Cambridge University Press, 1981), 17. Hubert Lamb, *Climate, History and the Modern World*, 260. Jean M. Grove, 'The Century Time-Scale'. In *Time-Scales and Environmental Change*, eds. Thackwray S. Driver and Graham P. Chapman. (Oxford: Routledge, 1996), 40. Geoffrey Parker, *Global Crisis: War, Climate Change and Catastrophe in the Seventeenth Century*. (London: Yale University Press, 2013), 26. Ljungqvist, 'A New Reconstruction of Temperature Variability in the Extra-Tropical Northern Hemisphere during the Last Two Millennia', 445.

[5] Piet H. Nienhuis, *Environmental History of the Rhine-Meuse Delta: An Ecological Story on Evolving Human-Environmental Relations Coping with Climate Change and Sea Level Rise*. (New York: Springer, 2008), 54, 87. M. van Tielhof and P. J. E. M. van Dam, *Waterstaat in Stedenland: het Hoogheemraadschap van Rijnland voor 1857*. Utrecht: Matrijs, 2006. William TeBrake, *Medieval Frontier: Culture and Ecology in Rijnland*. (College Station: Texas A&M University Press, 1985). Audrey M. Lambert, *The Making of the Dutch Landscape: An Historical Geography of the Netherlands*. (London: Academic Press, 1985), 203.

skills and infrastructure that permitted the rise of new industries on land and at sea. When the Spanish Habsburg Empire absorbed the Low Countries late in the fifteenth century, the region's cities had become hubs in a continent-straddling commercial network. Yet they were also divided by a bewildering patchwork of local laws and customs, and frayed by the spread of Protestantism. Spanish attempts to centralize the region under Catholic rule ignited a revolt that eventually united the northern provinces of the Low Countries within a radical new kind of political structure: a loose confederation largely governed by councils of urban merchants.[6]

This 'Dutch Republic' gave rise to a remarkably dynamic economy that thrived while its competitors faltered amid the chilliest decades of the Little Ice Age. Dutch entrepreneurs invented or implemented technologies that sharply increased the efficiency of, for example, shipping, shipbuilding, firefighting, and land reclamation. Merchants, many of them immigrants from the war-torn southern Low Countries, cultivated new industries and circumvented Spanish embargoes by establishing the Dutch East and West India Companies. The East India Company quickly came to dominate the lucrative trade that sent precious metals to Asia in exchange for spices and textiles. Burgeoning Amsterdam became the financial and commercial capital of Europe; a major hotbed for mapmaking and publishing; and the first truly global nexus for importing, trading, and exporting goods. For decades, the republic's level of urbanization, rates of literacy, robust fiscal system, stable and effective governments, diverse commercial economy, and efficient sources of energy set it apart within contemporary Europe. Its economic booms and busts, frequently triggered by financial speculation and accompanied by environmental degradation, resembled those of present-day capitalism. The precocious dynamism of the Dutch economy made the republic a great power with global reach, but it was not to last. By the middle of the seventeenth century, Dutch commercial success provoked protectionist legislation, costly wars, and – worst of all – emulation in France and especially England. Meanwhile, falling commodity prices, increasing labour costs, and a series of natural disasters undermined the republic's agricultural productivity.

[6] Louis Sicking, *Neptune and the Netherlands: State, Economy, and War at Sea in the Renaissance*. (Leiden: Brill, 2004), 209. Jonathan Israel, *The Dutch Republic: Its Rise, Greatness, and Fall, 1477–1806*. (Oxford: Clarendon Press, 1998), 209. Maarten Prak, *The Dutch Republic in the Seventeenth Century*. (Cambridge: Cambridge University Press, 2005), 8. Alastair Duke, *Reformation and Revolt in the Low Countries*. (London: Hambledon Press, 1990), 11.

In the face of these challenges, the republic's economy changed and ultimately declined in the eighteenth century, just as Earth's climate started warming.[7]

There was something about the Dutch Republic that let its citizens thrive during the coldest decades of the Little Ice Age. This book demonstrates, first, that weather was a dynamic natural agent that shaped the history of the Dutch Golden Age. It shows, second, that weather trends in the chilliest phases of the Little Ice Age had mixed but overall beneficial consequences for distinctively Dutch ways of conducting commerce and waging war, which the culture of the republic registered and reinforced. Climate changes that led to particularly cold stretches of the Little Ice Age certainly presented challenges for Dutch citizens, but they also offered opportunities that merchants, sailors, soldiers, and inventors aggressively exploited.

Most histories of the Little Ice Age focus on agriculture. Yet domestic agricultural production was less important for the prosperity and security of the Dutch Republic than it was for most other states. This book therefore explores diverse and, until now, largely unstudied links between climate change and early modern history. It shows that complex relationships

[7] Violet Barbour, *Capitalism in Amsterdam in the 17th Century*. (Ann Arbor: University of Michigan Press, 1963), 12. Bas van Bavel, 'Manors and Markets. Economy and Society in the Low Countries (500–1600): A Synopsis'. *Tijdschrift voor Sociale en Economische Geschiedenis* 8:2 (2011): 63. J. L. Price, *Dutch Society, 1588–1713*. (New York: Longman, 2000), 70. Jan de Vries and Ad van der Woude, *The First Modern Economy: Success, Failure, and Perseverance of the Dutch Economy, 1500–1815*. (Cambridge: Cambridge University Press, 1997), 357. C. A. Davids, 'De technische ontwikkeling in Nederland in de vroeg-moderne tijd. Literatuur, problemen en hypothesen'. *Jaarboek voor de Geschiedenis van Bedrijf en Techniek* 8 (1991): 9. Oscar Gelderblom, *Zuid-Nederlandse kooplieden en de opkomst van de Amsterdamse stapelmarkt (1578–1630)*. (Hilversum: Uitgeverij Verloren, 2000), 114. Victor Enthoven, 'Early Dutch Expansion in the Atlantic Region, 1585–1621'. In *Riches from Atlantic Commerce: Dutch Transatlantic Trade and Shipping, 1585–1817*, eds. Johannes Postma and Victor Enthoven. (Leiden: Brill, 2003), 23. Gerrit Knaap and Ger Teitle, eds., *De Verenigde Oost-Indische Compagnie: Tussen Oorlog en Diplomatie*. (Leiden: KITLV Uitgeverij, 2002), 4. Jonathan Irvine Israel, *Dutch Primacy in World Trade, 1585–1740*. (New York: Oxford University Press, 198), 213. Clé Lesger, *Handel in Amsterdam ten tijde van de Opstand: kooplieden, commerciële expansie en verandering in de ruimtelijke economie van de Nederlanden ca. 1550 – ca. 1630*. (Hilversum: Uitgeverij Verloren, 2001). P. C. Emmer, *The Dutch in the Atlantic Economy, 1580–1880*. (Aldershot: Ashgate, 1998), 14. Jan Luiten van Zanden, 'Economische Groei in Holland tussen 1500 en 1800'. *NEHA-Bulletin* 16:2 (2001): 65. J. L. van Zanden, *Arbeid tijdens het handelskapitalisme: Opkomst en neergang van de Hollandse economie 1350–1850*. (Hilversum: Uitgeverij Verloren, 1991), 11. E. M. Jacobs, *In Pursuit of Pepper and Tea: The Story of the Dutch East India Company*. (Walburg: Walburg Pers, 2009), 11.

between global climatic trends and local environments influenced the transportation networks that sustained the Dutch trading empire. Weather that became common in cooler climates encouraged new discoveries and industries in distant seas, quickened the journeys of departing East India Company ships, hampered some elements of Baltic commerce while possibly enriching others, and altered how travellers moved within the republic.

The book also demonstrates that climate change affected how the Dutch defended their republic and expanded its commercial empire. From 1568 to 1688, Dutch military operations generally benefitted from cold, wet, and stormy weather that became more common in especially chilly phases of the Little Ice Age. However, in the 1630s and 1650s, weather typical of an interruption in the Little Ice Age aided Dutch offensives in the Spanish Netherlands and then thwarted the republic's naval operations during the First Anglo-Dutch War.

Finally, the book reveals that climate change influenced the dynamic culture of the Dutch Golden Age. By tracing weather patterns through time, some Dutch citizens developed a vague awareness of what we would call climate change. Dutch artistic responses to weather expressed the conviction that even the extremes of a frigid climate could be endured and, occasionally, exploited. Little Ice Age weather encouraged social spaces and technologies that contributed to the resilience of the republic in the face of climate change.

That concept – 'resilience' – is notoriously difficult to define. Other scholars have used it to refer to an adaptive social capacity that mitigates loss amid changing environmental conditions. According to that definition, 'vulnerability' means the potential for loss. In this book, 'resilience' also encompasses the largely unavoidable natural circumstances that can make shifting environmental conditions more or less damaging in a particular place, for a particular society. Resilience, therefore, is not just about what humans decide to do, but also about the choices environmental circumstances allow them to make. A society that is vulnerable to climate change could simply be in the wrong place, at the wrong time.[8]

[8] Grove, 'The Century Time-Scale'. 80. Georgina H. Endfield, 'Exploring Particularity: Vulnerability, Resilience, and Memory in Climate Change Discourses'. *Environmental History* 19 (2014): 305. Christian Pfister, 'Climatic Extremes, Recurrent Crises and Witch Hunts: Strategies of European Societies in Coping with Exogenous Shocks in the Late Sixteenth and Early Seventeenth Centuries', *The Medieval History Journal* 10:1&2 (2007): 44. Field et al., 'Climate Change 2014: Impacts, Adaptation, and Vulnerability, Summary for Policymakers', 5.

We can therefore imagine resilience to climate change as a negotiation between environmental fluctuations, on the one hand, and the characteristics of a society, on the other. If a climatic shift is too extreme, no society can endure. If a society depends on a particularly delicate environmental equilibrium, even a hint of climatic variability can be dangerous. Societies can be vulnerable for very different reasons. Today, developed states strain or exceed the capacity of environments that climate change will make less hospitable. In the early modern world, by contrast, many societies depended on the meagre yields and slight surpluses of agricultural systems that could rarely cope effectively with shifting climatic conditions. As we will see, the Dutch Republic was not one of those civilizations.

A NEW APPROACH TO THE HISTORY OF CLIMATE CHANGE

Scientists have long understood that Earth's climate has never been entirely stable, yet most historians have only recently accepted that climate changes influenced human history. The Little Ice Age in particular belatedly entered the mainstream of the historical profession owing to the pioneering work of scholars such Emmanuel Le Roy Ladurie, Hubert Lamb, and Christian Pfister, who first developed rigorous methods for reconstructing past climate changes and tying them to human histories.[9] In recent years, scholars have drawn on these methods and used a broadening range of textual and scientific sources to write increasingly sophisticated histories of the Little Ice Age. Still, nearly all conclude that cooling made life more difficult for just about everyone in the early modern world. They focus on examples of decline and disaster: admittedly the most common fate of premodern societies confronted with sudden or severe shifts in the environments they exploited. Yet most ignore societies that prospered in cold periods of the Little Ice Age, which means that they

[9] Rudolf Brázdil et al., 'Historical Climatology in Europe – the State of the Art'. *Climatic Change* 70:3 (2005): 366. Hubert Lamb, *The English Climate*. (London: English Universities Press, 1964), 12. Emmanuel Le Roy Ladurie, *Times of Feast, Times of Famine*, 10. Gustaf Utterström, 'Climatic Fluctuations and Population Problems in Early Modern History', *Scandinavian Economic History Review* 3:1 (1955): 3. Behringer, *A Cultural History of Climate*, 86. Emmanuel Le Roy Ladurie, *Times of Feast, Times of Famine: A History of Climate since the Year 1000*. (Garden City, NY: Doubleday & Company, Inc., 1971), 293. Lamb, *Climate, History and the Modern World*, 232. Christian Pfister, 'The Little Ice Age: Thermal and Wetness Indices for Central Europe', *The Journal of Interdisciplinary History* 10:4 (1980): 665. Christian Pfister, 'The Climate of Switzerland in the Last 450 Years'. *Geographica Helvetica* 35 (1980): 15.

rarely consider how individuals and communities could endure, adapt to, and exploit changes in the natural world.[10]

I therefore began my research for this book by searching for weather references, not disaster stories, in early modern Dutch documents. Occasionally, I specifically sought texts written during weather extremes, but even then I did not concentrate solely on the kinds of weather that other historians have associated with societal crises. By approaching my sources with an open mind, I found that relationships between climate change and human activity were, and perhaps remain, more complex and counterintuitive than narratives that stress decline, or 'declension' typically allow. There were winners and losers in the early modern struggle with climate change, just as there are today and will be in the future.

To trace the human consequences of climate change, in this book I carefully measure percentages and gauge probabilities. One of the book's most important principles is that seemingly slight changes in environmental conditions or human arrangements can have disproportionate consequences for people and their societies. The reason lies in the relationship between long-term trends and short-term events. A trend need only trigger one event for it to have major historical significance. More importantly, superficially slight trends are often expressed in short-term extremes. For instance, although Earth's average temperature has, as of 2017, risen by just over one degree Celsius since the conclusion of the Little Ice Age, severe heat waves are now four times more common around the world than they were in 1850. To take another example, a 30 per cent

[10] Fred Pearce, *Climate and Man: From the Ice Ages to the Global Greenhouse*. (London: Vision Books, 1989), 31. Neville Brown, *History and Climate Change: A Eurocentric Perspective*. (London: Routledge, 2001), 262. Bauernfeind and Woitek, 'The Influence of Climatic Change on Price Fluctuations in Germany during the 16th Century Price Revolution', *Climatic Change* 43:1 (1999): 307. Pfister, 'Climatic Extremes, Recurrent Crises and Witch Hunts', 39. Leo Noordegraaf, 'Dearth, Famine and Social Policy in the Dutch Republic at the End of the Sixteenth Century'. In *The European Crisis of the 1590s: Essays in Comparative History*, ed. Peter Clark. (London: George Allen & Unwin, 1985), 67. Joëlle Gergis, Don Garden, and Claire Fenby, 'The Influence of Climate on the First European Settlement of Australia: A Comparison of Weather Journals, Documentary Data and Palaeoclimate Records, 1788–1793'. *Environmental History* 15(3) (2010): 485. Wolfgang Behringer, *A Cultural History of Climate*. (Cambridge: Polity Press, 2010), 141. Adam R. Hodge, '"In Want of Nourishment for to Keep Them Alive": Climatic Fluctuations, Bison Scarcity, and the Smallpox Epidemic of 1780–82 on the Northern Great Plains'. *Environmental History* 17(2) (2012): 400. See also Sam White, Richard Tucker, and Ken Sylvester, 'Climate and American History: The State of the Field'. In *Cultural Dynamics of Climate Change and the Environment in Northern America*, ed. Bernd Sommer. (Leiden: Brill, 2015). Sam White, *The Climate of Rebellion in the Early Modern Ottoman Empire*, 12–14.

decline in the grain harvest could double the price of bread in many parts of early modern Europe, yet a 50 per cent reduction quintupled it. All of this should give us pause as we contemplate our warmer future.[11]

To write a book about such a vast topic, I had to draw some sharp and at times painful limits. The Little Ice Age undoubtedly affected land reclamation, agricultural production, pastoralism, and industry within the Dutch Republic. It influenced Dutch fisheries within the waters of the republic, the North Sea, and beyond. It helped cause catastrophic storm and river flooding, and it altered the efficiency of the West India Company, the Levantine trade, the Archangel trade, and other profitable but often brutal expressions of Dutch commercial might that are not covered in this book. Some scholars have either examined or started to examine how climate change influenced these and other aspects of the Dutch Golden Age. All the same, I was tempted to write a book that briefly touched on all these topics, one that was, in other words, a mile wide but an inch thick. Such a book, however, would have reflected a problematic trend in histories of climate change.

These histories can be wonderfully broad, covering a dizzying array of possible interactions between climate change and human affairs. But many also skip lightly over the ways in which global environmental change really affected people on the level of the transient local activities that ultimately shape human history. By ignoring how the influence of climate change cascades across different scales of space, place, and time, such books can also rest on one-dimensional understandings of causation. Ultimately, big histories like this one can either attempt to cover every aspect of a historical relationship, or give examples that reflect a broader pattern. I opt for the latter approach by exploring some of the best-sourced interactions between climate change and the history of the Dutch Golden Age. That has led me to examine weather patterns and social arrangements rarely examined by other historians, and it has, I hope, provided a novel perspective on humanity's long experience with climate change.

PREVIOUS SCHOLARSHIP AND FRESH SOURCES

The coastal regions of the Low Countries have long been especially susceptible to climate changes. They lie so far beneath sea level that even

[11] Parker, *Global Crisis*, 20. Fischer and Knutti, 'Anthropogenic Contribution to Global Occurrence of Heavy-Precipitation and High-Temperature Extremes', 1.

minor fluctuations in average temperature, precipitation, and storminess have made them vulnerable to flooding. Their average winter temperatures have usually lingered near freezing, so modest cooling or warming has dramatically altered the duration and extent of the ice that can form on their many waterways. They are relatively close to major extremes in atmospheric pressure, so they can endure profound changes in prevailing wind directions. Scholars have long studied how farmers and engineers have shaped the unusual environments of the Low Countries. Yet strangely, very few have investigated how the Little Ice Age changed those environments during the best-known period in the history of the Low Countries: the Golden Age of the Dutch Republic.

The reasons may lie in the dominant themes that run through historiographies of both Dutch environmental history and climate change. Historians of the Low Countries usually focus not on how environmental changes have influenced human actions, but rather on how human actions have led to environmental changes. They may mention weather, especially when describing life at sea, but they rarely describe how weather patterns changed over time in ways that mattered for people.[12] Meanwhile, historians of the Little Ice Age are often especially interested in the destructive consequences, for human beings, of climatic cooling or variability. From that perspective, the relative success of the Dutch Republic during decades of cooling and crisis might suggest that it was scarcely affected by climate changes. The prosperous Dutch appear only briefly in histories of the Little Ice Age, when they are mentioned at all.[13]

[12] For descriptions of how storms affected Dutch voyages to and within Asia, for example, see Jaap R. Bruijn, 'Between Batavia and the Cape: Shipping Patterns of the Dutch East India Company'. *Journal of Southeast Asian Studies*, 11:2 (1980): 260. Femme S. Gaastra, *The Dutch East India Company: Expansion and Decline*. (Zutphen: Uitgeversmaatschappij Walburg Pers, 2003), 114. Robert Parthesius, *Dutch Ships in Tropical Waters: The Development of the Dutch East India Company (VOC) Shipping Network in Asia 1595–1660*. (Amsterdam: Amsterdam University Press, 2010), 52. Maarten Hell and Wilma Gijsbers, 'Geborgen of gezonken, gered of verdronken: Papieren getuigen van scheepsrampen rond Texel (1575–1795)'. *Tijdschrift voor Zeegeschiedenis* 31:2 (2012): 45. This book draws from two erudite collections of weather-related primary sources and histories: J. Buisman and A. F. V. van Engelen (ed.), *Duizend jaar weer, wind en water in de Lage Landen, Vol. IV 1575–1675*. (Franeker: Uitgeverij Van Wijnen, 2000). J. Buisman and A. F. V. van Engelen (ed.), *Duizend jaar weer, wind en water in de Lage Landen, Vol. V 1675–1750*. (Franeker: Uitgeverij Van Wijnen, 2006).

[13] Behringer, *A Cultural History of Climate*, 111. Lamb, *Climate, History, and the Modern World*. 2nd ed., 228. Brian M. Fagan, *The Little Ice Age: How Climate Made History, 1300–1850*. (Boulder: Basic Books, 2000), 113. Brooke, *Climate Change and the Course of Global History: A Rough Journey*, 422.

The few scholars who have examined the experiences of the Dutch during the Little Ice Age have tackled one of three big topics. The first involves the long, characteristically Dutch struggle against the sea. For decades, scientists have debated the extent to which medieval warming and early modern cooling influenced the historical geography of the Low Countries. They have recently reached a rough consensus. Climate changes, it seems, played a decidedly secondary role in the hydraulic history of the Dutch Republic, one that was always mediated by human activities. Scholars in many disciplines are still struggling to sketch the precise character of these relationships, and this book draws on their efforts.[14]

The second big topic focuses not on the material consequences of water, but rather on the famous art of the Golden Age. For decades, interdisciplinary scholars have argued that winter scenes painted by Dutch artists in the sixteenth, seventeenth, and eighteenth centuries depicted real landscapes in a frigid climate. Very recently, scholars such as Ingrid Sager and Alexis Metzger have reinterpreted such paintings in light of the most recent scholarship on the Little Ice Age. This book draws on their findings, but takes a more sceptical approach to the relationship between cooling and art.[15]

The third and final topic – the one that most concerns this book – deals with whether the Little Ice Age helped or hindered the Dutch during their Golden Age. One group of scholars has tried to incorporate Dutch history within bigger narratives of disaster during the Little Ice Age. In 1985, Leo Noordegraaf wrote a short but groundbreaking article that connected cool, wet conditions in the Low Countries during the late sixteenth century to harvest failures, high food prices, decreases in the purchasing power of wages, and ultimately crisis. More recently, Adam Sundberg has examined the consequences of environmental disasters in the Low Countries that overlapped with climate changes in the early eighteenth century. Most famously, Geoffrey Parker wrote a landmark book that

[14] Nienhuis, *Environmental History of the Rhine-Meuse Delta*, 240. Gottschalk, *Stormvloeden en rivieroverstromingen in Nederland, Vol. II*, 817. Gottschalk, *Stormvloeden en rivieroverstromingen in Nederland, Vol. III*, 414.

[15] Alexis Metzger, 'Le froid en Hollande au Siècle d'or. Essai de climatologie culturelle'. (PhD diss., University of Paris, 2016). Ingrid D. Sager, *The Little Ice Age and 17th Century Dutch Landscape Painting, a Study on the Impact of Climate on Art*. (Dominguez Hills: California State University, 2006). Alexis Metzger, *Plaisirs de Glace: Essai sur la peinture hollandaise hivernale du Siècle d'or*. (Paris: Editions Hermann, 2012). Peter Robinson, 'Ice and Snow in Paintings of Little Ice Age Winters'. *Weather* 60:2 (2005): 37.

blames seventeenth-century cooling for catastrophes around the world, including three Dutch coups d'état. As this book shows, the weather that accompanied the chilliest phase of the Little Ice Age certainly did end lives and ruin livelihoods across the Dutch Republic. Yet, climate change also offered important commercial, military, and even cultural benefits for Dutch citizens.[16]

A second group of scholars has therefore viewed the Dutch Republic as a rare success story in the calamitous seventeenth century. In 1978 and 1980, Jan de Vries argued that the chilly and erratic climate of the Little Ice Age did not spell disaster for important elements of the Dutch economy. Years later, Louwrens Hacquebord found correlations between climatic cooling, bowhead whale behaviour, and years of plenty for the Dutch Arctic whaling industry. In 1996, J. R. Jones consulted scientific literature to conclude that easterly winds – that is, winds that blow from the east – and storms during the Little Ice Age aided Dutch attempts to leave port, and hindered English blockades, during the Anglo-Dutch Wars. In the following year, De Vries and Ad van der Woude briefly speculated that 'longer-term manifestations of the [Little Ice Age] offered, on balance, more benefits to the Dutch than they imposed costs'. This book sides with that view, focusing not only on long-term correlations but also short-term relations between climate change, weather, and human affairs.[17]

[16] Noordegraaf, 'Dearth, Famine and Social Policy in the Dutch Republic at the End of the Sixteenth Century', 75. Adam Sundberg, 'Claiming the Past: History, Memory, and Innovation Following the Christmas Flood of 1717'. *Environmental History* 20:2 (2015): 238. Parker, *Global Crisis*, xvi. Jan de Vries, 'The Crisis of the Seventeenth Century: The Little Ice Age and the Mystery of the "Great Divergence"'. *Journal of Interdisciplinary History* 44:3 (2013): 369. See also Parker and Smith, *The General Crisis of the Seventeenth Century*. Maria A. Schenkeveld, *Dutch Literature in the Age of Rembrandt: Themes and Ideas.* (Amsterdam: John Benjamins Publishing, 1991), viii. Israel, *The Dutch Republic*, 20.

[17] Parker did describe Dutch successes (and Portuguese failures) in Asia, but argued that they cannot be linked to climate change. Parker, *Global Crisis*, 417. Recently, articles in a volume on Dutch admiral Michiel de Ruyter briefly linked cold winters during the Little Ice Age to events in the military and economic histories of the Dutch Republic. Prud'homme van Reine, 'Michiel Adriaenszoon de Ruyter and his Biographer Gerard Brandt'. In *De Ruyter: Dutch Admiral*, eds. Jaap R. Bruijn and Ronald Prud'homme van Reine. (Rotterdam: Karwansaray BV, 2011), 38. Jaap Jan Zeeberg summarized some scientific reconstructions of the polar environment in the late sixteenth century, in his description of Dutch polar expeditions. Jaap Jan Zeeberg, *Terugkeer naar Nova Zembla: de laatste en tragische reis van Willem Barents*. (Zutphen: Walburg Pers, 2007), 75. Jan de Vries, 'Measuring the Impact of Climate on History: The Search for Appropriate Methodologies'. *Journal of Interdisciplinary History*, 10:4 (Spring 1980): 626. Jan De Vries, *Barges and Capitalism. Passenger Transportation in the Dutch Economy, 1632–1839.* (Utrecht: HES Publishers, 1978), 295. Louwrens Hacquebord,

This book reaches fresh conclusions because it relies on a combination of the newest scientific scholarship and diverse textual sources, such as letters, intelligence reports, diary entries, and logs kept aboard ships, which explicitly show how weather affected human affairs. People whose lives and livelihoods depended on the weather wrote most of these documents. For example, the author of a particularly important diary, Claas Ariszoon Caeskoper, lived on the western coast of the Zaan near Amsterdam, where he worked a windmill that pressed oil. Wind and temperature influenced both the efficiency of his mill and, more substantially, the transportation of the commodities it helped produce. By affecting the extent of sea ice in the far north, weather even influenced the success of Caeskoper's investments in Arctic whaling. It is no surprise that he kept a daily record of changes in weather.

Few relied on weather more than sailors. When European mariners embarked on journeys that took them far from familiar coastlines, they started to keep detailed logs that meticulously recorded weather. One reason was that the leaders of increasingly bureaucratized admiralties and merchant companies wished to evaluate the performance of their officers. Wind direction and velocity not only provided the power supply of a sailing ship, but also constrained the ship's capacity to move where its crew desired it to go. By the fifteenth century, ships and their crews had acquired the ability to 'tack' (that is, sail) against the wind, but this was usually difficult, time-consuming work, and it was often impossible in high winds. In storms, coasts and underwater sandbanks, known as shoals, imperilled ships when they were in a 'lee' position relative to that vessel, which means that the wind blew towards the shoals and therefore pushed the ship in that direction. To a far greater extent than it does today, competent command of a merchant vessel or warship depended on exploiting, enduring, and at times anticipating the weather.[18]

The more important reason that sailors kept logs, however, had to do with the limits of early modern navigation. From the mid-seventeenth century, sailors could determine latitude with reasonable accuracy, but they could not easily discern longitude once they left behind known coastal landmarks. To estimate their longitude, most sailors relied on

'The Hunting of the Greenland Right Whale in Svalbard, Its Interaction with Climate and Its Impact on the Marine Ecosystem'. *Polar Research* 18:2 (1999): 155. J. R. Jones, *The Anglo-Dutch Wars of the Seventeenth Century*. (London: Longman, 1996), 18. De Vries and van der Woude, *The First Modern Economy*, 23.

[18] Jaap R. Bruijn, *The Dutch Navy of the Seventeenth and Eighteenth Centuries*. (Columbia: University of South Carolina Press, 1990), 44.

'dead reckoning', a technique that required knowledge of three essential variables: a ship's speed, measured by log line; its course, determined by compass; and any drift by the ship from its course. That last variable responded primarily to the direction and velocity of the wind. A ship sailing from east to west would drift south, for example, if the wind blew from the north. To have even a rough sense of where they were, sailors needed to obsessively keep track of the wind. Most ship logbooks therefore abound with reliable, detailed, and almost unbroken weather observations that sailors wrote down whenever the wind changed.[19]

Many landlubbers also had the means, training, and time to meticulously record even those environmental conditions that only indirectly influenced their lives. They also described how weather helped shape human activities. For instance, Adriaen van der Goes, a lawyer for the Court of Holland in The Hague, wrote letters to his brother that included detailed reports of weather in towns across the Low Countries. Meanwhile, less privileged artists and authors sketched, painted, or wrote about weather in ways that appealed to their customers.

Finally, the leaders of the republic managed affairs of state that, in a maritime country, frequently depended on weather. They are the final group of Dutch citizens whose records inform this book. The most important were the civil servants who set the agenda for the provincial council of Holland, and thereby often shaped national policy for the entire republic. Some of these officials, called 'Land's Advocates' until 1619, and thereafter 'Grand Pensionaries', received thousands of letters during their careers. Many described how weather influenced the movement of the Republic's fleets, the conduct of its diplomats, and the commerce of its merchants.[20]

METHOD AND MEANING

It is very hard to clearly link climate changes, which are always gradual and global, to a local weather event that comes and goes in a matter of

[19] Dennis Wheeler, 'British Naval Logbooks from the Late Seventeenth Century: New Climatic Information from Old Sources'. *History of Meteorology* 2 (2005), 136. H. E. Lansberg, 'Past Climates from Unexploited Written Sources', *Journal of Interdisciplinary History*, No. 10 (1980), 631. See also R. García-Herrera et al., 'CLIWOC: A Climatological Database for the World's Oceans 1750–1854', *Climatic Change* 73 (2005): 1–12.

[20] Bert Koene, *De Caeskopers: Een Zaanse koopmansfamilie in de Gouden Eeuw*. (Hilversum: Uitgeverij Verloren, 2011), 11. C. J. Gonnet, 'Inleiding'. In *Briefwisseling tusschen de gebroeders van der Goes (1659–1673) Vol. I*, ed. C. J. Gonnet. (Amsterdam: Johannes Müller, 1899), XXIV.

hours or days. That makes it equally difficult to connect climatic trends to human activities on similarly short and local scales. Scientists can establish these relationships as they play out today by using supercomputers that help them interpret meteorological data collected by thousands of weather stations the world over. Since historians work with relatively limited sources, we do not have that luxury. We must wrestle with the reality that, while climate change can make some kinds of weather more or less likely to occur, all but the most extreme kinds of weather can happen in any climate, warm or cold. A weather event made more common by climate change may have altered the course of human history, yet it was not necessarily caused by climate change. The atmospheric conditions that made it possible might have been entirely anomalous. Moreover, weather that was unusual in a climatic regime could influence human history as significantly as weather that conformed to the climatic norm.[21]

I use a three-step method to address these issues of scale and causation. First, I figure out how long-term global climate changes during the Little Ice Age influenced local environments across short timeframes. For instance, I might discover that climatic cooling increased the frequency of autumn storms in the North Sea. Second, I uncover many examples of such short-term, local environmental changes affecting human activities on similar temporal and geographic scales. I might find that shipwrecks usually coincided with storms, and that survivors or weather observers often blamed them on storms. Third, I establish the big relationships between climate change and human history as they played out across decades, often in large regions. I might conclude that climatic cooling, by increasing the frequency of storms, also increased the risks associated with travel through the North Sea. The second step of this method varies with each topic I explore in this book. When I examine commerce, I connect local environments to voyages and voyagers; when I investigate war, I link them to battles; when I turn to culture, I consider distinct cultural responses, like the creation of a painting or poem. The details differ, but the method stays the same.[22]

[21] Tapio Schneider, Tobias Bischoff, and Hanna Plotka, 'Physics of Changes in Synoptic Midlatitude Temperature Variability', *American Meteorological Society* 28:6 (March 2015): 2312. Edwards, *A Vast Machine*, 289.

[22] Bernstein et al., *Climate Change 2007: Synthesis Report*, 30. Fernand Braudel, *The Mediterranean and the Mediterranean World in the Age of Philip II, Vol. I.* (California: University of California Press, 1995), 102. *The Global Climate 2001–2010: A Decade of Climate Extremes – Summary Report.* (Geneva: World Meteorological Organization, 2013), 2.

Even after taking these steps, historians who study climate change – 'climate historians' – are still left to confront one of the thorniest concepts in climate scholarship: probability. Of course, most historical narratives deal in probability, because historians can rarely establish beyond doubt all the little connections that together link historical trends and events. They use the best evidence they can find to write the most plausible narratives that bind the general to the particular. Yet in climate scholarship, the trends are especially vast, and connecting them to distinct events on a human scale is particularly daunting. Some of the steps in my method therefore yield more probable relationships than others. The connections between weather and human activities that I trace in this book, which unfold on similar scales, rest on firmer ground than those I establish between weather and climate change, or between climate change and the grand sweep of human history.

There is also another kind of probability that climate historians should consider. Historians of all stripes can fall into simplistic determinism – the idea that a single force or set of forces predetermined the course of human history – but that trap may be especially dangerous for climate historians. Historians have only recently had access to scientific climate reconstructions and methods for deciphering weather information in old documents that permit them to track the consequences of climate change at the local level. In past decades, scholars in various disciplines repeatedly made sweeping assumptions about relationships between climate changes and human history on century timescales that provoked deep and enduring scepticism among mainstream historians.[23] In fact, the big structures that give shape to human history – cultural, socioeconomic, and political – have always mediated, or channelled, how weather influenced by climate change affected individual people. Decisions made by individuals in the face of these pressures then reshaped historical structures in ways that transformed how they registered climate change. Ultimately, this book shows that climate changes led to weather that limited or expanded the choices open to people, but did not determine their actions.[24]

[23] For a classic example, see Robert Claiborne, *Climate, Man and History*. (London: Angus and Robertson, 1973).

[24] Helge Salvesen, 'The Climate as a Factor of Historical Causation'. In *European Climate Reconstructed from Documentary Data: Methods and Results*, ed. Buckhard Frenzel. (Stuttgart: Gustav Fischer Verlag, 1992), 219. Elizabeth Jones, 'Climate, Archaeology, History, and the Arthurian Tradition: A Multiple-Source Study of Two Dark-Age Puzzles'. In *The Years without Summer: Tracing AD 536 and Its Aftermath*, ed. J. D. Gunn. (Oxford: Archaeopress, 2000), 31.

Climate historians deal with quantified data that reflect gradual and often global shifts in environmental conditions. For that reason, it might seem appropriate that they consider human activities only by using quantitative evidence on a similar scale. For example, a climate historian examining a country or continent might connect century-scale climatic cooling to an overlapping decrease in the length of the growing season, and a corresponding decline in living standards in agricultural economies. Climate historians can certainly make good use of big data, but they should try to support their analyses of vast quantitative trends with qualitative accounts of short-term events on a local level. Quantitative records, after all, do not necessarily provide a more accurate or objective picture of the past. They still reflect the subjective judgements of human beings, and their meaning is always determined by their context. It is therefore problematic for historians to link quantitative datasets based solely on the presence of overlapping statistical trends. Correlation need not imply causation.

Climate historians should instead attempt to link climate change to local, short-term human activities by establishing a chain of probable causality that binds the general to the particular. To grasp how a big trend affected human history, historians need to understand how that trend manifested on the small scale that mattered to individual people. This book therefore reaches firm conclusions only when convincing qualitative sources are available to connect different quantitative trends by providing first-hand accounts of how weather influenced human affairs. To gain further insight into these interactions, most chapters in the book compare trends or events in colder, wetter, stormier decades of the Little Ice Age with those in warmer, drier, and more tranquil periods. Such comparisons can make it easier to isolate the influence of climate change in human history.[25]

The history of climate change is closely linked to the history of energy. The chilliest phase of the Little Ice Age unfolded in an era of organic economies. In them, human or animal muscles joined technologies such as the sail and mill to harness energy only recently released by the sun. Most people lived off the land, in dispersed communities that had little to trade with one another. It took the extensive exploitation of ancient solar

[25] Fernand Braudel, *The Mediterranean and the Mediterranean World in the Age of Philip II*, 355. Edwards, *A Vast Machine*, 4. Jan de Vries, 'The Economic Crisis of the Seventeenth Century after Fifty Years'. *Journal of Interdisciplinary History* 40:2 (2009): 164.

energy bound up in fossil fuels to transform these conditions. Historians have debated whether the Dutch Republic exceeded the limits of the organic economy. The republic's high levels of urbanization, extensive networks of trade, thriving industrial centres, and commercialized agriculture are often perceived as symptoms of, and stimulus for, an unusually efficient energy supply.[26]

This book finds that the resilience of the republic in the face of the Little Ice Age partly reflected how the Dutch used energy, and how much they had to use. In organic economies, cool temperatures, precipitation extremes, and unpredictable weather ruin harvests and thereby reduce the dominant source of useable energy, often with disastrous consequences for human beings. Many climate historians accordingly assume that climate change most directly impacted human history by altering the growth and health of staple crops. Yet the Dutch imported a substantial share of their food in the same way that they established a world-straddling commercial empire: by exploiting the energy of wind on the relatively friction-free surface of water. Often, weather that undermined the supply of useable energy for farmers and pastoralists actually increased how much energy the Dutch could use on their ships. Dutch admirals even developed strategies to exploit as much of this energy as possible. Entrepreneurs also invented technologies that helped the Dutch efficiently harness energy from wind, water, and peat during the chilliest decades of the Little Ice Age. The impacts of climate change on Dutch commerce and conflict, at least, do not seem to have been less direct or less important than the impacts on agriculture. A focus on energy therefore calls into question some long-standing assumptions in climate history.[27]

[26] E. A. Wrigley, *Continuity, Chance and Change: The Character of the Industrial Revolution in England.* (Cambridge: Cambridge University Press, 1988), 57. R. W. Unger, 'Energy Sources for the Dutch Golden Age; Peat, Wind and Coal'. *Research in Economic History* 9 (1984): 228. C. A. Davids, *The Rise and Decline of Dutch Technological Leadership: Technology, Economy and Culture in the Netherlands, 1350–1800, Vol. I.* (Leiden: Brill, 2008), 17. Karel Davids, 'Technological Change and the Economic Expansion of the Dutch Republic, 1580–1680'. In *The Dutch Economy in the Golden Age: Nine Studies*, eds. C. A. Davids and L. Noordegraaf. (Amsterdam: Nederlandsch Economisch-Historisch Archief, 1993), 83. Vaclav Smil, *Energy in World History.* (Boulder: Westview, 1994), 248. John Landers, *The Field and the Forge: Population, Production and Power in the Pre-Industrial West.* (New York: Oxford University Press, 2003), 7.

[27] Chantal Camenisch et al., 'The 1430s: A Cold Period of Extraordinary Internal Climate Variability during the Early Spörer Minimum with Social and Economic Impacts in North-Western and Central Europe'. *Climate of the Past* 12 (2016): 2118.

THE STRUCTURE OF THIS BOOK

Chapter 1 introduces the human and environmental histories that frame this book. It describes why climates change, explains how scholars reconstruct past changes, and surveys what the Little Ice Age looked like globally and across the Low Countries. The book then unfolds in three parts, each with two chapters that establish connections between climate change and a pillar of Dutch prosperity.

The first part of the book traces how the Little Ice Age affected Dutch commerce by altering the ability of mariners and merchants to move through their world. It argues that climate changes occasionally hampered but often benefitted different kinds of Dutch trade and travel. Chapter 2 shows that the Little Ice Age influenced Dutch attempts to establish and maintain commercial connections with Asia. It starts by examining Dutch expeditions to the Arctic in the sixteenth and early seventeenth centuries, which were undertaken to map a new route to Asia. The local consequences of climatic cooling helped thwart attempts to chart a passage, but also led to discoveries that transformed understandings of the Arctic and encouraged the growth of a lucrative but ecologically destructive whaling industry. Next, the chapter considers trade undertaken by the Dutch East India Company (*Vereenigde Oostindische Compagnie*, or VOC) along the southern passage to Asia. It concludes that changes in atmospheric circulation over the Atlantic Ocean increased the risks, but also the speed, by which goods, people, and information moved between the republic and Asia.

Chapter 3 begins by examining how climate change influenced Dutch commerce in the Baltic Sea. The chapter traces how winter freezing and frequent storms hampered travel through the Baltic during the chilliest periods of the Little Ice Age. Yet it demonstrates that the republic's merchants also responded creatively to the risks imposed by frequent gales, and profited when climatic shocks contributed to higher grain prices elsewhere in Europe. The chapter continues by investigating travel within the republic's borders. It reveals that the Dutch Republic's diverse networks of transportation helped its citizens maintain their mobility during even the coldest phases of the Little Ice Age.

The second part of this book investigates how climate changes affected Dutch armies and fleets in the wars that established the Republic and preserved its commercial primacy. It argues that complex relationships between global climate changes and regional environments provided important advantages to Dutch forces during the chilliest decades of the

Little Ice Age. Chapter 4 finds connections between a shifting climate and the Dutch struggle for independence from the Spanish Empire, known as the Eighty Years' War (1568–1648). It describes how climatic cooling exacerbated existing vulnerabilities in Spain's control of the Low Countries and thereby helped provoke a rebellion in 1568. It continues by examining relationships between climate change and different phases of the Eighty Years' War. Cold, wet, and stormy conditions, common during a chillier climate, impeded offensive operations from the escalation of the Dutch rebellion in 1572 to the signing of the Twelve Years' Truce in 1609. Such weather usually offered important advantages to Dutch soldiers and sailors as they fought to defend their rebellion from Spain. Yet in the late 1620s and the 1630s, a warmer, drier break in the Little Ice Age provided advantages for offensive campaigns just as France allied with the republic and as the Spanish Empire entered another war. Dutch armies then expanded the republic's borders by exploiting both favourable strategic circumstances and beneficial weather.

Chapter 5 investigates hostilities between the Dutch Republic and its rising commercial competitor, England, during the onset of the Maunder Minimum. It explains that key differences between English and Dutch naval systems led each to respond differently to climatic cooling and its associated changes in atmospheric circulation. It shows that, in the first Anglo-Dutch War (1652–1654), prevailing westerly winds granted crucial advantages to English fleets. Yet easterly winds grew more common as the Maunder Minimum deepened, benefitting Dutch fleets, which had adopted English tactics and technology. Frequent and persistent easterlies would later aid the republic's invasion of England during the Glorious Revolution of 1688.

The third part of this book argues that the culture of the Dutch Golden Age responded to the Little Ice Age in ways that contributed to the resilience of the republic in the face of climate change. Chapter 6 shows that some of the republic's citizens developed a vague awareness of climate change, which may have informed commercial and military strategies aimed at exploiting the opportunities it offered. The chapter then explains how the paintings of the Golden Age occasionally depicted the real consequences of climate change and often reflected the pragmatic attitudes of the Dutch amid the weather of the Little Ice Age.

Chapter 7 traces how climate changes influenced texts and technologies. It reveals that symbols in many maps and pamphlets partly registered the weather of the Little Ice Age. It then investigates weather metaphors in Dutch poetry and the rise of a poetic genre that responded to real weather-related disasters. Next, the chapter traces the development of ice cultures that emerged in frigid winters, and explains the reluctance of Dutch citizens to persecute so-called witches for weather-related disasters, restraint unusual in early modern Europe. Finally, it reveals how and why the Dutch invented or implemented technologies that helped them thrive amid the chilliest phases of the Little Ice Age.

1

The Little Ice Age

Climate change is today closely associated with the greenhouse effect. The sun emits short-wave radiation in the form of ultraviolet rays and visible light, which easily pass through Earth's atmosphere. Dark surfaces with low albedo, or reflectivity, such as snow-free land or ice-free water, absorb a large percentage of this radiation, while surfaces with high albedo, such as clouds or ice, absorb a relatively small percentage and reflect the rest into space. As surfaces both dark and light absorb solar radiation, their temperature increases. In order to be at thermal equilibrium, they release extra heat as long-wave, or infrared, radiation, which does not easily pass through Earth's atmosphere. Greenhouse gases, such as carbon dioxide and methane, absorb some of it and radiate it back to Earth's atmosphere and surface. Even minute changes in the atmospheric concentration of these gases can dramatically change Earth's temperature. Over the last two centuries, industrial civilizations have released more than a trillion tons of carbon dioxide into the atmosphere, a number that expands by over 30 billion tons a year. As a result, atmospheric carbon dioxide concentrations are now higher than they have been for millions of years, and Earth is warming fast.[1]

Past climate changes had very different causes, many of which unfolded simultaneously. The amount of carbon dioxide in our atmosphere, for

[1] John Cook et al., 'Consensus on Consensus: A Synthesis of Consensus Estimates on Human-Caused Global Warming'. *Environmental Research Letters* 11 (2016): 1–7. Myles R. Allen, 'Warming Caused by Cumulative Carbon Emissions towards the Trillionth Tonne'. *Nature Letters* 458 (2009): 1163. Brooke, *Climate Change and the Course of Global History*, 477.

example, also fluctuates in response to volcanic activity and land use changes that alter vegetation patterns on large scales. Big volcanic eruptions send huge quantities of sulphur dioxide into the stratosphere, which is quickly converted into aerosols that reflect a share of incoming short-wave solar radiation. Volcanic aerosols can linger in the atmosphere for years, creating dust veils that warm the stratosphere but cool the surface. Sulphur injected into the atmosphere by tropical eruptions can cause global cooling when circulated by the prevailing winds of both the Northern and Southern Hemispheres. While the cooling effect of volcanic eruptions does not scale proportionately with the size of the eruption, consecutive big eruptions at the right latitude can lower Earth's average temperature for many years.[2]

Some causes of climate change register small but significant fluctuations in the amount of radiation that reaches Earth from the Sun. Over thousands of years, the characteristics of Earth's orbit and rotation change in ways that periodically trigger deep ice ages when Earth's average temperature is already sufficiently low. The Sun's activity also fluctuates according to both a roughly 11-year cycle and a much longer, 2,400-year Hallstatt cycle. In decades-long periods of low solar activity, the Sun enters a grand solar minimum, which is detectable on Earth through the near absence of sunspots and solar flares. In periods of high solar activity, the Sun reaches a grand solar maximum distinguished by plentiful sunspots and flares.[3]

Even minor temperature fluctuations can trigger so-called positive feedback loops in Earth's climate system. The effect resembles audio feedback, where a microphone picks up a modest amount of noise, broadcast by a speaker, and amplifies it by rebroadcasting it through the speaker. Similarly, a slight increase in Earth's average temperature melts sea ice, for example, which reduces Earth's albedo and causes it to reflect more heat, which then triggers more warming, more melting, and so on.[4] Similarly, warming in the Arctic melts permafrost, which releases

[2] Jihong Cole-Dai, 'Volcanoes and Climate'. *Wiley Interdisciplinary Reviews: Climate Change* 1:6 (2010): 824. Thomas J. Crowley, 'Causes of Climate Change over the Past 1000 Years'. *Science* 289:5477 (2000): 271.

[3] Brooke, *Climate Change and the Course of Global History*, 67, 115, 155.

[4] Of course, sea ice – like any terrestrial surface – does not have a homogenous albedo. Gregory Flato et al., 'Evaluation of Climate Models', in *Climate Change 2013: The Physical Science Basis. Contribution of Working Group I to the Fifth Assessment Report of the International Panel on Climate Change*, eds. T. F. Stocker et al. (Cambridge: Cambridge University Press, 2014), 751.

methane, a potent greenhouse gas that further warms temperatures, and again leads to more melting, more warming, and on.[5]

Atmospheric and oceanic circulation, together with associated lows and highs in atmospheric pressure, can amplify, prolong, or even cause lasting changes in Earth's average temperature. Some of the biggest currents push warm, salty water to the poles from the equator, which is closer to the Sun than the rest of our planet. Atlantic Meridional Overturning Circulation (AMOC), for example, drives warm, salty water past Europe and into the Arctic. As this water evaporates, it grows saltier and therefore denser. Once it reaches high latitudes, it starts to sink beneath lighter, fresher water. This chillier water then flows south past North America to replace the salty water meandering north. Circular, wind-driven currents, known as gyres, contribute to this so-called thermohaline circulation.[6]

Changes in the strength of the northern polar vortex, a low-pressure zone that rotates clockwise over the Arctic, can affect the overturning of warm saltwater and cold freshwater off southeastern Greenland. They can also affect the state of the North Atlantic Oscillation (NAO), which consists of a low-pressure zone near Iceland and a high-pressure zone near the Azores. When pressure around Iceland is especially low, and very high around the Azores, the NAO is considered to be in a positive setting. Westerly winds strengthen and flow at high latitudes across the Northern Atlantic and Europe. Since water responds more slowly to changes in temperature than land, a positive NAO can bring milder winters and cooler summers to northern Europe, with more storms and precipitation. When the difference in pressure between the Icelandic low and the Azores high is less pronounced, the NAO enters a negative setting. Westerly winds are weaker and now blow over more southerly latitudes of the Mediterranean. Temperatures in both winter and summer can be more extreme, but storms and precipitation less common across Northern Europe.[7]

[5] Brooke, *Climate Change and the Course of Global History*, 68. Judith A. Curry, Julie L. Schramm, and Elizabeth E. Ebert, 'Sea Ice-Albedo Climate Feedback Mechanism'. *Journal of Climate* 8:2 (1995): 240.

[6] Rui Xin Huang, *Ocean Circulation: Wind-Driven and Thermohaline Processes.* (Cambridge: Cambridge University Press, 2010), 5. Agatha M. de Boer, 'Oceanography: Sea Change'. *Nature Geoscience* 3:10 (2010): 669. Hendrik M. van Aken, *The Oceanic Thermohaline Circulation: An Introduction.* (New York: Springer, 2007), 2.

[7] Thomas Reichler et al., 'A Stratospheric Connection to Atlantic Climate Variability'. *Nature Geoscience* 5:11 (2012): 783. Kirien Whan and Francis Zwiers. 'The Impact of ENSO and the NAO on Extreme Winter Precipitation in North America in Observations and Regional Climate Models'. *Climate Dynamics* (2016): 2. Brooke, *Climate Change and*

The NAO is strongly correlated to the Arctic Oscillation, a similar seesaw of atmospheric pressure between the Arctic and lower latitudes. True to its name, the Arctic Oscillation is more centred on the Arctic than the NAO, and has a stronger relationship with surface air temperatures at high latitudes. When it is in a positive setting, atmospheric pressure is low over the Arctic and relatively high at more southerly latitudes. Cold, stormy conditions stretch across very high latitudes, yet warmer weather prevails further south. When the Arctic Oscillation is in a negative setting, the atmospheric seesaw is reversed, and chillier, stormy conditions reach down to lower latitudes across the Northern Hemisphere.[8]

Climatologists have identified yet another oscillation in the Northern Atlantic, this one a roughly 70-year seesaw between warm and cold phases in North Atlantic sea surface temperatures. Model simulations suggest that the state of this Atlantic Multidecadal Oscillation (AMO) may be influenced by the strength of AMOC, but there is still no observational evidence of this relationship. The engine driving the AMO cycle may be something entirely different. We do know that changes in the AMO affect average global temperatures and atmospheric circulation. They lead to fluctuations in the frequency of Atlantic hurricanes, the quantity of precipitation across India and Africa, and storminess over Europe.[9]

the Course of Global History, 168. See also James W. Hurrell et al., eds., *The North Atlantic Oscillation: Climatic Significance and Environmental Impact, 1st Edition.* (Washington, DC: American Geophysical Union, 2003).

[8] 'Patterns in Arctic Weather and Climate'. National Snow and Ice Data Center. Accessed 27 June 2016, https://nsidc.org/cryosphere/arctic-meteorology/weather_climate_patterns.html#arctic_oscillation. David W. J. Thompson and John M. Wallace, 'The Arctic Oscillation Signature in the Wintertime Geopotential Height and Temperature Fields'. *Geophysical Research Letters* 25:9 (1998): 1297. Maarten H. P. Ambaum et al., 'Arctic Oscillation or North Atlantic Oscillation?' *Journal of Climate* 14:16 (2001): 3496. Brooke, *Climate Change and the Course of Global History*, 168.

[9] Jeff R. Knight, Chris K. Folland, and Adam A. Scaife, 'Climate Impacts of the Atlantic Multidecadal Oscillation'. *Geophysical Research Letters* 33:17 (2006): 1. Gerard D. McCarthy et al., 'Ocean Impact on Decadal Atlantic Climate Variability Revealed by Sea-Level Observations'. *Nature* 521:7553 (2015): 508. Ken Drinkwater et al., 'The Atlantic Multidecadal Oscillation: Its Manifestations and Impacts with Special Emphasis on the Atlantic Region North of 60° N'. (Paper presented at the ESSAS Annual Science Meeting, Copenhagen, Denmark 7–9 April 2014). Richard A. Kerr, 'A North Atlantic Climate Pacemaker for the Centuries'. *Science* 288:5473 (2000): 1985. Michael E. Schlesinger and Navin Ramankutty, 'An Oscillation in the Global Climate System of Period 65–70 Years'. *Nature* 367 (1994): 723. Mingfang Ting et al., 'Forced and Internal Twentieth-Century SST Trends in the North Atlantic'. *Journal of Climate* 22 (2009): 1470. Roward T. Sutton and Daniel L. R. Hudson, 'Atlantic Ocean Forcing of North American and European Summer Climate'. *Science* 309 (2005): 115.

Over land and far to the east, another variable feature of Earth's atmosphere can strengthen or weaken to influence weather across Eurasia. This is the Siberian High, a pressure cell over northern Asia that responds to the regional extent of snow and especially sea ice. A strong Siberian High unleashes cold, dry winds across Asia and expands deep into Western Europe, pushing back the otherwise temperate climate in the region that is made possible by the warm waters of AMOC. Not only does a strong Siberian High bring frigid winter weather to Europe, but it may also disturb the usual flow of westerly winds across the continent.[10]

These are the key engines of atmospheric and oceanic circulation in the parts of the world that this book primarily examines. There is one more crucial source of variability, however, and it takes us far beyond the Atlantic region to a vast belt of water that stretches across much of the tropical Pacific Ocean. When this water warms, El Niño conditions prevail, and when it cools, La Niña sets in. Although warm or cold states of the El Niño Southern Oscillation (ENSO) only last for about a year, they can alter weather patterns the world over. This is because fluctuations in the temperature of so much water alter convection and precipitation on huge scales across the Pacific. The frequency and strength of warm or cool phases in ENSO varies across long timescales, in response to cooling or warming trends. Severe El Niño or La Niña conditions can dramatically increase the frequency of weather events – such as heat waves or hurricanes – already made more common in a given climatic regime. Earth's climate is a fantastically complex jigsaw puzzle, and every part contributes to the whole.[11]

RECONSTRUCTING PAST CLIMATE CHANGES

Scholars use increasingly diverse methods to piece together how the constituent elements of Earth's climate have fluctuated in the past. Many scientists gather and interpret so-called proxy data from natural 'archives' that include tree rings, lakebed sediments, ice cores, animal middens, and

[10] Brooke, *Climate Change and the Course of Global History*, 168. BingYi Wu, JingZhi Su, and RenHe Zhang, 'Effects of Autumn-Winter Arctic Sea Ice on Winter Siberian High'. *Chinese Science Bulletin* 56:30 (2011): 3220. Judah Cohen, Kazuyuki Saito, and Dara Entekhabi, 'The Role of the Siberian High in Northern Hemisphere Climate Variability'. *Geophysical Research Letters* 28:2 (2001): 299.

[11] For much more detail, see Edward S. Sarachik and Mark A. Cane, *The El Niño-Southern Oscillation Phenomenon*. (Cambridge: Cambridge University Press, 2010).

many other natural sources that respond to weather. By measuring the thickness of tree rings, for example, or layers deposited in ancient glacial ice, scientists can reconstruct temperature or precipitation trends going back hundreds or thousands of years. Other scientists develop computer simulations based on the physics of interactions between the atmosphere, hydrosphere, cryosphere, and biosphere. Their digital models can simulate past, present, and future climates. Some of the most comprehensive scientific reconstructions of past climate change combine model simulations with proxy data. Inevitably, these reconstructions shimmer within error margins, as inconsistencies emerge between different models and proxies. Areas of consensus may strengthen over time, but scientific understandings of past climates are never entirely stable.[12]

Scholars in the human sciences can complement and at times challenge climate reconstructions compiled using natural archives by tracing how peoples of the past actually experienced and recorded past weather. Archaeologists, for example, can investigate developments in human material culture that partly reflect the social consequences of weather and climate change. Researchers in other disciplines can make use of direct weather observations, compiled as early as the late sixteenth century, using meteorological instruments. However, they must carefully compensate for the technical limitations of early instruments, which did not record weather as reliably as their present-day equivalents. Moreover, until the eighteenth century, observers rarely used them to record weather for long stretches of time. Even when they did, they only measured weather in small corners of the world. For most of the Little Ice Age, many of the best documentary sources for climate reconstruction therefore describe weather without using meteorological instruments, or alternatively, they report on human activities that depended on particular weather conditions, such as ice breaking. Ship logbooks, written by sailors who accurately recorded wind direction and velocity without using sophisticated meteorological instruments, provide a bridge between such documents and early instrumental measurements.[13]

For the purposes of reconstructing past climate changes, documents can have advantages over proxy data from natural archives or model

[12] Brazdil et al., 'Historical Climatology in Europe – The State of the Art', 364. Gergis, Garden, and Fenby, 'The Influence of Climate on the First European Settlement of Australia', 504. Brown, *History and Climate Change*, 315. Lamb, *Climate, History and the Modern World*, 148. Edwards, *A Vast Machine*, xv.

[13] Brazdil et al., 'Historical Climatology in Europe – The State of the Art', 370.

simulations. Many provide meteorological information with a much higher precision, or resolution, than most scientific evidence. Low-resolution climate reconstructions measure weather over long time frames or across large geographic dimensions. Ice cores, for example, can provide annual or seasonal information on temperature, precipitation, and even the composition of the atmosphere across vast regions for hundreds of thousands of years. Climate reconstructions at this resolution give deep context to short-term climatic variability. However, to find connections between climate changes and human affairs, historians ideally need local weather data at a much higher resolution, over months, days, and (if possible) even hours. Diary entries or letters, for example, can give precise information about the short-term, local consequences of bigger climatic trends. Moreover, documentary sources usually provide equally good weather information for every season, whereas proxy data from ancient organisms often reveals trends only in summer weather conditions. Even then, it is hard to know whether the trends registered by organic proxy data are relevant to temperature, precipitation, or cloudiness (which influences sunniness), since different plants in different regions need a different combination of all of these variables in order to thrive. Many documents, by contrast, easily distinguish between diverse weather conditions.[14]

Nevertheless, documentary evidence has its weaknesses. Some observers merely copied second-hand accounts of weather and passed them off as their own experiences. Others incorrectly or imprecisely gave the dates and times of weather events, if they mentioned these details at all. Most did not feel obliged to keep unbroken records of weather, and their meteorological records therefore have frustrating gaps. Some described weather metaphorically, in ways that communicated ideas but cannot be linked to real events. Many exaggerated the severity or impact of weather in order to provoke, or excuse, human activities. Finally, few observers enjoyed the lifespans most of us take for granted today, so their weather records were short-lived.[15]

These problems are serious, but they are not insurmountable. Starting in the 1970s, historical climatologists started to critically assess the

[14] Brazdil et al., 'Historical Climatology in Europe – The State of the Art', 370. Chantal Camenisch, 'Endless Cold: A Seasonal Reconstruction of Temperature and Precipitation in the Burgundian Low Countries during the 15th Century Based on Documentary Evidence'. *Climate of the Past* 11:8 (2015): 1050.

[15] Brazdil et al., 'Historical Climatology in Europe – The State of the Art', 374.

reliability of weather information in different sources. They then quantified accounts of temperature and precipitation in the most reliable sources on simple, ordinal scales.[16] To do so, they first judged whether surviving texts described warm, average, or cold temperatures, or dry, average, or wet conditions, over the course of a month. Then, they created monthly indices of temperature and precipitation on a scale from negative one (cold or dry) to plus one (warm or rainy). Finally, they determined seasonal conditions by adding monthly values. They expanded three-value monthly or seasonal indices by assigning more weight to weather descriptions calibrated with early instrumental data, or to weather recorded by an unusual number of documents. The sheer quantity of Dutch weather observations has allowed researchers to reconstruct temperature trends in the Low Countries on a nine-grade scale. These seasonal statistics are continuous from the sixteenth century, and they have made this book possible.[17]

However, Dutch citizens in the Golden Age often cared more about wind direction and velocity, which affected the course and speed of sailing ships, than they did about temperature and precipitation. Whenever possible, this book leans on surviving ship logbooks to reconstruct changes in prevailing winds. Logbooks recorded unusually detailed weather information, but they do present peculiar problems for climate historians. First, it can be difficult to know where exactly mariners wrote many of their logbook entries. Once they left familiar seas and landmarks, they could no longer precisely judge longitude or even, in the sixteenth and early seventeenth centuries, latitude. Often, modern scholars must painstakingly reconstruct the course and speed of early modern ships to estimate where they were on a particular day of their journeys. Second, mariners judged direction – of their ships or the winds they encountered – with reference to the north magnetic pole, not the north geographic pole. At lower latitudes, this made little difference. However, it started to

[16] Cornelis Easton might have been the first to come up with this idea, in 1928. M. V. Shabalova and A. F. V. van Engelen, 'Evaluation of a Reconstruction of Temperature in the Low Countries AD 764–1998'. *Climatic Change* (March 2000), 220.

[17] Pfister, 'Climatic Extremes, Recurrent Crises and Witch Hunts', 44. A. F. V. van Engelen, J. Buisman, and F. IJnsen, 'A Millennium of Weather, Winds and Water in the Low Countries', in *History and Climate: Memories of the Future?*, eds. P. D. Jones et al. (New York: Kluwer Academic/Plenum Publishers, 2001), 112. Shabalova and Van Engelen, 225. Brazdil et al., 'Historical Climatology in Europe – The State of the Art', 378. Rüdiger Glaser et al., 'Seasonal Temperature and Precipitation Fluctuations in Selected Parts of Europe during the Sixteenth Century'. *Climatic Change* 43:1 (1999): 171. Camenisch, 'Endless Cold', 1053.

matter a great deal once their ships reached very high latitudes. The north magnetic pole, to a much greater extent than the north geographic pole, drifts over time, in response to the complex dynamics of Earth's core, ionosphere, radiation belts, and magnetosphere. In the sixteenth and seventeenth centuries, it was much farther from the north geographic pole than it is today. Scholars must therefore use historical magnetic variation databases to determine the precise course of early modern ships in the Arctic that strayed far from the shore, and the exact direction of the winds their crews encountered.[18]

Third, mariners recorded wind velocities using dozens of now-obsolete nautical terms that referred to the sails that could be furled or unfurled in different winds. Fortunately, scholars with the multinational Climatological Database for the World's Oceans (CLIWOC) project created a dictionary that translates early modern wind velocity terms into modern Beaufort (BF) readings. Even so, some wind terms cannot be deciphered using the BF scale.[19]

Fourth, not all ship logbooks were alike. Flag officers kept narratives of their time aboard warships, but they were not required to record wind direction or velocity (although most did anyway). By contrast, their immediate subordinates usually measured these conditions without fail, but their logbooks have, for earlier periods, survived in smaller quantities. Dutch naval logbooks are in fact rare, since a fire destroyed the archives of the republic's admiralties in 1844.[20]

Finally, even when all these problems are overcome, there are still basic limitations to the climate information that early ship logbooks can provide. To measure climate change today, scientists rely not only on satellites but also on weather buoys and stations, distributed in huge quantities across Earth's surface. However, in the sixteenth and seventeenth centuries, ships simply did not simultaneously sail in sufficient numbers, with sufficient distribution, for scholars to use surviving logbooks for

[18] Matthew Ayre et al., 'Ships' Logbooks from the Arctic in the Pre-Instrumental Period'. *Geoscience Data Journal* 2 (2015): 57. Nils Olsen and Mioara Mandea, 'Will the Magnetic North Pole Move to Siberia?' *Eos* 88:29 (2007): 294.

[19] Ricardo García-Herrera et al., *CLIWOC Multilingual Meteorological Dictionary: An English-Spanish-Dutch-French Dictionary of Wind Force Terms Used by Mariners from 1750 to 1850*. (Den Haag: Koninklijke Nederlands Meteorologisch Instituut, 2003), 5.

[20] Clive Wilkinson, 'British Logbooks in UK Archives, 17th–19th Centuries – A Survey of the Range, Selection and Suitability of British Logbooks and Related Documents for Climatic Research'. (Norwich: Climatic Research Unit School of Environmental Sciences University of East Anglia, 2009), 9.

comprehensive regional weather reconstructions. At best, we can use local meteorological observations in ship logbooks to infer regional weather patterns, suggest possible connections between weather and human activities, and provide imperfect evidence for scientific climate reconstructions. Overall, we should always appreciate the complexities climate historians encounter when reconstructing climate changes using even relatively robust documentary sources.

The most accurate climate reconstructions are therefore those that combine the strengths and weaknesses of diverse natural and textual sources. In recent decades, historians have increasingly used these reconstructions to investigate how climate change influenced human history. Their studies are particularly persuasive for civilizations that left behind abundant weather information on media hardy enough to survive the centuries and accessible enough to interpret easily today. In the high medieval centuries, on the eve of the Little Ice Age, such civilizations emerged or matured around the world.[21]

CAUSES AND CONSEQUENCES OF THE LITTLE ICE AGE

Climate reconstructions can take us millions or even billions of years back in time. Yet our story begins late in the thirteenth century, when the Little Ice Age dawned amid catastrophic volcanic eruptions, declining solar activity, and gradual changes in Earth's orbit that lowered how much solar energy reached the Northern Hemisphere in late summer. Expanding sea ice triggered positive feedbacks in the Arctic and may have weakened AMOC, the pump that pushes saltwater into the Northern Atlantic. Atmospheric circulation and pressure responded in ways that altered precipitation patterns around the world. In the fourteenth century, torrential rains and catastrophic droughts coincided with generally falling temperatures across much of Earth. Yet only in the fifteenth century did the Little Ice Age reach its first great cold phase: the Spörer Minimum (1450–1530). It is named after a low point in solar activity that astronomer Gustav Spörer pieced together by compiling ancient sunspot observations.[22]

[21] Brazdil et al., 'Historical Climatology in Europe – The State of the Art', 377. A. Pauling, J. Luterbacher, and H. Wanner. 'Evaluation of Proxies for European and North Atlantic Temperature Field Reconstructions'. *Geophysical Research Letters* 30:15 (2003), 4.

[22] Y. Zhong et al., 'Centennial-Scale Climate Change from Decadally-Paced Explosive Volcanism: A Coupled Sea Ice-Ocean Mechanism'. *Climate Dynamics* 37 (2011): 2373. David C. Lund et al., 'Gulf Stream Density Structure and Transport during the Past

The Spörer Minimum was cold, but in many regions the coldest stretch of the Little Ice Age began in the early 1560s, when a series of severe winters culminated in the frigid winter and chilly summer of 1565. Across much of the world, average annual temperatures fell at least 0.5 degrees Celsius below the twentieth-century norm until the aftermath of a brutally cold year without summer in 1628. Across continental Europe in particular, temperatures were usually chilliest during the winter and spring, owing perhaps to the consequences of a long fall in the amount of heat carried north by the subpolar gyre. This second great Little Ice Age cold phase is occasionally called the Grindelwald Fluctuation, since it coincided with the expansion of a glacier bordering the Swiss town of Grindelwald. Solar activity was not nearly as low as it had been during the Spörer Minimum, and at first, cooling may have been triggered by the natural variability that affects all complex systems, including Earth's climate. Later, volcanic eruptions made it even colder. Nevado del Ruiz blew up in 1595, and then Huaynaputina exploded just five years later in one of the most powerful eruptions of the past 2,500 years.[23]

Millennium'. *Nature* 444 (2006): 602. Gifford Miller et al., 'Abrupt Onset of the Little Ice Age Triggered by Volcanism and Sustained by Sea-Ice/Ocean Feedbacks'. *Geophysical Research Letters*, 39:2 (2012), 4. Flavio Lehner et al., 'Amplified Inception of European Little Ice Age by Sea Ice–Ocean–Atmosphere Feedbacks'. *Journal of Climate* 26:19 (2013): 7586. Stefan Rahmstorf et al., 'Exceptional Twentieth-Century Slowdown in Atlantic Ocean Overturning Circulation'. *Nature Climate Change* 5 (2015): 477. Eduardo Moreno-Chamarro, 'An Abrupt Weakening of the Subpolar Gyre as Trigger of Little Ice Age-Type Episodes'. *Climatic Dynamics* (2016). DOI: 10.1007/s00382-016–3106-7. Alan D. Wanamaker Jr. et al., 'Surface Changes in the North Atlantic Meridional Overturning Circulation during the Last Millennium'. *Nature Communications* 3 (2012): 3. Markus Stoffel et al., 'Estimates of Volcanic-Induced Cooling in the Northern Hemisphere over the Past 1,500 Years'. *Nature Geoscience* 8 (2015): 786. Jean M. Grove, 'The Initiation of the "Little Ice Age" in Regions Round the North Atlantic'. In *The Iceberg in the Mist: Northern Research in Pursuit of a 'Little Ice Age'*, eds. Astrid E. J. Ogilvie and Trausti Jónsson. (Dordrecht: Springer Netherlands, 2001): 53. Yaotiao Jiang and Zhentao Xu, 'On the Spörer Minimum'. *Astrophysics and Space Science* (1986): 159. E. H. Lee at al., 'The Sunspot and Auroral Activity Cycle Derived From Korean Historical Records of the 11th–18th Century'. *Solar Physics* 224: 1–2 (2004): 375. Gavin A. Schmidt et al., 'Climate Forcing Reconstructions for Use in PMIP Simulations of the Last Millennium (v1. 0)'. *Geoscientific Model Development* 4:1 (2011): 34. Camenisch, 'Endless Cold', 1058.

[23] Sigl et al., 'Timing and Climate Forcing of Volcanic Eruptions', 546. Brooke, *Climate Change and the Course of Global History*, 441. William Atwell, 'Volcanism and Short-Term Climatic Change in East Asian and World History c. 1200–1699', *Journal of World History* 12 (2001): 56. K. Briffa et al., 'Influence of Volcanic Eruptions on Northern Hemisphere Summer Temperature over the Past 600 Years', *Nature* 393 (1998): 454. Jürg Luterbacher et al., 'European Summer Temperatures since Roman Times'. *Environmental Research Letters* 11:12 (2016): 7. Samuel U. Nussbaumer and Heinz

The various pieces of Earth's climate puzzle responded to the falling temperatures, but not always as we might expect. The AMO only cooled around 1580, but from the start the Siberian High strengthened considerably. By 1600, AMOC – the Atlantic saltwater pump – reached its weakest state in centuries. At around the same time, the NAO switched into a strongly negative phase, and there it would remain until the late 1620s. As it returned to a persistently positive state, AMOC strengthened again.[24]

Strong El Niño conditions prevailed for much of the seventeenth century, weakening South Asian monsoons. In many regions, precipitation regimes responded in complex ways to changes in atmospheric circulation. For instance, precipitation declined during the Grindelwald Fluctuation along the shores of the Mediterranean, but it probably rose

J. Zumbühl, 'The Little Ice Age History of the Glacier des Bossons (Mont Blanc massif, France): A New High-Resolution Glacier Length Curve Based on Historical Documents'. *Climatic Change* 111 (2012): 318. K. R. Briffa, T. J. Osborn and F. H. Schweingruber, 'Large-Scale Temperature Inferences from Tree Rings: A Review'. *Global and Planetary Change* 40:1–2 (2004): 23. See also Michael Sigl et al., 'A New Bipolar Ice Core Record of Volcanism from WAIS Divide and NEEM and Implications for Climate Forcing of the Last 2000 Years', *Journal of Geophysical Research: Atmospheres* 118 (2013): 1151–1169. Shanaka L. de Silva and Gregory A. Zielinski, 'Global Influence of the AD 1600 Eruption of Huaynaputina, Peru'. *Nature* 393:6684 (1998): Lamb, *Climate, History and the Modern World*, 2nd ed., 260. K. R. Briffa et al., 'European Tree Rings and Climate in the 16th Century', *Climatic Change* 43:1 (1999): 166. D. Rind, 'The Sun's Role in Climate Variations'. *Science* 296 (2002): 675. William Atwell, 'Volcanism and Short-Term Climatic Change in East Asian and World History c. 1200–1699', *Journal of World History* 12 (2001): 56. K. Briffa et al., 'Influence of Volcanic Eruptions on Northern Hemisphere Summer Temperature', 454. Jean M. Grove, *Little Ice Ages: Ancient and Modern, Vol. I.* (London: Routledge, 2004), 181. Hans W. Linderholm et al., 'Fennoscandia Revisited: A Spatially Improved Tree-Ring Reconstruction of Summer Temperatures for the Last 900 Years'. *Climate Dynamics* 45 (2015): 944. Lea Schneider et al., 'Revising Midlatitude Summer Temperatures Back to AD600 Based on a Wood Density Network', *Geophysical Research Letters* 42 (2015): 4556. Rüdiger Glaser, *Klimageschichte Mitteleuropas. 1000 Jahre Wetter, Klima, Katastrophen.* (Darmstadt: Buchgesellschaft, 2001), 58. Christian Pfister and Rudolf Brázdil, 'Climatic Variability in Sixteenth-Century Europe and Its Social Dimension: A Synthesis', *Climatic Change* 43:1 (1999): 32. Eduardo Moreno-Chamarro et al., 'Winter Amplification of the European Little Ice Age Cooling by the Subpolar Gyre', *Nature Scientific Reports* 7 (2017): 3.

[24] Pablo Ortega et al., 'A Model-Tested North Atlantic Oscillation Reconstruction for the Past Millennium'. *Nature* 523:7558 (2015): 72. Rahmstorf et al., 'Exceptional Twentieth-Century Slowdown in Atlantic Ocean Overturning Circulation', 477. Gray, 'A Tree-Ring Based Reconstruction of the Atlantic Multidecadal Oscillation since 1567 AD', 2. Rosanne D'Arrigo et al., 'A Reconstructed Siberian High index since AD 1599 from Eurasian and North American Tree Rings'. *Geophysical Research Letters* 32:5 (2005): 2.

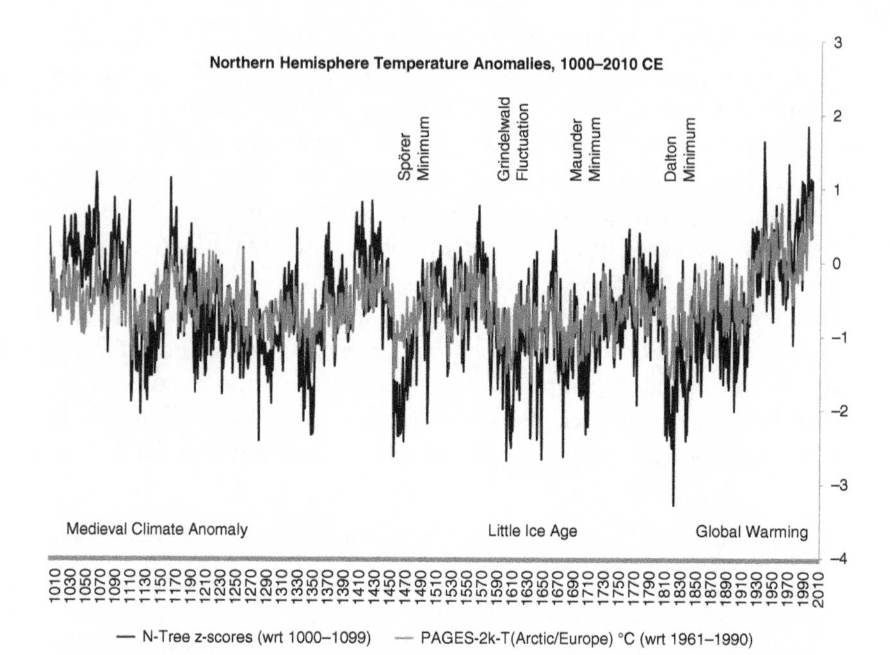

FIGURE 1.1 Northern Hemisphere tree growth anomalies relative to the 1000–1099 CE average (black) and European and Arctic summer temperature anomalies relative to the 1961–1990 average (grey) over the past millennium. Source: M. Sigl et al., 'Timing and Climate Forcing of Volcanic Eruptions for the Past 2,500 Years', *Nature* 523 (2015): 545.

across parts of Northwestern Europe, especially during spring and autumn. Early in the Grindelwald Fluctuation, the very warm state of the AMO, and the weakly positive setting of the NAO, may have been partially responsible.[25]

During the coldest years of the Grindelwald Fluctuation (Figure 1.1), the growing season in Northern Europe declined by as many as six weeks. That encouraged farmers to abandon wheat, which thrives in warm, dry conditions, for cold-weather crops like barley, oats, or rye. In sixteenth-century Northwestern Europe, agricultural commercialization and

[25] Christopher M. Moy et al., 'Variability of El Niño/Southern Oscillation Activity at Millennial Timescales during the Holocene Epoch'. *Nature* 420:6912 (2002): 163. Jeff R. Knight, Chris K. Folland, and Adam A. Scaife, 'Climate Impacts of the Atlantic Multidecadal Oscillation'. *Geophysical Research Letters* 33:17 (2006): 3. Joëlle Gergis and Anthony Fowler, 'A History of ENSO Events since A.D. 1525: Implications for Future Climate Change', *Climatic Change* 92 (2009): 343–387.

increasingly sophisticated networks of transportation lowered the risk of starvation. Yet across Europe, harvest failures could still provoke famines, especially when wars coincided with extreme weather in economically underdeveloped areas. Food shortages and malnutrition again contributed to the spread of disease in animals and their human masters. For Europeans, the perception of worsening weather was nearly as important as the reality. Witch hunts found scapegoats in women and men blamed for the related ills of harmful weather, famine, and 'unnatural' diseases.[26]

Conditions were no less severe beyond Europe. In the Ottoman Empire, then encroaching on Europe, the onset of the Grindelwald Fluctuation brought dry, frigid winters and springs that contributed to devastating famines and cattle plagues. Owing perhaps to the strengthening Siberian High, frigid temperatures and a truly catastrophic drought stretched across Anatolia in the early 1590s. At the same time, the Ottomans embarked on costly military campaigns that strained their capacity to extract resources from overpopulated hinterlands. Famines and then banditry devastated the Anatolian countryside, while starvation sapped the strength of the Ottoman army. In Africa, dramatic swings between wet and dry conditions temporarily opened a pathway through the Sahara from Morocco to Timbuktu, the capital of the vast but declining Songhai Empire. Moroccan soldiers, equipped with European firearms, used this path to sack the Songhai capitol of Timbuktu.[27]

The first decades of the seventeenth century were bitterly cold across much of the Northern Hemisphere, yet solar activity was on the rise. In the fourth decade of the seventeenth century, average temperatures increased while storm frequency decreased in most of the hemisphere, despite fresh volcanic eruptions. The Siberian High weakened dramatically and the NAO switched into a strong positive phase, bringing more westerly winds to Europe. The AMO remained cool, however, which may have reduced precipitation across the continent. Across much of the

[26] Behringer, *A Cultural History of Climate*, 117. Wolfgang Behringer, 'Climatic Change and Witch-Hunting: The Impact of the Little Ice Age on Mentalities', *Climatic Change* 43:1 (1999), 345. Pfister, 'Climatic Extremes, Recurrent Crises and Witch Hunts', 37. Bauernfeind and Woitek, 'The Influence of Climatic Change on Price Fluctuations in Germany', 307. Parker, *Global Crisis*, 18.

[27] Sam White, *The Climate of Rebellion in the Early Modern Ottoman Empire*. (Cambridge: Cambridge University Press, 2011), 72. Parker, *Global Crisis*, 197. Brooke, *Climate Change and the Course of Global History*, 449. Matthew D. Jones et al., 'A High-Resolution Late Holocene Lake Isotope Record from Turkey and Links to North Atlantic and Monsoon Climate'. *Geology* 34:5 (2006): 361.

world, slightly warmer and more stable conditions would last into the 1640s.[28]

By 1645, solar activity, measured by sunspot counts, started to decline, and average annual temperatures fell with them, especially in winter and spring. Volcanic eruptions again contributed to the cooling, and before long average temperatures across much of the Northern Hemisphere slipped to roughly 1 degree Celsius below the twentieth-century average. Atmospheric and oceanic circulation responded and caused significant regional shifts in average annual precipitation and storm frequency. This third great cold phase of the Little Ice Age is called the Maunder Minimum. It is named after Edward Maunder, a nineteenth-century astronomer who, like Spörer, reconstructed sunspot observations. Both the NAO and the AO gradually shifted into a negative position that endured, with some variations, until the early eighteenth century. The Siberian High, by contrast, fluctuated for the entire Maunder Minimum, while the AMO actually reached a warm state that lingered until around 1710.[29]

In the northern periphery of Europe, cooler temperatures and shifting vegetation ranges again complicated pastoral and agricultural systems. In Iceland, cooler temperatures encouraged destructive overgrazing, and that combined with increasing storminess to cause rapid erosion. In the northern reaches of continental Europe, more farmers reared sheep instead of cows, which were harder to support in chilly temperatures. Many struggled to adapt as the cultivation limit of common crops shifted

[28] Gray, 'A Tree-Ring Based Reconstruction of the Atlantic Multidecadal Oscillation since 1567 AD', 2. Ortega et al., 'A Model-Tested North Atlantic Oscillation Reconstruction for the Past Millennium', 72. Jee-Hoon Jeong et al., 'Recent Recovery of the Siberian High Intensity'. *Journal of Geophysical Research: Atmospheres* 116:D23 (2011): 3.

[29] Rosanne D. D'Arrigo et al., 'Tree-Ring Reconstructions of Temperature and Sea-Level Pressure Variability Associated with the Warm-Season Arctic Oscillation since AD 1650'. *Geophysical Research Letters* 30:11 (2003): 3. John A. Eddy, 'The Maunder Minimum'. *Science* 192:4245 (1976): 1190. John A. Eddy, 'Climate and the Changing Sun'. *Climatic Change* 1 (1977): 181. Stuiver and Quay, 'Changes in Atmospheric Carbon-14', 11. José M. Vaquero et al., 'Revisited Sunspot Data: A New Scenario for the Onset of the Maunder Minimum'. *The Astrophysical Journal Letters* 731:2 (2011): 1. Briffa et al., 'Influence of Volcanic Eruptions on Northern Hemisphere Summer Temperature', 454. Sigl, et al., 'Timing and Climate Forcing of Volcanic Eruptions', 546. Ortega et al., 'A Model-Tested North Atlantic Oscillation Reconstruction for the Past Millennium', 72. Briffa, Osborn and Schweingruber, 'Large-Scale Temperature Inferences from Tree Rings: A Review', 23. Gray, 'A Tree-Ring Based Reconstruction of the Atlantic Multidecadal Oscillation since 1567 AD', 2. Moinuddin Ahmed et al., 'Continental-Scale Temperature Variability during the Past Two Millennia'. *Nature Geoscience* 6:5 (2013): 341.

further south. Wild plant diversity probably decreased at high altitudes and latitudes. Wild animals behaved differently, too. Scavenging wolves, for example, invaded villages during cold winters, while vultures departed the frigid Alps. Northern European rivers froze over completely during the coldest winters of the period, halting lines of trade and communication by water. In many winters, temperatures stayed so low, for so long, that the ice was thick enough and lasted long enough to support festivals called 'frost fairs'. The sense of solidarity in these fairs stood in sharp contrast to the feelings that animated European witch-hunts, which resumed again during the 1690s, a decade of volcanic eruptions that, in many regions, was the chilliest of the Maunder Minimum.[30]

Not all places endured a distinct Grindelwald Fluctuation and Maunder Minimum, with a warmer interlude in between. Across much of North America, for example, temperature fluctuations in the seventeenth century may not have closely mirrored those in Europe. There was also considerable diversity in the climatic trends that played out in different North American regions. Still, the seventeenth century was overall chillier in North America than the preceding or subsequent centuries, and landmark cold seasons – such as the frigid winter of 1657/1658 – affected both shores of the Atlantic. The consequences of such weather could be as devastating in North America as they were in Europe. The first settlers to Jamestown, Virginia, for example, had the misfortune of arriving during some of the chilliest and driest weather of the Little Ice Age in that region. Crop failures contributed to the dreadful mortality rates endured by the colonists, and to the brief abandonment of their settlement in 1610.[31]

[30] Behringer, *A Cultural History of Climate*, 96. Hubert Lamb, *Historic Storms of the North Sea, British Isles, and Northwest Europe*. (Cambridge: Cambridge University Press, 1991), 22. Jürg Luterbacher, 'The Late Maunder Minimum (1675–1715) – Climax of the "Little Ice Age" in Europe'. In *History and Climate: Memories of the Future?*, eds. P. D. Jones et al. (New York: Kluwer Academic/Plenum Publishers, 2001), 30.

[31] V. Trouet et al., 'A 1500-Year Reconstruction of Annual Mean Temperature for Temperate North America on Decadal-to-Multidecadal Time Scales'. *Environmental Research Letters* 8:2 (2013): 6. Parker, *Global Crisis*, 6. David W. Stahle and Malcolm K. Cleaveland, 'Tree-Ring Reconstructed Rainfall over the Southeastern U.S.A. during the Medieval Warm Period and Little Ice Age'. *Climatic Change* 26 (1994): 206. R. D. D'Arrigo and G. C. Jacoby Jr., 'Dendroclimatic Evidence from Northern North America'. In *Climate Since A.D. 1500*, eds. Raymond S. Bradley and Philip D. Jones. (New York: Routledge, 2003), 302. Mann, 'The Little Ice Age', 1259. John P. Cropper and Harold C. Fritts, 'Tree-Ring Width Chronologies from the North American Arctic'. *Arctic and Alpine Research* 13:2 (1981): 249. H. C. Fritts and X. M. Shao, 'Mapping Climate Using Tree-Rings from Western North America', in *Climate Since A.D. 1500*, 279. W. R. Baron, 'Historical Climate Records from the Northeastern United States,

Central China also did not enjoy a mid-seventeenth century reprieve from the Little Ice Age. In fact, it was bitterly cold in the 1630s and early 1640s, just as average temperatures warmed modestly elsewhere. Chilly weather and precipitation extremes ruined crops on a vast scale, worsening famines that caused particular distress in overpopulated regions. The ruling Ming Dynasty seemed to have lost the 'mandate of heaven', the divine sanction that, according to Confucian doctrine, kept the weather in check. Deeply corrupt, riven by factional politics, undermined by an obsolete examination system for aspiring bureaucrats, and scornful of martial culture, the regime could neither adequately address widespread starvation nor the banditry it encouraged. Climatic cooling caused even more severe suffering in neighbouring, militaristic Manchuria. There, the solution seemed clear: to invade China and plunder its wealth. The Manchus raided and ultimately conquered China, founding the Qing Dynasty in 1644. In some regions, then, cooling and crises endured well past 1628 and continued with no interruption into the late seventeenth century, with profound social consequences. Yet average temperatures in Northeast and Northwest China did rise during the middle of the seventeenth century. The notion that the Grindelwald Fluctuation and Maunder Minimum were distinct cold periods has value well beyond Europe and the Arctic, but should be applied with caution outside these regions.[32]

Attempts to precisely date the beginning and end of just about any recent climatic regime are sure to set off controversy. This is not only because global climate changes had diverse manifestations from region to region, but also because climate changes involved much more than shifts

1640 to 1900', in *Climate Since A.D. 1500*, 83. T. M. Cronin et al., 'Medieval Warm Period, Little Ice Age and 20th Century Temperature Variability from Chesapeake Bay'. *Global and Planetary Change* 36:1–2 (2003): 17. David W. Stahle et al., 'The Lost Colony and Jamestown Droughts'. *Science* 280:5363 (1998): 564. Dennis B. Blanton, 'Drought as a Factor in the Jamestown Colony, 1607–1612'. *Historical Archaeology* (2000): 76. See also: Sam White, Richard Tucker, and Ken Sylvester, 'Climate and American History: The State of the Field'. In *Cultural Dynamics of Climate Change and the Environment in Northern America*, ed. Bernd Sommer. (Leiden: Brill, 2015), pp. 109–136.

[32] Parker, *Global Crisis*, 142. Q. Ge et al., 'Temperature Changes over the Past 2000 Yr in China and Comparison with the Northern Hemisphere'. *Climate of the Past* 9:3 (2013): 1156. Keyan Fang et al., 'Tree-Ring Based Reconstruction of Drought Variability (1615–2009) in the Kongtong Mountain Area, Northern China'. *Global and Planetary Change* 80 (2012): 195. Pingzhong Zhang et al., 'A Test of Climate, Sun, and Culture Relationships from an 1810-Year Chinese Cave Record'. *Science* 322:5903 (2008): 942. Weihong Qian and Yafen Zhu, 'Little Ice Age Climate near Beijing, China, Inferred from Historical and Stalagmite Records'. *Quaternary Research* 57:1 (2002): 117.

in average annual temperature. Changes in oceanic and atmospheric circulation, for example, rarely responded immediately or simply to changes in average global temperatures. It is therefore hard to figure out whether the Maunder Minimum reached Northwestern Europe when average annual temperatures declined, when storminess increased, when average annual precipitation rose, or when weather became less predictable from year to year.

Wolfgang Behringer and other historians have argued that scholars should consider the 'subjective factor' of human responses to weather when dating past climatic regimes. According to this view, the Maunder Minimum, for example, did not begin when temperatures started declining, but when that decline was, for the first time, deep enough to trigger weather that profoundly altered human lives. When we consider climate changes in this way, we may be more inclined to subjectively date climatic regimes using extreme events, such as 'years without summer'. Dating climate changes with an eye to social consequences does take us away from the statistical methods and conclusions pioneered by scientists, but it draws us closer to the human subjects of historical research. In this book, the dates for climatic regimes reflect, first and foremost, long-term and large-scale changes in average annual temperature and, importantly, their causes. Yet they also take into account distinct regional chronologies for changes in prevailing weather, and changes in atmospheric or oceanic circulation that often meant more to the Dutch than shifts in average annual temperatures.[33]

Whatever methods we use to date climate changes, and whatever regional variations we may unearth, it seems certain that the years between 1560 and 1720 constituted the chilliest stretch, or nadir, of a worldwide Little Ice Age. In Europe, changes in prevailing weather contributed to ruined harvests, food shortages, commodity price increases, human and animal epidemics, social unrest, and ultimately outbreaks of violence that destabilized one society after another. According to a growing group of historians, this calamitous sequence of events amounted to a 'general crisis' that followed from a tragic intersection of dramatic climate change and acute societal vulnerability. Endemic religious wars compounded the effects of inflation created by imports of gold and silver from the New World, just as rising populations strained the limits of contemporary agriculture. Societies that in the best of times relied on meagre agricultural surpluses simply lacked the technology and flexibility to quickly adapt to new environmental

[33] Behringer, 'Climatic Change and Witch-Hunting', 345.

circumstances. In France, the Holy Roman Empire, Iberia, Scotland, and many other countries or regions, the psychological, economic, and demographic consequences were staggering.[34]

Recently, Geoffrey Parker argued that the seventeenth-century general crisis engulfed the whole world. During this global crisis, a third of Earth's population died in disasters either triggered or worsened by climatic cooling. In Russia, for example, droughts and subsequent food shortages probably helped incite bloody popular revolts that empowered nobles to entrench exploitative serfdom. In Mughal India, monsoon failures led to devastating famines that compounded the deprivations of military campaigns. Droughts and locust plagues in western Africa created ideal conditions for outbreaks of disease that helped destabilize Kongo, one of the few African states that had been powerful enough to resist European encroachment. Overall, according to Parker, the global crisis saw 'more cases of simultaneous state breakdown around the globe than any previous or subsequent age'. Regional specialists have taken issue with some of Parker's claims, emphasizing instead the political ideals and ambitions that provoked many rebellions, and the complex aspirations of ordinary people in crowds that rioted amid, but not necessarily because of, subsistence crises. Nevertheless, the global crisis concept helps unify hundreds of books and articles in climate history that all deal with examples of disaster in the Little Ice Age.[35]

[34] White, *The Climate of Rebellion in the Early Modern Ottoman Empire*, 7. Sam White, 'Animals, Climate Change, and History'. *Environmental History* 19 (2014): 322. Bell, 'The Little Ice Age and the Jews', 12. Behringer, *A Cultural History of Climate*, 105, 146. Brown, *History and Climate Change*, 251. Karen J. Cullen, *Famine in Scotland: The "Ill Years" of the 1690s*. (Edinburgh: Edinburgh University Press Ltd., 2010), 2. Pfister, 'Climatic Extremes, Recurrent Crises and Witch Hunts', 50. Christian Pfister and Rudolf Brazdil, 'Social Vulnerability to Climate in the "Little Ice Age": An Example from Central Europe in the Early 1770s'. *Climate of the Past Discussions* 2.2 (2006): 123. Lamb, *Climate, History, and the Modern World*, 199. Erich Landsteiner, 'Wenig Brot und saurer wein: Kontinuität ud Wandel in der zentraleuropäischen Ernährungskulter im letzen Drittel des 16. Jahrhunderts'. In *Kulturelle Konsequenzen der 'Kleinen Eiszeit'*, eds. Wolfgang Behringer, Hartmut Lehmann, and Christian Pfister. (Göttingen: Vandenhoeck & Ruprecht, 2005), 109. Brazdil et al., 'Historical Climatology in Europe – the State of the Art', 404. De Vries, 'The Economic Crisis of the Seventeenth Century', 160. Parker, *Global Crisis*, 249. Geoffrey Parker, 'Crisis and Catastrophe: The Global Crisis of the Seventeenth Century Reconsidered'. *American Historical Review* 113 (2008): 1056. Brooke, *Climate Change and the Course of Global History*, 447.

[35] John Brooke, *Climate Change and the Course of Global History*, 446. Parker, *Global Crisis*, xix, 166, 410, 479. Parker, 'Crisis and Catastrophe: The Global Crisis of the Seventeenth Century Reconsidered', 1053. William M. Cavert, 'Winter and Discontent in Early Modern England'. In *Governing the Environment in the Early Modern World:*

Temperatures across the Northern Hemisphere recovered by around 1720. In subsequent decades, only frigid winters in the early 1740s interrupted a warmer and in many places drier and more tranquil climatic regime. Then, beginning in the 1760s, Earth's average temperature started falling again. Volcanic eruptions compounded the cooling influence of dropping solar radiation, the NAO switched to a strongly negative position, the AMO cooled considerably, and the Siberian High strengthened. This final cold phase of the Little Ice Age is called the Dalton Minimum (1760–1850), after yet another sunspot-tracking astronomer. At last, between 1850 and 1900, the world escaped from the Little Ice Age, although it soon fell into the human-made crisis of global warming.[36]

THE LITTLE ICE AGE IN THE DUTCH REPUBLIC

Changes in average annual temperatures in the Low Countries roughly mirrored broader Northern Hemisphere trends. Average annual temperatures in the region declined sharply with the onset of the Spörer Minimum, rose in the early sixteenth century, and collapsed in all seasons with the coming of the Grindelwald Fluctuation in around 1561. Average spring, summer, autumn, and winter temperatures were especially frigid in the final decade of the sixteenth century and the first decade of the seventeenth century. Thereafter, both summers and winters slowly started to warm. Yet the chilly, unpredictable weather of the Grindelwald Fluctuation endured in the Low Countries, as it did across the Northern Hemisphere, until the 'year without summer' in 1628 (Figure 1.2).[37]

Theory and Practice, eds. Sara Miglietti and John Morgan. (London: Routledge, 2017), 117.

36 Robert M. Wilson, 'Volcanism, Cold Temperature and Paucity of Sunspot Observing Days (1818–1858): A Connection?' The Smithsonian/NASA Astrophysics Data System, 1998. Accessed 7 July 2012, http://ntrs.nasa.gov/archive/nasa/casi.ntrs.nasa.gov/19980233233.pdf. Fredrik Charpentier Ljungqvist, 'A New Reconstruction of Temperature Variability in the Extra-Tropical Northern Hemisphere during the Last Two Millennia', *Geografiska Annaler: Series A, Physical Geography* 92:3 (2010): 344. Sebastian Wagner and Eduardo Zorita, 'The influence of Volcanic, Solar and CO2 Forcing on the Temperatures in the Dalton Minimum (1790–1830): A Model Study', *Climate Dynamics* 25 (2005): 210. Ortega et al., 'A Model-Tested North Atlantic Oscillation Reconstruction for the Past Millennium', 72. Gray, 'A Tree-Ring Based Reconstruction of the Atlantic Multidecadal Oscillation since 1567 AD', 2. Jeong et al., 'Recent Recovery of the Siberian High intensity', 3.

37 Shabalova and Van Engelen, 'Evaluation of a Reconstruction of Temperature in the Low Countries', 236. Van Engelen, Buisman and IJnsen, 'A Millennium of Weather, Winds and Water in the Low Countries', 112.

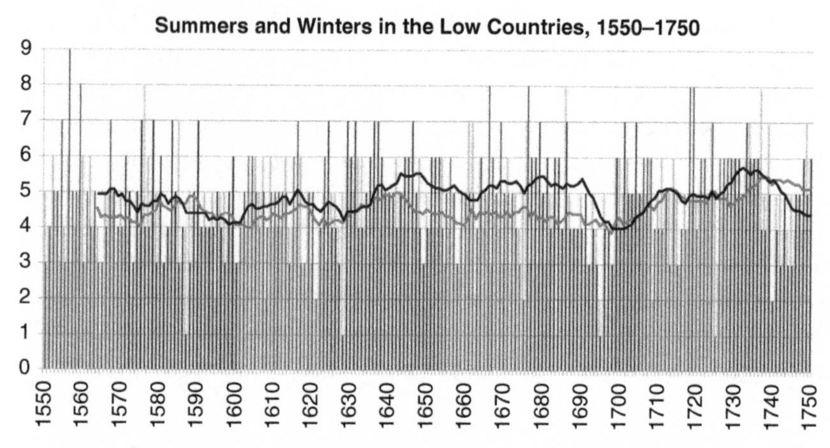

FIGURE 1.2 A graph, compiled using documentary evidence, showing winter (grey) and summer (black) temperature changes in the Low Countries from 1550 to 1750. Higher readings for summer (May, June, July, August, and September) and winter (November, December, January, February, and March) correspond to higher temperatures. A 15-year moving average shows the trends.
Source: Van Engelen, Buisman, and IJnsen, 'A Millennium of Weather, Winds and Water in the Low Countries', 112.

After 1628, average temperatures across the Low Countries warmed in all seasons until the onset of the Maunder Minimum in around 1645. Then, average seasonal temperatures gradually declined until around 1660. Yet summers remained far hotter relative to twentieth-century averages than winters were colder, and both seasons were warmer from 1629 to 1660 than they were for the two centuries between 1550 and 1750. Both year-to-year winter and summer temperatures in the Grindelwald Fluctuation and the heart of the Maunder Minimum also varied much more than they did from 1629 to 1660 (Appendix 1).[38]

We can therefore think of the period from 1645 to 1660 as an 'Early Maunder Minimum' in the Low Countries and the surrounding region. Only after around 1660 did average winter temperatures fall to very low levels, where they remained until the end of the Maunder Minimum. Average temperatures in spring and fall were also low until the eighteenth

[38] Van Engelen, Buisman and IJnsen, 'A Millennium of Weather, Winds and Water in the Low Countries', 112.

century. By contrast, summers remained relatively warm, despite major fluctuations from year to year, until around 1690. Average temperatures in all seasons started to climb after around 1709, until the regional conclusion of the Maunder Minimum with the remarkably hot summer of 1718. In the wake of the very warm year of 1758, average regional temperatures again declined with the coming of the Dalton Minimum. The final cold phase of the Little Ice Age lasted in the Low Countries, as elsewhere, until at least 1850.[39]

Global temperature trends that manifested in the Low Countries undoubtedly reflected and helped cause changes in atmospheric and oceanic circulation. Yet regional manifestations of large-scale circulation changes can be difficult to trace using documents written in the Low Countries. Most Dutch observers only rarely mentioned ordinary rainfall and snowfall; and when they did, they did not record how much precipitation actually fell. Many did make note of floods and droughts, yet both extremes reflected not only weather and perhaps climate change but also human practices and infrastructure. Still, weather diaries and ship logbooks do provide hints that torrential downpours were more common in the Low Countries during the coldest phases of the Little Ice Age than they were before or after. Tree-ring evidence suggests that the Dutch Republic often avoided droughts that swept across Western Europe during the Little Ice Age, but usually shared in especially wet years that affected the whole continent. However, trees in northern Europe respond more strongly to variations in temperature and sunlight than precipitation.[40]

Overall, Northern European winters during the Maunder Minimum were, on average, colder and drier than they were in the twentieth century, while summers were cooler and wetter. This is what we would expect in a persistently negative NAO. In this book, I link increases in spring, summer, and autumn wetness across the Low Countries to the climate

[39] Shabalova and Van Engelen, 'Evaluation of a Reconstruction of Temperature in the Low Countries', 236. H. M. van den Dool, H. J. Krijnen and C. J. E. Schuurmans, 'Average Winter Temperatures at De Bilt (the Netherlands) 1634–1977', *Climatic Change* 1 (1978): 327. Buisman, *Duizend jaar Vol. IV*, 707.

[40] Raible, 'Climate Variability – Observations, Reconstructions, and Model Simulations for the Atlantic-European and Alpine Region', 19. Dennis Wheeler, 'British Naval Logbooks from the Late Seventeenth Century', 142. Andreas Pauling et al., 'Five Hundred Years of Gridded High-Resolution Precipitation Reconstructions over Europe and the Connection to Large-Scale Circulation'. *Climate Dynamics* 26:4 (2006): 392. 'The Old World Drought Atlas'. The International Research Institute for Climate and Society, Columbia University. Accessed 28 June 2016, http://iridl.ldeo.columbia.edu/expert/home/.jennie/.PDSI/.OWDA/.pdsi/figviewer.html.

of the Grindelwald Fluctuation and the Maunder Minimum, except where documentary evidence points in a different direction.[41]

The coldest periods of the Little Ice Age may also have increased the frequency and severity of storms across Northwestern Europe. Scientists had assumed that lower sea levels in the chilliest stretches of the Little Ice Age would lead to fewer storm inundations, or 'surges', in the region. Beginning in 1975, however, Elisabeth Gottschalk published compelling evidence for a rise in storm surges across the Low Countries during the Grindelwald Fluctuation, a decline after 1630, and a sharp increase in the Maunder Minimum. In 1984, Hubert Lamb argued that severe gales were especially common in the North Sea region during the Maunder Minimum. According to Lamb, seven such storms ravaged the shores of the North Sea in the 1660s alone, compared with six in the entire first half of the seventeenth century.[42]

Fifteen years later, historical geographer Adriaan de Kraker tested these conclusions by examining the maintenance accounts of Flemish dikes and dunes. He found that severe storms in coastal Flanders were four times more common during the Grindelwald Fluctuation than they had been, although weaker storms were actually less frequent. According to De Kraker, storm activity diminished during warm or moderate winters, while intensifying in frigid winters. Yet in 2005, De Kraker tempered some of these findings. He again used accounts of dike and dune maintenance in coastal towns, but this time he analyzed only continuous, uniform data gathered over many decades. He confirmed that the Grindelwald Fluctuation was particularly stormy, but uncovered no clear link between cold winters and increases in gale frequency or severity.[43]

These conclusions are valuable, but they should be treated with caution. Maintenance accounts do not directly document storms but rather

[41] Glaser, *Klimageschichte Mitteleuropas*, 58. Buisman *Duizend jaar Vol. V*, 927.

[42] Elisabeth M. K. Gottschalk, *Stormvloeden en rivieroverstromingen in Nederland, Vol. II: de periode 1400–1600*. (Assen: Van Gorcum, 1975), 817. Elisabeth M. K. Gottschalk, *Stormvloeden en rivieroverstromingen in Nederland, Vol. III: de periode 1600–1700*. (Assen: Van Gorcum, 1977), 414. Andreas Pauling et al., 'Five hundred years of gridded high-resolution precipitation reconstructions', 392. Lamb, *Historic Storms of the North Sea, British Isles, and Northwest Europe*, 22. See also: J. P. Bakker, 'Transgressionsphasen und Sturmflutfrequenz in den Niederlanden in historischer zeit', *Verhandlungen des Deutschen Geographentages*, 232–237. Würzburg, 1957. Nienhuis, *Environmental History of the Rhine-Meuse Delta*, 240.

[43] Adriaan M. J. de Kraker, 'Reconstruction of Storm Frequency in the North Sea Area of the Preindustrial Period, 1400–1625 and the Connection with Reconstructed Time Series of Temperatures', *History of Meteorology* 2 (2005), 66. Pfister and Brázdil, 'Climatic Variability in Sixteenth-Century Europe and Its Social Dimension', 32.

the damage storms inflicted on human infrastructure. This damage registered not only the strength of a storm but also a host of local environmental and social conditions. In particular, maintenance accounts overrepresent gales that blew from the sea because such storms inflicted greater damage to dikes, dunes, and coastal towns in Flanders. The same storms were also more likely to produce the devastating surges traced by Gottschalk and Lamb.[44]

Logs kept aboard early modern ships can be much more useful than maintenance accounts for measuring changes in storm frequency and severity, because most naval officers recorded every storm that came their way. On the modern Beaufort scale of nautical wind velocity, wind speeds during a gale blow at or above BF 8 (at least 63 kilometres/hour), which creates waves more than 5.5 metres high.[45] Dennis Wheeler has studied English logbooks kept aboard ships travelling through the English Channel during the late Maunder Minimum. They suggest that winds at or above BF 8 became more common during the late Maunder Minimum. Most evidence, including some examined for the first time in this book, therefore suggests that storms were more frequent in Northwestern Europe during both the Grindelwald Fluctuation and the Maunder Minimum than they were before or after.[46]

Across the region, the climatic trends of the Little Ice Age led to changes not only in the frequency of extremes in wind velocity, but also prevailing wind direction. In today's climate, regional winds blow overwhelmingly from the west, but it was not always that way. In the 1960s, Lamb was among the first to chart gradual trends in wind direction across early modern Europe. He used weather diaries to conclude that the frequency of westerly winds over England rose in relatively warm decades of the Little Ice Age, but declined during its coldest phases.[47]

[44] Tim Soens, 'Floods and Money: Funding Drainage and Flood Control in Coastal Flanders from the Thirteenth to the Sixteenth Centuries'. *Continuity and Change* 26:3 (2011): 334. Tim Soens, 'Explaining Deficiencies of Water Management in the Late Medieval Flemish Coastal Plain, 13th–16th Centuries'. In *Water Management, Communities, and Environment: The Low Countries in Comparative Perspective, C. 1000 – C. 1800*, ed. Hilde Greefs. (Hilversum: Academia Press, 2006), 36. Nienhuis, *Environmental History of the Rhine-Meuse Delta*, 234.

[45] Ricardo García-Herrera et al., *CLIWOC Multilingual Meteorological Dictionary*, 44.

[46] Dennis Wheeler et al., 'Atmospheric Circulation and Storminess Derived from Royal Navy Logbooks: 1685 to 1750'. *Climatic Change* 18 (2009): 257. Adriaen van der Goes, 'Hage, den 8 December 1665'. In *Briefwisseling tusschen de gebroeders van der Goes (1659–1673) Vol. I*, ed. C. J. Gonnet. (Amsterdam: Johannes Müller, 1899), 221.

[47] Lamb, *Climate, History and the Modern World*, 198. Siegismund and Schrum, 'Decadal Changes in the Wind Forcing over the North Sea', 44. C. G. Korevaar, *North Sea*

Ship logbooks allow us to revisit Lamb's conclusions with more robust documentary sources. English logbooks show that westerly winds in the English Channel were rare in the Maunder Minimum from January to May, and again in September, although there were big year-to-year changes in the frequency of these winds. Logs also suggest that easterly winds were common during colder winters, and overall more frequent in winter than they are today. In particular, there seems to have been a strong correlation between northeasterly winds and chilly weather. Oceans cool or warm more slowly than land, and the warm currents brought north by AMOC flow past Europe. In cold months, westerly winds bring heat into Western Europe, but in warm months those same winds can bring cooler temperatures. If easterly winds grew more common in winter spring during the Little Ice Age, they probably brought cooler weather to the North Sea region.[48]

Dutch temperature reconstructions therefore suggest that westerly winds were usually rare in cold winters. Similarly, in the Baltic, warmer decades in the Little Ice Age probably brought more westerly winds, while colder weather after 1654 in particular ushered in more easterly winds.[49] Dutch and English sources written during the chilliest phases of the Little Ice Age confirm these relationships. For example, in 1673 the English diplomat William Temple wrote that the air above the Republic

> would be all Fog and Mist, if it were not clear'd by the sharpness of their Frosts, which never fail with every East-wind for about four Months of the year, and are much fiercer than in the same Latitude with us, because that Wind comes to them

Climate, Based on Observations from Ships and Lightvessels. (Dordrecht: Kluwer Academic Publishers, 1990), 65. 'Northeast England: Climate', Met Office. Accessed 2 February 2013, www.metoffice.gov.uk/climate/uk/ne. 'Eastern England: Climate', Met Office. Accessed 2 February 2013, www.metoffice.gov.uk/climate/uk/ee. Wheeler, 'Understanding Seventeenth-Century Ships' Logbooks', 12.

[48] Wheeler, 'British Naval Logbooks from the Late Seventeenth Century', 140. Wheeler et al., 'Atmospheric Circulation and Storminess Derived from Royal Navy Logbooks', 13. Wheeler, 'Understanding Seventeenth-Century Ships' Logbooks', 16. S. D. Outten and I. EsauI. Esau, 'A Link between Arctic Sea Ice and Recent Cooling Trends over Eurasia'. *Climatic Change* 110:3–4 (2011): 1069. See also Rüdiger Glaser and Gerhard Koslowski, 'Variations in Reconstructed Ice Winter Severity in the Western Baltic from 1501 to 1995, and Their Implications for the North Atlantic Oscillation'. *Climatic Change* 41 (1999): 188.

[49] Van Engelen, Buisman and IJnsen, 'A Millennium of Weather, Winds and Water in the Low Countries', 112. Rüdiger Glaser and Gerhard Koslowski, 'Variations in Reconstructed Ice Winter Severity in the Western Baltic from 1501 to 1995, and Their Implications for the North Atlantic Oscillation'. *Climatic Change* 41 (1999): 184.

over a mighty length of dry Continent, but is moistned by the Vapours, or softned by the warmth of the Seas motion, before it reaches us.[50]

Many other observers on both shores of the English Channel noted these same connections between freezing temperatures and easterly winds during the Maunder Minimum, especially during the winter. Either the relationship was more pronounced in winter or observers cared more, since winter freezing affected their ability to travel.[51]

The Dutch and English ship logbooks I introduce in this book support other textual evidence that shows a rise in the frequency of easterly winds and storms across the North Sea region during the Maunder Minimum. Unfortunately, very few logbooks survive from the Grindelwald Fluctuation, and we therefore have a foggier picture of regional wind directions and velocities during the late sixteenth and early seventeenth centuries. Scientific data can help fill this gap. Diverse proxy evidence has revealed that atmospheric and oceanic circulation in the Northern Atlantic changed profoundly over the course of the seventeenth century. Persistent atmospheric blocking events, for example, diverted the normal flow of westerly winds across Northern Europe. The NAO was often in a negative setting during the coldest periods of the Little Ice Age, at least in winter and autumn. That would have decreased the frequency of westerly winds, and increased the frequency of easterlies, across the northeastern Atlantic. It may also have opened the Baltic and North Sea regions to frigid meridional (that is, longitudinal) winds flowing down from the Norwegian Sea. However, a negative NAO can lead to fewer storms and less precipitation across Northwestern Europe, and as we have seen, documentary evidence suggests that just the opposite trend actually played out.[52]

[50] William Temple, *Observations upon the United Provinces of the Netherlands*, ed. George Clark. (Oxford: Clarendon Press, 1972), 79.

[51] Narbrough, 'Journal of John Narbrough, Captain of the *Fairfax*. September 18, 1672, to July 1, 1673', 95. Adriaen van der Goes, *Briefwisseling tusschen de gebroeders van der Goes (1659–1673) Vol. I*, 198. Buisman, *Duizend jaar Vol. IV*, 611.

[52] Dennis Wheeler, 'Understanding Seventeenth-Century Ships' Logbooks: An Exercise in Historical Climatology'. *Journal for Maritime Research* (2004), 16. Glaser and Koslowski, 'Variations in Reconstructed Ice Winter Severity in the Western Baltic', 188. Jürg Luterbacher et al., 'Reconstruction of Monthly NAO and EU Indices Back to AD 1675'. *Geophysical Research Letters* 26:17 (1999): 2746. Jürg Luterbacher et al., 'Extending North Atlantic Oscillation Reconstructions Back to 1500'. *Atmospheric Science Letters* 2:1–4 (2002): 120. C. Schmutz, 'Can We Trust Proxy-Based NAO Index Reconstructions?' *Geophysical Research Letters* 27:8 (2000): 1138. Heinz Wanner et al., 'North Atlantic Oscillation – Concepts and Studies'. *Surveys in*

The culprit might have been the Arctic Oscillation. It was in a negative phase during much of the Maunder Minimum, which probably brought more storms to much of Europe. In the chilliest decades of the Little Ice Age, extensive sea ice in the Greenland Sea may have also brought more storms to Northern Europe by pushing the North Atlantic storm track to the south. That would have compensated for the southward diversion of prevailing westerly winds, and the storms they brought with them, when the NAO was in a positive setting. Northwestern Europe may have been especially stormy when a strong polar vortex coincided with a negative NAO.[53]

Other changes in Northern Hemisphere circulation undoubtedly mediated the influence of the NAO on wind directions across the North Sea region. The Siberian High was very intense at the start of the seventeenth century, which probably disrupted prevailing westerly winds in Northern Europe. It then weakened for several decades, before teetering between strong and weak states during the Maunder Minimum. The AMO cooled during the Grindelwald Fluctuation, which may have strengthened westerly winds across Europe. When it warmed in the Maunder Minimum, easterlies could have become more common. Recent model simulations suggest that changes to the subpolar gyre resulted in weaker northward heat transport through the Iceland-Scotland Ridge, which in turned cooled the Nordic and Barents Seas in ways that created persistent atmospheric blocking events across Northern Europe. Scientists are still working to determine exactly how all of these pieces fit together to alter atmospheric circulation across the Northern Hemisphere.[54]

Geophysics 22:4 (2001): 322. Jürg Luterbacher et al., 'European Seasonal and Annual Temperature Variability, Trends, and Extremes since 1500'. *Science* 303:5663 (2004): 1501. Edward R. Cook, 'Multi-Proxy Reconstructions of the North Atlantic Oscillation (NAO) Index: A Critical Review and a New Well-Verified Winter NAO Index Reconstruction Back to AD 1400'. In *The North Atlantic Oscillation: Climatic Significance and Environmental Impact*, eds. James W. Hurrell et al. (Washington, DC: American Geophysical Union, 2003), 63. Valérie Trouet et al., 'Persistent Positive North Atlantic Oscillation Mode Dominated the Medieval Climate Anomaly'. *Science* 324:5923 (2009): 79.

[53] Kathrin Walter and H-F. Graf, 'The North Atlantic Variability Structure, Storm Tracks, and Precipitation depending on the Polar Vortex Strength'. *Atmospheric Chemistry and Physics* 5:1 (2005): 239. Alastair G. Dawson et al., 'Complex North Atlantic Oscillation (NAO) Index Signal of Historic North Atlantic Storm-Track Changes'. *The Holocene* 12:3 (2002): 363. D'Arrigo et al., 'Tree-Ring Reconstructions of Temperature and Sea-Level Pressure Variability Associated with the Warm-Season Arctic Oscillation since AD 1650', 3.

[54] Ortega et al., 'A Model-Tested North Atlantic Oscillation Reconstruction for the Past Millennium', 72. Reichler et al., 'A Stratospheric Connection to Atlantic Climate Variability', 783. Jeong, 'Recent Recovery of the Siberian High Intensity', 3. Gray,

All the same, scholars in many disciplines have assembled a convincing picture of how the Little Ice Age affected weather in the Low Countries and across the broader North Sea region. They have shown that the climates of both the Grindelwald Fluctuation and the Maunder Minimum were distinguished not only by very low average temperatures, but also by changes in interannual weather variability, seasonal storm frequency, average precipitation, and prevailing wind directions. As we will see, trends in these weather conditions often mattered more for Dutch citizens than gradual shifts in average temperatures.

'A Tree-Ring Based Reconstruction of the Atlantic Multidecadal Oscillation since 1567 AD', 2. Alexis Metzger and Martine Tabeaud, 'Reconstruction of the Winter Weather in East Friesland at the Turn of the Sixteenth and Seventeenth Centuries (1594–1612)'. *Climatic Change* 141:2 (2017): 333. Moreno-Chamarro et al., 'Winter Amplification of the European Little Ice Age Cooling by the Subpolar Gyre', 3.

PART ONE

COMMERCE AND CLIMATE CHANGE

Part I Preface

Fernand Braudel wrote that distance was 'the first enemy' for sixteenth-century Europeans. Even using the best technology of the day – the full-rigged sailing ship – it took months or even years to reach ports in distant continents. After spending so long in transit, goods, messages, and people rarely arrived when needed. Time spent in transit was also time exposed to the hazards of travel, such as crime, disease, deprivation, and a volatile environment. In sum, travel was dangerous, expensive, poorly planned, and, above all, time-consuming.[1]

Two big variables limited the speed and efficiency of contemporary travel: weak government authority and insufficient technology. Most governments could not collect the resources necessary to build and maintain major 'improvements' to the dirt paths and winding rivers used for transportation across most of early modern Europe. Ramshackle infrastructure exacerbated the constraints of early modern technology, which, on roads and modest waterways, primarily harnessed only the modest energies derived from human or animal muscles. European mobility was therefore hampered by the inefficiency with which energy was siphoned

[1] Braudel, *The Mediterranean and the Mediterranean World in the Age of Philip II*, Vol. I, 355. Landers, *The Field and the Forge*, 4. Peter M. Solar, 'Opening to the East: Shipping between Europe and Asia, 1770–1830'. *The Journal of Economic History* 73:3 (2013): 625. See also Bethany Aram, 'Distance and Misinformation in the Conquest of America'. In *The Limits of Empire: European Imperial Formations in Early Modern World History: Essays in Honor of Geoffrey Parker*, eds. Tonio Andrade and William Reger. (Farnham: Ashgate Publishing, 2013).

from and then applied to environments only lightly touched by human activity.[2]

Dutch citizens fuelled their republic's rise to global commercial primacy by engaging in and improving modes of travel that could either access more energy, or could use modest amounts of energy more efficiently. Dutch merchant vessels usually harnessed the power of wind, not muscle, and together constituted a greater share of total energy use in the republic than they did elsewhere in Europe. The transportation of people, goods, and information across significant distances within the republic's coastal provinces was overwhelmingly undertaken by boat or barge. Even vessels without sails used the limited energy provided by human or animal muscles to drag heavy cargo easily across the relatively frictionless surface of water.[3]

In the seventeenth-century Dutch Republic, human activity and changing environmental conditions created a vast hybrid of natural and artificial transportation networks that sustained the relatively modern economy of the coastal provinces. Ships sailing through these networks hauled commodities on a scale that still impresses. The VOC, for example, manufactured and equipped 1,581 vessels in its lifetime, and its biggest ships – its East Indiamen – displaced well over 1,000 tons. In 1636, perhaps 1,750 smaller but still substantial merchant vessels supported Dutch trade in European waters. By then, Dutch merchants dominated seaborne trade in ports from Archangel in the far north to Constantinople in the south. Another 450 ships of no more than 80 tons plied the sea trades near the republic's home waters.[4]

By the middle of the seventeenth century, Dutch ocean-going vessels had a total carrying capacity of over 400,000 tons. In the cities of the republic, some of the raw materials carried by this immense fleet were consumed, refined, and worked into finished goods. A correspondingly huge number of light vessels ferried goods, people, and information through the lakes, rivers, channels, and creeks of the republic itself. Comprehensive figures dating from the Golden Age are not available,

[2] Catherine Delano-Smith, 'Milieus of Mobility: Itineraries, Route Maps and Road Maps'. In *Cartographies of Travel and Navigation*, ed. James R. Akerman. (Chicago: University of Chicago Press, 2006), 29. Smil, *Energy in World History*, 229.

[3] Richard Unger, 'Energy Sources for the Dutch Golden Age: Peat, Wind and Coal', 228. Frits H. Horsten, *Doorgaande wegen in Nederland, 16e tot 19e eeuw: Een historische wegenatlas*. (Amsterdam: Uitgeverij Aksant, 2005), 47.

[4] De Vries and Van der Woude, *The First Modern Economy*, 404. Israel, *The Dutch Republic*, 314, 940. Stevens, *Dutch Enterprise and the VOC*, 25.

yet statistics compiled in 1808 reveal that 18,421 inland commercial vessels, from small boats to 60-ton barges, possessed a total carrying capacity of more than 250,000 tons. Given the economic stagnation of the Low Countries in the eighteenth century, that number had probably changed little since the seventeenth century. The volume of travel over the republic's dirt roads was insignificant by comparison, except in the poor, dry, and hilly provinces and territories that surrounded the coastal provinces.[5]

Travel through much of the republic was not necessarily faster than it was elsewhere in Europe. Rather, it was the reliability, frequency, and flexibility of transportation services in the coastal provinces that impressed travellers. Transportation costs were also low overall, while carrying capacity was very high. Many of these advantages ultimately flowed from the efficiency with which waterborne travel harnessed energy.[6]

Climate change profoundly affected the republic's remarkable transportation network. The following chapters give a representative analysis of interactions between climate change, weather, and movement through the republic's expanding commercial world. They begin by examining celebrated voyages at the periphery of the Dutch trading empire, but ultimately consider humbler trips across muddy paths, over frozen lakes, and through winding creeks. They show that climate changes during the Little Ice Age aided some kinds of movement but hindered others, in ways that, overall, offered more advantages than disadvantages for Dutch merchants and mariners. 'In the sixteenth century', Braudel wrote, 'all timetables were completely dependent on the weather. Irregularity was the rule'. Certainly, but changes in prevailing weather could rewrite that rule on a grand scale.[7]

[5] De Vries and Van der Woude, *The First Modern Economy*, 191.
[6] De Vries and Van der Woude, *The First Modern Economy*, 192.
[7] Braudel, *The Mediterranean and the Mediterranean World in the Age of Philip II*, Vol. I, 360.

2

Reaching Asia in a Stormy, Chilly Climate

In the 1570s and '80s, war in the southern Low Countries devastated Antwerp and forced many of its leading merchants to flee abroad. Then, in the 1590s, a series of military victories by the newly founded Dutch Republic convinced many of these merchants to settle in the burgeoning commercial cities of its coastal provinces. Meanwhile, Spanish embargoes disrupted a lucrative Dutch trade in the spices, textiles, and other Asian commodities brought to Europe aboard Iberian ships. Merchants newly arrived in the republic aimed to circumvent the embargoes by establishing their own direct commercial connections with Asian markets. At first, their prospects for success did not seem promising. The Portuguese Empire had dominated commerce between Asia and Europe since the fifteenth century, and in 1580 its crown had been united with that of Spain. The same Iberians who threatened the republic's very survival were firmly ensconced in Asia, and Dutch merchants lacked the Asian allies and cartographical knowledge necessary to challenge them.[1]

Many merchants therefore looked north. Cartographers in the republic's coastal cities guessed that sailing to Asia through the Russian Arctic would shorten the journey by two-thirds. Yet this route, widely called the 'Northeast Passage', was for the moment uncharted. Dutch merchants believed that finding it would earn them great profits and, at a stroke, alter the strategic balance between Spain and the Dutch Republic. Today, rising traffic through the Northeast Passage demonstrates the fundamentally sound logic behind these ambitions. Yet whereas modern exploitation of

[1] Gaastra, *The Dutch East India Company*, 12. Israel, *The Dutch Republic*, 324. G. V. Scammell, *The First Imperial Age: European Overseas Expansion c. 1400–1715*. (Abingdon: Routledge, 1989), 97.

the Arctic is made possible by a warming climate, the Dutch quest for the Northeast Passage coincided with the cooling of the Grindelwald Fluctuation. At first glance, the environmental circumstances for northern exploration could not have been worse.

In 1594, 1595, and 1596, Dutch entrepreneurs and explorers launched their most ambitious expeditions in search of the Northeast Passage. All succumbed either to sea ice or the threat of sea ice before they had pressed far into the Arctic. Yet the journeys were not simple failures, foiled by cold weather. Each expedition actually responded to a suite of occasionally counterbalancing, sometimes mutually reinforcing interactions between the Arctic and subarctic atmosphere, hydrosphere, cryosphere, and biosphere. In 1594, an unusually warm summer helped the first expedition penetrate deeply into the Arctic. Its sailors did not uncover the Northeast Passage, but their discoveries suggested to them that such a passage would be possible. Dutch merchants therefore financed two more expeditions, in 1595 and 1596. Both faced sea ice and frigid temperatures more typical of the Grindelwald Fluctuation, which blocked access to the Northeast Passage. Yet a cooler climate also interacted with diverse regional environments to encourage the exploration of previously uncharted islands.

New discoveries helped revolutionize European understandings of the Arctic, and uncovered lucrative resources that were later exploited by economically important and ecologically transformative new industries. The Dutch soon dominated an Arctic whaling industry that centred on newly discovered islands. Its history was also influenced by shifts in sea-ice extent that responded to changing temperatures. In a sense, dynamic interactions between global climate change and regional Arctic environments meant that, in the far north, dynamic environments helped shape their exploration, interpretation, and ultimately exploitation by European adventurers.

Arctic exploration did not end with the Barents expeditions, yet from the mid-1590s Dutch merchants increasingly invested in the southern route to Asia. They formed small, so-called precursor companies that quickly exposed both the weak hold of the Iberians over Asian commerce and the disadvantages of competition among Dutch mercantile interests. On 20 March 1602, the republic's highest body, the States-General, therefore issued a charter that merged these companies to form the VOC. The operations of the VOC, like the journeys in search of the Northeast Passage, were influenced by the climatic shifts of the Little Ice Age.[2]

[2] Gaatstra, *The Dutch East India Company*, 119. Harm Stevens, *Dutch Enterprise and the VOC: 1602–1799*. (Zutphen: Walburg Pers, 1998), 16.

For the VOC to exploit price fluctuations in different ports while defending its control of Asian waters, the traffic in goods and information carried aboard its biggest ships – its East Indiamen – needed to be reliable, inexpensive, and swift. These necessities were linked: the price of commerce rose if vessels were lost, while the possibilities for disaster increased the longer a ship was at sea.[3] The dependability, expense, and duration of VOC voyages all responded to evolving relationships between climate changes, patterns of prevailing wind, and daily weather. During the frigid Maunder Minimum (1645–1720), changes in atmospheric circulation across the northern Atlantic likely increased the sailing speed of vessels departing the republic, relative to the velocity of outbound ships in preceding, warmer decades. Ships returning to the republic from Asian ports, however, took a different route than ships sailing from the republic and were more ambiguously affected by new wind patterns. Overall, the influence of changes in prevailing wind during the Maunder Minimum probably decreased the duration of VOC voyages.

During the Maunder Minimum, VOC crews also encountered more storms, especially in the North Sea region (Map M2). Most storms do not appear to have directly imperilled the largest VOC vessels. They were bigger and sturdier than most other merchant ships, and usually sailed far from potentially threatening lee shores. Nevertheless, storms had an important but complex influence on VOC journeys. Gales routinely scattered fleets and damaged individual ships. Yet, when high winds blew in a favourable direction, storms could propel vessels at high speeds, shortening their time in transit between Europe and Asia. All things considered, weather that became more common during the Maunder Minimum benefitted the VOC, although these benefits were fickle and, to some extent, shared by other merchant companies.

PLANNING THE BARENTS EXPEDITIONS IN THE GRINDELWALD FLUCTUATION

In the 1590s, a group led by merchant Jan Huyghen van Linschoten and publisher-cartographer Lucas Waghenaer formed in the town of Enkhuizen (Map M1), its purpose dedicated to exploring and exploiting the Northeast Passage to Asia. Another circle committed to the passage coalesced in Amsterdam under the leadership of publisher Cornelis Claes, cartographer-clergyman Petrus Plancius, and cartographer-navigator Willem Barents. The entrepreneurs hoped to secure exclusive rights to

[3] Gaastra, *The Dutch East India Company*, 111.

northern trade route, and planned to build fortresses amid the ice that would defend these routes from Iberian usurpers.[4] At first, the wealthy and ambitious merchant Balthasar de Moucheron financed these expeditions. De Moucheron drew on his friendship with celebrated cartographer Gerard Mercator to provide the latest cartographical information. Mercator's first maps of the Arctic depicted a polar continent that was joined to the European mainland and thus afforded no passage by sea to Asia. Yet by the late sixteenth century, Mercator had become convinced that the Northeast Passage was not only possible but in fact 'doutlesse verie easie and short'. Finding it would yield a new map – in effect, a key – that would unlock Dutch trade with Asia through the far north.[5]

In the sixteenth century, European descriptions of the Arctic still entertained readers with accounts of exotic civilizations, fearsome monsters, and fantastic treasures. Yet among scholars and mariners, understandings of the far north were steadily improving. Midway through the century, cartographers revised ancient maps that depicted a vast Arctic continent. New maps had four continents that surrounded a towering magnetic mountain. That concept was inspired by newly popularized observations made by Nicholas of Lynn in 1360, which had outlived the more reliable records of earlier Norse explorers. Then, from the middle of the sixteenth century, forays into the waters north of Europe charted parts of the Scandinavian and Russian coast with increasing accuracy. This allowed the Dutch entrepreneurs to focus on the newly discovered realm of Novaya Zemlya, which lay in the possible path of the Northeast Passage.[6]

Long known to Russian hunters, Novaya Zemlya was discovered for the Dutch by the merchant Olivier Brunel in the cold 1570s. The fragmentary records that survive to document his voyages reveal that further progress east

[4] Peter van der Krogt, *Joan Blaeu, Atlas Major of 1665*. (Cologne: Taschen, 2010), 35. Zeeberg, *Terugkeer naar Nova Zembla*, 26. Hellinga, *Pioniers van de Gouden Eeuw*. (Zutphen: Walburg Pers, 2007), 31. Kees Zandvliet, *Mapping for Money: Maps, Plans and Topographical Paintings and Their Role in Dutch Overseas Expansion during the 16th and 17th Centuries*. (Amsterdam: Batavian Lion International, 2002), 62.

[5] Marijke Spies, *Arctic Routes to Fabled Lands: Olivier Brunel and the Passage to China and Cathay in the Sixteenth Century*. (Amsterdam: Amsterdam University Press, 1997), 41. J. Braat, 'Dutch Activities in the North and the Arctic during the Sixteenth and Seventeenth Centuries'. *Arctic* 37:4 (1984), 473.

[6] Novaya Zemlya was discovered for sixteenth-century Europeans by the explorers of the English Muscovy Company in 1553. Zeeberg, *Terugkeer naar Nova Zembla*, 36. Rayner Unwin, *A Winter Away from Home: Willem Barents and the North-East Passage*. (Seafarer Books: London, 1995), 4. Samuel Bawlf, *The Secret Voyage of Sir Francis Drake, 1577–1580*. (Vancouver: Douglas & McIntyre, 2003), 48.

had been blocked by extensive sea ice.[7] In 1580/1581, the English Muscovy Company sponsored an expedition by Arthur Pet and Charles Jackman. They managed to find a way through the Yugor Strait, a narrow passage that separated the island of Vaygatsch, south of Novaya Zemlya, from the Russian mainland (Map M4). The explorers became the first Western Europeans to enter the Kara Sea, but they stayed only briefly before turning back in the face of ice and fog. Years later, De Moucheron strongly supported Dutch exploration of the passage around Vaygatsch. He insisted to the States-General that the republic was playing a 'dangerous game' without a firm foothold in the Yugor Strait. At any moment, explorers from other nations might swoop in and uncover a passage for themselves.[8]

By contrast, Plancius and his associates in Amsterdam deduced from the failure of the English expedition that the straits around Vaygatsch were too shallow to afford passage into the seas beyond.[9] Like other advocates for a northern passage, Plancius believed that deep water in rough, open seas could not freeze. The English explorer John Davis even deduced that, since ice was frozen freshwater, it must form on land, not in the salty sea. It was this conviction that encouraged earlier explorers and cartographers to infer the existence of land from the distribution of Arctic sea ice. If ice was visible, land must be nearby. Polar continents in maps therefore overlapped with the typical extent of Arctic sea ice during the Little Ice Age. Both Dutch and English explorers also believed that ice actually generated cold conditions, because winds sweeping off ice were usually frigid. Sea ice at high latitudes accordingly did not suggest that the Arctic was inaccessible. In fact, many European scholars deduced that, in the summer, continuous sunlight at high latitudes made the poles about as warm as the tropics. Plancius and his fellow Arctic enthusiasts concluded that belts of cold weather and ice surrounded the balmy poles, and tapered

[7] Braat, 'Dutch Activities in the North and the Arctic', 473. V. Ye. Borodachev, V. Yu. Alexandrov, 'History of the Northern Sea Route'. In *Remote Sensing of Sea Ice in the Northern Sea Route: Studies and Applications*, ed. Ola M. Johannessen. (New York: Springer Praxis Books, 2007), 1. Jaap Jan Zeeberg, *Into the Ice Sea: Barents' Winter on Novaya Zemlya – A Renaissance Voyage of Discovery*. (Amsterdam: Rozenberg Publishers, 2005), 57. See also Marijke Spies, *Bij noorden om. Olivier Brunel en de doorvaart naar China en Cathay in de zestiende eeuw*. Amsterdam, 1994). V. D. Roeper and G. J. D. Wildeman, *Ontdekkingsreizen van Nederlanders (1590–1650)*. (Utrecht: Kosmos Uitgevers, 1993). P. T. G. Horensma, 'Olivier Brunel and the Dutch Involvement in the Discovery of the Northeast Passage'. *Fram* 2:1 (1985): 121–128.

[8] 'Heeft U [in the Yugor Strait] niet onmiddellijk vaste voet, dan speelt U gevaarlijk spel'. Zeeberg, *Terugkeer naar Nova Zembla*, 41. Hellinga, *Pioniers van de Gouden Eeuw*, 31.

[9] William J. Mills, *Exploring Polar Frontiers: A Historical Encyclopedia*, Vol. II. (Santa Barbara: ABC CLIO, 2003), 521.

off in the deep waters just north of Novaya Zemlya. If only they could find a way through.[10]

Of course, they were badly mistaken. In the summer, the Arctic does receive continuous sunlight, but that light reaches the region at a more oblique angle than it does at the equator. This is the primary reason for the difference in temperature between the Arctic and the tropics. Even now, ice cover is virtually unbroken at very high northern latitudes. In the sixteenth century, ice above northern Eurasia was overall far more extensive than it is today. Many forces influenced the extent, movement, and consistency of this ice, but the most important by far were regional temperatures, ocean currents, and atmospheric circulation.[11]

Arctic and European temperature trends over the past millennium did not exactly mirror each other. When the onset of the Grindelwald Fluctuation started to cool Europe, average air surface temperatures across the Arctic actually increased. The Arctic only started cooling by the 1580s, very likely under the cumulative influence of small volcanic eruptions. In the Arctic, as in the Low Countries, cooling was much more pronounced in the spring, autumn, and winter than in the summer.[12]

Yet Arctic sea ice responds not only to air surface temperatures but also to sea surface temperatures. Sea surface temperatures may actually have increased across the Arctic in the first decades of the Grindelwald Fluctuation, before a cooling Atlantic Multidecadal Oscillation (AMO) and a slowing Atlantic Meridional Overturning Circulation (AMOC) led to chillier temperatures after around 1590. Model simulations and

[10] Captain Jansen, 'Notes on the Ice between Greenland and Nova Zembla: Being the Results of Investigations into the Records of Early Dutch Voyages in the Spitzbergen Seas'. *Proceedings of the Royal Geographical Society of London* 9:4 (1864–1865): 175. Sam White, 'Unpuzzling American Climates: New World Experience and the Foundations of a New Science'. *Isis* 106:3 (2015): 555.

[11] 'Dynamics'. National Snow & Ice Data Center. Accessed 4 Jan 2013, http://nsidc.org/cryosphere/seaice/processes/dynamics.html#wind. Peter Lemke, Markus Harder, and Michael Hilmer. 'The Response of Arctic Sea Ice to Global Change'. *Climatic Change*, 46 (2000): 278.

[12] Iver Murdmaa et al., 'Paleoenvironments in Russkaya Gavan' Fjord (NW Novaya Zemlya, Barents Sea) during the last millennium'. *Palaeogeography, Palaeoclimatology, Palaeoecology* 209 (2004): 153. Raymond S. Bradley and Philip D. Jones, '"Little Ice Age" Summer Temperature Variations: Their Nature and Relevance to Recent Global Trends'. *The Holocene* 3 (1993): 367. E. Crespin et al., 'The 15th Century Arctic Warming in Coupled Model Simulations with Data Assimilation'. *Climate of the Past* (2009): 394. Jaap Jan Zeeberg, *Climate and Glacial History of the Novaya Zemlya Archipelago, Russian Arctic: With Notes on the Region's History of Exploration.* (Amsterdam: Rozenberg Publishers, 2002), 99. Nicholas P. McKay and Darrell S. Kaufman, 'An Extended Arctic Proxy Temperature Database for the Past 2,000 Years'. *Scientific Data* 1 (2014): 6.

evidence from ice cores, lake sediments, and other proxy sources all suggest that the annual average extent of Arctic sea ice only started expanding after the mid-1590s.[13]

Of course, the Arctic is vast, and regional trends there do not always dictate local realities. Proxy sources can also suggest conflicting trends on diverse temporal and geographic scales. Changes in the concentration of microscopic organisms in marine sediments suggest that the water off northern Svalbard, and to a lesser extent western Svalbard, cooled from 1500 until the end of the Little Ice Age. Lakebed sediments, by contrast, indicate that the West Spitsbergen Current in the Fram Strait warmed starting in around 1600. They also provide evidence that glaciers on Svalbard expanded owing to rising precipitation, not declining temperatures. A sediment core unearthed from northwestern Novaya Zemlya suggests that glaciers there expanded from around 1400 to 1600, but then retreated in the seventeenth century. Increased glaciation probably enhanced cyclonic activity in the Novaya Zemlya area, which may have affected regional sea ice. Logbooks kept by explorers and whalers, meanwhile, record a sharp increase in sea ice across the Barents Sea during the Grindelwald Fluctuation. Local and regional studies compiled with diverse scientific and historical evidence therefore all confirm that the 1590s was a decade of profound environmental change in the far north.[14]

[13] Christophe Kinnard et al., 'Reconstructed Changes in Arctic Sea Ice over the Past 1,450 Years'. *Nature* 479:7374 (2011): 511. McKay and Kaufman, 'An Extended Arctic Proxy Temperature Database for the Past 2,000 Years', 6. Rueda et al., 'Coupling of Air and Sea Surface Temperatures in the Eastern Fram Strait during the Last 2,000 Years'. *The Holocene* 23:5 (2013): 695. Gray, 'A Tree-Ring Based Reconstruction of the Atlantic Multidecadal Oscillation since 1567 AD', 2. Rahmstorf et al., 'Exceptional Twentieth-Century Slowdown in Atlantic Ocean Overturning Circulation', 477. Moreno-Chamarro, 'An Abrupt Weakening of the Subpolar Gyre as Trigger of Little Ice Age-Type Episodes', 8. D'Arrigo, 'A Reconstructed Siberian High Index since AD 1599 from Eurasian and North American Tree Rings', 2. Årthun, Marius, Tor Eldevik, Lars Henrik Smedsrud, Øystein Skagseth, and R. B. Ingvaldsen. 'Quantifying the Influence of Atlantic Heat on Barents Sea Ice Variability and Retreat'. *Journal of Climate* 25:13 (2012): 473–64743. Marie-Alexandrine Sicre et al., 'Decadal Variability of Sea Surface Temperatures Off North Iceland over the Last 2,000 Years'. *Earth and Planetary Science Letters* 268: 1–2 (2008): 140.

[14] Patrycja Jernas et al., 'Palaeoenvironmental Changes of the Last Two Millennia on the Western and Northern Svalbard Shelf'. *Boreas* 42:1 (2013): 245. Torgny Vinje, 'Barents Sea Ice Edge Variation over the Past 400 Years', in *Extended Abstracts, Workshop on Sea-Ice Charts of the Arctic.* WMO/TD 949 (1999): 5. Leonid Polyak, Ivar Murdmaa, and Elena Ivanova, 'A High-Resolution, 800-Year Glaciomarine Record from Russkaya Gavan', a Novaya Zemlya Fjord, Eastern Barents Sea'. *The Holocene* 14:4 (2004): 633. E. Crespin et al., 'Arctic Climate over the Past Millennium: Annual and Seasonal Responses to External Forcings'. *The Holocene* 23 (2013): 327. J. Overpeck et al., 'Arctic Environmental Change of

THE FIRST EXPEDITION: FRUSTRATION AND PROMISE

In the midst of these changes, the first expedition for the Northeast Passage organized by the Enkhuizen and Amsterdam entrepreneurs departed the Zuiderzee on 5 June 1594. The fleet sailed under the command of Admiral Cornelis Nay aboard the *Zwaan* and Vice Admiral Cornelis Rijp on the *Mercurius*, and it carried Jan Huyghen van Linschoten, whose journal provides the best account of its voyage. Barents captained a smaller, third vessel with the unassuming name *Het Boot* ('The Boat'). Like others in the Amsterdam group, Barents believed that the expedition would most likely find open seas well north of Novaya Zemlya. However, De Moucheron, who financed the voyage, had ordered the explorers to avoid these waters. He directed them to seek open sea, and thus a passage to Asia, near the island of Vaygatsch.[15]

The expedition braved storms and then a calm to reach Kildin Island on 21 June, where Barents convinced Nay to divide the fleet. On 29 June, Barents ordered his crew to set sail for the north coast of Novaya Zemlya. Sailors aboard the other two ships left Kildin for Vaygatsch on 2 July. Three days later, sea ice surrounded them for the first time. The explorers escaped the ice by evening, but on 8 July they encountered massive icebergs near the town of Svyatoi Nos on the eastern coast of Murmansk Oblast. On 9 July they arrived at Svyatoi Nos and anchored in a nearby harbour to await the retreat of the ice. A week later, Nay finally commanded the crews to weigh anchor. Aided by high, favourable winds, they made rapid progress from Kolokolkovaya Bay to Novaya Zemlya, and on 21 July they approached Vaygatsch. They discovered

the Last Four Centuries'. *Science* 278:1251 (1997): 1253. Hilary Birks, 'Holocene Vegetational History and Climatic Change in West Spitsbergen – Plant Macrofossils from Skardtjørna, an Arctic Lake'. *The Holocene* 1:3 (1991): 216. Zeeberg, *Climate and Glacial History of the Novaya Zemlya Archipelago*, 66 and 105. William J. D'Andrea et al., 'Mild Little Ice Age and Unprecedented Recent Warmth in an 1,800-Year Lake Sediment Record from Svalbard'. *Geology* 10.1130 (2012): 1007.

[15] Jan Huyghen van Linschoten, 'Voyagie, of Schipvaart, van Ian Huyghen van Linschoten, van bijnoorden om lans Noorwegen, de Noordkaap, Lapland, Finland, Rusland, &c. Anno 1594 en 1595'. Franeker: Gerard Ketel, 1601. In *Reizen van Jan Huyghen van Linschoten naar het noorden (1594–1595)*. (The Hague: Martinus Nijhoff, 1914), 38. Hellinga, *Pioniers van de Gouden Eeuw*, 32. Jan Huyghen van Linschoten, 'Voyagie, of Schipvaart, van Ian Huyghen van Linschoten, van bijnoorden om lans Noorwegen, de Noordkaap, Lapland, Finland, Rusland, &c. Anno 1594 en 1595'. Franeker: Gerard Ketel, 1601. In *Terugkeer naar Nova Zembla*, 142. A. van der Moer, *Een zestiende-eeuwse Hollander in het verre oosten en het hoge noorden*. (The Hague: Martinus Nijhoff, 1979), 20.

shipwrecks and trees far inland, which convinced them that storms must have recently thrashed the island.[16]

Van Linschoten reported no sea ice from 19 July until 24 July, when the *Zwaan* and *Mercurius* were the first Dutch vessels to approach Yugor Strait in over two decades. As the explorers entered the strait on 25 July, however, they encountered more ice than ever drifting with the wind and current through the strait from east to west. To the leaders of the expedition, the parallel course of the current and the wind suggested that a passage existed to the Kara Sea and, in turn, to Asia. To find it, however, they would have to survive the icebergs streaming through the strait. In stormy weather, the vice admiral's vessel narrowly escaped the strait, sustaining only minor damage. Icebergs continued to drift west from the Kara Sea, driven by remarkably consistent winds from the east. On 29 July, a half-mile long iceberg forced even the admiral's ship to abandon the Yugor Strait.[17]

Yet in the following week, most of the icebergs and sea ice melted. On 9 August, the explorers sailed east, and the weather cleared. Before long, the mariners passed into the Kara Sea, where they encountered high waves and a sea so ice-free that Van Linschoten believed beyond doubt that they had found their passage to China. On 11 August, the explorers, now approximately 300 kilometres east of Vaygatsch, reached the rivers Morzhovka, Saltintayu, and Nyodati. From there, they believed that the coast curved south towards China. Before long, the wind encouraged them to abandon the coast and head further to sea. There, massive icebergs, some home to aggressive walruses, combined with heavy fog to again imperil their expedition. The explorers decided to turn back while it was still possible.[18]

On 15 August, their ships returned through the Yugor Strait and found their colleagues on *Het Boot*. Barents had sailed north of Novaya Zemlya before running into impassable sea ice. By 10 September, the returning fleet entered the North Sea, and six days later it arrived off Texel after a journey of more than three months. The expedition of 1594 was among the most successful polar voyages of its time. Nevertheless, Barents and Plancius did not share the subsequent enthusiasm of De Moucheron and the Enkhuizen circle. They still believed that the northerly route around

[16] Van Linschoten, 'Voyagie, of Schipvaart, van Ian Huyghen van Linschoten', 63. Hellinga, *Pioniers van de Gouden Eeuw*, 32.

[17] Van Linschoten, 'Voyagie, of Schipvaart, van Ian Huyghen van Linschoten', 79.

[18] Van Linschoten, 'Voyagie, of Schipvaart, van Ian Huyghen van Linschoten', 100.

Novaya Zemlya was more easily navigable than the one that passed through the Yugor Strait.[19]

The expedition's success had been made possible by the culture, economy, and technology of the Dutch Republic at the dawning of its Golden Age. Yet it also owed much to the decisions the explorers made as they confronted an Arctic environment in flux. They recorded environmental conditions that should have marked an increase in the extent of regional sea ice. According to Van Linschoten's journal, current and wind alike drove ice west through the Yugor Strait, into the Barents Sea. An easterly current (that is, flowing west) through the Straits usually corresponds to a weak westerly current of warm water from the Atlantic Ocean. Indeed, AMOC was slowing down over the course of the 1590s, and it may well have been especially slow in 1594. Why, then, did the explorers enjoy unusually ice-free seas?

There are many possible explanations. Arctic sea surface temperatures did not start declining exactly when AMOC began to slow down, so they may have been warm in 1594. Storms of the kind recorded by the explorers can also break up sea ice. The most compelling explanation, however, has to do with the warmth of the summer around Novaya Zemlya in 1594. In that year, the summer in Northwestern Europe was only slightly cooler than the twentieth-century average. The lack of ice encountered by the Dutch explorers suggests that summer temperatures in the Russian Arctic were equally moderate. That may be why sea ice, which seemed so daunting when the explorers arrived off Novaya Zemlya, quickly melted away. It left behind the open seas that enabled the explorers to leverage the resources of the Dutch Republic and explore the Arctic as Europeans rarely had before.[20]

THE SECOND EXPEDITION: FAILURE AND DISCOURAGEMENT

Buoyed by the successes of 1594, De Moucheron financed a second, even larger expedition in the summer of 1595. On 2 July, seven vessels from Amsterdam, Enkhuizen, and Zeeland departed Texel under Nay's command. Barents served as lead pilot of the Amsterdam ships, while Van

[19] Van Linschoten, 'Voyagie, of Schipvaart, van Ian Huyghen van Linschoten', 136. Hellinga, *Pioniers van de Gouden Eeuw*, 32. Van Linschoten, 'Voyagie, of Schipvaart, van Ian Huyghen van Linschoten', in *Terugkeer naar Nova Zembla*, 155.

[20] Zeeberg, *Climate and Glacial History of the Novaya Zemlya Archipelago*, 66. Van Engelen, Buisman and IJnsen, 'A Millennium of Weather, Winds and Water in the Low Countries', 112. Shabalova and Van Engelen, 'Evaluation of a Reconstruction of Temperature in the Low Countries', 225.

Linschoten was head merchant on account of his experiences in Asia. With Barents was the young Jacob van Heemskerk, later among the most celebrated explorers and admirals of the Dutch Golden Age. After braving high winds, the fleet approached the North Cape – the northernmost tip of Norway – on 5 August. Nearly two weeks later, Gerrit de Veer, an explorer aboard the Dutch vessels, wrote that they had reached the coast of Novaya Zemlya, which was lined with a 'great mass of ice'.[21]

The quantity of sea ice persuaded the mariners to reconsider their options. After a debate, they resolved to follow De Moucheron's instructions by attempting to enter the Yugor Strait. Broken sea ice forced the crews to alter course, yet the fleet sailed into the strait on 19 August. Its sailors quickly found the water near the so-called *Afgodenhoek*, or 'Idol Point', closed because of ice. Varnek Bay, however, was relatively ice-free and provided shelter from the windblown icebergs of the strait. For nearly a week the vessels anchored in the bay. A small boat sent to scout the Kara Sea could not get past the Yugor Strait on account of the ice. Then, on 23 August, the explorers encountered a party of Russians preparing to set sail for the sea. The Russians claimed that, before long, much of the Kara Sea would be frozen, even to its southern coast. Prompted perhaps by the Russian warning, on 25 August the Dutch sailors made a renewed attempt to enter the sea. Yet at 'Twist Point', sea ice forced them to turn back.[22]

In the next week, Barents and the other mariners spent several days among the inhabitants of the southern shore of Vaygatsch. On 2 September, their vessels completed a treacherous journey through the ice to reach 'Cross Point', a gently protruding stretch of the coast. On 3 September, the explorers again attempted to enter the Kara Sea, but dense sea ice forced them to retreat once more. De Veer described 'the great quantitie of Ice, and the mist that then fell, at which time the Winde blew so uncertaine, that we hold no course, but were forced continually to winde and turne about, by reason of the Ice, and the unconstantnesse of the wind'. After hours of such desperate manoeuvring in variable wind, the mariners correctly guessed that they had sailed back towards the southern coast of Vaygatsh in the Yugor Strait. With the season growing perilously late, on 4 September the explorers tied their vessels

[21] Hellinga, *Pioniers van de Gouden Eeuw*, 32. Zeeberg, *Terugkeer naar Nova Zembla*, 46. Gerrit de Veer, *The True and Perfect Description of Three Voyages by the Ships of Holland and Zeeland*. (London, 1609), 7. Gerrit de Veer, *Reizen van Willem Barents, Jacob van Heemskerck, Jan Cornelisz. Rijp en Anderen Naar het Noorden (1594–1597), Eerste Deel*. (The Hague: Martinus Nijhoff, 1917), 32.

[22] De Veer, *The True and Perfect Description of Three Voyages*, 9. De Veer, *Reizen van Willem Barents*, 36.

to the so-called States Island, which afforded some protection from the ice. The island was actually southeast of the Yugor Strait and in the Kara Sea, but the ice prohibited progress beyond this forward position.[23]

With their way blocked, the sailors foraged on the island for game and crystals, hoping that the ice would soon shift to open a passage to Asia. Polar bears hunted nearby, but the Dutch did not yet understand the danger they posed. Then, on 6 September, a thin and apparently famished bear ambushed two men as they wandered far inland. According to the English translation of De Veer's account, the first man cried, 'who is that that pulles me so by the necke[?]' whereupon the second helpfully responded with, 'oh mate, it is a Beare'. The second man hurried back to his ship, where a party of some twenty sailors armed themselves with firearms brought along to deal with Iberian soldiers. They approached the bear and opened fire, but the bear charged into the barrage, killed one sailor, and scattered the rest. Delays caused by sea ice had exposed the crew to an alien and unforgiving biosphere.[24]

Some of the frightened and frustrated sailors staged a short-lived mutiny that was quelled only after five of its instigators were hanged. Then, between 9 and 12 September, the explorers launched three desperate attempts to break through the ice that drifted east of States Island. Yet it afforded no passage, and the expedition was forced to return to the Yugor Strait. As if to confirm that it was now too late to linger near Novaya Zemlya, a severe storm struck the fleet on 13 and 14 September, and on the morning of the 15 September, an easterly wind pushed thick sea ice into the Yugor Strait, driving the explorers west into the Barents Sea. With any passage to Asia now clearly blocked by ice, Nay, Barents, and their subordinates agreed to return to the republic. On 26 October, the expedition returned to Amsterdam having never left the immediate vicinity of Novaya Zemlya.[25]

Compared to the voyage of 1594, the expedition of 1595 probably endured hydrological and atmospheric conditions that more clearly reflected the late onset of the Grindelwald Fluctuation in the far north. The explorers observed easterly currents driving sea ice through the Yugor Strait that were probably made possible by another year in which warm Atlantic water flowed only weakly into the Arctic. Whereas the ice had

[23] De Veer, *The True and Perfect Description of Three Voyages*, 13. De Veer, *Reizen van Willem Barents*, 40.

[24] De Veer, *The True and Perfect Description of Three Voyages*, 14. De Veer, *Reizen van Willem Barents*, 41. Hellinga, *Pioniers van de Gouden Eeuw*, 32.

[25] De Veer, *Reizen van Willem Barents*, 43. Hellinga, *Pioniers van de Gouden Eeuw*, 32. Spies, *Arctic Routes to Fabled Lands*, 139.

melted and opened a passage to the Kara Sea in 1594, it persisted in the summer of 1595, owing in part to cold sea surface and surface atmosphere temperatures that may have registered the volcanic eruption of Nevado del Ruiz in March. High winds and storms likely also funnelled more ice west from the frigid Kara Sea into the Yugor Strait.[26]

In the spring of 1595, the explorers and their supporters made decisions that compounded the influence of environmental conditions that were far less favourable than they had been in 1594. The second voyage left later in the year than the other expeditions, arriving at the Yugor Strait halfway through August. In the same month a year earlier, the first fleet had already sailed deep into the Kara Sea. In leaving later in the year, the commanders of the second expedition failed to take advantage of a likely quirk in seasonal temperatures across the Arctic during the Grindelwald Fluctuation. Average Arctic summer temperatures probably declined significantly less than they did in other seasons, while average autumn temperatures declined more. The adventurers in 1595 probably endured a much sharper fall in temperature from summer to autumn than one would experience around Novaya Zemlya today. That may have reduced the usual melting of sea ice in August and accelerated its expansion in September and October.

Thick sea ice forced the explorers to wait in pockets of open water around the Yugor Strait, which increased the likelihood of deadly encounters with polar bears. The resulting death toll, coupled with the frustration caused by impenetrable sea ice, provoked dissension. Indirectly, it led to executions that poisoned already frayed relations between the Enkuizen and Amsterdam groups. In the final months of 1595, the passage through the Yugor Strait therefore appeared far less promising than it had a year earlier. De Moucheron declined to finance further Arctic exploration, and Enkhuizen would not contribute any more ships.[27]

THE THIRD EXPEDITION: DISCOVERY, DISASTER, AND SURVIVAL

Not all advocates of the Northeast Passage were so discouraged. Van Linschoten, for example, believed that 'we will learn by additional

[26] Zeeberg, *Climate and Glacial History of the Novaya Zemlya Archipelago*, 66. Van Engelen, Buisman and IJnsen, 'A Millennium of Weather, Winds and Water in the Low Countries', 112. Shabalova and Van Engelen, 'Evaluation of a Reconstruction of Temperature in the Low Countries', 225.

[27] Spies, *Arctic Routes to Fabled Lands*, 140. Zeeberg, *Terugkeer naar Nova Zembla*, 46.

investigation of the Vaygach [sic] area the right time to avoid the ice and conquer the obstacles that now, for lack of experience, appear insurmountable'. Plancius and Barents, for their part, were eager to pursue the northerly course they had long proposed. On 25 March 1596, Plancius obtained a grant from townships in Holland, Zeeland, and Utrecht to launch an expedition that would, at last, lie under the unquestioned authority of the Amsterdam 'merchant-adventurers'.[28]

On 16 May 1596, two vessels destined for the far north attempted to leave the Zuiderzee. Shipwrights had fortified their hulls with a double layer of outer planking, an adaptation to sea ice that may also have been used in earlier journeys to the far north. Barents was firmly ensconced as the intellectual leader of his third expedition, but Heemskerck captained his vessel, and Jan Cornelisz Rijp commanded the second ship. Once again, De Veer documented their voyage. Barents intended to sail far to the north and its presumably deep, ice-free waters, before bearing east to avoid the supposed polar continent. Promisingly, the expedition encountered no sea ice even after De Veer reported that it had sailed so far north that 'wee had no night'.[29]

Before long, Rijp's pilot insisted that they had drifted too far to the east and would in fact soon encounter the Yugor Strait. Barents and Heemskerck consented to steer even further to the north. On the following day, De Veer reported a troubling sign: sea ice on the horizon, 'which from afar looked like an oncoming flock of swans'. The crews managed to manoeuvre through on 5 June, but by the next day, the ice had become so solid that passing through was impossible. The explorers therefore steered southwest before resuming their north-northeast course along the great mass of ice. They were now as far north as they had ever journeyed. The ice towered around them and, by 8 June, again forced them to alter course. They soon spotted an island, which they approached to avoid the ice. They named it 'Bear Island' to commemorate a polar bear they slew there. After Rijp and Barents argued about their position a second time, the expedition left the island on 13 June. Four days later, it again encountered thick sea ice.[30]

[28] Hellinga, *Pioniers van de Gouden Eeuw*, 33. Zeeberg, *Terugkeer naar Nova Zembla*, 46. Zeeberg, *Into the Ice Sea*, 60.

[29] De Veer, *The True and Perfect Description of Three Voyages*, 3. De Veer, *Reizen van Willem Barents*, 48. Hellinga, *Pioniers van de Gouden Eeuw*, 33. Zeeberg, *Terugkeer naar Nova Zembla*, 46. Zeeberg, *Into the Ice Sea*, 61. Jerzy H. G. Gawronski and Jaap Jan Zeeberg, 'The Wrecking of Barents' Ship'. In *Northbound with Barents: Russian-Dutch Integrated Archaelogical Research on the Archipelago Novaya Zemlya*, eds. Pyotr Boyarsky and Jerzy Gawronski. (Amsterdam: Uitgeverij Jan Mets, 1997), 90.

[30] De Veer, *The True and Perfect Description of Three Voyages*, 6. De Veer, *Reizen van Willem Barents*, 51. Zeeberg, *Into the Ice Sea*, 61. Spies, *Arctic Routes to Fabled Lands*, 143.

Once more, ice forced the sailors to alter course. At just under 80° N on 19 June, the explorers spotted land, although the wind, blowing from the Northeast, hindered their attempts at drawing near. Barents insisted that they had reached the coast of Greenland, but Rijp thought it was *terra incognita* and appropriately designated it 'the New Land'. Their crew called it *Spitsbergen*, 'Sharp Mountains', because its peaks seemed to scrape the clouds. Rijp was, in fact, finally correct in a navigational dispute with Barents. Now halfway between Norway and the North Pole, the explorers had discovered the largest island of what is today called the Svalbard archipelago (Map M4). On 21 June, they reached the shore, where they wrote detailed accounts of the island's diverse fauna and flora. Two days later, they hoisted anchor. For the following week, they explored up and down the coast, their course routinely blocked by sea ice. Ultimately, sea ice thwarted all attempts to sail around Spitsbergen's northern coast. Yet because the ships were near land, the ice did not prove that deep water could freeze. On 1 July, the explorers returned to Bear Island, no closer to the Northeast Passage.[31]

Rijp insisted on pressing north, beyond 80° N, to search again for an opening in the ice. Barents, however, believed that no passage would be possible through the great landmass of Greenland. After a heated argument, the two agreed to part ways and attempt different passages: Rijp in the ice north of Spitsbergen, Barents around the northern coast of Novaya Zemlya. In later testimony before the States-General, Rijp recalled that he had returned to the waters off Spitsbergen, where his ship penetrated the ice pack to 79° N. According to a journal kept by crewmember Thenis Claeszoon, impenetrable ice blocked their progress and then tore a hole in Rijp's vessel. As water poured into the ship, the crew raised the leak above sea level by shifting their cargo. Working from boats, they repaired the hull, and after leaving messages nearby, sailed to Novaya Zemlya in pursuit of Barents.[32]

The expedition of 1596 departed nearly a month earlier than even the first expedition had in 1594. On the one hand, average summer temperatures that, in the Arctic, cooled far less than average temperatures in other seasons during the Grindelwald Fluctuation likely aided its initial discoveries. On the other hand, the summer was not so balmy that the mariners could avoid sea ice altogether to sail wherever they liked. Water temperatures around parts of Spitsbergen were probably cold during the 1590s,

[31] De Veer, *The True and Perfect Description of Three Voyages*, 9. De Veer, *Reizen van Willem Barents*, 55. Spies, *Arctic Routes to Fabled Lands*, 143.

[32] Zeeberg, *Into the Ice Sea*, 62.

although the West Spitsbergen Current may have been warming. There was just enough sea ice to redirect the expedition towards previously undiscovered islands.

After Rijp and his crew departed on 1 July, Heemskerck and Barents commanded their sailors to bear east, towards Novaya Zemlya. They were now less certain that deep water had to be free of ice. De Veer reported that, given their high latitude, they 'much wondered' about a short-lived lack of sea ice on 4 July. Twelve days later, they arrived off Novaya Zemlya and began to sail up the island's western coast. On 19 July, they reached 'Cross Island' (Cape Dyakanova) at roughly 76° N, yet found their way blocked by ice. While waiting for an opening, they survived many close encounters with polar bears. At last, they manoeuvred around the ice on 4 August. After two days, they passed the *Hoeck van Nassouwen* or 'Point of Nassau'. Rijp reached Cape Dyakanova on the same day, but now the way forward was entirely sealed by ice.[33]

On 7 August, the ice took a more dangerous form for Barents and his crew. Vast icebergs constrained the movement of their ship, and drifted perilously close in an easterly wind. The crew attached their vessel to an iceberg to avoid colliding with other ice masses, yet on 10 August that iceberg splintered on the seabed. It was only by sailing over and through shards of broken ice that the explorers narrowly escaped. Barents and Heemskerk guided their ship nearer the shore, because the largest icebergs could not enter shallow water. For several days, it was shallow water, not deep water, which was ice-free. Before long, they reached the so-called island of Orange, where they survived a now-routine polar bear encounter. On the following day, there was cause for relief. A scouting party climbed a hill on Novaya Zemlya and discovered open water to the southeast and east-southeast. According to De Veer, 'we were much comforted, thinking we had won our voyage'.[34]

After rounding the tip of Novaya Zemlya, on 20 August the explorers braved icebergs to reach a bay they called 'Ice Haven', on the northeastern coast of the island. They pressed south, but soon faced storms and thick sea ice. Finally, on 26 August, Barents decided that the expedition should abandon its quest for a passage and retrace its steps. Yet when the crew

[33] De Veer, *The True and Perfect Description of Three Voyages*, 14. De Veer, *Reizen van Willem Barents*, 60. Zeeberg, *Into the Ice Sea*, 62.

[34] Zeeberg, *Into the Ice Sea*, 62. De Veer, *The True and Perfect Description of Three Voyages*, 17. De Veer, *Reizen van Willem Barents*, 62. Zeeberg, *Terugkeer naar Nova Zembla*, 47.

returned to Ice Haven later that day, ice pressed in from the sea with a southeast wind and entirely surrounded their ship. On 27 August, grinding sea ice lifted the whole ship four feet above the water. According to De Veer, the ship, crushed by the ice, 'seemed to burst in a 100 pieces [sic], which was most fearfull both to see and heare and made all the haire of our heads to rise upright with feare'. It was clear that there would be no imminent escape from Novaya Zemlya.[35]

Faced with this terrifying reality, Barents, Heemskerck, and their crew decided to build a shelter on land. There, they could endure the winter while safe from the unstable sea ice. Fortunately, on 11 September a scouting party found dead trees strewn on the tundra coast, uprooted and washed ashore in a storm. With wood hewn from these trees the crew began the long and desperate struggle to erect a shelter before the onset of the polar winter, with its daytime darkness, frigid temperatures, and incessant storms. On 23 September, the expedition's carpenter died, likely from overwork. Yet despite frequent bear attacks and worsening blizzards, the crew finished most of their shelter by 12 October. They called it the *Behouden Huys*, or 'Saved House'. The sailors who had remained aboard the ship moved in on 24 October.[36]

On 3 November, the sun vanished beneath the horizon, and the crew would not see it again for months. Thereafter, the shimmering light of stars, the moon, and the aurora borealis, reflecting off the snow, allowed the explorers to forage when it was not too cold or stormy. The sporadic thundering of sea ice on the coast broke the silence. Bears that had routinely attacked the house disappeared with the sun. The crew manufactured pelts from foxes that had become more common around the same time. Still the temperatures continued to fall, and storms grew more frequent. Neither fur nor boiling water could long defend against the cold. In a blizzard on 6 December, De Veer wrote that the cold was 'almost not to be indured, whereupon we lookt pittifully one upon the other, being in greate feare, that if the extremity of the cold grew to be more and more, we should all die there with cold'. By late December, a barrage of severe blizzards brought frigid temperatures and heavy snowfall that completely buried the Saved

[35] De Veer, *The True and Perfect Description of Three Voyages*, 23. De Veer, *Reizen van Willem Barents*, 70. 'Charctic Interactive Sea Ice Graph'. National Snow & Ice Data Center. Available at: http://nsidc.org/arcticseaicenews/charctic-interactive-sea-ice-graph.

[36] De Veer, *The True and Perfect Description of Three Voyages*, 31. De Veer, *Reizen van Willem Barents*, 79. Louwrens Hacquebord, 'In Search of *Het Behouden Huys*: A Survey of the Remains of the House of Willem Barentsz on Novaya Zemlya'. *Arctic* 48:3 (1995): 248–256.

House. Such storms had become routine. Remarkably, the crew experienced blizzards on 49 days from the beginning of December to the end of March. On 24 January, their spirits were lifted when the sun appeared to rise after nearly three months of darkness. It was the first recorded observation of what was thereafter known as the 'Novaya Zemlya effect', a polar mirage created by the atmospheric refraction of sunlight.[37]

Before long, the sun returned in truth. The weather remained cold and stormy for months to come, but by May open water was visible from the coast. The ship, however, could not be dislodged, and storms with easterly winds repeatedly forced thick sea ice back into the harbour. At last, the explorers lost hope that their ship would ever sail again. On 15 May, Heemskerck and Barents ordered the crew to prepare small boats for a desperate journey home.[38] On 14 June, the crew departed Novaya Zemlya aboard these boats. In the following months, they journeyed south and west in the face of shifting sea ice, bears, walruses, storms, and navigational blunders. Shortly after their departure, Barents, long sick with scurvy, died alongside crewman Claes Adrians while they huddled on the windswept ice. Four days later, crewman Jan Franszoon perished after the boats capsized in the bitterly cold water. Nevertheless, most of the explorers arrived at Kildin on 25 August, where to their astonishment they encountered Jan Cornelisz Rijp and his crew. Reunited, the survivors reached Amsterdam on 1 November, where their homemade fur coats created a sensation.[39]

Adventurers seeking the Northeast Passage could have been trapped by ice even in the warm twentieth-century climate. Still, the onset of the Grindelwald Fluctuation in the Arctic greatly increased the odds that Barents and his crew would find themselves imprisoned off Novaya Zemlya in 1596. A new pattern of moderate atmospheric cooling in summer, but dramatic cooling in other seasons, helped lure the explorers further into the Arctic. Sparse sea ice initially allowed Barents and his crew to slip past Cape Dyakanova, but the gate would soon close. The Arctic summer was not warm enough, and seas not open enough, to allow Rijp to find a way through. Perhaps Rijp would have convinced Barents to attempt an earlier return to the republic. Yet, in 1595, Barents had unsuccessfully argued for an

[37] De Veer, *The True and Perfect Description of Three Voyages*, 37, 47. De Veer, *Reizen van Willem Barents*, 87, 99. Unwin, *A Winter Away from Home*, 111, 125.

[38] De Veer, *The True and Perfect Description of Three Voyages*, 77. De Veer, *Reizen van Willem Barents*, 122.

[39] De Veer, *The True and Perfect Description of Three Voyages*, 127. De Veer, *Reizen van Willem Barents*, 178. Unwin, *A Winter Away from Home*, 229. Hellinga, *Pioniers van de Gouden Eeuw*, 37.

overwintering near the island of Vaygatsch, south of Novaya Zemlya. In 1596, the explorers were again well provisioned for that possibility.[40]

Surviving a winter in northern Novaya Zemlya was an entirely different prospect. Few Western Europeans had ever lived through an Arctic winter, and the northern tip of Novaya Zemlya is nearly halfway between the North Pole and the Arctic Circle. The unusually sharp shift in temperature between summer and autumn likely increased the difficulty of avoiding and escaping a sudden thickening of sea ice off Novaya Zemlya. Thereafter, a frigid winter punctuated by relentless storms conspired with a relatively cold spring to deepen and lengthen the hardships endured by the explorers in their Saved House. Looming over these atmospheric changes was the slowing AMOC, which may have increased the amount of sea ice that the survivors needed to navigate as they struggled to leave Novaya Zemlya in the summer of 1597. Because their vessels never entered the Yugor Strait, however, they did not observe the direction of the current there.[41]

FURTHER VOYAGES AND ARCTIC WHALING

Between 1594 and 1597, Dutch expeditions helped revolutionize European understandings of the Arctic. They strongly suggested that even very deep water could freeze, thereby undermining popular notions of polar kingdoms inhabited by fantastical beings. They showed that the Arctic ice sighted by adventurers in previous centuries was no indication of nearby land, and thereby challenged the idea of an Arctic continent. Accordingly, Dutch maps depicted Arctic geography and fauna with increasing accuracy, and new lands that actually existed appeared to the European imagination. The expeditions led to important discoveries about the behaviour of sea ice, the distribution of Arctic fauna and flora, and the physics of light. Moreover, the journals kept by De Veer and Van Linschoten were translated into many languages, published by Dutch printing houses, and read in the republic's coastal cities. The voyages became enduring symbols of the ambition and resilience of the Dutch Republic in its Golden Age.[42]

[40] Unwin, *A Winter Away from Home*, 40.

[41] Crespin et al., 'Arctic climate over the past millennium', 327. Crespin et al., 'The 15th Century Arctic Warming in Coupled Model Simulations With Data Assimilation', 394.

[42] See, for example, N. Veldhorst, and A. Blommensteijn, 'De overwintering op Nova Zembla in het negentiende-eeuwse kinderboek'. In *Behouden uit het Behouden Huys: catalogus van de voorwerpen van de Barentsexpeditie (1596), gevonden op Nova Zembla*, ed. J. Braat. (Amsterdam: De Bataafsche Leeuw, 1998), 62–74.

Yet the voyages did not persuade all European entrepreneurs and scholars that a northern passage was impossible. Remarkably, Plancius still insisted that deep water could not freeze, and that summer temperatures near the North Pole were too high for sea ice. Moreover, the potential profits of a northern passage continued to entice merchants to finance polar expeditions. In 1607, the English Muscovy Company, for example, commissioned a mariner, Henry Hudson, to chart a passage to Asia through the Arctic. Some Dutch merchants feared that Hudson would find a northern passage for their English competitors that would then be inaccessible to the republic's commercial interests. These fears persisted even after Hudson's first and second expeditions encountered impenetrable sea ice around Svalbard and Novaya Zemlya. Amsterdam merchants therefore hired Hudson in the winter of 1608–1609. On 25 March 1609, Hudson and a crew of 16 Dutch and English sailors departed Amsterdam aboard the *Halve Maan* ('Half Moon'). Their express orders were to seek a route to Asia in the vicinity of Novaya Zemlya.[43]

When the explorers reached the northernmost point of Norway in the third week of May, Robert Juet, who kept their journal, wrote that they had 'much trouble, with fogges sometimes, and more dangerous of ice'. In a blizzard on May 19, dissent bordering on mutiny erupted among the crew. Hudson responded by suggesting that they undertake the search for a passage in milder latitudes, far to the southwest. He had, in fact, secretly lost interest in the Northeast Passage, and he was eager to find the Northwest Passage in the Americas. The *Half Moon* ultimately sailed into what is now called the Hudson River in New York State. Its crew did not uncover a passage to Asia, but they did chart the future site of the city of New Amsterdam and the colony of New Netherlands, for the Dutch. Hudson was forced by his English sailors to stop at Dartmouth on his return voyage to Amsterdam. While there, he was ordered by King James to remain in the country and cease his service to the Dutch.[44]

[43] Robert Juet, 'The Third Voyage of Master Henry Hudson, toward Nova Zembla ... '. In *Henry Hudson the Navigator: The Original Documents in Which His Career Is Recorded.* (London: Hakluyt Society, 1860), 45. Hen C. Murphy, *Henry Hudson in Holland: An Inquiry into the Origin and Objects of the Voyage Which Led to the Discover of the Hudson River.* (New York: Burt Franklin, 1909), 17. George Malcolm Thomson, *The North-West Passage.* (London: Secker & Warburg, 1975), 66.

[44] Juet, 'The Third Voyage of Master Henry Hudson', 48. Murphy, *Henry Hudson in Holland*, 33. Thomson, *The North-West Passage*, 68. McCoy, *On the Edge*, 99. Douglas Hunter, *Half Moon: Henry Hudson and the Voyage that Redrew the Map of the World.* (New York: Bloomsbury Press, 2009), 38.

Documentary sources suggest that the summer of 1609 was, in the context of the Grindelwald Fluctuation, unusually warm across northwestern Europe. Nevertheless, Hudson's third expedition left very early in the year, before rising temperatures could fully melt the sea ice off the Norwegian coast. Moreover, AMOC was reaching its slowest state of the Little Ice Age. Perhaps the explorers could have found a way through anyway, but Hudson sought any excuse to abandon his search for the Northeast Passage. The reaction of his crew to the first sign of sea ice provided it. Relationships between global climatic trends, local environmental circumstances, and human decisions therefore helped shape the outcome of his voyage. For the Dutch Republic, the consequences were both lucrative and counterintuitive. Strangely, meteorological conditions in the far north had contributed to the discovery of a potentially profitable site for a settlement in a much warmer and more southerly environment.[45]

After Hudson's voyages, European activities across the Arctic gradually gathered pace. Rather than seeking passage to Asia, Dutch merchants and mariners increasingly concentrated on harvesting what many came to see as the largely untapped natural resources of the Arctic. The industries they created were inspired by earlier voyages in search of a northern passage. In his journal, De Veer had vividly described the natural abundance of Spitsbergen, although he made only one reference to a whale. Then, in 1604, an English crew under Captain Stephen Bennet reached Bear Island and found a vast herd of more than 1,000 walruses. They slaughtered 15, and returned in 1606 and 1607 to continue the killing. Also in 1607, Hudson, using charts composed by Barents, reached Spitsbergen and first reported the extraordinary quantity of bowhead whales in its fjords. Scientists now understand that the whales were drawn to the region by the mingling of warm and cold water from the East and West Spitsbergen currents, which created rich feeding grounds near the edge of drift ice. In 1610, Jonas Poole, an Englishman, journeyed to Spitsbergen and, like Hudson, described a 'great store of whales' off its coast. These accounts encouraged English whalers to visit Svalbard in 1611, and Dutch whalers followed one year later. For them, bowhead whales were ideal prey. Unlike many other whales, they are slow, docile, and relatively easy to kill. They are also enormous, often weighing more than 100 tons, with thick reserves of blubber that help them endure the Arctic cold. Whalers

[45] Van Engelen, Buisman, and IJnsen, 'A Millennium of Weather, Winds and Water in the Low Countries', 112.

hunted whales primarily for their blubber, which they rendered into lamp oil, soap, leather, or wax.[46]

In 1614, the Dutch *Noordsche Compagnie* or 'Northern Company' won a monopoly over the slaughter of whales and walruses from Novaya Zemlya to the Davis Strait. The consolidation of Dutch commercial interests in the Arctic took place amid similar developments that led to the creation of the East and West India Companies. The Northern Company and its English, Danish, and French competitors quickly set up factories at nearly every accessible coastal site along northwestern Spitsbergen. Dutch whalers established their infamous slaughterhouse of Smeerenburg – 'blubber town' – on Amsterdamøya, a little island just off Spitsbergen. Almost immediately, the whalers, divided by nationality and based in different factories, used theft and violence to undermine their rivals. Already in 1614, representatives of the English Muscovy Company insisted that Dutch whalers had no right to hunt the waters off Spitsbergen. They argued that a Portuguese map apparently showed that an Englishman, Sir Willoughby, had discovered the island for the company more than 40 years before the third Barents voyage. In 1614, three warships therefore escorted Dutch whalers to their Spitsbergen hunting grounds. In subsequent whaling seasons, escorting warships chased away their competition and safeguarded the lucrative plunder of oil and bone, while whalers established fortresses around their factories. Spitsbergen had become another frontier in a global struggle between growing European empires. Occasionally, rival factions within the same merchant companies sought to deceive one another by plundering secret hunting grounds. All of these machinations complicated the lives of whalers who also endured many of the hazards that had confronted Barents and his crew. Signs of scurvy riddle the skeletons of most whalers who died on or near Spitsbergen and were buried in its icy soils. Many skeletons have tibia and

[46] McCoy, *On the Edge*, 96. Ian Gjertzand and Øystein Wiig, 'Past and Present Distribution of Walruses in Svalbard'. *Arctic* 47:1 (1994): 34. De Veer, *The True and Perfect Description of Three Voyages*, 5. De Veer, *Reizen van Willem Barents*, 51. Louwrens Hacquebord, 'Three Centuries of Whaling and Walrus Hunting in Svalbard and Its Impact on the Arctic Ecosystem'. *Environment and History* 7 (2001): 172. Louwrens Hacquebord, Frits Steenhuisen and Huib Waterbolk, 'English and Dutch Whaling Trade and Whaling Stations in Spitsbergen (Svalbard) before 1660'. *International Journal of Maritime History* 15:2 (2003): 117. Jansen, 'Notes on the Ice between Greenland and Nova Zembla', 167. John F. Richards, *The World Hunt: An Environmental History of the Commodification of Animals*. (Oakland: University of California Press, 2014), 129. W. O. van der Knaap, 'Human Influence on Natural Arctic Vegetation in the 17th Century and Climatic Change since A.D. 1600 in Northwest Spitsbergen: A Paleobotanical Study'. *Arctic and Alpine Research* 17:4 (1985): 372.

clavicle fractures, which were probably caused by slips and falls aboard ice-coated whaling vessels.[47]

The climatic fluctuations of the Little Ice Age probably shaped the history of the whaling industry, just as they had influenced the exploratory journeys that made it possible. The few surviving ship logbooks kept by Dutch whalers during the Grindelwald Fluctuation reveal that extensive sea ice frustrated, and at times imperilled, voyages to the Arctic. The author of one of these logbooks, for example, reported on 7 June 1615 that sea ice was too thick for the crew to find a way through. They spotted a whale three days later, but the ice soon turned them around. In the evening, the wind started to rise, so they raised their sails. Just then, thick sea ice again surrounded them. They tried but failed to anchor themselves to an iceberg, and the wind stiffened into a storm that brought torrential rain. The ship might have been destroyed, according to the journal author, 'had God not saved us'.[48]

Extensive sea ice in the Grindelwald Fluctuation may have threatened whalers, but it probably also helped them find their quarry. Scientists have suggested that, as sea ice in the vicinity of Spitsbergen expanded, bowhead whales congregated near its edge. While grouped together, they were relatively easy to track down and kill, and that may actually have benefitted whalers who found their way through the ice. By the early 1620s, English and Dutch whalers annually dispatched some 30 vessels, collectively, to the waters off Spitsbergen.[49]

Then, regional summer temperatures rose during the warmer seventeenth-century interruption in the Little Ice Age. In the vicinity of

[47] Louwrens Hacquebord, 'The Hunting of the Greenland Right Whale in Svalbard, Its Interaction with Climate and Its Impact on the Marine Ecosystem'. *Polar Research* 18:2 (1999): 375. J. M. Węsławski et al., 'Greenland Whales and Walruses in the Svalbard Food Web before and after Exploitation'. *Oceanologia* 42.1 (2000): 40. Hacquebord, Louwrens and Nienke Boschman. *A Passion for the Pole: Ethological Research in Polar Regions*. (Casemate Publishers, 2008). Louwrens Hacquebord and Nienke Boschman. *A Passion for the Pole: Ethological Research in Polar Regions*. (Philadelphia: Casemate Publishers, 2008), 89. George J. R. Maat, 'Osteology of Human Remins from Amsterdamoya and Ytre Norskoya', in *Smeerenburg Seminar: Report from a Symposium Presenting Results from Research into Seventeenth Century Whaling in Spitsbergen*. Norsk Polarinstitutt Rapportserie 38 (1987): 45. Martin Conway, *I. 1596–1617 Spitsbergen*. Notes from Collection of Notes and Printed Items on the History of Spitzbergen & Its Exploration. Reference code: SSC/23. Royal Geographical Society, London, United Kingdom. Louwrens Hacquebord, *De Noordse Compagnie (1614–1642): Opkomst, Bloei en Ondergang*. (Zutphen: Walburg Pers, 2014), 22, 117.

[48] Journaal van een Groenlandvaarder, 1615. Walvisvaarders. Oud archief stad Enkhuizen 1353–1815 (1872). Reference Code: 0120. Westfries Archief (Hoorn, Netherlands).

[49] Hacquebord, 'The Hunting of the Greenland Right Whale in Svalbard', 378. Hacquebord, *De Noordse Compagnie (1614–1642)*, 111.

Spitsbergen, this interlude started early, in 1625, and lasted until 1645, as it did in most other places. As sea ice retreated, whales spread across the open sea to the west and north of the island. Less extensive ice made for safer sailing and lengthened the hunting season. Slippery, icy conditions became less common aboard whaling vessels, and whalers may have avoided falls and bone fractures. However, it was now much harder for them to find their quarry. Of course, not all summers were warm in the vicinity of Svalbard, despite the generally milder climate. Michael Adriaenszoon de Ruyter, later one of the republic's most celebrated admirals, worked as a pilot aboard whaling vessels in 1633 and 1635. He reported extensive sea ice and storms off Jan Mayen Island that kept the whalers from reaching land. Still, temperatures were often warmer than they had been, and both the Northern Company and its English counterpart suffered as whale populations dispersed. Moreover, individual whalers increasingly violated company monopolies. In 1642, the Northern Company lost its privileges.[50]

Just three years later, average annual temperatures declined once more, as the Maunder Minimum came to Svalbard. Bowhead whales again congregated along the edge of the pack ice north of Spitsbergen. Whaling was more profitable than ever. In some years, more than 300 whaling vessels sailed for the seas off Svalbard, where they could kill more than 2,500 whales. Dutch whalers now dominated the hunting grounds off Spitsbergen, and oil and bone harvested from bowhead whales occupied an increasingly important place in the republic's economy. In 1670, some 8,000 seamen worked in Dutch whaling fleets, nearly as many as served on VOC ships, and far more than sailed in the herring fishery. Yet, as temperatures warmed in the wake of the Maunder Minimum, whales again dispersed in ways that made them difficult to hunt. By then, the regional bowhead whale population was considerably smaller than it had been, and the Svalbard whaling industry began a long decline.[51]

[50] Hacquebord, *De Noordse Compagnie (1614–1642)*, 111. Hacquebord, 'The Hunting of the Greenland Right Whale in Svalbard', 378.

[51] Hacquebord, 'The Hunting of the Greenland Right Whale in Svalbard', 379. De Vries and Van der Woude, *The First Modern Economy*, 257. Jaap Bruijn, 'The Maritime World of the Dutch Republic'. In *De Ruyter: Dutch Admiral*, eds. Jaap R. Bruijn and Ronald Prud'homme van Reine. (Rotterdam: Karwansaray BV, 2011), 27. L. Hacquebord, 'Twenty-Five Years of Multi-Disciplinary Research into the17th Century Whaling Settlements in Spitsbergen'. Available at: www.rug.nl/research/portal/files/14531514/07.pdf. See also Louwrens Hacquebord, 'Smeerenburg: het verblijf van Nederlandse walvisvaarders op de Westkust van Spitsbergen in de zeventiende eeuw'. (PhD diss., Universiteit van Amsterdam, 1984). Robert D. Everitt and Bruce D. Krogman. 'Sexual Behavior of Bowhead Whales Observed Off the North Coast of Alaska'. *Arctic* 32:3

Before Europeans charted and started exploiting Spitsbergen, some 46,000 bowhead whales swam through the seas off its western coast. Annually, they consumed around four million tons of plankton. As their numbers collapsed in the eighteenth century, the food web off Svalbard changed in response. Seabirds and polar cod filled the ecological niche formerly occupied by whales. Walruses, butchered alongside whales, had annually ingested roughly 400,000 tons of benthic organisms, such as molluscs, before Barents mapped Spitsbergen. When their population plummeted, bearded seals and eiders, a species of sea duck, replaced their ecological role. By unlocking a new world to European mariners, the quest for the Northeast Passage set in motion a transformation of a major Arctic ecosystem that was faster and had bigger consequences than perhaps any previously undertaken by human beings. Indigenous communities and Basque whalers had long hunted bowhead whales in other Arctic environments, but together they had killed no more than several hundred animals annually.[52]

Increased Dutch and English activity in polar seas led to further discoveries, and additional attempts at a northern passage. Crews aboard whaling vessels and their escorts drafted increasingly accurate maps to meet a growing demand, in the republic, for accurate depictions of the waters north of Europe. Some adventurers won financial backing from the Northern Company to follow English and French mariners into what is today the Canadian Arctic. However, few were as well equipped as the expeditions of the 1590s, and none yielded the discoveries that so distinguished the earlier voyages.[53]

(1979): 279. Israel, *The Dutch Republic*, 623. Maat, 'Osteology of Human Remains from Amsterdamoya and Ytre Norskoya', 44. Hacquebord, *De Noordse Compagnie (1614–1642)*, 120.

[52] J.M. Węsławski et al., 'Greenland Whales and Walruses in the Svalbard Food Web', 40. See also Louwrens Hacquebord and Jurjen R. Leinenga, 'The Ecology of Greenland Whale in Relation to Whaling and Climate Change in 17th and 18th Centuries'. *Tijdschrift voor Geschiendenis* 107 (1994): 415–438.

[53] Günter Schilder, 'Development and Achievements of Dutch Northern and Arctic Cartography in the Sixteenth and Seventeenth Centuries'. *Arctic* 37:4 (1984): 508. Jansen, 'Notes on the Ice between Greenland and Nova Zembla', 167. Martin Conway, *No Man's Land: A History of Spitsbergen from Its Discovery in 1596 to the Beginning of the Scientific Exploration of the Country.* (Cambridge: Cambridge University Press, [first published 1906], 2012), 76.

ARCTIC EXPLORATION AND EXPLOITATION IN THE LITTLE ICE AGE

The Little Ice Age transformed the Arctic environment in ways that influenced how Dutch mariners explored and later exploited the waters north of Europe. Yet it was actually seasonal warmth, which was less common during the colder climate of the late sixteenth century, that contributed to the success of the Dutch voyage to Novaya Zemlya in 1594. The promise of that expedition inspired a second in 1595, but conditions were now more typical of the Grindelwald Fluctuation. The explorers left late in the season, exposing their voyage to a sharp drop between average summer and autumn temperatures. Heavy sea ice therefore thwarted their attempts to investigate the Kara Sea.

This reversal only encouraged entrepreneurs in Amsterdam to attempt the more northerly passage for which they had long advocated. Early in the summer of 1596, a third expedition initially benefitted from weather that likely reflected the relative warmth of Arctic summers in the Grindelwald Fluctuation. Yet after its sailors discovered Bear Island and Spitsbergen, they were trapped off Novaya Zemlya when temperatures and sea ice manifested the sharp transition to autumn in a cooler climate. Sea ice and storms subsequently worsened the misery of their overwintering and imperilled their desperate escape from the Arctic.

The Barents expeditions unlocked new possibilities for European explorers and entrepreneurs. They also opened a new theatre of competition between English and Dutch merchants and mariners. Ironically, Dutch commercial interests scored a major victory when abundant sea ice encouraged Henry Hudson, an Englishman hired by the VOC, to chart the future site of New Amsterdam rather than scouting the Northeast Passage. The picture was more mixed around Svalbard. Dutch sailors long dominated the whaling industry set in motion by the Barents and Hudson voyages. Surprisingly, the frigid climates of the Grindelwald Fluctuation and Maunder Minimum actually benefitted whalers around Spitsbergen. Yet unsustainable whaling combined with further climate changes to doom the industry, and Dutch whalers proved less capable than their English counterparts of finding new hunting grounds.

Global climatic trends have diverse regional and local consequences, even in Arctic environments that react dramatically to small fluctuations in average temperatures. Dutch activities in the far north did not simply fail as temperatures cooled, but rather responded to complex, local interactions between the atmosphere, hydrosphere, cryosphere, and biosphere.

Conditions that prevailed during the Grindelwald Fluctuation might have hampered Dutch attempts to chart a northern passage to Asia, but they also encouraged new discoveries and industries, with important human and environmental consequences.

THE SOUTHERN ROUTE TO ASIA

For many Dutch merchants, the Barents expeditions proved that a northern passage was unlikely to exist, and even if it did, it would be prohibitively expensive to exploit. Merchants such as De Moucheron therefore invested heavily in small companies that organized expeditions to Asia along the southern route, around the Cape of Good Hope. Most returned with lucrative cargo, but all flirted with disaster. Delays caused by calm winds or storms lengthened the time that crews endured cramped, unsanitary conditions and spoiled rations, which in turn led to outbreaks of disease. By damaging and scattering fleets, storms also left crews more vulnerable to privateers. The companies that financed the early expeditions to Asia were too small to comfortably endure these risks, and competition among them destabilized prices for Asian commodities. The States-General therefore united the companies to form the VOC, which they gave a monopoly over Dutch trade from the Red Sea to Japan. A governing board known as the *Heren XVII* ('Seventeen Lords') would have the authority to conduct diplomacy, field troops, construct warships, and impose governors on indigenous populations across Asia. De Moucheron, who was not among the lords, would die bankrupt.[54]

The VOC had two related purposes: first, to profit from the lucrative trade in spices, textiles, and other high-value, low-volume Asian commodities; and second, to undermine the Iberian commercial economy.[55] In 1619, the

[54] De Vries and Van der Woude, *The First Modern Economy*, 384. Harm Stevens, *Dutch Enterprise and the VOC: 1602–1799*. (Zutphen: Walburg Pers, 1998), 16. Femme S. Gaastra, *The Dutch East India Company: Expansion and Decline*. (Zutphen: Uitgeversmaatschappij Walburg Pers, 2003), 119. Gerrit Knaap and Ger Teitler (eds.), *De Verenigde Oost-Indische Compagnie: Tussen Oorlog en Diplomatie*. (Leiden: KITLV Uitgeverij, 2002), 1. Tonio Andrade, 'The Company's Chinese Pirates: How the Dutch East India Company Tried to Lead a Coalition of Pirates to War against China, 1621–1662'. *Journal of World History* 15:4 (2004): 422. Hellinga, *Pioniers van de Gouden Eeuw*, 130. Israel, *The Dutch Republic*, 320. Günter Schilder and Hans Kok, *Sailing for the East: History & Catalogue of Manuscript Charts on Vellum of the Dutch East India Company (VOC), 1602–1799*. (Houton: Hes & De Graaf Publishers, 2010), 14, 45.

[55] To Grand Pensionary Johan van Oldenbarnevelt, the VOC was founded 'to damage the enemy and to secure the homeland'. Stevens, *Dutch Enterprise and the VOC*, 16. Scammell, *The First Imperial Age*, 21.

VOC's governor general in Asia, Jan Pieterszoon Coen, seized the small settlement of Batavia, which then became the centre of Dutch power in Asia. In the following decades, the VOC established fortified factories across Asia at the expense of both European and indigenous powers. With over 30,000 employees at its peak, it ultimately dominated trade not only between Asia and Europe but also between major Asian ports, which made it an increasingly important part of the republic's economy and culture.[56]

The company's activities at sea required intimate knowledge of ocean currents and especially the trade winds, which blow persistently from the northeast in the Northern Hemisphere and from the southeast in the Southern Hemisphere (Map M3). In both hemispheres, these winds result from warm air flowing at high altitudes from the equator, descending at subtropical high pressure regions, and tilting back along the surface towards the low pressure equator through the force of Earth's rotation. To fully exploit trade winds, VOC sailors experimented with different routes to Asia until the Seventeen Lords laid down 'sailors orders' that mandated a standardized course. Ships sailed south through the English Channel, except when they took a so-called back way that curved north and then south around Scotland and Ireland. Pieter van Dam, a long-serving member of the Seventeen Lords, estimated that this route added about a month to the duration of VOC voyages, so it was obligatory only when VOC ships needed to avoid the channel in times of war. Eventually, all ships sailed past the Bay of Biscay and, after crossing the equator, followed a precisely marked *wagenspoor* ('cart track'). Crews anchored at Table Bay near the Cape of Good Hope to resupply and repair any damage to their ships. In 1652, the company set up a fortified way station at Cape Town that resupplied its passing ships. After leaving the settlement, sailors usually followed the winds by sailing directly east, curving north off the coast of Australia, and making for Batavia.[57]

[56] Israel, *The Dutch Republic*, 324. Gaastra, *The Dutch East India Company*, 12 and 109. Ernst van Veen, 'De Portugees-Nederlandse concurrentie op de vaart naar Indië (1596–1640)' *Tijdschrift voor Zeegeschiedenis* 22:1 (2003): 3. Scammell, *The First Imperial Age*, 21. C. R. Boxer, *The Portuguese Seaborne Empire*. (Manchester: Carcanet in association with the Calouste Gulbenkian Foundation, 1991). J. R. Bruijn, F. S. Gaastra and I. Schöffer, with assistance from A. C. J. Vermeulen, *Dutch-Asiatic Shipping in the 17th and 18th Centuries: Introductory Volume*. (The Hague: Martinus Nijhoff, 1987), 19. Jaap R. Bruijn, 'The Dutch East India Company as Shipowner, 1602–1796'. *American Neptune* 47:4 (September 1987): 240. Gaastra, *The Dutch East India Company*, 134. Knaap and Teitle, *De Verenigde Oost-Indische Compagnie*, 4.

[57] The risk of being shipwrecked on Australia's western coast was real, but in the VOC's history, only six vessels were lost there. Gaastra, *The Dutch East India Company*, 114.

For much of the seventeenth century, the VOC organized its Asia-bound vessels into two fleets: the Christmas Fleet, which set sail in the winter, and the Easter Fleet, which departed in the spring. When the English Channel was at peace, these fleets referred not to convoys but rather individual ships that participated in a biannual exodus from many Dutch ports. If harbour ice let them leave port, outbound vessels in the Christmas Fleet had to brave conditions in the North Sea region that were stormy in both warmer and cooler climates. Yet they could arrive in the Indian Ocean just before the end of the summer monsoon, which gave rise to winds that aided travel from Batavia to the Company's other strongholds in Asia. After 1636, other ships were organized into a third Fairs Fleet that departed in September and October and could more consistently harness the winds of the monsoon. By the eighteenth century, so many ships departed the republic for Asia that the idea of separate fleets had become obsolete.[58]

Logistics in Asia forced most vessels sailing from Batavia to the republic to leave between November and January, and none of these ships ever arrived in Dutch ports later than November of the following winter. That was still too late for the Seventeen Lords. They aimed to hold the company's autumn auction when all expected inbound vessels had arrived, but arrivals later than October required a second auction that drove down prices. Despite repeated instructions from the Seventeen Lords to dispatch ships earlier in the year, the governors general of Batavia never deemed that feasible. Even in times of peace, VOC ships returning to the republic usually sailed in convoys, and joined escorting warships when they arrived in the North Sea region.[59]

The passage through the northeastern Atlantic often determined the success or failure of VOC journeys. In these waters, crews coped with many variables that could impact the timely completion of their voyages. For example, it was in the waters off Europe that hostile ships most imperilled VOC crews. Ice could delay sailors trying to leave Dutch

Harm Stevens, *Dutch Enterprise and the VOC*, 9. Hamish Scott, *The Oxford Handbook of Early Modern European History, 1350–1750: Cultures and Power*. (Oxford: Oxford University Press, 2015), 233. Bruijn et al., *Dutch-Asiatic Shipping in the 17th and 18th Centuries*, 58, 64.

[58] Gaastra, *The Dutch East India Company*, 111.

[59] *Generale missiven van gouverneurs-generaal en raden aan Heren der Verenigde Oostindische Compagnie, Vol. 3*, ed. W. P. H. Coolhaas. (The Hague: Martinus Nijhoff, 1980), 314. Pieter van Dam, *Beschryvinge van de Oostindische Compagnie* Vol. 3., ed. F. W. Stapel. (The Hague: Martinus Nijhoff, 1927; orig. 1701), 499. Femme Gaastra, *Bewind en beleid bij de VOC: de financiële en commerciële politiek bij de bewindhebbers, 1672–1702*. (Zutphen: Walburg Pers, 1989), 49.

harbours in the winter, especially during the coldest phases of the Little Ice Age. The most important variables of all were wind direction and velocity, which were less predictable in the northeastern Atlantic than they were along the rest of the cart track. Nevertheless, wind patterns in the region responded to decadal trends in atmospheric circulation that ultimately benefitted the VOC's trading empire.[60]

CLIMATE CHANGES AND STORMS IN VOC CORRESPONDENCE AND JOURNALS

Service aboard a VOC ship was a dangerous occupation, and more frequent storms in the coldest decades of the Little Ice Age made it riskier still. Approximately 3 per cent of outbound and 5 per cent of inbound VOC ships were lost due to storms or enemy action. Over the lifetime of the VOC, losses amounted to 144 ships, many overflowing with people and priceless commodities. Losing even one of these ships could inflict an immense financial and human toll on the VOC, and in turn on the economy of the Dutch Republic.[61]

Journals that recorded the major outlines of voyages from the republic to Asia reveal that death was routine aboard company ships (Appendix, Section II). Many sailors died due to disease and falling overboard, risks that rose during storms at sea. Deaths peaked during years of abundant shipwrecks, which occurred in storms that blew towards a lee shore (Figure 2.1). Shipwrecks were especially frequent during the coldest stretches of the Little Ice Age, and more than half occurred in the North Sea region. Wrecks declined during the warmer 1630s and '40s, so they did not correlate to changes in the total number of VOC ships at sea.[62]

[60] Frank Siegismund and Corinna Schrum, 'Decadal Changes in the Wind Forcing over the North Sea'. *Climate Research* 18:39–45 (2001): 44.

[61] Bruijn, 'The Dutch East India Company as Shipowner, 1602–1796', 134. Bruijn, 'Shipping Patterns of the Dutch East India Company', 261. Parthesius, *Dutch Ships in Tropical Waters*, 52. Jan De Vries, 'Connecting Europe and Asia: A Quantitative Analysis of the Cape-Route Trade, 1497–1795'. In *Global Connections and Monetary History, 1470–1800*, eds. Dennis O. Flynn, Arturo Giraldez, and Richard von Glahn. (Aldershot: Ashgate, 2003), 34–106, 54. See also P. G. M. Diebels, '"Op papier vergan". Onderzoek naar vergane schapen in de archieven van de Verenigde Oostindische Compagnie'. *Nederlandsch Archievenblad* 95 (1991): 174–190.

[62] Jaap van Overbeek, 'Database VOC Schepen'. *De VOC Site*. Bruijn, *Dutch Asiatic Shipping in the 17th and 18th Centuries*. Bruijn, 'Shipping Patterns of the Dutch East India Company', 261. Bruijn, 'The Maritime World of the Dutch Republic', 30.

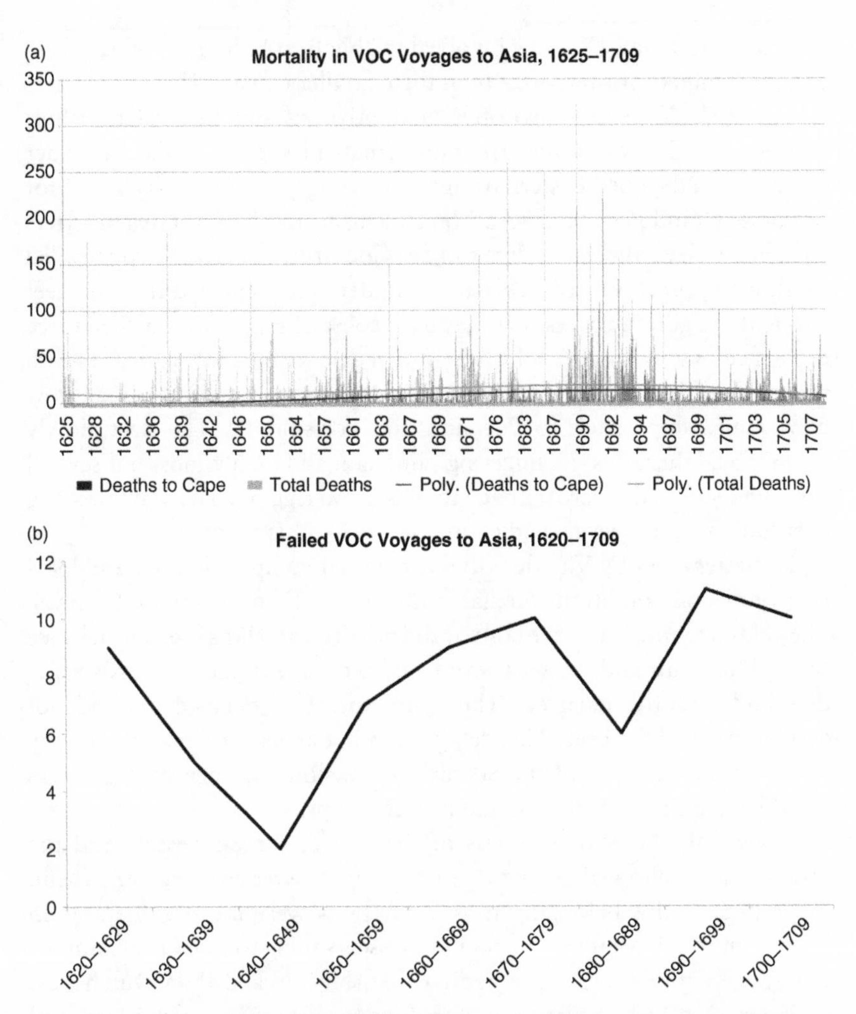

FIGURE 2.1 Top: total mortality, by year, recorded in 1,472 journals written aboard vessels travelling from the republic to the Cape (black), and from the republic to Asia (grey), 1625–1709. Order 3 polynomial regression reveals trends in the graph. Bottom: failed VOC voyages, by decade, in journals that describe trips from the republic to Asia, 1620–1709.

Occasionally, gales wrecked VOC ships in the republic's home waters. East Indiamen were too big to enter Amsterdam's shallow harbour without the assistance of tugboats and external floatation tanks, so most loaded and unloaded their cargo on the island of Texel (Map M1). Letters and diaries reveal that shipwrecks off Texel were more frequent in the Maunder Minimum than they were before or after, and that storms were often to blame. Yet few involved the big East Indiamen, which seem to have handled storms better than their smaller cousins.[63]

Correspondence can also offer qualitative insights into relationships between VOC voyages and the more frequent storms of the Maunder Minimum in the northeastern Atlantic. In January and February 1707, for example, Grand Pensionary Anthonie Heinsius received a series of letters written by Vice Admiral Philips van der Goes from a VOC convoy headed south from Texel. On 10 February, Van der Goes reported that the fleet was making good progress off the south coast of England. Yet then three days of calm winds slowed the fleet until a gale with winds from the south scattered all but its warships and East Indiamen. Westerly winds now blew many ships back to Portland and Portsmouth. The fleet slowly reassembled there despite lingering rain, hail, and high winds, but several ships had suffered severe damage to masts and rigging. The warships and East Indiamen, however, had endured only light damage.[64]

The letters sent by Van der Goes reveal that complex human and local environmental conditions mediated the effect of storms on VOC crews. The gale encountered by the convoy did not drive its ships into a nearby lee shore, but south and westerly winds did blow them back towards ports they had recently departed. The storm therefore delayed but did not destroy most of the fleet. This delay was still dangerous since the convoy sailed during the War of the Spanish Succession, and nearby privateers could have targeted scattered and isolated ships.

In general, the seaworthiness of the VOC's largest vessels and the routes they followed ensured that storms wrecked few of them. By contrast, ships belonging to other nations were more vulnerable in the face of rough weather. Portuguese vessels sailing to Asia, for example, were nearly four times more likely to be shipwrecked than Dutch East Indiamen. Yet Lisbon was easier for ships to enter than Amsterdam, and its port bordered a less stormy sea. Portuguese officials worried that their ships might be overburdened with cargo, or that they left too late in the season to exploit favourable winds. Danish ships bound for Asia did not sink at the rate of their Portuguese counterparts, but they still shipwrecked at twice the rate of Dutch East Indiamen. The British East India Company

[63] 'Wrecks in Documents'. *Maritiem programma Nederland, Rijksdienst voor het Cultureel Erfgoed.* Accessed 24 June 2013, www.maritiemprogramma.nl/WID_00.htm. Parthesius, *Dutch Ships in Tropical Waters*, 52.

[64] Van der Goes, 'Van Van Der Goes, 10 februari 1707'. *De Briefwisseling van Anthonie Heinsius*, 71.

lost a far smaller share of its ships than the Portuguese or Danish, but it still lost more than the VOC.[65]

Dutch ships were sturdier than their Portuguese counterparts, and their crews may have been more capable of handling gales than their European colleagues, at least until the early eighteenth century. When VOC shipwrecks did occur, they could be tremendously costly for the Dutch East India Company. Even when vessels survived, they usually required expensive repairs. Overall, wear and tear caused by rough weather in the northeastern Atlantic probably raised costs of maintaining all East Indiamen that survived the passage to and from Asia. For VOC employees, service at sea was a dangerous business, and it became even riskier during the coldest phases of the Little Ice Age. Still, for a long time the Dutch coped with this danger more effectively than their European rivals.[66]

WINDS, STORMS, AND CLIMATE CHANGE IN VOC SHIP LOGBOOKS

Logbooks written aboard VOC ships recorded not only wind velocity but also wind direction, often with daily or even hourly updates. Many logbooks paired these observations with detailed descriptions of a vessel's speed and course. Combined, this information reveals how changes in atmospheric circulation affected VOC journeys across the northern Atlantic Ocean.

The earliest Dutch logbook that both chronicled a voyage to Asia and recorded weather in the Atlantic provides an account of a journey undertaken in 1601, by three vessels under the command of Joris van Spilberghen. This expedition, financed by the ill-fated De Moucheron, just predated the establishment of the VOC. Its mariners were among the first Dutch sailors to arrive at the island of Ceylon (present-day Sri Lanka), later a major Dutch possession. On 5 May, they left Zeeland with a favourable northeasterly wind. Four days later, a storm blowing from the south drove them into the haven of Dartmouth. According to the logbook, one of the ships sprang a leak in the storm, and salt water flooded its stores of bread. New provisions were brought aboard as the fleet waited for the wind to subside. It was not until 15 May that the vessels could leave port. That evening, the expedition passed Plymouth. As no further setbacks hampered its voyage in the

[65] Gillian Hutchinson, 'Threats to Underwater Cultural Heritage'. *Marine Policy* 20:4 (1996): 290. De Vries, 'Connecting Europe and Asia', 54. Parker, *Global Crisis*, 416.

[66] Solar, 'Opening to the East', 642. Van Veen, 'De Portugees-Nederlandse concurrentie op de vaart naar Indië', 14.

northeastern Atlantic, the log's next entry reported the fleet's arrival at Cape Verde off the western coast of Africa on 10 June.[67]

The log suggests that easterly winds aided crews sailing southwest through the North Sea region, and it confirms that storms could delay, if not necessarily imperil, the largest merchantmen bound for Asia. Logbooks with fewer interruptions that documented later voyages to Asia provide further evidence for those relationships. The log kept aboard the *Wapen van Hoorn* in 1627 recorded daily distance travelled and morning wind direction on virtually every day between the ship's departure from the republic on 19 March and its arrival at Cape Verde on 12 April. Fully 82 per cent of the logbook's morning measurements described some variation of easterly winds, owing in part to the ship encountering the northeastern trade winds. In the present climate, they blow from around 30° N down to the equator between October and April. In other months, they shift far to the southeast. Still, the *Wapen van Hoorn* did benefit from easterlies further north as it passed through the North Sea region. Its voyage confirms that such winds increased the speed of vessels travelling south from the republic. On days with easterly winds, the *Wapen van Hoorn* travelled, on average, 218 kilometres per day, while in days with westerlies it covered just 167 kilometres. Company ships could sail only six points of the compass against the wind, and when they did, their journeys slowed down considerably. Sailors therefore needed favourable winds to travel quickly out of the northern Atlantic Ocean.[68]

Few logbooks with continuous meteorological data survive to document weather in the northeastern Atlantic during the warmer decades that separated the Grindelwald Fluctuation from the Maunder Minimum. There is, however, a meticulous logbook that was kept in 1662: an unusually warm year in the context of the Maunder Minimum, but one that coincided with a shift in the North Atlantic Oscillation (NAO) to a negative position. Crewman Gerrits Boos wrote the log while he served as navigator aboard the East Indiaman *Maarseveen* on a journey from Rotterdam to Batavia.[69]

[67] Joris van Spilbergen, ''T historiael journael, van tgene ghpaseert is van whegen dry schepen, ghenaemt den Ram, Schaep ende het Lam, ghevaren wt zeelandt vander stadt Camp-Vere naar d'Oost-Indiën, onder t'beleyt van Joris van Spilberghen, Generael anno 1601'. In *De reis van Joris van Spilbergen naar Ceylon, Atjeh en Bantam 1601–1604*. ('s-Gravenhage: Martinus Nijhoff, 1933), 1.

[68] 'Journal vant schip Wapen van Hoorn op sijn 3de voyagie'. Verenigde Oost-Indische Compagnie Collectie, Reference code: 1.04.02. Nationaal Archief (Den Haag, Netherlands). Bruijn et al., *Dutch-Asiatic Shipping in the 17th and 18th Centuries*, 58.

[69] Herman Ketting, *Leven, werk en rebellie aan boord van Oost-Indiëvaarders (1595–±1650)*. (Amsterdam: Het Spinhuis, 2005), 57.

The ship left port on 9 October and for the next two weeks struggled against calms and winds from the southwest and southeast. Over these 14 days the ship travelled 1,200 kilometres, or just 86 kilometres on the average day. It did not sail in a straight line, but rather dithered near the Celtic Sea. By contrast, from 29 October to 6 November, the *Maarseveen* surged forwards in winds that increasingly blew from the northeast. In just seven days of favourable weather, it had travelled 1,678 kilometres in a straight line, averaging some 187 kilometres per day.[70]

As it closed on the Canary Islands on 7 November 1662, the *Maarseveen* again endured a stretch of low, westerly winds. The ship travelled a mere 833 kilometres from 7 until 15 November, averaging just 93 kilometres per day. Then, one month after the *Maarseveen*'s first recorded log, the ship's pace quickened once more. Strong trade winds from the northeast propelled the vessel down through the cart track and towards the equator. Overall, from 15 October to 30 November, the *Maarseveen* travelled nearly 6,220 kilometres, from the mouth of the English Channel to a position just west of Guinea. Its log reveals that, when the wind was high and blew from the north, east, and especially the northeast, the ship could travel over 30 times faster than it did in weak and contrary winds from the southwest.[71]

The *Maarseveen* ultimately encountered the northeastern trade winds off Africa. It is therefore not surprising that, in the first six weeks of his journey, Boos observed easterlies in 57 per cent of his morning logbook entries, and westerly winds in just 43 per cent. Yet it is striking that he recorded more southeasterly than southwesterly winds in the first two weeks of his journey, well before the *Maarseveen* reached the trade winds. Other VOC journeys during the Maunder Minimum also encountered abundant easterlies, even while north of the northeastern trades.

Take, for example, the *Vosmaar*, which left Wielingen in convoy on 26 April 1696, and the *Boor*, which left Texel on 17 July 1699. The *Vosmaar* departed in a season distinguished by relatively abundant easterlies, even in the twentieth-century climate. Its logbook records easterly winds on 34 per cent of morning entries written in the Atlantic north of 40° N. Easterlies were only slightly more common during the voyage of the *Vosmaar* than their annual regional average in the twentieth

[70] Gerritsz Boos, *Maarseveen* logs, records 69243–69251, 29 October–6 November. Entered by Rolf de Weijert. CLIWOC Database. Accessed 24 June 2013, www.knmi.nl/cliwoc.

[71] Gerritsz Boos, *Maarseveen* logs, records 69261–69277, 16 November – 2 December. Entered by Rolf de Weijert. CLIWOC Database. Accessed 24 June 2013, www.knmi.nl/cliwoc.

century.[72] However, during the first 18 days of the journey of the *Boor*, 44 per cent of logbook morning observations reported easterlies. This despite the vessel's departure in the summer: a season then, as now, characterized by abundant westerlies. The difference in the amount of easterlies experienced by each crew correlates with a difference in the speed of their ships. The *Vosmaar* travelled a daily average of 104 kilometres in the first leg of its journey, while the *Boor* covered an average of 128 kilometres per day.[73]

Other VOC ship logbooks written during the coldest part of the Maunder Minimum also recorded frequent easterly winds in the North Sea region. For example, the log kept aboard the *Unie* in the winter of 1699/1700 listed easterlies in 44 per cent of morning and 67 per cent of evening observations. In the winter of 1701, the log of the *Berkel* recorded easterlies in 49 per cent of morning entries. Both logbooks contain only broken references to daily distance covered. They nonetheless hint that the speed of ships sailing from the republic peaked in easterly and especially northeasterly winds. They also suggest that wind direction was a more important influence than wind velocity on the speed of VOC ships. The *Vosmaar* sailed through winds that averaged roughly 13 kilometres/hour before the ship reached 40° N, while the *Boor* weathered average winds of just 5.5 kilometres/hour. Nevertheless, the journey of the *Boor* was quicker than that of the *Vosmaar*.[74]

We can isolate the influence of changes in prevailing wind direction and velocity on VOC ship voyages by looking at Company voyages during the warmer climate that followed the Maunder Minimum, when westerly winds were again common in the North Sea region. The regional frequency of

[72] Siegismund and Schrum, 'Decadal Changes in the Wind Forcing over the North Sea', 44. Korevaar, *North Sea Climate*, 65. 'Northeast England: Climate', Met Office, accessed 2 February 2013, www.metoffice.gov.uk/climate/uk/ne. 'Eastern England: Climate', Met Office, accessed 2 February 2013, www.metoffice.gov.uk/climate/uk/ee.

[73] Korevaar, *North Sea Climate*, 21.

[74] 'Journal vant schip Wapen van Hoorn op sijn 3de voyagie'. Verenigde Oost-Indische Compagnie Collectie, Reference code: 1.04.02. Nationaal Archief (Den Haag, Netherlands). 'Journaal gehouden op het schip Vosmaar van de kamer Zeeland door schipper Jacob Lantsheer'. Verenigde Oost-Indische Compagnie Collectie, Reference code: 1.04.02. Nationaal Archief (Den Haag, Netherlands). 'Journaal gehouden op het schip Boor door schipper Jan van Wijck'. Verenigde Oost-Indische Compagnie Collectie, Reference code: 1.04.02. Nationaal Archief (Den Haag, Netherlands). 'Journaal gehouden op het schip Unie door schipper Jan Vrelant'. Verenigde Oost-Indische Compagnie Collectie, Reference code: 1.04.02. Nationaal Archief (Den Haag, Netherlands). 'Journaal gehouden op het schip Berkel'. Verenigde Oost-Indische Compagnie Collectie, Reference code: 1.04.02. Nationaal Archief (Den Haag, Netherlands).

westerlies peaked in the late 1730s, declined in the colder 1740s, picked up in the early 1750s, and fell sharply with the onset of the Dalton Minimum after 1755. Logbooks kept aboard 10 VOC vessels – the *Africaensche Galey, Admiraal de Ruyter, Akerendam, Bos en Hoven, Landskroon, Oud Haarlem, Schagen, Scholtenburg, Spaarzaamheid*, and *Westerveld* – reveal the consequences of these fluctuations for sailors at sea.[75]

All sailed through the North Sea region between 1750 and 1775. For the first two weeks of their journeys, officers aboard the company ships observed an average of 58 per cent easterly winds, 39 per cent westerly winds, and 3 per cent calms, variable winds, or purely northerly or southerly winds. However, the three ship logbooks that describe voyages in the early 1750s overwhelmingly recorded westerly winds, while the seven logbooks written in or after 1755 listed far more easterlies. The weather data in these logs therefore confirm that, in the 1750s, westerlies grew less common, and easterlies more frequent, across the North Sea region.[76]

Nevertheless, atmospheric circulation changes with the seasons, in ways that fluctuate within and between climatic regimes. As a result, it would be hard to compare VOC ship voyages in warmer and colder years, if these voyages took place in different seasons. Luckily, the seventeenth-century vessels considered in this chapter all departed in the spring or fall, with just one exception: the *Boor*. In the 1760s, crews aboard the *Admiraal de Ruyter* and *Bos en Hoven*, which left the republic in the spring, both experienced easterlies during most of their passage through the northeastern Atlantic. The weather observations in their logs are

[75] Lamb, *Historic Storms of the North Sea, British Isles, and Northwest Europe*, 31. Grove, *Little Ice Ages Ancient and Modern*, 8. Wheeler et al., 'Atmospheric Circulation and Storminess Derived from Royal Navy Logbooks', 13.

[76] C. Mattijsen, *Africaensche Galey* logs, records 11389–11403, 6 January–20 January. Entered by Maarten Koek. Cornelis van de Putte, *Admiraal de Ruyter* logs, records 9242–9256, 11 March–25 March. Entered by Renate Meijer. Cornelis van de Stam, *Akerendam* logs, records 12689–12704, 5 January–20 January. Entered by Frank Boekhorst. Cornelis van der Stam, *Bos en Hoven* logs, records 29025–29039, 30 March–13 April. Entered by Rolf de Weijert. J. W. v/d Velden, *Landskroon* logs, records 65874–65888, 22 December–5 January. Entered by Toni Spek-Font Pallares. Jan Siereveld, *Oud Haarlem* logs, records 85717–85731, 28 December–11 January. Entered by Pauline Beckers. Jacob Leertouwer, *Schagen* logs, records 105316–105330, 27 August–10 September. Entered by Frank Boekhorst. Pieter Clement, *Scholtenburg* logs, records 106280–106294, 26 December–9 January. Entered by Bruni Oehlers. Willem Vrugt, *Spaarzaamheid* logs, records 109396–109410, 28 October–11 November. Entered by Frank Boekhorst. Lieve van Rentergem, *Westerveld* logs, records 132726–132740, 25 November–9 December. Entered by Frank Boekhorst. CLIWOC Database. Accessed 24 June 2013, www.knmi.nl/cliwoc.

similar to those recorded aboard the *Wapen van Hoorn*, which of course also sailed in a cold climate.[77]

No such parallels existed between autumn voyages in different climatic regimes. The *Spaarzaamheid* in 1751, and the *Westerveld* in 1764, both departed in the fall. Crews aboard both vessels experienced far more westerlies in the first two weeks of their journeys than did the sailors of the *Maarseveen*, which also left port in autumn. Still, VOC logbooks overall record an unusually high frequency of easterlies in the North Sea region during coldest periods of the Little Ice Age, which coincided with a negative NAO. In these frigid decades, VOC mariners experienced different wind patterns than we would today.[78]

The eighteenth-century logbooks confirm that easterlies quickened the voyages of VOC vessels sailing south through the English Channel. The three ships that left port in the early 1750s, when westerly winds were more common, sailed an average daily distance of 143 kilometres. For the six vessels sailing after 1755, that average increased to 164. This 14 per cent rise in average distance covered reflects a more than 30 per cent leap in the number of easterlies VOC logbooks recorded after 1755. The strong influence of wind direction is especially clear when the journeys of these ten ships are categorized according to the prevailing winds experienced, rather than the year of their travels. Crews that endured westerly winds for at least half of the first two weeks of their voyages travelled an average speed of just 126 kilometres per day. By contrast, sailors who enjoyed easterly winds for more than half of their first two weeks travelled a daily average of 181 kilometres.[79]

[77] Cornelis van de Putte, *Admiraal de Ruyter* logs, records 9242–9256, 11 March–25 March. Entered by Renate Meijer. Cornelis van der Stam, *Bos en Hoven* logs, records 29025–29039, 30 March–13 April. Entered by Rolf de Weijert. Jacob Leertouwer, *Schagen* logs, records 105316–105330, 27 August–10 September. Entered by Frank Boekhorst. CLIWOC Database. Accessed 24 June 2013, www.knmi.nl/cliwoc.

[78] Willem Vrugt, *Spaarzaamheid* logs, records 109396–109410, 28 October–11 November. Entered by Frank Boekhorst. Lieve van Rentergem, *Westerveld* logs, records 132726–132740, 25 November–9 December. Entered by Frank Boekhorst. CLIWOC Database. Accessed 24 June 2013, www.knmi.nl/cliwoc.

[79] C. Mattijsen, *Africaensche Galey* logs, records 11389–11403, 6 January–20 January. Entered by Maarten Koek. Cornelis van de Putte, *Admiraal de Ruyter* logs, records 9242–9256, 11 March–25 March. Entered by Renate Meijer. Cornelis van de Stam, *Akerendam* logs, records 12689–12704, 5 January–20 January. Entered by Frank Boekhorst. Cornelis van der Stam, *Bos en Hoven* logs, records 29025–29039, 30 March–13 April. Entered by Rolf de Weijert. J. W. v/d Velden, *Landskroon* logs, records 65874–65888, 22 December–5 January. Entered by Toni Spek-Font Pallares. Jan Siereveld, *Oud Haarlem* logs, records 85717–85731, 28 December–11 January. Entered by Pauline Beckers. Jacob Leertouwer, *Schagen* logs, records 105316–105330, 27 August–10 September. Entered by Frank Boekhorst. Pieter Clement, *Scholtenburg*

Long-term shifts in prevailing wind could also set the stage for short-term extremes, in which winds overwhelmingly blew from one direction for several weeks at a time. Such winds dramatically affected ship voyages. For example, 93 per cent of the winds encountered by the crew of the *Africaensche Galey* in the first two weeks of their journey in 1750 issued from the west, and their ship travelled a daily average of just 90 kilometres. However, during the first 14 days of their travels in 1766, the crew of the *Scholtenburg* experienced easterly winds 93 per cent of the time, and their vessel sailed an extraordinary 215 kilometres per day.[80]

For VOC ships sailing south through the English Channel, changes in wind direction could shorten or prolong journeys through the northeastern Atlantic by as many as two weeks. Crews taking the back way, however, spent far more time in the northeastern Atlantic, and winds there had a correspondingly bigger impact on the overall duration of their voyages. Adriaen Jongekoe, a navigator aboard the *Afrika*, wrote one of the most illuminating logbooks to chronicle such a journey. The East Indiaman departed the republic on 12 April 1677, during the final year of a long conflict with France. It therefore travelled in convoy around Scotland and Ireland. Jongekoe reported that the ship covered 207 kilometres on 22 April, as it rounded the northern coast of Scotland in strong winds from the north-northeast. However, on 23 April, it sailed just 81 kilometres against a contrary wind from the west-southwest. The wind shifted again to blow from the southeast for much of 24 April, and by evening it had

logs, records 106280–106294, 26 December–9 January. Entered by Bruni Oehlers. Willem Vrugt, *Spaarzaamheid* logs, records 109396–109410, 28 October–11 November. Entered by Frank Boekhorst. Lieve van Rentergem, *Westerveld* logs, records 132726–132740, 25 November–9 December. Entered by Frank Boekhorst. CLIWOC Database. Accessed 24 June 2013, www.knmi.nl/cliwoc.

[80] C. Mattijsen, *Africaensche Galey* logs, records 11389–11403, 6 January–20 January. Entered by Maarten Koek. Cornelis van de Putte, *Admiraal de Ruyter* logs, records 9242–9256, 11 March–25 March. Entered by Renate Meijer. Cornelis van de Stam, *Akerendam* logs, records 12689–12704, 5 January–20 January. Entered by Frank Boekhorst. Cornelis van der Stam, *Bos en Hoven* logs, records 29025–29039, 30 March–13 April. Entered by Rolf de Weijert. J. W. v/d Velden, *Landskroon* logs, records 65874–65888, 22 December–5 January. Entered by Toni Spek-Font Pallares. Jan Siereveld, *Oud Haarlem* logs, records 85717–85731, 28 December–11 January. Entered by Pauline Beckers. Jacob Leertouwer, *Schagen* logs, records 105316–105330, 27 August–10 September. Entered by Frank Boekhorst. Pieter Clement, *Scholtenburg* logs, records 106280–106294, 26 December–9 January. Entered by Bruni Oehlers. Willem Vrugt, *Spaarzaamheid* logs, records 109396–109410, 28 October–11 November. Entered by Frank Boekhorst. Lieve van Rentergem, *Westerveld* logs, records 132726–132740, 25 November–9 December. Entered by Frank Boekhorst. CLIWOC Database. Accessed 24 June 2013, www.knmi.nl/cliwoc.

stiffened while veering to issue from the east-northeast. The *Afrika* crossed 141 kilometres in the favourable wind. Yet strong gusts soon strengthened into a ferocious storm that raged throughout the next day. Surprisingly, the logbook of the *Afrika* did not report damage and death. Instead, it revealed that high winds from the northeast propelled the vessel a remarkable 341 kilometres to the west. On 26 April, strong winds continued to blow from the north, and the *Afrika* travelled another 252 kilometres. Overall, for the 16 days in April during which the distance covered was either recorded or decipherable, the *Afrika* crossed a total of 2,778 kilometres, averaging a swift 173 kilometres per day. By 30 April, the ship reached the vicinity of Porto, Portugal. From there, the trade winds carried it on to the Cape.[81]

Jongekoe listed easterly winds in 68 per cent of his morning logbook entries. For his crew, persistent easterlies and a severe storm shortened the usual month-long detour of the backway by two weeks, and helped them avoid French privateers. Storms, as we have seen, could threaten and occasionally delay VOC ships, but the logbook of the *Afrika* reveals that sailors could also exploit their ferocity. Crews in the open sea coped with a storm by 'scudding' before the wind. They reduced their sails to preserve their masts and struggled to position their vessel so the wind was astern, which meant that high waves would not impact the hull broadside. A ship that survived a storm at sea was therefore transported far in the direction of the storm's winds. More VOC sailors enjoyed these benefits of storms than did sailors from other trading companies, since fewer VOC ships wrecked in storms. Indeed, the gale of 25 April does not seem to have imperilled the *Afrika*, which was far from a lee shore. Several sailors fell overboard and drowned during the first weeks of the ship's voyage, but such tragedies were sadly routine aboard East Indiamen.[82]

Hubert Lamb has argued that, in the North Sea, severe storms with northerly winds grew more common in the late Little Ice Age. This trend may have played out in the waters north of Scotland and Ireland, although Lamb worked from a small sample of surviving documents that he did not always interrogate with a historian's critical eye. Nevertheless, it may be that all of the meteorological conditions endured by the mariners aboard

[81] Adriaen Jongekoe, *Afrika* logs, records 11248–11266, 12 April–30 April. Entered by Rolf de Weijert. CLIWOC Database. Accessed 24 June 2013, www.knmi.nl/cliwoc. Unger, 'Introduction', in *Cogs, Caravels and Galleons*, 27.

[82] Lawrence Otto Goedde, *Tempest and Shipwreck in Dutch and Flemish Art: Convention, Rhetoric, and Interpretation*. (Philadelphia: The Pennsylvania State University Press, 1989), 166.

the *Afrika* in the first leg of its journey were precisely those that the Maunder Minimum had made more common.[83]

Relatively few eighteenth-century ships took the back way, and therefore few logbooks from a warmer climate can contextualize the journey of the *Afrika*. Still, four VOC vessels did take the northern route between 1750 and 1760: the *Hercules* in 1756, the *Jerusalem* in the same year, the *Sloterdijk* in 1759, and the *Noordbeveland* in 1760. The logbooks kept aboard these ships all noted plentiful easterly winds. However, while the *Afrika* sailed in persistent northerly winds, the eighteenth-century ships endured abundant southerly winds. None of the four ship logbooks written in the 1750s recorded a single storm, let alone a storm with winds from the north. Yet in 1769, a log kept aboard the *Agatha*, a whaling vessel bound for Svalbard, recorded three days of uninterrupted gustiness from the north as it sailed just east of the back way. Meanwhile, in the late eighteenth century, crews aboard the frigates *Dregterlandt, Braave*, and *Bellone* survived gales and squalls issuing from the north, as their vessels passed through the waters north of Scotland and Ireland. It may be that a rise in the frequency of storms accompanied the onset of the Dalton Minimum in the waters north of the British Isles during the late eighteenth century. The storm encountered by the crew of the *Afrika* may well have been typical of conditions in a chilly climate.[84]

It is easy to assume that changes in wind speed and direction affected VOC ships returning to the republic from Asia in just the opposite way as they did departing vessels. However, the course taken by most returning crews swerved far west of the route used by departing sailors (Map M3). Returning sailors took this path to exploit the westerly winds that usually prevailed across much of the northern Atlantic Ocean. Some inbound

[83] Lamb, *Historic Storms of the North Sea, British Isles, and Northwest Europe*, 30.

[84] Adriaen Jongekoe, *Afrika* logs, records 11248–11266, 12 April–30 April. Entered by Rolf de Weijert. *Hercules* logs, records 54537–54546, 9 July–18 July. Entered by Ronald Schurink. Godfried Wargijn, *Jerusalem* logs, records 61167–61178, 4 August–15 August. Entered by Frank Boekhorst. Jacob Rijzik van den Briel, *Noordbeveland* logs, records 84254–84270, 18 May–1 June. Entered by Florie Barnhoorn. Cornelis van der Stam, *Sloterdijk* logs, records 108144–108169, 23 May–16 June. Entered by Rolf de Weijert. Adam Ooms, *Agatha* logs, records 11656–11676, 3 August–23 August. Entered by Frank Boekhorst. Jacobus Arkenbout, *Dregterlandt* logs, records 40721–40818, 20 April–2 August. Entered by Pim Vente. J. Zoeteman, *Braave* logs, records 29252–29381, 24 February–6 August. Entered by Simone Pathuis. H. C. Albers, *Bellone* logs, records 27427–27555, 24 February–7 August. Entered by Simone Pathuis. CLIWOC Database. Accessed 24 June 2013, www.knmi.nl/cliwoc.

ships actually sailed southeast for several weeks before bearing north at the entrance to the English Channel.[85]

Few logbooks kept aboard VOC ships returning from Asia survive from the seventeenth century. Eighteenth-century logbooks therefore provide the best glimpses into how changes in prevailing winds affected inbound journeys. These logs suggest that wind velocity could have a greater impact than wind direction on the duration of returning voyages. For example, on 31 April 1757, the East Indiaman *Akerendam* covered 189 kilometres in brisk southwesterly winds, but on 1 May it traversed 211 kilometres in a stiff breeze from the north-northeast. The ship covered 122 kilometres when northerly winds moderated on the following day, and just 93 kilometres on 3 May, in relatively calm conditions. Wind velocity may have mattered more than direction because vessels could sail in many directions and still travel closer to home.[86]

Officers aboard the ships *Hercules, Jerusalem, Sloterdijk*, and *Noordbeveland* wrote logbooks while using the back way to return to the republic from Asia. During their journey around the British Isles, their vessels travelled a relatively sluggish daily average distance of 105 kilometres. They may have been slowed by a lack of high, squally winds, but this time it seems that wind direction was the more important influence on their speed. In particular, southerly winds appear to have accelerated ships taking the back way to the republic. While traversing the back way, inbound crews sailed north around the British Isles for much longer than they travelled south in the North Sea. It therefore stands to reason that southerlies benefitted these sailors more than northerlies.[87]

Ultimately, logbooks clearly show that easterly and especially northeasterly winds greatly increased the speed of outbound VOC ships as they sailed through the northeastern Atlantic on their way to Asia. They also support reconstructions of winds and atmospheric circulation that show

[85] Bruijn, *Dutch Asiatic Shipping in the 17th and 18th Centuries*, Vol. I, 24.

[86] Cornelis van de Stam, *Akerendam* logs, records 12672–12685, 22 April–5 May. Entered by Frank Boekhorst.
Pieter Grijp, *Alkemade* logs, records 14282–14295, 9 June-22 June. Entered by Rolf de Weijert. CLIWOC Database. Accessed 24 June 2013, www.knmi.nl/cliwoc.

[87] Entered by Rolf de Weijert. *Hercules* logs, records 54537–54546, 9 July–18 July. Entered by Ronald Schurink. Godfried Wargijn, *Jerusalem* logs, records 61167–61178, 4 August–15 August. Entered by Frank Boekhorst. Jacob Rijzik van den Briel, *Noordbeveland* logs, records 84254–84270, 18 May–1 June. Entered by Florie Barnhoorn. Cornelis van der Stam, *Sloterdijk* logs, records 108144–108169, 23 May–16 June. Entered by Rolf de Weijert. CLIWOC Database. Accessed 24 June 2013, www.knmi.nl/cliwoc.

a rise in the frequency of easterlies during the Maunder Minimum. As a result, VOC ships departing the republic in this period usually sailed more quickly than they did before or after. Storms in the northeastern Atlantic may have occasionally delayed, damaged, or even imperilled VOC vessels, but at least some also sped up outbound VOC vessels. Logbooks therefore suggest that the climate of the Maunder Minimum largely benefitted journeys to Asia from the republic. Well to the west of the North Sea region, prevailing westerly winds helped VOC ships return to the republic from Asia. Wind velocity seems to have been at least as important for such inbound journeys as wind direction, and some may have been quickened by storms. Still, it seems that inbound journeys were overall ambiguously affected by the Maunder Minimum.

THE BIG PICTURE: CLIMATE CHANGES, WINDS, AND THE SPEED OF VOC SHIPS

The treasure trove of texts left behind by the VOC lets us interrogate these relationships on the largest scales. Did climate change in the Northern Atlantic affect the broader efficiency of the VOC? Thousands of journals that described voyages between Texel and Batavia (Appendix, Section III) reveal, above all, that the time it took for VOC ships to travel between Europe and Asia fluctuated dramatically from the expeditions of the precursor companies through the final years of the Maunder Minimum (Figure 2.2).[88]

Even ships that sailed in the same year could take wildly different times to reach Batavia or Texel. Exceptionally long journeys were always more common for ships departing to Batavia than they were for ships returning to Texel. As a result, the standard deviation of outbound voyages to Batavia is 77.5, far higher than the standard deviation of inbound voyages from Batavia, which is 41.9. Extremely long voyages to Batavia were especially frequent in the early decades of Dutch trade with Asia, before the standardization of the cart track.

[88] Bruijn et al., *Dutch Asiatic Shipping in the 17th and 18th Centuries*, Vol. I, 24. *Dutch Asiatic Shipping in the 17th and 18th Centuries*, Vol. II, *Outward-Bound Voyages from the Netherlands to Asia and the Cape (1595–1794)*, eds. J. R Bruijn et al. (The Hague: Martinus Nijhoff, 1979), 1–459. *Dutch Asiatic Shipping in the 17th and 18th Centuries*, Vol. III: *Homeward-Bound Voyages from the Asia and the Cape to the Netherlands (1597–1795)*, eds. J. R Bruijn et al. (The Hague: Martinus Nijhoff, 1979), 1–343. Van Overbeek, 'Database VOC Schepen'. De VOC Site, accessed 24 June 2013, www.vocsite.nl/schepen/lijst.html.

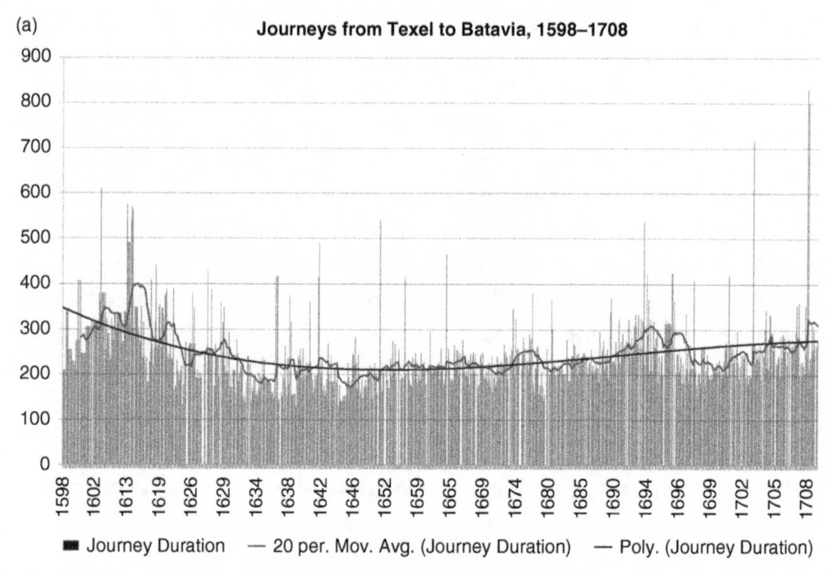

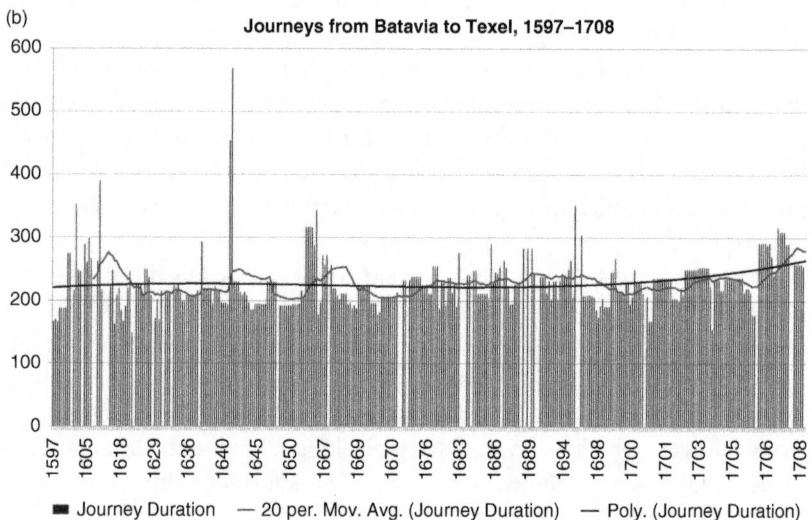

FIGURE 2.2 Top: journey duration, in days, of VOC voyages from Texel to Batavia between 1595 and 1708. Bottom: journey duration from Batavia to Texel between 1597 and 1708. An Order 3 polynomial regression and a 20-year moving average reveal trends in both graphs.

Inbound and outbound journey statistics show very different long-term trends in the length of average voyages. Outbound trips were long in the first decades of the seventeenth century, shortened in the 1630s and 1640s, and then lengthened gradually until the 1690s. If easterly winds in the northeastern Atlantic grew more common in both cold periods of the Little Ice Age and thereby shortened VOC voyages – as logbooks suggest – we might expect precisely the opposite trend. Inbound voyage duration did not fluctuate as much. Returning journeys were slightly longer in the first decades of the seventeenth century, slightly shorter in the final decades of the century, and slightly longer in the first decade of the eighteenth century. Since the influence on inbound journeys of changes in prevailing wind directions seemed ambiguous in ship logbooks, this trend is less surprising.[89]

Trends in VOC journey times reflected more than just shifting patterns of weather. Fortunately, some of these competing influences can be safely ruled out. Early seventeenth-century attempts to standardize the route of VOC voyages to Asia do not appear to have been the primary cause of declining journey durations. After all, the average length of journeys actually increased in the first years of Dutch trade with Asia. Moreover, technological improvements to East Indiamen were modest between 1598 and 1708, and could not have had much influence on voyage times. Trends in the average age and tonnage of VOC ships over the same period also do not match those in journey durations.[90]

By contrast, a steady rise in the number of days that VOC crews spent at the Cape of Good Hope and other secondary ports in the Atlantic Ocean surely did affect total journey durations. Although the Seventeen Lords had decreed in 1616 that crews could call only at the cape while sailing to and from Asia, in practice sailors often visited other ports by the end of the seventeenth century. In particular, many stopped at the Cape Verde islands to resupply their stores of freshwater. The islands are today on the fringes of the Intertropical Convergence Zone (ITCZ), which brings summer rains when it moves north every year. During the Maunder Minimum, however, the whole ITCZ shifted to the south, bringing long droughts to the islands. That might have been why crews called there infrequently, except when they ran low on supplies after

89 Bruijn et al., *Dutch Asiatic Shipping in the 17th and 18th Centuries*, Vol. II, 1–459. Bruijn et al., *Dutch Asiatic Shipping in the 17th and 18th Centuries*, Vol. III, 1–343. Van Overbeek, 'Database VOC Schepen'. De VOC Site, accessed 24 June 2013, www.vocsite.nl/schepen/lijst.html.

90 Partly because most VOC ships did not make more than four journeys. Solar, 'Opening to the East', 635. George M. Welling, 'De zin en onzin van schepen tellen'. *Tijdschrift voor Zeegeschiedenis* 28:1 (2009): 24. Bruijn et al., *Dutch Asiatic Shipping in the 17th and 18th Centuries: Introductory Volume*, 58.

taking the back way towards the end of the seventeenth century. Sailors who resorted to entering other ports of call often did so to escape storms or repair storm damage. Climate change, therefore, both discouraged and encouraged crews to use secondary ports of call along the cart track.[91]

At least some of the rise in average journey duration in the late seventeenth century therefore did not reflect changes in how much time crews actually spent in the dangerous environment of the open ocean. We can focus on these changes by subtracting the number of days that Dutch vessels spent in secondary ports from the total duration of their voyages (Figure 2.3). Once at sea, company crews usually tried to minimize how much time it took for them to reach their next port of call. To further isolate the influence of weather in the Atlantic, we can distinguish between the time it took for crews to reach the Cape of Good Hope and the time it took them to complete their entire journey to either Texel or Batavia. The results are striking. First, the total duration of voyages from Texel to Batavia correlates with statistical significance to the duration of their journeys from Texel to the Cape of Good Hope. The passage through the Atlantic Ocean, which included the region in which winds changed dramatically in the seventeenth century, was therefore the most important part of most VOC voyages.

Second, the dominant trend in the graph is now the sharp drop in journey duration from the early seventeenth century until the 1640s. We can further isolate the influence of weather by looking only at peacetime voyages. Some VOC ships still took the longer back way in times of peace, but it was used far more frequently during wars. Restricting our focus to peacetime voyages leaves us with six relatively isolated periods, because the Dutch Republic was so often at war in the seventeenth century. Journeys in these periods reflect the same trend as before, but now it is even more striking. The time that VOC ships spent at sea declined dramatically over the course of the early to mid-seventeenth century.[92]

[91] Bruijn et al., *Dutch Asiatic Shipping in the 17th and 18th Centuries*, Vol. II, 1–459. Bruijn et al., *Dutch Asiatic Shipping in the 17th and 18th Centuries*, Vol. III, 1–343. Van Overbeek, 'Database VOC Schepen'. De VOC Site, accessed 24 June 2013, www.vocsite.nl/schepen/lijst.html. Bruijn et al., *Dutch Asiatic Shipping in the 17th and 18th Centuries: Introductory Volume*, 67. David K. Patterson, 'Epidemics, Famines, and Population in the Cape Verde Islands, 1580–1900'. *The International Journal of African Historical Studies* 21:2 (1988): 291.

[92] Bruijn et al., *Dutch Asiatic Shipping in the 17th and 18th Centuries*, Vol. II, 1–459. Van Overbeek, 'Database VOC Schepen'. De VOC Site, accessed 24 June 2013, www.vocsite.nl/schepen/lijst.html. Bruijn et al., *Dutch Asiatic Shipping in the 17th and 18th Centuries: Introductory Volume*, 64.

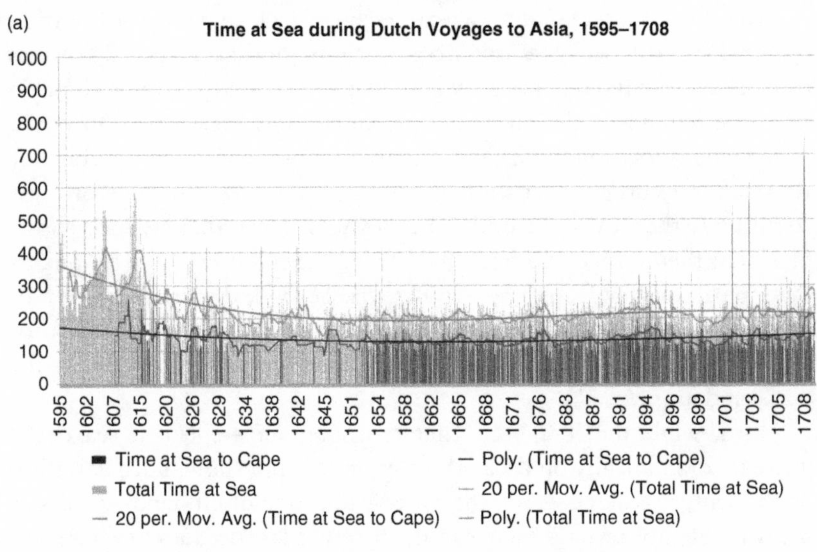

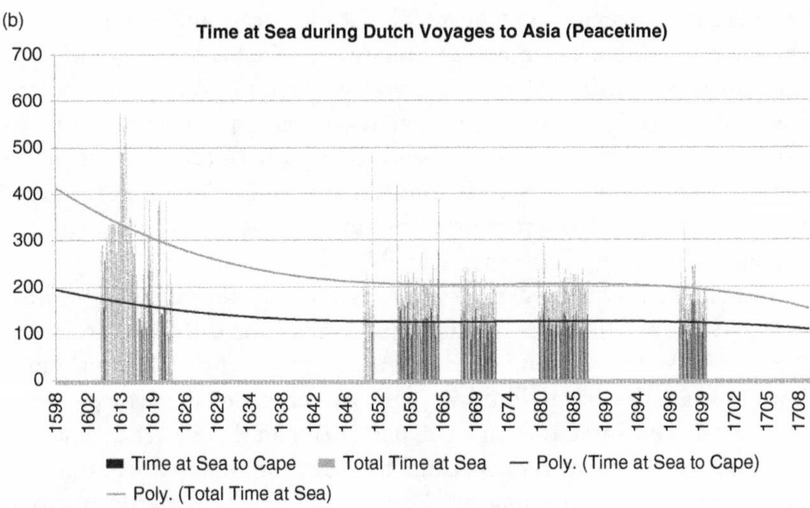

FIGURE 2.3 Top: time spent at sea, in days, from Texel to the Cape of Good Hope (black), and to Batavia (grey), for Dutch ships sailing from Texel to Batavia between 1595 and 1708. Bottom: the same graph shows only journeys in peacetime. Order 3 polynomial regression and 20-year moving averages highlight trends in the top graph. Because the bottom graph has large gaps, it does not use moving averages (but it does have an order 3 polynomial regression).

Using the same techniques, we can reconstruct changes in the duration of returning VOC voyages (Figure 2.4). More journals recorded voyages from Texel to Batavia, partly because many ships that arrived in Batavia from the republic ended up hauling commodities between Asian ports. In some decades, roughly half of the VOC ships that left the republic for Asia never returned. Statistics of inbound journeys are therefore less continuous than those of outbound voyages. Nevertheless, they show, first, that the average trip from Batavia to Texel did not take as long as the typical journey from Texel to Batavia. Second, the total duration of returning passages from Batavia to Texel correlates to the duration of their trips through the Atlantic Ocean, but not as strongly as it does for outbound journeys.[93]

Third, while the total time that returning ships spent at sea could fluctuate dramatically on decadal scales, it does not show much variation on the century scale. Overall, the average duration of inbound voyages at sea was roughly 20 days higher in the first and last decades of the seventeenth century than it was in the middle decades. Peacetime voyages reflect the same trend, but much more dramatically. Trends in the duration of inbound versus outbound VOC ship voyages therefore differ in important ways. Whereas the amount of time that outbound journeys spent at sea was very high in the early seventeenth century but declined later in the century, inbound voyages took only slightly longer in the early seventeenth century, and lengthened again late in the century. How can we explain these sharply different trends?[94]

Climate history provides possible answers, but they are at first difficult to come by. Since the frequency of winds from different directions fluctuated by the season, we can further refine the VOC outbound journey statistics by dividing voyages by season of departure. There were far more winter and spring departures than there were in summer and fall, which means that the statistics for those first two seasons are a good deal more continuous. Looking at winter departures alone reveals a negative correlation between winter temperatures and outbound voyage duration in the first half of the seventeenth century. However, this correlation does not meet the threshold for statistical significance, and it weakened in the 1630s before disappearing after the

[93] De Vries, 'Connecting Europe and Asia', 51.

[94] Bruijn et al., *Dutch Asiatic Shipping in the 17th and 18th Centuries*, Vol. III, 1–343. Van Overbeek, 'Database VOC Schepen'. De VOC Site, accessed 24 June 2013, www.vocsite.nl/schepen/lijst.html.

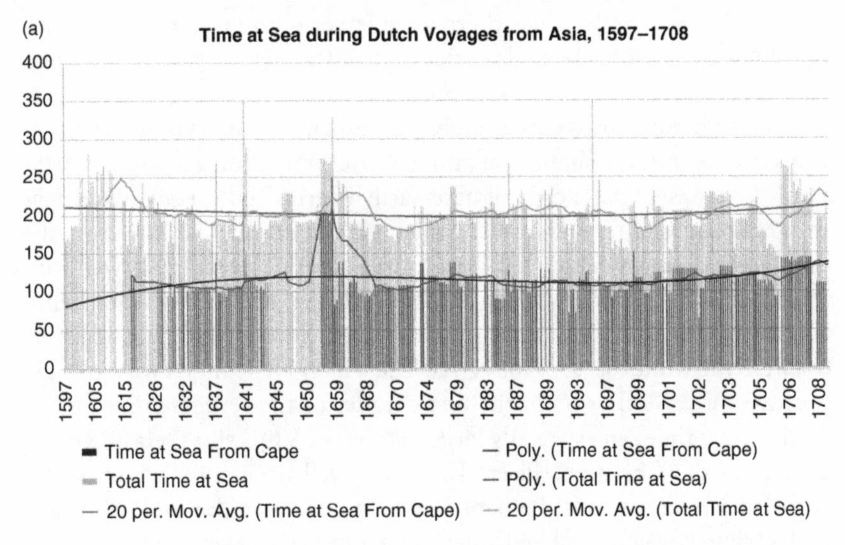

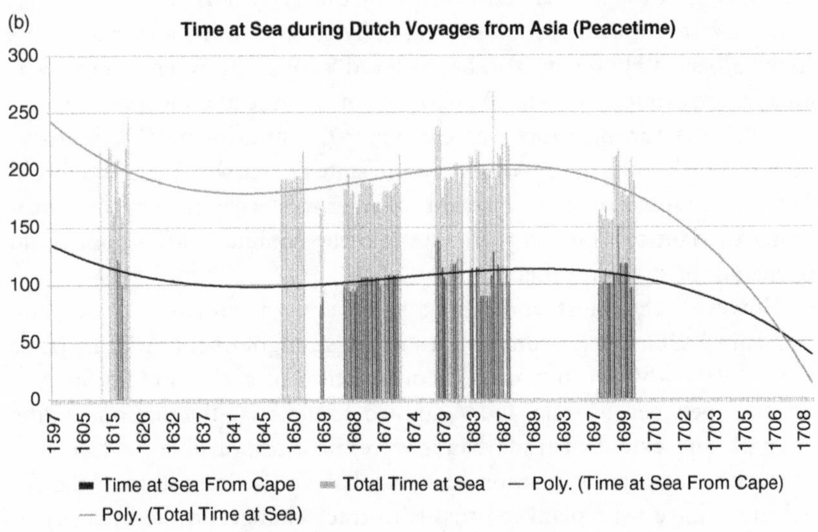

FIGURE 2.4 Top: Time spent at sea, in days, from Batavia to the Cape of Good Hope (black), and to Texel (grey), for Dutch ships sailing from Batavia to Texel between 1597 and 1708. Order 3 polynomial regression and 20-year running averages reveal trends. Bottom: the same graph with only journeys in peacetime. Order 3 polynomial regression highlights the trends.

1660s. Unfortunately, since there were fewer inbound journeys, dividing them by season yields data that is too fragmentary to be of much use.

Although easterly winds usually accompanied cold winter temperatures in the republic, changes in atmospheric circulation across the northern Atlantic as a whole did not necessarily overlap with regional changes in average annual temperatures. At first glance, gradual variations in the amount of time that VOC ships spent at sea also do not correlate well with fluctuations in the annual state of the NAO. Yet in the early seventeenth century, changes in the duration of outbound voyages did coincide with a shift in the winter state of the NAO. The winter NAO index was strongly positive for several years in the first decades of the seventeenth century. At the same time, an especially large number of VOC ships left in winter, as part of the Christmas Fleet. They may well have endured unusually frequent westerly winds. Perhaps it is telling that the duration of winter and spring voyages declined quickly in the early seventeenth century, while summer journeys took substantially longer until the 1670s. Shifts in the Siberian High may also have played a role. The Siberian High was weak from around 1610 until 1640, which influenced atmospheric circulation across Europe. Moreover, changes in the duration of VOC journeys coincide with shifts in the AMO. Its cold state during the late Grindelwald Fluctuation may well have brought stronger westerly winds to the northeastern Atlantic, while its warm state in the Maunder Minimum could have had the opposite effect.[95]

However, the most compelling link between climate changes and trends in VOC voyage duration lies in the strength of the Atlantic trade winds. Recently, a trailblazing reconstruction of early modern Spanish voyages between Manila and Acapulco found that fluctuations in the strength and extent of trade winds were most responsible for trends in journey times. Similar relationships may have played out in the Atlantic. Scientists have used plankton fossils to trace changes in the intensity of ocean upwelling in the southern Caribbean, which is driven by the trade winds. They have uncovered striking evidence for an increase in

[95] Luterbacher et al., 'Extending North Atlantic Oscillation Reconstructions Back to 1500'. *Atmospheric Science Letters* 2:1–4 (2002): 120. Ortega et al., 'A Model-Tested North Atlantic Oscillation Reconstruction for the Past Millennium', 72. Gray, 'A Tree-Ring Based Reconstruction of the Atlantic Multidecadal Oscillation since 1567 AD', 2. Bruijn et al., *Dutch Asiatic Shipping in the 17th and 18th Centuries*, Vol. II, 1–459. *Dutch Asiatic Shipping in the 17th and 18th Centuries*, Vol. III, 1–343. Jeong, 'Recent Recovery of the Siberian High Intensity', 3.

upwelling, and therefore trade wind strength, from 1410 to 1590, and from around 1640 to 1880. The beginning of this second surge in the strength of trade winds overlaps with both the start of the Maunder Minimum and a drop in outbound VOC journey times.[96]

A mix of scientific and documentary sources therefore suggests that the Maunder Minimum shortened the duration of Dutch trips to Asia in three ways. First, changes in the state of the NAO, Siberian High, and AMO may have raised the frequency of easterly winds in the North Sea region. Second, both the quicker passage of departing journeys through the northeastern Atlantic and the southward movement of the ITCZ dissuaded sailors from stopping at the most popular port of call. Third, the rising strength of the trade winds likely increased the speed of ships across the entire Atlantic. Voyages from Asia may well have been slowed by fluctuations in the NAO and AMO, but strengthening trade winds probably quickened them.

For crews aboard VOC vessels, journey duration was a matter of life, death, and profit. Time spent at sea was time spent exposed to storms and enemy combatants in unsanitary and typically disease-ridden conditions. Already high death rates peaked during storms and wars, both common during the Maunder Minimum. Mortality also increased in years that coincided with unusually long voyages to or from Batavia. If escaping the high odds of dying at sea was not motivation enough for a speedy passage to Asia, the Seventeen Lords offered lucrative bounties for outbound journeys that arrived at their destinations within six months. These bounties were a testament to the unequal importance for the VOC of outbound versus inbound journey times.[97]

The Little Ice Age affected different elements of the VOC's trading empire differently. However, changes to distinct aspects of the company's commercial network did not counteract one another to cancel out the influence of climatic changes. First, shifts in prevailing weather shortened outbound voyages more than they lengthened inbound journeys. Second, departing and returning vessels carried different goods and sailed to different ports for different purposes. Outbound ships typically

[96] David E. Black, Larry C. Peterson, Jonathan T. Overpeck, Alexey Kaplan, Michael N. Evans, and Michaele Kashgarian. 'Eight Centuries of North Atlantic Ocean Atmosphere Variability'. *Science* 286:5445 (1999): 1711.

[97] Bruijn et al., *Dutch Asiatic Shipping in the 17th and 18th Centuries: Introductory Volume*, 103. *Dutch Asiatic Shipping in the 17th and 18th Centuries*, Vol. II, 1–459. Van Overbeek, 'Database VOC Schepen'. De VOC Site, accessed 24 June 2013, www.vocsite.nl/schepen/lijst.html. Bruijn, 'The Maritime World of the Dutch Republic', 30.

transported silver, information, and instructions, essential prerequisites for sustaining the company's trade in Asia and defending its monopoly from other European powers. Inbound ships, on the other hand, carried the profits of the commerce enabled by their outbound counterparts. As we have seen, the Seventeen Lords fretted about inbound journey times, because late arrivals could not take part in the VOC's autumn auction. Nevertheless, changes to outbound travel times were more influential to the success of the VOC's commercial operations than shifts in inbound journey durations. Information about regional prices or newly hostile entities was most effective if it arrived quickly, and could be entirely irrelevant if delayed. Precious metals could be employed most effectively if used with the most current market information to maximize profits.[98]

Rapid passage along the cart track also allowed outbound VOC vessels belonging to the Christmas Fleet to arrive in Batavia before the conclusion of the summer monsoon. The monsoon's southwest winds let company officials redistribute goods brought to Batavia by ships travelling in both the Christmas and Fairs fleets. The summer monsoon weakened during the coldest decades of the Little Ice Age, yet its winds were still strong enough to power the company's intra-Asian trade if vessels arrived in Batavia on time. The weather of the Maunder Minimum in the northeastern Atlantic therefore provided important commercial advantages to the VOC.[99]

As the republic declined relative to other European powers in the final decades of the seventeenth century, the VOC accounted for an ever-larger share of the Dutch economy. Yet as the company's revenues rose, its profits declined. Its bloated infrastructure in Asia struggled to remain competitive against English and Scandinavian East India companies that increasingly traded coffee, tea, and other commodities even more lucrative than spices. In 1741, the VOC's governor general in Batavia, Gustaaf Willem van Imhoff, submitted an urgent recipe for reform to the Seventeen Lords. Some of his 'considerations' recommended increased bounties for rapid passage to Batavia. He wrote additional proposals in the following year that advocated smaller, quicker ships and improved training for company mariners.[100]

[98] Gaastra, *The Dutch East India Company*, 111. Jacobs, *In Pursuit of Pepper and Tea*, 60.

[99] Anil K. Gupta et al., 'Abrupt Changes in the Asian Southwest Monsoon during the Holocene and Their Links to the North Atlantic Ocean'. *Nature* 421 (2003): 356.

[100] Gustaaf Willem van Imhoff, 'Consideratiën over den tegenwoordigen staat van de Nederlandsche O.I.C'. Verenigde Oost-Indische Compagnie Collectie, Reference code: 1.04.02. Nationaal Archief (Den Haag, Netherlands). Peter Stearns, 'The Essence of

Did Van Imhoff perceive and respond to changes in ship journeys that were, in turn, influenced by shifting climatic conditions? His recommendations did not explicitly mention wind patterns, so it is hard to know for sure. They were certainly inspired by a series of shipwrecks off the Cape of Good Hope, yet these tragedies cannot be linked to climate change. They also reacted to the speed of Scandinavian, French, and English East Indiamen, which increasingly outpaced their Dutch counterparts. Yet the gradual increase in westerly winds over the northeastern Atlantic since the end of the Maunder Minimum, which would have slowed outbound ships, may also have played a role. The leaders of the VOC, after all, could access decades of weather observations in archived ship logbooks, and they could consult long-serving veterans of the passage to Asia.[101]

Van Imhoff's recommendations were only the most detailed entry in a long, fraught history of VOC governors general arguing about the duration of VOC voyages with their masters in the republic. Weather, shaped by climate changes, prompted discussions and responses from Europe to Asia among officials in the world's wealthiest company.

CONCLUSIONS: EXPLORING AND EXPLOITING DISTANT SEAS IN A CHANGING CLIMATE

Climate changes influenced Dutch efforts to establish, control, and exploit commercial connections with Asia. The chilly Grindelwald Fluctuation affected how Dutch explorers seeking a northern passage to Asia encountered, mapped, and interpreted Arctic and subarctic environments. Manifestations of the Little Ice Age in the far north blocked the route to Asia but encouraged discoveries that later contributed to the prosperity and culture of the Dutch Golden Age. They also helped convince the republic's merchants to focus on securing a southern sea route to Asia, and affected the first Dutch journeys around Africa. Storminess associated with both the Grindelwald Fluctuation and the Maunder Minimum increased the likelihood of death and disaster during VOC voyages.

Commodification: Caffeine Dependencies in the Early Modern World'. *Journal of Social History* 35 (2001): 269. Bruijn et al., *Dutch Asiatic Shipping in the 17th and 18th Centuries: Introductory Volume*, 103. Richard W. Unger, 'Ship Design and Energy Use, 1350–1875'. In *Shipping and Economic Growth, 1350–1850*, eds. Jan Lucassen and Richard W. Unger. (Leiden: Brill, 2011), 249–267, 250.

[101] Van Imhoff, 'Consideratiën over den tegenwoordigen staat van de Nederlandsche O.I.C'. Solar, 'Opening to the East', 636.

It may also have increased maintenance costs for Company vessels. However, Dutch East Indiamen were less frequently wrecked by storms than vessels aligned with other European states. Moreover, changes in wind velocity and direction during the Maunder Minimum reduced the amount of time spent at sea by ships travelling to Asia. Quicker journeys not only increased the efficiency of VOC operations, but also decreased the amount of time that VOC personnel were exposed to the hazards of being at sea.

Dutch merchants and mariners may have coped more successfully with the cold phases of the Little Ice Age than did their European competitors, yet they were not alone in benefitting – and at times suffering – from changes in prevailing weather during the Little Ice Age. Still, travel at sea was more important to the economy and culture of the republic's coastal provinces than it was to most other European regions. From the final decade of the sixteenth century to the collapse of the Dutch Republic, more Dutch vessels departed for Asia than ships belonging to any other European nation. Hence, weather associated with climate changes that affected all shipping actually had a greater influence on the Dutch Republic than the rest of Europe. That was true both for journeys that took Dutch sailors far from their republic, and for those that kept them much closer to home.[102]

[102] De Vries, 'Connecting Europe and Asia', 40.

3

Sailing, Floating, Riding, and Skating through a Cooler Europe

The merchants and mariners of the Dutch Republic expanded their commercial network to Asia by using the wealth and expertise they had gained from trade in European waters. All Dutch trade, in turn, depended on the web of canals and roads that connected the towns of the republic. Journeys in or near the heart of the Dutch commercial empire were no less affected by climate change than voyages in more distant seas, and that helped shape the history of the republic's dynamic economy.

Centuries before the Golden Age, herring exports allowed merchants in the northern Low Countries to purchase wine, salt, textiles, and other goods in western France, only to sell them in the same year for Baltic bulk commodities such as timber, metals, and grain. By the sixteenth century, people in the northern Low Countries widely referred to their Baltic commerce as the *moeder negocie*, or 'mother of all trades'. In 1666, Baltic commerce still accounted for around 75 per cent of the capital active on the Amsterdam bourse. By then, nearly all of the ships that hauled goods between the Baltic and the rest of Europe were Dutch. Grains, especially rye, were the most significant commodities returned to the republic, since Dutch farmers grew cash crops for external markets and could not by themselves feed the republic. Early in the seventeenth century, at least 75 per cent of the grain imported from the Baltic arrived in Amsterdam.[1]

[1] Maarten Prak, *Gouden Eeuw*, 105. Price, *Dutch society*, 70. De Vries and Van der Woude, *The First Modern Economy*, 357. Sicking, *Neptune and the Netherlands*, 6. Milja van Tielhof, *The Mother of All Trades: The Baltic Grain Trade in Amsterdam from the Late 16th to the Early 19th Century*. (Leiden: Brill, 2012), 7, 68. Barbour, *Capitalism in Amsterdam in the 17th Century*, 27. Christensen, *Dutch Trade to the Baltic about 1600*, 20.

For sailors engaged in this essential commerce, weather that became more common in the coldest decades of the Little Ice Age threatened lives and livelihoods. Extensive sea ice that expanded rapidly in frigid winters and melted slowly in cool springs repeatedly kept their ships in port, and occasionally trapped them at sea. Frequent and severe storms imperilled crews aboard the relatively small vessels that worked the Baltic trades, which typically sailed near lee shores. In the Baltic, cold and violent weather also provoked legal wrangling, complicated diplomatic relations, and disrupted supply lines for armies in the field. The Little Ice Age therefore influenced the profitability and preservation of Dutch commercial and political relationships in the Baltic.

However, the Dutch were rarely powerless in the face of a changing climate. New weather patterns may have actually benefitted the entrepreneurial merchants who worked as individuals or in small businesses to control the republic's trade with the Baltic. Merchants adopted innovations that helped them mitigate the risk of dangerous weather to commodities at sea. During the coldest periods of the Little Ice Age, they also exploited vast inventories of Baltic grain, stored in Amsterdam warehouses. When cold weather or precipitation extremes contributed to harvest failures, commodity price increases, and starvation elsewhere in Europe, Dutch merchants could sell grain at a handsome profit. Still, frigid weather in autumn, winter, and spring could lead to freezing that would stop Dutch ships from arriving in port and thereby raise grain prices for Dutch consumers while keeping Dutch merchants from exporting their inventories. Overall, climatic cooling was largely beneficial for merchants in the mother of all trades, but often harmful for the mariners they employed.[2]

Within the republic, commodities, information, and people from across an expanding commercial empire journeyed from major harbours to industrial, cultural, and political centres. They travelled on roads, creeks, canals, rivers, lakes, and coastal stretches of the sea, to cities such as Amsterdam, Rotterdam, The Hague, Leiden, and Haarlem. There, labourers refined commodities or used them to build finished products, regents interpreted information from far-flung informants, and mariners assumed new socioeconomic roles. Before long, the internal transportation system of the republic accommodated products, correspondence, and

[2] Werner F. Y. Scheltjens, 'The Changing Geography of Demand for Dutch Maritime Transport in the Eighteenth Century'. *Histoire & mesure* 27:2 (2012): 3.

people as they returned to the sea. Transportation networks enabled and supported this steady heartbeat of Dutch capitalism.[3]

Because these networks were diverse and intricately connected, they provided Dutch citizens with many options for travel. In the context of early modern Europe, such redundancies gave a distinct resiliency to movement through the Dutch Republic in the face of the coldest, wettest, and stormiest decades of the Little Ice Age. This resilience increased during the seventeenth century, but it was not absolute. Movement through the Dutch transportation system ground to a halt when major storms coincided with either severe freezing or flooding. Such weather was common during the Grindelwald Fluctuation (1560–1628) and Maunder Minimum (1645–1720). Overall, shifting weather patterns consistently enabled or facilitated some forms of transportation through the Dutch Republic, while hampering others. In the process, they helped shape the efficiency and culture of movement through the Low Countries.

CLIMATE CHANGES AND SEA ICE IN THE SOUND TOLL REGISTERS

In 1429, King Eric VII of Denmark ordered officials at Elsinore tollhouse near Copenhagen to collect dues from passing sailors. Elsinore overlooked the Sound, a narrow passage that connects the Baltic Sea to the *Kattegat*, or 'Cat Gate' – so named because only a cat could easily fit through – and in turn the North Sea. Tolls levied on ships entering the Sound would eventually account for 10 per cent of Danish crown revenues.[4]

Officials in Elsinore tollhouse meticulously recorded the dues they exacted on vessels sailing through the Sound. Their registers preserve quantified and almost unbroken information about 1.8 million passages through the Sound between 1497 and 1857 (Appendix, Section III). They reveal that the monthly quantity of dues paid by captains passing the Sound changed as winters cooled during the chilliest phases of the Little Ice Age. In particular, the coldest winters of the Maunder Minimum in the Baltic coincided with a sharp reduction, or even a complete cessation, of winter traffic through the Sound (Figure 3.1). From the warmer 1630s through the end of the Maunder Minimum, a strong and statistically significant (0.45)

[3] De Vries and Van der Woude, *The First Modern Economy*, 179.

[4] J. W. Veluwenkamp, 'Sound Toll Registers: Concise Source Criticism', 1. Accessed 10 August 2013, www.soundtoll.nl/images/files/STRpdf.pdf. Hill, *The Danish Sound Dues and the Command of the Baltic*, 11. Nicholas, *The Northern Lands*, 56.

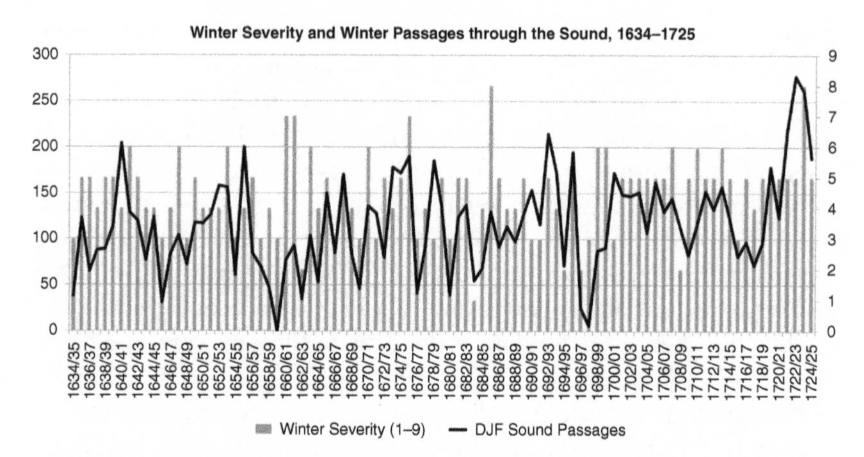

FIGURE 3.1 Winter severity and ship passages through the Sound from the winter (December, January, and February) of 1634/1635 to the winter of 1724/1725. Winter passages through the Sound plummeted in cold winters. Compiled using statistical tools available through the Sound Toll Registers Online database.

correlation existed between winter traffic and winter warmth. Winters cooled over the course of the Maunder Minimum, of course, but varied from year to year. Statistics of passages through the Sound therefore have a high standard deviation of 0.53. Severe winters also corresponded with an unusually late resumption of passages through the Sound in the spring.[5]

These statistics suggest compelling relationships between climate change and Baltic commerce, but they do not quite capture how frigid winters could take many forms. The winters of 1673/1674 and 1691/1692, for example, were distinguished less by bitter cold than by unusually long freezing. By contrast, the winters of 1683/1684, 1694/1695, 1697/1698, and 1708/1709 were not only exceptionally cold but also very long, with sub-zero temperatures that lasted deep into the spring. In all of these winters, traffic through the Sound ceased for at least two months. In most of them, passages resumed in April, and only reached high volumes in May.[6]

Sea ice almost certainly caused these changes in Baltic shipping. Sea ice extent in the Baltic closely correlated to regional winter temperatures, which cooled during the Maunder Minimum and warmed considerably in

[5] 'The Sound Toll Registers', Sound Toll Registers Online. Accessed 2 July 2013, www.soundtoll.nl/index.php/en/over-het-project/sonttol-registers. See also Nina Ellinger Bang, *Tabeller over Skibsfart og Varetransport gennen Øresund 1497–1660*, Vol. I–III. (Copenhagen: Gyldendalske Boghangel, 1906–1933).

[6] 'The Sound Toll Database', Sound Toll Registers Online. Accessed 1 April 2015, www.soundtoll.nl/index.php/en/over-het-project/sonttol-registers.

the eighteenth century. Not only did sea ice in cold winters close the Sound to Dutch mariners, but it also spread across the harbours of port cities in both the Baltic and the republic. Sailors in icebreakers and labourers on foot struggled keep the harbours free of ice. To support their work, authorities imposed taxes on ship owners, so shipping became more expensive in cold weather. However, even crews in icebreakers could not keep harbours open when sea ice grew too thick and too extensive. In the especially frigid winters of the Grindelwald Fluctuation and the Maunder Minimum, thick sea ice along the coast of the republic extended beyond the Zuiderzee and accumulated along the North Sea shore. Travel by ship was all but impossible.[7]

Mild winters coincided with a very different pattern of trade in the Baltic. Traffic through the Sound did not stop at all in the winters of 1636/1637, 1638/1639, 1660/1661, 1685/1686, 1723/1724, and 1736/1737, which were at least as warm, and at least as short, as average twentieth-century winters. Two of these winters coincided with the Maunder Minimum, but again, this should not surprise us. Just as cold weather can still happen in our era of rapid warming, mild winters and hot summers could occur in Europe even during the chilliest phases of the Little Ice Age. However, mild winters were much more common in warmer stretches of the Little Ice Age.[8]

In mild winters, ships in substantial quantities traded in Baltic ports, especially in December. In December of 1640, for example, 188 Dutch ships sailed through the Sound, and 218 passed through in

[7] Luterbacher et al., 'European Seasonal and Annual Temperature Variability', 1500. Van Engelen, Buisman and IJnsen, 'A Millennium of Weather, Winds and Water in the Low Countries', 112. Buisman, *Duizend jaar* Vol. V, 213. Claas Arisz. Caescoper, 'Jornael 1695'. *Nootijsye Boeck, anno 1669–1678, ofte Joernael.* Gemeente Archief Zaanstad, 129. Staten van ontvangst van het klompwachtsgeld. 1680–1794. Reference code: 502. Gemeente Amsterdam Stadsarchief (Amsterdam, Netherlands). Glaser and Koslowski, 'Variations in Reconstructed Ice Winter Severity in the Western Baltic from 1501 to 1995', 184. Glaser, *Klimageschichte Mitteleuropas*, 52. Petra J. E. M. van Dam, 'Water, Steam, Ice. Environmental Perspectives on Historical Transitions of Water in Northwestern Europe'. *Nova Acta Leopoldina* 98:360 (2009): 37. Van der Goes, 'Hage, den 27 February 1670'. *Briefwisseling tusschen de gebroeders van der Goes (1659–1673)* Vol. II, 113. D. Hansson and A. Omstedt, 'Modelling the Baltic Sea Ocean Climate on Centennial Time Scale: Temperature and Sea Ice'. *Climate Dynamics*, 30: 768. Milja van Tielhof and Jan Luiten van Zanden, 'Freight rates between Amsterdam and various port cities 1500–1800, and factors costs of shipping industry 1450–1800'.

[8] Van Engelen, Buisman and IJnsen, 'A Millennium of Weather, Winds and Water in the Low Countries', 112. 'The Sound Toll Database', Sound Toll Registers Online. Accessed 1 April 2015, www.soundtoll.nl/index.php/en/over-het-project/sonttol-registers.

December 1722. Dues paid by captains passing through the Sound in the winter never approached their spring, summer, and autumn levels. Yet in the wake of mild winters, traffic in the spring surged much earlier in the year than it did after cold winters. Whereas passages through the Sound did not reach high volumes until April or even May in the wake of cold winters, it approached peak volume as soon as early March after warm winters. When temperatures lingered above freezing, the Baltic and its ports stayed open and ice-free. Dutch merchants and mariners could sail and trade at will. Cold weather during the Little Ice Age therefore disrupted Baltic commerce and made shipping more expensive for merchants. By contrast, milder weather permitted shipping year-round, which made it cheaper. Curiously, there was no statistically significant correlation between winter temperatures and annual traffic through the Sound. Severe winters may have caused short-term disruptions in Dutch trade with the Baltic, but merchants and mariners compensated by shipping more commodities later in the year.[9]

Nevertheless, dues paid at the tollhouse of Elsinore did decline at the beginning and end of the Maunder Minimum, and again during the chilly winters of the early 1740s. They also rarely reached decadal peaks during frigid winters. Moreover, the price of chartering a ship to ports in northern Europe seems to have increased during the Maunder Minimum, though year-to-year fluctuations in prices were substantial, and substantial gaps interrupt surviving accounts. In any case, social developments that cannot easily be linked to climate change also affected the flow of ships through the Sound. In particular, passages through the Sound and therefore dues paid at Elsinore declined during wars that economically or directly involved the Baltic region, such as the Anglo-Dutch Wars (1652–1654, 1664–1667, 1672–1674), the Second Northern War (1655–1660), the War of the Spanish Succession (1701–1714), and the Great Northern War (1700–1721). Overall, passages through the Sound rose steadily during the eighteenth century, mirroring the economic and demographic expansion of contemporary Western Europe. Climate change was therefore just one among many variables that contributed to gradual trends in Baltic commerce, and in turn the history of the Dutch economy.[10]

[9] 'The Sound Toll Database', Sound Toll Registers Online. Accessed 1 April 2015, www.soundtoll.nl/index.php/en/over-het-project/sonttol-registers. For a visualization of these trends, see: www.dagomardegroot.com/frigid.html.

[10] 'The Sound Toll Database', Sound Toll Registers Online. Accessed 13 July 2013, www.soundtoll.nl/index.php/en/over-het-project/sonttol-registers. Michael Flinn, *The European Demographic System, 1500–1820*. (Baltimore: Johns Hopkins University

CLIMATE CHANGES AND SEA ICE IN BALTIC CORRESPONDENCE

We can use quantitative data to identify correlations between historical and environmental trends, but only qualitative sources can firmly establish how these trends were connected. Unfortunately, sailors active in Baltic commerce did not keep logbooks that remain with us today. Luckily, Dutch diplomats stationed in Baltic ports sent thousands of letters to their political masters in the republic that shed further light on relationships between trade and sea ice during the chilliest decades of the Little Ice Age.[11]

For example, on 11 January during the so-called Great Winter of 1708/1709, a letter to Grand Pensionary Heinsius from Marinus van Vrijbergen reported that temperatures were so cold across the Baltic that ink froze in pens and people refused to leave their homes. A day later, Robert Goes, a Dutch envoy and long-time resident of Copenhagen, wrote that letters from Hamburg had been much delayed by the cold. Indeed, correspondence between Dutch officials between ports in northern Europe often suffered long delays in frigid winters. Ships carrying letters could not leave frozen harbours, so couriers used routes on land that were treacherous in the cold. Goes also revealed that 67 Dutch merchant vessels bound for the republic had been trapped by ice in the Sound. On 14 January, correspondence from Johan Hulft mentioned that supplies could not reach allied troops fighting the ongoing War of the Spanish Succession, owing to 'severe and violent frost' in the Baltic. Cold temperatures and sea ice in 1708/1709 therefore undermined the flow of information, commodities, and military supplies across the Baltic.[12]

On 15 January, Goes wrote again to inform Heinsius that the cold had ebbed enough for most of the republic's merchantmen to retreat into Copenhagen's harbour, where they would wait until winter passed. Yet on 18 January, renewed freezing kept the ships from entering port. On 26 January, Goes reported that Danish labourers were trying to free the ships from the ice, but the work was going more slowly than expected, owing in part to the disunity and insubordination of Dutch captains. Goes

Press, 1981), 101. Frits Snapper, *Oorlogsinvloeden op de Overzeese Handel van Holland, 1551–1719*. (Amsterdam: Dukkerijen vh Ellerman Harms, 1959), 35.

[11] Maria Bogucka, 'Amsterdam and the Baltic in the First Half of the Seventeenth Century'. *The Economic History Review* 26:3 (1973): 435.

[12] Van Vrijbergen, 'Van Van Vrijbergen, 11 Januari 1709', Goes, 'Van Goes, 12 Januari 1709', Hulft, 'Van Hulft, 14 Januari 1709', *De Briefwisseling van Anthonie Heinsius, 1702–1720. Deel 8: 1 oktober 1708–30 juni 1709*, ed. A. J. Venendaal Jr. ('s-Gravenhage: Martinus Mijhoff, 1986), 188, 191.

did not mention how exactly the captains had undermined attempts to free them. On 2 February, he wrote only that the work continued. A week later, he reported that the last of the Dutch ships had finally reached Copenhagen.[13]

In the spring, letters from Goes vindicated the apparent unease of Dutch captains. On 13 April, Goes revealed that, owing to the extreme cold and ice, the captains had not been able to enlist the Copenhagen sailors' guild to free their ships. They had therefore agreed to a contract with a Danish naval officer, which bound them to pay a modest fee for every ship brought into harbour by Danish sailors. That officer now demanded nearly four times the total fee that the Dutch had originally agreed to pay. Apparently the ice had been so thick, and the cold so severe, that extricating the Dutch vessels had been much more gruelling and expensive than anticipated. Yet the Dutch captains refused to amend their original contract. Dutch proposals for mediation were dismissed, since Danish ministers did not want to involve the States-General.[14]

On 23 April, Goes reported that the sea around Copenhagen had finally opened for shipping. Dutch crews, however, could not leave until they had resolved their contractual dispute. On 11 May, nearly five months after the rescue of the Dutch merchant fleet, Goes wrote that both parties remained deadlocked. In fact, the Danish officer now insisted that no contract had ever been drafted. Dutch captains were raising funds through merchants to cover the outstanding payment, and on 18 May a large convoy that included seven warships arrived from the republic. Under the protection of the warships, on 25 May the long-delayed merchant fleet finally left for home. Frigid weather had provoked legal wrangling that interrupted the flow of Dutch ships through the Sound long after the last sea ice melted.[15]

Although written during the moderate winter of 1718/1719, letters sent to Heinsius by Jacob de Bie Jr., the republic's special envoy to Sweden, reflect the full range of possible links between climate changes, winter

[13] Goes, 'Van Goes, 15 Januari 1709', Goes, 'Van Goes, 26 Januari 1709', Goes, 'Van Goes, 2 Februari 1709', Goes, 'Van Goes, 9 Februari 1709', *De Briefwisseling van Anthonie Heinsius, 1702–1720. Deel 8*, 192, 232, 249.

[14] Goes, 'Van Goes, 12 Maart 1709', Goes, 'Van Goes, 24 Maart 1709', Goes, 'Van Goes, 13 April 1709', *De Briefwisseling van Anthonie Heinsius, 1702–1720. Deel 8: 1 oktober 1708–30 juni 1709*, 333, 369, 436.

[15] Goes, 'Van Goes, 23 April 1709', Goes, 'Van Goes, 27 April 1709', Goes, 'Van Goes, 30 April 1709', Goes, 'Van Goes, 11 Mei 1709', Goes, 'Van Goes, 18 Mei 1709', Goes, 'Van Goes, 21 Mei 1709', Goes, 'Van Goes, 25 Mei 1709', *De Briefwisseling van Anthonie Heinsius, 1702–1720. Deel 8*, 458, 472, 479, 506, 522, 527, 536.

weather, and Baltic transportation. De Bie set out on a secret diplomatic voyage to secure restitution for Dutch ships seized by the new Swedish regime of Queen Regent Ulrika Eleonora. On 21 February, De Bie wrote to Heinsius from Hamburg and explained the cause of delays in what had become a traumatic first leg of his voyage. Flooding had hindered De Bie's journey over land, and sudden freezing kept him from pressing on by boat. At Winsen, sea ice had blown in from the Baltic with southwesterly winds, and that required long detours. Thereafter, bouts of heavy rain, freezing, blizzards, and fog each contributed something different to delays in the voyage to Hamburg. De Bie promised that he would consult with others for guidance on the remainder of his journey, but for the moment he was stuck in Hamburg.[16]

On 23 February, De Bie wrote that the Sound had frozen over. The sea ice had reached this extent around two months later in the year than it had in the frigid winter of 1708/1709. Still, it was sufficient to dissuade De Bie from travelling near Copenhagen. Instead, he resolved to take an inland boat to Lübeck with the first favourable wind. From there, he hoped to travel north through the Danish islands to the town of Ystad, east of Copenhagen and just beyond the Sound, and then on to Stockholm. On 2 March, De Bie wrote again to announce that he had arrived at Lübeck on February 25th and arranged transport to Ystad aboard a small merchant vessel. Yet variable winds and a combination of rain and snow kept the ship in port until the 28th. On 1 March, the mixed weather yielded to steady freezing with a northwesterly wind. Departure was impossible under such circumstances.[17]

As De Bie wrote, however, the wind turned to blow from the southwest, a direction favourable for vessels departing the port of Lübeck. After sending his letter, De Bie resolved to discover if the ship could set sail. He insisted that he would ask the captain to attempt a passage either through the Sound or through the more treacherous Great Belt, should the ice allow it. However, on 6 March, De Bie reported that he was still in Lübeck, because the wind had shifted just before his ship could depart. Now, however, the wind turned to again issue from the southwest.

[16] De Bie, 'Van De Bie, 21 Februari 1719', *De Briefwisseling van Anthonie Heinsius, 1702–1720. Deel 14: 2 oktober 1718–22 juli 1720*, ed. A. J. Venendaal Jr. (Den Haag: Instituut voor Nederlandse Geschiedenis, 2001), 105. Michael F. Metcalf, 'Conflict as Catalyst: Parliamentary Innovation in Eighteenth-Century Sweden'. *Parliaments, Estates and Representation* 8:1 (1988): 66.

[17] De Bie, 'Van De Bie, 23 Februari 1719', *De Briefwisseling van Anthonie Heinsius, 1702–1720. Deel 14*, 116.

The skipper intended to take to the river on the following day and sail from there to Travemünde, a nearby port that bordered the Baltic. These plans suited De Bie, but he worried: sea ice in the Sound was apparently now so extensive that it delayed correspondence.[18]

De Bie fell silent until 30 March, when he sent a long letter from Stockholm that detailed the unhappy last leg of his journey. He had departed for Travemünde on 7 March, but his progress had slowed to a crawl in the face of difficulties with Danish officials at sea and a contrary wind. By the following day, De Bie and the sailors aboard his ship encountered drift ice. When they reached Landskrona on the morning of the 12th, they found the entire coast beleaguered by sea ice. With great difficulty, they found a way through the ice and reached the vicinity of the town, only to find its harbour choked with even more ice.[19]

De Bie somehow reached the coast despite a contrary northeasterly breeze, but further travel north by sea would clearly be impossible. De Bie had had to leave his carriage in Lübeck, however, since the ship that took him to Landskrona was too small to carry it. That forced him to buy passage through the Swedish countryside on a series of rented wagons. At last, after a 'long and miserable journey', he arrived in Stockholm no earlier than 27 March. In his letter, De Bie begged Heinsius to understand why it had taken so long to reach the city. His concern was understandable, because the delays were ruinous. The captured vessels had just been sold to repair the battered finances of the Swedish crown. On 1 April, De Bie wrote that the ships and their cargo were probably lost for good.[20]

Sea ice in the winter of 1718/1719 was far less extensive than it had been a decade earlier. Still, De Bie's journey reveals that sea ice hampered Baltic transportation even during moderate winters in the Little Ie Age. Moreover, the seesaw of freezing and thawing, typical of a milder winter in the Baltic, undermined De Bie's attempts to travel by land. Flooding might have been easier to overcome had temperatures stayed above freezing, and snow might have been less bothersome had rain and fog not immediately followed. The same likely did not apply for Baltic seaborne commerce, as thawing of any sort was indisputably better than continued freezing. Indeed, for much of the winter of 1718/1719, a trickle of vessels

[18] De Bie, 'Van De Bie, 2 Maart 1719', De Bie, 'Van De Bie, 6 Maart 1719', *De Briefwisseling van Anthonie Heinsius, 1702–1720. Deel 14*, 108, 121.

[19] De Bie, 'Van De Bie, 30 Maart 1719', *De Briefwisseling van Anthonie Heinsius, 1702–1720. Deel 14*, 149.

[20] De Bie, 'Van De Bie, 30 Maart 1719', De Bie, 'Van De Bie, 1 April 1719', *De Briefwisseling van Anthonie Heinsius, 1702–1720. Deel 14*, 150, 154.

continued to pass through the Sound. Still, the nature of De Bie's diplomatic mission reveals that the republic's Baltic trade intersected with the many other reasons its citizens travelled through the region. Success for De Bie would have returned substantial capital to Dutch merchants in a time of economic stagnation. That success eluded De Bie because of complex interactions between climatic trends, local environmental conditions, human infrastructure, and spur-of-the-moment decisions.

The technologies and practices that allowed the Dutch to dominate Baltic commerce remained vulnerable to climate changes in ways that changed little from the beginning of the Grindelwald Fluctuation to the end of the Maunder Minimum. Descriptions of sea ice and its consequences in the Heinsius correspondence therefore echo through letters, diaries, and chronicles compiled during the entire history of the Dutch Golden Age. Many of these documents describe how sea ice and weather that we today associate with the Little Ice Age hindered sailors plying the Baltic trades, in their attempts to leave or return to the republic. For example, on 12 February during the cold winter of 1585/1586, Velius, the famed chronicler of Hoorn, wrote that a sudden onset of high winds and freezing temperatures had trapped 18 ships in ice that rapidly spread near the harbour. The town's citizens used axes to break through the ice and free most of the beleaguered vessels, which they subsequently brought into port. In March, the farmer Abel Eppens reported that the harbour of Delfzijl had been blocked by sea ice that pressed forward in persistent easterly winds, trapping the ships within.[21]

During the long and remarkably cold winter of 1620/1621, the Zuiderzee froze over entirely amid persistent easterly winds, and sea ice extended far into the North Sea. In February, the ice trapped a ship heavily laden with commodities between the northwestern coast of Friesland and the island of Terschelling. Labourers carried the vessel's cargo in wagons across the frozen Zuiderzee to Amsterdam, Hoorn, and Enkhuizen. Pieter van Winsem, a lawyer at the Court of Friesland, reported that another merchant vessel was frozen in the ice at the same location, and would have to be unloaded. Meanwhile, sea ice trapped Jan Hanszoon and his crew as their ship approached Vlieland, one of the islands that divided the North Sea from the Zuiderzee. With staff in hand, Hanszoon, and presumably his crew, travelled by foot to the town of Harlingen. Even in the southerly

[21] Th. Velius, *Kroniek van Hoorn Band 2: 1560–1629*, eds. Jan Plekker and Rob Resoort. (Hoorn: Publicatiestichting Bas Baltus, 2007), 602. Buisman, *Duizend jaar Vol. IV*, 87 and 93.

city of Middelburg, citizens struggled to break the ice in their harbour. Correspondence therefore confirms that the coldest years and decades of the Little Ice Age brought extensive sea ice to Northern Europe that undermined many expressions of the Dutch relationship with the Baltic.[22]

WIND VELOCITY, WIND DIRECTION, AND BALTIC COMMERCE

Gales may have been even more dangerous than sea ice for sailors engaged in Baltic commerce. Crews leaving the republic for the Baltic often waited for favourable winds near Texel, where they were vulnerable to storms that blew in from the sea. Archaeological and textual evidence indicates that the number of wrecks on the coast of Texel peaked during the coldest years of the Maunder Minimum. Letters suggest that storms were often to blame. On 6 January 1654, for example, over 20 merchant vessels, most returning from the Baltic, foundered when a catastrophic storm struck an anchored Dutch convoy near Texel. On 12 December 1659, Adriaen van der Goes reported that many merchant ships had been stranded on the coast amid relentless gales. On 18 August, 11 years later, he wrote that a merchant vessel leaving Rotterdam had been being struck by lightning. The blast ruined much of the vessel's lucrative cargo and may have killed some of its crew. On 9 September 1695, a series of storms disrupted regional commerce, and as many as 1,000 mariners perished in shipwrecks across the North Sea. On the evening of 21 September, a fierce gale tore ships from their anchors in English harbours and drove them into the channel. The wind stranded many vessels along the shores of France and the Low Countries. Worse, it shattered 70 English coal freighters on the coast of Norfolk.[23]

In October of the following year, intermittent freezing and thawing coincided with gales that wrecked countless Dutch and English merchant

[22] Buisman, *Duizend jaar Vol. IV*, 340. Pier Winsemius, *Chronique ofte historische geschiedenisse van Vrieslant, Vol. 20. (Franeker, 1622)*, 910.

[23] 'Wrecks in Documents'. Maritiem programma Nederland, Rijksdienst voor her Cultureel Erfgoed. Accessed 24 June 2013, www.maritiemprogramma.nl/WID_00.htm. Hell and Gijsbers, 'Geborgen of gezonken, gered of verdronken', 46. C. Ahlmström, *Looking for Leads: Shipwrecks of the Past Revealed by Contemporary Documents and the Archaeological Record.* (Fairbanks: University of Alaska Press, 1997). Van der Goes, 'Hage, den xij December 1659'. *Briefwisseling tusschen de gebroeders van der Goes (1659–1673)* Vol. I, 51. Van der Goes, 'Hage, den 18 Augusti 1659'. *Briefwisseling tusschen de gebroeders van der Goes (1659–1673)* Vol. II, 146. Buisman, *Duizend jaar* Vol. V, 352, 255, and 267. Lamb, *Historic Storms of the North Sea, British Isles, and Northwest Europe*, 55.

vessels in the North Sea. In December, John Evelyn marvelled in his diary that such 'exceeding greate storms wrecking many at sea' had not 'ben knowne in any mans [sic] memory'.[24] Variable temperatures soon yielded to a bitterly cold winter and thick sea ice. In January and February, frequent storms joined these icy conditions to threaten shipping across the North Sea region. In January, a Dutch warship under the command of Captain Jacob Schoon rescued the beleaguered survivors of a merchant vessel that had shipwrecked on the Norwegian coast nine days earlier. Most of the passengers and crew had already perished, but those who lived may have resorted to cannibalism to survive. Stormy weather continued into the summer. In a diary entry written on 30 August 1697, Claas Ariszoon Caescoper blamed four days of unremitting storminess on a series of shipwrecks off Texel. Storms from the west were especially dangerous for sailors off the republic, because their winds exposed them to a lee shore. While westerly winds in the North Sea were overall less common in the Maunder Minimum than they were before or after, that fortunate change was offset by a simultaneous rise in the frequency and severity of storms. Moreover, easterly winds created lee shores in other parts of a Baltic journey.[25]

Storms could not only kill sailors in shipwrecks but also delay their journeys by keeping them from leaving port. For example, on 20 November 1670, Van der Goes informed his brother that 14 days of unrelenting gales had flooded nearby polders and prevented many ships from departing. Delays were even worse when gales scattered fleets at sea. It could take weeks to reunite a merchant convoy, and in the meantime isolated ships were vulnerable to enemy fleets or privateers.[26]

Sailors risked their lives when they took to sea. Merchants, by contrast, risked only their investments, and over time they found ways to minimize that risk. Many Dutch merchants active in the Baltic trades divided or 'parcelled' their shipments in different vessels. European merchants had used the practice since at least the Middle Ages. More frequent and more severe storms in the Grindelwald Fluctuation, however, may have encouraged Dutch merchants to refine the parcelling system. When Dutch merchants had the means, they distributed the most valuable shipments

[24] Buisman, *Duizend jaar* Vol. V, 242.

[25] Claas Arisz. Caescoper, '30 Augustus 1697'. *Nootijsye Boeck, anno 1669–1678, ofte Joernael*. Gemeente Archief Zaanstad.

[26] Van der Goes, 'Hage, den 20 November 1670'. *Briefwisseling tusschen de gebroeders van der Goes (1659–1673)* Vol. II, 160.

in as many ships as possible, and they further divided these shipments in particularly stormy seasons. They routinely parcelled even small shipments of cheap commodities into multiple vessels. After the first decades of the seventeenth century, parcelling increasingly separated those responsible for shipping from those who handled commercial activity. Most merchants now chartered vessels from shipmasters, and hired 'factors' in Baltic ports to manage their business.[27]

The parcelling system was far from foolproof. Parcelled goods travelled in separate ships but often sailed within the same fleet, so big storms could still threaten a merchant's entire investment. It was accordingly more expensive to charter a ship in autumn, since that season was always notorious for its storms, and therefore its risks to sailors and the cargoes they ferried. As storm frequency and severity rose in the late seventeenth century, merchants and shipmasters therefore increasingly acquired marine insurance. The volume of insurance cases handled by the republic's Chamber of Insurance and Average actually climbed in the wake of severe winters.[28] Surviving documents do not mention whether merchants and shipmasters detected long-term changes in storm frequency. Yet consciously or unconsciously, they certainly used a combination of old and new innovations to creatively respond to the Little Ice Age.[29]

Despite the ingenuity of merchants and mariners, toll accounts suggest that traffic through the Sound diminished during particularly stormy years in the Maunder Minimum. For example, after the winter of 1694/1695, among the coldest of the Little Ice Age, shipping through the Sound only reached peak volume long after the last ice had melted in the Baltic. Severe and persistent storms in the spring of 1695 may have encouraged some sailors to remain in port, while wrecking those who might otherwise have paid dues at the tollhouse of Elsinore. Four years later, temperatures matched their twentieth-century averages, yet repeated storms in the winter of 1698/1699 beached whales and ruined ships along the republic's coast. In the Sound, winter shipping persisted, but at an abnormally low rate for such a mild winter, possibly because gales interfered with voyages from the republic.[30]

[27] Christensen, *Dutch Trade to the Baltic about 1600*, 177.

[28] Notably in 1709, 1726, 1729, 1740, 1763, 1784, and 1795. Sabine Go, *Marine Insurance in the Netherlands, 1600–1870: A Comparative Institutional Approach*. (Amsterdam: Askant, 2009), 117.

[29] Christensen, *Dutch Trade to the Baltic about 1600*, 145.

[30] Buisman, *Duizend jaar* Vol. V, 352, 255 and 267. 'The Sound Toll Database', Sound Toll Registers Online. Accessed 12 July 2013, www.soundtoll.nl/index.php/en/over-het-project/sonttol-registers.

Without ship logbooks, we cannot systematically determine how shifts in prevailing wind directions and velocities affected the duration of voyages to and from the Baltic. However, other documents provide tantalizing hints of the importance of small variations in wind for Baltic voyages. Legal texts, for example, implicitly recognized the importance of wind for the success of journeys to and from the Baltic. For example, in 1673, a typical contract written by a captain off Stockholm promised the delivery of his cargo in Amsterdam 'when God provides a favourable wind'. Unfortunately, his vessel shipwrecked and never made it to Amsterdam.[31] Two years earlier, Adriaen van der Goes wrote that persistent easterly winds prohibited travel northeast from the republic, hampering Dutch trade with Archangel, a Russian port in the White Sea. Frequent easterly winds during the Maunder Minimum may have helped ships leave most Dutch ports, arrive in Amsterdam's harbour from the Zuiderzee, and travel out of the Baltic.[32]

Surviving correspondence supports that hypothesis. On 2 April 1709, Marinus van Vrijbergen in Copenhagen complained to Heinsius that he had received no letters from Holland, despite a persistent easterly wind. Such a wind delayed ships as they approached Copenhagen but aided departure from most Dutch harbours, and perhaps that was more important. On 29 June, another letter written in the same city by Goes reported that, five days earlier, a French merchant fleet carrying grain had been hindered by contrary winds as it struggled to leave the Baltic. France, Britain, and the republic were among the European powers then embroiled in the War of the Spanish Succession. The wind had also thwarted a British convoy pursuing the French fleet, which meant that it probably blew from the west. Three French ships returned to port, but set sail again on 26 June. Once more, they evaded the British squadron, this time by using favourable winds that now must have issued from the east. Letters therefore reveal that changes in the direction of wind could help shape the fate of ships plying the Baltic trades.[33]

[31] 'Documents regarding the recovery by Joseph Deutz of 48% insurance on 100 lasts of tar and 20 lasts of pitch on the ship *Ridderhuys*, of which only part was saved after foundering of the ship, 1673'. Deutz Family 1613–1878. Reference code: 234. Gemeente Amsterdam Stadsarchief (Amsterdam, Netherlands).

[32] Van der Goes, 'Hage, den 7 May 1671'. *Briefwisseling tusschen de gebroeders van der Goes (1659–1673)* Vol. I, 221. *Briefwisseling tusschen de gebroeders van der Goes (1659–1673)* Vol. II, 205.

[33] Van Vrijbergen, 'Van van Vrijbergen, 2 April 1709', Goes, 'Van Goes, 29 juni 1709', *De Briefwisseling van Anthonie Heinsius, 1702–1720, Deel 8: 1 oktober 1708–30 juni 1709*, 408, 664. Goes, 'Van Goes, 9 juli 1709', *De Briefwisseling van Anthonie Heinsius,*

One month later, Goes relayed Danish displeasure over the presence of a large Anglo-Dutch fleet amassed in the city's harbour. Goes explained that, to depart, the British warships did not require a wind as favourable as the one needed by the 160 merchant vessels in the Dutch convoy. The British ships set sail on 25 July, but the Dutch fleet was forced to wait for weeks, much to the consternation of Danish officials eager to maintain their state's neutrality. Different winds could therefore affect different ships in distinct ways.[34]

Changes in atmospheric circulation and the extent of sea ice in Northern European waters affected the flow of people, commodities, and information through the Baltic, which was dominated by Dutch merchants and mariners. Overall, Dutch merchants responded creatively and effectively to the challenges posed by the coldest decades of the Little Ice Age. The sailors they employed, however, endured greater risks to their lives and livelihoods than they did in warmer climates. A shifting climate had an unequal effect on people of different means, and different degrees of protection from its most ferocious weather.

CLIMATE CHANGES, HARVEST FAILURES, AND BALTIC COMMERCE

The coldest phases of the Little Ice Age influenced not only how commodities moved through the Baltic, but also how many commodities there were to move. Winter temperatures that lingered long into spring and even summer repeatedly contributed to harvest failures across the Baltic. In northwestern Europe, cold years during the Little Ice Age shortened by more than one month a growing season that, on average, lasted just over six months in the late twentieth century. Not surprisingly, grain prices rose sharply in the Dutch Republic during the coldest, rainiest, and stormiest decades of the Little Ice Age. For example, chilly years during the Little Ice Age clearly corresponded to spikes in the price of wheat on the Amsterdam bourse (Figure 3.2).[35]

1702–1720, Deel 8: 1 juli 1709–31 december 1709, ed. A. J. Venendaal Jr. ('s-Gravenhage: Martinus Mijhoff, 1988), 29.

[34] Goes, 'Van Goes, 27 Juli 1709', Goes, 'Van Goes, 6 augustus 1709', Goes, 'Van Goes, 10 augustus 1709', *De Briefwisseling van Anthonie Heinsius, 1702–1720, Deel 8: 1 juli 1709–31 december 1709*, 99, 129, 147.

[35] De Vries and Van der Woude, *The First Modern Economy*, 200. Van Tielhof, *The Mother of All Trades*, 298. Allen and Unger, 'Database by Commodity'. Accessed 2 April 2015,

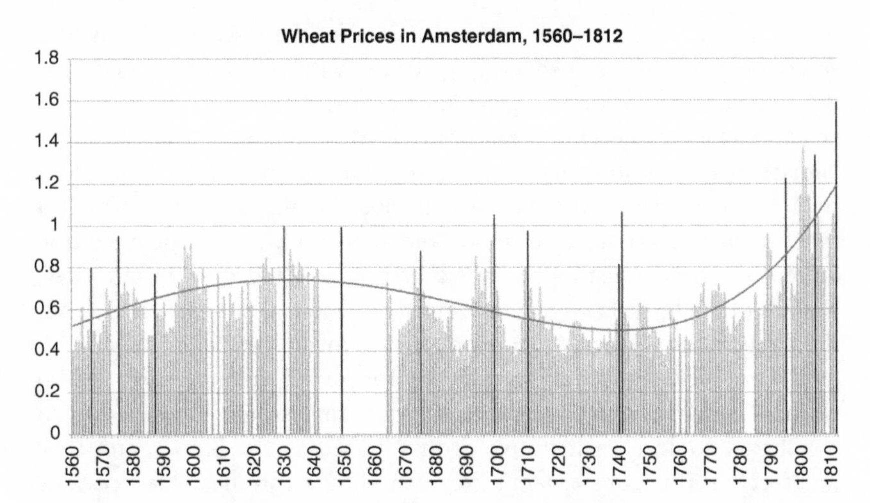

FIGURE 3.2 Amsterdam wheat prices, in grams of silver per litre, during the Little Ice Age. Particularly cold years that coincided with high wheat prices are in black. Very warm years – such as 1686 – often coincided with low wheat prices. Order 4 polynomial regression shows that wheat prices roughly responded to changes in average temperature. Robert C. Allen and Richard W. Unger, 'Database by Commodity', *Allen-Unger Global Commodity Prices Database*, accessed 2 April 2015, http://www.gcpdb.info/data.html.

Yet these relationships should be approached with caution. Ties between global climate changes, regional weather patterns, and long-term trends in commodity prices were always complex. For farmers, variability in season-to-season, year-to-year weather was probably more disruptive than gradual cooling or warming. Many could and did cope with climatic trends by planting different crops – rye in place of wheat, for example – but they could not easily adapt to weather they could not anticipate. Less predictable weather did accompany the coldest phases of the Little Ice Age, but it is hard to gauge how increased weather variance helped shape gradual trends in grain prices. Moreover, the socio-economic characteristics, military demands, and political imperatives of different European societies always mediated the impact of weather on grain prices. Overall, the demographic expansion of Europe inflated grain prices and reduced the value of labour until the middle of the seventeenth century. Thereafter, grain prices declined and labour's real wage increased

www.gcpdb.info/data.html. Thomas Rötzer and Frank M. Chmeilewski, 'Phenological Maps of Europe'. *Climate Research* 18 (2001): 253.

until the 1740s. Commodity prices shaped by these secular trends also responded to short-term shocks, especially wars, which demanded steadily increasingly taxes and growing bureaucracies in many European states, including the Dutch Republic. In this context, the influence of climate change is difficult to quantify. Still, letters, diaries, and other texts written across early modern Europe do suggest that harvests of many staple crops suffered amid cold temperatures and precipitation extremes. Climate historians have therefore concluded that the coldest periods of the Little Ice Age undermined agricultural production in societies already destabilized by wars or political mismanagement.[36]

When overlapping human and environmental circumstances led to regional food shortages, commodity price spikes, and famines, Dutch merchants could earn lucrative profits by selling the Baltic grain they had stockpiled in Amsterdam's great warehouses. In the coldest periods of the Little Ice Age, they sold their inventories on a vast scale. In December 1593, for instance, around 150 Dutch merchant vessels waited for favourable weather to deliver grain shipments to ports across western and southern Europe. Early in the eighteenth century, and again in the frigid 1740s, French merchants bought grain from Amsterdam in huge quantities when crop failures led to food shortages. In many years, dozens of ships bound for southern destinations and laden with Baltic grain bypassed Amsterdam entirely, yet Dutch merchants largely controlled even this trade.[37]

It is impossible to separate how climate change influenced grain prices across Europe from the ways in which it more directly affected the flow of Dutch ships through the Baltic. In Amsterdam, shipping costs for victuals rose sharply in years distinguished by frigid winters and extensive sea ice, and indeed trends in shipping costs and winter severity roughly mirrored one another during the Maunder Minimum. On 26 December 1662, in a particularly chilly winter, Adriaen van der Goes wrote a letter to his brother that clearly articulated these relationships. After describing the bitter cold, he reported that grain ships returning from the Baltic had been trapped for two weeks in thick sea ice near Vlieland. Their cargo could not be unloaded and taken across the ice by sled or wagon, perhaps because

[36] De Vries and Van der Woude, *The First Modern Economy*, 26 and 200. De Vries, 'Measuring the Impact of Climate on History', 626.

[37] Parker, *The Dutch Revolt*, 128. Barbour, *Capitalism in Amsterdam in the 17th Century*, 27. 366. De Vries and Van der Woude, *The First Modern Economy*, 366. Van Tielhof, *The Mother of All Trades*, 71, 74, 298. White, *The Climate of Rebellion in the Early Modern Ottoman Empire*, 131.

the ice was too unstable or uneven for transportation. Van der Goes hoped that the vessels were still seaworthy, and that thawing would soon bring open water. Grain prices had climbed sharply, and, like many others in The Hague, Van der Goes trusted that they would fall once the vessels were unloaded in port. However, on 9 February 1663 he wrote that the grain ships had now been stuck in the ice for two months. Clearly, informed Dutch citizens believed that disruptions in Baltic shipping caused by extensive sea ice raised the price of grain. It might seem that climate change could scarcely affect Dutch grain prices because merchants could relieve shortages in domestic supply by importing Baltic grain. In fact, domestic increases in the price of grain could actually get worse when extensive sea ice blocked Baltic imports. A great strength for the republic in the chilliest decades of the Little Ice Age – its maritime lifelines to distant grain-producing regions – then became a weakness.[38]

When grain prices rose in the republic, the purchasing power of wages collapsed for many Dutch citizens. High grain prices can therefore be tied to periods of economic crisis in the history of the Dutch Republic. Yet stockpiles in Amsterdam, and to a lesser extent Rotterdam – which received grain imports from England, Rhineland, and Zeeland – did insulate Dutch citizens to some degree from the acute grain shortages that caused starvation elsewhere in Europe. Wheat was indeed far more plentiful in the affluent cities of the coastal provinces than it was in most other parts of Europe. Less expensive rye, which yielded coarser and less desirable bread, was usually more abundant than wheat only in the poorer, inland communities of the republic. Even in the wealthiest Dutch cities, however, disruptions in the transport of grain and in turn the price of wheat led many to resort to rye, which of course further increased its price.[39]

[38] Richards, *The Unending Frontier*, 75. De Vries, 'Measuring the Impact of Climate on History', 613. Van der Goes, 'Hage, den 26 December 1662'. *Briefwisseling tusschen de gebroeders van der Goes (1659–1673)* Vol. I, 166. Van der Goes, 'Hage, den 9 February 1663'. *Briefwisseling tusschen de gebroeders van der Goes (1659–1673) Vol.* I, 171. Peter Clark, 'Introduction'. In *The European Crisis of the 1590s: Essays in Comparative History*, ed. Peter Clark. (London: George Allen & Unwin, 1985), 9. Noordegraaf, 'Dearth, Famine and Social Policy in the Dutch Republic at the End of the Sixteenth Century', 78. Milja van Tielhof and Jan Luiten van Zanden, 'Freight Rates between Amsterdam and Various Port Cities 1500–1800, and Factors Costs of Shipping Industry 1450–1800'.

[39] Van Tielhof, *The Mother of All Trades*, 88, 91. Jan Luiten van Zanden, 'The Prices of the Most Important Consumer Goods, and Indices of Wages and the Cost of Living in the Western Part of the Netherlands, 1450–1800'. Available at: www.iisg.nl/hpw/data.php#netherlands.

Overall, milk, butter, cheese, peas, beans, vegetables, and various kinds of fish all accounted for a much higher share of the Dutch diet than the diets of people elsewhere in Europe. For example, children in the *Burgerweeshuis*, an Amsterdam orphanage established for the middle classes, received no more than 45 per cent of their calories from grains. Since it is unlikely that these orphans would have received a very different diet than other children in their socioeconomic class, it is safe to conclude that the republic's urban middle classes received less than half of their calories from grains. Towards the end of the final decade of the seventeenth century – the coldest of the Maunder Minimum – the municipal government of Amsterdam started brainstorming how best to preserve the city's food supply. Their calculations tell us that, in a typical year, the average Amsterdammer ate only around half the bread that people in the Southern Netherlands consumed. The diverse caloric intake of citizens in the republic's coastal provinces ensured that their diet was unusually resilient to disruptions in the supply of grain.[40]

The food supply of the republic's coastal cities was therefore relatively secure during the Golden Age, despite occasional fluctuations in the price of grain. The profitability of the Baltic grain trade, however, was less stable. For Dutch merchants, a high supply of Baltic grain led to low grain prices on the Amsterdam bourse and low profits for Dutch merchants, although they did at least have large quantities of grain to export. A low supply, by contrast, led to high prices and high profits for Dutch merchants, yet they had little to export beyond what was stockpiled in grain inventories. Not only the production failures brought about by poor harvests, but also distribution failures that followed from abundant sea ice in the Sound, may have occasionally benefitted Dutch merchants by limiting the supply of grain and thereby raising its prices. More frequently, however, extensive sea ice kept Dutch merchants from exploiting a winter rise in grain prices, because their exports could not take to sea. That was especially true in landmark winters, when sea ice suffocated every Dutch harbour. As a result, food shortages and price spikes in ice-free parts of spring, summer, and autumn were more reliably profitable for Dutch merchants than the same conditions in winter.[41]

[40] Van Tielhof, *The Mother of All Trades*, 84. Ken Albala, *Food in Early Modern Europe*. (Westport, CT: Greenwood Press, 2003), 10.

[41] Haley, *The Dutch in the Seventeenth Century*, 153. Noordegraaf, 'Dearth, Famine and Social Policy in the Dutch Republic at the End of the Sixteenth Century', 77. Van Tielhof, *The Mother of All Trades*, 81, 85.

These relationships may not have worked the same way over time. For much of the seventeenth century, a negative correlation existed between the price of rye in Amsterdam and the amount of rye shipped through the Sound. When traffic through the Sound declined and grain imports were low, prices in Amsterdam increased sharply. This correlation weakened in the late seventeenth century and then turned positive in the eighteenth century. Now, changes in the demand for grain – and in turn its price – seem to have provoked shipments from the Baltic. Changes in the supply of Baltic grain were no longer the most important influence on its price in Amsterdam. As both the Dutch Golden Age and the Maunder Minimum came to a close, the climate changes that helped shape Baltic commerce were less economically important for the republic than they had been.[42]

THE LITTLE ICE AGE AND BALTIC COMMERCE: CONCLUSIONS AND CONSEQUENCES

The merchants and mariners who worked the mother of all trades often suffered during weather associated with the chilliest decades of the Little Ice Age. Extensive sea ice caused by long or severe freezing halted Baltic shipping in winter, delayed its resumption in spring, and hastened its conclusion in autumn. By interrupting travel through the Baltic, the environmental manifestations of climatic cooling strained relationships between port officials and Dutch mariners, which ultimately provoked legal disputes. They also disrupted efforts by Dutch diplomats and armies to defend the republic's commercial interests in the region.

In the chilliest phases of the Little Ice Age, frequent storms also threatened the ships and crews that serviced the republic's Baltic commerce. However, Dutch merchants adapted to changing climatic circumstances by inventing or refining methods of mitigating the risks to their investments. The same merchants exploited harvest failures across Europe that followed, in part, from cooler weather and precipitation extremes. Dutch merchants could then exploit the vast grain inventories in Amsterdam's warehouses to reap impressive profits, but only if Dutch harbours were free of sea ice. Rising grain prices could bring hardships to ordinary people across the

[42] Van Tielhof, *The Mother of All Trades*, 96. See also P. W. Klein, 'Kwantitatieve aspecten van de Amsterdamse roggehandel in the 17e eeuw en de Europese economische geschiedenis'. In *Ondernemende geschiedenis: 25 opstellen geschreven bij het afscheid van Mr. H. van Riel.* (The Hague: M. Nijhoff, 1977), 75–88.

republic, yet most of them did not depend on grains to the same extent as other European commoners.

The climate histories of Dutch commerce with the Baltic, and in turn the republic's broader economy, therefore do not follow straightforward narratives of hardship and decline. Many Dutch citizens adapted to and exploited an environment in flux. They may not have been aware that their climate was changing, yet consciously or unconsciously, they responded in ways that benefitted their interests, and in turn those of their society.

CLIMATE CHANGE AND TRANSPORTATION WITHIN THE REPUBLIC

For the Dutch economy to function efficiently, goods, people, and information needed to move with relative ease between centres of industrial, agricultural, and knowledge production in the republic. Already in 1529, Amsterdam and Hoorn established a service in which licensed skippers ferried passengers, goods, and correspondence between the cities according to standard tariffs, aboard small sailing ships that left at regular intervals, whether empty or full, and stopped at previously agreed-upon locations. This *beurtveer* or 'turn ferry' system expanded rapidly across the coastal provinces in the final decade of the sixteenth century.[43]

In the first decades of the seventeenth century, the turn ferry network connected most Dutch population centres that could be accessed by water. Skippers serviced some of these locations many times per day. By the eighteenth century, some 800 turn ships departed each week from Amsterdam alone, bound for 121 destinations across the republic. However, high or contrary winds could still wreak havoc on the sailing vessels of the turn ferry.

Accordingly, city governments and merchants in the seventeenth century financed new canals bordered by paths that could be used by horses to pull barges. These *trek*, or 'pull', ferries did not need sails and were

[43] Klompmaker, *Handel in de Gouden Eeuw*, 70. Audrey M. Lambert, *The Making of the Dutch Landscape*, 203. De Vries and Van der Woude, *The First Modern Economy*, 181. R. Pots and J. Knoester, *Blauwe ader van de Bollenstreek: 350 jaar Haarlemmertrekvaart-Leidsevaart, 1657–2007. Geschiedenis, betekenis en toekomst.* (Leiden: Primavera Pers), 11. Horsten, *Doorgaande wegen in Nederland, 16e tot 19e eeuw*, 50. See also: Frderik Lambertus van Holk, 'Archeologie van de binnenvaart: wonen en werken aan boord van binnenvaartschepen (1600–1900)'. (PhD Diss., University of Groningen, 1997). Nienhuis, *Environmental History of the Rhine-Meuse Delta*, 100.

therefore less vulnerable to the wind. In 1632, the first *trekveer* opened between Amsterdam and Haarlem. It offered hourly departures, a steady and reliable speed of around seven kilometres per hour, and a total transit time of just over two hours. By the middle of the seventeenth century, it accommodated more than 300,000 travellers per year. Before long, the network spread across the full breadth of the coastal provinces. Its main function was to move people, although many barges also carried goods or correspondence in small volumes. The ferries were, in the words of Adriaan de Kraker, the 'forerunners of trains during the industrial era'. Passengers enjoyed refreshments in first- or second-class compartments, and they brought along their children for half price.[44]

By the middle of the seventeenth century, even minor centres in the republic's maritime provinces had been plugged into the overlapping turn or pull ferry systems. In the context of contemporary Europe, they provided an unusually flexible, reliable, inexpensive, and safe system for transporting commodities, correspondence, and people. Intersecting and extending beyond this extensive infrastructure were humbler networks, plied by small boats individually or collectively owned by farmers and petty industrialists. Some of their routes wound through creeks and ditches, but others crossed the same waterways navigated by much larger vessels. They carried essential commodities, such as buttermilk, hay, fish, and even freshwater, between rural communities, or more frequently rural and urban areas. The boats that serviced them, called *schuiten*, reached around 10 metres long, displaced roughly two tons, and often made use of sails. Among the most common and essential of these boats were *melkschuiten*, or 'milk boats', so named because they carried dairy products that accounted for a sizable share of the average Dutch citizen's caloric intake.[45]

[44] H. Klompmaker, *Handel in de Gouden Eeuw*, 66. Lambert, *The Making of the Dutch Landscape*, 204. De Vries and Van der Woude, *The First Modern Economy*, 183. Pots and Knoester, *Blauwe ader van de Bollenstreek*, 11. Davids, *The Rise and Decline of Dutch Technological Leadership Vol. I*, 84. J. J. J. M. Beenakker, 'De Trekvaart tussen Leiden en Haarlem'. *Dever Bulletin* (1994): 18. S. J. Fockema Andreae, 'De trekvaart Haarlem-Leiden driehonderd jaar'. In *Haerlem jaarboek*. (Haarlem: Erven F. Bohn, 1959), 76. Nienhuis, *Environmental History of the Rhine-Meuse Delta*, 100. Adriaan de Kraker, 'Ice and Water. The Removal of Ice on Waterways in the Low Countries, 1330–1800'. *Water History*, 2.

[45] Anton Wegman, *De Waterlandse Melkschuit: varende boeren tussen Waterland en Amsterdam 1600–1900*. (Amsterdam: Stichting de Waterlandse Melkschuit, 2011), 21. Marjolein 't Hart, 'The Dutch Republic: The Urban Impact upon Politics'. In *A Miracle Mirrored, A Miracle Mirrored: The Dutch Republic in European Perspective*, eds.

The vast majority of traffic through the Dutch Republic travelled by water, but roads did exist, including big *herenwegen* that connected major centres and *hessenwegen* that accommodated the transport of commodities. Many travellers rode horses or simply walked to reach nearby destinations, even in wealthy, urbanized, waterlogged Holland. The Dutch Republic actually had more roads in 1600 than the Kingdom of the Netherlands did in 1848. Yet these earlier roads were not paved streets but rather poorly maintained paths of rutted dirt or sand. Most meandered along circuitous routes, owing to the ubiquitous presence of water, and that forced travellers into long delays at ferry crossings. For that reason, at least 95 per cent of all travellers between Amsterdam and Haarlem, for example, took the pull ferry after it was established. For the rest of the seventeenth century, its share of travellers between the cities never dipped far below 80 per cent. However, it was impractical to build canals in parts of the republic's relatively poor and sparsely populated eastern hinterland. There, unhardened and unpaved roads were all that connected many communities. These roads were easily compromised in weather associated with the coldest decades of the Little Ice Age.[46]

TURN AND PULL FERRIES IN WARM AND COLD CLIMATES

Sailors in the turn ferry network, like their colleagues in the Baltic trades, could not travel when cold weather brought thick ice to the waterways of northern Europe. The consequences could be profound. In a letter sent on 13 January 1637, for instance, Nicolaes van Reigersbech informed Hugo de Groot that the States-General could not assemble due to sustained freezing, which had halted turn ferry traffic. Temperatures during the winter of 1636/1637 matched the twentieth-century norm and were therefore typical of the interlude between the Grindelwald Fluctuation and Maunder Minimum. Yet a long stretch of highly variable weather meant that conditions in January were as cold as they were during some of the chilliest winters of the Little Ice Age. The correspondence to De Groot suggests that travel by land on a large scale could be impractical during periods of sustained freezing in the republic. When turn ferries could not

Karel Davids and Jan Lucassen. (Cambridge: Cambridge University Press, 1996), 62. Van Tielhof, *The 'Mother of All Trades'*, 81.

[46] Michiel H. Bartels, 'Zeven keer door de Zuiderdijk'. *Jaarboek* 78 (2011): 72. Horsten, *Doorgaande wegen in Nederland, 16e tot 19e eeuw*, 47. De Vries and Van der Woude, *The First Modern Economy*, 187. Nienhuis, *Environmental History of the Rhine-Meuse Delta*, 102.

travel, the payment of river tolls also dropped considerably. The finances of towns that relied on 'local privileges' such as the collection of tolls therefore suffered during periods of sustained freezing temperatures.[47]

Freezing conditions kept ice on the waterways of the republic for months at a time during the coldest years of the Little Ice Age. In the frigid winter of 1662/1663, for example, letters sent by Adriaen van der Goes reported that sustained ice cover had halted the turn ferry for nearly three months. During the equally severe winter of 1683/1684, Claas Caescoper wrote that ice had stopped the turn ferry between Zaandam and Amsterdam for more than nine weeks. Even longer disruptions to the turn ferry network afflicted the republic during the similarly cold winters of 1694/1695 and 1708/1709.[48]

When the long winters of the Little Ice Age finally gave way to springtime thawing, the thick ice on Dutch rivers melted, broke up, and floated to sea. However, pieces could be trapped on sandbanks, along dikes, and at other chokepoints of rivers that had become narrower and more winding with time. If the ice did not melt quickly enough, it could create enormous dams that held back more and more melt water, until it threatened to flood the surrounding countryside. Centuries of hydraulic engineering had made the landscape of the Rhine-Meuse Delta particularly vulnerable to such flooding. Sediments deposited between dikes made rivers shallower than they had been, while accelerating attempts to drain the surrounding landscape with windmills and sluices caused it to fall beneath the level of most riverbanks. Dutch labourers built higher and higher dikes to compensate, but these dikes faced ever more pressure from the waters they held back. Ice dams therefore raised the prospect of catastrophic flooding, and they spread panic through the republic whenever they formed. Toll accounts written in the moderate winter of 1635/1636 suggest that ice dam flooding could also disrupt travel through the turn ferry network. Although floods increased the surface area of the watery networks that spanned the republic's coastal provinces, their rapid currents and opaque water could make them unsafe for turn ferries. However, the same thawing that caused ice dams to form usually melted them within a week, which stopped the flooding and resumed the turn

[47] Buisman, *Duizend jaar* Vol. IV, 439.

[48] Claas Arisz. Caescoper, '5 Maart 1684'. *Nootijsye Boeck, anno 1669–1678, ofte Joernael*. Gemeente Archief Zaanstad. Van der Goes, 'Soude syn van 6 Maert 1670'. *Briefwisseling tusschen de gebroeders van der Goes (1659–1673)* Vol. II, 117. Egbert Alting, *Diarium van Egbert Alting, 1553–1594*, eds. W. J. Formsma and R. van Roijen. (The Hague: Nijhoff, 1964), 254. Buisman, *Duizend jaar* Vol. V, 328.

ferry. Dutch engineers also constructed means of diverting floodwater, such as cross-dikes and sideways diversions, which created more protection behind river dikes.[49]

Skippers aboard turn ferries did not keep logbooks that have been preserved, so we cannot determine exactly how traffic through their networks responded to shifts in atmospheric circulation. As easterly winds grew more frequent in the Maunder Minimum at the expense of westerlies, average journey times probably decreased along some turn ferry routes, but increased in others. On average, some routes were probably faster for ships when they travelled in one direction than when they travelled back along the same course. That mattered, because traffic departing from and returning to a city like Amsterdam did not necessarily have equal socioeconomic importance. Some routes did use rowboats, not sailing ships. In other cases, people or horses could pull ships by rope in contrary winds. Often, however, travel in one direction along some turn ferry networks was not just slower but actually impractical in contrary winds, especially when those winds blew at high velocities. On 17 December 1665, for example, Adriaen van der Goes suggested in a letter that a ship could only reach Delft with an easterly wind. Luckily for the passengers aboard that ship, a wind soon rose from the east. By contrast, in the first week of July 1686, Claas Caescoper wrote that his turn ferry had been delayed by high and presumably contrary winds as it prepared to embark for Zeeland. Changes in the frequency of such winds during the chilliest decades of the Little Ice Age had profound consequences for at least some turn ferry routes.[50]

Stormy weather also hampered the turn ferry. Gales frustrated passengers when they delayed journeys by keeping ships in port. They could be deadly when vessels were already on their way, especially when their routes crossed over large bodies of water. For instance, in the frigid winter of 1586, a severe storm wrecked a ferry carrying many passengers between Amsterdam and Leiden. In 1589, letters reveal that another storm delayed the travels of Johan van Oldenbarnevelt, the new Land's Advocate of the States-General. In autumn of 1671, a turn ferry travelling from Rotterdam

[49] Buisman, *Duizend jaar* Vol. IV, 220. Gottschalk, *Stormvloeden en rivieroverstromingen in Nederland*, Vol. II, 818. Gottschalk, *Stormvloeden en rivieroverstromingen in Nederland, Vol. III*, 417. Tol and Langen, 'A Concise History of Dutch River Floods', 361.

[50] Caescoper, '1 Julij 1686'. *Nootijsye Boeck, anno 1669–1678, ofte Joernael*. Gemeente Archief Zaanstad. Van der Goes, 'Hage, den 17 December 1665'. *Briefwisseling tusschen de gebroeders van der Goes (1659–1673)* Vol. I, 229.

to Middelburg stranded in what Van der Goes referred to as a 'hurricane', although its crew eventually harnessed favourable winds to get underway again. Changes in the average velocity and direction of winds during the chilliest decades of the Little Ice Age may have had an impact on the turn ferry network rivalling that of severe and long-lasting winter freezing.[51]

Letters written by travellers through the Dutch Republic register complicated relationships between the actions of Dutch sailors and the weather that accompanied Little Ice Age cold periods. For example, in the generally chilly year of 1595, Fynes Moryson, a wealthy Englishman, reached the Friesian town of Leeuwarden on the first leg of a long journey to Jerusalem. On the following morning, he attempted to take a turn ferry to Groningen, but 'the covetous Marriners [sic] had over-loaded it, and the winds were boisterous'. A combination of human error and storminess had temporarily foiled Moryson's travel plans. Yet the Dutch transportation network provided many options for travel between cities. For a reasonable fare, Moryson reported, 'we foure consorts hired a private boate'. That day, they travelled most of the distance to Groningen, pushed forward by a favourable westerly wind that was nevertheless 'so boysterous, as we were in no small feare'. After eating supper and sleeping at an inn, they boarded their boat in the morning, with the wind still so high that they remained 'in the same ... danger'. Near Groningen, 'in a great tempest of wind', they lost their rudder and might have succumbed 'had not the waves of the water (by God's mercy) driven it to us'. Despite their harrowing experiences, all aboard the boat survived and reached their destinations.[52]

The horse-drawn barges of the pull ferry were less reliant on weather than sailing vessels, which meant that the network was more dependable. Yet it also meant that the service could not benefit from weather that accelerated journeys by sail. On a chilly, rainy morning in 1667, Prince Cosimo de Medici and his followers, having just started a trip through the Low Countries, endured high winds while on a sailing vessel they had

[51] Johan van Oldenbarnevelt, 'Rapport van Oldenbarnevelt als Gecommitteerde der Staten van Holland, 12–22 Maart 1589'. In *Bescheiden betreffende zijn staatkundig beleid en zijn familia, Eerste Deel: 1570–1601*, ed. S. P. Haak. (The Hague: Martinus Nijhoff, 1934), 160. Buisman, *Duizend jaar* Vol. IV, 87 and 640.

[52] Fynes Moryson, *An Itinerary Containing His Ten Yeeres Travell through the Twelve Dominions of Germany, Bohmer- land, Sweitzerland, Netherland, Denmarke, Poland, Italy, Turky, France, England, Scotland, and Ireland*, Vol. I. Centre for Reformation and Renaissance Studies, Victoria University, Toronto. Available at: https://archive.org/stream/fynesmorysons01moryuoft/fynesmorysons01moryuoft_djvu.txt.

hired. The howling winds were, according to their travel journal, 'not entirely favourable', yet the crew of their boat manipulated its sails to effectively harness the wind. As a result, they quickly left behind a horse-drawn barge. The pull ferry was safer in the violent weather of the Little Ice Age, but it was not always faster.[53]

Moreover, traffic along the pull ferry network responded to military, economic, and environmental developments that affected all travel through the republic. For example, pull ferry traffic declined during the Second Anglo-Dutch War (1664–1667) and plummeted in the first year of the third war, as French and German armies occupied large swaths of the republic. However, in 1673, when the immediate threat to the republic faded, passengers returned in large numbers. More devastating were the economic consequences of increasingly competitive English commerce, which compounded the effects of an agricultural crisis in the late 1670s to help trigger the first sharp fall in pull ferry passengers, between 1674 and 1679. From 1686/1687 to 1691, a second steep decline probably reflected the economic consequences of the Glorious Revolution and the Nine Years' War. These severe reversals punctuated a general slump in pull ferry passages that deepened into the eighteenth century and ultimately mirrored the stagnation of the Dutch economy.[54]

Traffic through the pull ferry network therefore registered military and economic challenges. Yet these human variables cannot be extricated from the influence of climatic trends. Take, for example, the first major collapse in pull ferry traffic. In November and December of 1675, a - cool year in the Maunder Minimum, two severe gales swept through the Low Countries. The force of wind and water destroyed dikes that had only recently been repaired after the defensive inundations of 1672. The result was one of the six most catastrophic storm floods in the history of the seventeenth-century republic. Floodwaters caused immensely expensive damage across the heartland of the republic, between Hoorn, Haarlem, Leiden, Utrecht, and Amsterdam. Saltwater floods increased the salinity of inundated farmland, lowering its productivity for years after the waters receded. At the same time, the republic's defences against the sea required urgent repairs, so the States-General approved onerous land taxes, which

[53] Filippo Corsini and Apollonio Bassetti, 'De eerste reis door Nederland van Cosimo de' Medici, winter 1667/1668 vastgelegd door kamerheer Filippo Corsini en secretaris Apollonio Bassetti'. In *Een Toscaanse prins bezoekt Nederland: De twee reizen van Cosimo de' Medici 1667–1669*, ed. Lodewijk Wagenaar, trans. Bertie Eringa. (Amsterdam: Bas Lubberhuizen), 34.

[54] De Vries, *Barges and Capitalism*, 280.

compounded agricultural crises, and in turn migration from affected regions. The economic, agricultural, and demographic shocks that followed from the flood of 1675 probably played a role in the subsequent reduction in pull ferry passengers. Only two years later, calamitous river flooding exacerbated the damage. Weather typical of a cooler climate may well have played a role in the first pronounced decline in pull ferry traffic.[55]

Relationships between flood events, infrastructural damage, economic stagnation, and lower pull ferry traffic were especially clear in the 1670s, but they were not confined to that decade. In 1652, during the early Maunder Minimum, a reduction in annual pull ferry passengers followed one year after storm and river floods. In 1655, another decline coincided with similarly widespread storm and river inundations. Particularly severe storm flooding in 1664 preceded a long fall in pull ferry passengers that overlapped with the Second Anglo-Dutch War. In 1682 and 1683, storm floods preceded a reduction in pull ferry traffic in 1684. Overall, low points in the popularity of the pull ferry usually followed major storm flooding by one year, perhaps because the full cost of these disasters took time to reach many of the pull ferry's regular travellers. Strangely, pull ferry traffic did not consistently decline during these floods, even though the footpaths used by horses that pulled the barges may well have been vulnerable to flooding and heavy rains. Moreover, the correlation between river flooding and changes in the popularity of the pull ferry is less clear. Storm surges inundated the heart of the pull ferry network in the coastal provinces, but many river floods devastated the republic's hinterland, where travellers often used roads.[56]

Floods may have ultimately reduced travel by pull ferry, but winter freezing could halt it altogether. Financial accounts reveal that ice closed pull ferry canals for an average of 28 days in the seventeenth and eighteenth centuries. When winters were mild – as they were in 1660/1661 and 1661/1662 – the service continued year-round. A relatively warm winter therefore increased the annual number of passengers who used the pull ferry, even if it coincided with a major flood, as it did in 1661. By contrast, in the frigid winter of 1662/1663, ice suspended travel through the pull

[55] Caescoper, 'November 1675'. *Nootijsye Boeck, anno 1669–1678, ofte Joernael.* Gemeente Archief Zaanstad. Buisman, *Duizend jaar* Vol. V, 24. Nienhuis, *Environmental History of the Rhine-Meuse Delta*, 237. Tol and Langen, 'A Concise History of Dutch River Floods', 365.

[56] Jan De Vries, *Barges and Capitalism*, 279. Gottschalk, *Stormvloeden en rivieroverstromingen in Nederland*, Vol. III, 414. Buisman, *Duizend jaar* Vol. IV, 640.

ferry network for more than 80 days. In letters to his brother, Van der Goes described widespread joy when thawing allowed the service to resume in early February. Yet after only three days temperatures fell below freezing, the ice returned, and travel by pull ferry ceased again.[57]

From 1660 to the end of the seventeenth century, five winters were so cold for so long that they suspended the pull ferry service for more than 70 days. Jan de Vries has shown that passenger volume fell from its long-term averages by nearly 7 per cent in the chilliest winters of the Little Ice Age. Years in which pull ferry traffic was low almost always had winters that were substantially colder than the seventeenth-century average, while years in which traffic was high had much warmer winters. Still, changes in the total annual volume of pull ferry and turn ferry traffic during cool winters may actually have been less important than more drastic shifts in the availability of both ferries. Even short interruptions in both services disrupted political deliberations and undermined municipal finances across the republic.[58]

Attempts to keep the pull ferry running in frigid winter weather confirm that the Dutch were not passive victims in the face of the Little Ice Age. When temperatures first dipped below freezing, operators simply used more horses to pull their barges through the thickening ice. When the ice became too thick – as it did in cold Little Ice Age winters – crews hitched horses to large icebreakers. In the heavily trafficked canals that strung together Amsterdam, Haarlem, and Leiden, icebreakers appeared at the beginning of winter. They cut through ice using thick iron plates and the pulling power of as many as forty horses. The plates often suffered damage during frigid winters, when the ice was heavy and hard. As a result, the costs of repairing the icebreakers and purchasing new iron plates roughly correlate to the severity of Little Ice Age winters. Despite their heavy iron, even icebreakers could not cope with the thickest ice that accompanied the coldest winters, and that accounted for long suspensions of pull ferry traffic.[59]

[57] Van der Goes, 'Hage, den xi January 1663'. Van der Goes, 'Hage, den 9 February 1663'. Van der Goes, 'Hage, den 23 February 1663'. *Briefwisseling tusschen de gebroeders van der Goes (1659–1673)* Vol. I, 168, 171, 173. Jan De Vries, *Barges and Capitalism*, 287. Buisman, *Duizend jaar* Vol. IV, 575.

[58] Jan De Vries, *Barges and Capitalism*, 287. Van Engelen, Buisman and IJnsen, 'A Millennium of Weather, Winds and Water in the Low Countries', 112. De Kraker, 'Ice and Water', 11.

[59] De Kraker, 'Ice and Water', 12.

Travel through transportation networks in the republic responded to weather events and climatic trends that affected all the activities pursued in the Dutch economy. Sometimes, weather associated with the Little Ice Age could have contradictory influences on Dutch transportation. For instance, both rye prices and pull ferry passages rose following cold winters. Although a large share of Dutch household income was spent on bread, traffic by pull ferry did not fall when Dutch citizens had less money to spend. This may seem confusing, but profits for some Dutch merchants rose in years of high grain prices, and perhaps that encouraged pull ferry travel by stimulating the Dutch economy. Ultimately, climate change affected Dutch ferry networks, but it was far from the only or even necessarily the most important influence, and Dutch citizens often found ways to adapt.[60]

CLIMATE CHANGE AND TRAVEL THROUGH THE REPUBLIC BY BOAT, ROAD, AND SKATE

Ferry networks accounted for most, but certainly not all, travel through the republic's coastal provinces. Many travellers moved through these provinces in their own small sailboats, often to deliver and sell agricultural commodities. While crews aboard the boats preferred to harness the wind, they could row if necessary, which allowed them to adapt more easily to changes in weather than sailors aboard turn ferries. Farmer-owned boats carrying agricultural goods were also more versatile than the barges of the pull ferry, since they could navigate both the rough seas of the Zuiderzee and the narrow spaces of Amsterdam's labyrinthine canals. The long, shallow rudder of a typical *schuit* allowed it to sail through very shallow water, while a leeboard[61] could be deployed amidships to mitigate the lateral force of wind. Weighed down by agricultural goods, ballast, or in rare occasions, passengers, these craft were usually stable in rough seas.[62]

[60] Jan de Vries, *Barges and Capitalism*, 291.

[61] In Dutch, *zijdzwaard*. Richard Unger, *Ships on Maps: Pictures of Power in Renaissance Europe*. (New York: Palgrave MacMillan, 2010), xxii.

[62] Wegman, *De Waterlandse Melkschuit*, 27. See also Maurice Kaak, *Vlaamse en Brabantse Binnenschepen uit de 18de en 19de eeuw: vergeten vaktaal en oude constructies*. (Ghent: Provinciebestuur Oost-Vlaanderen, 2010). F. Post, *Groninger Scheepvaart en Scheepsbouw vanaf 1600*. (Bedum: Profiel uitgeverij, 1997). P. J. V. M. Sopers and H. C. A. Kampen, *Schepen die verdwijnen*. (Haarlem: Uitgeverij Hollandia, 2000). G. C. E. Crone, *Nederlandsche binnenschepen*. (Amsterdam: Alert de Lange, 1944).

Nevertheless, records of voyages from agricultural Waterland to downtown Amsterdam reveal that storms imperilled milk boats during the Little Ice Age. To get to Amsterdam, farmers in early modern Waterland had to cross the IJ, which was then a wide saltwater bay off the Zuiderzee (Map M1). Amsterdammers had an insatiable demand for perishable dairy products, so milk boats sailed to the city even in dangerous weather. Once in the IJ, however, crews aboard the boats had little recourse when a storm arose. In February 1661, for example, a boat carrying an unusually high number of passengers foundered in a severe storm, drowning 20 people. On 9 November 1697, a boat transporting milk to Amsterdam capsized in a storm as it struggled to cross the IJ. Two years later, another vessel succumbed in similar circumstances.[63]

More milk boats sank in 1763, 1764, and 1788, in the colder, stormier weather that heralded the onset of the Dalton Minimum. In fact, such disasters exclusively coincided with the coldest phases of the Little Ice Age. While surviving sources suggest that very few of the thousands of voyages undertaken by farmers appear to have ended in catastrophe, this does not necessarily mean that such tragedies were rare. Newspapers and elite correspondence only registered the loss of a small, farmer-owned boat in exceptional circumstances: in 1661, for example, when many passengers drowned. Either way, for crews who operated milk boats, high winds caused delays more often than wrecks. Because voyages from Waterland to Amsterdam lasted no more than three hours, they could easily be postponed if conditions really seemed too severe for travel. Yet long delays during the frequent gales of Little Ice Age cold periods likely spoiled dairy products, and therefore cut into the profits of Dutch farmers. Perhaps some risked seas they should have avoided.[64]

In frigid winters during the chilliest decades of the Little Ice Age, the same severe freezing that halted travel by ferry also affected efforts by farmers to move their commodities to market. In the cold winter of 1586/1587, for example, Commander Van Vervou of the Dutch army reported that extensive ice cover on the Eem River had stopped boats from supplying pure water to brewers during an outbreak of plague, after local water had been contaminated. Correspondence and diary entries reveal that sustained freezing in the frigid winters of 1620/1621 and 1621/1622 led to extensive ice that prohibited travel by boat. In the cool winter of

[63] Wegman, *De Waterlandse Melkschuit*, 43. Buisman, *Duizend jaar* Vol. IV, 569.

[64] Caescoper, 'Januarij 1693'. *Nootijsye Boeck, anno 1669–1678, ofte Joernael*. Gemeente Archief Zaanstad. Wegman, *De Waterlandse Melkschuit*, 44.

1659/1660, letters sent by Adriaen van der Goes reported that boats could not set sail.[65]

During the equally chilly winter of 1671, Van der Goes on 19 November marvelled that ice had already forced boats to 'lie still before Leiden, Utrecht and Amsterdam'. In the landmark winters of 1683/1684 and 1694/1695, Caescoper suggested that, for more than three months, ice had made it impossible to travel by boat. In 1695, he reported that freezing and ice would continue to plague voyages by boat until August! Even in relatively moderate winters, such as those of 1661/1662, 1670/1671, 1685/1686, and 1698/1699, ice forced boats from the water. Yet sustained thawing interrupted freezing in each of these winters, and after February ice had largely disappeared from most waterways.[66]

Since dairy products accounted for such a large part of the Dutch diet, and such an important share of its agricultural production, the movement of dairy products into Dutch cities rarely stopped entirely. Farmers sailed whenever possible, and illustrations suggest that, even when ice blocked harbours, sailboats still carried milk if open water persisted in the IJ. When boats reached the ice, crews dragged them the rest of the way into port. If the ice expanded too far, however, farmers loaded their goods into sleds and continued their trade. Since individual milk boats were small, goods otherwise loaded onto boats could easily be transferred to a sled. As a result, most farmers in Waterland probably kept at least one sled. The kinetic friction of ice is higher than that of water, and early modern movement across a solid surface usually demanded human or animal muscle, so it was harder to travel by sled in cold winters than it was to travel by boat in warmer conditions. Still, despite minimal capital and access to only the most rudimentary transportation technologies, dairy farmers persisted in their trade during even the chilliest winters, when the republic's other waterborne networks could no longer function.[67]

Amsterdammers demanded not only dairy products but also regular shipments of fresh water. Over the course of the sixteenth century, the

[65] Van der Goes, 'Hage, den 22 January 1660'. *Briefwisseling tusschen de gebroeders van der Goes (1659–1673)* Vol. I, 51. Buisman, *Duizend jaar* Vol. V, 220.

[66] Caescoper, 'November 1698'. '10 March 1695'. *Nootijsye Boeck, anno 1669–1678, ofte Joernael*. Gemeente Archief Zaanstad. Van der Goes, 'Hage, den 11 December 1662'. *Briefwisseling tusschen de gebroeders van der Goes (1659–1673)* Vol. I, 160. Van der Goes, 'Hage, den 16 January 1661'. *Briefwisseling tusschen de gebroeders van der Goes (1659–1673)* Vol. II, 182. Buisman and Van Engelen, (ed.), *Duizend jaar weer, wind en water in de Lage Landen*, Vol. IV, 92.

[67] Wegman, *De Waterlandse Melkschuit*, 47. D. C. B. Evans et al., 'The Kinetic Friction of Ice'. *Proceedings of the Royal Society* 347:1651 (1976): 494.

water that flowed through Amsterdam became too salty and too polluted for consumption. Entrepreneurs therefore established a service that transported freshwater into Amsterdam by boat from nearby lakes and rivers. It expanded as the city's population grew in the seventeenth and eighteenth centuries. By 1781, more than 43 brewer ships, and 114 private water-company ships, delivered freshwater to Amsterdam's citizens. Winter freezing also disrupted this service. Yet the city's brewers could collectively access greater capital than small groups of dairy farmers, so they did not need to resort to using sleds. In 1651, during the early Maunder Minimum, they founded a company to deploy an icebreaker in Amsterdam's harbour. It could not open the harbour for shipping, but it could preserve a watery corridor to the river Weesp. Eight horses could usually pull it through the ice, but it required 12 in chilly winters, and it could not be used in the coldest winters of all, such as the ones between 1687 and 1690. In those frigid winters, labourers kept the water route from Amsterdam to the Weesp open by hand. The price of fresh water in Amsterdam therefore fluctuated according to winter severity, yet the brewers and the labourers they hired maintained its supply. In the cities of the republic, brewers and farmers alike adapted to the severe winters of Little Ice Age cold periods, because the consequences of abandoning some forms of mobility were simply too great.[68]

The weather that grew more frequent during the coldest phases of the Little Ice Age not only altered how existing transportation networks were used, but also contributed to modes of travel that encouraged new cultures and social spaces. Quintessentially Dutch paintings of winter landscapes reflect the popularity of skates and sleds when temperatures stayed below zero. However, they cannot do full justice to the scale of the icy thoroughfares that emerged when freezing lingered for as many as three months. In the frigid winter of 1620/1621, for example, chronicles and diaries recounted an ice fair near Harlingen that was visited by 1,300 sleds on just one day. Some had been pulled across the full breadth of the Zuiderzee.[69]

Diary entries written by Caescoper during the Maunder Minimum show that skaters flocked to the ice as soon as freezing conditions endured for more than a few nights. Many skated for pleasure, but others because skating provided the most efficient means of getting around. When the ice was thick enough, travellers on horseback or in carriages joined skaters on

[68] Davids, *The Rise and Decline of Dutch Technological Leadership*, Vol. I, 137. Van Dam, 'Water, Steam, Ice', 37.

[69] Buisman, *Duizend jaar* Vol. IV, 339.

frozen waterways. Ice on Dutch waterways could be used for transportation even in moderate winters, but it endured much longer, and supported more weight, during the coldest decades of the Little Ice Age.[70]

Yet not all ice was alike. On 7 March during the cold winter of 1683/1684, Caescoper wrote that ice on regional waterways had grown very strong, but 'we have had no ice that can be crossed by skates'. The ice may have been rough and uneven, a product of high winds that whip up waves in sufficiently cold temperatures. During the winter of 1683/1684, Caescoper described storms in several diary entries, which may well have coincided with very cold temperatures. Blizzards could therefore have undercut some of the advantages for skaters of long, frigid winters during the chilliest stretches of the Little Ice Age. Yet ice can also become uneven when snow that has melted on the ice refreezes. These conditions require thawing and therefore warmer temperatures, which were of course less common in the coldest periods of the Little Ice Age. In any case, rough ice scarcely affected travel by carriages, horses, and sleds across frozen waters, except possibly in the Zuiderzee. There, thick shards of sea ice could converge in thawing and then refreeze in new formations when temperatures returned below zero.[71]

Even travel across smooth ice could be dangerous. Travellers routinely misjudged the thickness of ice, especially at the beginning and end of winters, or when conditions alternated between freezing and thawing. In March 1670, for example, Adriaen van der Goes wrote that a horse, a coach driver, and four women perished when they plunged through the ice at the Schie near Rotterdam. A chronicle kept by the St Elizabeth's covenant at Huissen, near the eastern border of the republic, reported that many monks fell through the ice on 10 March 1709, 'so that it was a wonder that they did not break their legs'. For travellers in the republic, sustained temperatures, whether cool or warm, were likely easier to adapt to and therefore less dangerous than variability. Still, it was difficult to travel safely when temperatures dropped too far below zero, as they did in cold spells during the landmark winters of the Little Ice Age.[72]

[70] Caescoper, '21 February 1695', '25 December 1695'. *Nootijsye Boeck, anno 1669–1678, ofte Joernael.* Gemeente Archief Zaanstad.

[71] D. A. Rothrock, 'The Energetics of the Plastic Deformation of Pack Ice by Ridging'. *Journal of Geophysical Research* 80:33 (1975): 4514. Caescoper, '7 Maert 1684', '29 February 1684', '28 Maert 1684'. *Nootijsye Boeck, anno 1669–1678, ofte Joernael.* Gemeente Archief Zaanstad.

[72] Buisman, *Duizend jaar* Vol. V, 252. Van der Goes, 'Soude syn van 6 Maert 1670'. *Briefwisseling tusschen de gebroeders van der Goes (1659–1673)* Vol. II, 118.

It is telling that many who journeyed by foot, horse, and carriage through the coastal provinces of the Dutch Republic in the winters of the Little Ice Age opted to travel on frozen water rather than on roads. Most of the republic's roads were as vulnerable to shifts in temperature as the waterways that intersected them. Freezing, for example, left many rutted paths impassable, either because they became too slippery or because mud and sand had frozen in uneven formations. In January 1586, the Earl of Leicester, then in The Hague, wrote that 'we cannot, till the wether break, send by water or land almost to any place'. He complained that he 'could not hear owt of Zeland but by long seas, all the rivers be ycie and frozen', but not so frozen as to 'bear any horse or carriage'. Leicester did not even consider sending his messengers by road.[73]

Across Europe, ice cover on city streets imperilled those who ventured outside. Many who suffered injuries after slipping on ice could expect chronic pain, or even lifelong impediments to their mobility. For example, on 19 January during the cold winter of 1664/1665, Samuel Pepys in London recollected that he 'saw a woman that broke her thigh, in her heels slipping up upon the frosty streete'. Indeed, diaries written on both shores of the North Sea in the winter of 1694/1695 reveal that extreme cold could simply discourage travel altogether. On 23 January, John Evelyn in London wrote that 'so very fierce was the frost, as kept us still from church'. In the republic, popular songs performed during the frigid winter of 1708/1709, although perhaps apocryphal, nevertheless reflect widespread fears of being caught far from home when temperatures plummeted. Lyrics refer to a postman frozen on his horse, and a family frozen on the street. In early January, people did in fact freeze to death on roads and even in their homes amid a particularly sudden and severe cold snap. Song lyrics therefore reflected exaggerated popular responses to the very real dangers of a landmark winter in the Maunder Minimum.[74]

Wintry weather in the coldest decades of the Little Ice Age also hampered efforts to build new transportation infrastructure in the Dutch Republic. On 23 February 1663, for instance, Adriaen van der Goes

[73] Robert Dudley, 'Letter XV. The Earl of Leycester to Lord Burghley, 14th January 1585–6'. In *Correspondence of Robert Dudley, Earl of Leycester, during His Government of the Low Countries, in the Years 1585 and 1586*, ed. John Bruce. (London: John Bowyer Nichols and Son, 1844), 60.

[74] Samuel Pepys, 'Wednesday 9 January 1664/65', *Diary of Sir Samuel Pepys*. Accessed 25 July 2013, www.pepysdiary.com/archive/1665/01. Buisman, *Duizend jaar* Vol. IV, 213.

reported that icy conditions had inhibited the construction of new paths for post wagons, which functioned as a sort of miniature land-based turn ferry that connected major towns. Freezing during the severe winters of the Little Ice Age also hindered workers from maintaining roads that had already been built. For example, in the frigid winter of 1666/1667, ordinance drafted by Amsterdam city officials reveals that wintry weather postponed previously scheduled maintenance of the Overtoomseweg ('Overtoom road'). Because road maintenance may have taken longer during the chilliest decades of the Little Ice Age, its cost probably increased as well.[75]

In any season, heavy rain affected travel along the roads of the Dutch Republic. On 29 February 1684, Caescoper reported that a torrential downpour during an otherwise frigid winter had left the road he was walking on wet and very dangerous. Temporarily mild temperatures that permitted rain were not common during a severe Maunder Minimum winter, but a storm certainly was. On 5 August 1695, Christiaan Huygens wrote that a bout of rain had left one road so slippery that he had fallen on his way to lunch. Luckily, he escaped serious injury. Travellers coped with muddy roads by installing wider wheels on their wagons, or even by using sleds. Yet storm surges and torrential rains could cause floods that overwhelmed roads and stopped people from using them. On 8 December 1665, Van der Goes wrote that catastrophic storm flooding had prohibited all traffic along roads between Haarlem and The Hague.[76]

Snowstorms during severe winters could be equally disastrous for travellers on the republic's roads. A blizzard during the winter of 1662/1663 delayed many post wagons between Rotterdam and The Hague, while others vanished altogether. Perhaps some or even all of the missing travellers survived the blizzard, but many letters never reached their destinations. For months during the bitterly cold winter of 1708/1709,

[75] 'Akte van overeenkomst tussen de dijkgraaf en heemraden van Nieuwer-Amstel met de stad Amsterdam en de eigenaren van landerijen en huizen langs de Overtoomseweg inzake het onderhoud van deze weg 1666–1800'. Reference number: 5501. Archief van het Ambacht Nierwer-Amstel, met het Archief van de Ambachten Rietwijk, Rietwijkeroord en Rietwijkeroorderpolder. 'Keur van het Hoogheemraadschap van Rijnland tegen het zeilen in de Zuidbuurtse Watering'. Reference number: 1099. Regionaal Archief Leiden. Van der Goes, 'Hage, den 23 February 1663'. *Briefwisseling tusschen de gebroeders van der Goes (1659–1673)* Vol. IV, 173.

[76] Van der Goes, 'Hage, den 8 December 1665'. *Briefwisseling tusschen de gebroeders van der Goes (1659–1673)* Vol. IV, 221. Nienhuis, *Environmental History of the Rhine-Meuse Delta*, 102. Klompmaker, *Handel in the Gouden Eeuw*, 66.

heavy snowfall also accompanied bitterly cold conditions. Again, travel ground to a halt both on roads and in frozen waterways. Overall, stormy, wet weather during Little Ice Age cold periods hindered travel by land across the republic. Heavy precipitation slowed the trickle of people and correspondence along Dutch roads, and compounded the consequences of delays in waterborne transportation.[77]

Nevertheless, cold and wet weather in the chilliest stretches of the Little Ice Age did alter the usually lopsided balance between waterborne and land-based travel through the coastal Republic. When ice covered waterways in the winter, some travellers did indeed take to roads, so long as freezing was not too severe and did not coincide with heavy snow. When Delfzijl's harbour froze shut in March 1587, for example, labourers loaded 50 wagons with goods that would otherwise have travelled by ship. More significant, however, were shifts in annual precipitation and, in turn, water levels. Prolonged drought in December 1669 encouraged many to walk or ride along dried-up riverbeds. Droughts in the spring of 1672 allowed invading French and German armies to easily cross rivers that normally screened the republic's southeastern borders. In the summer of 1707, Caescoper reported that water levels had dropped lower than anyone could remember, which evidently led many people to ride their mules through dried-up creeks and ditches. These years of lower than average water levels coincided with relatively mild winters. Because plentiful precipitation accompanied some of the chilliest stretches of the Little Ice Age, travel on land through the Dutch Republic may have grown more common during warmer decades. Of course, travellers outside of the coastal provinces had to use roads – or else postpone their journeys – in all kinds of weather, during both warm and cold climates.[78]

Ultimately, small-scale travel through the Dutch Republic by water, ice, and road was more resilient than other kinds of movement to the climate changes of the Little Ice Age. Farmers on milk boats rarely foundered in storms, and they overcame freezing either by sailing through icy waters or by loading their goods on sleds. Brewers invested in icebreakers and even manual labour to preserve Amsterdam's supply of fresh water. Many travellers took to the ice using skates or sleds, especially during very

[77] Van der Goes, 'Hage, den 22 January 1660'. *Briefwisseling tusschen de gebroeders van der Goes (1659–1673)* Vol. I, 51. Caescoper, '29 February 1684'. *Nootijsye Boeck, anno 1669–1678, ofte Joernael.* Gemeente Archief Zaanstad. Buisman, *Duizend jaar* Vol. V, 219 and 352. Buisman, *Duizend jaar* Vol. IV, 581.

[78] Buisman, *Duizend jaar* Vol. IV, 93. Caescoper, 'June, July, August 1707'. *Nootijsye Boeck, anno 1669–1678, ofte Joernael.* Gemeente Archief Zaanstad.

cold or long winters. Some succumbed to thin ice or bitterly cold temperatures, but many moved quickly and easily through the republic. Weather associated with the coldest phases of the Little Ice Age could hamper attempts to maintain and use unhardened roads. Yet travel by land continued and even increased in the republic during very cold or very dry conditions. The flow of people, goods, and information through the republic never ceased entirely.

To preserve this flow, Dutch citizens of different social strata confronted the weather of the Grindelwald Fluctuation and Maunder Minimum with impressive physical and intellectual energy. It may not be a coincidence that, in the coldest decades of the Little Ice Age, Dutch governments, entrepreneurs, and labourers developed the pull ferry to free waterborne transportation from its dependence on shifts in wind direction and velocity. However, adaptation in the face of weather and climate change had limits. Prolonged freezing suspended most forms of travel across water while slowing or occasionally discouraging movement along roads. Overall, freezing impeded large-scale transportation in the northern Netherlands because the volume of goods or people that regularly passed through the waterways of the Dutch Republic could not be fully displaced onto wagons or skates. Storms also hindered all forms of travel, by land and water. In fact, heavy precipitation and flooding could entirely prevent movement through a region, overwhelming even the republic's remarkably flexible transportation network.

CONCLUSIONS: TRAVELLING THROUGH AND NEAR THE REPUBLIC IN THE LITTLE ICE AGE

Across early modern Europe, travel beyond the vicinity of major urban centres was a very uncertain prospect. Roads were sparse, poorly maintained, and often plagued by bandits. Travel by river was easier and safer, yet rivers could not reach every part of a country. Over time, merchants overcame some of these obstacles to ensure that trade increasingly connected European cities and towns. In the fifteenth, sixteenth, and seventeenth centuries, Dutch merchants seized control of seaborne trade in European waters. To a large extent, that achievement was made possible by, and helped to provoke, the creation of an intricate domestic transportation network that connected population centres across the Dutch Republic.

The many kinds of movement that carried Dutch sailors along overseas trade routes and carried travellers through the republic itself collectively yielded a transportation system that was distinct in early modern Europe. By applying the latest technical innovations to transportation on water, Dutch shipwrights and engineers created infrastructure that moved people, goods, and ideas with unprecedented efficiency. In no substantial state other than the Dutch Republic did canals accommodate the bulk of travellers, or did commerce by sea support such a large part of the economy. Yet the republic's ships, harbours, canals, and roads were vulnerable to changes in weather. Wet, stormy, and cold conditions in the chilliest decades of the Little Ice Age adversely affected some elements of this transportation infrastructure. Others, however, reflected conscious or unconscious adaptation to the regional manifestations of global climate changes.

Above all, the Dutch transportation system was diverse. It relied heavily on waterborne travel, yet it accommodated many modes of movement. Each responded differently to shifting weather patterns during the Little Ice Age. Changes in prevailing wind direction were more important for mariners in the Baltic and the North Sea than they were for travellers moving through the republic. Shifts in the extent and duration of ice on waterways mattered more for travellers using the ferry networks than they did for those who walked or rode along the republic's roads. Ice complicated travel for farmers in their boats, yet it accommodated quick and efficient movement across the republic by skate and sled. Heavy rain or snow was worse for travellers on land than it was for those at sea, yet storms, with their high winds, were more dangerous at sea.

For the Dutch domestic transportation system, diverse options for travel between locations gave a flexibility and resilience to movement in the face of climate changes. Sailors aboard vessels plying the Baltic trades were not as fortunate. They had few options when sea ice kept them from leaving port, or blocked entry to the Sound, and they faced terrible risks when stormy winds pushed them towards a lee shore. Yet, Dutch merchants safeguarded their profits by responding creatively to weather that imperilled the mariners they hired. Moreover, the diversity of the Dutch diet often allowed Dutch citizens to escape the worst consequences of the harvest failures and price increases that benefitted Dutch merchants and followed, in part, from Little Ice Age weather. The prosperity of the Dutch during the Little Ice Age reflected the ruthless entrepreneurialism of urban merchants, the resilience of travel within the republic, and perhaps especially the strengths of a diverse society.

The distinct characteristics of the Dutch transportation system therefore contributed to the mixed but overall beneficial consequences of climatic cooling for the Dutch. These relationships may have reflected characteristically Dutch understandings of nature. Dutch farmers, engineers, sailors, and labourers were used to living with, and systematically manipulating, a restless environment. They found creative solutions to travel in harsh weather, since movement was essential to their economy and culture. They would use similar ingenuity to navigate the advantages and disadvantages that the Little Ice Age would have for their conduct of war.

PART TWO

CONFLICT AND CLIMATE CHANGE

Part II Preface

Climate changes may have influenced the Dutch economy most directly by affecting the outcome of wars, since the very survival of the republic and the expansion of its commercial empire depended on military might. The Golden Age dawned amid a war of independence that gave rise to the republic in what had once been a province of the Spanish Empire. During the Eighty Years' Year, the military commanders and merchants of the republic revolutionized how war was fought on land, established a radically decentralized but effective naval system, and commercialized armed conflict. Soon after the republic at last earned its independence, France and especially England embarked on a series of wars aimed at destroying Dutch commercial preeminence and establishing a greater role for their own merchants in the world economy. Amid all these wars, Dutch merchants and mariners joined other Europeans in ruthlessly plundering the world. The very prosperity of the Golden Age at its height consequently made it an era of relentless violence. According to historian Jaap Bruijn, even in the wake of the Eighty Years' War the republic 'was a nation almost continuously involved in a war of independence'.[1]

[1] Glete, *Warfare at Sea*, 165. J. R. Hale, *War and Society in Renaissance Europe*. (London: Fontana, 1985), 22. Scammell, *The First Imperial Age*, 20. John A. Lynn, *Giant of the Grand Siècle: The French Army, 1610–1715*. (Cambridge: Cambridge University Press, 2006), 11. Ormrod, *The Rise of Commercial Empires*, 31. 't Hart, 'The Dutch Republic: The Urban Impact upon Politics', 68. Wantje Fritschy, 'Holland en de financiering van de Opstand (1568–1648): Deel I'. *Economisch Statistische Berichten* 89:4437 (2004): 328. Wantje Fritschy, 'Holland en de financiering van de Opstand (1568–1648): Deel II'. *Economisch Statistische Berichten* 89:4438 (2004): 353. Bruijn, *The Dutch Navy of the*

The following two chapters are part of a new wave of scholarship that explores the environmental context of past wars. They argue that Dutch forces usually benefitted from weather common in cold phases of the Little Ice Age. To make that case, they find relationships between climate change, weather, and tactical operations. In military parlance, tactics relate to the conduct of battle, while strategy refers to the process of manipulating resources and manoeuvring forces so they are best positioned to damage the enemy. By focusing on tactics, these chapters trace the military influence of climate change from the global to the local, from the century timescale to the minute and hour.[2] Success in war ultimately hinges on how much energy a military force can harness and apply to the destruction of its enemy. In the Eighty Years' War, the Anglo-Dutch Wars, and the Glorious Revolution, shifts in prevailing weather altered how belligerents could exploit and consume energy. Long, frigid winters during the Grindelwald Fluctuation (1560–1628) and Maunder Minimum (1645–1720) increased the energy demands of troops in the field and labourers in shipyards. However, freezing also allowed armies to march across waterways that otherwise served as barriers to invasion. Heavy precipitation jeopardized military campaigns by forcing armies to use excessive energy while travelling over flooded or muddy roads. Over the course of the Anglo-Dutch Wars and the Glorious Revolution, changes in atmospheric circulation ultimately allowed Dutch mariners to more effectively harness the energy of wind. Storms unleashed great energy, yet interacted in different ways with distinct military systems to unevenly affect how much of that energy the combatants could use. Ultimately, it was by changing how belligerents could locally exploit energy to move and fight that global climate changes most clearly influenced the wars that shaped the Dutch Golden Age.

Seventeenth and Eighteenth Centuries, 18. Jaap R. Bruijn, 'Introduction'. In *De Ruyter: Dutch Admiral*, eds. Jaap R. Bruijn and Ronald Prud'homme van Reine, 7–16. (Rotterdam: Karwansaray BV, 2011), 8.

[2] Glete, *Warfare at Sea*, 17.

4

Cooling, Warming, and the Wars of Independence, 1564–1648

The Dutch Wars of Independence, collectively called the Eighty Years' War, were so costly that they repeatedly bankrupted one of the world's richest empires and so revolutionary that they transformed how Europeans fought at home and abroad. Already in the 1550s, the futile brutality of the Inquisition in the Low Countries kindled talk of insurrection against Spanish rule. In 1566, widespread unrest spilled into mob violence that provoked a heavy-handed Spanish response. The first battles between Spanish and rebel armies erupted in 1568. Yet only in 1572 did the rebellion establish a strong foothold in the northern Low Countries. It was not until 1581 that its largely Protestant provinces abandoned hope of compromise with the Spanish crown. By the late 1590s, the rising economic clout of the republic meant that its rebellion had become a global contest of rival great powers. In a sense, the Dutch won their independence in 1609, with the signing of a Twelve Years' Truce that legitimized the republic. Yet fighting resumed in the 1620s and soon took on an even more international character amid the Thirty Years' War then raging in the neighbouring Holy Roman Empire. In the late 1620s and 1630s, the republic allied with France and assumed the offensive against a distracted Spanish Empire. The conflict would simmer until 1648, when peace treaties formally secured Dutch independence and ended the Thirty Years' War.[1]

Climate change profoundly influenced this long and complicated struggle. In the early 1560s, frigid, stormy weather associated with the onset of the Grindelwald Fluctuation contributed to food shortages and deadly

[1] Graham Darby, 'Introduction'. In *The Origins and Development of the Dutch Revolt*, ed. Graham Darby. (London: Routledge, 2003), 1.

flooding across the Low Countries. These disasters exacerbated widespread unrest that had already been provoked by Spanish religious persecution, economic mismanagement, and attempts at political centralization.[2] Then, after the revolts of 1568 and 1572, offensive operations undertaken by both Spain and the rebellious republic were more difficult and thus less likely to succeed in the weather of the Grindelwald Fluctuation. Storms and heavy precipitation undermined sieges, impeded the movement of armies, and increased the effectiveness of floods deliberately unleashed to thwart invasions. At sea, gales repeatedly thwarted Dutch and Spanish fleets attempting offensive operations near the coast. Freezing temperatures allowed Spanish troops to invade over ice-covered rivers and lakes that otherwise protected the republic, but campaigns in such weather rarely succeeded. Sieges often dragged deep into winters that had become much colder on average, especially in places protected by star-shaped fortifications recently introduced from Italy. The consequences were often devastating for invading soldiers.

Even in the first decades of the Wars of Independence, the armies of the Dutch rebellion and later the republic launched many offensives, some of which failed in cold, wet, or stormy weather. Yet in a broad strategic sense, the Grindelwald Fluctuation initially benefitted rebels whose primary concern was to defend their emerging country against Spanish invasions. Then, in the aftermath of a 'year without summer' in 1628, average temperatures temporarily rebounded, while precipitation likely declined, across the Low Countries. At around the same time, Spain entered the war of the Mantuan Succession in Italy and its finances collapsed, while France allied with the republic. Subsequently, a combined Dutch and French offensive in the Spanish-controlled Southern Netherlands benefitted from weather that was overall warmer and drier than it had been. Environmental conditions therefore shifted in ways that multiplied the military consequences of human decisions and policies. The result was to encourage and aid Dutch military operations against Spain.

Dutch and Spanish combatants and political leaders closely followed the ways in which weather transformed different environments across the Low Countries. Officers and soldiers on both sides appreciated that weather could play a crucial role on the battlefield. Yet the soldiers and

[2] Geoffrey Parker, *The Dutch Revolt*. (London: Penguin Books, 1985), 57. Geoffrey Parker, *The Army of Flanders and the Spanish Road, 1567–1659*. (Cambridge: Cambridge University Press, 1971), 195. Prak, *The Dutch Republic in the Seventeenth Century*, 8. Martin van Gelderen, *The Political Thought of the Dutch Revolt 1555–1590*. (Cambridge: Cambridge University Press, 2002), 32.

sailors of the Dutch Republic usually responded more creatively to changing meteorological conditions than their Spanish counterparts. Their flexibility contributed to their unlikely success in the face of the most powerful empire in early modern Christendom.

ENVIRONMENTAL CONDITIONS AND MILITARY PRACTICES

For military commanders, water both networked and divided the Low Countries. Bodies of water provided environmental barriers for invading armies that could be fortified by defending forces. Even lightly garrisoned towns or fortresses were difficult to besiege when surrounded by water. Coastal towns in particular could not be invested (a military term meaning besieged) without establishing local naval supremacy. Marshes could slow the progress of armies and undermine attempts at establishing a siege around a town or fortress. In desperate circumstances, sluices could be opened and dikes breached to inundate city surroundings and relieve sieges. However, supplies, equipment, and even information could also travel more efficiently and often more quickly by water than land. Entire armies could use ships to quickly invade places that would have been time consuming or even impossible to reach by land. Water therefore provided some logistical advantages for invading armies, but on the whole it offered greater benefits to defending garrisons.[3]

At the beginning of the Dutch revolt, Spanish commanders worried that every rebel-held town and fortress would take months to besiege, especially in watery regions. Invading armies could bypass garrisoned strongholds, but only by risking their supply lines. Over time, both rebels and Habsburgs protected strategic positions with the *Trace Italienne*, an expensive, star-shaped fortress that allowed defenders to fire on attackers from every angle, and featured sloped, muddy walls that absorbed artillery fire. Besieging such a fortress could take years. Both environmental conditions and changing technologies and strategies therefore conspired to lengthen sieges so that they stretched into the winter months, when armies would otherwise be disbanded or quartered in cities. These armies expanded dramatically over the course of the Eighty Years' War owing to

[3] De Vries and Van der Woude, *The First Modern Economy*, 14. Parker, *The Dutch Revolt*, 22. Marjolein 't Hart, *The Dutch Wars of Independence: Warfare and Commerce in The Netherlands, 1570–1680*. (London: Routledge, 2014), 12. Colin Martin and Geoffrey Parker, *The Spanish Armada: Revised Edition*. (Manchester: Manchester University Press, 1999), 48.

a host of reasons that included population growth, the widespread introduction of firearms, the rising fiscal sophistication of Spanish and Dutch governments, and the difficulty of besieging the *Trace Italienne*. Mercenaries from across Europe swelled the ranks of armies on both sides, until the Low Countries became known as the continent's 'School of War'. Trailing behind armies, 'campaign communities' of prostitutes, families, and merchants outnumbered all but the largest cities.[4]

Sieges were among the most complex and expensive public works of the sixteenth and seventeenth centuries. Most unfolded according to a predictable sequence. First, soldiers or conscripted labourers would build two fortified rings just beyond artillery range from the target city: a circumvallation, which faced inward to repel the town's garrison, and a contravallation, which faced outward to defend against a relieving field army. Coastal towns could only be invested with a fleet. Even when entirely encircled, towns could communicate with the outside world by using carrier pigeons, fire signals, and occasionally trained dogs and secret passageways. Food, fuel, and ammunition, however, were harder to come by.[5]

Next, the besieging army opened trenches just outside the reach of muskets fired from the 'outerworks' of the town's fortifications. By digging in zigzags and employing small redoubts, soldiers survived raids and bombardment from the town while inching towards the outerworks. Once their trenches were close enough, sappers burrowed even closer while soldiers deployed siege cannons to level artillery in the town. After the outerworks fell, volunteers built bridges across the interior ditch that protected most fortifications. Artillery and sappers then undermined the remaining walls.

[4] Rudi de Graaf, *Oorlog, mijn arme schapen. Een andere kijk op de Tachtigjarige Oorlog.* (Franeker: Van Wijnen, 2004), 16. Olaf van Nimwegen, *The Dutch Army and the Military Revolutions, 1588–1688.* (Woodbridge: The Boydell Press, 2010), 120, 135. 't Hart, *The Dutch Wars of Independence*, 17. Hale, *War and Society in Renaissance Europe*, 47, 206. Geoffrey Parker, *The Army of Flanders and the Spanish Road*, 8. Lynn, *Women, Armies, and Warfare in Early Modern Europe*, 33. See also Charles van den Heuvel, 'De verspreiding van de Italiaanse vestingbouwkunde in de Nederlanden in de tweede helft van de zestiende eeuw'. In *Vesting: Vier eeuwen vestingbouw in Nederland*, eds. J. Sneep, H. A. Treu and M. Tydeman. (The Hague: Stichting Menno van Coehoorn, 1982).

[5] Van Nimwegen, *The Dutch Army and the Military Revolutions*, 144. Pieter Christiaanszoon Bor, *Oorsprongk, begin, en vervolgh der Nederlandsche oorlogen, Vol. I.* (Amsterdam: Joannes van Someren, Abraham Wolfgangh, Hendrick en Dirck Boom, 1679), 550, 558. J. O. H. Brouwer (ed.), *Kronieken van Spaansche Soldaten uit het Begin van den Tachtigjarigen Oorlog.* (Zutphen: B. V. W. J. Thieme & Cie, 1980), 240. Willem van Oranje aan commissarissen tot het ontzet van Leiden, 8 October 1574. De Correspondentie van Willem van Oranje nr. 9408, 15 December 2014. http://resources.huygens.knaw.nl/wvo/brief/9408.

At last, the besieging army prepared for the final assault. According to informal rules of war, the defending garrison now had one last chance to surrender. Besieging troops usually spared those who capitulated but slaughtered any who resisted before plundering the town they had defended.[6]

Persistent rain could wreak havoc on besiegers trying to follow these steps. Rain thwarted attempts to dig trenches, and interfered with movement along supply lines. Rain and storms could also worsen the impact of floods unleashed by the defending garrison. Bitterly cold temperatures could be even more dangerous to besieging armies. Soldiers routinely froze to death in the field or even in camp when they ran out of fuel. The combination of cold and wet weather could be particularly dangerous to both besiegers and the besieged because it often encouraged the spread of diseases that afflicted digestive and respiratory systems. Moreover, since the aim of many sieges was to starve beleaguered populations into submission, and since military supply lines were usually tenuous, especially in rainy weather, malnutrition ran rampant among encamped armies and defending garrisons alike. Malnourished bodies have fewer fat-storing cells that produce the hormone leptin, which modulates the strength of parts of the human immune system. Starving soldiers and civilians were therefore particularly susceptible to epidemic disease, especially the kinds that thrived in chilly, humid weather. The wartime migration and mobilization of huge numbers of people and animals in turn helped spread these diseases.[7]

Campaigns on land during the Wars of Independence often coincided with battles at sea. High winds and strong currents in the English Channel and North Sea threatened oar-driven galleys, while shallow water and shifting sandbanks near the coast imperilled taller galleons. Only sailing vessels of shallow draught could navigate effectively through both kinds of water. While Spanish commanders long relied on a mix of galleys and heavy galleons, the rebels from the start used light and nimble sailing ships that could cope with any kind of sea. Rebel captains preferred to grapple and board enemy vessels, while Spanish captains at least initially favoured artillery bombardment.[8]

[6] Van Nimwegen, *The Dutch Army and the Military Revolutions*, 144.

[7] Camenisch et al., 'The 1430s: A Cold Period of Extraordinary Internal Climate Variability during the Early Spörer Minimum', 2117. Graham M. Lord et al., 'Leptin Modulates the T-cell Immune Response and Reverses Starvation-Induced Immunosuppression' *Nature* 394:6696 (1998): 897.

[8] David Goodman, *Spanish Naval Power: Reconstruction and Defeat.* (Cambridge: Cambridge University Press, 1997), 4. R. A. Stradling, *The Armada of Flanders: Spanish Maritime Policy and European War, 1568–1668.* (Cambridge: Cambridge University Press,

Government-sanctioned piracy, called privateering, accounted for most hostilities at sea. Investors usually financed privateering to compensate for commercial activities disrupted by war. Small privateering crews typically used light vessels that could overwhelm isolated merchant ships but posed little threat to escorted convoys. This posed a dilemma for merchants, since prices for commodities collapsed when a convoy carrying them made it to port, but sailing alone was dangerous business. Privateers divided their profits between crews, investors, and the crown. Some merchants therefore hoped for wars that could present profitable but ideally one-sided opportunities for privateering, and some governments anticipated these profits when planning to finance naval campaigns.[9]

Spanish and Dutch naval systems coevolved over the course of the Eighty Years' War, yet they always shared key vulnerabilities. The Dutch Republic and the Spanish Empire both depended on seaborne trade, and the fleets they fielded both needed favourable weather to be effective. In battle, every fleet in the age of sail struggled to acquire the 'weather gage', the upwind position from a downwind enemy. Ships upwind of their opponents gained the initiative in attack, which allowed them to set the order of battle and deploy their preferred tactics. By contrast, sailors aboard leeward vessels usually had to await the decisions of their upwind counterparts. Sometimes, neither fleet had clearly acquired the weather gage when a battle began. In such cases, their sailors tried to outmanoeuvre one another to claim it. Yet because fleets departing the Low Countries usually sailed west into the English Channel or North Sea when they left port, they normally had the weather gage when winds blew from the east. Conversely, fleets sailing from England, and often Spain or France, typically had the weather gage in westerly winds. Moreover, it could be hard for sailors to leave port without favourable winds, and in the Low Countries these usually blew from the east.[10]

1992), 6. Martin and Parker, *The Spanish Armada*, 48. Bruijn, 'The Maritime World of the Dutch Republic', 20. Wantje Fritschy, 'A "Financial Revolution" Reconsidered: Public Finance in Holland during the Dutch Revolt, 1568–1648', *Economic History Review* LVI:1 (2009): 58. Hellinga, *Zeehelden van de Gouden Eeuw*, 55. Bruijn, *The Dutch Navy of the Seventeenth and Eighteenth Centuries*, 20.

[9] Virginia W. Lunsford, *Piracy and Privateering in the Golden Age Netherlands*. (Basingstoke: Palgrave Macmillan, 2005), 10. Gijs Rommelse, *The Second Anglo-Dutch War: International Raison D'état, Mercantilism and Maritime Strife*. (Hilversum: Uitgeverij Verloren, 2006), 114. David J. Starkey, 'Voluntaries and Sea Robbers: A Review of the Academic Literature on Privateering, Corsairing, Buccaneering and Piracy'. *The Mariners Mirror* 97:1 (2001): 130. Glete, *Warfare at Sea*, 41. Bruijn, *The Dutch Navy of the Seventeenth and Eighteenth Centuries*, 73. Bruijn, 'The Maritime World of the Dutch Republic', 31.

[10] A. T. Mahan, *The Influence of Sea Power upon History 1660–1783*. (Boston: Little, Brown and Company, 1890), 4, 21. J. Oliver and J. A. Kington, 'The Usefulness of Ships'

Wind direction not only affected whether and how captains could attack, but also their possibilities for retreat. Favourable winds usually helped fleeing sailors make rapid progress back to friendly harbours, where ships could be repaired and the wounded tended to. Yet contrary or calm winds occasionally offered advantages by temporarily pausing the pursuit, or by aiding skilled crews that could tack against them. Storms could drive retreating ships towards safety or destruction, depending on the direction of their winds and the seaworthiness of ships that had often been badly damaged. If retreating ships approached a friendly harbour while their pursuers were out to sea, storms could scatter and sink many ships in the victorious fleet.

Storms affected just about every aspect of war at sea. Since officers used rowed boats to exchange orders or discuss plans, storms could paralyze a fleet by making it impossible to use these boats. Gales also routinely damaged ships by, for example, severing anchor cables or collapsing masts. As equipment failed, sailors suffered. Aboard most ships, many sailors fell ill, some endured serious injury, and a few fell overboard. All faced the prospect of death by shipwreck, especially when near a lee shore or sailing in perilously close proximity to other wind-blown ships.[11]

In their cultures, compositions, tactics, and technologies, the diverse militaries that fought in the wars of the Dutch Republic coevolved over more than a century of relentless conflict. Through it all, their campaigns on land and at sea registered the influence of distinct environments in the Low Countries and the broader North Sea region. As these environments responded to climate changes, they provided a shifting balance of advantages and disadvantages for the combatants.

ONSET OF THE WARS IN A COOLING CLIMATE, 1564–1568

In the early sixteenth century, Charles V united the thrones of the Low Countries and the Catholic Spanish Empire just as the emergence of Christian humanism laid the groundwork for the rapid and divisive spread of Protestantism through the provinces that would become the Dutch Republic. In 1555, Philip II succeeded Charles and, in 1559, moved to

Log-Books in the Synoptic Analysis of Past Climates'. *Weather* 25:12 (1970): 521. R. E. J. Weber, 'The Introduction of the Single Line Ahead as a Battle Formation by the Dutch, 1665–1666'. *Mariner's Mirror* 73 (1987): 5–19. Glete, *Warfare at Sea*, 68.

11 Jones, *The Anglo-Dutch Wars*, 191. Vonk, *De Victorieuze Zeeslag op Schoneveld*, 112. Thomas Allin and Jeremy Smith, 'Report of Their Work on the Movement of Ships, Present Bad Weather'. ADM 106/288, Folio 52. National Archives at Kew (London, United Kingdom).

centralize his rule in the Low Countries by imposing new taxes, limiting the legal privileges of towns and nobles, and launching a brutal Inquisition against Protestantism. In the early 1560s, these measures motivated the great nobility of the Low Countries to petition the Spanish regime in Brussels for more authority to manage affairs in the Low Countries, and greater religious toleration. Hundreds of lesser nobles soon joined them to advocate for the suspension of religious prosecutions.[12]

As closely linked political and religious crises worsened in the Low Countries, average annual temperatures declined across the Northern Hemisphere. In 1565, in the wake of the first landmark winter of the Grindelwald Fluctuation, frost in spring and summer delayed the planting of seeds and ultimately ruined harvests in the Low Countries just as war between Denmark and Sweden shut the Sound for Dutch shipping. Food prices climbed and work dried up for the many sailors, merchants, and labourers who otherwise participated in the mother of all trades. Across the northwestern Low Countries, rye prices nearly doubled, while real wages fell sharply. In Amsterdam, meanwhile, freight rates for shipping victuals surged. Some communities endured particularly devastating commodity price increases. The price of wheat in Diksmuide, Flanders, for example, tripled between March and December. At the convent of Leeuwenhorst in Holland, prices for rye, oats, barley, and hempseed all soared.[13]

In August, a riot broke out at the corn market in Ghent. In its wake, the town's magistrates fretted about 'the evident danger from the dearth of corn and the large number of paupers, coupled with the arrival in this town of about 300 people from the region of Armentières who, it is to be feared, are

[12] Parker, *The Dutch Revolt*, 78. Israel, *The Dutch Republic*, 147. Peter Arnade, *Beggars, Iconoclasts, and Civic Patriots: The Political Culture of the Dutch Revolt*. (Ithaca: Cornell University Press, 2008), 80. Van Gelderen, *The Political Thought of the Dutch Revolt*, 37. Henk van Nierop, '*Alva's Throne* – Making Sense of the Revolt of the Netherlands'. In *The Origins and Development of the Dutch Revolt*, ed. Graham Darby. (London: Routledge, 2003), 36. Graham Darby, 'Narrative of Events'. In *The Origins and Development of the Dutch Revolt*, ed. Graham Darby. (London: Routledge, 2003), 17. Alastair Duke, *Reformation and Revolt in the Low Countries*. (London: Hambledon Press, 1990), 16.

[13] Van Tielhof, *The Mother of All Trades*, 81. Van Engelen, Buisman and IJnsen, 'A Millennium of Weather, Winds and Water in the Low Countries', 112. Milja van Tielhof and Jan Luiten van Zanden, 'Freight Rates between Amsterdam and Various Port Cities 1500–1800, and Factors Costs of Shipping Industry 1450–1800'. Geertruida de Moor, 'Wages and Prices from the Convent Leeuwenhorst, 1410–1570'. Jan Luiten van Zanden, 'The Prices of the Most Important Consumer Goods, and Indices of Wages and the Cost of Living in the Western Part of the Netherlands, 1450–1800'. Available at: www.iisg.nl/hpw/data.php#netherlands.

infected with heresy'. In November, a government minister in Brussels worried that high unemployment and 'the shortage of grain which grows worse every day' would make it impossible to 'restrain the common people, who are discontented and protest loudly'. He feared that 'if the people rise up ... the religious issue will become involved'. In the same month, ministers in the provincial parliament (or 'State') of Holland mentioned that food shortages had set the people 'murmuring and voicing criticisms which might tend towards sedition'. According to contemporary historian Pieter Christiaanszoon Bor, high grain prices had indeed provoked unrest that targeted Spain's regime in Brussels. Further riots erupted in Breda, Mechelen, Ter Goes, and other towns across the Low Countries. While it is difficult now to reconstruct the motivations of the rioters, high food prices may well have provoked protests that soon turned to violent demonstrations against the broader injustices of Spanish rule.[14]

In the following year, nobles succeeded in suspending religious persecution. Massive, open-air Calvinist services, outlawed by Brussels, coincided with lingering unemployment and high food prices. Then, in August, groups of as many as 200 people broke into Catholic churches across the Low Countries and shattered religious iconography. Philip II reacted to this 'Iconoclastic Fury' by ordering an army to the Low Countries under the notoriously ruthless Duke of Alba. Dutch nobles mustered only ineffective resistance, and the greatest of them – William of Orange – fled to Germany. When Alba assumed the office of governor general in Brussels, he set up a Council of Troubles that executed over 1,000 people. Its brutality only inflamed tensions across the Low Countries.[15]

In 1568, William launched a four-pronged invasion of the Low Countries that quickly ended in ignominious defeat. Yet punishing taxes

[14] Parker, *The Dutch Revolt*, 78. Bor, *Oorsprongk, begin, en vervolgh der Nederlandsche oorlogen*, Vol. I, 30. Van Tielhof, *The Mother of All Trades*, 81. Van Engelen, Buisman and IJnsen, 'A Millennium of Weather, Winds and Water in the Low Countries', 112. Milja van Tielhof and Jan Luiten van Zanden, 'Freight Rates between Amsterdam and Various Port Cities 1500–1800, and Factors Costs of Shipping Industry 1450–1800'. Geertruida de Moor, 'Wages and Prices from the Convent Leeuwenhorst, 1410–1570'. Jan Luiten van Zanden, 'The Prices of the Most Important Consumer Goods, and Indices of Wages and the Cost of Living in the Western Part of the Netherlands, 1450–1800'. Available at: www.iisg.nl/hpw/data.php#netherlands.

[15] Parker, *The Dutch Revolt*, 109. Israel, 161. 't Hart, *The Dutch Wars of Independence*, 14. Arnade, *Beggars, Iconoclasts, and Civic Patriots*, 217. Van Gelderen, *The Political Thought of the Dutch Revolt*, 40. Graham Darby, 'Narrative of Events', 18. Bruijn, *The Dutch Navy of the Seventeenth and Eighteenth Centuries*, 3. S. Groenveld, H. L. Ph. Leeuwenberg, M. E. H. N. Mout, and W. M. Zappey, *De Tachtigjarige Oorlog: Opstand en Consolidatie in de Nederlanden (ca. 1560–1650)*. (Zutphen: Walburg Pers, 2008), 92.

imposed by Alba provoked renewed unrest that was again worsened by weather associated with a cooler, stormier climate. On 1 November 1570, a ferocious gale on All Saints' Day brought a storm surge that breached dikes and killed thousands along the entire coastline of the northern Low Countries. Many survivors resented a regime that seemed unable to prioritize the economy and safety of the Low Countries. The flood also exacerbated rising tensions between Protestants and Catholics. In Hoorn, for example, scornful Protestants drove off a Catholic priest who tried to exorcise the rising waters in the town square.[16]

Sweden and Denmark resolved their war in 1570, opening the Baltic for trade. Yet in each of the following two years, harvests across the Eastern Baltic failed amid bitterly cold weather, and grain imports to the Low Countries dried up. Soaring grain prices and plummeting real wages helped sustain popular discontent with the regime in Brussels. On 16 March 1572, seditious parodies of the Lord's Prayer littered the streets of Ghent. 'Hellish father who in Brussels doth dwell', the prayer began, 'Thou takest away daily our daily bread / While our wives and our children lie starving or dead'. In many towns, the circumstances for rebellion had rarely looked better.[17]

Nevertheless, the weather of the Grindelwald Fluctuation nearly proved disastrous for the rebellion. Storms in the winter of 1571/1572 forced 10 rebel ships and an equal number of merchant prizes onto the isle of Vlieland. A small company of soldiers could have easily captured the wounded crew and their battered ships, but disagreements between Alva and his provincial governors meant that troops were only dispatched in early March. By then, rebel sailors had repaired their ships, and they fled to sea with minimal losses. They joined the rest of the rebel fleet and, on 1 April, sent shockwaves

[16] Velius, *Kroniek van Hoorn*, 439. Van Engelen, Buisman and IJnsen, 'A Millennium of Weather, Winds and Water in the Low Countries', 112. Nienhuis, *Environmental History of the Rhine-Meuse Delta*, 248. 't Hart, *The Dutch Wars of Independence*, 19. Parker, *The Dutch Revolt*, 155. Th. Velius, *Kroniek van Hoorn: Band 2 1560–1629*. (Hoorn: Publicatiestichting Bas Baltus, 2007), 451. Hale, *War and Society in Renaissance Europe*, 185. Martin and Parker, *The Spanish Armada: Revised Edition*, 48. Fritschy, 'A "Financial Revolution" Reconsidered', 59. Graham Darby, 'Narrative of Events', 18.

[17] Parker, *The Dutch Revolt*, 127. J. Buisman and A. F. V. van Engelen, eds., *Duizend jaar weer, wind en water in de Lage Landen, Vol. III 1450–1575*. (Franeker: Uitgeverij Van Wijnen, 1998), 665. Van Engelen, Buisman and IJnsen, 'A Millennium of Weather, Winds and Water in the Low Countries', 112. Bauernfeind and Woitek, 'The Influence of Climatic Change on Price Fluctuations in Germany during the 16th Century Price Revolution', 303. Van Tielhof and Van Zanden, 'Freight Rates between Amsterdam and Various Port Cities 1500–1800'. De Moor, 'Wages and Prices from the Convent Leeuwenhorst, 1410–1570'. Van Zanden, 'The Prices of the Most Important Consumer Goods'. Available at: www.iisg.nl/hpw/data.php#netherlands.

through the Low Countries by seizing the port town of Brill. Spontaneous revolts in other coastal villages helped the rebels take control of trade routes across the northern Netherlands, which forced other cities to join their movement. However, grain and in turn bread remained in perilously short supply. As hunger spread through the rebellious towns in autumn, Dutch grain ships gathered in the Baltic. Storms and thickening sea ice in the late season at first convinced crews to delay their return until the spring. Yet Velius in Hoorn wrote that, 'by God's grace', crews aboard two or three ships broke the consensus and set sail for the republic, whereupon everyone else followed. Sea ice trapped some ships in the Zuiderzee, but most reached their destinations and starvation was averted.[18]

The onset of the Grindelwald Fluctuation increased the likelihood of weather that threatened lives and livelihoods in the Low Countries just as religious tensions, economic crises, and heavy-handed repression kindled widespread discontent. Food shortages and unemployment caused, in part, by cold snaps and storms did not send mindless mobs spilling into the streets of towns across the Low Countries. Yet many ordinary people clearly blamed the regime in Brussels for worsening poverty and hunger. That could only strengthen the suspicion, fanned by rebel propaganda, that the Low Countries were governed in the interests of Spain, not the Low Countries themselves. In many towns, acute shortages of life's basic necessities provided the initial motivation for demonstrations that assumed a violent and rebellious character when crowds brought up the other alleged abuses of the regime in Brussels. Storms, floods, and frost therefore subtly contributed to currents of social unrest that gradually pushed the Low Countries into open revolt. In 1572, storms also very nearly doomed the rebellion by threatening, or appearing to threaten, the navigation of ships. Yet sailors aboard makeshift warships and merchant vessels alike endured great risks to launch and sustain a lasting rebellion in the Low Countries.

CONDUCT OF THE WARS IN THE EARLY GRINDELWALD FLUCTUATION, 1572–1575

In July 1572, the States of Holland and Zeeland appointed William of Orange as their Stadholder, a position roughly equivalent to the English

[18] Velius, *Kroniek van Hoorn*, 476. Arnade, *Beggars, Iconoclasts, and Civic Patriots*, 217. Graham Darby, 'Narrative of Events', 19. 't Hart, *The Dutch Wars of Independence*, 14. Parker, *The Dutch Revolt*, 131. Buisman, *Duizend jaar* Vol. III, 667. Frits Snapper, *Oorlogsinvloeden op de Overzeese Handel van Holland, 1551–1719*, 26.

'Lord Lieutenant'. The title originally denoted a representative of the sovereign, but it would now be given to patriarchs of the House of Orange who commanded the armed forces. In a matter of weeks, the rebellion had firmly established itself in the northern Netherlands.[19]

Alba's response was swift. On 12 November, Spain's famed Army of Flanders besieged the rebel-held town of Zutphen on the IJssel River. Bitterly cold temperatures had covered the town's moat with ice, and Spanish soldiers approached with ease. Prospects for the defending garrison were bleak. According to Bernardino de Mendoza, a high-ranking Spanish commander, the garrison's soldiers fled just two days into the siege, many by boat across the partially frozen IJssel. Spanish troops then massacred most of Zutphen's inhabitants, some by exposure to the icy waters of the IJssel. The atrocity in Zutphen, combined with further massacres in Mechelen, Naarden, and Utrecht, drove the municipal governments of Hasselt, Kampen, and Zwolle to capitulate without a siege. Yet Alba's brutality stiffened resistance across the coastal towns of the northern Netherlands, where Calvinism had deeper roots. In fact, following the fall of Zutphen, rebels attempted to prevent a Spanish invasion by breaking the ice that surrounded their territories in Friesland and Holland. It is therefore difficult to determine whether the killings at Zutphen, made possible in part by frigid weather, benefitted or threatened the broader rebellion against Spain.[20]

In December 1572, Alba and the Army of Flanders approached the city of Haarlem, which bordered Holland's coastal sand dunes. In order to invest the city, Spanish soldiers needed to seize the nearby village of Spaarndam, which surrounded a dam at the intersection of the river Spaarne and the IJ. For armies approaching from Spanish-held Amsterdam, the dam provided access to the higher hinterland of Haarlem along the North Sea coast, where a major road provided an easy way for the rebels to supply the city. As Alba dispatched a force to take Spaarndam, rebel defenders reinforced its garrison and opened sluices to inundate its surroundings. Yet on 6 December, temperatures plunged well below

[19] 't Hart, *The Dutch Wars of Independence*, 19. Parker, *The Dutch Revolt*, 155. Velius, *Kroniek van Hoorn: Band 2 1560–1629*, 451. Hale, *War and Society in Renaissance Europe*, 185. Martin and Parker, *The Spanish Armada: Revised Edition*, 48. Van Gelderen, *The Political Thought of the Dutch Revolt*, 43.

[20] Brouwer, *Kronieken van Spaansche Soldaten*, 220. Velius, *Kroniek van Hoorn*, 479. Hale, *War and Society in Renaissance Europe*, 185. 't Hart, *The Dutch Wars of Independence*, 15. Parker, *The Dutch Revolt*, 136. Van Gelderen, *The Political Thought of the Dutch Revolt*, 43. Graham Darby, 'Narrative of Events', 19. Buisman, *Duizend jaar Vol. III*, 677.

freezing, and the waters around Spaarndam froze so thoroughly that the Spanish could attack across the ice. Despite suffering heavy losses, Spanish-led troops captured the village and used its wooden houses as fuel to protect themselves from the cold. The army now besieged Haarlem. Its soldiers nearly outnumbered the city's inhabitants.[21]

Until 7 December, frigid weather typical of the Grindelwald Fluctuation had largely benefitted the Spanish, but that would soon change. Haarlem's small garrison repulsed several Spanish attempts at storming the city, and the Army of Flanders could not seal the Haarlemmermeer, a nearby lake. The Spanish therefore prepared for a long siege in what would be one of the coldest winters of the Grindelwald Fluctuation. As the months dragged on, Bor wrote, the soldiers became 'destitute, [for] the cold caused much discomfort and sickness'. Dutch jurist Hugo de Groot later wrote that thousands died owing to both the fighting and the 'severe winter'. Diego Nuñez de Alba, an eyewitness with the Spanish army, reported that its soldiers 'suffered in the great frosts and went up to three or four leagues in search of firewood'.[22]

In January, a rebel army tried but failed to relieve the town, while another Spanish storm assault also failed. William had hoped for prolonged winter thawing, which was common before the 1560s and occurred even during the Grindelwald Fluctuation. Persistent melting would allow the locally superior rebel fleet to intercept supplies reaching the besieging army from Amsterdam and Utrecht, which had not yet joined the revolt. On 5 January, temperatures did climb above freezing, but thawing persisted for only 10 days before the cold returned. Rebel soldiers therefore adapted by using skates to pillage Spanish supply lines that cut across frozen waterways. Most carried a spear that they used to cross partly frozen creeks, or gaps in the ice on larger bodies of water. When the ice melted, they took to rowboats and continued their raids.[23]

[21] Willem van Oranje aan admiraal N. N. De Correspondentie van Willem van Oranje nr. 3245, 14 December 2014. http://resources.huygens.knaw.nl/wvo/brief/3245. Bor, *Oorsprongk, begin, en vervolgh der Nederlandsche oorlogen*, 423. Petra van Dam, *Vissen in Veenmeren*, 2. Brouwer, *Kronieken van Spaansche Soldaten*, 230. Buisman, *Duizend jaar Vol. III*, 678.

[22] Bor, *Oorsprongk, begin, en vervolgh der Nederlandsche oorlogen*, 433. Parker, *The Army of Flanders*, 140. Van Engelen, Buisman and IJnsen, 'A Millennium of Weather, Winds and Water in the Low Countries', 112. Buisman, *Duizend jaar Vol. III*, 678. Hugo de Groot, *Kroniek van de Nederlandse Oorlog, De Opstand 1559–1588'*. (Nijmegen: Uitgeverij Vantilt, 2014), 81.

[23] Velius, *Kroniek van Hoorn*, 489. 't Hart, *The Dutch Wars of Independence*, 15. Parker, *The Dutch Revolt*, 158. Buisman, *Duizend jaar Vol. III*, 680.

In the meantime, Alba recognized the advantage that naval superiority would soon give the rebels. He therefore commissioned the construction of new warships in Amsterdam. In the spring, his expanded fleet confronted a reinforced rebel flotilla on equal terms. Velius wrote that stormy weather hindered the rebel fleet as it struggled to meet the Amsterdam armada. The rebel flagship, blown by the winds, sailed far ahead of the rest of the fleet. When it tacked to rejoin the other vessels, the sight of the flagship sailing away from the enemy convinced the other captains to retreat. The Amsterdam fleet pursued and even seized one of the rebel ships. This bizarre victory allowed the Spanish to seal the Haarlemmermeer and completely invest Haarlem. The town finally capitulated in July, whereupon the Army of Flanders massacred its garrison.[24]

During the siege, the stormy, frigid weather of the Grindelwald Fluctuation yielded a complex pattern of advantages and constraints for both belligerents. Cold temperatures that would have been unusual in a warmer climate initially helped Alba invest the town, but then contributed to the high rates of mortality and desertion that weakened his army and undermined his broader offensive in Holland. Persistent cold also thwarted large-scale rebel attempts to plunder Spanish supply lines, but the rebels quickly adapted by launching small-scale raids that exploited the ice. At sea, however, high winds undermined the rebellion's best change of defending Haarlem.

The town's fall was ultimately a Pyrrhic victory for Alba. The gruelling siege had killed many of his soldiers and given other rebellious towns many months to prepare their defences. The slaughter of Haarlem's garrison also stiffened resistance in these towns, since it now seemed that there was little hope in surrender. Worse, Spanish soldiers had not been paid despite their suffering, owing perhaps to the high costs of the siege. They mutinied when Alba wisely kept them from sacking Haarlem. After two weeks, Alba finally suppressed the uprising by paying substantial arrears to every soldier. Yet dissent continued to fester in the Army of Flanders. In the following year, Spanish troops mutinied again, rather than spend another winter in the field. Their terms stipulated that 'during the time when the enemy is not campaigning or is not besieging places, Your Excellency should order us to

[24] Velius, *Kroniek van Hoorn*, 494. Bor, *Oorsprongk, begin, en vervolgh der Nederlandsche oorlogen*, 433. Willem van Oranje aan admiraal N. N. De Correspondentie van Willem van Oranje nr. 2547, 14 December 2014. http://resources.huygens.knaw.nl/wvo/brief/2547. Willem van Oranje aan magistraat van Gouda. De Correspondentie van Willem van Oranje nr. 9460, 14 December 2014. http://resources.huygens.knaw.nl/wvo/brief/9460. Buisman, *Duizend jaar Vol. III*, 683.

winter-quarters in walled and populous towns'. Had the winter of 1572/1573 been milder, the demands of the mutineers might have been different, and their mutinies would have been far less likely to occur.[25]

Rebel soldiers and sailors quickly adapted to frigid winter weather, especially when it trapped their vessels in sudden accumulations of sea ice. For example, in February during the frigid winter of 1571/1572, ice trapped sailors under the command of Willem van Trelongh near the island of Wieringen in the Zuiderzee. On 3 March, the loyalist Admiral Jan Symonszoon Rol gathered a group of soldiers and travelled to Wieringen by sled. Rol commanded two assaults on the ship, once by using his sleds as shields against cannon fire. Yet his guns made little impression on the hull, and the rebels repelled both attacks. The rebels used a reprieve in the fighting to cut their ship free of the ice, and then sailed out towards the North Sea while taunting Rol and his soldiers.[26]

In the winter of 1572/1573, more sudden and even more severe freezing in early December trapped seven rebel warships in sea ice within sight of Spanish-held Amsterdam. The ice that benefitted the Spanish attack on nearby Spaarndam would also have allowed loyalist forces to seize these ships with relative ease. Civilians quickly gathered from nearby rebel towns to cut through the ice, which was now some 45 centimetres thick. Spanish troops adopted a Dutch innovation by tying plates with iron spikes to their boots, which helped them march across the ice to attack the ships. Yet they found that the rebels had broken enough ice to make the vessels unassailable by an army. After the Spanish retreated, strong winds rose from the west and pressed the ice against the ships. Nevertheless, the rebels continued their work, and the Spanish did not return. At last, a wind from the northwest raised water levels and briefly opened the ice. The ships arrived safely in the ports of Enkhuizen and Hoorn, just as the wind shifted and closed the ice once more. Severe winter freezing in 1572 suspended naval operations and trapped rebel vessels, but challenging environmental conditions did not determine military outcomes. Both Spanish and particularly Dutch forces nimbly adapted to changing weather conditions.[27]

After the capitulation of Haarlem, the cold, stormy weather of the Grindelwald Fluctuation would more clearly benefit rebel defenders (Map 4.1). On 21 August 1573, for example, the Army of Flanders arrived

[25] Parker, *The Dutch Revolt*, 162. Parker, *The Army of Flanders*, 169. Israel, *The Dutch Republic*, 180.

[26] Velius, *Kroniek van Hoorn*, 447.

[27] Velius, *Kroniek van Hoorn*, 478. Brouwer, *Kronieken van Spaansche Soldaten*, 222.

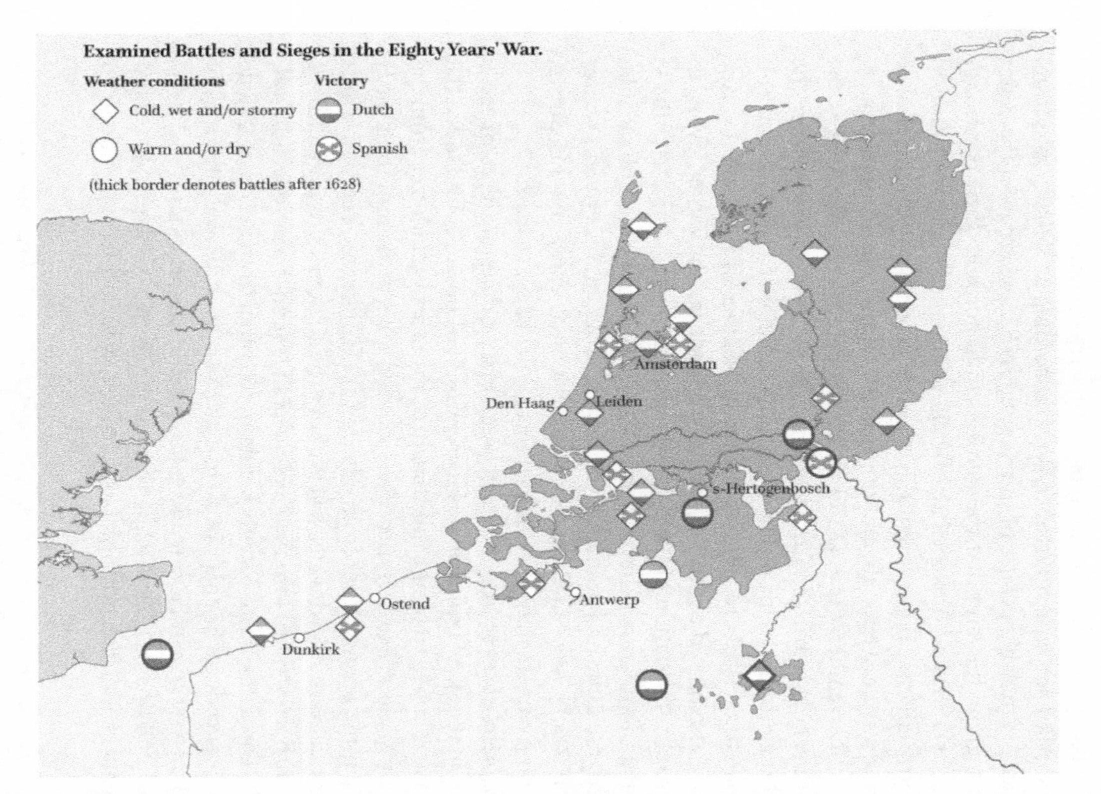

MAP 4.1 Locations of battles and sieges examined in this chapter. Diamonds represent battles fought in weather associated with the Grindelwald Fluctuation; circles depict battles that coincided with weather associated with a warmer interlude in the Little Ice Age. Flags represent the victors in each battle. Symbols with dark borders depict battles after 1628, the final year of the Grindelwald Fluctuation. The map reveals both that cold, wet, and stormy weather was very common during the Eighty Years' War, and that Dutch soldiers often prevailed in these conditions. Hans van der Maarel, Red Geographics.

before Alkmaar, a town to the north of Haarlem that was already defended by the *Trace Italienne*. The Spanish beleaguered the town and repeatedly attempted to seize it, but the rebel garrison repulsed every assault. When Alba ordered another attack on 20 September, his soldiers refused because they had not been paid. Nevertheless, the army continued to invest Alkmaar until 8 October, when according to Velius, '[the siege] collapsed ... mostly because of unrelenting rain... whereupon the water rose so high on the land that the soldiers could not keep their positions'. In fact, the rebels had breached nearby dikes, and the floods that followed were more effective in persistent rain. A rebel fleet relieved Alkmaar once the water was deep enough, and the Spanish army fled to Amsterdam.[28]

On 17 November 1573, Don Luis de Requeséns replaced Alba at the head of the largest army in Christendom. The costly siege of Haarlem, the mutinies within the Army of Flanders, and the failure to seize Alkmaar all contributed to Alba's recall. Yet the frigid weather of the Little Ice Age may have also played a role. According to Mendoza, 'the winter, owing to the climate and location of the Netherlands, was so damaging to [Alba's] health that his doctors believed another winter would be fatal'. Even if he survived, the duke had gout, and the 'bitterly cold, and very wet', winter weather would have made it painful for him to carry out his duties. A changing climate may have helped force Alba back to Spain.[29]

In September 1573, the Spanish assembled a daunting fleet of large galleons in the IJ. Maximilian de Henin, Count of Bossu, commanded the armada and hoped to retake full control of the nearby Zuiderzee from the rebels. By William's orders, the rebels scuttled ships in the mouth of the IJ to prevent the Spanish fleet from entering the Zuiderzee. Yet high winds and the tide soon raised water levels above the sunken ships and allowed the Spanish fleet to sail into the Zuiderzee. In response, the rebel admiral, Cornelis Dirckszoon van Monnickendam, retreated from the coast. A gale rose and forced the Spanish back to port, just as ships were frantically pressed into service in Hoorn and other rebel-held port cities.[30]

Rebel and Spanish fleets engaged each other on 5 October. The wind had weakened sufficiently for battle, but it was still strong enough to

[28] Velius, *Kroniek van Hoorn*, 511. 't Hart, *The Dutch Wars of Independence*, 15. Parker, *The Dutch Revolt*, 162. Bor, *Oorsprongk, begin, en vervolgh der Nederlandsche oorlogen*, 454. Buisman, *Duizend jaar Vol. III*, 690.

[29] De Groot, *Kroniek van de Nederlandse Oorlog*, 84. Brouwer, *Kronieken van Spaansche Soldaten*, 229. 't Hart, *The Dutch Wars of Independence*, 19. Parker, *The Dutch Revolt*, 155. Van Gelderen, *The Political Thought of the Dutch Revolt*, 44.

[30] Velius, *Kroniek van Hoorn*, 515. Groenveld et al., *De Tachtigjarige Oorlog*, 98.

prevent outgunned rebel crews from grappling and boarding the larger Spanish vessels. Both sides suffered major losses. On 11 October, they engaged again in the Battle of the Zuiderzee. While outgunned, the rebels were continually reinforced and resupplied from the shore. Moreover, the southeasterly wind had given them the weather gage, which they exploited by grappling the Spanish fleet. Crews aboard no fewer than three rebel vessels surrounded and eventually overwhelmed Bossu's flagship, the *Inquisition*. At last, Bossu surrendered, and the rebels prevailed. Control of the Zuiderzee, which connected rebellious towns and enabled their maritime commerce, continued to elude the Spanish. For the rebels, the advantages provided by high winds probably outweighed the drawbacks, which were quickly erased by a change in wind direction.[31]

In the same month, the Army of Flanders besieged the heavily fortified city of Leiden, located between Amsterdam and The Hague at the crossing of two major waterways, the Old Rhine and the Vliet. As the siege dragged on into the following spring, William of Orange and his subordinates grasped that their only chance of relieving the city would be to transform the environment that surrounded it. In the summer of 1574, William mustered a fleet of nearly 200 flat-bottomed boats and sent a carrier pigeon to starving Leiden, with a letter that announced his intent to flood the city's hinterland. The bird escaped interception, and its message overjoyed members of the municipal government. On 3 August, the rebels hired experienced 'dike diggers' to pierce the dikes that bordered the Hollandse IJssel and the Maas.[32]

As farmland flooded for many kilometres between Leiden and the town of Delft, the rebel fleet took to the rising waters. However, light winds slowed the pace of the flooding, and Spanish defences forced the rebels to redirect the waters along a new route, which required still more dike breaches. With hundreds starving to death within the city walls, many citizens begged their government to capitulate. However, morale rose when another encouraging message arrived by pigeon from

[31] Velius, *Kroniek van Hoorn*, 529. Parker, *The Dutch Revolt*, 162. Charl Lavell, 'De slag op de Zuiderzee: Een vergeten geschiedenis gezien door tijdgenoten, geschiedschrijvers en dichters', West-Friesland 'oud en nieuw' 53 (1986): 43. Anton van der Lem, *De Opstand in de Nederlanden, (1555–1609)*. (Utrecht: Kosmos-Z&K Uitgevers, 1995), 78. Gonnie Koek, 'Hoorn en Monnickendam: De herinnering van de slag op de Zuiderzee (1573–1800)' (MA diss., Leiden University, 2012), 3. Buisman, *Duizend jaar Vol. III*, 691.

[32] Robert Tiegs, 'Hidden Beneath the Waves: Commemorating and Forgetting the Military Inundations during the Siege of Leiden'. *Can. J. of Netherlandic Studies/Rev. can. d'études néerlandaises* 35 (2014): 10. Bor, *Oorsprongk, begin, en vervolgh der Nederlandsche oorlogen*, 489. Parker, *The Dutch Revolt*, 164. Parker, *The Army of Flanders*, 169. Israel, *The Dutch Republic*, 181.

Orange. At last, on 1 October a storm and heavy rain drove the water forward.[33]

The inundations that brought the rebel fleet to Leiden created a 'militarized landscape': an environment mobilized for the purpose of making war. In their struggle for independence, the rebels repeatedly used floodwaters to create these landscapes and even the odds against numerically superior Spanish forces. The Spanish, by contrast, rarely deployed artificial inundations. Francisco de Valdes, the Spanish commander directing the siege of Leiden, had learned that Holland could be flooded if the sluice at Maaslandsluis were breached. 'At any time you might wish to flood this country', Valdes wrote to Philip II, 'it is in your power'. Yet, Philip decided against it, as it would leave Holland 'lost and ruined for ever' and 'earn for us a reputation for cruelty which would be better avoided'. There were limits, after all, to Spanish brutality.[34]

According to an eyewitness of the siege of Leiden, many rebels, by contrast, believed that spoiled land was better than lost land. Many farmers understandably did not agree, and the inundations provoked bitter resentment across the Dutch countryside. Rebel propaganda therefore played up the providential nature of the weather that aided their inundations. 'The wind and rain stood at your service', one pamphlet concluded, 'driving back the enemy in dishonour'. Perhaps swayed by such pamphlets, Hugo de Groot wrote that the wind wondrously combined with the tide to aid the advance of the floodwaters. Before long, Spanish soldiers deserted their positions in advance of the floodwaters, and the rebel fleet relieved Leiden on 3 October.[35]

Weather and climate change influenced the siege of Leiden in complicated ways that overall favoured the rebels. Calm weather in a stormy climate

[33] Willem van Oranje aan burgerij van Leiden, kapiteins van de schutterij van Leiden, en magistraat van Leiden. De Correspondentie van Willem van Oranje nr. 10582, 15 December 2014. http://resources.huygens.knaw.nl/wvo/brief/10582. Willem van Oranje aan commissarissen tot het ontzet van Leiden, 8 October 1574. De Correspondentie van Willem van Oranje nr. 9408, 15 December 2014. http://resources.huygens.knaw.nl/wvo/brief/9408. Bor, *Oorsprongk, begin, en vervolgh der Nederlandsche oorlogen*, 559. 't Hart, *The Dutch Wars of Independence*, 17. Parker, *The Dutch Revolt*, 164. Parker *The Army of Flanders*, 198. Israel, *The Dutch Republic*, 181. Lambert, *The Making of the Dutch Landscape*, 178. Arnade, *Beggars, Iconoclasts, and Civic Patriots*, 241. Buisman, *Duizend jaar Vol. III*, 691. 'The Old World Drought Atlas'. Accessed 28 June 2016, http://iridl.ldeo.columbia.edu/expert/home/.jennie/.PDSI/.OWDA/.pdsi/figviewer.html.

[34] Tiegs, 'Hidden Beneath the Waves', 12. Geoffrey Parker, 'Early Modern Europe'. In *The Laws of War: Constraints on Warfare in the Western World*, eds. Michael Howard, George J. Andreopoulos, and Mark R. Shulman. (New Haven: Yale University Press, 1997), 47.

[35] De Groot, *Kroniek van de Nederlandse Oorlog*, 90. Tiegs, 'Hidden Beneath the Waves', 12.

allowed carrier pigeons with promising news to arrive in the town as the siege entered its desperate final weeks. Yet a gale compounded the impact of the spring tide, bringing floodwaters to the town with a speed that panicked its besiegers. Spanish troops abandoned their positions in disarray, leaving behind precious supplies and equipment. In 1575, Philip II declared bankruptcy, Requeséns died, and Spanish troops mutinied on a vast scale.[36]

ESCALATION AND TRUCE IN A FRIGID CLIMATE, 1576–1609

On 4 November 1576, mutinous Spanish troops sacked Antwerp with cruelty that shocked observers across Europe.[37] Both loyal and rebellious provinces quickly agreed to the Pacification of Ghent, a treaty that condemned the previous regime in Brussels and called for the removal of all Spanish troops from the Low Countries. The treaty left the status of Calvinism undecided, however, and it quickly unravelled once the mutineers departed in 1577. In the same year, Philip resolved to resume his war in the Low Countries. From October 1578, Alexander Farnese, later Duke of Parma and Governor General in Brussels, took command of the Army of Flanders. On 6 January 1579, the States of Hainaut and Artois recognized the authority of Philip and Parma by signing the Union of Arras. The Walloon provinces of the southern Low Countries soon followed.[38]

In response, the provinces of the northern Netherlands signed the Union of Utrecht on 23 January 1579, which effectively established an independent Republic in defiance of Spain. It immediately faced long odds. Despite generally chilly weather, Parma in the 1580s brilliantly exploited the overwhelming quantitative and qualitative superiority of his army, relative to its rebel counterpart, to retake no fewer than 83 formerly rebellious towns. Then, in 1584, a Spanish agent assassinated William of Orange. With prospects for the rebellion bleak, the republic's States-General looked to its reluctant ally, England, for a new head of state. Late in 1585, Queen Elizabeth ordered Robert Dudley, Earl of Leicester, to the Low Countries at

[36] Van Engelen, Buisman and IJnsen, 'A Millennium of Weather, Winds and Water in the Low Countries', 112. 't Hart, *The Dutch Wars of Independence*, 19. Parker, *The Dutch Revolt*, 155. Hale, *War and Society in Renaissance Europe*, 185. Tiegs, 'Hidden Beneath the Waves', 12.

[37] See, for example, George Gascoigne, *A Larum for London, or The Siedge of Antwerpe.* (London: William Ferbrand, 1602).

[38] Parker, *The Dutch Revolt*, 196. 't Hart, *The Dutch Wars of Independence*, 19. Henk van Nierop, 'Similar Problems, Different Outcomes: The Revolt of the Netherlands and the Wars of Religion in France', 40. Martin van Gelderen, *The Political Thought of the Dutch Revolt*, 52.

the head of 7,000 troops. Still the military situation continued to deteriorate. The balance of military power so strongly favoured the Spanish offensive that cool, wet weather did not provide a sufficient defensive advantage for the rebellion's forces to prevail.[39]

Amid these major and, for the new republic, discouraging developments, small-scale raids and skirmishes helped shape the course of the war. Many raged in regions contested by the opposing armies, as competing garrisons scoured the countryside and imposed crippling 'fire taxes' on unfortunate civilians. The sparse documentary record of these raids suggests that they were as influenced by weather, and in turn climate change, as battles and sieges. For example, in early December 1585, three Spanish infantry regiments entered the Bommelerwaard, a region surrounded by rivers that lies just east of 's-Hertogenbosch, then a major Spanish-held town. Antonio Carnero, a Spanish chronicler, wrote that the soldiers used boats to cross a river and arrive at an island. To their surprise, they discovered that Dutch raiders had earlier seized provisions the Spanish had cached there. When the Spanish attempted to leave, a Dutch fleet appeared to starve them on the island. The soldiers hungered for several days. Then, on the evening of 8 December, extraordinary flash freezing, extreme even in the winters of the Grindelwald Fluctuation, covered the water with three inches of ice. The rebel fleet fled as the river froze, and the Spanish reached the mainland by carrying their boats across the ice.[40]

Networks of communication and transportation also shaped the outcome of the Eighty Years' War. Surviving letters occasionally demonstrate that contemporaries keenly understood that shifting weather conditions affected correspondence, and thereby military planning. Take, for example, the many letters sent between Leicester and English nobles during the frigid winter of 1585/1586. Soon after Leicester arrived in the Low Countries, the wind turned to blow from the east. Winds from that direction hamper the progress of sailing vessels travelling east, from England to mainland Europe. On 26 December, Leicester wrote to Francis Walsingham, Queen Elizabeth's principal secretary and spymaster. Leicester explained that he urgently required the services of Robert Killegrew and William Pelham. They carried a copy of the Treaty of

[39] Israel, *The Dutch Republic*, 209. 't Hart, *The Dutch Wars of Independence*, 21. Van Nimwegen, *The Dutch Army*, 170. Parker, *The Army of Flanders*, 8, 211. Parker, *The Dutch Revolt*, 224. Graham Darby, 'Narrative of Events', 20. See also Rolf Hendrik Bremmer, *Reformatie en rebellie: Willem van Oranje, de calvinisten en het recht van opstand: tien onstuimige jaren, 1572–1581*. (Franeker: Wever, 1984).

[40] Brouwer, *Kronieken van Spaansche Soldaten*, 301.

Nonsuch, which stipulated the terms of English financial and military support for the Dutch rebellion. Leicester had sent for the officers on 15 December, yet they had not yet arrived. Also on the 26 December, William Cecil, Lord Burghley, Elizabeth's chief advisor and lord high treasurer, sent a letter to Leicester. Cecil wrote that 'we have not hard from your lordship, nether I thynk hath your lordship hard from hence [sic]'. When he finally received Leicester's letter, Walsingham wrote that Killegrew and Pelham had long been delayed at sea by contrary winds. Leicester may not have received Walsingham's response until after Killegrew and Pelham had at last arrived in the republic.[41]

The weeks surrounding the turn of the year in 1585/1586 were crucial not just for relations between England and the new republic, but also for the course of the rebellion in the Low Countries. According to the Treaty of Nonsuch, England would send a governor general to the republic with sweeping military, legal, and economic powers. Leicester had therefore received a monarch's welcome, and the States-General offered him the lofty title of governor general. If he accepted, Elizabeth would gain sovereignty over the republic. Some of her advisors had long advocated for just such an 'open and whole-hearted commitment' to what they perceived as the rebellion's Protestant cause. The rebellion would gain legitimacy in the eyes of European nobles, but England could easily find itself directly at war with the Spanish Empire. Elizabeth therefore favoured a middle path that would keep England between two disastrous fates: the failure of the Dutch revolt on the one hand, and outright war with Spain on the other. Between 1585 and 1588, she opened five separate peace negotiations with Philip, all while supporting the Dutch rebellion.[42]

Leicester may not have understood the nuances of Elizabeth's policy towards the revolt. In letters to London, he asked for orders and reported

[41] Robert Dudley, 'Letter XV. The Earl of Leycester to Mr. Secretary Walsyngham. 26th December 1585', Francis Walsingham, 'Mr. Secretary Walsyngham to the Earl of Leycester. December, 1585', William Cecil, 'Lord Burghley to the Earl of Leycester. 26th December, 1585', Dudley, 'Letter XV. The Earl of Leycester to Mr. Secretary Walsyngham. 22 January, 1585–6', Stephen Burrough, 'A Journal of My Lord of Leycesters proceading in the Lowe Countries', in *Correspondence of Robert Dudley*, 30, 37, 38, 69, 464. Hugh Dunthorne, *Britain and the Dutch Revolt 1560–1700*. (Cambridge: Cambridge University Press, 2013), 71.

[42] 'A Treaty between Elizabeth Queen of England, and the States of the United Provinces, by which the said Queen engages to assist the States on certain Conditions. Made at Nonsuch the 10th of August, 1585', *A General Collection of Teatys, Manifesto's, Contracts of Marriage, Renunciations, and other Publick Papers, from the Year 1495, to the Year 1712, Vol. 2*, 2nd ed. (London: J. J. and P. Knapton, 1732), 87. Dunthorne, *Britain and the Dutch Revolt 1560–1700*, 71.

that he felt compelled to accept the governor-generalship. For nearly a month, his letters went unanswered. On 12 January, Cecil wrote a letter to Leicester explaining that persistent easterly winds and frosts were keeping English vessels from leaving for the Low Countries. According to Cecil, 'ther is no on thyng that more annoyeth [your] expedition than the advers wyndes, that somtyme kepeth us from understandying of your procedynges, not many dayes but manny wekes [sic]'. According to Cecil, the wind not only thwarted the sending of letters but also of 'men, horse, victells and money'.[43]

On 22 January, Leicester sent an embittered letter to Walsingham. He begged for supplies to fight the Spanish, made an impassioned plea for Elizabeth to accept sovereignty over the Low Countries, and finally complained, 'the wynd kepes back all hearing from ye, being [42] days since I hard from England [sic]'. Three days later, Leicester, having still not heard from London, yielded to Dutch pressure and accepted the governor-generalship. He then dispatched a flurry of letters to England that explained his decision and begged for more financial support. On 7 February, Cecil wrote that he was glad to receive news from Leicester, which confirmed that Leicester had obtained the most recent correspondence from London. However, ongoing military operations had made these 'old letters' owing to 'contrary wynd, which of late ... holdeth strongly ether west, which pleseth us to send, but not to heare; or els in the [East], which discontenteth ether of us in contrary manner [sic]'. Cecil informed Leicester that the queen had flown into a rage when she learned that the earl had accepted the governor-generalship. In subsequent months, Elizabeth poisoned her relationship with the States-General by undermining Leicester's position in the Low Countries and withholding desperately needed troops and money. Later in the year, Leicester left the republic's war effort in great confusion when he abruptly returned to England.[44]

[43] Cecil, 'Lord Burghley to the Earl of Leycester. 12th January 1585–6', Dudley, 'The Earl of Leycester to Mr. Secretary Walsyngham. 15th January 1585–6', in *Correspondence of Robert Dudley*, 50, 64. Johan van Oldenbarnevelt, 'De Nederlandsche Gedeputeerden in Engeland, 21 Augustus 1585'. In *Bescheiden Johan van Oldenbarnevelt 1570–1620, Eerste Deel: 1570–1601*, ed. S. P. Haak. (The Hague: Martinus Nijhoff, 1934), 105.

[44] Dudley, 'The Earl of Leycester to Mr. Secretary Walsyngham', Dudley, 'The Earl of Leycester to Mr. Secretary Walsyngham', Dudley, 'The Earl of Leycester to the Lord Treasurer, The Lord Chamberlain, the Vice Chamberlain, and Mr. Secretary Walsyngham', Cecil, 'Lord Burghley to the Earl of Leycester', in *Correspondence of Robert Dudley*, 76, 88, 96, 104. Derek Wilson, *Sweet Robin: A Biography of Robert Dudley, Earl of Leicester 1533–1588*. (London: Allison & Busby LTD, 1981), 211. De Groot, *Kroniek van de Nederlandse Oorlog*, 196.

In the winter of 1585/1586, the freeze in correspondence between English officials and the subsequent souring of Anglo-Dutch relations may have reflected the influence of the Little Ice Age. Changes in wind direction, as we have seen, cannot be convincingly linked to the Grindelwald Fluctuation in the Low Countries, but storminess can. For sixteenth-century sailors, leaving port was very difficult without favourable winds, but at sea they could usually make some progress against all but the most contrary winds. It is therefore likely that, for nearly two months, North Sea winds blew too hard to tack against. Fortunately for the republic, in some respects Leicester's departure from the Low Countries actually brightened the rebellion's prospects. Johan van Oldenbarnevelt skilfully assumed Leicester's political responsibilities, while William's son Maurice and his nephew, William Louis of Nassau, capably succeeded him as military commanders.

Despite Elizabeth's reluctance to claim sovereignty over the Dutch Republic, Philip II and his ministers always viewed the Treaty of Nonsuch as a declaration of war. In January 1586, English privateering provoked them into action. Philip asked Parma and the marquis of Santa Cruz, admiral of Spain's Atlantic fleet, to draft proposals for an attack on England. Santa Cruz responded first, with a plan for a vast armada that would defeat the English fleet and then land an invading army. Months later, Parma suggested a very different approach: a surprise invasion. Troops would board barges that could, with 'a following wind', cross the channel in just eight hours. If they managed to evade the English fleet, they could march swiftly to London. In the end, Philip chose both options. A great armada would be assembled in Spain. It would sail to the coast of Flanders, escort Parma's men to England, and defeat any opposition it encountered at sea.[45]

In theory, Spain's conquest of the Portuguese Empire in 1580 had finally provided the Spanish naval system with the rugged galleons, naval infrastructure, and skilled personnel it needed to defeat English and Dutch fleets in the Atlantic Ocean. Yet by 1587, it was obvious that the extraordinary armada envisioned by Santa Cruz outstripped even the impressive resources of the Spanish Empire. Then, in April, an English squadron under Francis Drake sacked Cadiz and made for Spanish treasure galleons returning from the Indies. Santa Cruz took his fleet to sea, but

[45] Jonathan I. Israel and Geoffrey Parker, 'Of Providence and Protestant Winds: The Spanish Armada of 1588 and the Dutch Armada of 1688'. In *The Anglo-Dutch Moment: Essays on the Glorious Revolution and Its World Impact*, ed. Jonathan I. Israel. (Cambridge: Cambridge University Press, 1991), 350.

gales quickly inflicted such damage to its ships that it could no longer set sail for England that year.[46]

At last, in the stormy summer of 1588 the armada set sail for Flanders. With 130 ships and perhaps 20,000 sailors, soldiers, and staff, it was still an enormous undertaking. On 6 August, the fleet waited within sight of Parma's army. Yet on 7 August, the English scattered the Armada with 'fireships', vessels set alight and released amid enemy warships to burn them. The English fleet then defeated the armada in the Battle of Gravelines. For the Spanish, the worst was yet to come. Severe storms plagued the armada's retreat around the coasts of Scotland and Ireland, inflicting by far the greatest damage to its ships and their crews. Navigational errors had left Spanish crews much closer to the Irish coast than they had anticipated, and westerly gales exposed them to a lee shore. Many vessels were shattered on the coast. Changes in patterns of atmospheric circulation caused by abundant sea ice and chilly temperatures in the northern Atlantic may well have caused these storms.[47]

While English fleets and Atlantic storms are usually credited with the armada's defeat, Dutch mariners and weather off the Low Countries also played a crucial role. After English fireships scattered the armada, Dutch vessels seized at least two stray Spanish galleons. Spanish officers wrote that storms also stranded some of their vessels on the coast of Flanders, well before the armada's retreat. Most importantly, Justin of Nassau blockaded Dunkirk with a fleet of 30 to 40 heavily armed but shallow-draughted vessels. That prevented Parma's army from reaching the nearby Armada and invading England. Perhaps they were unnecessary, since high, westerly winds would have kept Parma from even leaving the shore, had he decided to make the attempt. Still, Parma appealed for light vessels from the Armada that could engage the Dutch fleet in the shallow seas off Flanders. With the English fleet nearby, these could not be spared. Moreover, Parma could not seize Vlissingen, a port in which the

[46] Israel and Parker, 'Of Providence and Protestant Winds', 348.

[47] Garrett Mattingly, *The Defeat of the Spanish Armada*. (London: Random House, 1959), 270. Lamb, *Climate, History, and the Modern World*, 218. K. S. Douglas and H. H. Lamb, *Weather Observations and a Tentative Meteorological Analysis of the Period May to July 1588*. (Norwich: University of East Anglia Climatic Research Unit, 1979), 25. CRU Research Paper 61 (Norwich, 1979). Parker, *The Dutch Revolt*, 219. Patrick Gallagher and Don Cruickshank, eds., *God's Obvious Design: Papers for the Spanish Armada Symposium, Sligo, 1988: with an Edition and Translation of the Account of Francisco de Cuéllar*. (London: Tamesis Books, 1990), 108. Norman Longman, *Defending the Island: Caesar to the Armada*. (London: Pimlico, 1989), 482. Martin and Parker, *The Spanish Armada: Revised Edition*, 173. Graham Darby, 'Narrative of Events', 24.

Armada could have sheltered. Without an army and without safe harbour from storms, the Spanish invasion of England could not succeed.[48]

In 1588, stormy winds that were common in a cooler climate therefore compounded the disastrous consequences for the Spanish war effort of poor strategic decisions and navigational errors. Relationships between the atmosphere, cryosphere, and hydrosphere that increased the frequency of gales in the North Sea region continued to confound Spanish naval operations. In 1596 and 1597, storms drove back smaller fleets ordered to the Low Countries from Spain.[49]

Following the costly failure of the Spanish Armada, the death of Henry III of France embroiled Spain in a war over his succession. With the Spanish crown distracted, Dutch armies under Maurice and William Louis won sweeping gains in the 1590s that encircled the new republic's core provinces with easily defendable territories. Frequent storms and heavy rain, however, repeatedly slowed the progress of both Dutch offensives and Spanish counterattacks. For example, on 28 May 1592, Maurice and the Dutch field army invested the Spanish-held town of Steenwijk, a nest of Zuiderzee privateers that guarded the entrance to Friesland. According to Anthonie Duyck, a member of the Council of State who accompanied Maurice on his campaigns, continuous and often torrential rain hampered the siege. Steenwijk only capitulated on 5 July. The Dutch army then besieged the crucial fortress of Coevorden, which lay between two marshes in the far east of the northern Low Countries, and guarded the approach to Groningen. From late August until Coevorden surrendered on 12 September, the army, camped in swamps, endured outbreaks of disease worsened by the difficulty of transporting victuals over poor and often flooded roads.[50]

Heavy rain associated with the Grindelwald Fluctuation slowed military offensives, but could not determine their outcome. The tactical

[48] Brouwer, *Kronieken van Spaansche Soldaten*, 417. Gallagher and Cruickshank, *God's Obvious Design*, 108. Buisman, *Duizend Jaar Vol. IV*, 108. Neil Hanson, *The Confident Hope of a Miracle: The True Story of the Spanish Armada.* (New York: Knopf Doubleday Publishing Group, 2007), 299. James McDermott, *England and the Spanish Armada: The Necessary Quarrel.* (New Haven: Yale University Press, 2005), 287. Martin and Parker, *The Spanish Armada: Revised Edition*, 47.

[49] Parker, *The Army of Flanders*, 2.

[50] Anthonis Duyck, *Journaal van Anthonis Duyck, advokaat-fiscaal van den Raad van State, 1591–1602, Eerste Deel.* (The Hague: Martinus Nijhoff and D.A. Thieme, 1862), 132. Buisman, *Duizend Jaar Vol. IV*, 131. Parker, *The Army of Flanders*, 2, 207. Nimwegen, *The Dutch Army and the Military Revolution*, 154. 't Hart, *The Dutch Wars of Independence*, 21. Puype, 'Victory at Nieuwpoort, 2 July 1600', 70. Graham Darby, 'Narrative of Events', 25.

consequences of such weather might have been decisive only if the defending Spanish army had been equal to the attacking force commanded by Maurice. Yet in 1592, the Dutch so outnumbered the Spanish that they could overcome the hindrance even of torrential rain. That likely came as little consolation for Dutch troops suffering in the muck.

On 28 March in the following year, Maurice and the Dutch army invested Geertruidenberg, a town near Gorinchem on the republic's southern perimeter. Once again, continuous rain undermined the siege, but this time Dutch soldiers adapted to challenging conditions by building wooden foundations for heavy artillery that otherwise sank into the mud. After a long siege, Geetruidenberg fell on 25 June. Unrelenting rain continued to plague military operations until the winter, hampering, for example, the passage of Dutch troops through Groningen in October. In the same month, an army under Spanish commander Francisco Verdugo invested Coevorden. Verdugo mistakenly believed that the residents of Coevorden, now loyal to the republic, had nearly exhausted their victuals and would soon capitulate. His army therefore arrived with insufficient supplies of food and firewood. Even as the weather cooled, Verdugo continued to believe that Coevorden teetered on the verge of surrender. In parts of the chilly, wet winter of 1593/1594, as many as 40 of his soldiers died per day, and many more deserted. Finally, Verdugo abandoned the siege on 7 May, with the approach of the Dutch field army under Maurice.[51]

For an army that was already outnumbered, poor tactical decisions were especially devastating in the rainy, stormy, frigid weather that was typical of the Grindelwald Fluctuation. Still, such weather did not directly determine the outcome of Spanish campaigns. Two years after Verdugo ended his siege, an army under Archduke Albert, another one of Philip's nephews and the new governor general of the Spanish Netherlands, besieged Hulst, a fortress town in southern Zeeland. According to the merchant Jan de Pottre in Brussels, continuous rain temporarily impeded and ultimately discouraged the first investment of the town in May. Yet a renewed siege led the town's garrison to capitulate on 18 August. Shortly thereafter, however, the Spanish crown again declared bankruptcy. To add insult to injury, De Pottre wrote that, in September, torrential

[51] Buisman, *Duizend Jaar Vol. IV*, 144. Van Nimwegen, *The Dutch Army and the Military Revolutions*, 160. 'The Old World Drought Atlas'. Accessed 28 June 2016, http://iridl.ldeo.columbia.edu/expert/home/.jennie/.PDSI/.OWDA/.pdsi/figviewer.html.

rain ruined Albert's triumphant – and very expensive – entry into Brussels.[52]

Weather is, of course, prone to variability under any climatic regime. Even in the cold and wet 1590s, unusually warm, dry conditions occasionally influenced military operations. For example, in January 1597, Maurice gathered an army at Geertruidenberg by using waterways that were still navigable in unusually warm winter weather. On 23 January, Maurice and his army marched approximately 40 kilometres south along muddy roads to surprise a Spanish force of some 6,000 men at Turnhout. Varax, the Spanish commander, ordered a retreat to the nearby town of Herentals, yet to get there his army needed to pass across the river Aa. The weather was dry but meltwater had swollen the river, so the Spanish crossing was difficult and slow. On 24 January, the Dutch cavalry caught up to the Spanish army while it was scattered in disorganized groups in the forest of Turnhout. Some 2,200 Spanish soldiers were killed, approximately 500 were taken as prisoners, and the prospects for a Spanish offensive in 1597 were extinguished. Only 12 Dutch cavalrymen perished. William Louis reflected that thawing and then unusually dry conditions had made the ambush possible, because cavalry could not easily use the unhardened roads of the Low Countries if they were wet or frozen.[53]

Relationships between global climate change, local environmental conditions, and military operations were therefore complex during the Eighty Years' War. Yet the strategic significance of weather made more likely in the Grindelwald Fluctuation outweighed that of meteorological exceptions to the cold, wet, stormy trend. The extraordinary Dutch campaign of 1600 provided some of the most dramatic examples. Its roots stretched back to May 1598, when the French and Spanish crowns agreed to the Peace of Vervins. In the winter, the States of Holland and West Friesland planned a massive operation to break the ice in key rivers, and so hamper an

[52] Van Nimwegen, *The Dutch Army and the Military Revolutions*, 163. Jan de Pottre, *Dagboek van Jan de Pottre, 1549–1602*, ed. B. de St. Genois. (Ghent: C. Annoot-Braeckman, 1861), 197.

[53] Van Nimwegen, *The Dutch Army and the Military Revolutions*, 165. Ubbo Emmius, *Willem Lodewijk, graaf van Nassau (1560–1620)*. (Zutphen: Uitgevrij Verloren, 1994), 138. Buisman, *Duizend Jaar Vol. IV*, 171. Anthonis Duyck, *Journaal van Anthonis Duyck, advokaat-fiskaal van den Raad van State: 1591–1602, Vol. III*. (The Hague: Nijhoff, 1866), 222. Puype, 'Victory at Nieuwpoort, 2 July 1600', 72. 'The Old World Drought Atlas'. Accessed 28 June 2016, http://iridl.ldeo.columbia.edu/expert/home/.jennie/.PDSI/.OWDA/.pdsi/figviewer.html.

expected Spanish offensive. Yet the Spanish attack never came, and in the summer mutinies paralyzed the Army of Flanders.[54]

In the spring of 1600, the republic's Stadholders, members of its States-General, and leaders of its provincial states debated how best to exploit these mutinies, which temporarily kept the Spanish Empire from concentrating its full resources on the Low Countries. The States of Zeeland lobbied for an offensive into the southern Netherlands that would halt Spanish privateering. The States-General agreed and ordered Maurice to land his field army at the Dutch fortress town of Ostend, in Flanders. From there, Maurice would surprise the nearby Spanish-held seaport of Nieuwpoort, before besieging the port town of Dunkirk and eliminating its notorious privateers. Once he had taken both towns, he would impose a crippling tax on their inhabitants. The scheme was fraught with risk. Maurice's maritime lines of supply would be very long and vulnerable not only to Spanish raids, but also to storms and contrary winds. His chances of achieving surprise depended on weather that would bring his army quickly and safely to Ostend. At Flushing on 20 June, Maurice only grudgingly led his army into nearly 1,000 transport vessels.[55]

When stormy winds delayed their departure, Maurice decided that a long journey by sea would be too risky. Instead, he ordered the army to land near an estuary of the Scheldt, a week's march from Ostend. After it disembarked, storms indeed threatened its shipments of victuals from the republic. Dutch soldiers endured great hardships while crossing through swamps with little drinkable water, but they arrived before Ostend on 1 July. Maurice left 2,000 soldiers near the town before pressing on towards Nieuwpoort. Yet most Spanish troops had by now ceased their mutiny, and a large army under Albert closed in. That army soon surprised the small Dutch force near Ostend, which suffered heavy losses but gave Maurice the time he needed to organize the bulk of his troops on the beach near Nieuwpoort.[56]

[54] Buisman, *Duizend Jaar Vol. IV*, 195. 'Stukken betreffende de doorbraak in de Lekdijk Bovendams onder 't Waal, en de maatregelen daartegen, 1624. Met een kaart en retroacta, 1323–1600', Rijnland, Oude Archieven van het hoogheemraadschap van, Inventory Number 9020–9021, Hoogheemraadschap van Rijnland (Leiden, Netherlands).

[55] Van Nimwegen, *The Dutch Army and the Military Revolution*, 167. Buisman, *Duizend Jaar Vol. IV*, 195. Puype, 'Victory at Nieuwpoort, 2 July 1600', 73. Paul Allen, *Philip III and the Pax Hispanica, 1598–1621: The Failure of Grand Strategy*. (New Haven: Yale University Press, 2000), 44. On Dunkirk privateering, see, for example, A. P. van Vliet, 'Kapers op de kust: Maassluis en de Duinkerker kapers'. *Tijdschrift voor Zeegeschiedenis* 6:1 (1987): 3–12.

[56] Paul Allen, *Philip III and the Pax Hispanica*, 45. Van Nimwegen, *The Dutch Army and the Military Revolution*, 170. Parker, *The Army of Flanders*, 212.

On 2 July, the Spanish pressed forward, blocking lines of retreat to Ostend and thus threatening to annihilate the Dutch field army. Stiff northwesterly winds whipped up sand and blinded the Spanish as they marched in from the east, but Dutch soldiers initially gave way. When Spanish troops had advanced far enough to expose their flanks, Maurice ordered his waiting cavalry into the fray. The Spanish scattered. Approximately 3,000 Spanish soldiers perished, compared to at least 1,000 Dutch troops. The battle largely turned on the superior discipline and organization of Dutch forces. Driving winds blowing from the beach, however, certainly hampered Spanish soldiers. Moreover, the battle might not have unfolded at all had the Dutch army arrived at Ostend by sea. Ironically, gales born of a stormier climate had aided the Dutch war effort by limiting the tactical options its commanders perceived as feasible.[57]

In the immediate aftermath of the battle, high northwesterly winds prevented Dutch ships carrying wounded soldiers from leaving the harbour of Ostend and returning to the safety of the republic. The States-General now instructed Maurice to besiege Nieuwpoort and, from there, press on to Dunkirk. Yet according to Duyck, torrential and unrelenting rain slowed the army's advance on Nieuwpoort and threatened its supply of bread, likely by hampering travel over the roads from Ostend. On 7 July, Duyck reported, 'It continues to rain. So much water has fallen that the army at Nieuwpoort can scarcely do anything. [After Maurice] ordered the soldiers to build shelters, they stayed busy by protecting themselves against the driving rain.'[58]

Two days later, Duyck wrote that persistent and torrential rain had flooded trenches and kept the troops from building their shelters. Worse, Spanish soldiers had opened sluices around the town, creating a flood that was all the more devastating in the rain. On 10 July, a storm damaged Dutch vessels blockading the hostile harbour of Nieuwpoort, because they

[57] Van Nimwegen, *The Dutch Army and the Military Revolution*, 170. Buisman, *Duizend Jaar Vol. IV*, 196. 't Hart, *The Dutch Wars of Independence*, 19. Israel, *The Dutch Republic*, 259. Leen Dorsman, *1600, Slag bij Nieuwpoort*. (Zutphen: Uitgeverij Verloren, 2000), 15. Parker, *The Army of Flanders*, 212. Maurice of Nassau, 'A True Relation of the Famous & Renowmed [sic] Victorie Latelie Atchieued by the Counte Maurice of Nassau, Neere to Newport in Flaunders against the Arch-Duke Albertus', 1600. 'De Staten-General aan Prins Maurits, 27 Juni 1600'. In *Bescheiden Johan van Oldenbarnevelt 1570–1620, Eerste Deel: 1570–1601*, ed. S. P. Haak. (The Hague: Martinus Nijhoff, 1934), 105. Paul Allen, *Philip III and the Pax Hispanica*, 45. Werner Thomas, *De val van het Nieuwe Troje: Het beleg van Oostende 1601–1604*. (Oostende: Davidsfonds/Leuven, 2004), 42.

[58] Anthonis Duyck, *De slag bij Nieuwpoort: Journaal van de tocht naar Vlaanderen in 1600*. (Nijmegen: SUN, 2000), 81.

could not shelter within. Meanwhile, the rain continued with only fleeting interruptions. On 14 July, an exasperated Duyck wrote that establishing the siege was proving impossible, for the 'weather was so bad that it seemed as though God Himself was preventing the work'. With no prospect of victory in sight, on 17 and 18 July the Dutch army boarded vessels bound for Zeeland. After braving volatile and at times very high winds, its soldiers finally reached safe harbour on 2 August. The weather of the Grindelwald Fluctuation had ruined Dutch attempts to capitalize on the victory at Nieuwpoort, and probably helped convince Maurice and the States-General to retire the army to Zeeland.[59]

After the Battle of Nieuwpoort, both Dutch and Spanish commanders avoided open confrontations between field armies that could end in annihilation for the losing side. In the close quarters of the Low Countries, the destruction of a field army could mean the loss of vast territories, and possibly even the war. Moreover, mercenaries on both sides had a habit of deserting. Commanders hoped to delay battle until the army that opposed them had mostly melted away. After Nieuwpoort, sieges and relief operations would be even more central to the Eighty Years' War than they had been. In that new strategic reality, weather typical of a cooler climate continued to have great military significance.[60]

In 1601, the Spanish fully invested Ostend. Because Ostend could be resupplied from the sea and the harbour was nearly impossible to capture, the siege became a gruelling war of attrition. Storms repeatedly hindered the town's resupply from the republic, while heavy rain undermined its investment by Spanish troops. In November 1601, Maurice attempted to break the siege by encircling 's-Hertogenbosch, a Spanish-held city on the southern border of the republic that had crucial strategic and commercial significance. However, many of his troops froze to death in bitterly cold winter weather, which iced over local waterways and so prevented his army from efficiently receiving supplies by ship. According to Duyck, Maurice hoped for a change in the weather, but when this was not forthcoming he ordered a retreat to Gorinchem. The cold was so severe that a great deal of equipment, many horses, and perhaps even some sick soldiers were left behind.[61]

[59] Duyck, *De slag bij Nieuwpoort*, 102. Dorsman, *1600, Slag bij Nieuwpoort*, 21. Israel, *The Dutch Republic*, 259. Paul Allen, *Philip III and the Pax Hispanica*, 46. Thomas, *De val van het Nieuwe Troje*, 45. 'The Old World Drought Atlas'. Accessed 28 June 2016, http://iridl.ldeo.columbia.edu/expert/home/.jennie/.PDSI/.OWDA/.pdsi/figviewer.html.

[60] Van Nimwegen, *The Dutch Army and the Military Revolutions*, 171.

[61] 't Hart, *The Dutch Wars of Independence*, 25. Israel, Jonathan. *The Dutch Republic and the Hispanic World, 1606–1661*. (Oxford: Clarendon Press, 1982), 5. Parker, *The Army*

At last, in 1604, Spanish troops seized Ostend, after the cunning but ruthless Don Ambrogio Spínola took command of the besieging forces. It was a hollow victory. The Army of Flanders had lost as many as 70,000 soldiers in the siege, and the republic had taken Sluis, a nearby town of greater strategic importance that had served as a base for Spanish galleys. Yet in 1604 the Spanish and English crowns also signed the Peace of London, allowing Spain to devote even greater resources to the Low Countries. Over the following two years, the Army of Flanders seized several important towns on the republic's perimeter. Then, in the summer of 1606, a major Spanish invasion of the southeastern republic stalled in persistent rain. High water levels, and a strong current, increased the effectiveness of extensive Dutch river fortifications along the IJssel and Waal rivers, which prevented Spanish attempts at forcing a crossing. In October, another munity, the largest in the history of the Eighty Years' War, paralyzed the Spanish army for a year and reversed its momentum.[62]

Costly military successes had in fact badly stretched the finances of the Spanish crown. Moreover, the newly created VOC had started to spread through Asia, often at Spain's expense. On 14 December 1606, the Spanish Council of State therefore recommended that Spain's new ruler, Philip III, sharply reduce the size of the Army of Flanders. On 12 April 1607, the States-General and Archdukes Albert and Isabella, the governors general in Brussels, agreed to a ceasefire in which they exchanged recognition of the republic's sovereignty for vague oral assurances that the VOC would vacate its recent gains in Asia. In November, Philip III issued another Decree of Bankruptcy. On 7 July 1609, he grudgingly agreed to a twelve-year truce on terms that, he admitted, strongly benefitted the republic. Many Dutch citizens were relieved, for the winter of 1608/09 was among the coldest of the Little Ice Age. Spanish troops could have easily invaded across frozen rivers that no longer served as effective defensive barriers. For the Dutch, the ceasefire had come at just the right time.[63]

of Flanders and the Spanish Road, 213. Buisman, *Duizend Jaar Vol. IV*, 210. Paul Allen, *Philip III and the Pax Hispanica*, 65. Hale, *War and Society in Renaissance Europe*, 64. Van Nimwegen, *The Dutch Army and the Military Revolutions*, 179.

[62] Van Nimwegen, *The Dutch Army and the Military Revolution*, 196. Parker, *The Army of Flanders*, 11; 213. Paul Allen, *Philip III and the Pax Hispanica*, vii. Bruijn, *The Dutch Navy of the Seventeenth and Eighteenth Centuries*, 22. Thomas, *De val van het Nieuwe Troje*, 98.

[63] Brandt, *Historie der vermaerde zee- en koop-stadt Enkhuisen*, 277. Van Nimwegen, *The Dutch Army and the Military Revolutions*, 197. 't Hart, *The Dutch Wars of Independence*, 25. Israel, *The Dutch Republic and the Hispanic World*, 5. Parker, *The Army of Flanders and the Spanish Road*, 213. Buisman, *Duizend Jaar Vol. IV*,

CONCLUSION OF THE WARS IN A CHANGING CLIMATE, 1621–1648

When the Eighty Years' War resumed in 1621, it had fundamentally changed in character. On the one hand, Dutch merchants had expanded their global commercial reach, and their Republic could more easily match the forces mobilized by the Spanish Habsburgs. On the other hand, the ongoing Thirty Years' War, partly financed by both the Dutch Republic and the Habsburg Empire, repeatedly raised the spectre of invasion by a Catholic League army. In any case, the Eighty Years' War reignited with a reversal for the republic, when an army under Spínola seized Jülich, a town east of Maastricht, after a long and costly siege. However, in the following year, the Army of Flanders under Spínola lost perhaps 10,000 soldiers in a failed attempt to conquer Bergen op Zoom. After Spínola abandoned his siege on 2 October, some 2,500 of his soldiers deserted.[64]

In November, Maurice attempted to exploit this debacle by preparing a surprise amphibious assault on Antwerp. The city retained crucial military and economic significance for the Spanish Empire, and it was exceptionally difficult to besiege. On 21 November, temperatures plunged and threw Dutch plans into disarray. According to the diary of Jonkheer Alexander van der Capellen, a nobleman from Dordrecht, cavalry gathering for the attack had just crossed the Maas when they encountered 'sudden and severe freezing'. It 'was deemed unwise to press on with the horses', since their hooves had not been sharpened for winter, and they would not be able to handle the slippery conditions. The cold was also so severe that already 'three boys ... froze to death on their horses'. Cavalry officers feared that, if the cavalry waited one more day to return, the ice would break the anchors that supported the bridge over the Maas. In that case, there would be no cavalry available to repulse a Spanish assault on Friesland or the Veluwe. The cavalry therefore retreated. Still, Maurice did manage to assemble thousands of soldiers in Dordrecht. They boarded ships and set sail with easterly winds, which soon strengthened into a ferocious storm that brought another sudden fall in temperatures.

249. Paul Allen, *Philip III and the Pax Hispanica*, 232. See also W. J. M. van Eysinga, *De wording van het Twaalfjarig Bestand van 9 April 1609*. (Amsterdam: Noord-Hollandsche Uitgevers, 1959). Simon Groenveld, *Het Twaalf Jarig Bestand, 1609-1621: De Jongelingsjaren van de Republiek der Verenigde Nederlanden*. (The Hague: Haags Historisch Museum, 2009), 59.

[64] Nimwegen, *The Dutch Army and the Military Revolution*, 208. Parker, *The Army of Flanders*, 217. Israel, *The Dutch Republic*, 499.

The storm scattered the fleet, and ice then trapped most of its ships. Many soldiers drowned, and those who reached land were in great disorder. The attack on Antwerp failed before it even reached the city.[65]

Maurice, nearing the end of his life, was bedridden during the bitterly cold winter of 1623/1624. In February, Spanish armies under Spínola and Count Hendrik van den Bergh invaded the republic. Van den Bergh and 7,000 infantrymen braved the frigid weather to cross over the IJssel. Dutch labourers had not broken the thick ice that covered the river, as they normally did in cold winters. They were now hastily marshalled to break the ice in waterways across the inner Republic, while many farmers fled from the countryside. Suddenly, temperatures warmed. Melting ice threatened to sever the path of retreat for Van den Bergh's army. On 23 February, it therefore fled across the IJssel, after enduring perhaps 3,000 deaths. Most of those killed had succumbed to frigid weather, which returned even as Spanish forces completed their withdrawal. Subzero conditions therefore enabled but weakened the initial Spanish attack before short-lived thawing made it so risky that Van den Bergh decided to withdraw. Even in cold years, the random variability of weather ensured that a cooler climate never had a straightforward impact on military affairs.[66]

In April 1625, Maurice succumbed to illness and his brother, Frederik Hendrik of Orange, succeeded him as supreme commander of the army and fleet. In June, the Army of Flanders took advantage of the military confusion surrounding Maurice's illness and death to finally seize Breda, after a long siege in another frigid winter. The town, however, actually had minimal strategic significance, and its conquest had been so expensive that it harmed Spain more than the Dutch Republic. Ongoing Spanish blockades and privateering were certainly damaging the Dutch economy, but the Spanish crown could no longer sustain the rising costs of major offensives in the Low Countries. The new Spanish king, young Philip IV, therefore heeded the advice of his chief minister, the Count-Duke of Olivares, by assuming a defensive posture in the Low Countries. Herman van den Bergh replaced the aggressive Spínola as overall

[65] Jonkheer Alexander van der Capellen, *Gedenkschriften van Jonkheer Alexander van der Capellen, Heere van Aartsbergen, Vol. I*, ed. Robbert Lieve Jasper van der Capellen. (Utrecht, 1777/1778), 125. Buisman, *Duizend Jaar Vol. IV*, 350.

[66] Pieter Corneliszoon Hooft, *De briefwisseling van P. C. Hooft, deel 1, 1599–1630*, edited by H. W. Van Tricht. (Culemborg: Tjeenk Willink/Noorduijn, 1976), 483. Buisman, *Duizend Jaar Vol. IV*, 362. Van Engelen, Buisman and IJnsen, 'A Millennium of Weather, Winds and Water in the Low Countries', 112.

commander of the Army of Flanders. Yet in 1627, the Spanish crown was again forced to declare bankruptcy. Worse, in the following year it entered a costly conflict with France over who would rule the Duchy of Mantua in Italy. The War of the Mantuan Succession would severely weaken Spanish attempts to overcome the Dutch Republic.[67]

The military leaders of the republic could not immediately exploit these dramatic changes in the strategic situation of the Low Countries. Wet, stormy weather hampered Dutch offensives during the cool summer of 1626, and particularly during the extraordinary 'year without summer' in 1628. Moreover, most Dutch troops had gathered in the republic's north-east in the wake of a major Catholic League victory in the Thirty Years' War. A Catholic League army temporarily camped in East Friesland, frighteningly near the borders of the republic.[68]

Extensive sea ice during frigid winters also diminished the resources available to the Dutch fleet, which relied, in part, on harbour tolls. They plummeted in the republic's northern ports during cold winters, although fees in southern ports were hardly affected. For example, during the cool winter of 1626/1627, Amsterdam received £20,494 in toll revenue in January compared to £40,643 in March. The slightly more northerly towns of Hoorn and Alkmaar collected £66 and £0 in harbour dues during January, respectively. In March, tolls in both towns totalled £404 and £2,794, which in turn supported one of the five Dutch admiralties: that of Westfriesland and the Noorderkwartier. By contrast, in January the more southerly city of Middelburg collected £9,427 in harbour revenue for the Admiralty of Zeeland, but just £5,696 in March and £9,648 in April. Southerly Rotterdam, meanwhile, supported the powerful Admiralty of the Maas with £8,635 in harbour duties in January, compared to only £7,682 in March and £10,012 in April.[69]

Despite these financial difficulties, the Dutch fleet would win one of its most important victories late in frigid 1628. On 8 September, a Dutch flotilla off Cuba, led by Admiral Piet Pieterszoon Heyn, captured 16 ships

[67] Van der Capellen, Nimwegen, *The Dutch Army and the Military Revolution*, 217. 't Hart, *The Dutch Wars of Independence*, 28. Parker, *The Army of Flanders*, 218. Israel, *The Dutch Republic*, 506. Peter Wilson, *The Thirty Years War: Europe's Tragedy.* (Cambridge: Harvard University Press, 2009), 365.

[68] Israel, *The Dutch Republic*, 499. Nimwegen, *The Dutch Army and the Military Revolution*, 217. Buizman, *Duizend Jaar Vol. IV*, 397. *Gedenkschriften van Jonkheer Alexander van der Capellen Vol. I*, 511.

[69] Harold Edward Becht, *Statistische gegevens Betreffende den Handelsomzet van de Republiek der Vereenigde Nederlanden Gedurende de 17e Eeuw (1579–1715).* ('s-Gravenhage: Firma I.J.C. Boucher, 1908), xii.

belonging to the Spanish treasure fleet. They seized approximately 80,000 kilograms of silver, as well as furs, dyes, and spices collectively worth just as much. Heyn and his mariners lost some of their spoils after two of their ships foundered in a furious storm off the Bahamas, yet the rest of the fleet returned to the republic on 10 January.[70]

Heyn's theft spelled catastrophe for the Spanish Empire. Imports of precious metals to Spain were already in alarming decline amid crippling corruption, the deaths of indigenous labourers, and the exhaustion of easily accessible veins of ore. The Dutch triumph not only exacerbated this crisis but also undermined attempts by Olivares to restore confidence in the Spanish economy after the crown's bankruptcy in 1627. Moreover, Heyn's plundering, and earlier prowling by the so-called Nassau Fleet in the Caribbean, frightened Spanish mariners. Many feared that their shipping schedules made them vulnerable to Dutch privateering. Their captains responded by leaving the Caribbean later in the year, but that forced them to set sail during the Atlantic hurricane season. They fully understood that departing late from the Caribbean would 'tempt God', but for them the Dutch were a greater threat. Nevertheless, treasure fleets succumbed to hurricanes in 1631 and 1641, with devastating consequences for the Spanish economy.[71]

After 1628, the Grindelwald Fluctuation yielded to generally warmer weather across Europe. Storminess declined in the North Sea region, but it may have increased elsewhere. A sharp increase in the number of Caribbean shipwrecks in the 1630s and 40s, and a decline in the Maunder Minimum, suggests that hurricanes may have been more common in the region during warmer decades of the Little Ice Age. If so, climate change meant that Spanish sailors were taking even bigger risks than they probably realized. Still, not all early modern shipwrecks have

[70] Gerben Graddesz. Hellinga, *Zeehelden van de Gouden Eeuw*. (Zutphen: Walburg Pers, 2008), 105. Buizman, *Duizend Jaar Vol. IV*, 397. Wilson, *The Thirty Years War*, 435. Timothy R. Walton, The Spanish Treasure Fleets. (Sarasota: Pineapple Press, 2002), 121. Jonathan Israel, *Conflicts of Empires: Spain, the Low Countries and the Struggle for World Supremacy, 1585–1713*. (London: A&C Black, 1997), 41. Wendy de Visser, *Piet Hein en de zilvervloot: oorlog en handel in de West*. (Hilversum: Uitgeverij Verloren, 2001), 8. Schwartz, *Sea of Storms*, 39. Lunsford, *Piracy and Privateering in the Golden Age Netherlands*, 198.

[71] Gerben Graddesz. Wilson, *The Thirty Years' War*, 435. Jonathan Israel, *Conflicts of Empires: Spain, the Low Countries and the Struggle for World Supremacy, 1585–1713*. (London: A&C Black, 1997), 41. On the Nassau Fleet, see Anne Doedens and Henk Looijesteijn, *Op jacht naar Spaans Zilver: Het scheepsjournaal van Willem van Brederode, kapitein der mariniers in de Nassause vloot (1623–1626)*. (Hilversum: Uitgeverij Verloren, 2008). Scammell, *The First Imperial Age*, 28, 31.

been discovered, and either way shifts in the frequency of wrecks reflect both human and environmental variables. Correlations between trends in shipwrecks and weather should always be approached with caution.[72]

The summer of 1629 was among the hottest and driest of the Little Ice Age. In the watery Low Countries, the lack of rain provided ideal conditions for a military offensive on land. The spoils from the Spanish treasure fleet allowed Frederik Hendrik to contemplate seizing 's-Hertogenbosch, which had escaped Maurice and his field army during the siege of Ostend. Yet the city's surrounding marshes promised to complicate the construction of offensive siegeworks. Since 1578, they had been strengthened as defensive barriers by increasingly sophisticated means of artificial inundations, which could be engaged by the city's garrison. However, financial difficulties meant that the city's garrison in the summer of 1629 numbered no more than 4,000 soldiers, and their provisions were barely adequate for a long siege. Moreover, while the city's extensive fortifications required a besieging army to dig very long lines of circumvallation, they were undermined in places by medieval walls that would offer little resistance to artillery bombardment. For the defence of 's-Hertogenbosch, much would depend on water.[73]

On 1 May 1629, Frederik Hendrik and an army of around 28,000 infantry and cavalry arrived before the city. To get there, they had marched in 'extreme and unusual heat', according to contemporary Dutch historian Daniel Heinsius. Exhausted soldiers 'wandered off' and departed their ranks, disordering the army. Then, 'when our [soldiers] approached the city', Heinsius wrote, 'they could not imagine anything more daunting'. Its high towers and walls, looming up from the

[72] Some scholars have argued that, from the 1590s to the 1640s, hurricanes may have been less frequent in the Caribbean than they were before or after, owing to El Niño events that reduced hurricane activity. Valérie Trouet, Grant L. Harleyb, and Marta Domínguez-Delmásc, 'Shipwreck Rates Reveal Caribbean Tropical Cyclone Response to Past Radiative Forcing'. *Proceedings of the National Academy of Sciences*, doi: 10.1073/pnas.1519566113. Schwartz, *Sea of Storms*, 29, 39. See also Joëlle L. Gergis and Anthony M. Fowler, 'A History of ENSO Events since A. D. 1525: Implications for Future Climate Change'. *Climatic Change* 92:3–4 (2009): 343–87. César N. Caviedes, 'Five Hundred Years of Hurricanes in the Caribbean: Their Relationship with Global Climatic Variabilities'. *GeoJournal* 23:4 (1991); 301–10. César N. Caviedes, *El Niño in History: Storming through the Ages*. (Gainesville: University Press of Florida, 2001).

[73] Van Nimwegen, *The Dutch Army and the Military Revolution*, 140. Buisman, *Duizend Jaar Vol. IV*, 401. Parker, *The Army of Flanders*, 218. De Cauwer, *Tranen van bloed*, 69. P. H. Nienhuis, *Environmental History of the Rhine-Meuse Delta: An Ecological Story on Evolving Human-Environmental Relations Coping with Climate Change and Sea-Level Rise*. (Berlin: Springer Science and Business Media, 2008), 316.

surrounding water, resembled an enormous, oncoming ship. Nevertheless, Hendrik enlisted several thousand peasants to build a fortified line of circumvallation around the city and its waters. To bypass the city's fortifications and the lands its garrison could inundate, the circumvallation needed to be 35 kilometres long, among the longest in military history. Heinsius wrote that work continued day and night, and advanced with remarkable speed. Within eight days, the enlisted peasants completed the line of circumvallation, and by the end of the month they had erected many of its fortifications. To better connect parts of the besieging army, they even constructed a road through the marsh that surrounded 's-Hertogenbosch.[74]

Dry conditions typical of the interval between Little Ice Age cold periods therefore helped the Dutch field army avoid the fate it had suffered around Nieuwpoort in 1600. Three weeks after digging began, the besiegers finished establishing more than 116 cannons, which they used to systematically demolish the city's defences. Meanwhile, Frederik Hendrik ordered the construction of dikes that diverted the streams feeding the swamps around 's-Hertogenbosch. His soldiers then built windmills to drain the city's surrounding marshes, effectively creating a polder around 's-Hertogenbosch. Trenches could now be excavated in the dried land, and water diverted from the streams to surround the lines of circumvallation and thereby provide greater protection from relieving armies. Redirecting the streams, and draining the swamps they sustained, probably would have been far more challenging in the Grindelwald Fluctuation.[75]

Warm, dry weather lowered water levels in major rivers across the Low Countries. That raised the prospect of a diversionary Spanish invasion of the republic. Sure enough, in the night of 22 July 1629, a Spanish force crossed the IJssel at Westervoort, and the main army followed shortly after. Just five years earlier, high water levels had thwarted a Spanish

[74] Daniel Heinsius, *De gebeurtenissen die zich bij 's-Hertogenbosch en elders in de Nederlanden afspeelden in her jaar 1629*. (Leiden: Elsevier, 1631), 22.

[75] Heinsius, *De gebeurtenissen die zich bij 's-Hertogenbosch en elders in de Nederlanden afspeelden in her jaar 1629*, 25. Van der Capellen, *Gedenkschriften van Jonkheer Alexander van der Capellen Vol. I*, 546. Van Nimwegen, *The Dutch Army and the Military Revolution*, 140. Buisman, *Duizend Jaar Vol IV*, 401. Praak, *The Dutch Republic in the Seventeenth Century*, 67. Christopher Duffy, *Siege Warfare: The Fortress in the Early Modern World, 1494–1660*. (London: Routledge, 2013), 102. De Cauwer, *Tranen van bloed*, 74. J. Blaeu, 'Kaart van het Beleg van 's-Hertogenbosch in 1629', in *Atlas van Loon*, 1649. Constantijn Huygens, 'A. Van Hilten'. In *De briefwisseling van Constantijn Huygens, Eerste Deel*. (The Hague: Martinus Nijhoff, 1911), 260.

invasion over the same river. Panic now spread across the republic. Yet, at 3:00 a.m. on 19 August, 2,500 soldiers under Dutch colonel Otto van Gendt attacked and seized the town of Wesel, which housed a crucial supply depot for the Spanish army. With Spanish supply lines severed, Van den Bergh ordered a retreat, and on 14 September 's-Hertogenbosch finally capitulated to the republic. While warm, dry weather had overall benefitted offensive operations launched by both Dutch and Spanish commanders, the superior resources now commanded by the republic allowed its offensive to have greater military significance.[76]

In April 1632, Van den Bergh and other leading figures of the Southern, Spanish Netherlands secretly arrived in The Hague. They informed the States-General of widespread discontent with Spanish rule, and they divulged that resistance in the towns of Venlo, Stralen, and Roermond would collapse at the approach of the republic's field army. If those towns could be seized, Maastricht could be invested, and if Maastricht fell, the road would be open to a broader invasion of Brabant and Flanders. In response, and perhaps encouraged by warm, dry weather in the spring of 1632, Frederik Hendrik and an army of 28,000 men marched towards Maastricht. The Spanish-held towns on their route indeed capitulated with little provocation, but Maastricht was another matter. Very long lines of circumvallation were needed to invest the city, and persistent rain hindered the excavation of trenches by Dutch soldiers. However, Maastricht finally surrendered on 24 August, despite attempts by large Spanish and Imperial armies to relieve the city.[77]

Weather common in a warmer interval between Little Ice cold periods may have aided the progress of the Dutch army to Maastricht, but rains that would have been more frequent in chillier decades hampered, but did not thwart, its attempt at a siege. In 1635, offensive operations launched by Dutch and Spanish armies benefitted from weather that more clearly reflected the new, warmer climate. On 8 February, the States-General signed an alliance with the French crown, and in May, a French army of nearly 25,000 infantry and 5,000 cavalry joined a Dutch army of equal

[76] Van Nimwegen, *The Dutch Army and the Military Revolution*, 223. Van der Capellen, *Gedenkschriften van Jonkheer Alexander van der Capellen Vol. I*, 546. Buisman, *Duizend Jaar Vol. IV*, 401. Praak, *The Dutch Republic in the Seventeenth Century*, 67. De Cauwer, *Tranen van bloed*, 125. 't Hart, *The Dutch Wars of Independence*, 28. Parker, *The Army of Flanders*, 218.

[77] Barend Lampe, *Historisch Verhael aller gedenckwaerdiger geschiedenis, Vol. 21.* (Amsterdam: Jan Janszoon, 1635), 120. Van Nimwegen, *The Dutch Army and the Military Revolution*, 232.

size. Frederik Hendrik now commanded some 60,000 soldiers. In warm, dry conditions that favoured an offensive, he used his enormous army to invade the Southern Netherlands. On 8 June, it arrived before the village of Tienen. When its garrison unexpectedly resisted, Frederik Hendrik ordered an assault on the town. The attack succeeded, but rampaging soldiers sacked the village and murdered most of its inhabitants. The atrocity ruined any possibility of using Tienen for logistical purposes, or of garnering sympathy from the inhabitants of the Southern Netherlands. Despite the advantages of weather and numbers, the invasion ultimately failed. Meanwhile, a Spanish army surprised the fortress town of Schenkenschans in the eastern Republic. Its moat had dried up in the warm weather, and it quickly fell.[78]

On land, the war reached an uneasy stalemate. In the decade that followed, Dutch and French armies continued to encroach on the Spanish Netherlands, yet they did not seriously threaten its major towns. A powerful alliance of Dutch cities, led by Amsterdam, now called either for peace or a more vigorous prosecution of the war at sea, where Dutch forces repeatedly defeated their Spanish counterparts. The most spectacular Dutch victories unfolded over the summer and fall of 1639. In August, a large Spanish armada of more than 60 galleons, carrying as many as 24,000 soldiers, set out under the command of Antonio de Oquendo to deliver reinforcements to the Army of Flanders. A Dutch fleet of just 17 ships lay in wait, led by the new lieutenant admiral of the Dutch Republic: the young Maarten Harpertszoon Tromp. When the Spanish fleet heaved into sight on 15 September, Tromp arranged his small but nimble ships in single file. By outmanoeuvring the Spanish fleet, the Dutch managed to focus their fire on one galleon at a time. Crews aboard the sluggish Spanish ships could do little to respond. Oquendo's fleet sought shelter in the Downs, but the Dutch discovered it there on 30 September.[79]

For nearly a month, Dutch sailors blockaded the increasingly demoralized Spanish while waiting for a northwesterly wind that would give them

[78] Van Nimwegen, *The Dutch Army and the Military Revolution*, 249. Buisman, *Duizend Jaar Vol. IV*, 432.

[79] 't Hart, *The Dutch Wars of Independence*, 28. Simon Groenveld, 'The English Civil Wars as a Cause of the First Anglo-Dutch War, 1640–1652'. *The Historical Journal* 30:3 (1987): 542. Weber, 'The Introduction of the Single Line Ahead as a Battle Formation by the Dutch, 1665–1666', 6. Bruijn, *The Dutch Navy of the Seventeenth and Eighteenth Centuries*, 26. See also Michiel George de Boer, *Tromp en de Armada van 1639*. Nv Noord-Hollandsche uitgevers maatschappij, 1941. Parker, *The Army of Flanders*, 50.

the weather gage in an attack. Calm, easterly winds allowed reinforcements to arrive safely from the republic. Finally, on 31 October, a shift in the wind allowed Tromp to order an assault with the benefit of superior numbers. The weather gage allowed Tromp to deploy his fireships to devastating effect. At the cost of one ship, the Dutch fleet destroyed 40 vessels and killed perhaps 7,000 Spanish sailors. The bloody defeat ended Spanish attempts to establish naval supremacy in the North Sea region, and undermined its ability to reinforce the Army of Flanders. Since the French had blocked the routes that connected the southern Netherlands to the rest of the Habsburg Empire, soldiers from Spain could now reinforce the army only by sailing in isolated boats that slipped up the channel unnoticed. Increasingly, the army depended on local recruitment.[80]

Weather that had become common in the warmer and less stormy interval between Little Ice Age cold phases influenced the outcome of the Battle of the Downs. Although September and particularly October are usually tempestuous months in the English Channel and North Sea, few storms troubled the autumn of 1639. The Spanish fleet was relatively safe from storms in the Downs, but a severe gale would have been disastrous for the blockading Dutch fleet. In the North Sea region, such gales repeatedly scattered blockading fleets during the Grindelwald Fluctuation and Maunder Minimum.[81]

At last, in 1641, representatives of Spain, the republic, and the belligerents of the Thirty Years' War agreed in principle to begin negotiations that would settle the broader conflict between Catholics and Protestants in northern Europe. Seven years later, in 1648, Spain and the republic settled their long war. That spring, Spanish and Dutch representatives in Münster and The Hague ratified a peace treaty that formally recognized the republic's sovereignty, firmly established its new borders, and safeguarded Catholic worship, at least in private spaces. At great cost, the Dutch rebels, as Spanish nobles judged it, had prevailed against their heavenly and temporal lords.[82]

[80] 't Hart, *The Dutch Wars of Independence*, 28. Maarten Harpetsz. Tromp, *The Journal of Maarten Harpertszoon Tromp, Anno 1639*. (London: CUP Archive, 1930), 58. Hellinga, *Zeehelden van de Gouden Eeuw*, 136. Bruijn, *The Dutch Navy of the Seventeenth and Eighteenth Centuries*, 26.

[81] Tromp, *The Journal of Maarten Harpertszoon Tromp*, 197.

[82] Israel, *The Dutch Republic*, 598. Van Nimwegen, *The Dutch Army and the Military Revolution*, 282. Laura Manzano Baena, *Conflicting Words: The Peace Treaty of Münster (1648) and the Political Culture of the Dutch Republic and the Spanish Monarchy*. (Leuven: Leuven University Press, 2011), 245.

CONCLUSIONS: THE LITTLE ICE AGE AND THE EIGHTY YEARS' WAR

The Dutch Wars of Independence raged across unstable environments that reflected complex entanglements between global climate changes, local weather events, and human arrangements and decisions. In the 1560s, weather associated with the onset of the Grindelwald Fluctuation exacerbated existing socioeconomic and political vulnerabilities in the Spanish centralization of the Low Countries. Thereafter, the cooler climate aided defending armies while hindering military offensives. Frigid, stormy, wet weather often hampered invasions and sieges, though freezing did weaken the effectiveness of waterways as defensive barriers. At sea, gales repeatedly damaged Spanish fleets and foiled their attempts to land troops on both shores of the English Channel. The same storms hampered communications between military and political leaders. Weather typical of a cooler climate also affected small-scale raids in ways that frequently, but not invariably, benefitted rebels accustomed to the cold. Overall, the Dutch rebellion and the early republic were long on the defensive against Spanish aggression. The republic's survival was therefore made possible, in part, by climatic conditions that hindered military offensives across the distinct environments of the Low Countries.

Then, in the warmer, drier, and less stormy interval that prevailed across the Low Countries between the Grindelwald Fluctuation and the Maunder Minimum, military offensives were more likely to succeed. Climatic warming coincided with political and economic developments that together weakened Spain's strategic position in the Low Countries. A relatively warm and dry climatic break in the Little Ice Age therefore partly enabled the success of Dutch military operations between 1629 and 1639, and contributed to the triumph of the republic in 1648.

Over the course of the Eighty Years' War, the Dutch Republic and the Spanish Empire repeatedly seemed on the verge of victory. Yet, until the 1640s, the military pendulum always swung back the other way, with momentum sometimes slowed, and other times accelerated, by climate change. Climatic cooling contributed to the discontent that led to the Dutch revolt, and then helped that revolt survive its first decade. Its telltale weather slowed both the sweeping Spanish offensive of the 1580s, and the Dutch counteroffensive of the 1590s. After two decades of stalemate and truce, climatic warming strongly benefitted the Dutch offensive of the 1630s. Climate changes, in other words, were a catalyst for, but rarely a cause of, military victories and defeats.

5

Gales, Winds, and Anglo-Dutch Antagonism, 1652–1688

As the Dutch Republic reached its zenith in 1648, resentment mounted in the courts of Europe. Mercantilist ideology led many to believe that Holland in particular had enriched itself at the expense of foreign merchants. This feeling was perhaps strongest in England. By the early seventeenth century, English merchants were locked in an unequal commercial rivalry with their Dutch counterparts that stretched from the Arctic to Africa, the Americas to Asia. In October 1651, the so-called Rump Parliament of the new Commonwealth of England responded to pressure from London merchants by passing the protectionist Navigation Act, which aimed to extinguish Dutch trade with English territories. The act also authorized English warships to engage all vessels that did not acknowledge England's claim to 'sovereignty of the seas' by lowering their flags at the first sight of English vessels. As many within England had predicted, the States-General could not tolerate the insinuation that England controlled the North Sea and English Channel. The act therefore helped spark the first of four major seventeenth-century conflagrations between England and the Dutch Republic.[1]

[1] Lars Magnusson, *Mercantilism: The Shaping of an Economic Language*. (Oxford: Routledge, 2002), 8. Dirk Jan Struik, *The Land of Stevin and Huygens: A Sketch of Science and Technology in the Dutch Republic during the Golden Century*. (Leiden: Springer, 1981), 93. Jack S. Levy, 'The Rise and Decline of Anglo-Dutch Rivalry, 1609–1689'. In *Great Power Rivalries*, ed. William R. Thompson. (Columbia: University of South Carolina Press, 1999), 173. Jack S. Levy and Salvatore Ali, 'From Commercial Competition to Strategic Rivalry to War: The Evolution of the Anglo-Dutch Rivalry, 1609–52'. In *The Dynamics of Enduring Rivalries*, ed. Paul Francis Diehl. (Champaign: University of Illinois Press, 1998), 31. Ormrod, *The Rise of Commercial Empires*, 35. Glete, *Warfare at Sea*, 15. See also Simon Groenveld, 'The English Civil Wars as a Cause of the First

In 1651, most European observers believed that the Dutch Republic was the world's pre-eminent naval power. However, the English admiralty was actually on the verge of revolutionizing war at sea. It perfected 'line of battle' tactics in which ships gathered in single file and passed repeatedly by enemy fleets while firing broadsides at range. The line of battle made full use of English improvements to naval discipline and increases in ship size and armament. In the First Anglo-Dutch War (1652–1654), these developments coincided with the early Maunder Minimum, when average annual temperatures were chillier than they had been but winds often blew from the west. Such winds repeatedly helped English crews claim the weather gage they needed to deploy the line of battle. They may also have allowed English privateers to more easily leave their ports and seize the weather gage when attacking Dutch merchant shipping. The climate of the 1650s therefore enhanced English technological, tactical, and institutional advantages in naval warfare. English sailors won most of the battles in the First Anglo-Dutch War, and the Dutch Republic only narrowly salvaged a respectable peace.[2]

Climate change contributed to very different outcomes in the Second and Third Anglo-Dutch Wars. Before and during the second war (1664–1667), the Dutch naval system adopted many of the most successful elements of its English counterpart. Dutch vessels were now much bigger and more effectively sailed in the line of battle. Meanwhile, changing atmospheric and oceanic circulation increased the frequency of easterly winds and storms in the North Sea region. Easterlies helped Dutch commanders claim the weather gage in most battles, while the low design of Dutch ships made them less top heavy and therefore more stable than English vessels in stormy seas. These advantages in conditions that the deepening Maunder Minimum made more common helped the republic win a peace that preserved its commercial preeminence.

In the Third Anglo-Dutch War (1672–1674), easterly winds were less frequent than they had been in the second war, but more frequent than they had been in the first. After England aligned with France against the

Anglo-Dutch War, 1640–1652'. *The Historical Journal* 30:3 (1987): 541–566. Gijs Rommelse, 'English Privateering against the Dutch Republic during the Second Anglo-Dutch War (1664–1667)'. *Tijdschrift voor Zeegeschiedenis* 22:1 (2003): 22–31. John C. Appleby, 'Between the Bays: Anglo-Dutch Competition in the Chesapeake and Delaware Bay Regions from the 1620s to the 1660s'. *Tijdschrift voor Zeegeschiedenis* 24:1 (2005): 21–42.

[2] Angus Konstam, *Warships of the Anglo-Dutch Wars 1652–74*. (Oxford: Osprey Publishing, 2011), 7.

republic, Dutch naval commanders repeatedly exploited these winds to engage and defeat the allied fleet. A year of relentless storms also made it all but impossible for the allied fleet to exploit the republic's preoccupation with an invasion on land. Weather that only partly reflected the influence of climatic trends ultimately had an ambiguous impact on that invasion. Yet in both the Second and Third Anglo-Dutch Wars, easterly winds helped Dutch privateers leave their shores and engage English shipping. The many losses suffered by English merchants gradually diminished their enthusiasm for war and helped the republic win a convincing victory.

In 1688, a Dutch invasion fleet at least twice the size of the Spanish Armada forcibly changed England's government. Strong and persistent easterly winds brought the fleet quickly and safely to England, while keeping the English fleet from sailing out to meet it. This 'Protestant wind' would have been far less likely to occur outside of the Maunder Minimum. Ironically, the invasion it made possible would hasten the end of the Dutch Golden Age. Nevertheless, overall the weather that became more frequent with the deepening of the Maunder Minimum benefitted Dutch forces as they struggled to defend the republic's territorial integrity and its worldwide commercial pre-eminence.

ENVIRONMENTAL AND SOCIAL CONDITIONS IN THE ANGLO-DUTCH WARS

Most battles in the first two Anglo-Dutch Wars took place in the North Sea and English Channel, where sandbanks (called shoals) and currents created an unstable waterscape that naval officers competed to exploit (Map M2). The third war also raged across the amphibious, often militarized landscape that had served as a volatile setting for the Eighty Years' War. Dutch defenders engaged what is now remembered as the *Oude Hollandse Waterlinie* ('Old Hollandic Waterline'), a winding expanse of inundated farmland that effectively turned the province of Holland into an island. In the decisive months of the war, allied soldiers and sailors tried to reach this new island while the Dutch resisted as well as they could.[3]

[3] J. P. C. M. van Hoof, 'Met een vijand als bondgenoot. De rol van het water bij de verdediging van het Nederlandse grondgebied tegen een aanval over land'. *BMGN* 103 (1985): 624. For more on the Waterline, see Wim Klinkert, 'Water in oorlog. De rol van het water in de militaire geschiedenis van Holland na 1550'. In *Hollanders en het water. Twintig eeuwen strijd en profijt, Vol. II*, ed. Eelco Beukers. (Hilversum: Uitgeverij Verloren, 2007), 451–504.

On land and at sea, changes in the prevailing weather of the North Sea region shaped the diverse natural and artificial environments in which the Anglo-Dutch Wars played out. Average winter temperatures were not far removed from warm twentieth-century averages in the first war, but they responded to the deepening Maunder Minimum by cooling during the second and third wars, and during the Glorious Revolution. Average summer temperatures declined less steadily, and were actually higher in the second war than they had been in the first. However, by the third war they were far colder than they had been in the earlier wars. Meanwhile, average temperatures in autumn and particularly spring declined between the first and third wars. As temperatures cooled, precipitation increased and storms grew more common. However, even in the First Anglo-Dutch War storms were hardly rare, owing perhaps to the far-reaching effects of the strongest El Niño of the century.[4]

Naval ship logbooks confirm that the early Maunder Minimum brought more westerly winds to the North Sea region, while after around 1660 the later Maunder Minimum led to a discernable but hardly steady rise in the frequency of easterly winds. In 1653, Dutch Admiral Witte de With recorded easterly winds in just over a third of the wind measurements he made while sailing in the North Sea. From July 1664 to November 1666, the English naval officer Thomas Allin recorded easterlies in nearly half of the weather observations he wrote in the North Sea. From January 1672 to August 1673, English captain John Narbrough again recorded easterlies in slightly more than a third of the logbook entries he wrote while in the same region. Yet Narbrough sailed year-round while De With recorded most of his measurements in the spring and fall, when easterlies are more common across the region today. Since minor discrepancies occasionally existed in weather measurements in ship logbooks written aboard different ships in the same fleet, these statistics simplify the complexity of the 32-point compass used by most officers.[5]

[4] Jinbao Li, et al., 'Interdecadal Modulation of El Niño Amplitude during the Past Millennium'. *Nature Climate Change* 1 (2011): 114.

[5] De With, 'Journael off dagh register gehouden bij den Hr Vice Admiral Witte Cornelisz. de With, sedert 24 Aug. 1652 tot 5 Nov. 1658', Aanwinsten Eerste Afdeling, Reference code: 1.11.01.01, Nationaal Archief (The Hague, Netherlands). Korevaar, *North Sea Climate*, 65. Thomas Allin, *The Journals of Sir Thomas Allin, Vol. I, 1660–1666*, ed. R. C. Anderson. (London: Navy Records Society, 1939). John Narbrough, 'Journal of John Narbrough, Lieutenant and Captain of the *Prince*. January 7, 1671/2, to September 18, 1672. Pepysian MS. 2555'. In *Journals and Narratives of the Third Dutch War*, ed. R. C. Anderson, 108. Narbrough, 'Journal of John Narbrough, Captain of the *Fairfax*.

We can supplement logbook wind observations using diaries, letters, newspaper articles, and intelligence reports, all of which described weather during major battles in the Anglo-Dutch Wars. Taken together, historical sources suggest that westerly winds dominated in the North Sea region during the early Maunder Minimum, before declining in frequency in the 1660s and 1670s. They also show that this trend dramatically affected the weather that shaped naval battles (Figure 5.1).[6]

A shifting climate interacted with distinct English and Dutch naval cultures, technologies, and personnel, all of which had yielded opposing fleets with different environmental vulnerabilities. In 1652, the Dutch admiralties did not have easy access to iron, so they made use of small frigates and converted merchant vessels armed with light, bronze guns placed high above the water line and arranged in, at most, two tiers. Since the main function of the republic's navy had long been to escort merchant shipping, Dutch warships needed to operate in the shallow coastal waters and harbours of the Low Countries. Most Dutch warships therefore had very shallow draughts, which let them sail safely across sandbanks that grounded other warships. Most were smaller than English warships, and their hulls were lower and wider with fewer sharp lines.[7]

Collectively, the republic's admirals, captains, pilots, and common sailors were Europe's pre-eminent seamen. Many Dutch admirals and captains had learned their trade aboard merchant vessels, which gave them unparalleled knowledge of the North Sea environment. They divided their ships into groups, and had long used rudimentary line of battle tactics. However,

September 18, 1672, to July 1, 1673. Pepysian MS. 2556', in *Journals and Narratives of the Third Dutch War*, 200. Narbrough, 'Journal of John Narbrough, Captain of the *St. Michael*. July 1, 1673 to September 21, 1673. Pepysian MS. 2556', in *Journals and Narratives of the Third Dutch War*, 339. De Ruyter, Michiel Adriaanszoon. 'Journaal gehouden op het schip De gekroonde Liefde door denzelfde, in gelijke hoedanigheid, als voren, eigenhandig 29 April–13 Juni 1653'. Collectie de Ruyter, Reference code: 1.10.72.01, Nationaal Archief (The Hague, Netherlands). De With, 'Journal Kept by vice-Admiral Witte de With on Board Various Ships during the First Anglo-Dutch War, the Voyage to Norway to Escort the Merchant Fleet to the Republic, and the Voyage to the Sound to Secure the Baltic Sea and to Assist Denmark, 1652–1658', Aanwinsten Eerste Afdeling, Reference code: 1.11.01.01, Nationaal Archief (The Hague, Netherlands).

[6] Wheeler, 'Understanding Seventeenth-Century Ships' Logbooks', 16. Glaser and Koslowski, 'Variations in Reconstructed Ice Winter Severity in the Western Baltic', 188.

[7] Bruijn, *The Dutch Navy of the Seventeenth and Eighteenth Centuries*, 71. Konstam, *Warships of the Anglo-Dutch Wars*, 8. Richard W. Unger, *Dutch Shipbuilding before 1800*. (Assen/Amsterdam: Van Gorcum, 1978), 111. Alfred Staarman, 'De VOC en de Staten-Generaal in de Engelse Oorlogen: een ongemakkelijk bond-genootschap'. *Tijdschrift voor Zeegeschiedenis* 15:1 (1996): 19.

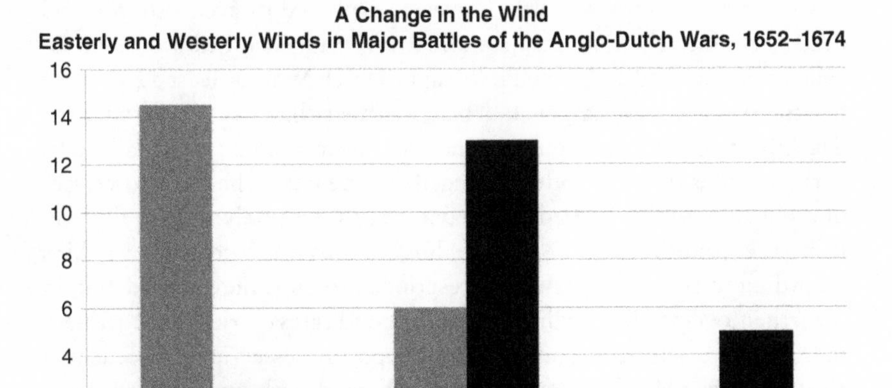

FIGURE 5.1 Easterlies and westerlies during the battles of the Anglo-Dutch Wars, recorded in Dutch and English ship logbooks, missives, intelligence reports, newspaper stories, and diaries.

Dutch vessels in large fleets were arranged in so many squadrons that they had difficulty remaining in good order once a battle was joined. Dutch ships usually started a battle in close formations that quickly unravelled when sailors acted to aid friendly ships in need, regardless of their position on the battlefield. Dutch warship design was also not standardized, although it followed some rough guidelines, so each ship had very different sailing characteristics. That made it even harder to regulate their movements in a line of battle. Dutch naval tactics therefore emphasized grappling and boarding: an approach that worked best in a confused melee. Dutch sailors trained their light guns at the rigging of nearby opponents, both to incapacitate ships before boarding and because thick wooden hulls absorbed all but the heaviest artillery fire. Overall, the republic's naval tactics were well suited for the small engagements familiar to Dutch sailors, but increasingly obsolete in large battles. The small size of Dutch ships was similarly outdated, but Amsterdam's regents believed that larger vessels would be impossible to control.[8]

[8] Hainsworth and Churches, *The Anglo-Dutch Naval Wars*, 22. Richard W. Unger, *Ships and Shipping in the North Sea and Atlantic, 1400–1800*. (Aldershot: Ashgate Publishing Limited, 1997), 28. Weber, 'The Introduction of the Single Line Ahead as a Battle Formation by the Dutch, 1665–1666', 5. Bruijn, *The Dutch Navy of the Seventeenth*

Cromwell's commonwealth, however, exploited its access to iron and deep harbours to construct a standing navy that included a core of so-called floating castles. By the First Anglo-Dutch War, at least 14 of these massive vessels were larger and better armed than the *Brederode*, the flagship of the Dutch Republic. They had deep draughts and tall hulls, with iron guns that were often arranged in three tiers. The third, lower tier of a big ship, which carried the heaviest guns, was only four to five feet from the waterline. In 1653, the English navy categorized warships according to six 'rates', which corresponded to guns they carried and, in turn, their overall size. English first and second rates carried more artillery than an entire field army and could sink opposing vessels at unprecedented range. However, they were usually overloaded with guns, which made them top heavy and therefore less stable than their Dutch counterparts, especially in rough seas, and they could not sail in shallow water.[9]

Many English admirals had been generals in the New Model Army, which had established the commonwealth. They drew on their expertise at war on land to maximize the effectiveness of large warships by refining line of battle tactics and requiring sailors to target hulls, not rigging, beyond the range of the inferior artillery fielded by opposing crews. They organized their fleets into three squadrons that could be easily manoeuvred using standardized signals. The English navy was therefore ideally designed to defeat its Dutch rival, yet its vessels had environmental vulnerabilities that the Dutch would ultimately exploit.[10]

These very different naval systems both depended on the direction and velocity of the wind. As we have seen, ships needed favourable winds both to leave port and to gain a tactical advantage in battle. The English in particular also preferred calm winds, and not only because their ships handled better in a light breeze. High winds tilted their ships to such an extent that they forced sailors to close the lower tier of guns, lest water

and Eighteenth Centuries, 52. Laura van 't Zand, 'Gehannes met een admiraalsschip: de bouw van de "Eendracht" (1652–1654)'. *Tijdschrift voor Zeegeschiedenis* 17:1 (1998): 143.

[9] N. A. M. Rodger, *The Command of the Ocean: A Naval History of Britain 1649–1815*. (London: Penguin Books, 2004), xxvii, 32, 648. Hainsworth and Churches, *The Anglo-Dutch Naval Wars*, 7.

[10] Jones, *The Anglo-Dutch Wars of the Seventeenth Century*, 59. Roger Hainsworth and Christine Churches, *The Anglo-Dutch Naval Wars*. (Stroud: Sutton Publishing Limited, 1998), 22. Konstam, *Warships of the Anglo-Dutch Wars*, 8. Weber, 'The Introduction of the Single Line Ahead as a Battle Formation by the Dutch, 1665–1666', 11. Bruijn, *The Dutch Navy of the Seventeenth and Eighteenth Centuries*, 70. Unger, *Dutch Shipbuilding before 1800*, 113.

flood through the open gun ports. If sailors dared to use their heaviest guns anyway, the angle of their ships sharply reduced the range of their artillery, if they had claimed the weather gage. Dutch ships with lighter guns then had greater range, although this was less important after battles deteriorated into confused melees (as they were prone to do). By contrast, on land temperature and precipitation most influenced the outcome of war. In the Second Anglo-Dutch War and the first months of the third war, the Dutch relied on these conditions even more than they had during their Wars of Independence. Soon after the Treaty of Münster, the patriarchs of the House of Orange died while attempting to seize power from the States-General, leaving behind only the infant William III. In subsequent decades of so-called True Freedom, Orangist sympathy lingered in the Dutch army. Invading armies during the Second and Third Anglo-Dutch Wars confronted dilapidated defences manned by an army that the States-General had deliberately neglected. For a time, only the waters that encircled and interlaced the Low Countries could muster a strong resistance.[11]

THE FIRST ANGLO-DUTCH WAR: 1652–1654

In the wake of the First Navigation Act, the republic's States-General passed a resolution that called for its fleet to be reinforced with no fewer than 150 ships by 1 April 1652.[12] The States hoped that this armada would intimidate the English into avoiding war. Yet the Dutch admiralties, long starved of funding, could not deliver, let alone crew, the required vessels. In May, Maarten Tromp left port with a ragtag fleet of just over 40 warships, most small and obsolete, many converted merchant vessels. It revealed weakness, not strength, and provoked rather than overawed the English. The States-General ordered Tromp to protect Dutch merchant convoys from inspection by English patrols, but to avoid the English coast and decide for himself whether to lower the flag for English warships.[13]

[11] Lynn, *Women, Armies, and Warfare in Early Modern Europe*, 20. Jones, *The Anglo-Dutch Wars*, 186. Hainsworth and Churches, *The Anglo-Dutch Naval Wars*, 172. Parker, *Global Crisis*, 238. Lynn, *Giant of the Grand Siècle*, 12.

[12] Samuel Rawson Gardiner, Ed. *Letters and Papers Relating to the First Dutch War, 1652–1654, Vol. I*, 57.

[13] J. C. De Jonge, *Het Nederlandsche Zeewezen, Vol. I*, 2nd ed. (Haarlem: A.C. Kruseman, 1858), 422. Hainsworth and Churches, *The Anglo-Dutch Naval Wars*, 4. Jones, *The Anglo-Dutch Wars*, 113. Bruijn, *The Dutch Navy of the Seventeenth and*

On 24 May 1652, the Dutch fleet anchored off Nieuwpoort. Before long, a gale rose from the north-northeast, exposing the fleet to a dangerous lee shore. Tromp decided to violate his orders by leading the fleet across the channel to the sheltered corner of Dover. There, an English fleet under Nehemiah Bourne also rode out the storm. As the Dutch and English fleets anchored in close proximity, word reached Tromp that an English squadron had attacked a Dutch convoy. Tromp ordered his fleet to face the English, yet the wind shifted to blow from the northwest. The English claimed the weather gage and fired first, at around 4:00 p.m. Early modern naval battles could not easily be fought in darkness, so this Battle of Dover ended in a matter of hours. Its outcome was technically inconclusive, but the English fared better than the Dutch. They had captured two vessels while losing none.[14]

These events, which instigated the First Anglo-Dutch War, reveal both the limitations and possibilities of tying weather and climate change to the origins and conduct of conflict. Westerly winds typical of the early Maunder Minimum helped the English claim the weather gage and therefore the tactical edge in battle, yet a gale with easterly winds convinced Tromp to seek shelter provocatively close to the English fleet. Weather undoubtedly influenced the origins and early character of the First Anglo-Dutch War, yet at most it only partly bore the signature of the early Maunder Minimum. Human decisions were, of course, at least equally important. Tromp had, after all, decided to violate his orders while commanding a fleet that antagonized the English, and the Commonwealth had earlier opted for a policy of naval confrontation while developing ships and tactics that could defeat the Dutch at sea.

The Battle of Dover alarmed the States-General, but both politicians and admirals on both sides of the Narrow Sea believed that the war would not be decided by large battles between state fleets.[15] The English aimed to attack Dutch merchant shipping, which the Dutch concentrated on

Eighteenth Centuries, 71. See also Johan E. Elias, *De vlootbouw in Nederland in the eerste helft der 17e eeuw, 1596–1655*. (Amsterdam: Noord-Hollandsche Uitgeversmaatschappij, 1933).

[14] Hainsworth and Churches, *The Anglo-Dutch Naval Wars*, 5. De Jonge, *Het Nederlandsche Zeewezen Vol. I*, 416. Hellinga, *Zeehelden van de Gouden Eeuw*, 137. Buisman, *Duizend jaar Vol. IV*, 522. Thomas White, 'An Exact and Perfect Relation Relation [sic] of the Terrible, and Bloudy Fight: Between the English and Dutch Fleets in the Downs, on Wednesday the 19 of May, 1652'. (London: Printed for Robert Wood, 1652), 5. 'Bloudy Newes from Holland: Being a True Relation of the Present Proceedings of the Dutch-Men against the English'. (London: Printed for E. Cotton, 1652).

[15] Jones, *The Anglo-Dutch Wars of the Seventeenth Century*, 115.

defending. In June and July, persistent westerly winds helped English squadrons leave port, surprise merchant convoys sailing up the channel, and claim the weather gage in combat with Dutch escorts. On 22 July, an English fleet under Admiral Robert Blake disrupted the massive Dutch herring fishery off the Shetland Islands. Blake then ordered his fleet to Fair Isle, where he believed incoming Dutch convoys would gather before continuing south. Tromp had assumed that Blake would position his fleet near Fair Isle. He approached roughly a week later, with a numerically impressive fleet that actually included many ships that were barely seaworthy. On 5 August, a northwesterly wind carried several inbound Dutch West Indiaman to the safety of Tromp's fleet, much to the elation of their crews. However, the wind soon strengthened into a furious gale. Sailors aboard the Dutch ships felt the full force of the storm, which pushed them towards a rocky lee shore. The English fleet, by contrast, found shelter in Bressay Sound on the east coast of the Shetlands. The gale's westerly winds therefore strongly favoured the English.

A Dutch survivor later wrote that 'the fleet being ... buried by the sea in the most horrible abysses, rose out of them, only to be tossed up to the clouds; here the masts were beaten down into the sea, there the deck overflowed ... the tempest was so much the mistress ... the ships could be governed no longer'. By the time the storm passed on 7 August, it had scattered Dutch warships and merchant vessels across the North Sea. Most would eventually find their way home, yet thousands of sailors had drowned and 16 warships and several merchantmen had been lost. Scurvy and malnutrition plagued the crews of the ships that limped home.[16]

Upon his return to port, the States-General replaced Tromp with his widely detested subordinate, Admiral Witte de With. On 5 October, De With sailed towards the Downs with a restored Dutch fleet. He hoped to lure the deep-draughted English vessels onto the shoals of nearby Goodwin Sands. However, De With's gambit failed just as the Downs appeared on his horizon. Southwesterly winds strengthened into a ferocious gale that pushed the Dutch fleet back into the North Sea. The storm persisted until 7 October, and forced the Commonwealth fleet under Robert Blake to remain in port. At sea, the Dutch fleet lost three warships. On the morning of 8 October, the southwesterly winds

[16] Hainsworth and Churches, *The Anglo-Dutch Naval Wars*, 30. Harald Appelboom, 'Harald Appelboom aan Axel Oxenstjerna, 27 July1652', in *Bescheiden uit Vreemde Archieven omtrent de Groote Nederlandsche Zeeoorlogen, Vol. 1*, 7.

finally slackened and the English set sail. Yet their headlong rush to sea scattered their fleet over many kilometres, and intermingled its three squadrons. Meanwhile, De With and his subordinates regrouped, claimed the weather gage, and attacked from the southeast.[17]

In the afternoon, English divisions under Blake and Admiral William Penn launched a counterattack. Blake tried to seize the weather gage by sailing along the eastern edge of the Kentish Knock shoal, but failed when two of his biggest ships ran aground. Penn's division had to screen the immobilized ships while Blake's squadron held off the entire Dutch fleet. The English appeared vulnerable, but the Dutch could not hold the weather gage. Light winds also allowed the English to deploy their lowest tier of guns, so Blake's division could use its superior armament to full effect. Before long, the English extricated their great ships, which then joined Penn's division to flank the battered Dutch divisions. As the light faded, many Dutch sailors kept their ships afloat only by pumping water from the hulls, while English ships had endured more superficial damage to their rigging. Sunrise found the fleets nearly 10 kilometres apart, drifting east in a westerly wind that, fortunately for the beleaguered Dutch, blew too feebly for battle. When the wind shifted to issue from the northwest, De With reluctantly ordered his captains to use it to retreat east, towards the republic. By the next day, the Dutch ships reached the safety of their home shoals. Many had been badly damaged, but only three had not returned.[18]

The Battle of the Kentish Knock revealed that English great ships, once deployed in the line of battle, could easily overwhelm smaller Dutch ships arranged in loose formations. Westerly winds could enhance this advantage. In a storm, westerlies thwarted De With's attempt to lure Blake into the Goodwin Sands. In battle, they helped English commanders claim the weather gage and thus the tactical initiative so crucial to line of battle tactics. Still, the influence of weather on each naval system was rarely straightforward. The storm's westerly winds scattered the Dutch fleet, and

[17] De Jonge, *Het Nederlandsche Zeewezen, Vol. I*, 416. Hainsworth and Churches, *The Anglo-Dutch Naval Wars*, 41. Jones, *The Anglo-Dutch Wars of the Seventeenth Century*, 118.

[18] Harald Appelboom, 'Harald Appelboom aan Christina van Zweden, 14 Oct 1652', *Bescheiden uit Vreemde Archieven omtrent de Groote Nederlandsche Zeeoorlogen, Vol. 1*, 27. Stoaks, 'A Great Victory Obtained by the English against the Dutch'. (London: Geo: Horton), 1652. De Jonge, *Het Nederlandsche Zeewezen*, 430. Hainsworth and Churches, *The Anglo-Dutch Naval Wars*, 44. Jones, *The Anglo-Dutch Wars of the Seventeenth Century*, 118. Buisman, *Duizend jaar Vol. IV*, 526.

the resulting confusion, along with the chaos of the English departure from port, helped delay hostilities until the afternoon. Because the battle started so late, neither side could win a decisive victory before nightfall. The quest for the weather gage in the face of southwesterly winds also temporarily grounded the largest vessels in the English fleet, and a northwest wind aided the Dutch escape on 9 October. Westerlies therefore benefitted the English overall, but also played a role in diminishing the scale of the English victory.

English privateering inflicted even costlier damage to the Dutch Republic than the defeat of its fleet. The republic would lose over 1,200 merchant vessels over the course of the war, most at the hands of English privateers. By contrast, Dutch privateers from Zeeland and Holland seized only around 400 English prizes. On the one hand, this imbalance was not quite as extreme as it initially appears, since the Dutch merchant fleet far outnumbered its English counterpart. On the other, Dutch privateers claimed most of their prizes in the final months of the war, when its outcome had been largely decided.[19]

Few within the Dutch Republic's governing circles believed that the Battle of the Kentish Knock had exposed structural weaknesses in Dutch ship construction or naval tactics. Rather, the States-General again blamed its commanding admiral for a defeat, and reinstated Tromp on 27 October. Tromp immediately planned to ease the pressure on the republic's commercial economy by escorting a convoy of nearly 400 merchant ships from Dutch ports to Mediterranean and Asian destinations. Blake and his subordinates took no action when informed of Dutch preparations. After all, in the seventeenth century most naval vessels sailing in northern waters were laid up by October. Their sailors could then serve on merchant vessels that would have otherwise taken to sea in the summer. Naval officers maintained a winter guard of greatly reduced strength until the spring, when the main fleet would be reassembled for the campaigning season. Blake may have believed that Tromp would or could not sortie with so many ships in a season notorious for its dangerous weather, especially in the 1650s, when storms that blew from the west, directly contrary to Tromp's intended course, were relatively common.[20]

[19] Rommelse, *The Second Anglo-Dutch War*, 115. Rommelse, 'English Privateering against the Dutch Republic'. *Tijdschrift voor Zeegeschiedenis* 22:1 (2003), 19. Jones, The Anglo-Dutch Wars, 143. J. R. Bruijn, 'Dutch Privateering during the Second and Third Anglo-Dutch Wars'. In *The Low Countries History Yearbook 1978*, ed. I. Schöffer. (Dordrecht: Springer, 1979), 80.

[20] Jones, *The Anglo-Dutch Wars*, 157.

For most of the Maunder Minimum, Baltic freezing would have limited the Dutch convoy to a southwesterly course. However, in 1652 mild conditions prevailed in October, November, and the first half of December. That probably led to less sea ice in the harbours of the republic, which would have helped Tromp prepare his fleet to set sail. New climatic reconstructions also suggest that westerly winds corresponded with reduced winter ice in the Baltic. English commanders may not have known where to ambush the Dutch fleet, because the lack of Baltic ice raised the prospect of the Dutch fleet taking a northerly route. A complex combination of weather that largely registered the climate of the early Maunder Minimum may therefore have encouraged the Dutch to undertake a rare winter convoy operation, while confusing the English response.[21]

In the first week of December, the Dutch convoy departed and took a southwesterly course down the English Channel. A northwesterly gale rose during the voyage. By 4:00 AM on 9 December, it had spirited Tromp's warships into the Dover Strait well ahead of their civilian charges. The warships had suffered little damage, and their crews were now unencumbered by escort duty. Blake departed the Downs on 10 December. Since he commanded only 52 ships to Tromp's 88, he sailed southwest to unite with hastily converted merchantmen bearing east from Portland. A southwesterly breeze rose on 11 December, as the English and Dutch fleets sighted one another. Both fleets tacked against the wind and sailed on parallel courses, temporarily separated by the Varne sandbank. However, the shingle ridges of Dungeness loomed ahead, cutting off Blake's course. If the English divisions could clear the sandbank before the Dutch, Blake would have the option of continuing on course to join with reinforcements from Portland. However, if the Dutch outraced the English, they would gain the weather gage while blocking the route to the Portland squadron. In that event, the most sensible option for the English would be to reverse course and retreat, leaving the sailors from Portland to their own devices.[22]

As Dungeness Point approached, Tromp took the weather gage. Yet Blake turned to port and took the leading edge of the English fleet directly into the waiting Dutch lines. Many English captains refused to follow. Thwarted by the wind, Blake made no attempt to use line of battle tactics,

[21] Glaser and Koslowski. 'Variations in Reconstructed Ice Winter Severity in the Western Baltic', 118. Buisman, *Duizend jaar Vol. IV*, 526. Jones, *The Anglo-Dutch Wars*, 157.

[22] Jones, *The Anglo-Dutch Wars*, 120. Buisman, *Duizend jaar Vol. IV*, 526.

and hostilities soon degenerated into small knots of conflict. Dutch sailors used the wind to fully exploit their superior numbers and nimbler ships. Reinforcements raced to any group of Dutch ships that seemed outgunned, and that turned the tide of battle. The English captured one Dutch ship, but the Dutch seized or destroyed three English vessels. One of these three had run aground, but Dutch mariners used the tide and the westerly winds to free it.[23]

The Battle of Dungeness was as indecisive a victory for the republic as the Battle of the Kentish Knock had been for the Commonwealth, yet it briefly allowed the Dutch to contain the English fleet. That provided a vital reprieve for the Dutch trading economy, and helped restore the republic's prestige in the courts of Europe. Tactical and strategic miscalculations by the English had nullified the advantages provided by their naval system, and westerly winds for once did not benefit but rather imperilled an English fleet caught badly out of position. The superior seamanship of the Dutch mariners earned them the weather gage, allowing Tromp to maximize the benefit of his greater numbers. Still, the Dutch were forced to manoeuvre desperately to seize that advantage. When the wind blew from the west, the weather gage did not come easily to fleets that sailed into battle from the east.

The storms that preceded both the Battle of Dungeness and the Battle of the Kentish Knock had very different consequences, because they occurred in distinct local environments that influenced but did not determine the decisions of the combatants. Before the Battle of the Kentish Knock, intense westerly winds pushed De With's fleet away from its destination and sank three of its ships, but similar winds before the Battle of the Dungeness left Dutch warships largely unscathed and spirited them towards the English fleet. Without the gale, escort duty would have forced Tromp to fight a defensive battle against a united English fleet. Luckily for the Dutch, Tromp's fleet in December 1652 was far from a lee shore, or indeed any shore, when it encountered the storm that blew it into the Dover Strait.

After the Battle of the Dungeness, Blake's damaged squadron limped back to the Downs before retiring to the greater security of the Thames.

[23] Hainsworth and Churches, *The Anglo-Dutch Naval Wars*, 53. Jones, *The Anglo-Dutch Wars*, 118. Harald Appelboom, 'Harald Appelboom aan Christina van Zweden, 23 December 1652', in *Bescheiden uit Vreemde Archieven omtrent de Groote Nederlandsche Zeeoorlogen, Vol. 1*, 37. Richard Harding, *Seapower and Naval Warfare, 1650–1830*. (London: UCL Press, 1999), 68. Bruijn, *The Dutch Navy of the Seventeenth and Eighteenth Centuries*, 72.

Tromp hoped to give chase while the English fleet was divided, but his pilots dissuaded him from entering the Thames. They felt that westerly winds, when combined with an ebbing tide, could easily strand even the shallow hulls of the Dutch vessels. Abundant westerly winds may well have affected what many mariners considered tactically possible. The Battle of Dungeness was therefore less decisive than it might have been. For two months, the English fleet regrouped in safety.[24]

Tromp's aborted raid was the last offensive operation planned by the Dutch in the First Anglo-Dutch War. After the Battle of Dungeness, persistent westerlies repeatedly helped English commanders seize the weather gage as they sailed from the English coast to engage Dutch fleets. In 1653, in battles off Portland and the Gabbard shoal, the English fleet exploited westerly winds to convincingly defeat the Dutch. After the Battle off the Gabbard, Dutch pamphlets blamed westerlies for the republic's defeat. Yet it had grown increasingly clear that English commanders used superior vessels and tactics to take advantage of those winds (Map 5.1).[25]

With English mastery of the North Sea temporarily uncontested, Blake imposed the war's first systematic blockade. However, shoals around the republic kept Dutch harbours safe from direct harassment. When hostile ships approached, an elaborate warning system alerted Dutch lookouts to remove buoys that marked safe entrances to harbours. Still, the blockade suffocated the republic's commercial economy. It could not endure for long, given the administrative weaknesses of contemporary naval systems, but it benefited from westerly winds that expedited supply shipments from England to the blockade.[26]

By early August, the remarkable productivity of Dutch shipyards allowed the republic's admiralties to restore their fleet and attempt to break the blockade. However, the Dutch fleet was divided into two relatively small squadrons: one commanded by Tromp, and the other by De With. Individually, each was no match for the English armada. On 6 August, while an English fleet blockaded De With's squadron in the harbour of Den Helder, Tromp's flotilla sailed over the southern horizon. The wind generally blew from the west, but occasionally shifted in ways that helped Dutch commanders unite their squadrons into

24 Hainsworth and Churches, *The Anglo-Dutch Naval Wars*, 56.

25 Downing, 'Downing aan Arlington, 19 Juni 1665'. *Bescheiden uit Vreemde Archieven omtrent de Groote Nederlandsche Zeeoorlogen, Vol. 1*, 209.

26 Sicking, *Neptune and the Netherlands*, 155. C. Postma, *Het hoogheemraadschap van Delfland in de middeleeuwen 1289–1589*. (Hilversum: Uitgeverij Verloren, 1989), 389. Hainsworth and Churches, *The Anglo-Dutch Naval Wars*, 82.

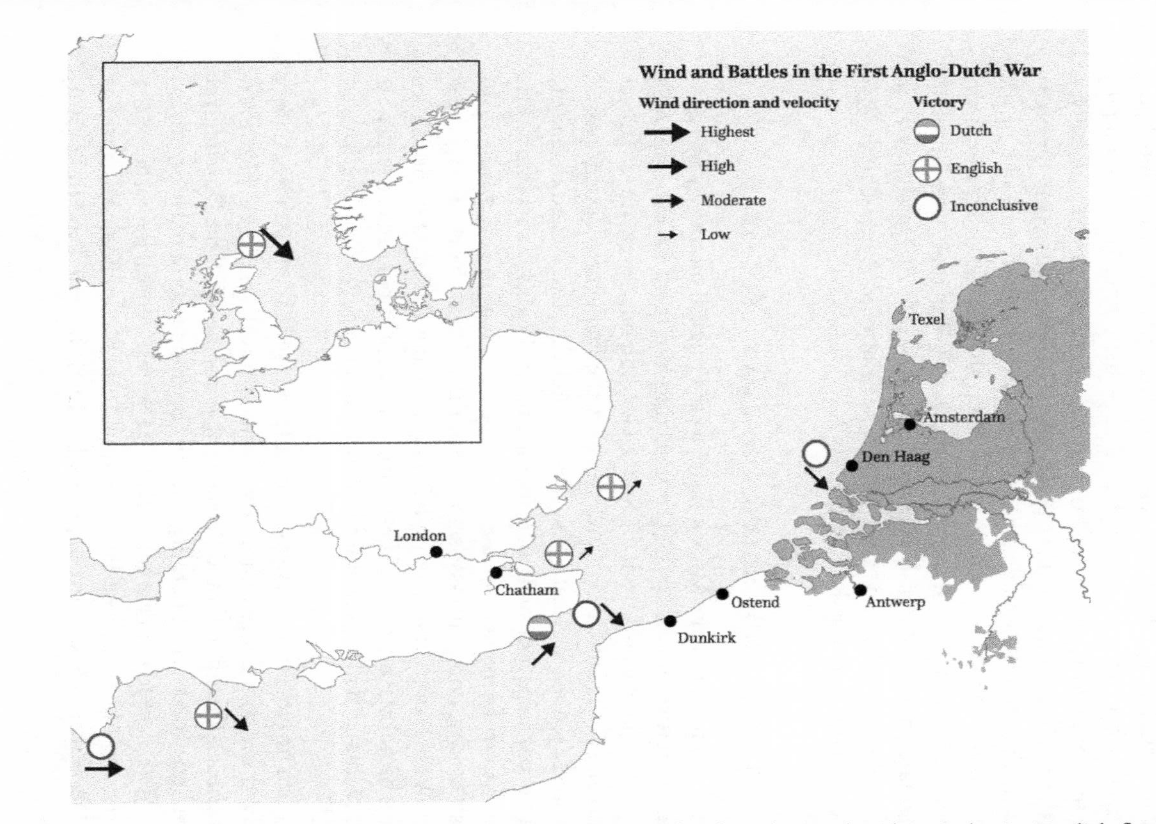

MAP 5.1 Battles and wind directions in the First Anglo-Dutch War. Every battle is depicted with a circle. An English flag in a circle represents an English victory, while a Dutch flag represents a Dutch victory. Arrows represent wind directions in each battle. The thicker the arrow, the higher the wind. The map reflects the extraordinary frequency of westerly winds in the war and their favourable consequences for English fleets. Hans van der Maarel, Red Geographics.

a combined fleet. In the First Anglo-Dutch War, weather did not always reflect the mid-century climatic norm, and this now had major consequences. On 8 August, the Dutch fleet inflicted so much damage to the English fleet that the English were forced to abandon their blockade. However, 3,000 Dutch seamen had died – including Tromp – and 15 ships had been lost, compared to at most 900 Englishmen and only 2 English vessels. Fortunately for the republic, Cromwell feared an Orangist revolt in the Dutch Republic, and the English suffered setbacks in the Baltic and the Mediterranean. In early 1654, that led English negotiators to conclude a peace so lenient that the war's outcome was closer to a stalemate than an English victory. Still, the scale of Dutch losses in commercial and military vessels meant that the First Anglo-Dutch War had been very costly for the republic.[27]

THE SECOND ANGLO-DUTCH WAR: 1664–1667

In 1660, Admiral George Monck restored the English monarchy by negotiating the return of Charles II. The new king had spent his exile in Breda and accepted lavish gifts from the States-General, but he remained implacably hostile to the Dutch Republic. In 1660, the English parliament passed a new and even more effective Navigation Act that threatened to end the lucrative participation of Dutch merchants in English commercial life. Shortly after Parliament passed the act, the Royal Adventurers, an English trading company associated with the Duke of York, engaged the Dutch West India Company (WIC) in an escalating series of hostilities over its brutal slave trade in West Africa. By September, a fleet under Sir Robert Holmes had nearly erased the presence of the WIC on the African coast.[28]

English provocations were as much a response to the Dutch Republic's perceived economic strength as its assumed naval weakness. However, under the leadership of Grand Pensionary Johan de Witt, the Dutch naval system had evolved considerably since the opening year of the First Anglo-Dutch War. Already in February 1653, the States-General had ordered the construction of 30 purpose-built warships, and it commissioned another 30 in December. These ships were equal to English second and third rates,

[27] De Vries and Van der Woude, *The First Modern Economy*, 465. Jones, *The Anglo-Dutch Wars of the Seventeenth Century*, 143.

[28] Jones, *The Anglo-Dutch Wars of the Seventeenth Century*, 150. Hainsworth and Churches, *The Anglo-Dutch Naval Wars*, 101.

and they formed the core of the republic's new standing navy. Moreover, as many as 90 smaller, quicker warships now protected Dutch assets from English raids. De Witt also simplified and centralized Dutch naval administration, ordered the construction of new naval infrastructure, and increased the financial resources available to the admiralties. Finally, he set up a permanent marine corps that addressed the difficulty of manning warships with volunteer crews.[29]

The republic's naval system had not improved in every respect. Tromp's remarkable seamanship had been among the republic's few advantages in the First Anglo-Dutch War. After his death, the equally capable De Ruyter declined De Witt's offer to serve as Lieutenant Admiral. De Witt, perhaps inspired by the success of English 'Generals at Sea', therefore turned to Jacob van Wassenaer lord of Obdam, an army officer with little experience in naval combat. Moreover, Dutch tactics did not yet emphasize the line of battle. They remained vague, and stipulated only that vessels should stay close, but that admirals should keep their squadrons separate. This was a daunting order, since the republic's fleet was, for political reasons, divided into no fewer than seven squadrons. Still, on balance, De Witt's changes improved both the overall morale of Dutch sailors, and the effectiveness of the republic's fleet. The Dutch naval system had adopted some of the most successful elements of its English counterpart.[30]

The composition of the English fleet had not changed much since 1654. Nevertheless, English *Fighting Instructions* had been further refined. They now specified that captains would fight in a single line during the entire battle, keeping the stations assigned to them before the commencement of hostilities. English tactics emphasized unity and discipline as never before, but pardoned republicans and staunch monarchists in practice divided the navy's leadership. The English naval system therefore benefitted from tactical sophistication but suffered from a lull in ship construction and the hubris and internal division of its commanders. It had assumed many of the worst institutional traits that had plagued the Dutch at the onset of the First Anglo-Dutch War. Moreover, it would now face similar environmental disadvantages brought about by a shifting climate.[31]

[29] Hainsworth and Churches, *The Anglo-Dutch Naval Wars*, 92. Bruijn, *The Dutch Navy of the Seventeenth and Eighteenth Centuries*, 78. Bruijn, 'Introduction', 9. Bruijn, 'The Maritime World of the Dutch Republic', 35.

[30] Hainsworth and Churches, *The Anglo-Dutch Naval Wars*, 92.

[31] Jones, *The Anglo-Dutch Wars of the Seventeenth Century*, 146.

At first, however, chilly weather undermined Dutch preparations for war. In the Low Countries, the winter of 1664/1665 was overall only slightly colder than the twentieth-century average. Yet temperatures plummeted in December and remained bitterly cold through February. On 6 February, officials at the Admiralty of the Maas, the most important Dutch admiralty, wrote a letter to the States-General that accounted for delays in a crucial shipbuilding programme. When complete, the programme would give the republic 24 ships that could finally fight toe to toe with all but the largest English first rates. According to the letter, prolonged freezing and 'other inconveniences', had slowed construction, and the vessels would not be completed on time. Unfortunately, neither the Admiralty's letter, nor subsequent missives written by members of the States-General, explained how cold winter weather affected shipbuilding.[32] It may be that the cold simply made it hard to work, or perhaps frozen waterways stopped or slowed the movement of materials to the shipyards.[33]

The most tantalizing hints of what may have happened actually come from the frigid winter of 1708/1709. On 30 March 1709, Grand Pensionary Heinsius received a letter from the Admiralty of Amsterdam. The admiralty informed him that sea ice prevented the collection of harbour duties for four months in the severe winter. As a result, the admiralties lacked both immediate cash reserves and ready credit to equip and supply warships. 'We can assure you', the letter concluded, 'that this [Admiralty] was never in such dire need of coin'. Similar circumstances may have slowed the construction of Dutch warships in 1665.[34]

The delay would have serious consequences. In April, the English main fleet under the Duke of York sortied from the Gunfleet in Essex before the Dutch armada could assemble. While stationed off Texel, the fleet captured eight Dutch merchant vessels inbound from Bordeaux and Lisbon. Thereafter, it was beset by gales. With no rich prizes expected for several months, James II commanded his captains to abandon the blockade and return to the Gunfleet. Soon after, the Dutch fleet finally gathered near Texel. With 120 mostly large vessels it was in some respects equal to the

[32] Bruijn, *The Dutch Navy of the Seventeenth and Eighteenth Centuries*, 78. Buisman, *Duizend jaar Vol. IV*, 592.

[33] Hainsworth and Churches, *The Anglo-Dutch Naval Wars*, 120.

[34] 'Admiraliteit van Amsterdam, 'Van de Admiraliteit van Amsterdam, 30 Maart 1709', 'Van Hop, 10 Maart 1709', *De Briefwisseling van Anthonie Heinsius, 1702–1720. Deel VIII: 1 oktober 1708 – 30 juni 1709*, 325, 395. Bruijn, *The Dutch Navy of the Seventeenth and Eighteenth Centuries*, 6.

fleet fielded by the English. Yet it had been weakened by the recent departure of a squadron under De Ruyter, and it consisted of wildly different ships crewed by sailors from across Europe and Asia. It would be hard to control relative to the English fleet, and not nearly as formidable as it would have been with the heavier ships still under construction. Nevertheless, in the first week of June De Witt responded to reports that the English armada had been scattered and damaged in a recent storm by convincing Obdam to seek out the English near their coast. On 12 June, the English ambassador, George Downing, lamented that 'the weather and wind have bin these 3 or 4 dayes as fit for [the Dutch fleet] goeing thither and for a fight as could be wished'. The Dutch were apparently 'exceeding confident . . . of getting the better' in battle.[35]

On 11 June, the Dutch armada encountered the English fleet 40 miles southeast of Lowestoft. However, Obdam did not command an attack, despite being upwind in the prevailing northeasterly. On 12 June, the English were just 10 miles distant, but again Obdam did not exploit his advantage. The winds were relatively light, but during the late Maunder Minimum gales were almost twice as common in June as they were in the twentieth century. Perhaps Obdam was waiting for rougher weather. The recently repaired English fleet would have been especially vulnerable to high winds, which would also have forced the English to close their lowest gun ports. More likely, Obdam hoped that fighting in a lee position would elevate his cannons, potentially giving them greater range despite the contrary winds. Still, Obdam's hesitation puzzled both Dutch and English sailors. One Dutch captain wrote, 'God Almighty took away the skill of our Commander in Chief, or never gave him any'.[36]

By the evening of 12 June, the wind shifted to blow from the south-southwest. By the next morning, the English had claimed the weather gage. The Duke of York promptly ordered his captains to attack. The English squadrons clustered together in their first pass, with some ships firing into friendly vessels. Yet, English lack of discipline paled in

[35] Appelboom, 'Harald Appelboom aan Adolf Johan van Zweden, Lowestoft, 13 June 1665', 'Nieuwsbericht uit Amsterdam, 25 Mei 1665', Downing, 'Downing aan Arlington, 26 Mei 1665', Downing, 'Downing aan Arlington, 2 Juni 1665', 'Verhaal van den slag bij Lowestoft, 13 Juni 1665', in *Bescheiden uit Vreemde Archieven omtrent de Groote Nederlandsche Zeeoorlogen, Vol. I*, ed. H. T. Colenbrander, 178, 180, 181, 183, 188.

[36] Hainsworth and Churches, *The Anglo-Dutch Naval Wars*, 120. Cornelis Tromp, 'Dutch Account Printed in Contemporary Broadsheet'. *The Second Dutch War: Described in Pictures & Manuscripts of the Time*, 12.

comparison to the chaotic conduct of Dutch captains. Many abandoned any semblance of order in their haste to disable, board, and seize English vessels. The Dutch could not use their fireships in the contrary wind, and both fleets bombarded one another. Thick smoke blew away from the English to envelop the Dutch, obscuring their sight. At 3:00 p.m., the powder magazine in Obdam's flagship exploded, killing all aboard. In the confusion that followed, the Dutch fleet scattered. Its warships were then over 112 kilometres from the safety of Dutch harbours, and they might have been annihilated but for the actions of the Duke of York's gentleman-in-waiting. Acting on prior orders from Anne Hyde, the Duchess of York, he commanded the captain of the English flagship to shorten sail while James was sleeping. The other English ships followed suit, so the fleet slowed down and abandoned its pursuit. This critical decision changed the character of the Dutch defeat. On the morning of 14 June, the bulk of the republic's fleet reached the safety of the shoals that screened the Dutch coast. The English lost 800 seamen and just one ship, while the Dutch lost 5,000 sailors and 17 ships. Both fleets counted two admirals and many captains among the dead.[37]

In the aftermath of the battle, months of persistent storminess frustrated English attempts to establish a blockade that might have suffocated the republic's economy. In the meantime, the Dutch completed their delayed great ships. A later English report to the Committee of Parliament concluded that the failure to press the English advantage after the battle had been the most important mistake of the war.[38]

The Battle of Lowestoft was fought in westerly winds, but weather typical of the Maunder Minimum influenced where, when, and how it unfolded. Prevailing westerly winds had prompted caution among Dutch pilots in the First Anglo-Dutch War, thwarting Tromp's hopes for a raid up the Thames. By contrast, in June 1665 a gale and persistent easterly winds encouraged most Dutch captains to hazard a battle far from the

[37] William Penn, 'Observations on the Battle'. In *The Second Dutch War: Described in Pictures & Manuscripts of the Time*, National Maritime Museum. (London: Her Majesty's Stationery Office, 1667), 12. 'Verhaal van den slag bij Lowestoft, 13 Juni 1665', in *Bescheiden uit Vreemde Archieven omtrent de Groote Nederlandsche Zeeoorlogen, Vol. I*, 188. Allin, *The Journals of Sir Thomas Allin, Vol. I*, 234. Jones, *The Anglo-Dutch Wars*, 158. Hainsworth and Churches, *The Anglo-Dutch Naval Wars*, 125.

[38] George Downing, 'Downing aan Arlington, 21 Juli 1665', 'The Heads of the Miscarriages of the Late Warr as They Lay before the Committee of Parliament, 1 Nov. 1667', in *Bescheiden uit Vreemde Archieven omtrent de Groote Nederlandsche Zeeoorlogen, Vol. I*, 272, 595. Buisman, *Duizend jaar Vol. IV*, 596.

safety of their home shoals. Obdam, by contrast, had been reluctant to depart Texel, and on 11 June he again hesitated to exploit steady easterlies by attacking the English with the weather gage. The inexperienced Obdam may have tried to compensate for the structural weaknesses of his fleet by using new tactics. Yet many Dutch citizens understood that Obdam had squandered weather that should have given him an advantage. They 'hardly give [Obdam] a good word', Downing reported in the wake of the battle. They blamed the loss on the English 'having the wind of them, and they say that if ever they should come to fight againe and have the wind of the English, they doubt not but they should give a better account of it'.[39]

By contrast, De Witt and the Dutch naval command did not solely blame Obdam or the weather for their defeat. Over the summer of 1664, they ceased the practice of using conscripted VOC ships in battle. They also developed new sailing instructions that finally emphasized the line ahead formation, and split all Dutch fleets into three squadrons. De Ruyter would himself introduce a signal by which captains would know to arrange their ships in the line, although this applied only to his squadron. Some Dutch captains worried that the length of the line of battle would leave it too vulnerable to the influence of wind and sea, but De Witt dismissed their objections. By making soundings of inlets to the Texel roadstead, De Witt even charted new ways of entering and exiting the republic's home waters. The republic's fleet would not be as vulnerable to wind direction as it had been when navigating these waters. Nevertheless, battle fleets gathered off the coast of the Low Countries still needed an easterly wind to cross the English Channel or North Sea.[40]

The Dutch Republic may have lost the first battle of the Second Anglo-Dutch War, but its privateers were making up for it. In the first war, English privateers devastated the republic's merchant shipping, and expectations of similar success had encouraged English provocations that led to the second war. Yet Dutch privateers seized as many prizes as their English rivals over the course of that war, and the larger size of the Dutch merchant fleet meant that English losses were far more damaging.

[39] Downing, 'Downing aan Arlington, 2 Juni 1665', in *Bescheiden uit Vreemde Archieven omtrent de Groote Nederlandsche Zeeoorlogen, Vol. I*, 184. Downing, 'Downing aan Arlington, 19 Juni 1665', in *Bescheiden uit Vreemde Archieven omtrent de Groote Nederlandsche Zeeoorlogen, Vol. I*, 209.

[40] Weber, 'The Introduction of the Single Line Ahead as a Battle Formation by the Dutch, 1665–1666', 15. Bruijn, *The Dutch Navy of the Seventeenth and Eighteenth Centuries*, 82. Staarman, 'De VOC en de Staten-Generaal in de Engelse Oorlogen', 16.

Moreover, Dutch privateers captured richly laden vessels returning from the colonies, while English privateers usually seized ships carrying only wine, brandy, and salt. The promise of profits through privateering also helped provoke the Third Anglo-Dutch War, but in that war the republic's privateers actually captured far more vessels than their English counterparts. While English merchants therefore initially supported all three Anglo-Dutch Wars, Dutch privateering in the second and third wars eventually convinced them to support peace negotiations.[41]

The growing success of Dutch privateering owed much to the decision of the States-General to forbid merchant shipping that did not service the oceanic rich trades. That forced many Dutch merchants and sailors to recoup their losses by taking up privateering. Yet the deepening of the Maunder Minimum may have also benefitted Dutch privateers (Map 5.2). Easterly winds probably helped them leave port to ambush merchant ships and granted them the initiative in battle. Moreover, privateers often lurked near sheltered coasts, and it is possible that more frequent, more severe storms inflicted damage to merchant ships at sea that privateers avoided. These merchant vessels could have been easier prey in the wake of such storms.[42]

In any case, only large fleets assembled to decisively defeat their counterparts could win or lose a naval war, despite the importance of privateering. Some merchant convoys were also too important and therefore too well defended to be taken by privateers. For example, on 10 July 1665 English agents reported that a heavily armed VOC fleet taking the back way had arrived at the port of Bergen in Norway. It carried riches that, if lost to the English, threatened to decide the war. An English armada under the Earl of Sandwich was already on its way. Meanwhile, the Dutch main fleet also sailed north to escort the VOC ships. On 9 August, Sandwich dispatched a squadron of 15 warships and two fireships under Sir Thomas Teddiman to engage the VOC fleet in Bergen. The rest of the English armada waited to ambush the Dutch main fleet when it arrived from the south. King Frederick of Denmark, who ruled southern Norway and nominally supported the republic, secretly agreed to surrender the VOC fleet into English hands, in return for half the spoils.[43]

[41] Jones, *The Anglo-Dutch Wars*, 30. Rommelse, *The Second Anglo-Dutch War*, 115. Bruijn, *The Dutch Navy of the Seventeenth and Eighteenth Centuries*, 87.

[42] Rommelse, *The Second Anglo-Dutch War*, 125. Rommelse, 'English Privateering against the Dutch Republic', 28.

[43] Hainsworth and Churches, *The Anglo-Dutch Naval Wars*, 131. Jones, *The Anglo-Dutch Wars*, 163.

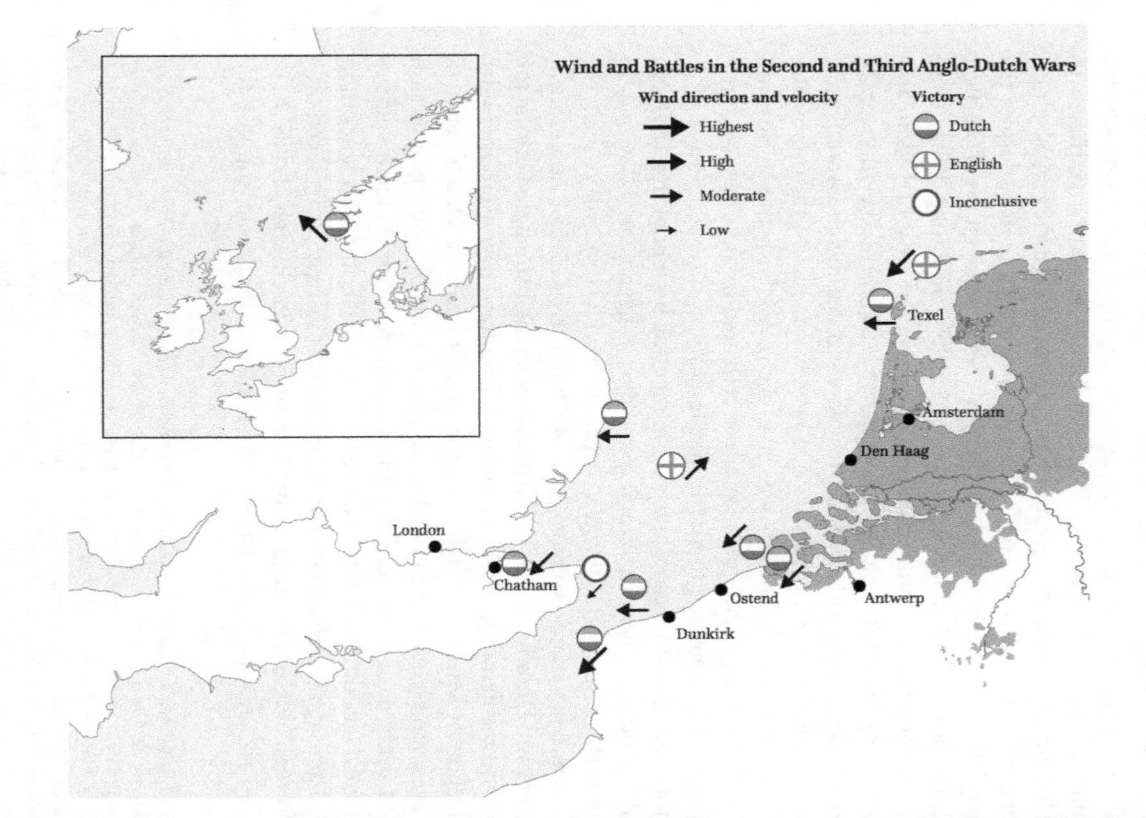

MAP 5.2 Battles and wind directions in the Second and Third Anglo-Dutch Wars. Every battle is depicted with a circle. An English flag in a circle represents an English victory, while a Dutch flag represents a Dutch victory. Arrows represent wind directions in each battle. The thicker the arrow, the higher the wind. The map reflects the remarkable frequency of high easterly winds in the wars, which often benefitted Dutch fleets. Hans van der Maarel, Red Geographics.

When Teddiman reached Bergen, however, Governor Claus von Aslefeldt denied all knowledge of a secret arrangement. High southeasterly winds that blew directly out of the harbour, also threatened to impede any attack. During the night, the Dutch repositioned their ships and fortified a garrison on the shore as negotiations dragged on between Teddiman's representative and Von Aslefeldt. The Danes continued to stall for time, but victuals were now running low aboard the English ships. At first light on the next day, Teddiman ordered an attack, despite the intense southeasterly wind. Eight English vessels engaged the VOC fleet while the others fired on a nearby Danish castle. Before long, Danish and Dutch cannon fire had badly damaged the rigging of most of Teddiman's warships. As the ships grew increasingly hard to control, they threatened to collide with one another in the driving wind. Sandwich wrote that 'if God had given us but few howers of a faire wind, against the opposition both of the Dane and Dutch wee had destroyed both the shipps and towne'.[44] Instead, Teddiman's squadron retreated from Bergen with 400 seamen killed, compared to 29 for the Dutch.[45]

Storms plagued the rest of the year, hampering both English and Dutch naval operations and discouraging a major engagement. However, in autumn the Bishop of Münster, Bernhard von Galen, allied with the English and led 20,000 soldiers into the Dutch territories of Achterhoek, Twente, and Drenthe. It was the first land campaign attempted during the wars, and the first large-scale intervention by a third party. Troops under the Bishop of Münster initially overran poorly prepared Dutch defences and even threatened the city of Groningen, but by October the invasion stalled in the face of torrential rains and severe storms. Dutch soldiers destroyed agricultural infrastructure in their retreat, and now starvation spread among the deluged invaders. Still, the Münsterite army faced only ineffectual military opposition until the new French king, Louis XIV, decided to act on a 1662 treaty that obligated France to support the

[44] 'Lord Sandwich's Narrative, 11 Juli-12 Oct 1665', in *Bescheiden uit Vreemde Archieven omtrent de Groote Nederlandsche Zeeoorlogen, Vol. I*, 258. 'Letter from Sir Thomas Teddiman to Sandwich, Copied into the Latter's Journal, Printed in Navy Records Society Vol. LXIV', in *The Second Dutch War*, National Maritime Museum, 15.

[45] 'Lord Sandwich's Narrative, 11 Juli-12 Oct 1665'. *Bescheiden uit Vreemde Archieven omtrent de Groote Nederlandsche Zeeoorlogen, Vol. 1: 1652–1667*, 258. 'Letter from Sir Thomas Teddiman to Sandwich, Copied into the Latter's Journal, Printed in Navy Records Society Vol. LXIV'. *The Second Dutch War: Described in Pictures & Manuscripts of the Time*, 15. Thomas Allin, *The Journals of Sir Thomas Allin, Vol. I*, 249. Hainsworth and Churches, *The Anglo-Dutch Naval Wars*, 131. Jones, *The Anglo-Dutch Wars*, 163.

republic in the face of English aggression. French troops routed Von Galen's demoralized army, and in January Louis XIV declared war on England. French intervention and the rains of a wetter climate, not Dutch troops, had saved the republic.[46]

On 15 February, English agents reported that frigid weather was again delaying the building and repairing of Dutch vessels. They projected that the cold would slow down the assembly and sortie of the republic's fleet in the spring. One source in Rotterdam conveyed that 'this last frost has hindered them much in the building; their business begins to loocke as it did last year when they said that in April they wold be ready to goe to sea but found themselves much disappointed ... by all appearance they wil be so late a coming to sea as they wer last yeare [sic]'.[47] The winter of 1665–1666 was no colder than the twentieth-century average, but the end of January and most of March were unusually chilly. Frigid weather again interfered with the republic's shipbuilding campaign, just as it had a year earlier.[48]

The correspondence of the Van der Goes brothers suggests that severe storms may have compounded the delays caused, in part, by chilly temperatures. In a letter to his brother on 8 December 1665, Adriaen van der Goes described a ferocious gale and a catastrophic storm surge. The storm was the dramatic conclusion to several days of tempestuous weather that had flooded polders, washed away dunes, stranded ships, and drowned animals and people across the republic's maritime provinces. On 17 December, Van der Goes emphasized that the loss of the polders in particular had been a 'major disaster' and a 'severe financial reversal'. This was especially unfortunate because 'meanwhile much money will be required for the urgent equipping of 170 warships, including 60 new vessels'. Indeed, on 4 June, an English source reported that ships belonging to North Holland and Friesland – the provinces most affected by

[46] De Witt, 'Aen de Heer Extr. Minister C. Van Beuningen, den 30 December 1665'. In *Brieven, Geschreven ende gewisselt tusschen den Heer John de Witt, Raedt-Pensionaris, ende de Gevolmghtigden van den Staedt der Vereenighde Nederlanden, so in Vranckryck, Engelandt, Sweden, Denemarcken, Poolen, enz: Beginnende met den jaere 1652 tot het jaer 1669 incluys, Vol. II.* (The Hague: Hendrick Scheurleer, 1723), 136. Rommelse, *The Second Anglo-Dutch War*, 147. Buisman, *Duizend jaar Vol. IV*, 600. Van der Goes, 'Hage, 17 December 1665', in *Briefwisseling tusschen de gebroeders van der Goes (1659–1673) Vol. I*, 228. 'The Old World Drought Atlas'. Accessed 28 June 2016, http://iridl.ldeo.columbia.edu/expert/home/.jennie/.PDSI/.OWDA/.pdsi/figviewer.html.

[47] 'Nieuwsbericht uit Rotterdam, 5 Febr. 1666', in *Bescheiden uit Vreemde Archieven omtrent de Groote Nederlandsche Zeeoorlogen, Vol. I*, 297.

[48] Buisman, *Duizend jaar Vol. IV*, 604.

the December storm – were late to join the republic's fleet, owing to a lack of money. Financial distress, exacerbated by the cost of repairs following the December gale, only worsened amid major storms that continued to afflict the republic between January and April 1666.[49]

Owing in part to chilly, stormy weather, the Dutch fleet would not leave the republic until June. The same weather also slowed English preparations, but not to an equal degree. The storms that devastated the low-lying coastal regions of the republic blew from the northwest and pushed water against coastal defences. They were therefore less damaging along the English shore. Moreover, cold snaps may have been more acute in the republic. During the Third Anglo-Dutch War, Sir William Temple wrote that freezing weather was the 'greatest disadvantage of Trade [the Dutch] receive from their Scituation [sic]'. After all, 'many times their Havens are all shut up for two or three Months with Ice, when ours are open and free'. The easterly winds that brought frigid temperatures to the republic apparently warmed as they crossed the North Sea or English Channel on their way to the British Isles. Yet there were other environmental influences at work in the winter of 1665/1666. England was in the midst of its worst wave of plague since the Black Death, especially in London, where some 100,000 people died by the summer of 1666. Economic shocks caused by the outbreak of plague probably contributed to the financial problems of the English crown, which were even more acute than those of the States-General. In the spring of 1666, a restless environment therefore also delayed the departure of the united English fleet.[50]

As the English armada finally prepared to sortie in May, the overriding concern of its leaders was to prevent a union of the Dutch fleet with squadrons belonging to a now openly hostile France. Both the English and Dutch knew that a French fleet had departed Toulon, a French port on

[49] Van der Goes, 'Hage, 17 December 1665', in *Briefwisseling tusschen de gebroeders van der Goes (1659–1673) Vol. I*, 221. Buisman, *Duizend jaar Vol. IV*, 602. Van der Goes, 'Hage, 17 December 1665', Van der Goes, 'Hage, den 5 February 1666', in *Briefwisseling tusschen de gebroeders van der Goes (1659–1673) Vol. I*, 229, 245. 'Nieuwsbericht uit Haarlem, 4 Juni 1666', in *Bescheiden uit Vreemde Archieven omtrent de Groote Nederlandsche Zeeoorlogen, Vol. I*, 313.

[50] Theophilus Garencières, a contemporary French apothecary, argued that the long, frigid winter of the previous year – 1664/1665 – was partly to blame for the outbreak of plague. Theophilus Garencières, *A Mite Cast into the Treasury of the Famous City of London: Being a Brief and Methodical Discourse of the Nature, Causes, Symptomes, Remedies and Preservation from the Plague, in this Calamitous Year, 1665*. (London: Thomas Ratcliffe, 1665), 8. Temple, *Observations upon the United Provinces of the Netherlands*, 79.

the Mediterranean coast, in late April. Prince Rupert, now co-commander of the English fleet with George Monck, later claimed to have received intelligence that French vessels were nearing the English Channel.[51] Much to Monck's surprise and distress, on 8 June Rupert selected 20 choice warships from the main English fleet and left with them to intercept the French before they could unite with the Dutch. Just before Rupert left port, Monck wrote a letter begging the admiralty for more ships. He revealed that he had received reports that the 'the Holland fleet will suddainly be out'. His intelligence was actually outdated, because all outgoing correspondence from the republic ceased when the Dutch fleet left port.[52]

Indeed, soon after Rupert's departure, the long-delayed Dutch fleet, now at last under the command of Admiral Michiel de Ruyter, used easterly winds to quickly cross the channel. When Monck finally received reports of the approaching armada, he sent urgent letters to Rupert, who had assumed that an easterly wind that would spirit the Dutch to England's coast would also bring him to the main English fleet before a battle started. However, he may have forgotten that he would only be aware of the oncoming Dutch fleet once a message had been brought to him by ship against contrary winds.[53]

On the morning of 11 June, Monck's remaining vessels were en route to the Swin from the Thames. Just then, the English warship *Bristol* sighted at least 80 Dutch warships riding out a strong wind that had shifted to blow from the southwest. While the English had the weather gage, Monck commanded just 54 vessels. His flag officers recommended retreat, citing not only the disparity in numbers but also the disadvantage of winds that blew 'so hard a gale that wee could not bear out our lower tire of gunns [sic]'.[54] Monck decided to ignore their advice and order an attack. His perplexing choice echoes Obdam's reluctance to engage in favourable

51 'Van Ruyven aan Williamson, 20 Mei 1666', *Bescheiden uit Vreemde Archieven omtrent de Groote Nederlandsche Zeeoorlogen, Vol. 1: 1652–1667*, 310. Hainsworth and Churches, *The Anglo-Dutch Naval Wars*, 139.

52 'Albemarle aan Arlington, 7 Juni 1666', 'Notes upon the June Fight, 1666', in *Bescheiden uit Vreemde Archieven omtrent de Groote Nederlandsche Zeeoorlogen, Vol. I*, 317, 340.

53 'Notes upon the June Fight, 1666', 'Albemarle aan Arlington, 7 Juni 1666', 'The Narratives of the Duke of Albemarle and Prince Rupert, of the miscariadges of the late dutch war, 1667', 'Nieuwsbericht uit Haarlem, 31 Mei 1666', 'Nieuwsbericht uit Haarlem, 4 Juni 1666', *Bescheiden uit Vreemde Archieven omtrent de Groote Nederlandsche Zeeoorlogen, Vol. 1: 1652–1667*, 312, 313, 317, 340, 602.

54 '"AN ACCOUNT OF THE BATTELL" between the English and Dutch Fleets, on the 11th, 12th and 14th Days of June 1666', *Bescheiden uit Vreemde Archieven omtrent de Groote Nederlandsche Zeeoorlogen, Vol. 1*, 334.

winds prior to the Battle of Lowestoft. Both decisions were opposed by subordinate officers and, in subsequent weeks, widely derided by people of diverse classes and occupations. Both exacerbated the environmental vulnerabilities of the tactics and technologies used by a major naval power. Both decisions, reached in weather typical of the deepening Maunder Minimum, revealed that military elites did not always reach decisions that appropriately exploited shifting environmental circumstances.

Following Monck's order to engage, the English squadrons rushed towards the republic's fleet. The speed of the English assault in such high winds forced many Dutch crews to cut cables and abandon their anchors. Yet the headlong charge allowed the Dutch, now fighting in line formation, to concentrate their fire on the leading English ships. By elevating Dutch cannons relative to the water, the wind may also have increased their range. Before long, several English warships had been disabled or captured.[55] Faster vessels around Monck's flagship separated from their slower counterparts, undermining the force of the initial assault and allowing the Dutch to manoeuvre for the weather gage. Squadrons under De Ruyter and Cornelis Tromp, Maarten's son, surrounded Monck's division as the English struggled to avoid the coast of Flanders. Overall, at least three English ships were lost to the Dutch before the coming of darkness.

At first light the battle resumed. The English now fielded at most 45 ships, while the Dutch retained 80. Although the wind had shifted to blow from the east, the English claimed the weather gage owing to the position of the fleets. For most of the day, the English and Dutch squadrons passed one another in line formation. By the evening, the English were left with just 28 heavily damaged vessels, while the Dutch retained 66. This time, Monck listened to his subordinates. He chose to retreat while the Dutch, tacking for another pass, were roughly five kilometres distant. The Dutch fleet gave chase. In the night, the wind shifted again to blow from the northeast, but in conditions of near calm neither the English survivors nor their Dutch pursuers made much progress.[56]

[55] Michiel Adriaanszoon de Ruyter, 'Journal Kept by de Ruyter', in *The Second Dutch War: Described in Pictures & Manuscripts of the Time*, 24. '"AN ACCOUNT OF THE BATTELL" between the English and Dutch Fleets, on the 11th, 12th and 14th days of June 1666', 334. Hainsworth and Churches, *The Anglo-Dutch Naval Wars*, 142.

[56] 'A True Narrative of the Engagement between His Majesty's Fleet and That of Holland, begun June 11th 1666 at 2 a Clocke Afternoone and Continuing till the 14th at 10 a Clocke at Night', in *Bescheiden uit Vreemde Archieven omtrent de Groote Nederlandsche Zeeoorlogen, Vol. I*, 346. Hainsworth and Churches, *The Anglo-Dutch Naval Wars*, 145.

The Dutch continued the chase on 13 June, growing closer but remaining just out of reach. Suddenly, at 4:00 p.m., Rupert's squadron sailed into view. Rupert tried to unite his squadron with Monck's, but three of his heaviest ships ran aground on the Galloper Shoal. Although two of the ships escaped, the biggest – the *Royal Prince* – was stuck. Meanwhile, the easterly wind and the force of the tide pressed the rest of the fleet away from the stricken ship, while bringing the Dutch closer. The republic's fleet soon surrounded and burned the *Prince*. As night fell, the Dutch made for their coast. The English fleet was finally united, although diminished by the loss of the *Prince*.[57]

On the fourth day of the battle, the English pursued the Dutch with a fleet that was now of roughly equal strength. Although winds blew from the south-southwest, the republic's fleet had the weather gage as the battle resumed. After hours of indecisive fighting, the Dutch, now benefitting from a shift in wind to the south-southeast, divided and finally routed the English fleet. Yet the Dutch could not give chase for long, owing to thick fog and De Ruyter's belief that his battered fleet could not sustain much more fighting. Nevertheless, the Dutch had prevailed in the bloodiest battle of the war. Although English sources maintained that only 10 English vessels were lost, Dutch and Danish sources claimed that as many as 36 English ships were seized or destroyed. The Dutch, meanwhile, lost between four and eight ships.[58]

The Four Days' Battle, as it came to be known in both England and the Dutch Republic, played a critical role in exhausting English finances in the Second Anglo-Dutch War. It was influenced by a complex pattern of weather events that reflected, in part, the deepening Maunder Minimum. Cold, stormy weather delayed Dutch fleet preparations until faulty intelligence convinced Rupert that the French would soon unite with their Dutch allies. After Rupert departed, a persistent easterly helped the Dutch quickly cross the channel, just as Monck's remaining vessels were en route from the Thames to the Swin, where the Dutch could not have trapped them.

[57] De Ruyter, 'Journal Kept by de Ruyter', 24.

[58] De Ruyter, 'Journal Kept by de Ruyter', 25. Hainsworth and Churches, *The Anglo-Dutch Naval Wars*, 148. Jones, *The Anglo-Dutch Wars*, 170. Buisman, *Duizend jaar Vol. IV*, 607. 'The Narratives of the Duke of Albermarle and Prince Rupert', 'A True Narrative of the Engagement between His Majesty's Fleet and That of Holland', 'Hans Svendsen's Journal, 10–30 Juni 1666', 'Loose Reports, 11–15 Juni 1666', '"AN ACCOUNT OF THE BATTELL" between the English and Dutch Fleets, on the 11th, 12th and 14th Days of June 1666', 'Notes upon the June Fight, 1666', 'Thomas Langley aan Williamson, 14 Juni 1666', in *Bescheiden uit Vreemde Archieven omtrent de Groote Nederlandsche Zeeoorlogen, Vol. I*, 342, 344, 348, 350, 363, 602.

Monck's letters and subsequent actions suggest that he genuinely believed that his fleet could not escape the Dutch, so he opted to attack with the element of surprise, even if his ships were less effective in high winds. His decision was disastrous, yet the arrival of Rupert's fresh squadron evened the odds. Because the fleets were now equally matched, the easterly that thwarted English attempts to aid the *Royal Prince*, a first-rate, was invaluable for the Dutch. Conversely, thick fog helped preserve what was left of the English fleet. Unlike the spring of 1665, the summer of 1666 had been unusually hot, a statistical outlier in the general trend of cool summers that characterized the deepening Maunder Minimum. Water both absorbs and loses heat more slowly than air. Heavy fog may have followed from interactions between unusually hot air brought north by the southwesterly wind, and water previously chilled by cooler weather.[59]

After the Four Days' Battle, the English naval system approached financial exhaustion. In late summer, the reassembled English fleet did manage to stalemate the Dutch in the St James' Day Battle, and raid Dutch merchant shipping near the republic's Zuiderzee islands. On 11 September, however, a severe easterly gale scattered the English fleet while the Dutch armada sheltered off the Flemish coast. As English crews struggled to reassemble their fleet on the following day, Thomas Allin wrote that he had 'heard ... of a great fire begun in London'. A blaze had indeed erupted in a bakery on the eastern fringe of London, and soon spread to nearby buildings. A heat wave and drought – conditions that should have been less likely in the climate of the Maunder Minimum – had dried the largely wooden infrastructure of cities across Europe.[60]

Moreover, the same persistent easterly winds that scattered the English fleet drove the fire west from eastern London along the shores of the Thames and deep into the city. Samuel Pepys in London wrote that the flames incinerated people, animals, and property, with 'the wind mighty high and driving [the fire] into the city'. According to John Evelyn, the fire ultimately resembled a 'hideous storm', with the flames thundering and the sky 'like the top of a burning Oven'. The Fire of London was largely extinguished by 16 September, although the rubble continued smouldering into March of the following year. More than 13,000 houses had been

[59] Van Engelen, Buisman, and IJnsen, 'A Millennium of Weather, Winds and Water in the Low Countries', 112.

[60] Franz Matthias Mauelshagen, *Klimageschichte der Neuzeit: 1500–1900*. (Darmstadt: Wiss. Buchges., 2010), 129. Parker, *Global Crisis*, 62.

destroyed across 400 acres. Coupled with the damage inflicted upon the English fleet, the financial toll of the fire crippled the English war effort.[61]

The long and severe winter of early 1667 yet again delayed the assembly and departure of the Dutch fleet. However, when the armada finally sortied on 6 June, it had no English rival to challenge its supremacy of the North Sea. Parliament had refused to approve new funds for the war. Naval vessels had been cannibalized for supplies during the cold winter, unpaid mariners deserted in droves, and the fleet's largest ships had been towed to apparent safety up the river Medway. Nevertheless, the crown continued to reject Dutch terms in peace negotiations, trusting that fortifications and a colossal chain at Gillingham near the mouth of the Medway would protect the core of the English fleet. De Witt, who had urged Tromp to raid the Thames in the First Anglo-Dutch War, now insisted that De Ruyter enter the Medway. On 17 June, the Dutch fleet arrived off the English coast and exploited a rising northeasterly wind to overwhelm the fortress of Sheerness on the mouth of the Medway. Too late, the English admiralty scrambled to reinforce its defences at Gillingham. To keep the Dutch from breaking through the chain, English sailors tried to create an underwater barrier by sinking ships in the shallow waters nearby. Yet they could not finish the barrier on time because the wind and tide kept them from sinking the *Sancta Maria* in the right place.[62]

A Dutch squadron under Admiral van Ghent arrived at Gillingham on 22 June. The easterly wind combined with the spring tide to press the Dutch ships against the chain. When it gave way, the squadron passed through the gap that might have been filled by the *Maria*. By the evening of 23 June, Dutch sailors had taken or burned the flagships of the English fleet. On the following day, Charles ordered his negotiators to drop outstanding English demands. On 31 July, English and Dutch diplomats signed a peace based on the pre-war status quo.[63]

[61] Thomas Allin, *The Journals of Sir Thomas Allin, Vol. I, 1660–1666*, 287. Samuel Pepys, 'Sunday 2 September 1666', *Diary of Sir Samuel Pepys*. Buisman, *Duizend jaar Vol. IV*, 608. Wenceslaus Hollar, 'Plan of London before the fire', map, 1665, Thomas Fisher Rare Book Library, University of Toronto, http://goo.gl/cqvf2U.

[62] Hainsworth and Churches, *The Anglo-Dutch Naval Wars*, 157.

[63] Jones, *The Anglo-Dutch Wars*, 177. Buisman, *Duizend jaar Vol. IV*, 615. 'Narratives of the Miscarriages in the Dutch War'. *The Second Dutch War: Described in Pictures & Manuscripts of the Time.* (London: Her Majesty's Stationery Office, 1667), 38. 'Dutch Account in Deposition to Dutch Magistrate'. *The Second Dutch War: Described in Pictures & Manuscripts of the Time.* (London: Her Majesty's Stationery Office, 1667), 40. 'Hans Svendsen's Journaal, 22 Juni-25 Aug. 1667', 'John Conny aan Williamson, 24

The Dutch largely benefitted from the weather of the deepening Maunder Minimum in their struggle with England. However, the Second Anglo-Dutch War in particular revealed that climate change and weather rarely influenced military activities in straightforward ways. In naval hierarchies, individuals could reach decisions that nuanced or even overturned the expected human consequences of global climate changes. Ironically, military histories that incorporate big, impersonal forces, such as climate change, can actually highlight the enduring importance of human choices on the smallest scales.

THE THIRD ANGLO-DUTCH WAR: 1672–1674

In the final year of the Second Anglo-Dutch War, French troops invaded the Spanish Netherlands and again raised the prospect of a strong army on the borders of the republic. Alarmed, the States-General threatened to intervene unless the French withdrew. Louis XIV consented in 1668, but he never forgave the supposed treachery of his former ally. In 1670, he convinced Charles II to sign the secret Treaty of Dover, which laid out how the English and French would support one another on land and at sea in a decisive war against the Dutch. The plan hatched by Louis, Charles, and their advisors imagined a massive French invasion, with English reinforcements, that would overwhelm the republic's long-neglected army. An allied armada would simultaneously defeat the outnumbered Dutch fleet and impose a blockade.[64]

By the time Charles and Louis were ready for war, seven new great ships strengthened the English fleet. By contrast, little had changed for the Dutch since the raid on the Medway five years earlier. The main difference for the combatants between the third and second wars was the nature of French involvement. In the Second Anglo-Dutch War, Louis XIV never seriously intended to risk his nascent fleet in battle, yet by 1670 the French naval system had matured. With Louis committed to joining the war at

Juni 1667', 'Chatham River. Narrative per Richard Tyler', 'Leijonbergh aan Karel XI, 24 Juni 1667', 'Adriaen de Haese aan zijn broeder in Indie,18 Juli 1667', 'Edward Gregory aan Pepys, 15 Aug. 1667', 'James Norman aan Pepys, 17 Aug. 1667', *Bescheiden uit Vreemde Archieven omtrent de Groote Nederlandsche Zeeoorlogen, Vol. 1*, 544, 549, 553, 568, 585, 587. Bruijn, *The Dutch Navy of the Seventeenth and Eighteenth Centuries*, 88.

[64] Paul Sonnino, *Louix XIV and the Origins of the Dutch War.* (Cambridge: Cambridge University Press, 2003), 23.

sea, the republic's fleet of 62 large vessels faced an allied flotilla that contained 74 ships of fourth rate and higher.[65]

On land, the unrivalled French army, which numbered 144,000 soldiers in 1672, faced the same prospect that had daunted the Army of Flanders exactly one century earlier. Any invasion from the south would be slowed by the tedious necessity of seizing one Dutch town after another. Dutch river defences, while badly neglected, could still transform any invasion into a grinding battle of attrition. The allied plan adopted in July of 1671 therefore imagined an invasion from the southeast that would outflank the bulk of the republic's static defences. Efforts to secure the neutrality of Cologne and Münster, vital for any attempt on the republic's eastern defences, culminated with both states pledging to join the invasion.[66]

In 1672, the Dutch Republic was utterly unprepared for war. A year earlier, abundant rain had raised water levels in the IJssel and Waal, the main tributaries of the Rhine, so that at least some Dutch citizens felt secure from invasion. Easterlies, storms, and frigid temperatures prevailed during the winter of 1671–1672. Yet in the spring, wet weather typical of the Maunder Minimum gave way to drought. Not even thawing ice could raise water levels, which according to Van der Goes were lower in March than anyone could remember. The IJssel was especially dry, as drought exacerbated gradual changes in the morphology of the river that had reduced its outflow and channelled more water into the Waal. The States-General conceded that the republic was open to invasion.[67]

In the second week of April 1672, England and France declared war within days of one another, plunging the republic into its *rampjaar*, the 'year of disaster'. Louis XIV personally led his army through the Spanish Netherlands, where dry roads quickened the advance of its 25,000 horses and 1,000 cannons. With scarcely a quarter of the soldiers fielded by the French, the republic's States Army could not defend the eastern frontier from concerted attack. Efforts to create an inundation zone around the

[65] Hainsworth and Churches, *The Anglo-Dutch Naval Wars*, 169. Jones, *The Anglo-Dutch Wars*, 184.

[66] Sonnino, *Louix XIV and the Origins of the Dutch War*, 12. Lynn, *Giant of the Grand Siècle*, 46.

[67] Claas Arisz. Caescoper, '10 Mart 1672', in *Nootijsye Boeck, anno 1669–1678, ofte Joernael*. Tol and Langen, 'A Concise History of Dutch River Floods', 363. Van der Goes, 'Hage, den 30 January 1671', in *Briefwisseling tusschen de gebroeders van der Goes (1659–1673) Vol. II*, 183. 'The Old World Drought Atlas'. Accessed 28 June 2016, http://iridl.ldeo.columbia.edu/expert/home/.jennie/.PDSI/.OWDA/.pdsi/figviewer.html.

IJssel, a tributary of the Rhine, failed due to low water levels and the resistance of farmers unwilling to sacrifice their land.[68]

Meanwhile, De Ruyter and De Witt understood that the republic's only hope for achieving superiority at sea lay in its fleet leaving port early in the year and defeating either the English or French fleets before they had a chance to unite. However, incessant gales kept the bulk of the Dutch fleet in port until the end of April. By the time the fleet crossed the channel, the English had already left for the Isle of Wight. With the Dutch nowhere in sight, the English and French fleets united on 7 May. Persistent easterly winds then delayed the allied fleet until 17 May, and De Witt urged his admirals to take advantage of the opportunity by again raiding the Medway. Yet when Admiral van Ghent led a squadron to the fortress of Sheerness, he found it far better defended than it had been in 1667. At last, on 5 June, the Dutch fleet used an easterly wind to surprise the allied fleet as it took on supplies off Sole Bay. Some sailors in the fleet had expected that the Dutch would attack if the wind blew from the east, yet their commanders were unprepared for battle. The Dutch lost two middling vessels but severely damaged the French squadron and sank the mammoth *Royal James* before deepening fog, a rising gale, and the coming of darkness ended the battle. It was a remarkable outcome, considering the numerical disparity between the fleets. In the first months of the Third Anglo-Dutch War, storms and easterlies typical of the Maunder Minimum often benefitted, but occasionally undermined, the republic's naval operations.[69]

De Ruyter understood that the allies needed to destroy the Dutch fleet before the republic could be invaded from the sea. Otherwise, their defenceless troop transports would be easy prey for Dutch warships. The Dutch fleet therefore needed only to survive and occasionally check the free reign of the allies in the North Sea. De Ruyter settled on a strategy that exploited

[68] Buisman, *Duizend jaar Vol. IV*, 645. Jones, *The Anglo-Dutch Wars*, 186. Rodger, *The Command of the Ocean*, 82. Israel, *The Dutch Republic*, 794. Tol and Langen, 'A Concise History of Dutch River Floods', 361.

[69] Narbrough, 'Journal of John Narbrough, Captain of the *Fairfax*. September 18, 1672, to July 1, 1673', 90. 'Hildebrand aan Williamson, 12 Mei 1672', in *Bescheiden uit Vreemde Archieven omtrent de Groote Nederlandsche Zeeoorlogen, Vol. II*, 93. Hainsworth and Churches, *The Anglo-Dutch Naval Wars*, 172. Robert Fruin, *De oorlog van 1672*. (Groningen: Wolters-Noordhoff 1972), 110. P. G. Vonk, *De Victorieuze Zeeslag op Schoneveld: het hol van de Ruyter*, 57. Jones, *The Anglo-Dutch Wars*, 191. Buisman, *Duizend jaar Vol. IV*, 646. Gerard Brandt, *Uit het Leven en Bedrijf van den here Michiel de Ruiter*, 236. 'Hildebrand aan Williamson, 12 Mei 1672', *Bescheiden uit Vreemde Archieven omtrent de Groote Nederlandsche Zeeoorlogen, Vol. II: 1667–1676*, ed. H. T. Colenbrander, 93. Bruijn, *The Dutch Navy of the Seventeenth and Eighteenth Centuries*, 89.

the shallow hulls of his ships by keeping the Dutch fleet behind shoals the allied ships could not pass over. The fleet would sail from these shoals to attack only in high, easterly winds, when it would have the weather gage and the allies would not be able to open all their gun ports.[70]

On land, the tactical situation was growing desperate. On 22 May, the French army under Louis and his general Condé used a bridge of ships to cross the shallow Maas at Visé, bypassing the fortifications of Maastricht. On the morning of 12 June, 6,000 French cavalry exploited low water levels to easily cross the Rhine. Hastily assembled Friesian defenders engaged them as soon as they reached the shore. The French prevailed and then built bridges to accommodate their army's artillery and infantry. Were the Rhine deeper, the French cavalry could only have crossed by bridge. The republic's defenders might have hindered its construction and so delayed a crossing.[71]

Upon hearing that the French had made it over the Rhine, the States-General and the States of Holland decided to abandon the IJssel line and concentrate their resources on defending the core provinces of Utrecht, Zeeland, and Holland. However, French armies quickly besieged Utrecht and approached the borders of Holland and Zeeland. The States-General sued for peace, offering the Generality Lands on the republic's southern border in addition to Maastricht and an extraordinary indemnity of 10 million livres. Louis, however, would agree to a separate peace only in exchange for Gelderland, Overijssel, and Utrecht. Since peace on those terms would have effectively ended the independence of the republic, peace negotiations came to nothing. On 8 June, the order was given to engage the Hollandic Water Line: a vast crescent of sluices, fortresses, and flooded land that would provide the coastal cities with their last and best defence. Engineers and labourers breached dikes and opened sluices in some areas while building new dikes in others. Brackish water inundated great swaths of farmland, diminishing their productivity long after they were drained.[72]

[70] Vonk, *De Victorieuze Zeeslag op Schoneveld: het hol van de Ruyter*, 113. Hainsworth and Churches, *The Anglo-Dutch Naval Wars*, 180. Bruijn, *The Dutch Navy of the Seventeenth and Eighteenth Centuries*, 89.

[71] 'Samuel Tucker aan Williamson, 17 Juni 1672', in *Bescheiden uit Vreemde Archieven omtrent de Groote Nederlandsche Zeeoorlogen, Vol. II*, 131. Buisman, *Duizend jaar Vol. IV*, 647. Israel, *The Dutch Republic*, 797. Jones, *The Anglo-Dutch Wars*, 187.

[72] Johan de Witt, 'Aan Cornelis de Witt. 20 Juni 1672'. In *Brieven van John de Witt: Vierde Deel, 1670–1672*, ed. Robert Fruin. (Amsterdam: Johannes Müller, 1913), 387. 'Nieuwsbericht uit Amsterdam, 20 Juni 1672', in *Bescheiden uit Vreemde Archieven omtrent de Groote Nederlandsche Zeeoorlogen, Vol. II*, 132. Buisman, *Duizend jaar*

Opening sluices and breaching dikes did not immediately engage the water line. Many peasants bitterly resisted the inundations, just as they had during the Wars of Independence. Fearing peasant mobs, the magistrate of Gouda delayed opening nearby sluices until the States-General finally threatened to use force. Farmers near the river Lek repeatedly drained inundated land under cover of darkness. Peasant resistance ended only when the States-General imposed the death penalty for sabotaging the water line. Even then, critical fortifications remained in poor repair, and low water levels in the enduring drought continued to slow the pace of flooding. For two critical weeks after its sluices were opened, the water line could be easily crossed while the French army waited just 20 kilometres from Amsterdam. As the French did nothing, drought yielded to rain, while favourable winds fanned the rising waters. Once again, human decisions interacted in counterintuitive ways with a web of environmental, social, and cultural conditions to shape the course of war. Louis XIV believed that he had already won and therefore continued to insist on unreasonable terms before ordering his army to press on. Yet the character of the war had fundamentally changed when the water line was finally ready. The amphibious struggle that characterized the rest of the *rampjaar* would be fought on terms more familiar to the Dutch.[73]

Still, social unrest swept through the republic. Refugees poured into coastal towns, farmers rioted against the floods, and city councils considered surrender. Popular fury at the republic's lack of preparation for invasion ultimately ended the period of True Freedom. In July, the States of Holland and Zeeland formally appointed William III as Stadtholder.

Vol. IV, 647. Israel, *The Dutch Republic*, 798. Jones, *The Anglo-Dutch Wars*, 188. Petra Dreiskämper, *Redeloos, radeloos, reddeloos: de geschiedenis van het rampjaar 1672*. (Hilversum: Uitgeverij Verloren, 1998), 47. Israel, *The Dutch Republic*, 798. Luc Panhuysen, *Rampjaar 1672. Hoe de republiek aan de ondergang ontsnapte*. (Amsterdam: Atlas, 2009), 12. 'Kaart van het ontwerp van een waterlinie tot dekking van de provincie Holland van Muiden aan de Zuiderzee langs de Vecht naar Weesp, Uitermeer, Hinderdam, langs Woerden, Oudenwater, Schoonhoven, Everdingen, Asperen tot Gorinchem aan de Mewede'. Kaartcollectie Ministerie van Oorlog, Situatiekaarten. Reference code: 4. Nationaal Archief (The Hague, Netherlands). Gottschalk, *Stormvloeden en rivieroverstromingen in Nederland, Vol. III*, 240. Lynn, *The Wars of Louis XIV 1667–1714*, 115.

[73] De Witt, 'Aan Cornelis de Witt. 20 Juni 1672', in *Brieven van John de Witt: Vierde Deel*, 387. Baron de W., 'Baron de W. aan Arlington, 14 Aug. 1672', in *Bescheiden uit Vreemde Archieven omtrent de Groote Nederlandsche Zeeoorlogen, Vol. II*, 174. Van der Goes, 'Den 1sten Augusti 1672', in *Briefwisseling tusschen de gebroeders van der Goes (1659–1673) Vol. II*, 389. Buisman, *Duizend jaar Vol. IV*, 649. Dreiskämper, *Redeloos, radeloos, reddeloos*, 46. Fruin, *De oorlog van 1672*, 174.

In the following month, a mob brutally murdered the De Witt brothers, probably with William's consent. Rainy weather prevailed for most of August, and strengthened the water line as a defensive barrier. German troops besieged the northern city of Groningen, yet cold, wet, and stormy conditions left local roads impassable and flooded trenches dug by the invaders. Inundations drowned as many as 2,000 Münsterite troops, and on 28 August their siege ended in failure. Torrential rain provided breathing room for the republic as its internal divisions violently resolved themselves.[74]

The water line turned Holland into an artificial island, flanked by the largely natural islands of Zeeland to the south, and Friesland, isolated by marshland, to the north. With the front temporarily stabilized, the most immediate danger came from the sea. A third of the Dutch fleet had been decommissioned so that its guns and marines could be used to resist the allied invasion. By 4 July, however, English shipyards had repaired the damage their fleet suffered at Sole Bay. The Anglo-French armada could now blockade the Dutch coast and support a naval invasion, and the Dutch fleet lacked the strength to confront it.[75]

On 4 July, Captain Narbrough reported that 'blowing weather hinders the taking in our provisions; otherwise the fleet might have been out [sooner]'. The wind relented on the following day, but when it resumed it blew at Beaufort 8 (between 63 km/h and 74 km/h). On 8 July, Rupert penned a letter to allied commanders with secret instructions should storms scatter their vessels. Ironically, for two days high winds kept Rupert's subordinates from boarding boats and taking the letter to other ships. On 11 July, the wind rose again to blow at 63 km/h to 74 km/h. It persisted until, on 14 July, a ferocious storm with winds at Beaufort 11 (103 to 117 km/h) drove the allied ships forward while inflicting damage and casualties. At sunset on the next day, with the gale continuing, Narbrough wrote that 'the clouds this evening ... were dark, heavy, hanging like great fleeces of wool ... throughout the whole hemisphere'.[76]

[74] Van der Goes, 'Den 1sten Augusti 1672', in *Briefwisseling tusschen de gebroeders van der Goes (1659–1673) Vol. II*, 388. Huneken, 'Huneken aan den Raad van Lubeck, 22 Aug. 1672', in *Bescheiden uit Vreemde Archieven omtrent de Groote Nederlandsche Zeeoorlogen, Vol. II*, 184. Buisman, *Duizend jaar Vol. IV*, 649. Israel, *The Dutch Republic*, 800.

[75] 'Samuel Tucker aan Williamson, 17 Juni 1672', *Bescheiden uit Vreemde Archieven omtrent de Groote Nederlandsche Zeeoorlogen, Vol. II*, 131.

[76] Narbrough, 'Journal of John Narbrough, Lieutenant and Captain of the *Prince*. January 7, 1671/2, to September 18, 1672 Pepysian MS. 2555', in *Journals and Narratives of the Third Dutch War*, 114.

The gales of early July badly disrupted allied attempts to get to sea, but they only provided a taste of what was to come. For nearly a year, unrelenting storminess would hamper allied naval operations. After an attempt to capture an inbound VOC fleet failed in incessant gales, on 6 August Narbrough described continued 'gusty, stormy weather' and concluded that 'never [was] such weather known in these seas at this time of the year before now'.[77] When the gale finally abated on 13 August, English commanders decided to return to port with nothing but damage and casualties to show for their time at sea. High winds and two further storms plagued the fleet until over a thousand sick men could be brought ashore on 23 August. On 24 August, a Dutch traitor informed his English masters that 'this foule weather by sea and land [the Dutch] attribut (as they have reason) to a great providence'.[78] Nevertheless, that evening Narbrough described 'a small air of wind at E.N.E. [East North East]', before concluding: 'thus ended this 24 hours – fair weather – a miracle'.[79] The respite ended just days later, and for much of September persistent stormy weather hampered English attempts to refit their fleet. When a squadron under Admiral Edward Spragge finally left port on 28 September, storms swiftly scattered it. In subsequent weeks, individual men of war returned with a total of only 20 small herring busses, a tiny portion of the Dutch fishing fleet and not nearly enough to improve the increasingly dismal condition of English finances.[80]

As autumn gave way to winter, storms continued to undermine the few naval operations still attempted by the allies. In October and November, Narbrough recorded at least 12 gales, all of which sustained winds at Beaufort (BF) 10 or 11 (89 km/h to 117 km/h) and forced his vessel from the Dutch coast. The autumn storminess of 1672 was exceptional even in the context of the Maunder Minimum. In December, as Narbrough sailed in convoys through the English Channel, he recorded ferocious storms that followed one another with little respite. On 28 December, his fleet

[77] Narbrough, 'Journal of John Narbrough, Lieutenant and Captain of the *Prince*. January 7, 1671/2, to September 18, 1672', 126. Hainsworth and Churches, *The Anglo-Dutch Naval Wars*, 179.

[78] Baron de. W., 'Baron de W. aan Arlington, 14 Aug 1672', *Bescheiden uit Vreemde Archieven omtrent de Groote Nederlandsche Zeeoorlogen, Vol. II*, 176.

[79] Narbrough, 'Journal of John Narbrough, Lieutenant and Captain of the *Prince*. January 7, 1671/2, to September 18, 1672', 146. Hainsworth and Churches, *The Anglo-Dutch Naval Wars*, 179.

[80] Narbrough, 'Journal of John Narbrough, Lieutenant and Captain of the *Fairfax*', 126. Hainsworth and Churches, *The Anglo-Dutch Naval Wars*, 179. Jones, *The Anglo-Dutch Wars*, 192.

survived a storm that raged for perhaps 13 days. During the gale, Narbrough's rushed entries offered little weather information. At last, on 10 January Narbrough wrote that it had been impossible to work owing to the heavy seas. 'On board fifty five men very sick of a violent fever', he reported, 'some distracted with it'. Relentless storms continued to scatter allied convoys into February.[81]

Overall, logbooks kept by English captains during the Third Anglo-Dutch War recorded a remarkable quantity of storms and high winds. Narbrough, Richard Haddock, George Legge, and the captain of the *Mary Rose* wrote 1,078 morning and evening weather observations between 7 January 1672 and 21 September 1673 that can be easily translated into modern Beaufort values. Of these measurements, more than half – 552, to be exact – recorded winds at or above BF 8, a bracing 63 to 74 km/h. Such winds would have prohibited battle and limited the possibilities open to naval commanders. Logs reported storms with winds at or above BF 10 – approximately 89 to 102 km/h – on 156 days, in over 14 per cent of entries. In other words, sailors in the war endured, on average, one truly ferocious storm every week.[82]

In the Low Countries, storms also hindered the first counteroffensives attempted by the States Army. Yet at the same time, heavy rain deepened the water line and made it more effective as a defensive barrier. In the winter, many within the republic feared that the water line would freeze more quickly than its ice could be broken, which would finally permit a French invasion. However, only in December did temperatures drop low enough for ice to support a French raid near The Hague, and thawing soon forced the French to withdraw. Both the moderate winter of 1672/1673

[81] Narbrough, 'Journal of John Narbrough, Lieutenant and Captain of the *Fairfax*. September 18, 1672, to July 1, 1673', 126.

[82] George Legge, 'Journal of George Legge, Captain of the *Royal Katherine*. March 9 1672/3 to September 14, 1673. Dartmouth MS. II', in *Journals and Narratives of the Third Dutch War*, 298. Richard Haddock, 'Journal of Richard Haddock, Captain of the *Royal Charles* and the *Sovereign*. May 11 1673 to June 29, 1673. Egerton MS 2521', in *Journals and Narratives of the Third Dutch War*, 334. Narbrough, 'Journal of John Narbrough, Lieutenant and Captain of the *Prince*. January 7, 1671/2, to September 18, 1672. Pepysian MS. 2555', in *Journals and Narratives of the Third Dutch War*, ed. 108. Narbrough, 'Journal of John Narbrough, Captain of the *Fairfax*. September 18, 1672, to July 1, 1673. Pepysian MS. 2556', in *Journals and Narratives of the Third Dutch War*, ed. 200. Narbrough, 'Journal of John Narbrough, Captain of the *St. Michael*. July 1, 1673 to September 21, 1673. Pepysian MS. 2556', in *Journals and Narratives of the Third Dutch War*, ed. 339. 'Mary Rose 1672–1675'. ADM 51/588. National Archives at Kew (London, United Kingdom). Herrera et al., *CLIWOC Multilingual Meteorological Dictionary*, 32.

and the dry spring of 1672 show that individual seasons during the Maunder Minimum rarely featured all the meteorological characteristics of a cooler climate. Weather that was less common in the Maunder Minimum influenced both the collapse of the republic's outer defences in the spring and the resilience of its inner defences in the winter.[83]

By the spring of 1673, the republic had survived its *rampjaar* and recovered some of its territorial losses. Meanwhile, the English crown could no longer finance a war that had grown increasingly unpopular at home. Charles therefore pinned his hopes on a decisive confrontation at sea, which would permit a naval invasion that would force the republic's surrender. As storms came less frequently in the summer, the Dutch armada returned to full strength. De Ruyter kept his fleet behind shoals and attacked only when easterly winds allowed him to compensate for the disparity in numbers by concentrating his forces where the allied fleet was strongest. In June, persistent easterlies allowed the republic's fleet to surprise the allies near Dutch waters, in engagements at Schooneveld off modern-day Flanders and, one week later, before the Schelde. Repeated gales and Dutch cannons damaged the allied ships and forced their crews back to English ports.[84]

As the English naval system neared financial exhaustion, the allied fleet returned to the waters off Schooneveld on 31 July before sailing north to intercept an incoming VOC convoy. Dutch admirals understood that to save the convoy, they would have to risk fighting the allies far from the safety of their shoals. On 2 August, William III instructed De Ruyter to engage anyway, believing that the English war effort would not survive another costly battle. When the fleets met off Texel on 18 August, the wind shifted to blow from the east. De Ruyter and his subordinates used the weather gage to divide and defeat the allies. Miscommunication between English and French squadrons during the battle poisoned allied relations, and the Dutch fleet seized control of the North Sea.

[83] Van der Goes, 'Hage, den 2 January 1673', in *Briefwisseling tusschen de gebroeders van der Goes (1659–1673) Vol. II*, 443. Buisman, *Duizend jaar Vol. IV*, 665. Israel, *The Dutch Republic*, 812. Vonk, *De Victorieuze Zeeslag op Schoneveld: het hol van de Ruyter*, 65.

[84] Edward Spragge, 'Journal of Sir Edward Spragge', in *Journals and Narratives of the Third Dutch War*, 319. Legge, 'Journal of George Legge', in *Journals and Narratives of the Third Dutch War*, 300. Gerard Brandt, *Uit het Leven en Bedrijf van den here Michiel de Ruiter*, 285. Jeremy Smith, 'Account of the Hoys and Boats taken Up by the Navy for the Landing of Soldiers'. ADM 106/281, Folio 52. National Archives at Kew (London, United Kingdom). Hainsworth and Churches, *The Anglo-Dutch Naval Wars*, 180. Jones, *The Anglo-Dutch Wars*, 206.

On 19 February 1674, the English government broke with Louis XIV by signing a separate peace that amounted to a humiliating confirmation of the status quo. Weather that bore the partial imprint of the Maunder Minimum made the republic's unlikely victory possible by enabling Dutch commanders to pursue audacious strategies on land and at sea.[85]

THE GLORIOUS REVOLUTION: 1688

The Dutch may have won the Third Anglo-Dutch War, but France remained at war with the republic. Privateers devastated Dutch merchant shipping, tariffs hindered Dutch commerce, and in 1677 a French army invaded the Spanish Netherlands. William countered by marrying Mary Stuart, Charles's daughter, and signing a treaty that established a closer bond between England and the Dutch Republic. At last, on 10 August 1678, the republic signed a peace treaty at Nijmegen that entrenched France in the southern Low Countries but reversed Dutch territorial losses, safeguarded Dutch merchant shipping, and lowered French tariffs.[86]

Meanwhile, colonial trades in the Americas and Asia started to transform England's economy so that it more closely resembled that of the republic. From 1640 to 1686, English merchant shipping doubled in tonnage. Between 1660 and 1700, imports and exports expanded by at least 600 per cent. Manufacturing and commerce boomed, so that by 1700 they together accounted for a third of England's national product, just as they did in the Dutch Republic. Industries firmly established in the Dutch Republic – such as shipbuilding and sugar refining – now took root and blossomed in England. English urbanization rose to 40 per cent in 1700, approaching the highest rates reached by the Dutch Republic at the peak of its Golden Age. Technological innovations that enabled

[85] Spragge, 'Journal of Sir Edward Spragge', in *Journals and Narratives of the Third Dutch War*, 329. Narbrough, 'Journal of John Narbrough, Captain of the *St. Michael*', in *Journals and Narratives of the Third Dutch War*, 361. 'Nieuwsbericht uit Amsterdam, 21 Aug. 1673', 'A Relation of the Battle Fought', 'A Breefe Relation of the Engagement', Narbrough, 'Captain Narbrough's Relation of the Battle', 'A Relation of the French Squadron', 'Nieuwsbericht uit Amsterdam', in *Bescheiden uit Vreemde Archieven omtrent de Groote Nederlandsche Zeeoorlogen, Vol. II*, 303, 306, 309, 312, 325, 330. Buisman, *Duizend jaar Vol. IV*, 664. Jones, *The Anglo-Dutch Wars*, 209. Hainsworth and Churches, *The Anglo-Dutch Naval Wars*, 187. Bruijn, *The Dutch Navy of the Seventeenth and Eighteenth Centuries*, 89.

[86] Israel, *The Dutch Republic*, 825. Lynn, *The Wars of Louis XIV*, 156. Dale Hoak, 'The Anglo-Dutch Revolution of 1688–89'. In *The World of William and Mary: Anglo-Dutch Perspectives on the Revolution, of 1688–89*, eds. Dale Hoak and Mordechai Feingold. (Stanford: Stanford University Press, 1996), 25.

everything from drainage projects to street lighting flowed from the republic to England. English observers clearly understood that they were 'going Dutch', as Lisa Jardine and Steve Pincus have put it, by adopting the most dynamic elements of an economy that had long outperformed its European rivals.[87]

Yet it was not English commercial successes but rather the prospect of England again allying itself with ascendant France that most concerned William. When Charles II died in 1685, his Catholic brother, James II, took the throne. The new king worked to repeal anti-Catholic legislation and installed Catholic supporters in positions of power. Surging crown revenues gave him a great deal of independence from parliament, and there was little prospect of him surrendering that freedom by joining William III in a costly war against Louis XIV, a fellow Catholic. Worst of all, in 1688 James's Catholic wife, Mary of Modena, gave birth to a son. Until then, Mary Stuart had been next in line to the English throne, and her reign would have brought England into close alliance with the Dutch Republic. Yet now it dawned on William that England had embarked on a permanent path towards Catholicism and perhaps even alliance with France. William and his advisors concluded that the only chance of saving the republic lay in a desperate invasion of England. They would force James to make the English 'useful to their friends and allies, and especially to this state'.[88]

Beginning in June, William and his subordinates began assembling a vast armament in the port cities of the republic. Preparations proceeded at a pace that astonished European observers. By October, the Dutch invasion fleet numbered 463 ships, which carried 40,000 soldiers and sailors along with 6,000 horses. In all, the fleet had nearly four times

[87] Steve Pincus, *1688: The First Modern Revolution.* (New Haven: Yale University Press, 2009), 82. C. G. A. Clay, *Economic Expansion and Social Change, Vol. I: England 1500–1700.* (Cambridge: Cambridge University Press, 1984), 170. Joyce Oldham Appleby, *Economic Thought and Ideology in Seventeenth-Century England.* (Princeton: Princeton University Press, 1978), 97. L. S. Multhauf, 'The Light of Lamp-Lanterns: Street Lighting in 17th-Century Amsterdam'. *Technology and Culture* 26 (1985): 236. John Houghton, 'England's Great Happiness'. (London: J. M. for Edward Croft, 1677). Edmund Gibson, *Camden's Britannia.* (London: F. Collins for A. Swalle and A. and J. Churchill, 1695), sig. [A2r].

[88] Craig Rose, *England in the 1690s: Revolution, Religion and War.* (Oxford: Blackwell Publishers Ltd., 1999), 3. Rodger, *The Command of the Ocean*, 136. Hoak, 'The Anglo-Dutch Revolution of 1688–89', 20. Israel, 'The Dutch Role in the Glorious Revolution', 120. Jonathan I. Israel, 'General Introduction'. In *The Anglo-Dutch Moment: Essays on the Glorious Revolution and Its World Impact*, ed. Jonathan I. Israel. (Cambridge: Cambridge University Press, 1991), 23.

as many ships, and twice as many soldiers, as the Spanish armada that had daunted England exactly one century earlier. It was 'a fleet the like of which has never been seen', marvelled contemporary Florentine historian Gregorio Leti. England's ambassador in The Hague agreed. The Dutch intended the 'absolute conquest' of England, he wrote, and had therefore made preparations on a scale 'never heard of in these parts of the world'.[89]

Yet from the start, the invasion had vanishingly slim odds of succeeding. First, James had assembled an army that, on paper, was nearly double the size of William's invasion force, although Dutch troops had greater experience and better equipment. William understood that the success of his invasion would depend on a popular uprising. He therefore hired thousands of disaffected English soldiers to give the impression that the invasion was a revolution that soldiers, nobles, and commoners could support without betraying their king. Powerful English dissidents also occupied important positions in the fleet, provided essential financial support, and helped William craft propaganda that appealed to English Protestants.[90]

Second, the English fleet, while outnumbered, remained formidable. Conventional military thinking held that an invasion could only succeed once the fleet had been decisively defeated. Yet William hoped to avoid battle with the English fleet, since it would undermine propaganda that framed his invasion as an indigenous revolution. He therefore added to his gamble by ordering Dutch troop transports to travel with the fleet. They would be helpless if a battle broke out at sea.[91]

Third, the French made it clear that they would view an invasion as an act of war against France. However, in September, the French army committed itself to an invasion of the Rhineland, and it would not be able to reach the republic until the following summer. Just in case, William hired mercenaries who quadrupled the size of the Dutch army. The new

[89] Lisa Jardine, *Going Dutch: How England Plundered Holland's Glory*. (New York: Harper Collins Publishers, 2008), 9. Hoak, 'The Anglo-Dutch Revolution of 1688–89', 17. Rose, *England in the 1690s*, 6. Rodger, *The Command of the Ocean*, 137. Israel and Parker, 'Of Providence and Protestant Winds', 351.

[90] Pincus, *1688: The First Modern Revolution*, 225, 234. Israel and Parker, 'Of Providence and Protestant Winds', 355. Jonathan I. Israel, 'The Dutch Role in the Glorious Revolution'. In *The Anglo-Dutch Moment: Essays on the Glorious Revolution and Its World Impact*, ed. Jonathan I. Israel. (Cambridge: Cambridge University Press, 1991), 125.

[91] Rodger, *The Command of the Ocean*, 136.

hires would stay behind to defend the borders of the republic from France.[92]

Fourth, merchants with little interest in supporting William's costly military adventures dominated the key legislative bodies of the republic: the States-General, the States of Holland, and the town councils of major coastal cities. Yet in 1687 and 1688, Louis banned most imports of Dutch herring into France, reintroduced tariffs he had scrapped in the Peace of Nijmegen, and seized Dutch ships in French ports. To many, war with France now seemed inevitable. Even Amsterdam's regents agreed that only an attack on England could prevent a second *rampjaar*.[93]

The fifth and most serious problem lay in the gales that usually wracked the North Sea region in late autumn. If far removed from a lee shore, the republic's warships might survive a storm, but less seaworthy troop transports would surely sink with their soldiers and horses. Stormy weather that we today associate with the Maunder Minimum may actually have convinced William's opponents that an invasion could never succeed. Yet the Dutch fleet needed another kind of weather that the chillier climate made more common: persistent easterly winds. Several days of such winds would allow the fleet to leave the Zuiderzee and reach England before a storm could destroy it. Perhaps the frequency of such weather persuaded William that his invasion could yet prevail. In any event, William and his naval commanders fully appreciated the risk they were taking. The invasion had to happen in the stormy autumn, however, because the French army threatened to enter the republic in the spring.[94]

By early October, the Dutch fleet was ready to leave port, but stormy, westerly winds kept it trapped off the republic. The English fleet grew by the day, so that by late October its warships were nearly as numerous as those in the Dutch armada. Morale plummeted within William's fleet, and among ordinary Dutch citizens who had been sure of success. With the fleet was Constantijn Huygens Jr., a member of the celebrated family that also included his brother, Christiaan, the most celebrated scientist of the Golden Age. On 21 and 22 October, Huygens wrote that the Dutch ships were being boarded, despite northwesterly winds. 'The wind is papist', went a common refrain – common, at least, until it was forbidden on pain

[92] Israel, 'The Dutch Role in the Glorious Revolution', 109, 119.

[93] Rose, *England in the 1690s*, 6. Jardine, *Going Dutch*, 41. Rodger, *The Command of the Ocean*, 136. Hoak, 'The Anglo-Dutch Revolution of 1688–89', 18. Pincus, *1688: The First Modern Revolution*, 227.

[94] Rodger, *The Command of the Ocean*, 138. Jardine, *Going Dutch*, 41.

of fine. According to the Polish ambassador in The Hague, the 'common thing every morning, which was most used, was first to go and see how the wind sate [sic], and if there were any probability of a change'.[95]

Finally, on 24 October, the wind shifted to blow from the southeast, and Huygens was 'very busy' with final preparations for departure. When he spoke with William two days later, he found the Prince burdened by 'thoughts of the strange journey that we were undertaking in winter, and with the consequences that it could have'. Nevertheless, on 27 and 28 October, the last horses boarded their troop transports, and parts of the fleet started congregating. At last, on 29 October, with winds still from the east, the armada left port. On the following day, disaster struck. As the fleet neared Goeree off Zeeland, the wind strengthened into a ferocious storm and shifted to blow from the northwest, 'with high seas and lightning'. The coast had become a treacherous lee shore. Amid the raging storm, most of the fleet managed to return to port. Yet on 1 November the scale of its losses became clear. Between 300 and 1,000 horses had died in the storm, and somehow they would need to be replaced. With the storm still howling on 3 November, Huygens met with senior leaders of the republic's army. It would be incredibly hard to reach England, they concluded, in a season plagued by such violent weather. Never had the risk of disaster seemed greater.[96]

Over the following days the storm gradually abated, while new horses arrived from across the republic. Huygens had frequent nightmares, and endured a fever that only broke on the evening of 8 November. As he looked out his window that night, he noticed that the wind had turned to blow from the east. On the next morning, with the wind now driving hard from the east, William and his advisors reached a decision: the fleet would sortie as soon as it could. That afternoon, 'many ships that we had feared were lost', Huygens wrote, 'showed up again'. On 10 November the wind shifted slightly to blow from the northeast, ideal for a Channel crossing. With difficulty, fresh horses arrived aboard Huygens's ship. The Amsterdam stock exchange crashed as investors responded to risk William was about to take. Finally, on 11 November, the fleet sailed out of Hellevoetsluis and made for England, with the wind still gusting from the

[95] Constantijn Huygens, *Journaal van Constantijn Huygens, den zoon, van 21 October 1688 tot 2 September 1696*. Accessed 27 May 2016, www.dbnl.org/tekst/huyg007jour02_01. Israel and Parker, 'Of Providence and Protestant Winds', 358.

[96] Huygens, *Journaal van Constantijn Huygens, den zoon*. Israel and Parker, 'Of Providence and Protestant Winds', 358. Rodger, *The Command of the Ocean*, 139.

northeast. On 13 November, the Dutch fleet reached the English coast. To overawe English onlookers, Dutch soldiers dressed in their parade regalia and played trumpets and drums above deck, while sailors aboard warships fired their guns. At a signal from William, the whole fleet stretched into a line that disappeared beyond the horizon. William had decided to leave his choice of landing to the wind. He opted, at first, to sail north to Yorkshire, but then changed his mind and decided instead to harness the full force of the wind by travelling southwest, to Plymouth (Map M2). Driven by the wind, the Dutch flotilla rushed past the Hampshire coast and only just managed to pull into Torbay, the last haven that could accommodate them, when the winds suddenly shifted to blow from the west. On 15 November, William's army landed.[97]

To get there, the Dutch armada twice sailed past the English fleet. George Legge, Baron of Dartmouth and Admiral of England's Channel Fleet, had gathered his ships in Gunfleet. English warships could easily assemble there from the Medway or Thames shipyards. Yet James had recommended that Dartmouth prepare his armada farther out to sea, lest he 'be surprised ... by the sudden coming of the Dutch fleet, as being a place he cannot well get out to sea from, while the wind remains easterly'. Indeed, the very wind that would bring the Dutch suddenly across the channel would keep the English from engaging them. Dartmouth ignored James's advice, possibly because his fleet was sheltered while in Gunfleet from the storms he anticipated. With westerly winds continuing in late October, he confided to James, 'I cannot see much sense in their attempt with the hazard of such a fleet and army at the latter end of October.' Yet the wind shifted. On 13 November, Dartmouth could just glimpse the Dutch fleet from his flagship, but his sailors could make no headway against the force of both the wind and tide. At last, on 14 November, the English fleet got to sea and pursued the Dutch. Hours later, the wind turned to blow from the southwest, blocking their progress and ending their chase. 'Tis strange', Dartmouth wrote forlornly to James, 'that such mad proceedings should have such success at this time a year'.[98]

To historians, the winds that enabled William's invasion were highly unusual, the kind of 'unexpected good fortunate', in the words of Jardine,

[97] Constantijn Huygens, *Journaal van Constantijn Huygens, den zoon*. Jardine, *Going Dutch*, 7. Rodger, *The Command of the Ocean*, 139. Israel and Parker, 'Of Providence and Protestant Winds', 361.

[98] Rodger, *The Command of the Ocean*, 139. Pincus, *1688: The First Modern Revolution*, 237. Israel and Parker, 'Of Providence and Protestant Winds', 359.

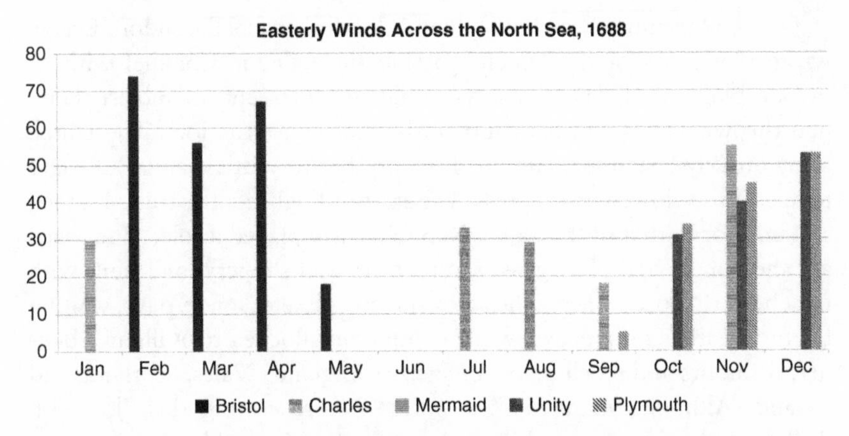

FIGURE 5.2 The percentage of easterly winds, relative to total wind measurements, recorded aboard the English warships *Bristol, Charles, Mermaid, Unity*, and *Plymouth* as they sailed through the North Sea region. Each monthly percentage reflects at least 10 days of weather observations. 'Variable' winds are not included in these statistics.

that seems to make a mockery of human planning. Yet this idea actually stems from William's propaganda, which played up the providential nature of the 'Protestant wind', but of course not the storm that had so nearly derailed the invasion. Wind measurements in ship logbooks written in the North Sea region during 1688 reveal that easterly winds were in fact common, relative to twentieth-century averages, during both spring and fall of that year (Figure 5.2). The extraordinary frequency of such winds in the spring may have influenced William's early thinking about the risks the republic would undertake in invading England. Certainly, the many easterlies in October and especially November should have convinced Dartmouth to move his fleet to sea. Prevailing winds in 1688 therefore reflected the climate of the Maunder Minimum even more dramatically than they did during the Second Anglo-Dutch War. It was the westerlies that delayed the Dutch invasion, not the easterlies that ultimately brought it quickly to England, which should have been unexpected.[99]

[99] 'Bristol 1685 June 4–1688 June 21'. ADM 51/124. 'Charles 1686 July 29–1688 Aug 28'. ADM 51/269. 'Mermaid 1686 Mar 25–1688 Oct 19 and Mermaid 1688 Oct 24–1688 Feb 12'. ADM 61/605. 'Unity 1688 Oct 12–1689 May 26'. ADM 51/1021. 'Plymouth 08 September 1688–31 December 1690'. ADM 52/88. National Archives at Kew (London, United Kingdom). Jardine, *Going Dutch*, 42. Pincus, *1688: The First Modern Revolution*, 237. Israel and Parker, 'Of Providence and Protestant Winds', 359. Wheeler, 'British Naval Logbooks from the Late Seventeenth Century', 140.

On 15 November, word of William's landing reached London. Evelyn wrote that news of the Dutch 'passing through the Channel with so favourable a wind, that our navy could not intercept, or molest them' had thrown James and his court into 'great consternation'. The Dutch army quickly began its march to London, but torrential rains and frigid temperatures slowed its progress. The state of English infrastructure, then still inferior to that of the Dutch Republic, also played a role. 'The roads are shockingly bad', Huygens wrote, 'dirty and slippery' and built with treacherous 'loose stones'. The army stayed at Exeter for 12 days, waiting for the weather to improve, while commoners flocked to William's banner. Rumours and rebellions swept across England, Wales, Scotland, and Ireland. Although many nobles waited before casting their lot with William or James, thousands of ordinary people, incited by Dutch propaganda, joined revolutionary armies. Reports that troops loyal to James had massacred Irish Protestants provoked an uprising of perhaps 100,000 people in London. As William's invasion turned into a popular insurrection, James abruptly fled London. William seized the opportunity to expand his ambitions. Rather than forcing James into an alliance against France, he now aimed to take direct political control of England alongside Mary Stuart. By delaying William, weather linked to the Maunder Minimum may have helped transform what his invasion could accomplish. Finally, on 28 December, William entered London. Despite torrential rain, the streets were ringed with cheering crowds. London would be under Dutch occupation until 1690. After more than 35 years of Anglo-Dutch hostility, the republic had, in a sense, finally prevailed.[100]

Yet by 1688, English and Dutch economies, cultures, and political systems were in many respects so similar, and so closely entangled, that William's conquest resembled the revolution described in Dutch propaganda. Ultimately, that revolution did not benefit the republic. For years, the new regime needed Dutch soldiers, sailors, and artillery in huge numbers to quell insurrections in England and to defeat invasions by 'Jacobite' forces loyal to James II. The close Anglo-Dutch alliance made possible by William's invasion also accelerated the flow of power and money from the republic to England. The wealth of the Prince of Orange now rested in London, not The Hague. The republic's low interest rates –

[100] Constantijn Huygens, *Journaal van Constantijn Huygens, den zoon*. Pincus, *1688: The First Modern Revolution*, 249. Rose, *England in the 1690s*, 7. Jardine, *Going Dutch*, 18. Hoak, 'The Anglo-Dutch Revolution of 1688–89', 21. Israel, 'The Dutch Role in the Glorious Revolution', 128.

at 3 per cent in the wake of William's invasion – drew enormous capital from Amsterdam to London. In the 1690s, investors financed the dramatic improvement of English roads and waterways for transportation, so that they more closely connected English population centres. Bankers adopted Dutch financial techniques, and established the Bank of England in 1694. Historians have debated the extent to which the Glorious Revolution stimulated the English economy, and whether it really led to a new political order. Yet it seems safe to conclude that the revolution hastened the process by which important aspects of England's economy came to mirror those of the republic.[101]

In a rivalry between two similar economies, England would prevail over the republic. It was far more populous, and its industries could more easily mine resources, such as iron and coal, that were less accessible in the republic. The republic's audacious invasion of England, complicated but ultimately made possible by the climate of the Maunder Minimum, would leave it economically and militarily overshadowed by its neighbour across the channel.

CONCLUSIONS: CLIMATE CHANGES, LOCAL ENVIRONMENTS, AND DUTCH WARS

In 1652, English captain Nicholas Foster was astonished that the republic would risk war, 'when (like an eagle's winds extended over her body) our coast surrounded theirs for 120 leagues ... and the wind blowing above three-quarters of the year westerly on the coast of England, made all our cape-lands and bays very good roads for ships to anchor at'.[102] His surprise was justified. In the First Anglo-Dutch War, frequent westerlies

[101] W. A. Speck, 'Some Consequences of the Glorious Revolution'. In *The World of William and Mary*, eds. Dale Hoak and Mordechai Feingold, 36. Jardine, *Going Dutch*, 345. Jonathan Israel, 'England, the Dutch, and the Mastery of World Trade', in *The World of William and Mary*, 84. Dan Bogart, 'Did the Glorious Revolution Contribute to the Transport Revolution? Evidence from Investment in Roads and Rivers'. *The Economic History Review* 64:4 (2011): 1073. Nuala Zahedieh, 'Regulation, Rent-Seeking, and the Glorious Revolution in the English Atlantic Economy'. *The Economic History Review* 63:4 (2010): 865. C. G. A. Clay, *Economic Expansion and Social Change: England 1500–1700, Vol. II: Industry, Trade, and Government*. (Cambridge: Cambridge University Press, 1984), 279. Alan Houston and Steve Pincus, 'Introduction: Modernity and Later Seventeenth-Century England'. In *A Nation Transformed: England after the Restoration*, eds. Alan Houston and Steve Pincus. (Cambridge: Cambridge University Press, 2001), 4. Israel, 'The Dutch Role in the Glorious Revolution', 151.

[102] Rodger, *The Command of the Ocean*, 11.

allowed English warships of unprecedented size, guided into line of battle tactics by artillery commanders, to bombard Dutch vessels at range with all their gun ports open. Not only did the English win more than twice as many major battles in the first war than in the latter wars combined, but prevailing westerlies also discouraged Dutch raids into the Thames estuary and beyond. Storms with westerly winds inflicted an unequal toll, and repeatedly scattered Dutch vessels, or destroyed them on lee shores while English armadas sheltered nearby. Westerlies also aided an English blockade and contributed to the success of English privateers. The weather of the early Maunder Minimum therefore helped the English fully exploit technological and tactical advantages that let them triumph in the First Anglo-Dutch War.

Yet by 1664, both the Dutch naval system and the environment of the North Sea region had changed. In the Second Anglo-Dutch War, frequent easterlies repeatedly helped the Dutch claim the weather gage during major battles and the spectacular raid on the Medway. The same winds fanned a fire that incinerated much of London and aided Dutch privateers. Storms persuaded English captains to repeatedly close their lower gun ports while engaging the Dutch, and heavy precipitation hampered an invasion of the republic by the Bishop of Münster. The shifting winds of the deepening Maunder Minimum added to the Dutch advantages of new ships, new tactics, and new naval administration.

In the Third Anglo-Dutch War, an extraordinary stretch of storminess thwarted allied attempts to exploit their superiority at sea after the Dutch fleet was partly dismantled. When the storms ebbed and the Dutch fleet was reassembled, its sailors exploited both easterlies and high winds to repel the larger allied armada. Drought at first undermined Dutch defences on land. Yet before long, torrential rains enhanced the effectiveness of the water line, which ultimately halted the allied invasion. A complex set of weather patterns that overall registered the Maunder Minimum again aided the defence of the republic.

Easterly winds were even more common in 1688. The 'Protestant wind' that carried William's invasion across the English Channel, and kept the English fleet from sailing out to meet it, probably reflected the influence of the Maunder Minimum. So did the rains that slowed the Dutch march to London until James abandoned his throne. The Glorious Revolution would have been far less likely to succeed in a warmer climate.

A cooling climate therefore gave advantages to Dutch forces that helped them prevail over the English. Yet as the republic adopted the most successful elements of the English naval system, the English economy adopted the economic and social innovations of the Dutch Golden Age. England soon eclipsed the Dutch Republic as a commercial, financial, and naval power.

No wars were ever won or lost solely because of climate change. The republic's victories in its wars with Spain, England, and France owed much to the extraordinary wealth generated by the republic's distinct economy, not to mention the decisions of commanders, ordinary soldiers, and civilians. Nevertheless, both civilian and military officials keenly appreciated the crucial importance of weather in shaping the fortunes of their armies and fleets. In 1622, Francis Bacon ended his *Historia Ventorum*, or 'History of the Winds', by advising that 'ways be found to predict the risings, fallings, and times of winds'. Forecasts of wind directions and velocities 'would be useful for navigation and agriculture, and most of all for choosing times for sea battles'. These recommendations would not be followed for some time, but Dutch commanders did repeatedly develop tactics that exploited prevailing weather. Did they perceive that weather patterns changed over the course of decades, in ways that gradually made some tactics and technologies more effective than others? As we will see, there is some evidence to suggest that they did.[103]

[103] Francis Bacon, *Historia Ventorum, Vol. 12*. (Oxford: Oxford University Press, 2007), 129.

PART THREE

CULTURE AND CLIMATE CHANGE

Part III Preface

The Dutch Golden Age was always precarious. The thriving commercial economy of the republic relied on a web of unstable relationships with foreign markets and a fleet that could secure the major sea-lanes to and from the Low Countries. The very survival of the republic depended on the improbable victories of a military financed by, and partly recruited from, a population that was far smaller than those of neighbouring rivals. No surprise, then, that the culture of the Golden Age was at first volatile but dynamic in ways that distinguished the republic from the rest of Europe. Religious and philosophical schisms provoked by the Reformation, the violent separation from Spain, and emerging scientific ideas entered public discourse and were never entirely resolved. Yet they gradually gave rise to a culture that prized discipline, education, applied science, relative religious toleration, and individual freedoms that startled foreign visitors but extended only to such activities that did not violate the demands of order and discipline. Civic culture loomed large in cities, where consumers and capitalists pursued rational self interest in ways that seemed at times to conflict with the demands of religious piety. All of these values underpinned the characteristic discipline of Dutch soldiers and sailors, the cleanliness and safety of Dutch cities, and the active participation of women in Dutch public life. They fostered technological innovation, permitted social mobility, inspired civic charity, and provoked a fascination for the arts that touched every stratum of society.[1]

[1] Israel, *The Dutch Republic*, 4, 353, 565, 637. Willem Frijhoff and Marijke Spies, *Dutch Culture in a European Perspective: 1650, Hard-Won Unity*. (Gorcum: Uitgeverij van

Today, the Dutch Golden Age is most closely identified with the genius of artists such as Rembrandt van Rijn, Frans Hals, Salomon van Ruysdael, and Johannes Vermeer, yet these masters are only the best-remembered representatives of a large and thriving industry. For the first time in the history of Western art, sixteenth- and seventeenth-century Dutch painters painted for the open market. They completed portraits for wealthy clients, just like other artists across Europe, but they also created realistic representations of the world that were prized by people of diverse socioeconomic backgrounds. Such art adorned not only the courts and estates of the wealthy and powerful, but also the humbler walls of middle class homes. Visitors to the republic reported with surprise that lavish paintings decorated even shops owned by otherwise impoverished artisans. Dutch painters also exported their work to European regions that shared elements of the republic's distinctively Protestant civic culture.[2]

Painters were only the most celebrated artists of the republic. Dutch mapmakers, pamphleteers, cartoonists, and poets also saw themselves as living in a golden age for their disciplines that mirrored the broader success of the republic. The rise of Amsterdam linked them all. Over the course of the seventeenth century, the city emerged as Europe's leading centre for publishing and cartography, as well as a booming staple market for writing and visual art. Much of what was sold depicted real environments and technologies that would have been familiar to Dutch customers. Such representations would also have resonated with foreign visitors. Many marvelled at Dutch technologies, particularly those that harnessed the energy of wind and water to sustain or transform the environments of the Low Countries. For more than a century, the coastal provinces of the republic were at the forefront of European technological innovation.[3]

Gorcum, 2004), 553. Simon Schama, *The Embarrassment of Riches: An Interpretation of Dutch Culture in the Golden Age*. (Berkeley: University of California Press, 1988), 331.

[2] Israel, *The Dutch Republic*, 555. De Vries and Van der Woude, *The First Modern Economy*, 116. Haley, *The Dutch in the Seventeenth Century*, 134. Lawrence Otto Goedde, *Tempest and Shipwreck in Dutch and Flemish Art*, 5. Wayne Franits, 'Introduction'. In *Looking at Seventeenth-Century Dutch Art: Realism Reconsidered*, ed. Wayne Franits. (Cambridge: Cambridge University Press, 1997), 1. Svetlana Alpers, 'Picturing Dutch Culture'. In *Looking at Seventeenth-Century Dutch Art: Realism Reconsidered*, ed. Wayne Franits. (Cambridge: Cambridge University Press, 1997), 57. Kahr, *Dutch Painting in the Seventeenth Century*, 20. Blankert, *Selected Writings on Dutch Painting*, 132.

[3] Davids, *The Rise and Decline of Dutch Technological Leadership, Vol. I*, 1.

The culture of the Dutch Republic was partly a product of the unusual mix of energy sources that fuelled the Golden Age and responded differently to climate change than those of predominantly agricultural economies. Dutch visual art in particular registered the influence of wind on sailing ships, which brought riches and foreign cultures to a coastal republic drained, in part, by windmills. Since the Little Ice Age influenced atmospheric circulation in a way that overall benefitted Dutch sailing vessels, important aspects of Dutch culture in a sense reflected the sources of the republic's resilience in the face of climate change.[4]

In the shadow of these big relationships between culture and climate change, artists, inventors, and ordinary people in the republic all responded to the Little Ice Age by writing about weather, creating art, occupying new social spaces, and devising technologies. In the chilliest decades of the period, some Dutch citizens traced gradual changes in the frequency of extreme weather events that reflected the influence of a cooler climate. At the same time, painters, poets, and pamphleteers in the republic pioneered new kinds of art that represented such weather. Frozen waterscapes in cold winters inspired 'ice cultures' that levelled already relaxed class distinctions in the republic. Urban inventors, meanwhile, developed technologies that helped the Dutch exploit or resist the environmental consequences of the Little Ice Age. The discourses, actions, and artefacts that constituted culture in the coastal cities of the republic therefore registered climate change in ways that overall reflected, and further contributed to, the resilience of the republic in the face of the Little Ice Age.

[4] See also Barry Lord, *Art & Energy: How Culture Changes*. (Chicago: University of Chicago Press, 2015).

6

Tracing and Painting the Little Ice Age

Between 1630 and 1670, more than 1,000 visual artists participated in the industry of Dutch painting. They were so productive that, by 1650, the citizens of Holland alone owned at least two and a half million paintings. While many were copies or works of dubious quality, roughly one in ten were original paintings of indisputable excellence. Other kinds of visual art, such as illustrations, pamphlets, cartoons, and maps, were more abundant still. Dutch artists responded to the demands of the open market, and a Protestant culture that discouraged representations of religious topics. They were among the first European artists to paint spontaneous portraits, realistic landscapes, stormy seascapes, and other scenes that captured elements of everyday life. Their art looked inward, at domestic scenes and ordinary objects, but also outward, at marine vistas and exotic locales, in ways that reflected the concentrated wealth and global reach of the Dutch trading empire.[1]

In the early seventeenth century, Amsterdam became the hub of trade not only in Dutch art, but also in paintings from the Spanish Netherlands, Italy, and the Holy Roman Empire. Artists gathered in the largest cities of the Dutch Republic and enrolled in municipal Guilds of St Luke that regulated their activities. Different artistic communities in different Dutch cities created distinct artistic cultures that tended to specialize in their own topics and techniques. The subjects they depicted and the styles they used coevolved with the military and economic histories of the republic. During

[1] Israel, *The Dutch Republic*, 557. Alan Jacobs, *17th Century Dutch and Flemish Painters*. (Amsterdam: McGraw-Hill Book Company Ltd. 1976), 9. Van der Woude, 'Schilderijproduktie', 25. Lawrence Otto Goedde, *Tempest and Shipwreck in Dutch and Flemish Art*, 30.

the overall prosperous Twelve Years' Truce, for example, many Dutch painters used brilliant dyes to depict sumptuous banquets and lavishly adorned companies. However, when the war with Spain resumed in the 1620s, the economy of the republic entered a prolonged slump. Dutch paintings generally grew smaller and less expensive. Increasingly, Dutch artists painted soldiers: in battle, in brothels, or in taverns. Dutch trade with Southern Europe and Pernambuco in South America temporarily collapsed, so it was harder for artists to acquire vibrant dyes such as indigo, cochineal, Campeche, and Brazil wood. Many adapted by painting in monochrome greys and browns. Others used brilliant hues only when crafting 'fine art' for wealthy connoisseurs. Then, after Dutch power reached its zenith with the conclusion of the Peace of Münster, many artists who had depicted the modest and austere now painted the spectacular and sophisticated. Large, vibrant, and meticulously detailed paintings of naval engagements, for example, reached the pinnacle of their popularity.[2]

Many Dutch artists therefore used changing techniques to depict the natural world at a time when it too was changing. Snowy winter landscapes and stormy seascapes in particular became artistic genres in the republic during the coldest and stormiest decades of the Little Ice Age. At the same time, Dutch weather observers used memories of the elderly, relevant landmarks, and even documentary evidence to compare weather in their present to similar weather in the past. Some even accurately identified long-term patterns in weather extremes, which was an important first step towards perceiving climate change, if not comprehending its physical causes and consequences. Dutch weather reconstructions suggest that, in the chilliest decades of the Little Ice Age, some Dutch artists may have consciously painted the local manifestations of a cooler, stormier climate. Even unwitting depictions of environments transformed by the Little Ice Age shed light on how the Dutch endured and at times exploited climate change.

PERCEIVING AND MEASURING CLIMATE CHANGES

Dutch culture most clearly registered climate change when the republic's citizens struggled to reconstruct weather patterns in their past. Letters, diary entries, and newspaper reports that recorded weather extremes in the Low Countries often concluded that no one could remember equally severe weather. The authors, and locals usually consulted for their recollections, apparently understood that weather events had happened, and

[2] Israel, *The Dutch Republic*, 556. Haak, *The Golden Age*, 152.

could perhaps happen again, that did not occur in decades past. Such reflections often concerned severe winters during the coldest decades of the Little Ice Age.

On 22 March 1586, for example, Abel Eppens in Emden wrote that even older people could not remember a winter as severe as the one they had just experienced. In 1608, Johan van de Sande in The Hague wrote that temperatures in January and February were colder than anyone could recall. In the February 1621, Dirck Janszoon in Friesland observed that ice cover was more extensive than anyone could remember or read about. In the same month and province, Pier Winsemius concluded that no one had ever heard of such severe winter freezing. In a winter just four years later, Van Wassenaer rhetorically asked if anyone had ever experienced such widespread ice cover. According to Caescoper, in March 1667 the Zuiderzee was still closed by ice, which even the very old could not recall. In November 1671, Adriaen van der Goes wrote that ink was freezing in his pen, 'which is unheard of'.[3]

References to unprecedented weather were not limited to reports of landmark winters. Jan de Pottre in Brussels wrote that the summer of 1590 was 'hotter than anyone could remember'. In 1599, the physician Dirck Velius in Hoorn wrote that the weather in April was warmer and more 'beautiful' than even the elderly could recall. Velius used a nearly identical phrase in his description of the warm autumn of 1616. Precipitation across all seasons provoked similar reflections. In 1615, Velius wrote that more snow had fallen on Hoorn in February than anyone could remember. In a letter sent on 25 November 1659, Van der Goes concluded that no autumn had ever been wetter. In December 1664, Tobias van Domselaer reported that freezing rain had covered trees in Amsterdam with a layer of ice that was thicker than anyone had seen before. Other atmospheric effects also prompted observers to scour their memories. Van Wassenaer wrote that, between 25 December 1625 and 17 January 1626, thick mist shrouded the sun from view in a way none could remember. He may have described the regional effects of aerosols released into the atmosphere by a volcanic eruption in Iceland.[4]

[3] Dirck Janszoon, *Het aantekeningenboek van Dirck Jansz. (1578–1636)*, ed. Pieter Gerbenzon. 120. (Hilversum: Uitgeverij Verloren, 1993), 120. Winsemius, Pier Winsemius, *Chronique ofte historische geschiedenisse van Vrieslant*, 910. Van Wassenaer, *Historisch Verhael Vol.* 12, 57. Van der Goes, 'Hage, den 19 November 1671'. *Briefwisseling tusschen de gebroeders van der Goes (1659–1673) Vol. II*, 305. Buisman, *Duizend Jaar Vol. IV*, 87, 612, 549.

[4] De Pottre, *Dagboek van Jan de Pottre, 1549–1602*, 185. Buisman, *Duizend Jaar Vol. IV*, 186, 301, 591. Van Wassenaer, *Historisch Verhael aller gedenckwaerdiger geschiedenis* … .

Severe storms frequently provoked reflection. A chronicle written in Flanders recalled that a ferocious gale on 5 May 1661 had been 'such a dreadful storm of wind, thunder, lightning and hail, as anyone could find depicted in writing'. In December 1665, an article in the *Hollantsche Mercurius* newspaper described a gale so severe that 'two of the oldest inhabitants near the Thames said they never heard of such a storm'. On 22 September 1671, Van der Goes described a storm that seemed to have no precedent.[5]

The frequent recurrence of Dutch claims that weather extremes had never happened before raises the possibility that such phrases were merely literary tropes. However, modern climatic reconstructions suggest that references to popular memory could be effective tools for contextualizing weather extremes. For example, the winter of 1585/1586 was indeed as frigid as any had been in two decades. The winters of 1594/1595, 1607/1608, and 1620/1621 were even chillier, in fact colder than any had been since the first landmark winter of the Grindelwald Fluctuation, in 1564/1565. The winters of 1657/1658, 1666/1667, and 1671/1672 were all as cold as any had been since 1620/1621.[6]

Moreover, extreme weather events became chronological landmarks for Dutch citizens, with lasting cultural significance that strengthened weather recollections.[7] During the Christmas Eve storm of 1593, for instance, a ship owned by an erudite merchant, Roemer Visscher, foundered on the coast of Texel. Shortly after the tragedy, Visscher's daughter was born. He gave her a morbid middle name: Tesselschade, or 'Texel Damage'. The memory of how severe the 1593 storm had been therefore became part of the identity of the Visscher family. Eventually it spread beyond the Visscher family, for Maria Tesselschade Visscher became an important member of the *Muiderkring*, a group of influential Dutch

Vol. 10, 116. Van der Goes, 'Hage, den 25 Novemb. 1659'. *Briefwisseling tusschen de gebroeders van der Goes (1659–1673) Vol. I*, 48. Atwell, 'Volcanism and Short-Term Climatic Change in East Asian and World History c. 1200–1699', 72. Van Wassenaer, *Historisch Verhael aller gedenckwaerdiger geschiedenis .... Vol. 12*, 57.

5 Buisman, *Duizend Jaar Vol. IV*, 186, 522, 601. *De Hollantsche Mercurius*. (Haarlem: Pieter Casteleun, 1666), 157. Van der Goes, 'Hage, den 8 October 1671'. *Briefwisseling tusschen de gebroeders van der Goes (1659–1673) Vol. II*, 279.

6 Van Engelen, Buisman and IJnsen, 'A Millennium of Weather, Winds and Water in the Low Countries', 112.

7 Christian Rohr, *Extreme Naturereignisse im Ostalpenraum: Naturerfahrung im Spätmittelalter und am Beginn der Neuzeit*. (Vienna: Böhlau Verlag, 2007), 56. Jacques Berlioz, *Catastrophes naturelles et calamités au Moyen Âge*. (Florence: Edizioni del Galluzzo, 1998), 25. Pfister, 'Climatic Extremes, Recurrent Crises and Witch Hunts', 57.

thinkers who helped shape the intellectual culture of the Golden Age. Other Dutch families tried to remember extreme weather in ways we might find more familiar today. Amid bitterly cold weather on 22 March 1658, contemporary Dutch historian Lieuwe van Aitzema wrote that, in The Hague, 'everyone let their children stand on the ice, so they could [later] say that the weather had really been that cold'. Dutch citizens who lived through extraordinary weather appreciated how rare that experience could be.[8]

Memories of seemingly unprecedented weather could be long lasting, but they never communicated much more than a vague awareness that weather extremes in the present were unusual in the context of the past. However, some Dutch observers contextualized exceptional weather by giving specific dates on which past weather had been equally unusual. They therefore developed an understanding of meteorological variability that was precise enough to be a rudimentary form of climate history. Sometimes, they even accessed documentary records of past weather that spanned several decades, just as a climate historian might do today.

Detailed references to dates were most common in descriptions of remarkably high or low water levels. That was especially true when water levels responded to extreme weather events, as they did in droughts, severe storms, and rapid thawing after frigid winters. For example, on 12 January 1594, with severe storms lashing the Zuiderzee region, pensionary Françoys Maelson informed Grand Pensionary Oldenbarnevelt that water levels 'have not been so high in eight years'. On 23 January 1610, Velius in Hoorn reported that 'high Northwesterly winds have driven the water to levels we have not seen in 40 years'. In the midst of massive river flooding across Holland in January 1624, Van Wassenaer wrote that the water had risen so high along the Maas near the city of Venlo that it topped a stone erected to commemorate high water levels in 1571.[9]

Natural or artificial landmarks such as that stone were not always mentioned in descriptions of water levels that referenced the past, but it is

[8] Lieuwe van Aitzema, *Saken van staet en oorlogh van Lieuwe van Aitzema*. (The Hague: Johan Veekym Johan Tongerlos and Jasper Doll, 1669), 125. Schama, *The Embarrassment of Riches*, 408. See also Milja van Tielhof, 'Texel, kerstavond 1593. De ramp die Tesselschade haar naam gaf'. In *Bourgondië voorbij. De Nederlanden 1250–1650. Liber alumnorum Wim Blockmans*, eds. M. Damen and L. Sicking, 311–324. (Hilversum: Uitgeverij Verloren, 2010).

[9] Buisman, *Duizend Jaar Vol. IV*, 141, 266. Van Wassenaer, *Historisch Verhael aller gedenckwaerdiger geschiedenis .... Vol. IV*, 74. Nienhuis, *Environmental History of the Rhine-Meuse Delta*, 250.

likely that they were normally consulted. Stones and other landmarks amounted to crude forms of instrumental record keeping that could supplement and improve oral and written histories of past water levels. In March 1625, for example, Van Wassenaer wrote that houses built on dunes had been swept away at Egmont aan Zee, a village on the Northwestern coast of Holland. He reported that survivors used the location of the houses to discern that water levels had risen higher in 1625 than they had in 1570. Meanwhile, in the nearby city of Enkhuizen, water levels crested the high-water mark recorded in 1610 on the tower of the Drommedaris, which defended the entrance to the harbour. During severe river floods in the generally frigid winter of 1650/1651, water levels in Nijmegen, observers noted, exceeded the highest level ever recorded on the town walls. On 5 December 1665, Adriaen van der Goes reported that waves fanned by a northwesterly storm swept across the coast at Scheveningen near The Hague until they reached the guesthouse at the Van der Goes estate. According to Van der Goes, water levels were therefore higher than they had been for exactly 80 years, since 1585, when the sea also rose that high.[10]

In some communities, governments systematically installed landmarks that helped them contextualize changes in water levels, and not only with reference to past extremes. In Amsterdam, the municipal government had long attempted to regulate the highly polluted water that flowed through the city's canals. Then, in 1675, a severe storm led to breaches in recently repaired but still vulnerable potions of dikes that had only just been rebuilt in the wake of the intentional inundations of 1672. Johannes Hudde, a scholar and the mayor of Amsterdam (a position then roughly equivalent to its director of public works), resolved to systematically determine the necessary height of the new dikes so that similar flooding could not happen again. He aimed to build dikes that were the same height everywhere and would therefore have no weak points, and he also hoped to flush clean water through the festering canals of Amsterdam. To that end, he needed to find a baseline, or control, for the water level around Amsterdam. New dikes would need to be substantially higher than this baseline, of course, while water in canals had to be just as deep.[11]

[10] Van Wassenaer, *Historisch Verhael aller gedenckwaerdiger geschiedenis .... Vol. III*, 150. Buisman, *Duizend Jaar Vol. IV*, 376, 511. Van der Goes, 'Hage, den 8 December 1665'. *Briefwisseling tusschen de gebroeders van der Goes (1659–1673) Vol. I*, 221.

[11] P. Van Dam and L. Murre, 'Van Amsterdams Peil naar Europees niveauvlak'. (forthcoming), 6.

In the winter of 1682/1683 or perhaps 1683/1684, Hudde ordered officials with the city water office at St Anthonispoort to measure water levels on the IJ, which then joined the Zuiderzee. By cutting through the ice that covered the IJ, they did not have to contend with waves. They found the average of their measurements, and that became the *Amsterdams Peil* ('Level of Amsterdam'). Under Hudde's direction, marble stones were then attached to eight sluices: the Eenhoornsluis, Nieuwe Haarlemmersluis, Oude Haarlemmersluis, Nieuwe Brugsluis, Kolksluis, Kraansluis, West-Indische sluis, and Scharrebiersluis. Not only did these stones give the desired height of the new dikes (at nine feet and five thumb-widths above the *Peil*), but they also laid out the standard depth for canal water in Amsterdam.[12]

While statistical thinking is usually identified with modernity, Lorraine Daston has argued that 'proto-quantification' played an important role in seventeenth-century thought. The Amsterdams Peil certainly reflected sophisticated statistical reasoning about water and weather averages, which is essential to present-day climatology. That allowed for the systematic improvement of flood defences across the coastal Republic just as climate change increased the frequency of storms. It did not, however, permit city officials to trace long-term fluctuations in storm frequency, severity, and sea levels.[13]

The Dutch precisely remembered the history and consequences of high water levels in their Republic using many different media. In 1696, contemporary historian Mattheus Smallegange and artist Jan Luyken collaborated on an illustration of the town of Reimerswaal. On 5 November 1530, catastrophic flooding overwhelmed the town, and it had never been reclaimed. The illustration depicted the town at its height, before the flood, and also in 1696, in its drowned, dilapidated state. Curiously, Smallegange and Luyken placed their representation of the flooded and abandoned town above their portrayal of the town in its heyday, which included a map. As we will see, such choices could communicate intricate parables on morality. Dutch citizens understood that floods were a consequence of both environmental stimulus and social vulnerability, which for them usually included immorality. Nevertheless, the illustration of Reimerswaal still reflected a detailed understanding of real, historical

[12] A. Waalewijn, *Drie eeuwen Normaal Amsterdams Peil.* (The Hague: Hoofddirectie van de Waterstaat, 1986), 14. Van Dam and Murre, 'Van Amsterdams Peil naar Europees niveauvlak', 8.

[13] Lorraine Daston, *Classical Probability in the Enlightenment.* (Princeton: Princeton University Press, 1988), xv.

water levels and flooding. It may have even registered a desire to compare past and present weather.[14]

Using landmarks, Dutch citizens contextualized water levels not only when they were abnormally high, but also when they were unusually low. On Christmas 1652, for instance, the painter Vincent Laurenszoon Van der Vienne remarked that the level of the Rhine had dipped beneath all the low water marks on city walls and ports. In December 1669, observers described water levels so low that previously submerged ruins had been exposed. Apparently, no one could remember seeing those ruins before. The Dutch most commonly described and contextualized unusually dry conditions by referring to travel across landscapes once covered by water. For example, in 1707, Caescoper wrote that June, July, and August were so dry that people could journey by mule along the beds of former waterways. Strangely, the specific references to past events that are common in descriptions of high water levels are absent in observations of unusual dryness. In 1672, reports of cows walking across dried up riverbeds on the eve of the French invasion, for instance, made no mention of the conditions described by Van der Vienne just three years earlier.[15]

Present-day flood reconstructions show that Dutch observers accurately contextualized water levels in their present by citing water levels on specific dates in their past. For example, regional storm surges did occur in 1586 and 1587, eight years before the flood Maelson experienced, although the more severe flooding in those years actually resulted from a dike breach near the city of Nijmegen, to the southeast. Velius's reference to floods 40 years before 1610 corresponds to the devastating All Saints' Flood of 1 November 1570, in which similarly high northwesterly winds coincided with the spring tide. Van Wassenaer used a stone to accurately recall high water levels during catastrophic river floods that followed the frigid and snowy winter of 1570/1571. When Van der Goes referred to surging water levels 80 years before 1665, he probably referenced storm floods that also swept across the northern coastal provinces in February 1585.[16]

[14] Nienhuis, *Environmental History of the Rhine-Meuse Delta*, 252. Mattheus Smallegange and Jan Luyken, 'Panorama op Reimerswaal', print, 1696, Amsterdam Museum, http://goo.gl/wort7d.

[15] Buisman, *Duizend Jaar Vol. IV*, 141, 629. Caescoper, *Dagboek van Claes Arisz. Caescoper*, 188.

[16] Gottschalk, *Stormvloeden en rivieroverstromingen Vol. II*, 700, 714, 771, 780. Nienhuis, *Environmental History of the Rhine-Meuse Delta*, 248.

Dutch observers generally did not commemorate especially severe or mild winters using the kind of memorial devices that helped people remember past water levels. Nevertheless, some Dutch citizens did use natural phenomena, such as the extent of ice on waterways, to accurately contextualize cold winters. During the frigid winter of 1599/1600, for example, Hugo de Groot reflected that Hollanders had not experienced such a winter in 35 years. De Groot, who was only 16, must have accessed oral or written histories of the landmark winter of 1564/1565, exactly 35 years earlier. In the grinding cold of December 1607, Velius observed that freezing had destroyed trees in Hoorn. He concluded that temperatures were lower than they had been for as long as those trees had lived. In a sense, he used the trees as proxy sources that helped him reconstruct past weather in a way that foreshadowed the much later scientific study of tree rings and ranges.[17]

Dutch observers sought historical parallels for severe freezing in their present by considering how it altered their options for travelling around the republic. During the winter of 1620/1621, for example, Pier Winsemius wrote that horse-drawn sleighs could now be taken to the republic's North Sea islands of Terschelling, Ameland, and Griend, which had not been possible since the equally frigid winter of 1607/1608. Winsemius marvelled that people could walk 12,000 steps west from Harlingen on the coast of Friesland before they glimpsed water. During the severe winter of 1657/1658, Van Aitzema reported that people could walk over ice that stretched from Zandvoort to Schagen along the coast of Holland. He concluded that it had been 50 years since this was last possible.[18]

Modern reconstructions of early modern winters indicate that Dutch references to past winters were generally accurate, but less precise than their attempts to contextualize water levels. The winter of 1599/1600 that De Groot described was indeed one of the coldest of the Little Ice Age, yet it was also slightly milder than the winter of 1572/1573. The winter of 1607/1608, observed by Velius, was as frigid as any that had affected the Low Countries since the beginning of the sixteenth century, except for the winter of 1564/1565. Winsemius correctly concluded that the winter of 1620/1621 had been the coldest since that of 1607/1608. The winter of 1657/1658, described by Van Aitzema, was among the chilliest since the landmark winter of 1607/1608, but it was actually slightly milder

[17] Hugo de Groot, *Batavi, Mirabilium Anni MDC*. Den Haag: 1600, 137. Buisman, *Duizend Jaar Vol. IV*, 246.

[18] Winsemius, *Chronique ofte historische geschiedenisse van Vrieslant*, 910. Van Aitzema, *Saken van staet en oorlogh*, 125.

than the winter of 1620/1621. The small mistakes made by De Groot and Van Aitzema probably reflect the limitations of ice cover as a proxy source for winter temperature. Sea ice along the coast, for instance, responds not only to air surface temperatures but also to sea surface temperatures, atmospheric and oceanic circulation, and other environmental conditions.[19]

The human consequences of the Little Ice Age therefore prompted Dutch citizens to think comparatively and accurately about weather across long timeframes. At the same time, Dutch natural philosophers pioneered the emerging science of meteorology, and one of their early goals was to track and measure weather with unprecedented precision. The mechanically minded scholar Isaac Beeckman, for example, received a weather observatory – the first of its kind in the Low Countries – from the town council of Dordrecht during the 'year without summer' in 1628. He used and refined new weather instruments in his observatory to keep detailed, quantitative weather observations. To uncover the causes for weather, he organized simultaneous weather observations – not only of temperature and wind but also 'rain, storms, snow, hail, etc.' – at observatories in different cities across the Low Countries.[20]

Despite Beeckman's innovations, Dutch scholars lacked the awareness of long-term statistical trends in average weather that today allows for a detailed, 'scientific' understanding of climate change and its causes. That did not stop some from seeking patterns in histories of weather. Already in 1597, Francis Bacon wrote that

> They say it is observed in the Low Countries (I know not in what part) that every five and thirty years the same kind and suit of years and weathers comes about again; as great frosts, great wet, great droughts, warm winters, summers with little heat, and the like; and they call it the *Prime*. It is a thing I do the rather mention, because, computing backwards, I have found some concurrence.[21]

At first glance, Bacon's suite of weather conditions contradicts itself. Winters are both mild and frigid; rain both plentiful and scarce. Yet the

[19] 'Van Engelen, Buisman and IJnsen, 'A Millennium of Weather, Winds and Water in the Low Countries', 112.

[20] Klaas Van Berkel, *Isaac Beckman on Matter and Motion: Mechanical Philosophy in the Making*. (Washington, DC: Johns Hopkins University Press, 2013), 51, 96. Isaac Beeckman, '10 September 1628'. In *Journal tenu par Isaac Beeckman de 1604 à 1634. Tome 3: 1627–1634 (1635)*, ed. Cornelis de Waard. (The Hague: Martinus Nijhoff, 1945), 85.

[21] Francis Bacon, 'Of Vicissitudes of Things'. In *Essays Civil and Moral*. The Harvard Classics, 1909–14. Accessed 14 December 2013, www.bartleby.com/3/1/58.html.

'Prime' he describes likely referred to a year of alternating meteorological extremes, with wild swings in temperature and precipitation. There is no scientific evidence for such a Prime, but extreme weather certainly accompanied the chilliest stretches of the Little Ice Age. If the concept of the Prime originated in the republic, it echoed many other attempts by Dutch observers to make sense of extreme weather in their present by finding parallels in the past. Yet in the case of the Prime, at least, these parallels mattered to Dutch scholars because they revealed patterns that could be used to predict the future. Successful strategies pursued by Dutch merchants and military commanders suggest but certainly do not prove that they too tried to trace and perhaps anticipate weather patterns in order to exploit them.

PAINTING RESPONSES TO LITTLE ICE AGE WINTERS

As at least some Dutch observers traced long-term changes in weather extremes and perhaps averages, Dutch artists tried their hand at an unusual scene: the icy winter landscape, often adorned with scenes of everyday life on frozen waterways. For scholars of past climate changes, these characteristically Dutch depictions of winter have long seemed like particularly clear representations of the Little Ice Age. In 1970, meteorologist Hans Neuberger first made that connection by analyzing more than 12,000 paintings created from 1400 to 1967, and today displayed in American and European museums. He concluded that depictions of cloudiness and darkness peaked in paintings completed between 1550 and 1849, which of course corresponds to three Little Ice Age cold phases that increased the frequency of wet, stormy weather. Hubert Lamb repeated and popularized these conclusions. Then, in 1980, another meteorologist, William Burroughs, published an article that expanded Neuberger's hypothesis. According to Burroughs, Dutch artists painted almost all of their winter landscapes in what he regarded as the coldest century of the Little Ice Age, between 1565 and 1665.[22]

Burroughs acknowledged, however, that not all winter landscapes represented contemporary weather. He insisted that Pieter Brueghel the Elder had been inspired by the frigid weather of 1565 when he painted a series of iconic winter landscapes. Yet his son, Pieter Brueghel the Younger, merely copied his father's work rather than painting real scenes from Dutch

[22] Hans Neuberger, 'Climate in Art'. *Weather* 25:2 (1970): 46. W. J. Burroughs, 'Winter Landscapes and Climatic Change'. *Weather* 36 (1981): 352. Lamb, *Climate, History and the Modern World*, 265.

winters.[23] By contrast, another painter, Hendrick Avercamp, did respond to frigid, Little Ice Age weather when he led a new artistic trend towards winter landscapes in the years that followed the cold winter of 1608. Burroughs further nuanced Neuberger's conclusions by allowing that changes in artistic convention led to the decline of winter landscapes after 1665. His conclusions are often repeated in cultural histories of the Little Ice Age. Today, many climate historians still argue that chilly winters played a role in the creation and popularity of winter landscapes.[24]

It is certainly tempting to imagine that the Dutch artists of winter landscapes faithfully depicted environments transformed by climate change. Brueghel the Elder was indeed the first artist to depict a wintry landscape without explicit religious imagery, and his early work quickly became famous. In subsequent decades, it inspired many other Dutch artists to paint depictions of activities on snow and ice-covered environments. At the same time, artists in the republic broke with European conventions by painting or sketching realistic landscapes and scenes that amounted to snapshots of everyday life. Until the 1940s, art historians in fact assumed that many sixteenth- and seventeenth-century Dutch paintings simply mirrored real life in the Dutch Golden Age.[25]

However, in the 1960s and 70s Jan Emmens and especially Eddy de Jongh deciphered the rich, metaphorical meanings embedded within the

[23] For examples, see Pieter Bruegel the Elder, 'Winter Landscape with a Bird Trap', painting, 1565, Musées Royaux des Beaux-Arts, www.wga.hu/frames-e.html?/html/b/bruegel/pieter_e/01/13winter.html. Pieter Brueghel the Elder, 'Hunters in the Snow', painting, 1565, Kunsthistorisches Museum Vienna, www.google.com/culturalinstitute/asset-viewer/hunters-in-the-snow-winter/WgFmzFNNN74nUg?hl=en. Pieter Brueghel the Younger, 'Winter Scene with Ice Skaters and Birds', painting, 1638, http://goo.gl/8rbqLX.

[24] W. J. Burroughs, 'Winter Landscapes and Climatic Change'. *Weather* 36 (1981): 352. Sam White, 'The Real Little Ice Age'. *The Journal of Interdisciplinary History* 44:3 (2014), 338. Adriaan M. J. de Kraker, 'The Little Ice Age: Harsh Winters between 1550 and 1650'. In *Hendrick Avercamp: Master of the Ice Scene*, ed. Pieter Roelofs. (Amsterdam: Rijksmuseum, 2009), 23. 'Ice and Snow in Paintings of Little Ice Age Winters', 38. Metzger, *Plaisirs de Glace: Essai sur la peinture hollandaise hivernale due Siècle d'or.* Ingrid D. Sager, *The Little Ice Age and 17th Century Dutch Landscape Painting, a Study on the Impact of Climate on Art.* (Dominguez Hills: California State University, 2006), 6. Douglas Macdougall, *Frozen Earth: The Once and Future Story of Ice Ages.* (Berkeley: University of California Press, 2004), 225. Behringer, *A Cultural History of Climate*, 139. Fagan, *The Little Ice Age*, 202. See also Emmanuel Le Roy Ladurie, *Histoire humaine et comparée du climat, Vol. I: Canicules et glaciers.* (Paris: Fayard, 2004).

[25] Haley, *The Dutch in the Seventeenth Century*, 134. Lawrence Otto Goedde, *Tempest and Shipwreck in Dutch and Flemish Art*, 5. Wayne Franits, 'Introduction', 1. Svetlana Alpers, 'Picturing Dutch Culture', 57. Kahr, *Dutch Painting in the Seventeenth Century*, 20. Blankert, *Selected Writings on Dutch Painting*, 132.

art of the Dutch Golden Age. Most scholars now believe that Dutch paintings were full of messages and metaphors that would have been clear to contemporary customers. Seventeenth-century artists and critics certainly understood that paintings did not necessarily represent things as they actually were. For example, in 1604, the artist Karel van Mander urged readers of his celebrated *Schilder-boeck* ('Painting Book') to paint 'from the imagination'. Even the realist artist and teacher Samuel van Hoogstraten of Dordrecht acknowledged that, while 'a perfect painting is like a mirror of Nature', it 'causes things that are not there to appear, and ... deceives', albeit 'in an acceptable, amusing, and praiseworthy way'. According to some contemporary art instructors, seemingly realistic landscapes actually gave artists greater room for invention than other genres of painting. For example, the late seventeenth-century art critic Roger de Piles wrote that, when painting landscapes, an artist 'has more opportunities, than in any of the other [genres], to please himself by the choice of his objects .... Thus painting, which is a kind of creation, is more particularly so with regard to landskip [sic]'.[26]

Accordingly, art historians have criticized the idea that early modern painters tried to represent the real weather of the Little Ice Age. Storms may have been more common in contemporary paintings, but then the golden backgrounds of medieval canvases, and the turn towards abstract art in the twentieth century, discouraged attempts to realistically depict weather. Moreover, landscape painting – the essential prerequisite for winter scenes –

[26] J. M. Nash, *The Age of Rembrandt and Vermeer: Dutch Painting in the Seventeenth Century*. (London: Phaidon, 1972), 48. Eddy de Jongh, 'Realism and Seeming Realism in Seventeenth-Century Dutch Painting'. In *Looking at Seventeenth-Century Dutch Art: Realism Reconsidered*, ed. Wayne Franits. (Cambridge: Cambridge University Press, 1997), 55. Eric J. Sluijter, 'Didactic and Disguised Meanings? Several Seventeenth-Century Texts on Painting and the Iconological Approach to Dutch Paintings of this Period', in *Looking at Seventeenth-Century Dutch Art*, 78. Joaneath A. Spicer, 'An Introduction to Painting in Utrecht, 1600–1650'. In *Masters of Light: Dutch Painters in Utrecht during the Golden Age*, eds. Joaneath A. Spicer and Lynn Federle Orr. (New Haven: Yale University Press, 1998), 15. E. de Jongh, 'The Iconological Approach to Seventeenth-Century Dutch Painting'. In *The Golden Age of Dutch Painting in Historical Perspective*, eds. Frans Grijzenhout and Henk van Veen, 200–223. (Cambridge: Cambridge University Press, 1999), 202. Kahr, *Dutch Painting in the Seventeenth Century*, 9. Israel, *The Dutch Republic*, 397. Westermann, *A Worldly Art*, 10. See also Christopher Brown, *Dutch Paintings*. London: National Gallery Publications, 1983. Svetlana Alpers, *The Art of Describing: Dutch Art in the Seventeenth Century*. (Chicago: University of Chicago Press, 1983). Willemijn C. Fock, 'Kunst en rariteiten in het Hollandse interieur'. In *De wereld binnen handbereijk: Nederlandse kunst- en rariteitenverzamelingen, 1585–1735*, eds. Ellinoor Bergevelt and Renee Kistemaker. (Zwolle: Waanders Uitgevers/Amsterdam Historisch Museum, 1992), 70–91.

only emerged as an established artistic genre in the early modern Dutch Republic. Icy landscapes did become popular during the Grindelwald Fluctuation but not during the chilliest decades of the Maunder Minimum, when Dutch consumers preferred bright, sunny scenes.[27]

It is in fact precisely because they appear like such clear cultural responses to climate change that Dutch winter landscapes can be a troublesome source for climate historians. To clearly link climate change to the production, subjects, and reception of art, scholars need to thoroughly contextualize how each artwork was created. They should endeavour to establish links between climate change and short-term variability in local environmental conditions, which includes weather. Next, they should seek to determine how these local environmental changes affected complex relationships between economic or military histories, marketplace dynamics, and the artist's ideas and perceptions. Leaving aside the unfathomable influence of the subconscious, scholars should then attempt to confirm either that the artist painted in response to a long-term weather trend that she or he had detected, or to short-term weather that reflected the influence of the Little Ice Age.[28]

It is hard for climate historians to follow all of these steps when examining most winter landscapes, given the sources that survive to document their creation. Some of what we do know about their production undermines the case for winter landscapes as clear responses to climate change. Take, for example, connections between local environments, the artist, and the production of art. Some sixteenth-century winter landscapes were the product of a team that included not only the lead artist but also his apprentices. They painted in a heated workshop, and most therefore did not see or experience real landscapes while they worked. Winter scenes therefore rarely depicted actual weather events, although they could still represent a generally cold season, or perhaps a weather trend that the lead artist had perceived.

Links between local environments, the market, and art could also be tenuous. Most winter landscapes were consumer products, painted for a marketplace that demanded seasonal portrayals of everyday life. In the

[27] David Huddart and Tim Stott, *Earth Environments Past, Present and Future*. (Chichester: John Wiley & Sons, 2013), 863. Kelly and Ó Gráda, 'The Waning of the Little Ice Age', 314. Albert Blankert, *Selected Writings on Dutch Painting: Rembrandt, Van Beke, Vermeer and Others*. (Zwolle: Waanders Publishers, 2005), 146.

[28] Molly Faries, 'Making and Marketing: Studies of the Painting Process'. In *Making and Marketing: Studies of the Painting Process in Fifteenth- and Sixteenth-Century Netherlandish Workshops*, ed. Molly Faries. (Turnhout: Brepols Publishers, 2006), 1.

sixteenth century, artists usually sold them alongside depictions of spring, summer, and autumn, which they painted in much warmer hues. Early in the frigid seventeenth century, winter scenes were less frequently packaged with other seasonal representations. They became darker, drearier, and often smaller. However, this shift in winter landscapes at least partly reflected trends not of climate, but rather in the artistic and commercial histories of the republic. Above all, winter was easier to paint with the monochrome hues that artists were forced to use when they could no longer access more vibrant dyes. Both consumers and artists also appreciated that all seasonal depictions had moral and metaphorical messages embedded in what look to modern observers like whimsical scenes from everyday life. By depicting skaters slipping on the ice, for example, artists communicated messages about tenuousness of human life and the dangers of sin.[29]

Yet winter landscapes still have great value for climate history. Individual artists painted some using accurate sketches that they had made during rambles in the countryside. Not all were heavy with metaphor, and some were sold alone, without other seasonal depictions. These paintings are a minority among winter landscapes, but they do reflect how artists perceived real relationships between people and the environmental manifestations of climate change. We can therefore consider them genuine cultural responses to the Little Ice Age. Some artists might also have painted their winter scenes because they perceived, consciously or unconsciously, that severe winters in their present were more common they had been. Regardless, even winter landscapes that were not painted in response to cooler winters in a chillier climate can still shed light on the climate history of the Dutch Republic. Depictions of winter activities reflect discourses between artists and consumers that reveal shared perceptions, or ideals, of how Dutch citizens coped with and exploited frigid weather. Even winter landscapes that were not created because of a cooler climate therefore still hint at relationships between the Little Ice Age and Dutch culture. Above all, most portray scenes of work and play and merriment on the ice that together suggest that cold weather could be

[29] Kelly and Ó Gráda, 'The Waning of the Little Ice Age', 314. Colin Coates, 'Seeing and Not Seeing: Landscape Art as a Historical Sources'. In *Method and Meaning in Canadian Environmental History*, eds. Alan MacEachern and William J. Turkel. (Toronto: Nelson Education, 2009), 155. Max J. Frieslaender, *Early Netherlandish Painting From Van Eyck to Bruegel*. (London: Phaidon Press, 1956), 135. De Jongh, 'Realism and Seeming Realism in Seventeenth-Century Dutch Painting', 27. Blankert, *Selected Writings on Dutch Painting*, 138.

endured, exploited, and even enjoyed. Clearly, this was a message that resonated with their intended audience.[30]

PAINTING WAR, WEATHER, AND CLIMATE CHANGE

Few artistic genres in the Dutch Republic represented real events, including weather, more accurately than the kind that dealt with military scenes. During the Dutch wars of independence, artists accompanied campaigns in the Low Countries to paint their major battles and sieges. Others represented these events in painstaking detail by listening to the recollections of soldiers and officers. Pieter Snaeyers, for example, drew from their memories to complete three paintings of the surrender of Breda in 1625. Jacques Callot used subsidies from the Spanish government in Brussels to create a massive and widely published map of the siege that he paired with an extensive index of relevant people and places.[31]

Paintings, illustrations, and maps of military confrontations could be used as propaganda alongside plays, poems, or pamphlets, but most faithfully reflected the major characteristics of battles or sieges. Many artistic representations of military operations in the Low Countries therefore included detailed depictions of local environments, especially when those environments influenced the outcome of campaigns. Soon after the Dutch Revolt, illustrators in rebel territories sketched both realistic and metaphorical portrayals of military inundations that relieved beleaguered towns. As we have seen, the stormy weather of the Grindelwald Fluctuation aided these deliberate floods. Artists also painted scenes of military operations in times of drought. During the *rampjaar* of 1672, for instance, Adam Frans van der Meulen accurately painted the French crossing of an unusually shallow Rhine. Since drought had lowered the Rhine, Van der Meulen's painting was partly a cultural response to weather, but not a climate change that actually decreased the frequency of such weather.[32]

Artists painted naval battles with even greater realism, and even more attention to weather, than campaigns on land. Their paintings, now

[30] De Jongh, 'Realism and Seeming Realism in Seventeenth-Century Dutch Painting', 28.

[31] Parker, *The Army of Flanders*, 104.

[32] 'Samuel Tucker aan Williamson, 17 Juni 1672', in *Bescheiden uit Vreemde Archieven omtrent de Groote Nederlandsche Zeeoorlogen, Vol. II*, 131. Buisman, *Duizend jaar, Vol. IV*, 647. Jones, *The Anglo-Dutch Wars*, 187. Frans Hogenberg, 'Leiden Ontzet in 1574', print, Prentenkabinet Museum Boijmans Van Beuningen, Het Geheugen van Nederland, http://goo.gl/Dg8TD5. Anonymous, 'Allegorie op de nood en het ontzet van Leiden', print, 1574, Rijksmuseum Amsterdam, www.rijksmuseum.nl/nl/collectie/RP-P-2001–149.

closely identified with the Dutch Golden Age, did not depict weather merely as a setting for human activity but also as a dynamic agent that shaped the outcome of battles. In the seventeenth century, Willem van de Velde the Elder and his son were arguably the most celebrated artists in the genre of marine painting. In the second half of the century, they completed a series of paintings and illustrations that chronicled the course of contemporary naval wars. Van de Velde the Elder was the official painter of the Dutch Admiralties during the first two Anglo-Dutch Wars, and he became the first painter known to have travelled with a war fleet as it campaigned at sea. In 1672, the Van de Veldes moved to England, and both artists worked for the English admiralty during the Third Anglo-Dutch War. After the war, Van de Velde the Younger continued his dangerous work for the admiralty by illustrating battles as they unfolded. During a battle, the Van de Veldes would sketch a rough outline of action from the lurching deck of a ship. Later, they refined and painted in their sketches from the safety of a studio. Many of their paintings of naval battles accordingly resemble photographs taken by present-day journalists 'embedded' with armies.[33]

The Van de Veldes laboured to accurately depict the technologies, environmental circumstances, and outcomes of naval confrontations. Willem van de Velde the Elder was born into a nautical family. His detailed paintings reflect a deep understanding of rigging and navigation, which he passed down to his son. Given their obsession with accuracy, and their presence in Dutch and later English fleets, it is no surprise that both artists depicted weather conditions that really affected naval engagements. For example, during the First Anglo-Dutch War, Van de Velde the Elder sketched high waves in an illustration of the Battle of Scheveningen. On 10 August 1653, that battle, the last of the First Anglo-Dutch War,

[33] Israel, *The Dutch Republic*, 875. Marleen Dominicus van Soest, *The Masterpieces Guide*. (Westzaan: Kunstdrukkerij Mercurius, 2009), 127. F. B. Cockett, *Early Sea Painters, 1660–1730*. (Suffolk: Antique Collectors' Club Ltd, 1995), 108. John Walsh Jr. and Cynthia P. Schneider, *A Mirror of Nature: Dutch Paintings from the Collection of Mr. and Mrs. Edward William Carter*. (New York: Los Angeles County Museum of Art, 1992), 105. Bob Haak, *The Golden Age: Dutch Painters of the Seventeenth Century*. (London: Thames and Hudson, 1984), 151. Kahr, *Dutch Painting in the Seventeenth Century*, 235. For an amusing depiction of Van de Velde the Younger painting in the Dutch fleet, see J. Dehoij, 'Willem van de Velde Sketching a Sea Battle', painting, 1845, State Hermitage Museum, www.arthermitage.org/Dehoij/Willem-van-de-Velde-Sketching-a-Sea-Battle.html. See also R. Daalder, *Van de Velde & Son, Marine Painters: The firm of Willem van de Velde the Elder and Willem van de Velde the Younger, 1640–1707*. (Leiden: Primavera Pers, 2016).

erupted soon after a gale. In subsequent wars, both artists repeatedly represented weather associated with the Maunder Minimum. In the Second Anglo-Dutch War, Van de Velde the Younger painted the English attack on a VOC fleet at Bergen, on 11 August 1665. In the painting, the harbour of Bergen and the VOC fleet are on the left, while the ocean and the English squadron are to the right. Clouds and smoke appear to blow from left to right, while flags flutter to the right of their masts. The depicted wind therefore blows from the east, out of their harbour. It was, of course, a high easterly wind that thwarted the English assault on the VOC fleet.[34]

Willem van de Velde the Younger and his father also completed several paintings of the Four Days' Battle, which raged from 11 to 14 June 1666. During the battle, high winds benefitted Dutch vessels, but a westerly initially allowed the English fleet to attack with the weather gage. Van de Velde the Elder was on the scene. His painting of the battle accurately portrayed English vessels attacking with the wind, despite very rough seas (Figure 6.1). His son painted the surrender of the *Royal Prince* on the fourth day of battle. The Dutch fleet had claimed the weather gage in easterly winds, which pushed them towards the grounded *Prince*. In the painting, the Dutch fleet sails towards the stricken ship from the left. Portrayals of smoke, flags, and sails all suggest that the wind blowing from left to right. Given the position of the Dutch fleet, Van de Velde accurately depicted an easterly breeze that we can now associate with the Maunder Minimum.[35]

Paintings by the Van de Veldes were therefore cultural responses not only to war, but also to weather shaped by a changing climate. Other artists who painted naval scenes similarly depicted weather that actually influenced battles at sea. One example is a seventeenth-century painting, by an anonymous artist, which portrayed the Battle of the Downs between Dutch and Spanish fleets on 21 October 1639. In the painting, smoke moves from the Dutch fleet, largely gathered on the left, to the Spanish fleet, on the right. The wind in the painting blows towards the English

[34] Willem van de Velde the Elder, 'The Battle of Terheide', painting, 1657, Rijksmuseum Amsterdam, www.rijksmuseum.nl/en/collection/SK-A-1365. Willem van de Velde the Younger, 'Action at Bergen', painting, 1666, National Maritime Museum, http://collections.rmg.co.uk/collections/objects/12190.html. Goedde, *Tempest and Shipwreck in Dutch and Flemish Art*), 1. Walsh and Schneider, *A Mirror of Nature*, 105.

[35] Willem van de Velde the Younger, 'The Capture of the Royal Prince', painting, 1666, Rijksmuseum Amsterdam, http://goo.gl/xeYBrs.

(a)

(b)

FIGURE 6.1 Painting the Little Ice Age. Top: taking to the ice during the frigid winter of 1607/1608. Hendrick Avercamp, 'Winter Landscape with Ice Skaters', painting, 1608, Rijksmuseum, Amsterdam, https://www.rijksmuseum.nl/en/collection/SK-A-1718. Bottom: Rough seas during the Four Days' Battle. Willem van de Velde the Elder, 'Episode uit de Vierdaagse Zeeslag, 11–14 Juni 1666, in de Tweede Engelse Zeeoorlog (1665–67)', painting, 1666, Rijksmuseum Amsterdam, www.rijksmuseum.nl/nl/collectie/SK-A-1392.

coast, which means that it must be an easterly. Indeed, an easterly benefitted the Dutch during the actual battle.[36]

Even some Dutch artists who did not normally paint naval battles and were not embedded with fleets strove to accurately represent weather. Willem Shellinks, for example, was a landscape artist who, in 1667, completed a painting of the republic's Raid on the Medway. In the painting, Dutch vessels sail up the Medway River, which meanders from the bottom left to the top right of the canvas. Plumes of smoke, and accordingly the wind, roughly follow the course of the river and therefore blow from the northeast. Wind in the painting therefore blows from the northeast, and corresponds to the actual wind that probably reflected the influence of the Maunder Minimum and definitely benefitted the Dutch raid.[37]

Other Dutch artists also attempted to accurately portray weather that influenced naval operations. Landscape artist Abraham Storck, for example, painted many seascapes, although naval conflict only featured in three of his works. His depictions of nautical technology reflect a rigorous concern for accurate detail that betrayed the influence of maritime artists such as the Van de Veldes. In 1670, Storck completed a painting of the Four Days' Battle that correctly portrayed high winds bending masts and fanning rough seas. He also accurately painted the bulk of the English fleet attacking with the weather gage, although he mistakenly portrayed English vessels with their lower gun ports open.[38]

Storck's painting is a cultural representation of and response to real weather, and probably the climatic cooling that made such weather more common. Like many Dutch artists who painted conflict at sea, however, Storck did not attempt to create a snapshot that depicted a single moment in the course of a battle. Rather, he gathered all the most spectacular and unusual aspects of the Four Days' Battle in a single scene. He depicted major events in the battle as if they all unfolded at the same time, although

[36] Anonymous (Netherlandish School), 'The Battle of the Downs, 21 October 1639', painting, seventeenth century, National Maritime Museum, London, http://collections.rmg.co.uk/collections/objects/11761.html.

[37] Willem Schellinks, 'The Dutch in the Medway', painting, 1667, Rijksmuseum, Amsterdam, www.rijksmuseum.nl/en/search/objecten?q=%22Willem+Schellinks%22&p=2&ps=12&ii=4#/SK-A-1393,16.

[38] Abraham Storck, 'The "Royal Prince" and Other Vessels at the Four Days Battle, 1–4 June 1666', painting, 1667, National Maritime Museum, http://collections.rmg.co.uk/collections/objects/11778.html. Willem Schellinks, 'The Dutch in the Medway', painting, 1667, Rijksmuseum, Amsterdam, www.rijksmuseum.nl/en/search/objecten?q=%22Willem+Schellinks%22&p=2&ps=12&ii=4#/SK-A-1393,16.

they really happened on different days. He therefore ignored the sequence in which relationships between weather and human activity actually played out. His painting shows only the stormy westerly winds that prevailed on the first day of battle, not the calmer easterlies of the second, third, and fourth days.

Many paintings of naval battles similarly distort time and space, and are therefore not fully reliable representations of reality. Moreover, most targeted audiences in one of the belligerent nations, and they occasionally served as mythmaking propaganda. In the republic, the demand for naval paintings accordingly declined in the late seventeenth century, as English naval power started to eclipse that of the republic, while the English appetite for naval scenes increased. Nevertheless, many Dutch paintings of naval conflict portray interactions between weather and human activity that are verified by ship logbooks, correspondence, and other documentary sources. They are undoubtedly clearer and more direct cultural responses to climate change than most winter landscapes.[39]

Many Dutch artists painted maritime scenes that did not necessarily represent historical events, but rather common views of life on the water. Paintings in this marine genre often portrayed vessels struggling through gales, usually near a lee shore that threatened their destruction. During the coldest, stormiest phases of the Little Ice Age, common reports of gales at sea and more frequent shipwrecks on the North Sea coast might have inspired artists to paint these 'stormscapes'. Dutch artists in fact invented the stormy sea as an independent theme for art, and only in the middle of the Grindelwald Fluctuation. However, they may have responded not to weather but rather the rising volume of Dutch trade, which exposed merchants and mariners to more storms and also created profits that ultimately supported the extraordinary rise of Dutch painting. Moreover, many artists, such as Jan Peeters, framed their stormscapes with exotic and often fanciful shores, and did not attempt to accurately depict Dutch naval technology. Their art therefore did not necessarily reflect real environmental conditions, let alone real ships and people affected by those conditions. The storm was also a powerful and highly complex metaphor in Dutch art. Stormscapes followed several recurring tropes, depicting either a ship in open water, a shipwreck on a rocky coast, a ship stranding on a beach, a ship threatened by a lee shore, ships framed by a gathering storm, or a storm over recognizably local waters. Each trope communicated a different meaning. Stormscapes that portrayed

[39] Haak, *The Golden Age*, 152.

ships approaching or breaking on a lee shore, for example, communicated familiar lessons about the danger of losing control and the importance of fortune. Paintings of ships weathering storms in the open sea illustrated the virtuous struggle for mastery in periods of uncertainty. The lightning that often cut across depictions of storms in Dutch waters represented warnings from God. Most stormscapes therefore had only tenuous connections to real places, experiences, and weather.[40]

Nevertheless, the desire to deploy storms as metaphors may have occasionally followed from the documented experiences of painters encountering real, local environmental manifestations of the Little Ice Age. Van de Velde the Younger, for instance, started painting more scenes of ships in gales only after crossing the channel and arriving in London in late 1672. As we have seen, that year was among the stormiest of the Little Ice Age in the North Sea region.[41] Storms probably hampered, and perhaps even threatened, Van de Velde's passage across the channel. Even paintings of storms at sea that did not depict real weather events could therefore have been cultural responses to experiences of weather, and in turn climate change. Stormscapes painted by the Van de Velde influenced many other artists, and more accurately depicted naval technologies and techniques than the paintings of Jan Peeters. Still, Van de Velde and others also painted many scenes of ships becalmed, drifting with limp sails in mirror-smooth seas. While Van de Velde painted more scenes of ships in stormy seas, his depictions of becalmed vessels suggest that portrayals of these very different meteorological extremes were often displayed

[40] Lawrence Otto Goedde, *Tempest and Shipwreck in Dutch and Flemish Art*, 20, 165, 190.

[41] Willem van de Velde the Younger, 'De Windstoot', painting, c. 1680, Rijksmuseum Amsterdam, Amsterdam, www.rijksmuseum.nl/nl/collectie/SK-A-1848. Willem van de Velde the Younger, 'An Indiaman in a Gale off a Rocky Coast', painting, c. 1650–1707, Private Collection, www.the-athenaeum.org/art/detail.php?ID=129724. Willem van de Velde the Younger, 'A Dutch Ship Scudding Before a Storm', painting, c. 1690, National Maritime Museum, http://collections.rmg.co.uk/collections/objects/12397.html. Willem van de Velde the Younger, 'A Mediterranean Brigantine Drifting Onto a Rocky Coast in a Storm', painting, c. 1700, National Maritime Museum, London, http://collections.rmg.co .uk/collections/objects/12398.html. Willem van de Velde the Younger, 'The Resolution in a Gale', painting, 1678, National Maritime Museum, London, http://blogs.rmg.co.uk/col lections/2014/10/20/queens-house-twitter-top-10/bhc3582/. Willem van de Velde the Younger, 'Ships in Distress off Rock', painting, c. 1700, Lancaster House, London, www .the-athenaeum.org/art/detail.php?ID=129826. Willem van de Velde the Younger, 'Three Ships in a Gale', painting, 1673, National Gallery, London, www.nationalgallery.org.uk /paintings/willem-van-de-velde-three-ships-in-a-gale. Willem van de Velde the Younger, 'Two English Ships Wrecked in a Storm on a Rocky Coast', painting, c. 1700, National Maritime Museum, London, http://collections.rmg.co.uk/collections/objects/12399.html.

together. In similar fashion, scenes of spring, summer, and fall often accompanied winter landscapes. Ultimately, the popularity of stormscapes in the Maunder Minimum therefore did not directly reflect a rise in the frequency or severity of gales. Such paintings were usually indirect and highly mediated cultural responses to climate change.[42]

Paintings that clearly reacted to specific weather events, or the consequences of those events, were therefore the clearest cultural responses to early modern climate change. It is harder to link the Little Ice Age to changes in the popularity and production of most winter landscapes and stormy seascapes. Nevertheless, Dutch weather observers and perhaps artists did accurately trace long-term changes in weather extremes, and some painters might therefore have consciously responded not merely to weather events, but to one aspect of what we would call climate change. Either way, Dutch paintings that represent frigid winters or storms illustrate how citizens of the republic lived with weather that became more common in the coldest phases of the Little Ice Age. They also offer insights into the relationships Dutch painters and their customers perceived between people and such weather.[43]

Some historians have argued that seventeenth-century Dutch painters depicted storms as straightforwardly negative cosmic disorders. According to Lawrence Otto Goedde, for example, Dutch painting de-emphasizes human agency and instead stresses the 'insignificance and impotence [of people] in the face of the overwhelming destructiveness of elemental nature'. In fact, while environmental conditions often challenge the

[42] Willem van de Velde the Younger, 'Schepen voor de kust tijdens windstilte', painting, c. 1650–1707, Rijksmuseum Amsterdam, Amsterdam, www.rijksmuseum.nl/nl/collectie/SK-A-722. Willem van de Velde the Younger, 'Windstilte', painting, c. 1650–1707, Rijksmuseum Amsterdam, Amsterdam, www.rijksmuseum.nl/nl/collectie/SK-A-436. Willem van de Velde the Younger, 'Het kanonschot', painting, 1680, Rijksmuseum Amsterdam, Amsterdam, www.rijksmuseum.nl/nl/collectie/SK-C-244. Willem van de Velde the Younger, 'Schepen voor anker', painting, c. 1650–1707, Rijksmuseum Amsterdam, Amsterdam, www.rijksmuseum.nl/nl/collectie/SK-A-3350. Willem van de Velde the Younger, 'Hollandse schepen op een kalme zee', painting, c. 1665, Rijksmuseum Amsterdam, Amsterdam, www.rijksmuseum.nl/nl/collectie/SK-C-1707. Willem van de Velde the Younger, 'Schepen voor de kust', painting, c. 1650–1707, Rijksmuseum Amsterdam, Amsterdam, www.rijksmuseum.nl/nl/collectie/SK-A-440. Aelbert Cuyp, 'River Scene with a Ferry Boat', painting, c. 1652, Auckland Art Galler, Toiotāmaki, www.aucklandartgallery.com/the-collection/browse-artwork/121/river-scene-with-a-ferry-boat.

[43] Haley, *The Dutch in the Seventeenth Century*, 134. De Vries and Van der Woude, *The First Modern Economy*, 116. Lawrence Otto Goedde, *Tempest and Shipwreck in Dutch and Flemish Art*, 5.

protagonists of Dutch seascapes and winterscapes, human activities and technologies almost always take centre stage. Moreover, weather in Dutch paintings less frequently inflicts disaster on passive victims than it is exploited or at least endured by active agents. In the majority of paintings that depict ships in storms, for example, Dutch artists showed vessels still under human control. In paintings of naval battles, mariners seize the advantage of the weather gage. In most winter landscapes, human beings thrive using technologies, such as skates and sleds, that help them master a frozen environment.[44]

Ultimately, in the paintings of the Dutch Golden Age, both metaphor and realism reflect the importance for Dutch citizens of weather associated with the chilliest decades of the Little Ice Age. By depicting the ways in which such weather could have ambiguous and sometimes exploitable consequences for human actors, Dutch paintings represented, and perhaps contributed to, the material history of the republic's experience with a colder climate.

CONCLUSIONS: TRACKING AND REPRESENTING THE LITTLE ICE AGE

In the Golden Age of the republic, Dutch observers compared the weather extremes of what we call the Little Ice Age to weather patterns in their past. Often, they concluded that weather in their present had no precedent, and they were usually right across timeframes of about a generation. Some observers, however, used natural or artificial landmarks and even precise measurements to more accurately track past weather extremes and occasionally even averages. Such thinking may well have helped the Dutch endure and exploit the weather of the Little Ice Age, and it certainly represents the most obvious way that climate change influenced Dutch culture.

Dutch artists may well have drawn from attempts to track past weather when they painted frozen landscapes and stormy seascapes. Yet Dutch winter landscapes in particular were not quite the straightforward representations of the Little Ice Age that they appear to be. By contrast, paintings that depict how weather common in Little Ice Age cold periods actually influenced real events, such as naval battles, did respond to concrete ramifications of a cooling climate. Both winter landscapes and naval scenes, however, reveal how Dutch artists and customers thought about weather, and in turn how they consciously or unconsciously perceived the consequences of climate change.

[44] Lawrence Otto Goedde, *Tempest and Shipwreck in Dutch and Flemish Art*, 180.

7

Texts, Technologies, and Climate Change

According to Ernst Kossmann, every historian interested in the culture of the Dutch Golden Age 'has had to answer the question as to whether, and if so how, art can be woven into the story'. While that is certainly the case for painting, it has been less true for mapmaking, pamphleteering, and poetry. Yet these less glamorous kinds of art all shaped and reflected the distinct characteristics of the Dutch Golden Age. Maps depicted Dutch discoveries, territorial claims, and technologies. Pamphlets represented debates and feuds that resonated in the Dutch Republic. Poems, like paintings, provided characteristically Dutch portrayals of everyday life.[1]

Diverse artistic genres therefore engaged with the social spaces, ideas, and innovations that were at the heart of the Dutch Golden Age. All responded to the Little Ice Age, occasionally in complementary ways. Maps, for example, registered the experiences of explorers in environments shaped by a shifting climate. They then helped subsequent explorers, and the merchants, fishermen, and whalers who followed in their wake, navigate those environments. Some of the clearest poetic

[1] Schenkeveld, *Dutch Literature in the Age of Rembrandt: Themes and Ideas*, viii, 470. Israel, *The Dutch Republic*, 477, 686. Ernst H. Kossmann, 'Seventeenth-Century Dutch Art in the Eyes of Historians'. In *The Golden Age of Dutch Painting in Historical Perspective*, eds. Frans Grijzenhout and Henk van Veen. (Cambridge: Cambridge University Press, 1999), 184. Reinder P. Meijer, *Literature of the Low Countries: A Short History of Dutch Literature in the Netherlands and Belgium*, 2nd ed. (The Hague: Martinus Nijhoff, 1978), 105. See also Deric Regin, *Traders, Artists, Burghers. A Cultural History of Amsterdam in the 17th Century*. (Assen: Koninklijke Van Gorcum, 1976). Thedoor Weever, *The Poetry of the Netherlands in Its European Context 1170–1930*. (London: Athlone Press, 1960).

responses to climate change, by contrast, expressed themes of loss and despair that contrasted with the emergence of energetic 'ice cultures' during the chilliest winters of the Little Ice Age. Yet overall Dutch culture reacted to climate change in ways that reflected the ambiguous but overall beneficial influence of the Little Ice Age across the Dutch trading empire.

CULTURAL RESPONSES TO CLIMATE CHANGE BETWEEN LITERATURE AND VISUAL ART

Some of the most widely reproduced and practically important art of the Dutch Golden Age applied written annotations to visual representations of the world. Maps, for example, richly labelled and described places that mapmakers depicted with the techniques of both visual art and contemporary science. From the early sixteenth century, publishers in the Low Countries printed sophisticated 'portolan' charts with sailing instructions for mariners that soon became common tools. Meanwhile, the profession of cartographer gained in prestige, and cartography increasingly influenced both literature and painting. By the early seventeenth century, most maps were commissioned by merchants, sketched by explorers, refined by cartographers, and either published in Amsterdam or hoarded by merchant companies. Family enterprises combined publishing and cartography to regularly print comprehensive atlases of the charted world. The intricately detailed maps in those atlases appealed not only to sailors but also to enthusiasts, collectors, and librarians. Yet because newly published atlases and maps usually incorporated the latest discoveries made by European explorers, they were especially valuable to merchants seeking new opportunities for profit. Hence, from the sixteenth to the eighteenth centuries, Dutch maps gradually grew more accurate.[2]

This was not a simple trend, however. Early modern mapmakers endeavoured to do more than accurately depict real environments and geographies. Many adorned their maps with symbols that communicated detailed messages. They placed ships, for example, in places that explorers

[2] Michael Jones, 'Tycho Brahe, Cartography and Landscape'. In *European Rural Landscapes: Persistence and Change in a Globalising Environment*, eds. H. Palang, H. Sooväli, M. Antrop, and G. Setten (Dordrecht: Springer Netherlands, 2004), 210. Leo Bagrow, *History of Cartography*. (New Brunswick: Transaction Publishers, 2010), 21. Sjoerd de Meer, 'De wereld van de zeekart'. In *Het Zeekarten Boek*, ed. Sjoerd de Meer. (Zutphen: Walburg Pers, 2007), 13. Zandvliet, *Mapping for Money*, 61. Sjoerd de Meer, 'Het kaartenmakersbedrijf van de Verenigde Oostindische Compagnie', in *Het Zeekarten Boek*, 57. Schilder and Kok, *Sailing for the East*, 68.

had recently charted and were now claimed by the state or corporate sponsors of those explorers. By the seventeenth century, they added sea monsters to maps to symbolize the presence of abundant marine resources, such as whales or walruses. Maps therefore advertised the imperial claims, mercantile ambitions, religious or magical assumptions, and scientific state-of-the-art with which Europeans approached the world.[3]

The places and the messages in every new map reflected reports written by explorers in expeditions that responded, as we have seen, to local environmental changes set in motion by the Little Ice Age. Three Dutch maps of the Arctic, published during and after the Barents and Hudson expeditions to the Arctic, revealed with particular clarity how climate change influenced mapmaking by affecting journeys of exploration. Gerard Mercator's son, Rumold, published the first in 1595, the year of the second Barents expedition (Map 7.1). In it, Greenland is connected to the polar continent, and a line of islands roughly matches the extent of the pack ice above northern Europe. Rivers flow north through four continents that surround a vast mountain at the geographic North Pole, while a smaller mountain at the magnetic North Pole rises from the water between Asia and North America.[4]

Shortly before his death, Barents drew and annotated a map that portrayed his discoveries in the far north. Two years later, in 1599, Cornelis Claeszoon of Harlem painted and published that map. Its boldness and relative accuracy are still startling. Barents replaced polar continents with open water, and rightly sketched Greenland as an island with a northern coastline that had not yet been mapped. He correctly placed both Spitsbergen and Bear Island relative to Norway and the geographic North Pole. He also depicted Novaya Zemlya with impressive precision, at least up to the point on the island's northeastern coast where Barents

[3] J. B. Harley, 'Maps, Knowledge, and Power'. In *The Iconography of Landscape: Essays on the Symbolic Representation, Design and Use of Past Environments*, eds. D. Cosgrove and S. Daniels (Cambridge: Cambridge University Press, 1988), 277. Unger, *Ships on Maps*, 178. Jones, 'Tycho Brahe, Cartography and Landscape', 211. Walter Mignolo, *The Darker Side of the Renaissance: Literacy, Territoriality, and Colonization*. (Ann Arbor: University of Michigan Press, 2003), 278. See also G. R. Crone, *Maps and Their Makers: An Introduction to the History of Cartography*, 5th Edition. (Dawson: Folkestone & Archon Books, 1978). R. V. Tooley and C. Bricker. *A History of Cartography: 2500 Years of Maps and Mapmakers*. (London: Thames and Hudson, 1969).

[4] See also W. A. Ligtendag, 'Willem Barentsz en de kartografie van het hoge noorden'. *Kartografisch tijdschrift* 23:1 (1997): 5.

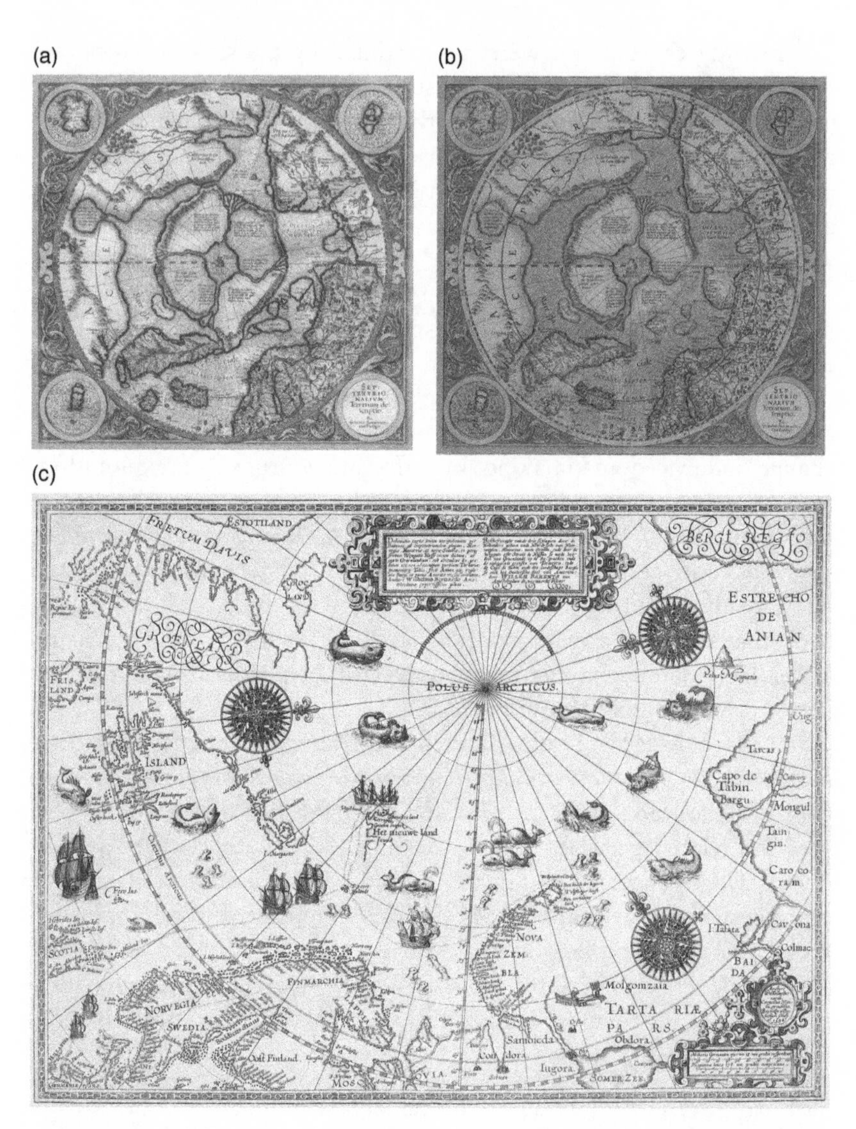

MAP 7.1 Top left: a map by Mercator depicts the Arctic as Dutch scholars understood it in 1595, on the eve of the third Barents voyage. Top right: a more accurate map of the Arctic, printed by Hondius and published nine years after the conclusion of the third Barents voyage. Bottom: map of the north drawn by Barents shortly before his death, and published in 1599. Rumold Mercator, *Atlantis Pars Altera: Geographia Nova Totius Mundi* (Duisburg, 1595), Willem Barents, *Deliniatio cartæ trium navigationum etc.* (The Hague: Cornelis Claeszoon, 1599). Jodocus Hondius, *Atlas.* (Amsterdam, 1606), Osher Map Library.

and his crew had overwintered. The local environmental manifestations of global climate change had influenced the nature of these discoveries and therefore the maps they made possible. They also indirectly killed Barents, which intensified popular interest in his final map and increased the impact of his findings.[5]

In 1604, Jodocus Hondius purchased the rights to Mercator's maps, and in 1606 published an atlas that included a new version of Mercator's Arctic map. It reflected an inconsistent mix of ancient conventions and new discoveries. Hondius kept some of the older map's rivers and continents, but replaced parts of two continents with open water. The existence of these continents now looked less like a certainty and more like a placeholder, pending further exploration. Hondius depicted Spitsbergen, Bear Island, and Novaya Zemlya as Barents had, while separating Greenland from the North Pole. For the first time, a major atlas released by an Amsterdam publishing house accurately depicted real Arctic environments, and showed that open water stretched across at least part of the far north.[6]

All three maps portrayed areas directly scouted by Europeans with great detail and precision. By contrast, they represented unexplored regions with simplified coastlines, blank spaces, and sparse labels. By affecting journeys of exploration, climate change affected when, and where, meticulously annotated depictions of real geography replaced vague unknowns. It also shaped narratives in maps that more explicitly communicated the values and purposes of explorers, cartographers, and their patrons. For example, Barents sketched an open sea teeming with monsters and ships to advertise the Arctic not only as an easier way of reaching Asia, but also as a region of abundant marine resources that had been claimed for the Dutch. His map, and especially Hudson's later reports from Spitsbergen, encouraged Dutch whalers to begin the slaughter of Arctic bowhead whales, which in turn influenced the republic's culture and economy. Whalers braved and occasionally exploited the weather of the Little Ice Age to help cartographers draft ever more accurate maps of the Arctic to aid their activities in the far north. That gradually led to the extirpation of bowhead whales from the seas near Svalbard, which altered how the regional ecosystem responded and

[5] Willem Barents, *Deliniatio cartæ trium navigationum etc.* (The Hague: Cornelis Claeszoon, 1599).

[6] Rumold Mercator and Jodocus Hondius, *Atlas.* (Amsterdam, 1606). Rumold Mercator, *Septentrionalium Terrarum descriptio 1595.* (Amsterdam, 1595).

contributed to climate change while undermining what had been an important aspect of the republic's economy and culture. In a small way, climate change and culture coevolved through mapmaking.[7]

Pamphlets were even more popular than maps in the sixteenth- and seventeenth-century Dutch Republic. Like maps, they usually annotated visual art so that it more clearly communicated ideas that were valuable to major commercial or state interests within the republic. In a sense, pamphlets were precursors to twenty-first century cartoons or comic books, and they only rarely featured straightforward representations of events as they actually unfolded.[8] Instead, most communicated patriotic or religious messages by using allegorical images, which usually had no discernable connections to real environmental conditions. Yet even such images were occasionally accompanied by text that reflected cultural receptions of weather and climate change.[9]

For example, a pamphlet published early in the Dutch wars of independence portrayed Catholic religious, military, and political leaders crushing a lion that represents the Dutch people. Broken artefacts beneath the lion represented the trammelled freedoms and privileges of Dutch towns and their citizens. A morbid poem accompanied the image. It compared the depredations of Spanish rulers to a stormy sea, and to strong currents that overwhelm a dike and flood the countryside. Adriaen Valerius published the pamphlet in a catalogue of sixteenth- and seventeenth-century Dutch songs. It preceded a lamentation that was set to music and dwelled on the misery imposed by Spanish rule. Valerius illustrated that dreary theme by referring to environmental

[7] See also W. A. Ligtendag, 'Willem Barentsz en de kartografie van het hoge noorden'. *Kartografisch tijdschrift* 23:1 (1997): 5–14.

[8] Dutch artists developed media that even more closely resembled comic books. See David Kunzle, *The Early Comic Strip: Narrative Strips and Picture Stories in the European Broadsheet from c.1450 to 1825*. (Berkeley: University of California Press, 1973).

[9] Israel, *The Dutch Republic*, 210. Haley, *The Dutch in the Seventeenth Century*, 73. P. A. M. Geurts, *De Nederlandse Opstand in de Pamfletten 1566–1584*. (Nijmegen: Centrale Drukkerij, 1956), 131. Femke Deen, David Onnekink, and Michel Reinders. 'Pamphlets and Politics: Introduction'. In *Pamphlets and Politics in the Dutch Republic*, eds. Femake Deen, David Onnekink and Michel Reinders. (Leiden: Brill, 2010), 3. Reinders, 'Burghers, Orangists and "good government", 316. Michel Reinders, 'Burghers, Orangists and "Good Government": Popular Political Opposition during the "Year of Disaster" 1672 in Dutch Pamphlets'. *The Seventeenth Century*, 23:2 (2013): 315. See also Michel Reinders, 'Printed Pandemonium: The Power of the Public and the Market for Poplar Political Publications in the Early Modern Dutch Republic'. (PhD Diss., Erasmus University Rotterdam, 2008).

conditions more common in a wetter, stormier climate. Some pamphlets therefore shaped and mobilized popular opinion by representing the local environmental manifestations of what we know as the Little Ice Age.[10]

Other pamphlets directly depicted how weather influenced political or military events. For instance, in 1673, in the immediate wake of the *rampjaar*, Romeyn de Hooghe and Govard Bibloo published a pamphlet that dramatically depicted a French raid. In December of 1672, the ice on the water near Meijepolder briefly froze more quickly than labourers could break it. At 10:00 p.m. on 27 December, French troops marched over the ice and made for The Hague. The ice was weak, however, and 12 French soldiers drowned near the town of Zegveld in the province of Utrecht. Nevertheless, in the afternoon the survivors reached and brutally sacked the towns of Zwammerdam and Bodegraven. Suddenly, the cold spell yielded to rain and thawing, which threatened to melt the ice and thereby isolate the French behind Dutch lines. The army quickly retreated back across the water line, where it would remain for the rest of the winter. In their pamphlet, De Hooghe and Bibloo vividly portrayed French soldiers marching over the ice to enter one of the villages they pillaged. Given the generally moderate temperatures that prevailed during the winter of 1672/1673, the temporary freezing that aided the French raid can probably not be linked to an overall cooler climate. Yet at the very least, the pamphlet, and others like it, reacted to and depicted an event clearly influenced by weather.[11]

Both mapmakers and publishers therefore responded to weather events and at times weather trends during the Little Ice Age, even though most probably did not perceive what we would call climate change. In general, maps more directly responded to climate changes than pamphlets. Local environmental circumstances, after all, clearly influenced journeys of exploration that ultimately shaped how maps represented the world. Still, pamphlets could also depict real environmental conditions that would have resonated with their intended audience. Climate changes only influenced the creation of maps and pamphlets, however, after affecting the commercial and political systems of the Dutch Republic.

[10] Adriaen Valerius, *Nederlandtsche gedenck-clank*, eds. P. J. Meertens, N. B. Tenhaeff, and A. Komter-Kuipers (Amsterdam: Wereldbibliotheek, 1942), 32. Marijke Barend-van Haeften, *Wilhemus en de anderen: Nederlandse liedjes, 1500–1700*. (Amsterdam: Amsterdam University Press, 2000), 73.

[11] Romeyn de Hooghe and Govard Bibloo, 'Franse wreedheden in Bodegraven en Zwammerdam', print, 1673, Rijksmuseum Amsterdam, http://goo.gl/5XjR8k.

LITERARY RESPONSES TO WEATHER AND CLIMATE CHANGE

Modern English drama, like realistic and characteristically Dutch winter and marine landscapes, emerged during the Grindelwald Fluctuation. The plays of Shakespeare in particular abound with references to extreme weather, such as severe winters and violent storms. Since the cold periods of the Little Ice Age increased the frequency of these extremes the North Sea region, 'ecocritical' approaches to Shakespeare's plays have interrogated whether, and how, they responded to environmental changes. Similar methodology can be used to explore weather references in the theatrical productions of the Dutch Golden Age.[12]

The most celebrated poet of the Dutch Golden Age, the republic's answer to Shakespeare, was undoubtedly Joost van den Vondel. In 1637, he premiered his magnum opus, *Gijsbrecht van Aemstel*, to inaugurate Amsterdam's first city theatre. The play dramatized a siege of Amsterdam in 1304 that bore some similarity to the ancient siege of Troy. Characters in the play occasionally refer to weather events that were more common in the chilliest decades of the Little Ice Age. In the third act, for example, Badeloch, the protagonist's wife, gives the play's most lucid description of weather. The siege around Amsterdam appears to have failed, but Badeloch's niece appears in a dream and urges her to flee. The enemy is only seemingly defeated, she warns, and will return soon. Later in the act, the dream turns out to be a premonition. Badeloch then envies the fortune of small, poor villages that are inconspicuous enough to escape the 'storms' and 'winds' that threaten large, rich cities. She takes comfort by remembering that 'Since my marriage, since my engagement: / What storms have not blown over my head? / What tower is high enough to let me see / The waves, the sea of all I have endured?'[13]

Badeloch's reflections in Van den Vondel's poetry were products of a maritime culture shaped by gales that threatened lives at sea and near the coast. Storms helped frame how Van den Vondel's characters perceived the world. They served as apt metaphors for violent and precarious lives. Because such storms were especially common during the coolest decades of

[12] Loretta Johnson, 'Greening the Library: The Fundamentals and Future of Ecocriticism'. *Choice* (December 2009): 10. Robert Markley, 'Summer's Lease: Shakespeare in the Little Ice Age'. In *Early Modern Ecostudies: From the Florentine Codex to Shakespeare*, eds. Thomas Hallock, Ivo Kamps, and Karen L. Raber. (Hampshire: Palgrave Macmillan, 2008), 132.

[13] Joost van den Vondel, *Gijsbrecht van Aemstel*, ed. Mieke B. Smits-Veldt. (Amsterdam: Amsterdam University Press, 1994), 70.

the Little Ice Age, climate changes may have influenced how writers expressed pain and suffering in Golden Age literature. Yet Van den Vondel's poetry also shows the limitations of this ecocritical approach. Neither 1637 nor the years that directly preceded and followed it were especially cold. At the time, prevailing weather actually registered the milder interval between Little Ice Age cold phases in the Low Countries. While a weak storm surge did flood some of Amsterdam's streets in 1637, no significant inundations affected Holland in either 1636 or 1635. Of course, it may be that Van den Vondel laid the intellectual groundwork for his play in earlier years that were distinguished by stormier conditions. However, such mental fermentation is as opaque to climate historians as the intentions with which Dutch artists painted most of their winter landscapes.[14]

More importantly, descriptions of weather in literature rarely reflect attempts by authors to accurately depict reality. Weather can serve the interests of plot, or, when used metaphorically, highlight a character's internal struggle. In Shakespeare's *The Tempest* (1611), for example, the sorcerer Prospero raises a storm that advances the plot while providing a metaphor for upheaval and confusion. Descriptions of storms in Van den Vondel's *Gijsbrecht van Aemstel* are also almost entirely metaphorical. Still, they contribute to a theme of besiegement that would have resonated in a prosperous, urbanized Republic whose citizens had literally walled themselves off from water, storms, and opposing armies. Meteorological descriptions in literature can therefore hint at past attitudes towards weather in ways that can be valuable to climate historians. It is nevertheless difficult to call them cultural responses to the Little Ice Age, because it is hard to discern whether climatic fluctuations encouraged poets to incorporate particular meteorological conditions in their writing. Neither the narrative decisions taken by Van den Vondel or Shakespeare, nor their significance for contemporary audiences, can be clearly tied to the climatic fluctuations of the Little Ice Age.[15]

By contrast, short poems crafted by amateurs or professionals in response to real weather events can be more convincingly linked to climate changes. On 23 February 1602, a northwesterly gale overwhelmed coastal defences and caused catastrophic storm flooding in the town of Edam, which in turn quickly ignited a major fire. The disaster inspired the town's

[14] Gottschalk, *Stormvloeden en rivieroverstromingen Vol. III*, 128. Van Engelen, Buisman and IJnsen, 'A Millennium of Weather, Winds and Water in the Low Countries', 112.

[15] Joost van den Vondel, Gijsbrecht van Aemstel, 70. William Shakespeare, *The Tempest*. (New York: Dover Publications, 1998).

chronicler to write 'Oh frightful night: that has swallowed the sweat / Of so many days, who would not take pity on the city? / That just yesterday stood so proudly, now has Fallen, / One storm, one flood, one fire destroyed it all'. Many short poems followed a similar template, and lamented the devastation or simple discomfort caused by extreme weather. During the unusually wet summer of 1648, the poet Reyer Anslo wondered, 'How could it be, / That raindrop after raindrop, / Crashes to the ground, / Day and night?'[16] After the frigid winter of 1666/67, the director of the Dutch herring fleet's guild of pilots hammered a long poem to his door. It read:

> In January sixteen hundred sixty seven,
> It froze and snowed severely,
> For six weeks shipping ceased,
> [Then] for three weeks people sailed as they pleased,
> [But] the most important thing commemorated here,
> Is how much ice there was in March.
> On the 16th [of March] it started to freeze again,
> On the 17th fishermen abandoned their trade,
> On the 18th many walked on the IJ[17] at the Laeg,
> On the 19th people crossed the IJ on the ice,
> On the 20th the weather and wind offered little relief,
> On the 21st it seemed that weather and wind might shift,
> On the 22nd the wind again ushered in freezing,
> On the 23rd the sun began to melt the ice,
> On the 24th the freezing lost its power,
> On the 25th many crossed the IJ with deliveries,
> On the 26th three people still walked across the IJ,
> After noon the boats sailed past the city,
> On the 27th the easterly wind piled the ice high on Pampus,[18]
> On the 29th [sic] shipping was therefore still delayed,
> On the 30th some managed to managed to sail and walk across the ice,
> On 1 April some people still walked on the Zuiderzee,
> On the 2nd a ship was trapped in ice at Urk,[19]
> This is recorded by M.T. the pilot's man,
> To keep God's wondrous power,
> In [everyone's] thoughts.[20]

[16] Anton van Duinkerken, *Het goud der gouden eeuw, bloemlezing uit de poëzie der zeventiende eeuw*. (Utrecht: Het Spectrum, 1955), 118. Buisman, *Duizend Jaar Vol. IV*, 212.

[17] The waterway before the IJ that led into the Zuiderzee.

[18] The sandbank before Amsterdam's harbour.

[19] An island, now part of the IJsselmeerpolders.

[20] Buisman, *Duizend Jaar Vol. IV*, 613.

Across the republic, extreme weather could encourage cultural responses that reflected and reinforced weather memories. Poetic responses to extreme winters, severe storms, and catastrophic flooding were especially common during the coldest phases of the Little Ice Age. Such poems therefore look like clear and direct cultural responses to the Little Ice Age. Admittedly, relationships between climate changes and poetic responses were mediated by cultural norms that encouraged poetry, for instance, or economic conditions that tied the republic to waterborne commerce. Moreover, the distinction between poetry that responded directly to weather, and poetry that employed descriptions of weather for narrative or metaphorical purposes, could be blurry. In a poem about the so-called 'wind prince', for example, Van den Vondel may have responded to storms and shifting wind patterns, but clearly used weather descriptions to serve patriotic Dutch narratives. Cultural reactions to climate change were never completely straightforward, but the creation and reception of some Dutch poems, at least, convincingly registered the Little Ice Age.[21]

ICE CULTURES AND WITCHCRAFT IN THE LITTLE ICE AGE

In the Dutch Republic, cultural responses to climate change emerged from, and helped shape, bonds between people. Exceptional weather in the chilliest decades of the Dutch Golden Age encouraged a feeling of shared experience among the republic's citizens that cut across social divides. The Dutch most clearly expressed this feeling by enthusiastically participating in icy new social spaces made possible by severe winters. On 25 January during the frigid winter of 1668/1669, for instance, Van der Goes marvelled to his brother that 'an unbelievable number of people are on the ice every day'. Other observers wrote that thousands of sleds took to the ice after large stretches of the Zuiderzee froze. The parallel experiences of so many people in landscapes transformed by the weather of Little Ice Age cold periods gave rise to an 'ice culture' that resembled carnivals elsewhere in Europe. On frozen waterways, women and men of every class and occupation mingled, social norms collapse, and merchants set up shop to sell their wares.[22]

[21] Joost van den Vondel, 'Aen den Leeuw van Holland', 1642. *Universiteit van Amsterdam.* Accessed 17 December 2013, http://cf.hum.uva.nl/dsp/ljc/vondel/1642/haarlemm.html. Joost van den Vondel, *Volledige dichtwerken en oorspronkelijk proza*, ed. Albert Verwey. (Amsterdam: Becht, 1937), 981.

[22] Van der Goes, 'Hage, den 25 January 1669'. *Briefwisseling tusschen de gebroeders van der Goes (1659–1673) Vol. II*, 22. Janszoon, *Het aantekeningenboek van Dirck Jansz,*

In the bitterly cold winter of 1608, for example, army commander Frederich van Vervou reported on 22 February that merchants had erected tents near the frozen Ems in the northeastern Republic. Crowds gathered there to drink beer and wine. Such scenes were common across the watery parts of the Low Countries. In the same winter, thousands of people drank beverages on the frozen Scheldt off Antwerp. Meanwhile, Hugo de Groot in The Hague marvelled at the egalitarian character of popular culture on the ice. De Groot was a sober observer of human nature. Just one year later, he would publish an influential treatise that helped establish the concept of freedom of the seas in international law. In 1608, he wrote that 'here [on the ice] people are honest and free, / Here the farmer pushes aside the nobleman'. He concluded that 'if anyone should ask from their heart who is really wise, / I say from my heart: only the ice'. De Groot's description suggests that, in a Republic where social stratification was already less pronounced than it was elsewhere in Europe, frozen waterways provided a reason to further level class distinctions, if only temporarily. This ice culture arose only in severe winters, when the ice was thick enough, and extensive enough, to support large social gatherings. It would have been far less likely to emerge outside the coolest phases of the Little Ice Age.[23]

Climatic cooling could therefore unite people across the Low Countries. Elsewhere, it also strengthened forces that divided them. Between 1560 and 1630, thousands of supposed witches across Europe were burned at the sake for alleged crimes that included conjuring precisely the kind of weather that had become common in the Grindelwald Fluctuation. In both Catholic and Protestant Europe, the persecution of witches was usually instigated by peasants, exacerbated by clergy, and encouraged by sympathetic magistrates. In the Dutch Republic, death sentences for witchcraft were only rarely imposed after 1595, following witch trials and executions in Amersfoort and Utrecht. In fact, accused witches from across Europe travelled to the *Hekenswaag* ('Witches' Scales') in the town of Oudewater to receive a fair trial, which they could not expect anywhere else in the continent.[24]

120. Buisman, *Duizend Jaar Vol. IV*, 192. Peter Burke, *Popular Culture in Early Modern Europe*. (Farnham: Ashgate Publishing, 2009), 256. Edward Muir, *Ritual in Early Modern Europe*. (Cambridge: Cambridge University Press, 1997), 92.

[23] Quoted in Buisman, *Duizend Jaar Vol. IV*, 252. Fredrich van Vervou, *Enige gedenckvveerdige geschiedenissen, tot narichtinge der nakomelingen*. (G. T. N. Suringar, 1841): 338.

[24] Claudia Swan, *Art, Science, and Witchcraft in Early Modern Holland: Jacques de Gheyn II (1565–1629)*. (Cambridge: Cambridge University Press, 2005), 3. Lene Dres-Coenders,

Both cultural and economic conditions muted the zeal for witch persecution in the republic. Across the rest of Europe, witch-hunts were usually rural tragedies fuelled by festering antagonisms over the rights to land. The coastal republic in particular was, by contrast, highly urbanized, with very high wages, robust civic charities, and vigilant neighbourhood watches. Moreover, cold, stormy weather that may have played a role in inciting witchcraft persecution elsewhere in Europe often benefitted the republic, although frigid weather had coincided with economic downturns in Amersfort and Utrecht during the witch trials there. Triggers for witch hunts beyond the republic's borders simply did not exist to the same extent within them.[25]

In fact, many Protestant priests in the seventeenth-century republic either doubted or rejected the existence of witches. Of these, the most influential was the Dutch Reformed pastor Balthasar Bekker. In 1691, he started to publish *The Enchanted World*, which in four volumes systematically deconstructed the dubious logic and Biblical misreadings that informed contemporary witch trials. To Bekker, belief in the Devil's overwhelming power on Earth was a pagan relic that undermined the true understanding of God's relationship with humanity. *The Enchanted World* ultimately helped end the persecution of witches across Europe. The culture of the republic therefore helped alter cultures in neighbouring countries that encouraged violence against accused witches amid the chilliest periods of the Little Ice Age.[26]

Het verbond van heks en duivel. Een waandenkbeeld aan het begin van de moderne tijd als symptoom van een veranderende situatie van de vrouw en als middel tot hervorming der zeden. (Baarn: Ambo, 1983), 227. Gary K. Waite, *Eradicating the Devil's Minions: Anabaptists and Witches in Reformation Europe, 1525–1600.* (Toronto: University of Toronto Press, 2007), 90. Henricus Institoris and Jacobus Sprenger, *Malleus Maleficarum Vol. II: The English Translation*, ed. Christopher Mackay. (Cambridge: Cambridge University Press, 2006), 43. For an alternative view, see Brian P. Levack, *The Oxford Handbook of Witchcraft in Early Modern Europe and Colonial America.* (Oxford: Oxford University Press, 2013).

[25] Dres-Coenders, *Het verbond van heks en duivel*, 196. Marijke Gijswijt-Hofstra, 'The European Witchcraft Debate and the Dutch Variant'. *Social History* 15:8 (2008): 186. Pfister, 'Climatic Extremes, Recurrent Crises and Witch Hunts', 57. Behringer, *A Cultural History of Climate*, 128. Alan Charles Kors and Edward Peters, eds., 'The Trail of Marie Cornu (1611)'. In *Witchcraft in Europe, 400–1700: A Documentary History.* (Philadelphia: University of Pennsylvania Press, 2001), 345. Stuart Clark, *Thinking with Demons: The Idea of Witchcraft in Early Modern Europe.* (Oxford: Oxford University Press, 1999), 543. Israel, *The Dutch Republic*, 354.

[26] Kors and Peters, 'Balthasar Bekker: *The Enchanted World* (1690)', in *Witchcraft in Europe*, 430. Benjamin J. Kaplan, 'Possessed by the Devil? A Very Public Dispute in Utrecht'. *Renaissance Quarterly* 49 (1996): 740. Koen Vermeir, 'Mechanical Philosophy

TECHNOLOGICAL INNOVATION IN A COOLING CLIMATE

The republic was not always more enlightened than its neighbours. Unlike governments elsewhere in Europe, for example, neither the States-General nor the provincial States directly encouraged inventions that did not have immediate military applications. Yet Dutch patentees still found inspiration in the rising influence of new scientific thinking in the republic and the publication of technical encyclopaedias, dictionaries, and journals in Dutch printing centres. For much of the seventeenth century, the republic therefore remained a hotbed for technological innovation.[27]

People of many professional and socioeconomic backgrounds requested patents, although merchants and artisans from the towns of Holland submitted the most applications. Trends in patent applications suggest that Dutch entrepreneurs invented technologies to exploit or cope with the weather of the Little Ice Age. For example, during the Grindelwald Fluctuation a relatively high percentage of patented inventions – reaching 10 per cent between 1580 and 1599 – involved heating applications. That percentage declined from the 1630s through 1660, rose sharply with the deepening of the Maunder Minimum, and then fell after 1680. These correlations hint that climatic cooling encouraged patentees to develop new heating technologies, at least until the end of the seventeenth century. Yet such technologies often had industrial purposes that had little to do with keeping people warm. Moreover, inventors increasingly owned just one patent over the course of the seventeenth century, and some did not submit patent applications at all, owing in part to the rise of new, institutionalized forms of knowledge production. Changes in patent statistics therefore did not necessarily reflect the need for heat in the chilliest decades of the Little Ice Age.[28]

in an Enchanted World: Cartesian Empiricism in Balthasar Bekker's Radical Reformation'. In *Cartesian Empiricisms*, eds. Mihnea Dobre and Tammy Nyden. (Dordrecht: Springer Netherlands, 2013), 275. Willem E. Burns, *Witch Hunts in Europe and America: An Encyclopedia.* (Portsmouth: Greenwood Publishing Corp. 2003), 23. Israel, *The Dutch Republic*, 925.

[27] C. A. Davids, *The Rise and Decline of Dutch Technological Leadership (2 Vols): Technology, Economy and Culture in the Netherlands, 1350–1800, Vol. I.* (Leiden: Brill, 2008), 4, 50. Karel Davids, 'Patents and Patentees in the Dutch Republic between c. 1580 and 1720'. *History and Technology: An International Journal* 16:3 (2000): 268. Israel, *The Dutch Republic*, 583. Ad van der Woude and Jan de Vries, *The First Modern Economy*, 349. De Vries, *The Economy of Europe in an Age of Crisis*, 92. Israel, *Dutch Primacy in World Trade*, 357. Price, *Dutch Society, 1588–1713*, 65.

[28] Davids, 'Patents and Patentees in the Dutch republic', 266. No. 511. 'Contract, waarbij Guy Libon een arbeider uit Dauphiné in dienst neemt om de oven in zijn glasblazerij te

The role of climate change in the development of transportation technologies is more convincing. During the Grindelwald Fluctuation, city councils advanced plans for pull ferries that allowed passengers to travel in unpredictable, stormy weather. The system expanded across the republic in the Maunder Minimum, when such weather was again common. By freezing waterways for months at a time, cooling may also have encouraged Dutch citizens to invent better ways of travelling on land. The percentage of patented inventions that involved land transportation declined with the conclusion of the Grindelwald Fluctuation, increased with the deepening of the Maunder Minimum, and fell again only after warming set in during the early eighteenth century.[29]

Correlations between inventions and climatic trends can hint at possible connections between climate change and technological innovation in the republic, but of course inventors responded to much more than weather. Every technological breakthrough emerged in the context of existing technologies, capital flows, and market pressures. Most took place in industrial and commercial centres that attracted hydraulic engineers, shipwrights, brewers, millers, smiths, and other professionals in a host of technical industries that all required direct engagement with the natural world. Inventors often benefitted from experience in these trades, as well as easy access to education and new publications. Patent statistics in particular cannot capture exactly how climate changes influenced those entangled social arrangements to provoke new inventions, so they are best used alongside other evidence.[30]

Letters and other qualitative sources suggest that some patents led to transportation technologies that did not involve land or liquid water and were clearly more effective during the coldest decades of the Little Ice Age. For example, on 17 January 1600, Adriaan Terrier received a patent for the construction of *ijsschuiten* or 'ice boats' that could navigate across frozen water. A decade later, Pieter Janszoon Twisck described seeing an 'ice-wagon' that resembled a sailboat on skates. Maurice of Nassau permitted the construction of two such craft, which astonished onlookers by reaching the then-extraordinary velocity of 80 kilometres/hour. Linking the development and representation of such vehicles to cool winters

bedienen', in *Bronnen tot de geschiedenis van het bedrijsleven en gildewezen van Amsterdam, Vol. III, 1633–1672.* (The Hague: Martinus Nijhoff, 1974), 272.

[29] Davids, 'Patents and Patentees in the Dutch republic', 266. De Vries and Van der Woude, *The First Modern Economy*, 183.

[30] De Vries and Van der Woude, *The First Modern Economy*, 345.

during the Little Ice Age is again not as straightforward as it at first appears. Dutch rivers can, after all, freeze even during warmer climatic regimes, and the ice wagon was soon adapted to function on land (Figure 7.1). Yet references to ice wagons appear in Dutch sources only after two of the coldest winters in the Grindelwald Fluctuation. Any technology dependant on ice was bound to be more practical when there was more ice, for longer. Ice wagons probably would not have been designed had mild winters been more common than they were.[31]

Surviving legal documents can provide still-deeper insights into relationships between climate change and technological culture within the republic. They reveal, for instance, that on 20 April 1667, Amsterdam citizens Hendrick Dirckszoon Block and Jacob Bosch agreed to a contract that spelled out their responsibilities for building a new icebreaker for the brewers' guild of Amsterdam. According to the contract, the icebreaker would ensure 'that boats could travel as quickly and unimpeded in the winter as they did in the summer, without being stopped by the ice'. The icebreaker already used by the brewer's guild was ineffective in cold winters, and, in the Low Countries, the winter of 1666/1667 had been frigid even for the Maunder Minimum. Weather common in a cooler climate seems to have encouraged entrepreneurs and inventors to develop an icebreaker more capable of cutting through thick ice.[32]

Primitive icebreakers had actually been used across the Low Countries since the fourteenth century. Yet it was only towards the end of the seventeenth century that they became specialized machines with little resemblance to other vessels in the Dutch Republic. An engraving of an icebreaker from the early eighteenth century depicted a strange craft, flat and wide at the prow with beams curving under the ship (Figure 7.1). Iron plates between these beams broke the ice into blocks, and pushed them below the boat. When the blocks surfaced at the stern, labourers pulled them from the water so they can be sold for use in cellars. The commercial value of ice therefore compensated for the costly expense of icebreaking. Ropes wrapped around sturdy, stubby masts connected the contraption to

[31] Buisman *Duizend Jaar Vol. IV*, 192. Swan, *Art, Science, and Witchcraft in Early Modern Holland*, 3. Israel, *Dutch primacy in world trade*, 357. Haley, *The Dutch in the Seventeenth Century*, 162.

[32] No. 1601, 'Contract betreffende voor her vervaardigen van een ijsbreker, 1667 April 20', in *Bronnen tot de geschiedenis van het bedrijsleven en gildewezen van Amsterdam, Vol. III*, 761. Van Engelen, Buisman and IJnsen, 'A Millennium of Weather, Winds and Water in the Low Countries', 112.

FIGURE 7.1 Technological responses to the weather of the Little Ice Age. Top: ice wagons on land. Bottom left: an icebreaker on the Amstel. Bottom right: A Jan van

large teams of horses. It was a noisy business – so noisy that the commander of the icebreaker used a kind of loudspeaker to communicate with his subordinates – yet in the engraving, skaters, sleds, and even carriages crowd the ice. It is a powerful scene of resilience and adaptation in the face of an overall chilly climate.[33]

Inventors in the Dutch Republic responded not only to the ice that came with a cooler climate, but also to urban fires linked in more complex ways to the weather of the Little Ice Age. The chilliest decades of the period were overall wet in the Low Countries, which would have eased the threat of urban fires. However, trends in both precipitation averages and the frequency of landmark precipitation events did not correlate perfectly with trends in average temperatures. Weather extremes accompanied the coldest decades of the Little Ice Age, and they included summer droughts that created ideal conditions for fires. Long, frigid winters also encouraged Dutch citizens to use fires or furnaces to keep warm, and to burn them longer, and hotter, than they would have in milder conditions. That too increased the risk of fire. Moreover, lightning strikes in the abundant storms of Little Ice Age cold periods ignited fires directly. Once a fire did break out, high winds could drive it towards nearby houses, transforming a small blaze into a major conflagration. Urban fires may therefore have become more common and more damaging during the chilliest decades of the Little Ice Age. Human practices and arrangements compounded the threat to early modern cities. Across Europe, combustible materials choked narrow city streets, and early attempts to

---

CAPTION FOR FIGURE 7.1 (cont.)

der Heyden's 'Fire Hose Book' depicts the inferno and storm of July 27, 1679. Willem Isaacszoon van Swanenburg, 'De zeilwagen van Simon Stevin', print, 1602, Rijksmuseum Amsterdam, http://hdl.handle.net/10934/RM0001.COLLECT.452721. Tieleman van der Horst and Petrus Schenk, 'Winter Vreugde op den Amstel en 't gaan des Ysbreekers en der Waterschuiten'. Collectie Atlas Dreesmann. Reference code 10094. Gemeente Amsterdam Stadsarchief (Amsterdam, Netherlands). 1730–1736. Jan van der Heyden, 'Oude brandspuiten en nieuwe slangbrandspuiten in de praktijk', print, 1690, Rijksmuseum Amsterdam, http://hdl.handle.net/10934/RM0001.COLLECT.438566.

[33] De Kraker, 'Ice and Water', 12.

control fires using bucket brigades and immobile pumps, for example, were rarely effective.[34]

Urban fires were therefore an ever-present danger in the republic's many cities. Occasionally, they threatened a city's very survival. In October 1576, for example, northeasterly winds fanned flames that incinerated hundreds of houses across Haarlem. Forty years later, lightning kindled a major conflagration in Zutphen. In April 1615, a fire spread through the combustible clay buildings of Lochem, and within hours, only four houses were left standing. After walking through the ruins, Willem Baudartius of Zutphen wrote that 'one can see only sadness, in people and in animals / All are mourning, the humblest with the mightiest'.[35] A fire had led to a darker version of the social equalizing otherwise provoked by thick, long-lasting ice. The size of Amsterdam meant that inhabitants of the republic's largest city were especially familiar with urban fires. Relatively small fires ignited in Amsterdam during the warm, dry summer of 1616, for example, and even in the cold, wet summer of 1622, although in that year arson was probably to blame. In the frigid winter of 1645 – the first of the Maunder Minimum – workers pouring lead in Amsterdam's Nieuwe Kerk ('New Church') forgot their melting pot near an open window. Hard, easterly winds kindled an inferno that destroyed much of the church. In the hot, dry summer of 1652, another fire gutted city hall just as its massive replacement was in the early stages of construction.[36]

In cities as in forests, fires cause creative destruction. New buildings, often constructed using fire-resistant materials, rose from the ashes of urban fires across early modern Europe. In the republic, legal documents suggest that technological innovation could be inspired not only by urban fires, but also by weather that made such disasters more likely. For

[34] Susan Donahue Kuretsky, 'Jan van der Heyden and the Origins of Modern Firefighting: Art and Technology in Seventeenth-Century Amsterdam'. In *Flammable Cities: Urban Conflagration and the Making of the Modern World*, eds. Greg Bankoff, Uwe Lübken, and Jordan Sand. (Madison: University of Wisconsin Press, 2012), 27. Buisman, *Duizend Jaar Vol. IV*, 481, 575.

[35] It was 'a city [but] not a city'. Willem Baudartius, *Memoryen ofte cort verhael der gedenck-weerdichste so kercklicke als werltlicke gheschiedenissen van Nederland, Vranckrijck, Hooghduytschland, Groot Britannyen, Hispanyen, Italyen, Hungaryen, Bohemen, Savoyen, Sevenburghen ende Turkyen, van den iaere 1603 tot in het Iaer 1624: Vol. 1.* (Arnhem: Ian Ianszoon, 1624), 19.

[36] Buisman, *Duizend Jaar Vol. IV*, 26, 238, 305, 311, 348, 481, 523. 'The Old World Drought Atlas'. Accessed 3 July 2016, http://iridl.ldeo.columbia.edu/expert/home/.jennie/.PDSI/.OWDA/.pdsi/figviewer.html.

instance, a bill of sale, written in May 1666, documented a transaction involving a patent for a new kind of fire hose. According to the bill, the inventor, the appropriately named Cornelis Janszoon Pomp,[37] sold a third of his patent to Adriaan Franszoon Pieck. Later that year, droughts would set the stage for a series of urban fires across Europe, most spectacularly in London. Yet Pomp and Pieck completed their exchange when drought was just beginning to increase the risk of such fires. The inventor, Pomp, actually received his patent on 28 July 1664, during another summer that was warm, dry, and stormy.[38]

The overwhelming scale of the Great Fire of London, not to mention its consequences for the course of the Second Anglo-Dutch War, shocked Dutch observers in a way that fires in the republic had not. It played a crucial role in the early development of fire insurance in England, although Dutch firms would be preoccupied with maritime insurance until late into the eighteenth century. It also provoked technological innovations in the republic, especially in Amsterdam, where the polymath Jan van der Heyden took the lead. Five years after the Great Fire of London, and three years after developing a new means of enclosed street lighting, Van der Heyden and his brother, Nicolaas, received patents for a technology they called the *slangpomp*, or 'snake pump'. Their invention was a long, flexible, leather hose that channelled pressurized water towards a fire. The brothers made it more effective by adding further innovations for pumping water, including a new kind of waterwheel and light, pressurized air tanks that could be easily mounted on nimble fire engines. New equipment inspired new social technologies. Amsterdam's municipal government reorganized its fire brigade, already the largest in Europe, into 60 divisions, each with 36 firefighters drawn from local guilds. Two 'firemasters' led each division, and kept track of their subordinates by using numbered badges. Fines discouraged firefighters from arriving late at a fire – especially at night – and homeowners from attempting to deal with fires themselves.[39]

[37] *Pomp* translates as 'pump'.

[38] Buisman, *Duizend Jaar Vol. IV*, 606. No. 1572. 'Akte betraffende de verkoop van een derde deel in de uitvinding van een houten brandspuit en enige materialen reeds vervaardigde spuiten', in *Bronnen tot de geschiedenis van het bedrijsleven en gildewezen van Amsterdam, Vol. III*, 746. Van Engelen, Buisman and IJnsen, 'A Millennium of Weather, Winds and Water in the Low Countries', 112. Mauelshagen, *Klimageschichte der Neuzeit*, 129. 'The Old World Drought Atlas'. Accessed 3 July 2016, http://iridl.ldeo.columbia.edu/expert/home/.jennie/.PDSI/.OWDA/.pdsi/figviewer.html.

[39] Jan van der Heyden, *Beschryving der nieuwlijks uitgevonden en geoctrojeerde slang-brand-spuiten, en haare wijze van brand-blussen tegenwoordig binnen Amsterdam in*

Van der Heyden's innovations first proved their worth on 12 January 1673, amid the ferocious storms that saved the republic from naval invasion. An admiralty storehouse burned so brightly that night that it illuminated all of Amsterdam, yet buildings near one of Van der Heyden's engines were saved. In subsequent years, the new technologies and practices started revolutionizing Amsterdam's fire brigade. By the hot and relatively dry summer of 1679, they were ready for the greatest fire in the history of Golden Age Amsterdam. Around midnight on July 27, lightning struck tanneries filled with whale oil and peat, and the resulting inferno incinerated some 50 houses before firefighters could respond. As the hours passed, however, firefighters armed with Van der Heyden's technologies gradually controlled the fire, saving Amsterdam from a far worse disaster.[40]

To sell his life-saving innovations, Van der Heyden created a vivid manual with matter-of-fact accounts of fires that contrasted with the allegorical depictions of fire in most Golden Age art (Figure 7.1). His detailed illustrations presented fires as comprehensible problems that could be prevented or extinguished by human ingenuity. Above all, this pragmatic attitude, typical of Golden Age culture, inspired the technologies that made Amsterdam more resilient to fires than other European cities. They also enriched the city. Van der Heyden exported his innovations across Europe and quickly became one of the republic's wealthiest citizens. Once again, Dutch entrepreneurs had profited from a likely consequence of the Little Ice Age.[41]

Occasionally, even the greatest minds of the republic invented technologies that were actually less effective in the chilliest periods of the Little Ice Age. For example, to help sailors calculate longitude, Christiaan Huygens developed a cycloidal variant of his earlier invention, the pendulum clock. In 1660, his younger brother Lodewijk took one of the new clocks on a ship to Spain and reported that it was useless in a storm. Christiaan

gebruik zijnde: Nevens beschryving der brand-ordres van de stad Amsterdam, Vol. I. (Amsterdam: Jan Rieuwertszoon, 1690), 6. De Vries and Van der Woude, *The First Modern Economy*, 138. Robert Evans, 'The Early History of Fire Insurance'. *The Journal of Legal History* 8:1 (1987): 88.

[40] Van der Heyden, *Beschryving der nieuwlijks uitgevonden en geoctrojeerde slang-brand-spuiten*, 6. Peter C. Sutton, *Jan Van Der Heyden (1637–1712)*. (New Haven: Yale University Press, 2006), 214. Kuretsky, 'Jan van der Heyden and the Origins of Modern Firefighting', 35. 'The Old World Drought Atlas'. Accessed 4 July 2016, http://iridl.ldeo.columbia.edu/expert/home/.jennie/.PDSI/.OWDA/.pdsi/figviewer.html.

[41] Michelle V. Packer, 'Rising from the Ashes: Fire Prevention as Social Transformation'. *Dutch Crossing* 39:2 (2015): 160. Parker, *Global Crisis*, 636.

reasoned that his clocks could be stopped and stowed in very high winds. Yet of course it was precisely in the wake of storms that crews aboard wayward ships most needed to know their location, and storms were common in the Maunder Minimum.[42]

Technological innovations were more direct responses to climate changes than most kinds of visual or literary art. As cold winters grew more common in the Grindelwald Fluctuation and Maunder Minimum, the economics of the marketplace did not necessarily encourage artists to paint more winter scenes. Yet the technology of icebreaking became increasingly essential for safeguarding the profits and nutrition of Dutch citizens. Convincing relationships therefore connected climate changes, weather events, cultural conditions, and the market for technologies that mitigated or exploited the manifestations of climate changes in local environments. By provoking innovation, climate changes contributed to the technological culture of the Dutch Republic. They also helped shape the social spaces and discourses in which inventors conceived and applied their technologies.

CONCLUSIONS: CULTURAL VULNERABILITY AND RESILIENCE DURING THE LITTLE ICE AGE

Relationships between climate change and a society's culture can be extremely difficult to pin down. In the loosely centralized Republic, cultures differed between distinct regions and cities. Yet all reflected the influence of cultures beyond the porous borders of the republic. There was still a distinctively Dutch culture, particularly in the port cities of the republic, yet many of its most important characteristics – its norms and traditions, for example – long predated the chilliest stretch of the Little Ice Age. These chapters have therefore focused on weather observers, art, social activities, and technology: well-documented aspects of Dutch culture that often registered both the influence of the Little Ice Age and the most peculiar elements of the Dutch Golden Age.

At least some Dutch observers grasped that the frequency and severity of extreme weather could shift on decadal scales. This limited awareness of climate change may have been more widespread than surviving written sources suggest. If so, it may have shaped artistic, technological, and social responses to climate change. However, individual weather events, rather than perceived changes in the frequency of these events, probably

[42] Israel, *The Dutch Republic*, 583.

provoked most cultural responses to climate change. Of course, cultural responses to climate change do not require explicit awareness of climate change. Shifts in prevailing weather may, in fact, have worked on the subconscious of those who created art, developed technology, and inspired social movements in the republic. Many who participated in the ice culture of the Dutch Golden Age, for instance, may not have connected it to winters that had become longer and more severe. All the same, they participated in a cultural response to climate change.

Dutch representations of weather during the Little Ice Age share a universal appreciation for its agency and power. Many also communicate a pragmatic conviction that the consequences of weather could be endured or exploited. Dikes could be rebuilt; ice could be used or removed; water could impede or improve military defences; and wind patterns could aid or hinder shipping. While Dutch art could express loss or bewilderment in the face of meteorological extremes, it more often depicted how weather could be mastered. Such cultural responses to weather and climate change in the republic may have contributed to the resilience of the Dutch in the face of the Little Ice Age.

CONCLUSION

Lessons from Ice and Gold

Two bitterly cold phases of the Little Ice Age – the Grindelwald Fluctuation and the Maunder Minimum – framed the Golden Age of the Dutch Republic. Societies around the world struggled as weather patterns changed, but the Dutch usually prospered. The reasons were complex, and included economic trends, social forces, or cultural developments that had little to do with weather. Yet one reason – one historians have, until now, left unexamined – surely involved the local manifestations of the Little Ice Age in the watery environments that sustained the Dutch trading empire, and in turn the ways in which the unusual society of the republic responded to those manifestations. Climate changes occasionally spelled disaster for Dutch farmers and soldiers, merchants, and mariners. Yet they also created opportunities that citizens of the republic's dynamic society were well positioned to exploit. Weather in the chilliest phases of the Little Ice Age ambiguously influenced the commercial, military, and cultural foundations of the Dutch Republic, but ultimately offered more advantages than disadvantages for most of its inhabitants. That contrasted with the more plainly disastrous consequences of Little Ice Age cold periods elsewhere.

The circulation of people, goods, and information through the Dutch trading empire continually expanded its frontiers and enriched the prosperity of its core cities. Climate changes most clearly influenced this circulation by occasionally imperilling but often aiding Dutch merchants, mariners, diplomats, and adventurers as they moved through their world. The local consequences of the Grindelwald Fluctuation in the Arctic redirected Dutch expeditions in search of a quicker passage to Asia, leading to discoveries that transformed how Europeans understood and exploited the far north. As atmospheric circulation changed across the Atlantic Ocean during the Maunder Minimum, journeys along the southern passage to Asia, long controlled by the Dutch East India Company, grew faster yet more dangerous. Closer to home, frequent storms and extensive sea ice in chilly phases of the Little Ice Age repeatedly disrupted Baltic commerce, communications, and diplomacy. Yet harvest failures partly triggered by unusually cold weather benefitted merchants who sold grain from vast inventories in Amsterdam and Rotterdam. Within the Dutch Republic itself, large-scale transportation networks were vulnerable to climate change, but humbler ways of getting around were much more resilient. Climatic cooling brought crises to agricultural economies, but its consequences for Dutch commerce were more diverse, and indeed often beneficial.

Weather associated with the coldest decades of the Little Ice Age also aided Dutch soldiers and sailors in the wars that established their Republic and prolonged its commercial primacy. Cooler, stormier, rainier weather, frequent in the Grindelwald Fluctuation, helped provoke the Dutch rebellion and then initially aided it by strengthening both natural and artificial defences against Spanish offensives. As the strategic balance across the Low Countries shifted in the late 1620s, so did the climate of the Northern Hemisphere. For nearly two decades, warm, dry, and tranquil weather was more common than it had been. These conditions benefitted Dutch offensives in the Spanish Netherlands, and helped the republic establish lasting independence. By 1645, the cooling of the Maunder Minimum was setting in. Yet in the North Sea region, it would be nearly two decades before this cooling was joined by greater seasonal weather variability, more common easterly winds, and increased storminess. In the First Anglo-Dutch War, westerly winds typical of the early Maunder Minimum benefitted English naval operations, multiplying English tactical and technological advantages. Thereafter, the frequency of storms and easterly winds increased just as the leaders of the republic transformed its navy and then its army. Together, environmental, intellectual, political, and technological changes helped the Dutch prevail in the Second and Third Anglo-Dutch Wars. The link between easterly winds and Dutch naval effectiveness was never more clear than in the Glorious Revolution, but the conquest of England would ultimately help bring an end to the Golden Age of Dutch naval and economic power.

Commercial and military responses to climate change across the Dutch trading empire were part of the culture for which the Golden Age is best remembered today. Some literate observers in the Dutch Republic used memories, written sources, and landmarks to discern long-term trends in extreme weather. They may not have traced fluctuations in average weather, yet they took a first step in perceiving climate change, and perhaps that was enough to influence Dutch economic and military strategies. The art, social spaces, and technologies of the Dutch Golden Age certainly registered climate change, in ways that helped Dutch citizens make sense of, and live with, the weather of the Little Ice Age.

Three essential concepts enabled and informed this book. The first is deceptively simple: climate change influences people through weather. To write a history that connects climatic trends to the fortunes of a society, we should try to consider the complex and occasionally counterintuitive ways that global, gradual climate changes manifest across short timescales in local environments. If we have the scientific and especially the historical sources, we should then link changes in those local environments to human activities. Only by looking at enough of these very particular relationships can we start to sketch broader connections between climate changes and human history. Not all of the steps in this method establish equally certain relationships. The small connections – the ones between an individual weather event and a discrete human response – are more probable than the broad links between big trends. By establishing many highly probable relationships on a small scale, however, climate historians can make their big conclusions more robust. Climate scientists wrestle with the concepts of probability and certainty all the time. Historians can profitably follow in their footsteps.

The second big concept, which more implicitly runs through this book, is that climate change influenced pre-industrial societies by affecting how much energy people could extract from local environments, and how they could use it. Energy that bore the imprint of weather, and over the course of decades climate change, sustained human lives and enabled complex civilizations. Energy constrained how people moved and therefore how they traded and fought one another. By altering the material world – including human bodies – it influenced how people thought and created culture. Climate historians rarely introduce concepts that unite the mechanisms by which very different kinds of weather influenced very different kinds of human history. The Dutch example suggests that we can find fresh relationships between human and climate histories by devoting more attention to flows and surpluses of energy.

The third and final concept is that interdisciplinary approaches can let us revisit established issues in history and other fields, while opening new topics for investigation. Work that links the topics and methods of science and history can lead us to novel perspectives on past, present, and future climate changes. Scientists can reconstruct environmental trends that mattered in the past and might matter in the future. Historians can build on these scientific reconstructions and tie them to human history in ways that enrich our understanding of the future. In many universities, the humanities and sciences are still imagined as utterly distinct fields of inquiry. Yet the more the disciplines of science and history are used together, the more scientists and humanists realize that at least some of their methods and interests are not so dissimilar, after all.

THE DUTCH EXCEPTION IN A WIDER CONTEXT

By exploring the Dutch Golden Age from a fresh perspective, this book has engaged in some very old debates about Dutch history. For Dutch historians, one of the biggest concerns the origins and character of the Dutch Golden Age. Historians have long suspected that the prosperity of the Dutch Republic was parasitic. Dutch citizens, according to such thinking, exploited weaknesses in larger states that, by virtue of the resources they could marshal, should have been more powerful. When those weaknesses ebbed, so did the Dutch Golden Age. This book suggests that part of the Dutch success story was the republic's resilience in the face of climate changes that contributed to disaster elsewhere in Europe. The Dutch did not just take advantage of disasters that troubled their neighbours, although they certainly did that too. The republic's prosperity and power also stemmed from its ability to avoid those disasters. In the final decades of the seventeenth century, wars became less destructive, states grew more capable, agricultural production increased, and commerce expanded across Northwestern Europe. Just as the Maunder Minimum entered its coldest phase, the republic's powerful neighbours, especially England, grew more resilient in the face of climate change. The ebbing of the Dutch advantage in a cooler, wetter, stormier climate may have been one reason for the conclusion of the Golden Age.[1]

Historians of the Dutch Republic have long understood that coastal environments in the early modern Low Countries were unusually malleable both by human and natural forces. Yet these historians have rarely studied the role of climate change. This book has traced how global climate change altered regional environments across the Dutch trading empire. Dutch citizens were accustomed to preparing for and living with

[1] Parker, *Global Crisis*, 619. Price, *Dutch Society*, 64.

environmental crises, and many – though by no means all – were comfortable with manipulating environments on a huge scale, for economic or military ends. The transformation of the coastal Low Countries into a networked, urbanized, and drained landscape some two metres below sea level was an environmental transition greater than any set in motion by the Little Ice Age. When climate change affected the Dutch Republic, many of its citizens simply endured and exploited yet another set of changing environmental circumstances. Perhaps this was one cause for their resilience in the face of the Little Ice Age.

Not only should climate change feature more prominently in histories of the Dutch Golden Age, but stories of societal resilience and adaptation should also play a bigger role in environmental histories of climate change. Clearly, the chilliest decades of the sixteenth, seventeenth, and eighteenth centuries were disastrous for civilizations the world over. The concept of a global crisis gives us a powerful device to make sense of the traumatic early modern period, and provides a clear warning about our future. Yet many societies joined the Dutch in coping more or less successfully with the coldest stretch of the Little Ice Age. The Mughal Empire in India, for example, responded to monsoon failures and catastrophic famine in 1630 and 1631 by organizing a vast social welfare programme. Droughts and famines persisted in the Maunder Minimum, but the empire continued to expand through military conquest. The inhabitants of the Indonesian archipelago, meanwhile, also endured catastrophic droughts, but they coped by relying on a mix of new crops and old transportation networks that helped them import rice. These imports grew more important as the growing spice trade encouraged Indonesian farmers to specialize in cash crops. Eventually, the prosperity of the Dutch Republic would be their downfall. Dutch merchants seized control of regional transportation networks and artificially raised food prices, and only then did famines afflict an archipelago that had thrived despite the Little Ice Age. Dutch traders were as ruthless in exploiting food crises in the Indian Ocean as they were in European waters. [2]

Globally, demographic and political disasters in the seventeenth century coincided with and were in part caused by the extraordinary spread of European explorers, settlers, and merchants around the globe. The European societies that best endured a changing climate – the Dutch Republic and eventually England – spearheaded the new age, one distinguished equally by discovery and depredation. Interactions between these

[2] Parker, *Global Crisis*, 411.

Northern Europeans and the inhabitants of diverse indigenous cultures, from the Indian Ocean to the Arctic, gave rise to new economies, new ways of thinking, and ultimately the modern world. Yet they also provoked immense human suffering, occasionally in communities that would otherwise have prospered in the Little Ice Age, but often in precisely those civilizations that struggled to adapt. By benefitting some societies, climate change therefore further undermined others, but always in ways channelled by human decisions and institutions. The human story of the Little Ice Age is therefore one of interconnected crisis and opportunity, misery and prosperity.

Broadly speaking, there were two approaches that helped large societies not just survive, but thrive during the chilliest decades of the Little Ice Age. The first was to 'go Dutch' by adopting the technologies, practices, and values that allowed the republic to prosper amid the global crisis. England followed this path so successfully that it eventually overtook the Dutch Republic as the world's leading commercial and financial centre. Around the world, English mariners and merchants explored, traded, and plundered alongside their Dutch counterparts. 'Going Dutch' inflicted a high toll on far-flung peoples and environments.[3]

The second approach was very different, and it was followed most closely by Japan. Like the Dutch Republic and to a lesser extent England, Japan under the shogunate established by Tokugawa Ieyasu prospered during the chilliest stretch of the Little Ice Age. Japan's population more than doubled in the seventeenth century, and its urban population nearly tripled. Japan did not go Dutch to escape the global crisis that unravelled neighbouring China. Instead, Japanese families and their shogunate pursued strategies that at least partly stressed conservation, not Dutch accumulation, and left Japan more closed, not more open, to the rest of the world.[4]

Ieyasu's grandson, Tokugawa Iemitsu, turned on three pillars of Dutch prosperity: open commerce, diversity, and toleration. In the 1630s, he outlawed Japanese citizens from conducting any foreign trade, and then expelled all Portuguese merchants. In 1641, he forced Dutch merchants to relocate to a previously uninhabited island. From there, they would be the

[3] Brooke, *Climate Change and the Course of Global History*, 462. Jardine, *Going Dutch*, 326.

[4] Parker, *Global Crisis*, 484. Conrad Totman, *Early Modern Japan*. (Berkeley: University of California Press, 1995), 140.

only Europeans to trade with Japan for nearly two centuries. Meanwhile, the regime promoted worship of the Tokugawa dynasty while brutally outlawing Christianity. Censors burned any and all texts associated with foreign religions. Japan diverged from the Dutch Republic in other ways, too. As Dutch soldiers and sailors fought war after war in battlefields that stretched from the Indian Ocean to the Caribbean to the North Sea, Japan avoided foreign entanglements. As a result, while taxation soared in the republic, it fell in Japan. Still, Japanese laws regulated consumption and the shogun advocated frugality, even as Dutch merchants pursued riches in every corner of the globe.[5]

Not all Japanese policies would dismay a Dutch regent. Ieyasu, for example, undertook a vast project to network Japan through a series of highways and couriers. Both literacy rates and the number of publishing houses rose sharply, just as they did in the cities of the republic. Urbanization climbed, and Japanese elites accumulated spectacular paintings and worldly goods. Scholars have also debated just how closed to the outside world the Japanese economy really was. Over the course of the seventeenth century, Dutch, Chinese, and Korean merchants ensured that the Japanese economy retained important commercial connections to foreign markets.[6]

Still, the bigger picture is clear: the shogunate increasingly isolated Japan from the rest of the world, just as the Dutch travelled, mapped, and exploited it. For very different reasons, both societies prospered: Japan through the growth of its domestic economy in a time of peace, the Dutch Republic through the expansion of its international commerce in a period of perpetual war. Jared Diamond famously (and controversially) distinguished between societies that pursued successful top-down and bottom-up approaches to environmental crises. Tokugawa Japan is a classic example of the former, but the republic is not as easy to classify. Ordinary Dutch merchants, soldiers, and inventors devised ingenious responses to the Little Ice Age that the decisions of elites and governing bodies repeatedly channelled in constructive ways. There seem to have been top-down, bottom-up, and middle-of-the-road approaches to coping with climate change.[7]

[5] Parker, *Global Crisis*, 495. Jared Diamond, *Collapse: How Societies Choose to Fail or Succeed*. (London: Penguin Books, 2006), 296.

[6] Parker, *Global Crisis*, 490. Totman, *Early Modern Japan*, 31. See also Michael S. Laver, *Japan's Economy by Proxy in the Seventeenth Century: China, the Netherlands, and the Bakufu*. (Amherst: Cambria Press, 2008).

[7] Diamond, *Collapse*, 277.

Crucially, neither Japan nor the republic assumed its distinct characteristics primarily because the Little Ice Age reached its chilliest point in the seventeenth century. Rather, both accidentally became more capable of weathering climate change in ways that further encouraged the emergence or consolidation of some of those characteristics. It is difficult to say which approach was more effective in the face of the Little Ice Age. Climate changes manifested in different ways across the Low Countries and Japan, and offered different opportunities and constraints for local communities. Yet the Japanese approach would not have worked for just about any other society, since it depended in part on the rich diversity and geographical isolation of Japanese environments. Going Dutch may have been a more accessible solution to climate change than going Japanese.

CAN PAST COOLING TEACH US ABOUT FUTURE WARMING?

Historians rarely feature in discussions about global warming. We study the past, not the future, and too many of us still assume that climates scarcely changed before the twentieth century. With some justification, most of us also hesitate to draw lessons or laws from our work that might shed light on the future. Yet a growing number of us are joining the growing community of scholars who investigate climate change. Often, we use sources that other researchers have difficulty accessing or interpreting. Occasionally, we explore topics that other academics have not considered, and we reach conclusions that can, in fact, provide fresh perspectives on humanity's future.[8]

Of course, often the societies we study were very different from our own. Relative to other cities in seventeenth-century Europe, Amsterdam was enormous, wealthy, and worldly, overflowing with an embarrassment of technological and cultural marvels. Most of us, however, would find it a small, shabby, smelly, primitive, and altogether weirdly alien place. Its people – with their extraordinary clothing, grotesque physical maladies, and (often) severe religion – confronted climatic cooling, not warming. Unlike us, they may not have been aware that average weather conditions were changing, and they certainly would not have appreciated the causes and global scale of those changes. What can such a place, at such a time, really teach us?

[8] For popular examples of such work, see HistoricalClimatology.com and ClimateHistory.net.

The frigid Golden Age of the Dutch Republic, it turns out, distils into a parable with three related lessons for our present and future. The first is that relationships between climate change and human activity are usually complex and occasionally counterintuitive. This book has suggested that we need to be careful in thinking of 'moderate' climate change – on the order of one or two degrees Celsius, relative to long-term averages – as a direct cause of social change. Instead, climatic variability works intricately through diverse environments, in ways that intrude on the tense dialogue between individual decisions and social arrangements. The character of these relationships reflects not only the scale of climate change but also the distinct characteristics of local environments, communities, and people.

This way of thinking about climate change is at odds with the kind of determinism that can enter assessments of the present-day and projected impacts of global warming. Doubtless, climate change is already adding to the pressures facing societies wracked by resource shortages and social unrest, yet we come no closer to understanding its impact when we view it as a straightforward cause of human events. We can only learn how we might adapt to climate change by understanding how its influence filters through the socioeconomic, cultural, and political systems in which humans structure their lives. To do that, our assessments of climate change would do well to incorporate a little history.[9]

The second lesson is that moderate climate changes can have very unequal consequences for different societies, owing not only to their indirect influence on human activities but also to the diverse ways in which they reshape local environments. We might assume that rich and powerful societies cope better with climate changes than less fortunate civilizations, which would make climate change a vehicle for social inequality. Yet the wealthiest empires of the early modern world – Ming China, the Ottoman Empire, the Spanish Empire, and Mughal India – all endured crises and in some cases even unravelled during the chilliest century of the Little Ice Age. Climate change, it seems, can imperil not only societies that have few resources to exploit, but also those that require abundant resources to prosper. The Dutch thrived in the seventeenth century not so much because their republic was rich, but because

[9] Mike Hulme, 'Reducing the Future to Climate: A Story of Climate Determinism and Reductionism', *Osiris* 26:1 (2011): 245. Chris D. Thomas et al., 'Extinction Risk from Climate Change'. *Nature* 427 (2004): 145. Mark Carey, 'Science, Models, and Historians: toward a Critical Climate History'. *Environmental History* 19 (2014): 354.

much of its wealth derived from activities that climate change either benefitted or affected ambiguously. Moreover, climate change influenced the distinct, watery environments of the Low Countries and North Sea region in ways that overall aided Dutch efforts in war and commerce. In that context, Dutch merchants, soldiers, and inventors worked hard to endure, and in many cases to aggressively exploit, the local environmental consequences of global climate change. In the near future, we can learn from the Dutch by investing in the opportunities afforded by renewable energy, expanding efforts to adapt coastlines and infrastructure to the demands of a warmer world, and strengthening commercial and intellectual connections between countries. Above all, those of us in developed countries should not assume that our collective wealth shields us from the consequences of global warming.

The first two lessons deal with 'moderate' climate changes, but the third concerns the severe change that will likely transform Earth later in the twenty-first century. On decadal and century timescales, average temperatures during the Little Ice Age did not drop more than one degree Celsius below twentieth-century averages. Yet even climate change on this relatively modest scale dramatically altered the frequency of weather extremes in ways that had indirect but often still dramatic consequences for societies the world over. Many Dutch citizens may have coped well with such weather, yet thousands still died in storms, floods, and severe winters. Elsewhere, foolhardy decisions in vulnerable societies imperilled millions when harvests failed, famine spread, and disease ran rampant. Perhaps the most important lesson is therefore the simplest: even moderate climate changes helped shape the course of human history, and what our future has in store is anything but moderate. If we are not careful, warming may eventually overwhelm even our best efforts to adapt to it.

Today, we therefore face a choice that could well shape the long-term prospects of our species. Will we embrace new technologies and sensible policies, thereby limiting climate change to a level that has some historical parallel? Or will we cling to the status quo, resigning ourselves to the uncharted dangers of potentially extreme warming? By the end of this century, the magnitude of the temperature change we have set in motion may well exceed that of the Little Ice Age by a factor of two, three, or more. If we do not act now, there may be no golden exceptions to the global crises of the future.

Appendix

1. SUMMER AND WINTER VARIANCE IN THE LOW COUNTRIES: 1630–1660

Using winter and summer intensity values compiled using documentary proxy data by A. F. V. van Engelen, J. Buisman, and F. IJnsen, Naresh Neupane, a climatologist at Georgetown University, calculated the variance of summers and winters between 1630 and 1660, relative to period from 1550 to 1750. According to the variance or F-test, summers between 1630 and 1660 were warmer than summers across the two-century (1550–1750) rest period. The value of summer variance for 1630–1660 is 1.24, while it is 2.2 for 1550–1750. Winters from 1630 to 1660 were colder than winters during the rest period, but the difference does not quite meet the threshold for statistical significance. The value of winter variance for 1630–1660 is 1.05, and for 1550–1750 it is 1.7.

I calculated the standard deviation of winter and summer temperatures in the Low Countries. The standard deviation of winter temperatures during the Grindelwald Fluctuation, from 1560 to 1628, is 1.2. Summer temperatures in the same period have a standard deviation of 1.4. Winter temperatures in the warmer decades from 1629 to 1660 have a standard deviation of 1. Summer temperatures have a standard deviation of 1.1. During the mature Maunder Minimum, from 1660 to 1718, winter temperatures have a standard deviation of 1.4. Summer temperatures have a standard deviation of 1.5.

II. VOC JOURNEY STATISTICS

Other historians have developed databases that standardize VOC journal data and track decade-scale changes in journey characteristics. To obtain higher resolution data on VOC journeys, I ran statistics on 6,000 voyages through a rigorous method for removing insufficiently continuous or inadequately precise information. Statistics of total journey times in Chapter 2 only include data for vessels that travelled along the approximate geography of the cart track, in voyages with precise, daily records. My statistics exclude journeys of ships that remained in a particular location for longer than a few months, for reasons that probably did not involve resupply.

I also needed to compensate for secondary ports visited by VOC ships sailing to or from Asia. Because of delays that accumulated when a ship lingered in or approached a port, secondary destinations could distort my statistics. Consequently, my journal statistics do not include journeys in which secondary destinations were visited, unless one of two conditions was met. First, the balance of evidence had to suggest that weather forced crews to resupply or delay their departure from a secondary port, although this does not include cases where crews had to return to their port of origin before departing a second time. In such cases, the relationship between weather and the return to port was too often unclear. For example, a leaky hull could force a return to port, yet the reasons for the leak were not always outlined explicitly in journals. A storm could have caused a leak, yet there were other possible culprits.

Second, the secondary destination had to be clearly positioned along the cart track, it had to be described with geographic precision, and time spent there had to be recorded to the day. Of approximately 6,000 VOC outbound and inbound entries dating from 1598 to 1709, nearly 2,000 remained after I applied my criteria.

III. VOC JOURNEY STATISTICS: TEXEL TO BATAVIA

VOC ships visited many ports in Asia, all of which took different times to reach. To uncover the influence of climate change on trends in VOC journey durations, I therefore focus on voyages between two crucial locations: Texel and Batavia. I included nearby Bantam, Bali, and Jacatra as substitutes for Batavia, yet excluded the more distant sites of Aceh and Johore.

IV. THE SOUND TOLLS

The Sound toll registers stored at the Danish National Archives have been digitalized and made freely available online, alongside powerful interpretive tools. Yet the information compiled within the digitized registers has its limits. Entries recorded ports of departure alongside intended destinations, but dates of departure were not provided, and journey times to the Sound are therefore impossible to plot using the registers. Moreover, the toll accounts provide no information of damage sustained in the voyage to the Sound, and there is no mention of failed journeys. The many ships and crews that foundered in storms or succumbed to piracy are not listed in any sufficiently continuous source, so mortality in Baltic commerce cannot be measured. Worse, the Sound toll registers compiled prior to 1634 have not yet been quantified in ways that readily enable statistical analysis.[1]

Fortunately, Dutch maritime culture and technology during the Golden Age did not change so dramatically as to prevent broad conclusions about the relationship between weather, climate, and shipping before 1634. The registers also faithfully reflect shifts in the flow of seaborne traffic into and out of the Baltic. Other routes granted access to the Baltic through the labyrinth of Danish islands, but these were barely navigable and only rarely attempted. Travel by land was also impractical for the large-scale transport of commodities. Some captains tried to avoid the dues altogether, but few could escape the notice of Kronborg castle and the patrolling guard ship nearby.[2]

[1] Veluwenkamp, 'Sound Toll Registers: Concise Source Criticism', 2. Christensen, *Dutch Trade to the Baltic about 1600*, 23, 25.

[2] Veluwenkamp, 'Sound Toll Registers: Concise Source Criticism', 2. Jan Glete, *Warfare at Sea, 1500–1650*. (New York: Routledge, 2000), 29.

Bibliography

ARCHIVED PRIMARY SOURCES

Claes Ariszoon Caescoper, Dagboek van Claes Arisz. Caescoper. PA-143. Gemeente Archief Zaanstad (Zaanstad, Netherlands).

Documents from Deutz Family 1613–1878. Reference code: 234. Gemeente Amsterdam Stadsarchief (Amsterdam, Netherlands).

Documents from Inventory Number 9020–9021, Oude Archieven van het Hoogheemraadschap van Rijnland (Leiden, Netherlands).

Documents from Reference Number: 5501. Archief van het Ambacht Nierwer-Amstel, met het Archief van de Ambachten Rietwijk, Rietwijkeroord en Rietwijkeroorderpolder.

Engraving from Collectie Atlas Dreesmann. Reference code 10094. Gemeente Amsterdam Stadsarchief (Amsterdam, Netherlands).

Maps from the Kaartcollectie Ministerie van Oorlog, Situatiekaarten. Reference code: 4. Nationaal Archief (The Hague, Netherlands).

Notes from Collection of Notes and Printed Items on the History of Spitzbergen & Its Exploration. Reference code: SSC/23. Royal Geographical Society (London, United Kingdom).

Ordinance and Correspondence from Ambachts en dorpsbestuur Zoeterwoude, Reference code: 0500A. Regionaal Archief Leiden (Leiden, Netherlands).

Ship Logbooks and Correspondence in Admiralty Records. Reference codes: ADM 51, ADM 51, ADM 61, ADM 106. National Archives at Kew (Richmond, United Kingdom).

Ship Logbooks and Correspondence in Collectie de Ruyter, Reference code: 1.10.72.01, Nationaal Archief (The Hague, Netherlands).

Ship Logbooks and Correspondence in the Verenigde Oost-Indische Compagnie Collectie, Reference code: 1.04.02. Nationaal Archief (The Hague, Netherlands).

Ship Logbooks in Aanwinsten Eerste Afdeling, Reference code: 1.11.01.01, Nationaal Archief (The Hague, Netherlands).

Ship Logbooks in Walvisvaarders. Oud archief stad Enkhuizen 1353–1815 (1872). Reference Code: 0120. Westfries Archief (Hoorn, Netherlands).

ONLINE PRIMARY AND SECONDARY RESOURCES

Allen, Robert C. and Richard W. Unger, 'Database by Commodity'. *Allen-Unger Global Commodity Prices Database*. Accessed 2 April 2015, www.gcpdb.info/data.html.

Avercamp, Hendrick. *Ice Landscape*. Painting. 1620. Staatliche Museen. Schwerin. www.ibiblio.org/wm/paint/auth/avercamp/ice-landscape-schwerin.jpg.

Winter Landscape with Ice Skaters. Painting. 1608. Rijksmuseum, Amsterdam, www.rijksmuseum.nl/en/collection/SK-A-1718.

Bacon, Francis. 'Of Vicissitudes of Things'. In *Essays Civil and Moral*. The Harvard Classics, 1909–14. Accessed 14 December 2013, www.bartleby.com/3/1/58.html.

Beerstraten, Jan Abrahamszoon. *Slag bij Ter Heijde*. Painting. 1653–1666. Rijksmuseum Amsterdam. Amsterdam. www.rijksmuseum.nl/en/collection/SK-A-22.

Bruegel, Pieter the Elder. *Hunters in the Snow*. Painting. 1565. Kunsthistorisches Museum. Vienna. www.google.com/culturalinstitute/asset-viewer/hunters-in-the-snow-winter/WgFmzFNNN74nUg?hl=en

Winter Landscape with a Bird Trap. Painting. 1565. Musées Royaux des Beaux-Arts. www.wga.hu/frames-e.html?/html/b/bruegel/pieter_e/01/13winter.html.

Brueghel, Pieter the Younger. *Winter Scene with Ice Skaters and Birds*. Painting. 1638. http://goo.gl/8rbqLX.

CLIWOC, 'CLIWOC Data Position Plots: *Afrika* (CLIWOC Meta Data)'. Accessed 24 June 2013, www.knmi.nl/cliwoc/cliwocmeta_africa.htm.

'CLIWOC Data Position Plots: *Maarseveen* (CLIWOC Meta Data)'. Accessed 24 June 2013, www.knmi.nl/cliwoc/cliwocmeta_maarseveen.htm.

'CLIWOC Ship Logbook Database'. Accessed 24 June 2013, www.knmi.nl/cliwoc

Dehoij, J. *Willem van de Velde Sketching a Sea Battle*. Painting. 1845. State Hermitage Museum. www.arthermitage.org/Dehoij/Willem-van-de-Velde-Sketching-a-Sea-Battle.html.

De Hooghe, Romeyn and Govard Bibloo. *Franse wreedheden in Bodegraven en Zwammerdam*. Print. 1673. Rijksmuseum Amsterdam. http://goo.gl/5XjR8k.

De Moor, Geertruida. 'Wages and Prices from the Convent Leeuwenhorst, 1410–1570'. *International Institute of Social History*. Accessed 8 September 2017, http://www.iisg.nl/hpw/data.php#netherlands.

Heinsius, Anthonie. 'De briefwisseling van Anthonie Heinsius'. Huygens ING. Accessed 8 March 2014, http://resources.huygens.knaw.nl/heinsiusrepublicpoliticswarfinance.

Hogenberg, Frans. *Leiden Ontzet in 1574*. Print. 16th Century. Prentenkabinet Museum Boijmans Van Beuningen. Het Geheugen van Nederland. http://goo.gl/Dg8TD5

Hollar, Wenceslaus. *Plan of London before the Fire*. Map. 1665. Thomas Fisher Rare Book Library. University of Toronto. http://goo.gl/cqvf2U.

Huygens, Constantijn. *Journaal van Constantijn Huygens, den zoon, van 21 October 1688 tot 2 September 1696*. Accessed 27 May 2016, www.dbnl.org/tekst/huyg007jour02_01.

Met Office. 'Eastern England: Climate'. Accessed 2 February 2013, www.metoffice.gov.uk/climate/uk/ee.

Met Office. 'Northeast England: Climate'. Accessed 2 February 2013, www.metoffice.gov.uk/climate/uk/ne.

Moryson, Fynes. *An Itinerary Containing His Ten Yeeres Travell through the Twelve Dominions of Germany, Bohmer-land, Sweitzerland, Netherland, Denmarke, Poland, Italy, Turky, France, England, Scotland, and Ireland, Vol. I*. Centre for Reformation and Renaissance Studies, Victoria University, Toronto. Accessed 28 January 2016, https://archive.org/stream/fynesmorysons01moryuoft/fynesmorysons01moryuoft_djvu.txt

National Snow & Ice Data Center. 'Dynamics'. Accessed 4 January 2013, http://nsidc.org/cryosphere/seaice/processes/dynamics.html#wind.

National Snow and Ice Data Center. 'Patterns in Arctic Weather and Climate'. Accessed 27 June 2016, https://nsidc.org/cryosphere/arctic-meteorology/weather_climate_patterns.html#arctic_oscillation.

Oranje, Willem van. 'De briefwisseling van Willem van Oranje'. Huygens ING. Accessed 12 April 2015, http://resources.huygens.knaw.nl/wvo.

Pepys, Samuel. *Diary of Samuel Pepys*. Accessed 10 January 2011, www.pepysdiary.com/archive/1665/01.

Smallegange, Mattheus, and Jan Luyken. *Panorama op Reimerswaal*. Print. 1696. Amsterdam Museum. http://goo.gl/wort7d.

Storck, Abraham. *The 'Royal Prince' and Other Vessels at the Four Days Battle, 1–4 June 1666*. Painting. 1667. National Maritime Museum. http://collections.rmg.co.uk/collections/objects/11778.html.

'The Old World Drought Atlas'. The International Research Institute for Climate and Society, Columbia University. Accessed 28 June 2016, http://iridl.ldeo.columbia.edu/expert/home/.jennie/.PDSI/.OWDA/.pdsi/figviewer.html.

'The Sound Toll Database', Sound Toll Registers Online. Accessed 3 July 2013, www.soundtoll.nl/index.php/en/over-het-project/sonttol-registers.

Van Dam, Petra J. E. M. 'De amfibische cultuur: Een visie op watersnoodrampen'. Accessed 1 February 2014, http://goo.gl/lCVlZD.

Van de Velde, Willem the Elder. *The Battle of Terheide*. Painting. 1657. Rijksmuseum Amsterdam. Amsterdam. www.rijksmuseum.nl/en/collection/SK-A-1365.

Episode uit de Vierdaagse Zeeslag, 11–14 Juni 1666, in de Tweede Engelse Zeeoorlog (1665–67). Painting. 1666. Rijksmuseum Amsterdam. Amsterdam. www.rijksmuseum.nl/nl/collectie/SK-A-1392.

Van de Velde, Willem the Younger. *A Dutch Ship Scudding Before a Storm*. Painting. C. 1690. National Maritime Museum. London. http://collections.rmg.co.uk/collections/objects/12397.html.

An Indiaman in a Gale off a Rocky Coast. Painting. C. 1650–1707. Private Collection. www.the-athenaeum.org/art/detail.php?ID=129724.

A Mediterranean Brigantine Drifting onto a Rocky Coast in a Storm. Painting. C. 1700. National Maritime Museum. London. http://collections.rmg.co.uk/collections/objects/12398.html.

Action at Bergen. Painting. 1666. National Maritime Museum. London. http://collections.rmg.co.uk/collections/objects/12190.html.

De Windstoot. Painting. C. 1680. Rijksmuseum Amsterdam. Amsterdam. www.rijksmuseum.nl/nl/collectie/SK-A-1848.

Het kanonschot. Painting. 1680. Rijksmuseum Amsterdam. Amsterdam. www.rijksmuseum.nl/nl/collectie/SK-C-244.

Hollandse schepen op een kalme zee. Painting. C. 1665. Rijksmuseum Amsterdam. Amsterdam. www.rijksmuseum.nl/nl/collectie/SK-C-1707.

Schepen voor anker. Painting. C. 1650–1707. Rijksmuseum Amsterdam. Amsterdam. www.rijksmuseum.nl/nl/collectie/SK-A-3350.

Schepen voor de kust. Painting. C. 1650–1707. Rijksmuseum Amsterdam. Amsterdam. www.rijksmuseum.nl/nl/collectie/SK-A-440.

Schepen voor de kust tijdens windstilte. Painting. C. 1650–1707. Rijksmuseum Amsterdam. Amsterdam. www.rijksmuseum.nl/nl/collectie/SK-A-722.

Ships in Distress off Rock. Painting. C. 1700. Lancaster House. London. www.the-athenaeum.org/art/detail.php?ID=129826.

The Capture of the Royal Prince. Painting.1666. Rijksmuseum Amsterdam. Amsterdam. http://goo.gl/xeYBrs.

The Resolution in a Gale. Painting. 1678. National Maritime Museum. London. http://blogs.rmg.co.uk/collections/2014/10/20/queens-house-twitter-top-10/bhc3582.

Three Ships in a Gale. Painting. 1673. National Gallery. London. www.nationalgallery.org.uk/paintings/willem-van-de-velde-three-ships-in-a-gale.

Two English Ships Wrecked in a Storm on a Rocky Coast. Painting. C. 1700. National Maritime Museum. London. http://collections.rmg.co.uk/collections/objects/12399.html.

Windstilte. Painting. C. 1650–1707. Rijksmuseum Amsterdam. Amsterdam. www.rijksmuseum.nl/nl/collectie/SK-A-436

Van den Vondel, Joost. 'Aen den Leeuw van Holland', 1642. Universiteit van Amsterdam. Accessed 17 December 2013, http://cf.hum.uva.nl/dsp/ljc/vondel/1642/haarlemm.html.

Van der Heyden, Jan. *Oude brandspuiten en nieuwe slangbrandspuiten in de praktijk*. Print. 1690. Rijksmuseum Amsterdam. http://hdl.handle.net/10934/RM0001.COLLECT.438566.

Van Overbeek, Jaap. 'Database VOC Schepen'. De VOC Site. Accessed 24 June 2013, www.vocsite.nl/schepen/lijst.html.

Van Swanenburg, Willem Issacszoon. *De zeilwagen van Simon Stevin*. Print. 1602. Rijksmuseum Amsterdam. http://hdl.handle.net/10934/RM0001.COLLECT.452721.

Van Tielhof, Milja and Jan Luiten van Zanden. 'Freight Rates between Amsterdam and Various Port Cities 1500–1800, and Factors Costs of

Shipping Industry 1450–1800'. *International Institute of Social History.* Accessed 8 September 2017, http://www.iisg.nl/hpw/data.php#netherlands.

Van Zanden, Jan Luiten. 'The Prices of the Most Important Consumer Goods, and Indices of Wages and the Cost of Living in the Western Part of the Netherlands, 1450–1800'. *International Institute of Social History.* Accessed 8 September 2017, http://www.iisg.nl/hpw/data.php#netherlands.

Veluwenkamp, J. W. 'Sound Toll Registers: Concise Source Criticism'. Accessed 10 August 2013, www.soundtoll.nl/images/files/STRpdf.pdf.

Wilson, Robert M. 'Volcanism, Cold Temperature and Paucity of Sunspot Observing Days (1818–1858): A Connection?' The Smithsonian/NASA Astrophysics Data System, 1998. Accessed 7 July 2012, http://ntrs.nasa.gov/archive/nasa/casi.ntrs.nasa.gov/19980233233.pdf.

'Wrecks in Documents'. *Maritiem programma Nederland, Rijksdienst voor het Cultureel Erfgoed.* Accessed 24 June 2013, www.maritiemprogramma.nl/WID_00.htm.

PUBLISHED PRIMARY SOURCES

A General Collection of Treatys, Manifesto's, Contracts of Marriage, Renunciations, and other Publick Papers, from the Year 1495, to the Year 1712, Vol. 2, 2nd ed. London: J. J. and P. Knapton, 1732.

A Perfect Relation of the Great Fight between the English and Dutch Fleets on Fryday and Satturday [sic] Last. London: Printed for George Horton, 1653.

Allin, Thomas. *The Journals of Sir Thomas Allin, Vol. I, 1660–1666.* Edited by R. C. Anderson. London: Navy Records Society, 1939.

Alting, Egbert. *Diarium van Egbert Alting, 1553–1594.* Edited by W. J. Formsma and R. van Roijen. The Hague: Nijhoff, 1964.

Bacon, Francis. *Historia Ventorum, Vol. 12.* Oxford: Oxford University Press, 2007.

Barents, Willem. *Deliniatio cartæ trium navigationum etc.* The Hague: Cornelis Claeszoon, 1599.

Baudartius, Willem. *Memoryen ofte cort verhael der gedenck-weerdichste so kercklicke als werltlicke gheschiedenissen van Nederland, Vranckrijck, Hooghduytschland, Groot Britannyen, Hispanyen, Italyen, Hungaryen, Bohemen, Savoyen, Sevenburghen ende Turkyen, van den iaere 1603 tot in het Iaer 1624: Vol. 1.* Arnhem: Ian Ianszoon, 1624.

Beeckman, Isaac. *Journal tenu par Isaac Beeckman de 1604 à 1634. Tome 3: 1627–1634 (1635).* Edited by Cornelis de Waard. The Hague: Martinus Nijhoff, 1945.

'Bloudy Newes from Holland: Being a True Relation of the Present Proceedings of the Dutch-Men against the English'. London: Printed for E. Cotton, 1652.

Brandt, Geeraert and Sebastiaan Centen. *Historie der vermaerde zee- en koopstadt Enkhuisen.* Hoorn: Jacob Duyn, 1747.

Brandt, Gerard. *Uit het Leven en Bedrijf van den here Michiel de Ruiter.* Amsterdam: G. Schreuders, 1687.

Brouwer, J. O. H., ed. *Kronieken van Spaansche Soldaten uit het Begin van den Tachtigjarigen Oorlog*. Zutphen: B. V. W. J. Thieme & Cie, 1980.

Bruijn, J. R., F. S. Gaastra, and I. Schöffer, with assistance from E. S. van Eyck. *Dutch-Asiatic Shipping in the 17th and 18th Centuries: Volume II, Outward-Bound Voyages from the Netherlands to Asia and the Cape (1595–1794)*. The Hague: Martinus Nijhoff, 1979.

Bruijn, J. R., F. S. Gaastra, and I. Schöffer, with assistance from E. S. van Eyck. *Dutch-Asiatic Shipping in the 17th and 18th Centuries, Volume III: Homeward-Bound Voyages from the Asia and the Cape to the Netherlands (1597–1795)*. The Hague: Martinus Nijhoff, 1979.

Colenbrander, H. T., ed. *Bescheiden uit Vreemde Archieven omtrent de Groote Nederlandsche Zeeoorlogen, Vol. I: 1652–1667*. The Hague: Martinus Nijhoff, 1919.

Colenbrander, H. T., ed. *Bescheiden uit Vreemde Archieven omtrent de Groote Nederlandsche Zeeoorlogen, Vol. II: 1667–1676*. The Hague: Martinus Nijhoff, 1919.

Coolhaas, W. P. H., ed. *Generale missiven van gouverneurs-generaal en raden aan heren XVII der Verenigde Oostindische Compagnie, Vol. 1–9*. The Hague: Martinus Nijhoff, 1980.

Corsini, Filippo and Apollonio Bassetti, 'De eerste reis door Nederland van Cosimo de' Medici, winter 1667/1668 vastgelegd door kamerheer Filippo Corsini en secretaris Apollonio Bassetti'. In *Een Toscaanse prins bezoekt Nederland: De twee reizen van Cosimo de' Medici 1667–1669*. Edited by Lodewijk Wagenaar, translated by Bertie Eringa, 31–157. Amsterdam: Bas Lubberhuizen.

De Groot, Hugo. *Batavi, Mirabilium Anni MDC*. Den Haag, 1600.

Kroniek van de Nederlandse Oorlog, De Opstand 1559–1588. Nijmegen: Uitgeverij Vantilt, 2014.

De Hollantsche Mercurius. Haarlem: Pieter Casteleun, 1666.

De Pottre, Jan. *Dagboek van Jan de Pottre, 1549–1602*. Edited by B. de St. Genois. Ghent: C. Annoot-Braeckman, 1861.

De Veer, Gerrit. *Reizen van Willem Barents, Jacob van Heemskerck, Jan Cornelisz. Rijp en Anderen Naar het Noorden (1594–1597), Eerste Deel*. The Hague: Martinus Nijhoff, 1917.

The True and Perfect Description of Three Voyages by the Ships of Holland and Zeeland. London, 1609.

De Witt, Johan. *Brieven, Geschreven ende gewisselt tusschen den Heer Johan de Witt, Raedt-Pensionaris, ende de Gevolmghtigden van den Staedt der Vereenighde Nederlanden, so in Vranckryck, Engelandt, Sweden, Denemarcken, Poolen, enz: Beginnende met den jaere 1652 tot het jaer 1669 incluys, Volume II*. The Hague: Hendrick Scheurleer, 1723.

De Witt, Johan. *Brieven van Johan de Witt, Derde Deel: 1665–1669*. Edited by Robert Fruin. Amsterdam: Johannes Müller, 1912.

Doedens, Anne and Henk Looijesteijn, *Op jacht naar Spaans Zilver: Het scheepsjournaal van Willem van Brederode, kapitein der mariniers in de Nassause vloot (1623–1626)*. Hilversum: Uitgeverij Verloren, 2008.

Dudley, Robert. *Correspondence of Robert Dudley, Earl of Leycester, during His Government of the Low Countries, in the years 1585 and 1586*. Edited by John Bruce. London: John Bowyer Nichols and Son, 1844.

Duyck, Anthonis. *De slag bij Nieuwpoort: Journaal van de tocht naar Vlaanderen in 1600*. Nijmegen: SUN, 2000.

Erasmus, Desiderius. *The Correspondence of Erasmus: Letters 1122 to 1251, 1520 to 1521*. Toronto: University of Toronto Press, 1974.

Garencières, Theophilus. *A Mite Cast into the Treasury of the Famous City of London: Being a Brief and Methodical Discourse of the Nature, Causes, Symptomes, Remedies and Preservation from the Plague, in this Calamitous Year, 1665*. London: Thomas Ratcliffe, 1665.

Gibson, Edmund. *Camden's Britannia*. London: F. Collins for A. Swalle and A. and J. Churchill, 1695.

Good Newes from General Blakes Fleet. London: Printed for Robert Ibbitson dwelling in Smithfield neer Hosier Lane, 1652.

Heinsius, Daniel. *De gebeurtenissen die zich bij 's-Hertogenbosch en elders in de Nederlanden afspeelden in her jaar 1629*. Leiden: Elsevier, 1631.

Hondius, Jodocus. *Atlas*. Amsterdam, 1606.

Hooft, Pieter Corneliszoon. *De briefwisseling van P. C. Hooft, deel 1, 1599–1630*. Edited by H. W. Van Tricht. Culemborg: Tjeenk Willink/ Noorduijn, 1976.

Houghton, John. *England's Great Happiness*. London: J. M. for Edward Croft, 1677.

Huygens, Constantijn *De briefwisseling van Constantijn Huygens, Eerste Deel*. The Hague: Martinus Nijhoff, 1911.

Janszoon, Dirck. *Het aantekeningenboek van Dirck Jansz. (1578–1636)*. Edited by Pieter Gerbenzon. 120. Hilversum: Uitgeverij Verloren, 1993.

Juet, Robert. 'The Third Voyage of Master Henry Hudson, toward Nova Zembla…'. In *Henry Hudson the Navigator: The Original Documents in Which His Career Is Recorded*, 45–93. London: Hakluyt Society, 1860.

Lampe, Barend. *Historisch Verhael aller gedenckwaerdiger geschiedenis…. Vol. 21*. Amsterdam: Jan Janszoon, 1635.

Mercator, Rumold. *Atlantis Pars Altera*. Duisburg, 1595.

Monck, George. *Two Letters from the Fleet: The One Written by Generall Monck to the Commissioners of the Admiralty Sitting at Whitehall. The Other by Capt Bourn, Captain of the Resolution to His Wife…*. London: Printed by Tho. Newcomb, dwelling in Thamestreet, over against Baynards-Castle, 1653.

Narbrough, John. 'Journal of John Narbrough, Captain of the Fairfax. September 18, 1672, to July 1, 1673. Pepysian MS. 2556'. In *Journals and Narratives of the Third Dutch War*. Edited by R. C. Anderson, 187–207. London: Publications of the Navy Records Society, 1945–1947.

National Maritime Museum, *The Second Dutch War: Described in Pictures & Manuscripts of the Time*. London: Her Majesty's Stationery Office, 1967.

Rawson Gardiner, Samuel, ed. *Letters and Papers Relating to the First Dutch War, 1652–1654, Vol. I*. London: Publications of the Navy Records Society, 1899.

Shakespeare, William. *The Tempest*. New York: Dover Publications, 1998.

Stoaks, *A Great Victory Obtained by the English against the Dutch*. London: Geo: Horton, 1652.

Temple, William. *Observations upon the United Provinces of the Netherlands*. Edited by Sir George Clark. Oxford: Clarendon Press, 1972.

Tromp, Maarten Harpetsz. *The Journal of Maarten Harpertszoon Tromp, Anno 1639*. London: CUP Archive, 1930.

Valerius, Adriaen. *Nederlandtsche gedenck-clank*. Edited by P. J. Meertens, N. B. Tenhaeff, and A. Komter-Kuipers. Amsterdam: Wereldbibliotheek, 1942.

Van den Vondel, Joost. *Gijsbrecht van Aemstel*. Edited by Mieke B. Smits-Veldt. Amsterdam: Amsterdam University Press, 1994.

Volledige dichtwerken en oorspronkelijk proza. Edited by Albert Verwey. Amsterdam: Becht, 1937.

Van der Capellen, Jonkheer Alexander. *Gedenkschriften van Jonkheer Alexander van der Capellen, Heere van Aartsbergen, Vol. I*. Edited by Robbert Lieve Jasper van der Capellen. Utrecht, 1777/1778.

Van der Goes, Adriaen, Martinus van der Goes, and Willem van der Goes, *Briefwisseling tusschen de gebroeders van der Goes (1659–1673) Vol. I*. Edited by C. J. Gonnet. Amsterdam: Johannes Müller, 1899.

'Hage, den 27 February 1670'. *Briefwisseling tusschen de gebroeders van der Goes (1659–1673) Vol. II*. Edited by C. J. Gonnet. Amsterdam, 1899.

Van der Heyden, Jan. *Beschryving der nieuwlijks uitgevonden en geoctrojeerde slang-brand-spuiten, en haare wijze van brand-blussen tegenwoordig binnen Amsterdam in gebruik zijnde: Nevens beschryving der brand-ordres van de stad Amsterdam, Vol. I*. Amsterdam: Jan Rieuwertszoon, 1690.

Van Linschoten, Jan Huyghen. *Voyagie, of Schipvaart, van Ian Huyghen van Linschoten, van bijnoorden om lans Noorwegen, de Noordkaap, Lapland, Finland, Rusland, &c. Anno 1594 en 1595*. Franeker: Gerard Ketel, 1601.

Van Oldenbarnevelt, Johan. *Bescheiden Johan van Oldenbarnevelt 1570–1620, Eerste Deel: 1570–1601*. Edited by S. P. Haak. The Hague: Martinus Nijhoff, 1934.

Van Spilbergen, Joris. *De reis van Joris van Spilbergen naar Ceylon, Atjeh en Bantam 1601–1604*, Edited by Wouter Nijhoff, S. P. L'Honoré Naber, F. W. Stapel, and F. C. Wieder. The Hague: Martinus Nijhoff, 1933.

Van Vervou, Fredrich. *Enige gedenckvveerdige geschiedenissen, tot narichtinge der nakomelingen*. G.T.N. Suringar, 1841.

Velius, Th. *Kroniek van Hoorn Band 2: 1560–1629*. Edited by Jan Plekker and Rob Resoort. Hoorn: Publicatiestichting Bas Baltus, 2007.

Venendaal Jr., A. J., ed. *De Briefwisseling van Anthonie Heinsius, 1702–1720. Deel VI: 1707*. The Hague: Martinus Mijhoff, 1984.

De Briefwisseling van Anthonie Heinsius, 1702–1720. Deel VXIX: 2 oktober 1718–22 juli 1720. Den Haag: Instituut voor Nederlandse Geschiedenis, 2001.

White, Thomas. *An Exact and Perfect Relation Relation [sic] of the Terrible, and Bloudy Fight: Between the English and Dutch Fleets in the Downs, on Wednesday the 19 of May, 1652*. London: Printed for Robert Wood, 1652.

Winsemius, Pier. *Chronique ofte historische geschiedenisse van Vrieslant, Vol. 20.* Franeker, 1622.

PUBLISHED SECONDARY SOURCES

Ahlmström, C. *Looking for Leads: Shipwrecks of the Past Revealed by Contemporary Documents and the Archaeological Record.* Fairbanks: University of Alaska Press, 1997.

Albala, Ken. *Food in Early Modern Europe.* Westport, CT: Greenwood Press, 2003.

Allen, Myles R., David J. Frame, Chris Huntingford, Chris D. Jones, Jason A. Lowe, Malte Meinshausen, and Nicolai Meinshausen. 'Warming Caused by Cumulative Carbon Emissions towards the Trillionth Tonne'. *Nature Letters* 458 (2009): 1163–1166.

Allen, Paul. *Philip III and the Pax Hispanica, 1598–1621: The Failure of Grand Strategy.* New Haven: Yale University Press, 2000.

Alpers, Svetlana. *The Art of Describing: Dutch Art in the Seventeenth Century.* Chicago: University of Chicago Press, 1983.

Ambaum, Maarten H. P., Brian J. Hoskins, and David B. Stephenson. 'Arctic Oscillation or North Atlantic Oscillation?' *Journal of Climate* 14:16 (2001): 3495–3507.

Anderson, R. C. 'Introduction'. In *The Journals of Sir Thomas Allin, Vol. II, 1667–1678.* Edited by R. C. Anderson, ix–xiii. London: Navy Records Society, 1939.

Andrade, Tonio. 'The Company's Chinese Pirates: How the Dutch East India Company Tried to Lead a Coalition of Pirates to War against China, 1621–1662'. *Journal of World History* 15:4 (2004): 415–444.

Andreae, S. J. Fockema. 'De trekvaart Haarlem-Leiden driehonderd jaar'. In *Haerlem jaarboek*, 76–83. Haarlem: Erven F. Bohn, 1959.

Appleby, Joyce Oldham. *Economic Thought and Ideology in Seventeenth-Century England.* Princeton: Princeton University Press, 1978.

Aram, Bethany. 'Distance and Misinformation in the Conquest of America'. In *The Limits of Empire: European Imperial Formations in Early Modern World History: Essays in Honor of Geoffrey Parker.* Edited by Tonio Andrade and William Reger, 223–236. Farnham: Ashgate Publishing, 2013.

Arnade, Peter. *Beggars, Iconoclasts, and Civic Patriots: The Political Culture of the Dutch Revolt.* Ithaca: Cornell University Press, 2008.

Årthun, Marius, Tor Eldevik, Lars Henrik Smedsrud, Øystein Skagseth, and R. B. Ingvaldsen. 'Quantifying the Influence of Atlantic Heat on Barents Sea Ice Variability and Retreat'. *Journal of Climate* 25:13 (2012): 4736–4743.

Atwell, William. 'Volcanism and Short-Term Climatic Change in East Asian and World History c. 1200–1699'. *Journal of World History* 12 (2001): 29–99.

Augustyn, Beatrijs. 'De evolutie van het duinecosysteem in Vlaanderen in de Middeleeuwen: antropogene factoren versus zeespiegelrijzingstheorie'. *Historisch-Geografisch Tijdschrift* 13:1 (1995): 9–19.

Ayre, Matthew, John Nicholls, Catharine Ward, and Dennis Wheeler. 'Ships' Logbooks from the Arctic in the Pre-Instrumental Period'. *Geoscience Data Journal* 2 (2015): 53–62.

Baena, Laura Manzano. *Conflicting Words: The Peace Treaty of Münster (1648) and the Political Culture of the Dutch Republic and the Spanish Monarchy*. Leuven: Leuven University Press, 2011.

Bagrow, Leo. *History of Cartography*. New Brunswick: Transaction Publishers, 2010.

Bakker, J. P. 'Transgressionsphasen und Sturmflutfrequenz in den Niederlanden in historischer zeit'. In *Verhandlungen des Deutschen Geographentages*, 232–237. Würzburg: F. Steiner Verlag, 1957.

Bamber, Jonathan L. and Antony J. Payne, eds. *Mass Balance of the Cryosphere: Observations and Modelling of Contemporary and Future Changes*. Cambridge: Cambridge University Press, 2004.

Bang, Nina Ellinger. *Tabeller over Skibsfart og Varetransport gennen Øresund 1497–1660, Vol. I–III*. Copenhagen: Gyldendalske Boghangel, 1906–1933.

Bankoff, Greg. 'The "English Lowlands" and the North Sea Basin: A History of Shared Risk'. *Environment and History* 19:1 (2013): 3–37.

Barbour, Violet. *Capitalism in Amsterdam in the 17th Century*. Ann Arbor: University of Michigan Press, 1963.

Barend-van Haeften, Marijke. *Wilhemus en de anderen: Nederlandse liedjes, 1500–1700*. Amsterdam: Amsterdam University Press, 2000.

Baron, W. R. 'Historical Climate Records from the Northeastern United States, 1640 to 1900'. In *Climate Since A.D. 1500*. Edited by Raymond S. Bradley and Philip D. Jones. New York: Routledge, 2003.

Bartels, Michiel H. 'Zeven keer door de Zuiderdijk'. *Jaarboek* 78 (2011): 69–77.

Bauernfeind, W. and U. Woitek, 'The Influence of Climatic Change on Price Fluctuations in Germany during the 16th Century Price Revolution'. *Climatic Change* 43:1 (1999): 303–321.

Bawlf, Samuel. *The Secret Voyage of Sir Francis Drake, 1577–1580*. Vancouver: Douglas & McIntyre, 2003.

Becht, Harold Edward. *Statistische gegevens Betreffende den Handelsomzet van de Republiek der Vereenigde Nederlanden Gedurende de 17e Eeuw (1579–1715)*. The Hague: Firma I. J. C. Boucher, 1908.

Beenakker, J. J. J. M. 'De Trekvaart tussen Leiden en Haarlem'. *Dever Bulletin* (1994): 18–21.

Behringer, Wolfgang. 'Climatic Change and Witch-Hunting: The Impact of the Little Ice Age on Mentalities'. *Climatic Change* 43:1 (1999), 335–351.

A Cultural History of Climate. Cambridge: Polity Press, 2010.

Benedict, Barbara M. *Curiosity: A Cultural History of Early Modern Inquiry*. Chicago: University of Chicago Press, 2001.

Berlioz, Jacques. *Catastrophes naturelles et calamités au Moyen Âge*. Florence: Edizioni del Galluzzo, 1998.

Birks, Hilary. 'Holocene Vegetational History and Climatic Change in West Spitsbergen – Plant Macrofossils from Skardtjørna, an Arctic lake'. *The Holocene* 1:3 (1991): 209–218.

Black, J. 'Was There a Military Revolution in Early Modern Europe?' *History Today* 58:7 (July 2008): 34–41.

Black, David E., Larry C. Peterson, Jonathan T. Overpeck, Alexey Kaplan, Michael N. Evans, and Michaele Kashgarian. 'Eight Centuries of North Atlantic Ocean Atmosphere Variability'. *Science* 286:5445 (1999): 1709–1713.

Blankert, Albert. *Selected Writings on Dutch Painting: Rembrandt, Van Beke, Vermeer and Others*. Zwolle: Waanders Publishers, 2005.

Blanton, Dennis B. 'Drought as a Factor in the Jamestown Colony, 1607–1612'. *Historical Archaeology* (2000): 74–81.

Bogart, Dan. 'Did the Glorious Revolution Contribute to the Transport Revolution? Evidence from Investment in Roads and Rivers'. *The Economic History Review* 64:4 (2011): 1073–1112.

Bogucka, Maria. 'Amsterdam and the Baltic in the First Half of the Seventeenth Century'. *The Economic History Review* 26:3 (1973): 433–447.

Bor, Pieter Christiaanszoon. *Oorsprongk, begin, en vervolgh der Nederlandsche oorlogen, Vol. I*. Amsterdam: Joannes van Someren, Abraham Wolfgangh, Hendrick en Dirck Boom, 1679–1684.

Borodachev, V. Ye. and V. Yu. Alexandrov, 'History of the Northern Sea Route'. In *Remote Sensing of Sea Ice in the Northern Sea Route: Studies and Applications*. Edited by Ola M. Johannessen, 1–23. New York: Springer Praxis Books, 2007.

Boxer, C. R. *The Portuguese Seaborne Empire*. Manchester: Carcanet in association with the Calouste Gulbenkian Foundation, 1991.

Braat, J. 'Dutch Activities in the North and the Arctic during the Sixteenth and Seventeenth Centuries'. *Arctic* 37:4 (1984): 473–480.

Behouden uit het Behouden Huys. Catalogus van voorwerpen van de Barentsexpeditie (1596), gevonden op Nova Zembla. De Rijksmuseumcollectie, aangevuld met Russische en Noorse vondsten. Amsterdam: De Bataaf sehe leeuw, 1998.

Bradley, Raymond S. and Philip D. Jones. '"Little Ice Age" Summer Temperature Variations: Their Nature and Relevance to Recent Global Trends'. *The Holocene* 3 (1993): 367–376.

Braudel, Fernand. *The Mediterranean and the Mediterranean World in the Age of Philip II, Vol. I*. California: University of California Press, 1995.

Brázdil, Rudolf, Christian Pfister, Heinz Wanner, Hans Von Storch, and Jürg Luterbacher. 'Historical Climatology in Europe – The State of the Art'. *Climatic Change* 70:3 (2005): 363–430.

Bremmer, Rolf Hendrik. *Reformatie en rebellie: Willem van Oranje, de calvinisten en het recht van opstand: tien onstuimige jaren, 1572–1581*. Franeker: Wever, 1984.

Briffa, K. R., P. D. Jones, F. H. Schweingruber, and T. J. Osborn, 'Influence of Volcanic Eruptions on Northern Hemisphere Summer Temperature over the Past 600 Years'. *Nature* 393 (1998): 450–455.

Briffa, K. R., P. D. Jones, R. B. Vogel, F. H. Schweingruber, M. G. L. Baillie, S. G. Shiyatov, and E. A. Vaganov. 'European Tree Rings and Climate in the 16th Century'. *Climatic Change* 43:1 (1999): 151–168.

Briffa, K. R., T. J. Osborn and F. H. Schweingruber. 'Large-Scale Temperature Inferences from Tree Rings: A Review'. *Global and Planetary Change* 40:1–2 (2004): 11–26.

Brokken, H. M. *Het ontstaan van de Hoekse en Kabeljauwse twisten*. Zutphen: Walburg Pers, 1982.

Brooke, John. *Climate Change and the Course of Global History: A Rough Journey*. Cambridge: Cambridge University Press, 2014.

Brown, Christopher. *Dutch Paintings*. London: National Gallery Publications, 1983.

Brown, Neville. *History and Climate Change: A Eurocentric Perspective*. London: Routledge, 2001.

Bruijn, Jaap R. 'Between Batavia and the Cape: Shipping Patterns of the Dutch East India Company'. *Journal of Southeast Asian Studies*, 11:2 (1980): 251–265.

'Dutch Privateering during the Second and Third Anglo-Dutch Wars'. In *The Low Countries History Yearbook 1978*. Edited by I. Schöffer, 67–83. Dordrecht: Springer, 1979.

'Introduction'. In *De Ruyter: Dutch Admiral*. Edited by Jaap R. Bruijn and Ronald Prud'homme van Reine, 7–16. Rotterdam: Karwansaray BV, 2011.

'The Dutch East India Company as Shipowner, 1602–1796'. *American Neptune* 47:4 (September 1987): 240–248.

The Dutch Navy of the Seventeenth and Eighteenth Centuries. Columbia: University of South Carolina Press, 1990.

'The Maritime World of the Dutch Republic'. In *De Ruyter: Dutch Admiral*. Edited by Jaap R. Bruijn and Ronald Prud'homme van Reine, 17–36. Rotterdam: Karwansaray BV, 2011.

Bruijn, J. R., F. S. Gaastra, and I. Schöffer, with assistance from A. C. J. Vermeulen. *Dutch-Asiatic Shipping in the 17th and 18th Centuries: Introductory Volume*. The Hague: Martinus Nijhoff, 1987.

Buisman, J. and A. F. V. van Engelen, ed. *Duizend jaar weer, wind en water in de Lage Landen, Vol. III 1450–1575*. Franeker: Uitgeverij Van Wijnen, 1998.

Duizend jaar weer, wind en water in de Lage Landen, Vol. IV 1575–1675. Franeker: Uitgeverij Van Wijnen, 2000.

Duizend jaar weer, wind en water in de Lage Landen, Vol. V 1675–1750. Franeker: Uitgeverij Van Wijnen, 2006.

Burke, Peter. *Popular Culture in Early Modern Europe*. Farnham: Ashgate Publishing, 2009.

Burns, Willem E. *Witch Hunts in Europe and America: An Encyclopedia*. Portsmouth: Greenwood Publishing Corp. 2003.

Burroughs, W. J. 'Winter Landscapes and Climatic Change'. *Weather* 36 (1981): 352–357.

Camenisch, Chantal. 'Endless Cold: A Seasonal Reconstruction of Temperature and Precipitation in the Burgundian Low Countries during the 15th Century Based on Documentary Evidence'. *Climate of the Past* 11:8 (2015): 1049–1066.

Camenisch, Chantal, Kathrin M. Keller, Melanie Salvisberg, Benjamin Amann, Martin Bauch, Sandro Blumer, Rudolf Brázdil, et al. 'The 1430s: A Cold

Period of Extraordinary Internal Climate Variability during the Early Spörer Minimum with Social and Economic Impacts in North-Western and Central Europe'. *Climate of the Past* 12:11 (2016): 2107–2126.

Carey, Mark. 'Science, Models, and Historians: Toward a Critical Climate History'. *Environmental History* 19 (2014): 354–364.

Cavert, William. 'Winter and Discontent in Early Modern England'. In *Governing the Environment in the Early Modern World: Theory and Practice*. Edited by Sara Miglietti and John Morgan, 114–133. London: Routledge, 2017.

Caviedes, César N. *El Niño in History: Storming through the Ages*. Gainesville: University Press of Florida, 2001.

'Five Hundred Years of Hurricanes in the Caribbean: Their Relationship with Global Climatic Variabilities'. *GeoJournal* 23: 4 (1991); 301–310.

Christensen, Aksel E. *Dutch Trade to the Baltic about 1600: Studies in the Sound Toll Register and Dutch Shipping Records*. Copenhagen: Einar Munksgarrd, 1941.

Claiborne, Robert. *Climate, Man and History*. London: Angus and Robertson, 1973.

Clark, Peter. 'Introduction'. In *The European Crisis of the 1590s: Essays in Comparative History*. Edited by Peter Clark, 3–22. London: George Allen & Unwin, 1985.

Clark, Stuart. *Thinking with Demons: The Idea of Witchcraft in Early Modern Europe*. Oxford: Oxford University Press, 1999.

Clay, C. G. A. *Economic Expansion and Social Change, Vol. I: England 1500–1700*. Cambridge: Cambridge University Press, 1984.

Economic Expansion and Social Change: England 1500–1700, Vol. II: Industry, Trade, and Government. Cambridge: Cambridge University Press, 1984.

Coates, Colin. 'Seeing and Not Seeing: Landscape Art as a Historical Source'. In *Method and Meaning in Canadian Environmental History*. Edited by Alan MacEachern and William J. Turkel, 140–157. Toronto: Nelson Education, 2009.

Cockett, F. B. *Early Sea Painters, 1660–1730*. Suffolk: Antique Collectors' Club Ltd., 1995.

Cohen, Judah, Kazuyuki Saito, and Dara Entekhabi. 'The Role of the Siberian High in Northern Hemisphere Climate Variability'. *Geophysical Research Letters* 28:2 (2001): 299–302.

Cole-Dai, Jihong. 'Volcanoes and Climate'. *Wiley Interdisciplinary Reviews: Climate Change* 1:6 (2010): 824–839.

Conway, Martin. *No Man's Land: A History of Spitsbergen from Its Discovery in 1596 to the Beginning of the Scientific Exploration of the Country*. Cambridge: Cambridge University Press, first published 1906, 2012.

Cook, Edward R. 'Multi-Proxy Reconstructions of the North Atlantic Oscillation (NAO) Index: A Critical Review and a New Well-Verified Winter NAO Index Reconstruction Back to AD 1400'. In *The North Atlantic Oscillation: Climatic Significance and Environmental Impact*. Edited by James W. Hurrell, Yochanan Kushnir, Geir Ottersen, and Martin Visbeck, 63–79. Washington, DC: American Geophysical Union, 2003.

Cook, John, Naomi Oreskes, Peter Doran, William Anderegg, Bart Verheggen, Ed Maibach, J. Stuart Carlton, Stephan Lewandowsky, Andrew G. Skuce, Sarah A. Green, Dana Nuccitelli, Peter Jacobs, Mark Richardson, Bärbel Winkler, Rob Painting, and Ken Rice. 'Consensus on Consensus: a Synthesis of Consensus Estimates on Human-Caused Global Warming'. *Environmental Research Letters* 11 (2016): 1–7.

Cook, Harold J. *Matters of Exchange: Commerce, Medicine, and Science in the Dutch Golden Age*. New Haven: Yale University Press, 2007.

Crespin, Elisabeth, Hugues Goosse, Thierry Fichefet, Aurélien Mairesse, and Yoann Sallaz-Damaz. 'Arctic Climate over the Past Millennium: Annual and Seasonal Responses to External Forcings'. *The Holocene* 23 (2013): 321–329.

Crespin, Elisabeth, Hugues Goosse, Thierry Fichefet, and Michael E. Mann. 'The 15th Century Arctic Warming in Coupled Model Simulations with Data Assimilation'. *Climate of the Past* (2009): 389–401.

Crone, G. C. E. *Nederlandsche binnenschepen*. Amsterdam: Alert de Lange, 1944.

Crone, G. R. *Maps and Their Makers: An Introduction to the History of Cartography*, 5th ed. Dawson: Folkestone & Archon Books, 1978.

Cronin, T. M., G. S. Dwyer, T. Kamiya, S. Schwede, and D. A. Willard. 'Medieval Warm Period, Little Ice Age and 20th Century Temperature Variability from Chesapeake Bay'. *Global and Planetary Change* 36:1 (2003): 17–29.

Cropper, John P. and Harold C. Fritts. 'Tree-Ring Width Chronologies from the North American Arctic'. *Arctic and Alpine Research* (1981): 245–260.

Crowley, Thomas J. 'Causes of Climate Change over the Past 1000 Years'. *Science* 289:5477 (2000): 270–277.

Cullen, Karen J. *Famine in Scotland: The 'Ill Years' of the 1690s*. Edinburgh: Edinburgh University Press Ltd., 2010.

Curry, Judith A., Julie L. Schramm, and Elizabeth E. Ebert, 'Sea Ice-Albedo Climate Feedback Mechanism'. *Journal of Climate* 8:2 (1995): 240–247.

Daalder, R. *Van de Velde & Son, Marine Painters: The Firm of Willem van de Velde the Elder and Willem van de Velde the Younger, 1640–1707*. Leiden: Primavera Pers, 2016.

D'Andrea, William J., David A. Vaillencourt, Nicholas L. Balascio, Al Werner, Steven R. Roof, Michael Retelle, and Raymond S. Bradley. 'Mild Little Ice Age and Unprecedented Recent Warmth in an 1800 Year Lake Sediment Record from Svalbard'. *Geology* 10.1130 (2012): 1007–1010.

Darby, Graham. 'Introduction'. In *The Origins and Development of the Dutch Revolt*. Edited by Graham Darby, 1–7. London: Routledge, 2003.

'Narrative of Events'. In *The Origins and Development of the Dutch Revolt*. Edited by Graham Darby, 8–28. London: Routledge, 2003.

D'Arrigo, Rosanne D. and G. C. Jacoby Jr. 'Dendroclimatic Evidence from Northern North America'. In *Climate Since A.D. 1500*. Edited by Raymond S. Bradley and Philip D. Jones, 296–311. New York: Routledge, 2003.

D'Arrigo, Rosanne, Gordon Jacoby, Rob Wilson, and Fotis Panagiotopoulos. 'A Reconstructed Siberian High Index since AD 1599 from Eurasian and North American Tree Rings'. *Geophysical Research Letters* 32:5 (2005): 1–4.

D. D'Arrigo, Rosanne, Edward R. Cook, Michael E. Mann, and Gordon C. Jacoby. 'Tree-Ring Reconstructions of Temperature and Sea-Level Pressure Variability Associated with the Warm-Season Arctic Oscillation since AD 1650'. *Geophysical Research Letters* 30:11 (2003): 1–4.

Daston, Lorraine. *Classical Probability in the Enlightenment*. Princeton: Princeton University Press, 1988.

Davids, C. A. 'De technische ontwikkeling in Nederland in de vroeg-moderne tijd. Literatuur, problemen en hypothesen'. *Jaarboek voor de Geschiedenis van Bedrijf en Techniek* 8 (1991): 9–37.

'Navigeren in Azië. De uitwisseling van kennis tussen Aziaten en navigatiepersoneel bij de voorcompagnieën en de VOC, 1596–1795'. *Tijdschrift voor Zeegeschiedenis* 9:1 (1990): 5–18.

'Patents and Patentees in the Dutch Republic between c. 1580 and 1720'. *History and Technology: An International Journal* 16:3 (2000): 263–283.

'Technological Change and the Economic Expansion of the Dutch Republic, 1580–1680'. In *The Dutch Economy in the Golden Age: Nine Studies*. Edited by C. A. Davids and L. Noordegraaf, 79–104. Amsterdam: Nederlandsch Economisch-Historisch Archief, 1993.

The Rise and Decline of Dutch Technological Leadership: Technology, Economy and Culture in the Netherlands, 1350–1800, Vol. I. Leiden: Brill, 2008.

Dawson, Alastair G., Kieran Hickey, Tom Holt, L. Elliott, S. Dawson, Ian D. L. Foster, Peter Wadhams, I. Jonsdottir, J. Wilkinson, J. McKenna, N. R. Davis, and D. E. Smith. 'Complex North Atlantic Oscillation (NAO) Index Signal of Historic North Atlantic Storm-Track Changes'. *The Holocene* 12:3 (2002): 363–369.

De Boer, Agatha M. 'Oceanography: Sea Change'. *Nature Geoscience* 3:10 (2010): 668–669.

De Boer, Michiel George. *Tromp en de Armada van 1639*. Nv Noord-Hollandsche uitgevers maatschappij, 1941.

De Cauwer, Peter. *Tranen van bloed: het beleg van 's-Hertogenbosch en de oorlog in de Nederlanden, 1629*. Amsterdam: Amsterdam University Press, 2007.

De Graaf, Rudi. *Oorlog, mijn arme schapen. Een andere kijk op de Tachtigjarige Oorlog*. Franeker: Van Wijnen, 2004.

De Jonge, J. C. *Het Nederlandsche Zeewezen, Vol. I*, 2nd ed. Haarlem: A.C. Kruseman, 1858.

De Jongh, Eddy. 'Realism and Seeming Realism in Seventeenth-Century Dutch Painting'. In *Looking at Seventeenth-Century Dutch Art: Realism Reconsidered*. Edited by Wayne Franits, 21–56. Cambridge: Cambridge University Press, 1997.

'The Iconological Approach to Seventeenth-Century Dutch Painting'. In *The Golden Age of Dutch Painting in Historical Perspective*. Edited by Frans Grijzenhout and Henk van Veen, 200–223. Cambridge: Cambridge University Press, 1999.

De Kraker, Adriaan M. J. 'Ice and Water. The Removal of Ice on Waterways in the Low Countries, 1330–1800'. *Water History*: 1–20.

'Reconstruction of Storm Frequency in the North Sea Area of the Preindustrial Period, 1400–1625 and the Connection with Reconstructed Time Series of Temperatures'. *History of Meteorology* 2 (2005), 51–70.

'The Little Ice Age: Harsh Winters between 1550 and 1650'. In *Hendrick Avercamp: Master of the Ice Scene*. Edited by Pieter Roelofs. Amsterdam: Rijksmuseum, 2009.

De Meer, Sjoerd. 'De wereld van de zeekart'. In *Het Zeekarten Boek*. Edited by Sjoerd de Meer, 11–30. Zutphen: Walburg Pers, 2007.

'Het kaartenmakersbedrijf van de Verenigde Oostindische Compagnie'. In *Het Zeekarten Boek*. Edited by Sjoerd de Meer, 47–58. Zutphen: Walburg Pers, 2007.

De Silva, Shanaka L. and Gregory A. Zielinski, 'Global influence of the AD 1600 eruption of Huaynaputina, Peru'. *Nature* 393:6684 (1998): 455–458.

De Visser, Wendy. *Piet Hein en de zilvervloot: oorlog en handel in de West*. Hilversum: Uitgeverij Verloren, 2001.

De Vries, Jan. *Barges and Capitalism. Passenger Transportation in the Dutch Economy, 1632–1839*. Utrecht: HES Publishers, 1978.

'Connecting Europe and Asia: A Quantitative Analysis of the Cape-Route Trade, 1497–1795'. In *Global Connections and Monetary History, 1470–1800*. Edited by Dennis O. Flynn, Arturo Giraldez, and Richard von Glahn, 34–106. Aldershot: Ashgate, 2003.

'Measuring the Impact of Climate on History: The Search for Appropriate Methodologies'. *Journal of Interdisciplinary History*, 10:4 (1980): 599–630.

'The Crisis of the Seventeenth Century: The Little Ice Age and the Mystery of the "Great Divergence". *Journal of Interdisciplinary History* 44:3 (2013): 369–377.

'The Economic Crisis of the Seventeenth Century after Fifty Years'. *Journal of Interdisciplinary History* 40:2 (2009): 151–194.

De Vries, Jan and Ad van der Woude. *The First Modern Economy: Success, Failure, and Perseverance of the Dutch Economy, 1500–1815*. Cambridge: Cambridge University Press, 1997.

Deen, Femke, David Onnekink, and Michel Reinders. 'Pamphlets and politics: introduction'. In *Pamphlets and Politics in the Dutch Republic*. Edited by Femake Deen, David Onnekink and Michel Reinders, 3–30. Leiden: Brill, 2010.

Delano-Smith, Catherine. 'Milieus of Mobility: Itineraries, Route Maps and Road Maps'. In *Cartographies of Travel and Navigation*. Edited by James R. Akerman, 16–68. Chicago: University of Chicago Press, 2006.

Diamond, Jared. *Collapse: How Societies Choose to Fail or Succeed*. London: Penguin Books, 2006.

Diebels, P. G. M. '"Op papier vergan". Onderzoek naar vergane schapen in de archieven van de Verenigde Oostindische Compagnie'. *Nederlandsch Archievenblad* 95 (1991): 174–190.

Douglas, K. S. and H. H. Lamb. *Weather Observations and a Tentative Meteorological Analysis of the Period May to July 1588*. Norwich: University of East Anglia Climatic Research Unit, 1979.

Dreiskämper, Petra. *Redeloos, radeloos, reddeloos: de geschiedenis van het rampjaar 1672*. Hilversum: Uitgeverij Verloren, 1998.

Dres-Coenders, Lene. *Het verbond van heks en duivel. Een waandenkbeeld aan het begin van de moderne tijd als symptoom van een veranderende situatie van de vrouw en als middel tot hervorming der zeden*. Baarn: Ambo, 1983.

Drinkwater, Ken, Martin Miles, Iselin Medhaug, Odd Helge Otterå, Trong Kristiansen, Svein Sundby, and Yongi Gao. 'The Atlantic Multidecadal Oscillation: Its Manifestations and Impacts with Special Emphasis on the Atlantic Region North of 60° N'. (Paper presented at the ESSAS Annual Science Meeting, Copenhagen, Denmark 7–9 April 2014).

Duffy, Christopher. *Siege Warfare: The Fortress in the Early Modern World, 1494–1660*. London: Routledge, 2013.

Duke, Alastair. *Reformation and Revolt in the Low Countries*. London: Hambledon Press, 1990.

Dunthorne, Hugh. *Britain and the Dutch Revolt 1560–1700*. Cambridge: Cambridge University Press, 2013.

Duyck, Anthonis. *De slag bij Nieuwpoort: Journaal van de tocht naar Vlaanderen in 1600*. Nijmegen: SUN, 2000.

Journaal van Anthonis Duyck, advokaat-fiskaal van den raad van state: (1591–1602) Uitgegeven op last van het departement van oorlog, met inleiding en aanteekeningen door Lodewijk Mulder, Vol. I. The Hague: Martinus Nijhoff, 1862.

Eamon, William. *Science and the Secrets of Nature: Books of Secrets in Medieval and Early Modern Culture*. Princeton, NJ: Princeton University Press, 1994.

Eddy, John A. 'The Maunder Minimum'. *Science* 192:4245 (1976): 1189–1202.

'Climate and the Changing Sun'. *Climatic Change* 1 (1977): 173–190.

Edwards, Paul. *A Vast Machine: Computer Models, Climate Data, and the Politics of Global Warming*. Cambridge: The MIT Press, 2010.

Elias, Johan E. *De vlootbouw in Nederland in the eerste helft der 17e eeuw, 1596–1655*. Amsterdam: Noord-Hollandsche Uitgeversmaatschappij, 1933.

Emmer, P. C. *The Dutch in the Atlantic economy, 1580–1880*. Aldershot: Ashgate, 1998.

Emmius, Ubbo. *Willem Lodewijk, graaf van Nassau (1560–1620)*. Zutphen: Uitgevrij Verloren, 1994.

Endfield, Georgina H. 'Exploring Particularity: Vulnerability, Resilience, and Memory in Climate Change Discourses'. *Environmental History* 19 (2014): 303–310.

Enthoven, Victor. 'Early Dutch Expansion in the Atlantic Region, 1585–1621'. In *Riches from Atlantic commerce: Dutch Transatlantic Trade and Shipping, 1585–1817*. Edited by Johannes Postma and Victor Enthoven, 17–47. Leiden: Brill, 2003.

Evans, D. C. B., J. F. Nye, and K. J. Cheeseman. 'The Kinetic Friction of Ice'. *Proceedings of the Royal Society* 347:1651 (1976): 493–512.

Evans, Robert. 'The Early History of Fire Insurance'. *The Journal of Legal History* 8:1 (1987): 88–91.
Everitt, Robert D. and Bruce D. Krogman. 'Sexual Behavior of Bowhead Whales Observed off the North Coast of Alaska'. *Arctic* 32:3 (1979): 277–280.
Fagan, Brian M. *The Little Ice Age: How Climate Made History, 1300–1850*. Boulder: Basic Books, 2000.
Fang, Keyan, Xiaohua Gou, Fahu Chen, Changzhi Liu, Nicole Davi, Jinbao Li, Zhiqian Zhao, and Yingjun Li. 'Tree-Ring Based Reconstruction of Drought Variability (1615–2009) in the Kongtong Mountain Area, northern China'. *Global and Planetary Change* 80 (2012): 190–197.
Faries, Molly. 'Making and Marketing: Studies of the Painting Process'. In *Making and Marketing: Studies of the Painting Process in Fifteenth- and Sixteenth-Century Netherlandish Workshops*. Edited by Molly Faries, 1–14. Turnhout: Brepols Publishers, 2006.
Fischer, E. M. and R. Knutti. 'Anthropogenic Contribution to Global Occurrence of Heavy-Precipitation and High-Temperature Extremes'. *Nature Climate Change* (2015): http://dx.doi.org/10.1038/nclimate2617.
Fix, Andrew C. *Prophecy and Reason: The Dutch Collegiants in the Early Enlightenment*. Princeton: Princeton University Press, 1991.
Flinn, Michael. *The European Demographic System, 1500–1820*. Baltimore: Johns Hopkins University Press, 1981.
Fock, Willemijn C. 'Kunst en rariteiten in het Hollandse interieur'. In *De wereld binnen handbereijk: Nederlandse kunst- en rariteitenverzamelingen, 1585–1735*. Edited by Ellinoor Bergevelt and Renee Kistemaker, 70–91. Zwolle: Waanders Uitgevers/Amsterdam Historisch Museum, 1992.
Franits, Wayne. 'Introduction'. In *Looking at Seventeenth-Century Dutch Art: Realism Reconsidered*. Edited by Wayne Franits, 1–7. Cambridge: Cambridge University Press, 1997.
Frieslaender, Max J. *Early Netherlandish Painting from Van Eyck to Bruegel*. London: Phaidon Press, 1956.
Frijhoff, Willem and Marijke Spies, *Dutch Culture in a European Perspective: 1650, hard-won unity*. Gorcum: Uitgeverij van Gorcum, 2004.
Fritschy, Wantje. 'A "Financial Revolution" Reconsidered: Public Finance in Holland during the Dutch Revolt, 1568–1648'. *Economic History Review* LVI:1 (2009): 57–89.
'Holland en de financiering van de Opstand (1568–1648): Deel I'. *Economisch Statistische Berichten* 89:4437 (2004): 328–330.
'Holland en de financiering van de Opstand (1568–1648): Deel II'. *Economisch Statistische Berichten* 89:4437 (2004): 353–355.
Fritts H. C. and X. M. Shao. 'Mapping Climate Using Tree-Rings from Western North America'. In *Climate Since A.D. 1500*. Edited by Raymond S. Bradley and Philip D. Jones, 269–295. New York: Routledge, 2003.
Fruin, Robert. *De oorlog van 1672*. Groningen: Wolters-Noordhoff 1972.
Gaastra, Femme S. *Bewind en beleid bij de VOC: de financiële en commerciële politiek bij de bewindhebbers, 1672–1702*. Zutphen: Walburg Pers, 1989.
The Dutch East India Company: Expansion and Decline. Zutphen: Uitgeversmaatschappij Walburg Pers, 2003.

Gallagher, Patrick and Don Cruickshank, eds. *God's Obvious Design: Papers for the Spanish Armada Symposium, Sligo, 1988: with an Edition and Translation of the Account of Francisco de Cuéllar*. London: Tamesis Books, 1990.

García-Herrera, Ricardo, Gunther P. Können, D. A. Wheeler, Maria R. Prieto, Philip D. Jones, and Frits B. Koek. 'CLIWOC: A Climatological Database for the World's Oceans 1750–1854'. *Climatic Change* 73 (2005): 1–12.

García-Herrera, Ricardo, Luis Prieto, David Gallego, Emiliano Hernández, Luis Gimeno, Gunther Können, Frits Koek, Dennis Wheeler, Clive Wilkinson, Maria Del Rosario Prieto, Carlos Báez, and Scott Woodruff. *CLIWOC Multilingual Meteorological Dictionary: An English-Spanish-Dutch-French Dictionary of Wind Force Terms Used by Mariners from 1750 to 1850*. Den Haag: Koninklijke Nederlands Meteorologisch Instituut, 2003.

Gawronski, Jerzy H. G. and Jaap Jan Zeeberg, 'The Wrecking of Barents' Ship'. In *Northbound with Barents: Russian-Dutch Integrated Archaelogical Research on the Archipelago Novaya Zemlya*. Edited by Pyotr Boyarsky and Jerzy Gawronski, 89–92. Amsterdam: Uitgeverij Jan Mets, 1997.

Ge, Q., Z. Hao, J. Zheng, and X. Shao. 'Temperature Changes over the Past 2000 yr in China and Comparison with the Northern Hemisphere'. *Climate of the Past* 9:3 (2013): 1153–1160.

Gelderblom, Oscar. *Zuid-Nederlandse kooplieden en de opkomst van de Amsterdamse stapelmarkt (1578–1630)*. Hilversum: Uitgeverij Verloren, 2000.

Gergis, Joëlle L. and Anthony M. Fowler, 'A History of ENSO Events since A. D. 1525: Implications for Future Climate Change'. *Climatic Change* 92:3–4 (2009): 343–387.

Gergis, Joëlle L., Don Garden, and Claire Fenby, 'The Influence of Climate on the First European Settlement of Australia: A Comparison of Weather Journals, Documentary Data and Palaeoclimate Records, 1788–1793'. *Environmental History* 15:3 (2010): 485–507.

Geurts, P. A. M. *De Nederlandse Opstand in de Pamfletten 1566–1584*. Nijmegen: Centrale Drukkerij, 1956.

Gijswijt-Hofstra, Marijke. 'The European Witchcraft Debate and the Dutch Variant'. *Social History* 15:8 (2008): 181–194.

Gjertzand, Ian and Øystein Wiig, 'Past and Present Distribution of Walruses in Svalbard'. *Arctic* 47:1 (1994): 34–42.

Glaser, Rüdiger. *Klimageschichte Mitteleuropas. 1000 Jahre Wetter, Klima, Katastrophen*. Darmstadt: Buchgesellschaft, 2001.

Glaser, Rüdiger and Gerhard Koslowski. 'Variations in Reconstructed Ice Winter Severity in the Western Baltic from 1501 to 1995, and Their Implications for the North Atlantic Oscillation'. *Climatic Change* 41 (1999): 175–191.

Glaser, Rüdiger, Rudolf Brázdil, Christian Pfister, Petr Dobrovolný, Mariano Barriendos Vallvé, Anita Bokwa, Dario Camuffo, Oldrich Kotyza, Danuta Limanówka, Lajos Rácz, and Fernando S. Rodrigo. 'Seasonal Temperature and Precipitation Fluctuations in Selected Parts of Europe during the Sixteenth Century'. *Climatic Change* 43: 1 (1999): 169–200.

Glete, Jan. *Warfare at Sea, 1500–1650*. New York: Routledge, 2000.

Global Humanitarian Forum. *The Anatomy of a Silent Crisis*. Geneva: Global Humanitarian Forum, 2009.

Go, Sabine. *Marine Insurance in the Netherlands, 1600–1870: A Comparative Institutional Approach*. Amsterdam: Askant, 2009.

Goedde, Lawrence Otto. *Tempest and Shipwreck in Dutch and Flemish Art: Convention, Rhetoric, and Interpretation*. Philadelphia: The Pennsylvania State University Press, 1989.

Goldgar, Anne. *Impolite Learning: Conduct and Community in the Republic of Letters, 1680–1750*. New Haven: Yale University Press, 1995.

Tulipmania: Money, Honor, and Knowledge in the Dutch Golden Age. Chicago: University of Chicago Press, 2008.

Gonnet, C. J. 'Inleiding'. In *Briefwisseling tusschen de gebroeders van der Goes (1659–1673), Vol. I*. Edited by C. J. Gonnet, i–xxxix. Amsterdam: Johannes Müller, 1899.

Goodman, David. *Spanish Naval Power: Reconstruction and Defeat*. Cambridge: Cambridge University Press, 1997.

Gottschalk, Elisabeth M. K. *Stormvloeden en rivieroverstromingen in Nederland, Vol II: de periode 1400–1600*. Assen: Van Gorcum, 1975.

Stormvloeden en rivieroverstromingen in Nederland, Vol III: de periode 1600–1700. Assen: Van Gorcum, 1977.

Gray, Stephen T., Lisa J. Graumlich, Julio L. Betancourt, and Gregory T. Pederson. 'A Tree-Ring Based Reconstruction of the Atlantic Multidecadal Oscillation since 1567 AD'. *Geophysical Research Letters* 31:12 (2004): 1–4.

Groenveld, Simon. *Het Twaalf Jarig Bestand, 1609–1621: De Jongelingsjaren van de Republiek der Verenigde Nederlanden*. The Hague: Haags Historisch Museum, 2009.

'The English Civil Wars as a Cause of the First Anglo-Dutch War, 1640–1652'. *The Historical Journal* 30:3 (1987): 541–566.

Grove, Jean M. *Little Ice Ages: Ancient and Modern, Vol. I*. London: Routledge, 2004.

'The Century Time-scale'. In *Time-Scales and Environmental Change*. Edited by Thackwray S. Driver and Graham P. Chapman, 39–87. Oxford: Routledge, 1996.

'The Initiation of the "Little Ice Age" in Regions Round the North Atlantic'. In *The Iceberg in the Mist: Northern Research in pursuit of a 'Little Ice Age'*. Edited by Astrid E. J. Ogilvie and Trausti Jónsson, 53–82. Dordrecht: Springer Netherlands, 2001.

Gupta, Anil K., David M. Anderson, and Jonathan T. Overpeck. 'Abrupt Changes in the Asian Southwest Monsoon during the Holocene and Their Links to the North Atlantic Ocean'. *Nature* 421 (2003): 354–357.

Haak, Bob. *The Golden Age: Dutch Painters of the Seventeenth Century*. London: Thames and Hudson, 1984.

Hacquebord, Louwrens. *De Noordse Compagnie (1614–1642): Opkomst, Bloei en Ondergang*. Zutphen: Walburg Pers, 2014.

'In Search of *Het Behouden Huys*: A Survey of the Remains of the House of Willem Barentsz on Novaya Zemlya'. *Arctic* 48:3 (1995): 248–256.

'Smeerenburg: het verblijf van Nederlandse walvisvaarders op de Westkust van Spitsbergen in de zeventiende eeuw'. PhD diss., Universiteit van Amsterdam, 1984.

'The Hunting of the Greenland Right Whale in Svalbard, Its Interaction with Climate and Its Impact on the Marine Ecosystem'. *Polar Research* 18:2 (1999): 375–382.

'Three Centuries of Whaling and Walrus Hunting in Svalbard and Its Impact on the Arctic Ecosystem'. *Environment and History* 7 (2001): 169–185.

'Twenty Five Years of Multi-Disciplinary Research into the 17th Century Whaling Settlements in Spitsbergen'. Available at: www.rug.nl/research/portal/files/14531514/07.pdf.

Hacquebord, Louwrens, Frits Steenhuisen and Huib Waterbolk. 'English and Dutch Whaling Trade and Whaling Stations in Spitsbergen (Svalbard) before 1660'. *International Journal of Maritime History* 15:2 (2003): 117–134.

Hacquebord, Louwrens and Nienke Boschman. *A Passion for the Pole: Ethological Research in Polar Regions*. Philadelphia: Casemate Publishers, 2008.

Hacquebord, Louwrens and Jurjen R. Leinenga, 'The Ecology of Greenland Whale in Relation to Whaling and Climate Change in 17th and 18th Centuries'. *Tijdschrift voor Geschiendenis* 107 (1994): 415–438.

Hainsworth, Roger and Christine Churches. *The Anglo-Dutch Naval Wars*. Stroud: Sutton Publishing Limited, 1998.

Hale, J. R. *War and Society in Renaissance Europe*. London: Fontana, 1985.

Haley, K. H. D. *The Dutch in the Seventeenth Century*. London: Thames and Hudson Ltd., 1972.

Hanson, Neil. *The Confident Hope of a Miracle: The True Story of the Spanish Armada*. New York: Knopf Doubleday Publishing Group, 2007.

Hansson, D. and A. Omstedt. 'Modelling the Baltic Sea Ocean Climate on Centennial Time Scale: Temperature and Sea Ice'. *Climate Dynamics*, 30: 763–778.

Harding, Richard. *Seapower and Naval Warfare, 1650–1830*. London: UCL Press, 1999.

Harley, J. B. 'Maps, Knowledge, and Power'. In *The Iconography of Landscape: Essays on the Symbolic Representation, Design and Use of Past Environments*. Edited by D. Cosgrove and S. Daniels, 277–312. Cambridge: Cambridge University Press, 1988.

Hell, Maarten and Wilma Gijsbers. 'Geborgen of gezonken, gered of verdronken: Papieren getuigen van scheepsrampen rond Texel (1575–1795)'. *Tijdschrift voor Zeegeschiedenis* 31:2 (2012): 42–59.

Hellinga, Gerben Graddesz. *Pioniers van de Gouden Eeuw*. Zutphen: Walburg Pers, 2007.

Zeehelden van de Gouden Eeuw. Zutphen: Walburg Pers, 2008.

Hill, Charles E. *The Danish Sound Dues and the Command of the Baltic*. Durham: Duke University Press, 1926.

Hoak, Dale. 'The Anglo-Dutch Revolution of 1688–89'. In *The World of William and Mary: Anglo-Dutch Perspectives on the Revolution, of 1688–89*. Edited by Dale Hoak and Mordechai Feingold, 1–26. Stanford: Stanford University Press, 1996.

Hodge, Adam R. '"In Want of Nourishment for to Keep Them Alive": Climatic Fluctuations, Bison Scarcity, and the Smallpox Epidemic of 1780–82 on the Northern Great Plains'. *Environmental History* (2012) 17(2): 365–403.

Horensma, P. T. G. 'Olivier Brunel and the Dutch Involvement in the Discovery of the Northeast Passage'. *Fram* 2:1 (1985): 121–128.

Horsten, Frits H. *Doorgaande wegen in Nederland, 16e tot 19e eeuw: Een historische wegenatlas*. Amsterdam: Uitgeverij Aksant, 2005.

Houston, Alan and Steve Pincus, 'Introduction: Modernity and Later Seventeenth-Century England'. In *A Nation Transformed: England after the Restoration*. Edited by Alan Houston and Steve Pincus, 1–19. Cambridge: Cambridge University Press, 2001.

Huang, Rui Xin. *Ocean Circulation: Wind-Driven and Thermohaline Processes*. Cambridge: Cambridge University Press, 2010.

Huddart, David and Tim Stott. *Earth Environments Past, Present and Future*. Chichester: John Wiley & Sons, 2013.

Hulme, Mike. 'Reducing the Future to Climate: A Story of Climate Determinism and Reductionism'. *Osiris* 26:1 (2011): 245–266.

Hunter, Douglas. *Half Moon: Henry Hudson and the Voyage that Redrew the Map of the World*. New York: Bloomsbury Press, 2009.

Hurrell, James W., Yochanan Kushnir, Geir Ottersen, Martin Visbeck, eds. *The North Atlantic Oscillation: Climatic Significance and Environmental Impact*, 1st ed. Washington, DC: American Geophysical Union, 2003.

Hutchinson, Gillian. 'Threats to Underwater Cultural Heritage'. *Marine Policy* 20:4 (1996): 287–290.

Ingram, M. J., G. Farmer and T. M. L. Wigley. 'Past Climates and Their Impact on Man: A Review'. In *Climate and History: Studies on Past Climates and Their Impact on Man*. Edited by M. J. Ingram, G. Farmer and T. M. L. Wigley, 3–50. Cambridge: Cambridge University Press, 1981.

IPCC. '2014: Summary for Policymakers'. In *Climate Change 2014: Impacts, Adaptation, and Vulnerability. Contribution of Working Group II to the Fifth Assessment Report of the Intergovernmental Panel on Climate Change*. Edited by C. B. Field, V. R. Barros, D. J. Dokken, K. J. Mach, M. D. Mastrandrea, M. D. Mastrndrea, T. E. Bilir, M. Chatterjee, K. L. Ebi, Y. O. Estrada, R. C. Genova, B. Girma, E. S. Kissel, A. N. Levy, S. MacCracken, P. R. Mastrandrea, and L. L. White. Cambridge: Cambridge University Press, 2014.

Israel, Jonathan Irvine. *Conflicts of Empires: Spain, the Low Countries and the Struggle for World Supremacy, 1585–1713*. London: A&C Black, 1997.

Dutch Primacy in World Trade, 1585–1740. New York: Oxford University Press, 1989.

'England, the Dutch, and the Struggle for Mastery of World Trade in the Age of the Glorious Revolution (1682–1702)'. In *The World of William and Mary: Anglo-Dutch Perspectives on the Revolution, of 1688–89*. Edited by Dale Hoak and Mordechai Feingold, 75–86. Stanford: Stanford University Press, 1996.

'General Introduction'. In *The Anglo-Dutch Moment: Essays on the Glorious Revolution and Its World Impact.* Edited by Jonathan I. Israel, 1–43. Cambridge: Cambridge University Press, 1991.

Radical Enlightenment: Philosophy and the Making of Modernity, 1650–1750. Oxford: Oxford University Press, 2001.

The Dutch Republic and the Hispanic World, 1606–1661. Oxford: Clarendon Press, 1982.

The Dutch Republic: Its Rise, Greatness, and Fall, 1477–1806. Oxford: Clarendon Press, 1998.

'The Dutch Role in the Glorious Revolution'. In *The Anglo-Dutch Moment: Essays on the Glorious Revolution and Its World Impact.* Edited by Jonathan I. Israel, 105–162. Cambridge: Cambridge University Press, 1991.

Israel, Jonathan Irvine and Geoffrey Parker. 'Of Providence and Protestant Winds: The Spanish Armada of 1588 and the Dutch Armada of 1688'. In *The Anglo-Dutch Moment: Essays on the Glorious Revolution and Its World Impact.* Edited by Jonathan I. Israel, 335–363. Cambridge: Cambridge University Press, 1991.

Jacobs, Alan. *17th Century Dutch and Flemish Painters.* Amsterdam: McGraw-Hill Book Company Ltd. 1976.

Jacobs, E. M. *In Pursuit of Pepper and Tea: The Story of the Dutch East India Company.* Walburg: Walburg Pers, 2009.

Jansen, Captain. 'Notes on the Ice between Greenland and Nova Zembla; Being the Results of Investigations into the Records of Early Dutch Voyages in the Spitzbergen Seas'. *Proceedings of the Royal Geographical Society of London* 9:4 (1864 – 1865): 163–181.

Jardine, Lisa. *Going Dutch: How England Plundered Holland's Glory.* New York: Harper Collins Publishers, 2008.

Jeong, Jee-Hoon, Tinghai Ou, Hans W. Linderholm, Baek-Min Kim, Seong-Joong Kim, Jong-Seong Kug, and Deliang Chen. 'Recent Recovery of the Siberian High intensity'. *Journal of Geophysical Research: Atmospheres* 116:D23 (2011): 1–9.

Jernas, Patrycja, Dorthe Klitgaard Kristensen, Katrine Husum, Lindsay Wilson, and Nalan Koç. 'Palaeoenvironmental Changes of the Last Two Millennia on the Western and Northern Svalbard Shelf'. *Boreas* 42:1 (2013): 236–255.

Jiang, Yaotiao and Zhentao Xu, 'On the Spörer Minimum'. *Astrophysics and Space Science* (1986): 159–162.

Johnson, Loretta. 'Greening the Library: The Fundamentals and Future of Ecocriticism'. *Choice* (December 2009): 7–13.

Jones, E. 'Climate, Archaeology, History, and the Arthurian Tradition: A Multiple-Source Study of Two Dark-Age Puzzles'. In *The Years without Summer: Tracing AD 536 and Its Aftermath.* Edited by J. D. Gunn, 25–34. Oxford: Archaeopress, 2000.

Jones, J. R. *The Anglo-Dutch Wars of the Seventeenth Century.* London: Longman, 1996.

Jones, Matthew D., C. Neil Roberts, Melanie J. Leng, and Murat Türkeş. 'A High-Resolution Late Holocene Lake Isotope Record From Turkey and

Links to North Atlantic and Monsoon Climate'. *Geology* 34:5 (2006): 361–364.

Jones, Michael. 'Tycho Brahe, Cartography and Landscape'. In *European Rural Landscapes: Persistence and Change in a Globalising Environment.* Edited by H. Palang, H. Sooväli, M. Antrop, and G. Setten, 209–226. Dordrecht: Springer Netherlands, 2004.

Jorink, Eric. *Reading the Book of Nature in the Dutch Golden Age.* Leiden: Brill, 2010.

Kaak, Maurice. *Vlaamse en Brabantse Binnenschepen uit de 18de en 19de eeuw: vergeten vaktaal en oude constructies.* Ghent: Provinciebestuur Oost-Vlaanderen, 2010.

Kahr, Madlyn Millner. *Dutch Painting in the Seventeenth Century.* New York: Harper & Row, Publishers, 1978.

Kaplan, Benjamin J. 'Possessed by the Devil? A Very Public Dispute in Utrecht'. *Renaissance Quarterly* 49 (1996): 738–759.

Kelly, Morgan and Cormac Ó Gráda. 'The Waning of the Little Ice Age: Climate Change in Early Modern Europe'. *Journal of Interdisciplinary History* 44:3 (2014), 301–325.

Kerr, Richard A. 'A North Atlantic Climate Pacemaker for the Centuries'. *Science* 288:5473 (2000): 1984–1985.

Ketting, Herman. *Leven, werk en rebellie aan boord van Oost-Indiëvaarders (1595–±1650).* Amsterdam: Het Spinhuis, 2005.

Keuning, J. *Willem Jansz. Blaeu: A Biography and History of His Work as a Cartographer and Publisher.* Revised and Edited by M. Donkersloot-De Vrij. Amsterdam: Theatrum Orbis Terrarum, 1973.

Kingra, Mahinder S. 'The *Trace Italienne* and the Military Revolution during the Eighty Years' War, 1567–1648'. *The Journal of Military History* 57 (July 1993): 431–446.

Kinnard, Christophe, Christian M. Zdanowicz, David A. Fisher, Elisabeth Isaksson, Anne de Vernal, and Lonnie G. Thompson. 'Reconstructed Changes in Arctic Sea Ice over the Past 1,450 Years'. *Nature* 479:7374 (2011): 509–512.

Kirtman, B., S. B. Power, J. A. Adedoyin, G. J. Boer, R. Bojariu, I. Camillioni, F. J. Doblas-Reyes, A. M. Fiore, M. Kimoto, G. A. Meehl, M. Prather, A. Sarr, C. Schär, R. Sutton, G. J. van Oldenborgh, G. Vecchi and H. J. Wang, '2013: Near-Term Climate Change: Projections and Predictability'. In *Climate Change 2013: The Physical Science Basis. Contribution of Working Group I to the Fifth Assessment Report of the International Panel on Climate Change.* Edited by T. F. Stocker, D. Qin, G. K. Plattner, M. Tignor, S. K. Allen, J. Boschung, A. Nauels, Y. Xia, V. Bex and P. M. Midgley, 953–1028. Cambridge: Cambridge University Press, 2014.

Klein, P. W. 'Kwantitatieve aspecten van de Amsterdamse roggehandel in the 17e eeuw en de Europese economische geschiedenis'. In *Ondernemende geschiedenis: 25 opstellen geschreven bij het afscheid van Mr. H. van Riel,* 75–88. The Hague: M. Nijhoff, 1977.

Klinkert, Wim. 'Water in oorlog. De rol van het water in de militaire geschiedenis van Holland na 1550'. In *Hollanders en het water. Twintig eeuwen strijd en profijt, Vol. II*. Edited by Eelco Beukers, 451–504. Hilversum: Uitgeverij Verloren, 2007.

Knaap, Gerrit and Ger Teitle, ed. *De Verenigde Oost-Indische Compagnie: Tussen Oorlog en Diplomatie*. Leiden: KITLV Uitgeverij, 2002.

Knight, Jeff R., Chris K. Folland, and Adam A. Scaife. 'Climate Impacts of the Atlantic Multidecadal Oscillation'. *Geophysical Research Letters* 33:17 (2006): 1–4.

Koek, Gonnie. 'Hoorn en Monnickendam: De herinnering van de slag op de Zuiderzee (1573–1800)'. MA diss., Leiden University, 2012.

Koene, Bert. *De Caeskopers: Een Zaanse koopmansfamilie in de Gouden Eeuw*. Hilversum: Uitgeverij Verloren, 2011.

Konstam, Angus. *Warships of the Anglo-Dutch Wars 1652–74*. Oxford: Osprey Publishing, 2011.

Korevaar, C. G. *North Sea Climate, Based on Observations from Ships and Lig htvessels*. Dordrecht: Kluwer Academic Publishers, 1990.

Kors, Alan Charles and Edward Peters. 'The Trail of Marie Cornu (1611)'. In *Witchcraft in Europe, 400–1700: A Documentary History*. Philadelphia: University of Pennsylvania Press, 2001.

Kossmann, Ernst H. 'Seventeenth-Century Dutch Art in the Eyes of Historians'. In *The Golden Age of Dutch Painting in Historical Perspective*. Edited by Frans Grijzenhout and Henk van Veen. Cambridge: Cambridge University Press, 1999.

Kuretsky, Susan Donahue. 'Jan van der Heyden and the Origins of Modern Firefighting: Art and Technology in Seventeenth-Century Amsterdam'. In *Flammable Cities: Urban Conflagration and the Making of the Modern World*. Edited by Greg Bankoff, Uwe Lübken, and Jordan Sand. Madison: University of Wisconsin Press, 2012.

Lamb, Hubert H. *Climate, History and the Modern World*, 2nd ed. Routledge: New York, 1995.

Historic Storms of the North Sea, British Isles, and Northwest Europe. Cambridge: Cambridge University Press, 1991.

The English Climate. London: English Universities Press, 1964.

'Volcanic Dust in the Atmosphere; with a Chronology and Assessment of Its Meteorological Significance'. *Philosophical Transactions of the Royal Society of London. Series A: Mathematical and Physical Sciences* 266:1178 (1970): 425–533.

Lambert, Audrey M. *The Making of the Dutch Landscape: An Historical Geography of the Netherlands*. London: Academic Press, 1985.

Landblad, J. Thomas. 'Foreign Trade of the Dutch Republic in the Seventeenth Century'. *Economic and Social History in the Netherlands* 4 (1992): 219–249.

Landers, John. *The Field and the Forge: Population, Production and Power in the Pre-Industrial West*. New York: Oxford University Press, 2003.

Landsteiner, Erich. 'Wenig Brot und saurer wein: Kontinuität ud Wandel in der zentraleuropäischen Ernährungskulter im letzen Drittel des 16. Jahrhunderts'. In *Kulturelle Konsequenzen der 'Kleinen Eiszeit'*. Edited by Wolfgang Behringer, Hartmut Lehmann, and Christian Pfister, 87–148. Göttingen: Vandenhoeck & Ruprecht, 2005.

Lansberg, H. E. 'Past Climates from Unexploited Written Sources'. *Journal of Interdisciplinary History*, No. 10 (1980), 631–642.
Lavell, Charl. 'De slag op de Zuiderzee: Een vergeten geschiedenis gezien door tijdgenoten, geschiedschrijvers en dichters'. *West-Friesland 'oud en nieuw'* 53 (1986): 43–68.
Laver, Michael S. *Japan's Economy by Proxy in the Seventeenth Century: China, the Netherlands, and the Bakufu*. Amherst: Cambria Press, 2008.
Lee, E. H., Y. S. Ahn, H. J. Yang, and K. Y. Chen. 'The Sunspot and Auroral Activity Cycle Derived From Korean Historical Records of the 11th–18th Century'. *Solar Physics* 224:1–2 (2004): 375–386.
Le Roy Ladurie, Emmanuel. *Histoire humaine et comparée du climat, Vol. I: Canicules et glaciers*. Paris: Fayard, 2004.
Times of Feast, Times of Famine: A History of Climate Since the Year 1000. Garden City, NY: Doubleday & Company, Inc., 1971.
Lehner, Flavio, Andreas Born, Christoph C. Raible, and Thomas F. Stocker. 'Amplified Inception of European Little Ice Age by Sea Ice-Ocean-Atmosphere Feedbacks'. *Journal of Climate* 26:19 (2013): 7586–7602.
Lemke, Peter, Markus Harder, and Michael Hilmer. 'The Response of Arctic Sea Ice to Global Change'. *Climatic Change*, 46 (2000): 277–287.
Lesger, Clé. *Handel in Amsterdam ten tijde van de Opstand: kooplieden, commerciële expansie en verandering in de ruimtelijke economie van de Nederlanden ca. 1550 – ca. 1630*. Hilversum: Uitgeverij Verloren, 2001.
Levack, Brian P. *The Oxford Handbook of Witchcraft in Early Modern Europe and Colonial America*. Oxford: Oxford University Press, 2013.
The Rise of the Amsterdam Market and Information Exchange: Merchants, Commercial Expansion and Change in the Spatial Economy of the Low Countries, C. 1550–1630. Farnham: Ashgate Publishing Ltd., 2006.
Levy, Jack S. 'The Rise and Decline of Anglo-Dutch Rivalry, 1609–1689'. In *Great Power Rivalries*. Edited by William R. Thomspon, 172–200. Columbia: University of South Carolina Press, 1999.
Levy, Jack S. and Salvatore Ali. 'From Commercial Competition to Strategic Rivalry to War: The Evolution of the Anglo-Dutch Rivalry, 1609–52'. In *The Dynamics of Enduring Rivalries*. Edited by Paul Francis Diehl, 29–63. Champaign: University of Illinois Press, 1998.
Li, Jinbao, Shang-Ping Xie, Edward R. Cook, Gang Huang, Rosanne D'Arrigo, Fei Liu, Jian Ma and Xiao-Tong Zheng. 'Interdecadal Modulation of El Niño Amplitude during the Past Millennium'. *Nature Climate Change* 1 (2011): 114–118.
Ligtendag, W. A. 'Willem Barentsz en de kartografie van het hoge noorden'. *Kartografisch tijdschrift* 23:1 (1997): 5–14.
Linderholm, Hans W., Jesper Björklundet, Kristina Seftigen, Björn E. Gunnarson, and Mauricio Fuentes. 'Fennoscandia Revisited: A Spatially Improved Tree-Ring Reconstruction of Summer Temperatures for the Last 900 Years'. *Climate Dynamics* 45 (2015): 933–947.
Ljungqvist, Fredrik Charpentier. 'A New Reconstruction of Temperature Variability in the Extra-Tropical Northern Hemisphere during the Last

Two Millennia'. *Geografiska Annaler: Series A, Physical Geography* 92:3 (2010): 339–351.

Longman, Norman. *Defending the Island: Caesar to the Armada.* London: Pimlico, 1989.

Lord, Barry. *Art & Energy: How Culture Changes.* Chicago: University of Chicago Press, 2015.

Lord, Graham M., Giuseppe Matarese, Jane K. Howard, and Richard J. Baker. 'Leptin modules the T-cell immune response and reverses starvation-induced immunosuppression'. *Nature* 394:6696 (1998): 897–901.

Lund, David C., Jean Lynch-Stieglitz, and William B. Curry. 'Gulf Stream Density Structure and Transport during the Past Millennium'. *Nature* 444 (2006): 601–604.

Lunsford, Virginia W. *Piracy and Privateering in the Golden Age Netherlands.* Basingstoke: Palgrave Macmillan, 2005.

Luterbacher, Jürg. 'The Late Maunder Minimum (1675–1715) – Climax of the "Little Ice Age" in Europe'. In *History and Climate: Memories of the Future?*. Edited by P. D. Jones, A. E. J. Ogilvie, T. D. Davies, and K. R. Briffa, 101–120. New York: Kluwer Academic/Plenum Publishers, 2001.

Luterbacher, Jürg, Daniel Dietrich, Elena Xoplaki, Martin Grosjean, and Heinz Wanner. 'European Seasonal and Annual Temperature Variability, Trends, and Extremes Since 1500'. *Science* 303:5663 (2004): 1499–1503.

Luterbacher, Jürg, E. Xoplaki, D. Dietrich, P. D. Jones, T. D. Davies, D. Portis, J. F. Gonzalez-Ruoco, H. von Storch, D. Gyalistras, C. Casty, and H. Wanner. 'Extending North Atlantic Oscillation Reconstructions Back to 1500'. *Atmospheric Science Letters* 2:1–4 (2002): 114–124.

Luterbacher, Jürg, Christoph Schmutz, Dimitrios Gyalistras, Eleni Xoplaki, and Heinz Wanner. 'Reconstruction of monthly NAO and EU indices back to AD 1675'. *Geophysical Research Letters* 26:17 (1999): 2745–2748.

Luterbacher, Jürg, J. P. Wener, J. E. Smerdon, L. Fernández-Donado, F. J. González-Rouco, D. Barriopedro, F. C. Ljungqvist, U. Büntgen, E. Zorita, S. Wagner, J. Esper, D. McCarroll, A. Toreti, D. Frank, J. H. Jungclaus, M. Barriendos, C. Bertolin, O. Bothe, R. Brázdil, D. Camuffo, P. Dobrovolný, M. Gagen, E. García-Bustamante, Q. Ge, J. J. Gómez-Navarro, J. Guiot, Z. Hao, G. C. Hegerl, K. Holmgren, V. V. Klimenko, J. Martín-Chivelet, C. Pfister, N. Roberts, A. Schindler, A. Schurer, O. Solomina, L. von Gunten, E. Wahl, H. Wanner, O. Wetter, E. Xoplaki, N. Yuan, D. Zanchettin, H. Zhang, and C. Zerefos, 'European Summer Temperatures since Roman Times'. *Environmental Research Letters* 11:12 (2016): 1–12.

Lynn, John A. *Giant of the Grand Siècle: The French Army, 1610–1715.* Cambridge: Cambridge University Press, 2006.

The Wars of Louis XIV 1667–1714. Oxon: Routledge, 1999.

Women, Armies, and Warfare in Early Modern Europe. Cambridge: Cambridge University Press, 2008.

Maat, George J. R. 'Osteology of Human Remins from Amsterdamoya and Ytre Norskoya'. In *Smeerenburg Seminar: Report from a Symposium Presenting*

Results from Research into Seventeenth Century Whaling in Spitsbergen. Norsk Polarinstitutt Rapportserie 38 (1987): 35–51.

Macdougall, Douglas. *Frozen Earth: The Once and Future Story of Ice Ages.* Berkeley: University of California Press, 2004.

Mackay, Christopher S. 'General Introduction'. In Institoris, Henricus and Jacobus Sprenger, *Malleus Maleficarum Vol. I: The Latin Text and Introduction.* Edited by Christopher Mackay, 1–188. Cambridge: Cambridge University Press, 2006. 37.

Magnusson, Lars. *Mercantilism: The Shaping of an Economic Language.* Oxford: Routledge, 2002.

Mahan, A. T. *The Influence of Sea Power upon History 1660–1783.* Boston: Little, Brown and Company, 1890.

Mann, Michael E. 'The Little Ice Age'. In *Encyclopedia of Global Environmental Change.* Edited by Michael C. MacCracken and John S. Perry, 504–509. Chichester: John Wiley & Sons, Ltd., 2002.

Marcott, Shaun A., Jeremy D. Shakun, Peter U. Clark, and Alan C. Mix. 'A Reconstruction of Regional and Global Temperature for the Past 11,300 Years'. *Science*, CCCIX (2013), 1198–1201.

Markley, Robert. 'Summer's Lease: Shakespeare in the Little Ice Age'. In *Early Modern Ecostudies: From the Florentine Codex to Shakespeare.* Edited by Thomas Hallock, Ivo Kamps, and Karen L. Raber, 131–142. Hampshire: Palgrave Macmillan, 2008.

Martin, Colin, and Geoffrey Parker. *The Spanish Armada.* Revised ed. Manchester: Manchester University Press, 1999.

Matthews, John A. and Keith R. Briffa. 'The "Little Ice Age": Re-evaluation of an Evolving Concept'. *Geografiska Annaler: Series A, Physical Geography*, 87:1 (2005): 17–36.

Mattingly, Garrett. *The Defeat of the Spanish Armada.* London: Random House, 1959.

McCarthy, Gerard D., Ivan D. Haigh, Joël J-M. Hirschi, Jeremy P. Grist, and David A. Smeed. 'Ocean Impact on Decadal Atlantic Climate Variability Revealed by Sea-Level Observations'. *Nature* 521:7553 (2015): 508–510.

McDermott, James. *England and the Spanish Armada: The Necessary Quarrel.* New Haven: Yale University Press, 2005.

McKay, Nicholas P. and Darrell S. Kaufman, 'An Extended Arctic Proxy Temperature Database for the Past 2,000 Years'. *Scientific Data* 1 (2014): 1–10.

Meijer, Reinder P. *Literature of the Low Countries: A Short History of Dutch Literature in the Netherlands and Belgium*, 2nd ed. The Hague: Martinus Nijhoff, 1978.

Metcalf, Michael F. 'Conflict as Catalyst: Parliamentary Innovation in Eighteenth-Century Sweden'. *Parliaments, Estates and Representation* 8:1 (1988): 63–75.

Metzger, Alexis. 'Le froid en Hollande au Siècle d'or. Essai de climatologie culturelle'. PhD diss., University of Paris, 2014.

Metzger, Alexis and Martine Tabeaud. 'Reconstruction of the Winter Weather in East Friesland at the Turn of the Sixteenth and Seventeenth Centuries (1594–1612)'. *Climatic Change* 141:2 (2017): 331–345.

Plaisirs de Glace: Essai sur la peinture hollandaise hivernale du Siècle d'or. Paris: Editions Hermann, 2012.

Mignolo, Walter. *The Darker Side of the Renaissance: Literacy, Territoriality, and Colonization*. Ann Arbor: University of Michigan Press, 2003.

Miller, Gifford H., Áslaug Geirsdóttir, Yafang Zhong, Darren J. Larsen, Bette L. Otto-Bliesner, Marika M. Holland, David A. Bailey, Kurt A. Refsnider, Scott J. Lehman, John R. Southon, Chance Anderson, Helgi Björnsson, and Thorvaldur Thordarson. 'Abrupt Onset of the Little Ice Age Triggered by Volcanism and Sustained by Sea-Ice/Ocean Feedbacks'. *Geophysical Research Letters*, 39:2 (2012), 1–5. Accessed January 14 2013. DOI: http://dx.doi.org/10.1029/2011GL050168

Mills, William J. *Exploring Polar Frontiers: A Historical Encyclopedia, Vol. II*. Santa Barbara: ABC CLIO, 2003.

Moreno-Chamarro, Eduardo, Davide Zanchettin, Katja Lohmann, and Johann H. Jungclaus. 'An Abrupt Weakening of the Subpolar Gyre as Trigger of Little Ice Age-Type Episodes'. *Climatic Dynamics* (2016). DOI: 10.1007/s00382-016-3106-7.

Moreno-Chamarro, Eduardo, Davide Zanchettin, Katja Lohmann, Jürg Luterbacher, and Johann H. Jungclaus. 'Winter Amplification of the European Little Ice Age Cooling by the Subpolar Gyre'. *Nature Scientific Reports* (2017). DOI: 10.1038/s41598-017-07969-0.

Morris, T. A. *Europe and England in the Sixteenth Century*. London: Routledge, 1998.

Moy, Christopher M., Geoffrey O. Seltzer, Donald T. Rodbell, and David M. Anderson. 'Variability of El Niño/Southern Oscillation Activity at Millennial Timescales during the Holocene Epoch'. *Nature* 420:6912 (2002): 162–165.

Muir, Edward. *Ritual in Early Modern Europe*. Cambridge: Cambridge University Press, 1997.

Multhauf, L. S. 'The Light of Lamp-Lanterns: Street Lighting in 17th-Century Amsterdam'. *Technology and Culture* 26 (1985): 236–252.

Murdmaa, Ivar, Leonid Polyak, Elena Ivanova, and Natalia Khromova. 'Paleoenvironments in Russkaya Gavan' Fjord (NW Novaya Zemlya, Barents Sea) during the Last Millennium'. *Palaeogeography, Palaeoclimatology, Palaeoecology* 209 (2004): 141–154.

Murphy, Henry C. *Henry Hudson in Holland: An Inquiry into the Origin and Objects of the Voyage which led to the Discover of the Hudson River*. New York: Burt Franklin, 1909.

Nash, J. M. *The Age of Rembrandt and Vermeer: Dutch Painting in the Seventeenth Century*. London: Phaidon, 1972.

Nienhuis, P. H. *Environmental History of the Rhine-Meuse Delta: An Ecological Story on Evolving Human-Environmental Relations Coping with Climate Change and Sea-Level Rise*. Berlin: Springer Science and Business Media, 2008.

Neuberger, Hans. 'Climate in Art'. *Weather* 25:2 (1970): 46–56.
Noordegraaf, Leo. 'Dearth, Famine and Social Policy in the Dutch Republic at the End of the Sixteenth Century'. In *The European Crisis of the 1590s: Essays in Comparative History*. Edited by Peter Clark, 67–83. London: George Allen & Unwin, 1985.
Nussbaumer, Samuel U. and Heinz J. Zumbühl, 'The Little Ice Age History of the Glacier des Bossons (Mont Blanc Massif, France): A New High-Resolution Glacier Length Curve Based on Historical Documents'. *Climatic Change* 111 (2012): 301–334.
Oliver, J. and J. A. Kington, 'The Usefulness of Ships' Log-Books in the Synoptic Analysis of Past Climates'. *Weather* 25:12 (1970): 520–528.
Olsen, Nils and Mioara Mandea. 'Will the Magnetic North Pole Move to Siberia?' *Eos* 88:29 (2007): 293–294.
Ormrod, David. *The Rise of Commercial Empires: England and the Netherlands in the Age of Mercantilism, 1650–1770*. Cambridge: Cambridge University Press, 2003.
Ortega, Pablo, Flavio Lehner, Didier Swingedouw, Valerie Masson-Delmotte, Christoph C. Raible, Mathieu Casado, and Pascal Yiou. 'A Model-Tested North Atlantic Oscillation Reconstruction for the Past Millennium'. *Nature* 523:7558 (2015): 71–74.
Outten, S. D. and I. Esau, 'A Link between Arctic Sea Ice and Recent Cooling Trends over Eurasia'. *Climatic Change* 110:3–4 (2011): 1069–1075.
Overpeck, J., K. Hughen, D. Hardy, R. Bradley, R. Case, M. Douglas, B. Finney, K. Gajewski, G. Jacoby, A. Jennings, S. Lamoureux, A. Lasca, G. MacDonald, J. Moore, M. Retelle, S. Smith, A. Wolfe, and G. Zielinski. 'Arctic Environmental Change of the Last Four Centuries'. *Science* 278:1251, (1997): 1251–1256.
Packer, Michelle V. 'Rising from the Ashes: Fire Prevention as Social Transformation'. *Dutch Crossing* 39:2 (2015): 160–185.
PAGES 2K Consortium, 'Continental-Scale Temperature Variability during the Past Two Millennia'. *Nature Geoscience* 6:5 (2013): 339–346.
Panhuysen, Luc. *Rampjaar 1672. Hoe de republiek aan de ondergang ontsnapte*. Amsterdam: Atlas, 2009.
Parker, Geoffrey. 'Crisis and Catastrophe: The Global Crisis of the Seventeenth Century Reconsidered'. *American Historical Review* 113 (2008): 1053–1079.
'Early Modern Europe'. In *The Laws of War: Constraints on Warfare in the Western World*. Edited by Michael Howard, George J. Andreopoulos, and Mark R. Shulman, 40–59. New Haven: Yale University Press, 1997.
Global Crisis: War, Climate Change and Catastrophe in the Seventeenth Century. London: Yale University Press, 2013.
The Army of Flanders and the Spanish Road, 1567–1659. Cambridge: Cambridge University Press, 1971.
The Dutch Revolt. London: Penguin Books, 1985.
'The Limits to Revolutions in Military Affairs: Maurice of Nassau, the Battle of Nieupoort (1600), and the Legacy'. *The Journal of Military History* 71:2 (2007): 331–372.

The Military Revolution: Military Innovation and the Rise of the West, 1500–1800. Cambridge: Cambridge University Press, 1996.

Parker, Geoffrey and Lesley M. Smith, eds. *The General Crisis of the Seventeenth Century*. Oxford: Routledge, 2005.

Parthesius, Robert. *Dutch Ships in Tropical Waters: The Development of the Dutch East India Company (VOC) Shipping Network in Asia 1595–1660*. Amsterdam: Amsterdam University Press, 2010.

Patterson, David K. 'Epidemics, Famines, and Population in the Cape Verde Islands, 1580–1900'. *The International Journal of African Historical Studies* 21:2 (1988): 291–313.

Pauling, Andreas, Jürg Luterbacher, and Heinz Wanner. 'Evaluation of Proxies for European and North Atlantic Temperature Field Reconstructions'. *Geophysical Research Letters* 30:15 (2003): 1–4.

Pauling, Andreas, Jürg Luterbacher, Carlo Casty, and Heinz Wanner. 'Five Hundred Years of Gridded High-Resolution Precipitation Reconstructions over Europe and the Connection to Large-Scale Circulation'. *Climate Dynamics* 26:4 (2006): 387–405.

Pearce, Fred. *Climate and Man: From the Ice Ages to the Global Greenhouse*. London: Vision Books, 1989.

Pfister, Christian and Rudolf Brazdil. 'Social Vulnerability to Climate in the "Little Ice Age": An Example from Central Europe in the Early 1770s'. *Climate of the Past Discussions* 2.2 (2006): 123–155.

'Climatic Variability in Sixteenth-Century Europe and Its Social Dimension: A Synthesis'. *Climatic Change* 43:1 (1999): 5–53.

Pfister, Christian. 'Climatic Extremes, Recurrent Crises and Witch Hunts: Strategies of European Societies in Coping with Exogenous Shocks in the Late Sixteenth and Early Seventeenth Centuries'. *The Medieval History Journal* 10: 1&2 (2007): 33–73.

'The Climate of Switzerland in the Last 450 Years'. *Geographica Helvetica* 35 (1980): 15–20.

'The Little Ice Age: Thermal and Wetness Indices for Central Europe'. *Journal of Interdisciplinary History* 10:4 (1980): 665–696.

Pickstone, John. *Ways of Knowing*. Chicago: Chicago University Press, 2001.

Pincus, Steve. *1688: The First Modern Revolution*. New Haven: Yale University Press, 2009.

Polyak, Leonid, Ivar Murdmaa and Elena Ivanova, 'A High-Resolution, 800-Year Glaciomarine Record from Russkaya Gavan', a Novaya Zemlya Fjord, Eastern Barents Sea'. *The Holocene* 14:4 (2004): 628–634.

Post, F. *Groninger Scheepvaart en Scheepsbouw vanaf 1600*. Bedum: Profiel uitgeverij, 1997.

Postma, C. *Het hoogheemraadschap van Delfland in de middeleeuwen 1289–1589*. Hilversum: Uitgeverij Verloren, 1989.

Pots, R. and J. Knoester. *Blauwe ader van de Bollenstreek: 350 jaar Haarlemmertrekvaart-Leidsevaart, 1657–2007. Geschiedenis, betekenis en toekomst*. Leiden: Primavera Pers, 2010.

Poulsen, Bo. *Dutch Herring: An Environmental History, C. 1600–1860*. Amsterdam: Amsterdam University Press, 2009.

Prak, Maarten. *Gouden Eeuw: Het raadsel van de Republiek*. Nijmegen: Uitgeverij SUN, 2002.

Price, J. L. *Dutch Society, 1588–1713*. New York: Longman, 2000.

Puype, J. P. 'Victory at Nieuwpoort, 2 July 1600'. In *Exercise of Arms: Warfare in the Netherlands, 1568–1648*. Edited by Marco van der Hoeven, 69–112. Leiden: Brill, 1997.

Qian, Weihong and Yafen Zhu. 'Little Ice Age Climate near Beijing, China, Inferred from Historical and Stalagmite Records'. *Quaternary Research* 57:1 (2002): 109–119.

Rahmstorf, Stefan, Georg Feulner, Michael E. Mann, Alexander Robinson, Scott Rutherford, and Erik J. Schaffernicht. 'Exceptional Twentieth-Century Slowdown in Atlantic Ocean Overturning Circulation'. *Nature Climate Change* 5 (2015): 475–480.

Raible, Christoph C. 'Climate Variability – Observations, Reconstructions, and Model Simulations for the Atlantic-European and Alpine Region from 1500–2100 AD'. *Climatic Change* 79 (2006): 9–29.

Regin, Deric. *Traders, Artists, Burghers. A Cultural History of Amsterdam in the 17th Century*. Assen: Koninklijke Van Gorcum, 1976.

Reichler, Thomas, Junsu Kim, Elisa Manzini, and Jürgen Kröger. 'A Stratospheric Connection to Atlantic Climate Variability'. *Nature Geoscience* 5:11 (2012): 783–787.

Reinders, Michel. 'Burghers, Orangists and "Good Government": Popular Political Opposition during the "Year of Disaster" 1672 in Dutch Pamphlets'. *The Seventeenth Century*, 23:2 (2013): 315–346.

'Printed Pandemonium: The Power of the Public and the Market for Poplar Political Publications in the Early Modern Dutch Republic'. PhD diss., Erasmus University Rotterdam, 2008.

Richards, John F. *The Unending Frontier*. Oakland: University of California Press, 2003.

The World Hunt: An Environmental History of the Commodification of Animals. Oakland: University of California Press, 2014.

Robinson, Peter. 'Ice and Snow in Paintings of Little Ice Age Winters'. *Weather* 60:2 (2005): 37–41.

Robock, Alan. 'Volcanic Eruptions and Climate'. *Reviews of Geophysics* 38:2 (2000): 191–219.

Rodger, N. A. M. *The Command of the Ocean: A Naval History of Britain 1649–1815*. London: Penguin Books, 2004.

Roeper, V. D. and G. J. D. Wildeman. *Ontdekkingsreizen van Nederlanders (1590–1650)*. Utrecht: Kosmos Uitgevers, 1993.

Rohr, Christian. *Extreme Naturereignisse im Ostalpenraum: Naturerfahrung im Spätmittelalter und am Beginn der Neuzeit*. Vienna: Böhlau Verlag, 2007.

Rommelse, Gijs. 'English Privateering against the Dutch Republic during the Second Anglo-Dutch War (1664–1667)'. *Tijdschrift voor Zeegeschiedenis* 22:1 (2003): 22–31.

The Second Anglo-Dutch War: International Raison D'état, Mercantilism and Maritime Strife. Hilversum: Uitgeverij Verloren, 2006.

Rose, Craig. *England in the 1690s: Revolution, Religion and War*. Oxford: Blackwell Publishers Ltd., 1999.

Rothrock, D. A. 'The Energetics of the Plastic Deformation of Pack Ice by Ridging'. *Journal of Geophysical Research* 80:33 (1975): 4514–4519.

Rötzer, Thomas and Frank M. Chmeilewski. 'Phenological Maps of Europe'. *Climate Research* 18 (2001): 249–257.

Rueda, Gemma, Susanne Fietz, and Antoni Rosell-Melé. 'Coupling of Air and Sea Surface Temperatures in the Eastern Fram Strait during the Last 2000 Years'. *The Holocene* 23:5 (2013): 692–698.

Sager, Ingrid D. *The Little Ice Age and 17th Century Dutch Landscape Painting, a Study on the Impact of Climate on Art*. Dominguez Hills: California State University, 2006.

Salvesen, Helge. 'The Climate as a Factor of Historical Causation'. In *European Climate Reconstructed from Documentary Data: Methods and Results*. Edited by Buckhard Frenzel, 219–255. Stuttgart: Gustav Fischer Verlag, 1992.

Sarachik, Edward S. and Mark A. Cane, *The El Niño-Southern Oscillation Phenomenon*. Cambridge: Cambridge University Press, 2010.

Scammell, G. V. *The First Imperial Age: European Overseas Expansion c. 1400–1715*. Abingdon: Routledge, 1989.

Schama, Simon. *The Embarrassment of Riches: An Interpretation of Dutch Culture in the Golden Age*. Berkeley: University of California Press, 1988.

Scheltjens, Werner F. Y. 'The Changing Geography of Demand for Dutch Maritime Transport in the Eighteenth Century'. *Histoire & mesure* 27:2 (2012): 3–48.

Schenkeveld, Maria A. *Dutch Literature in the Age of Rembrandt: Themes and Ideas*. Amsterdam: John Benjamins Publishing, 1991.

Schilder, Günter. 'Development and Achievements of Dutch Northern and Arctic Cartography in the Sixteenth and Seventeenth Centuries'. *Arctic* 37:4 (1984): 493–514.

Schilder, Günter and Hans Kok. *Sailing for the East: History & Catalogue of Manuscript Charts on Vellum of the Dutch East India Company (VOC), 1602–1799*. Houton: Hes & De Graaf Publishers, 2010.

Schlesinger, Michael E., and Navin Ramankutty. 'An Oscillation in the Global Climate System of Period 65–70 Years'. *Nature* 367 (1994): 723–726.

Schmutz, C., J. Luterbacher, D. Gyalistras, E. Xoplaki, and H. Wanner. 'Can We Trust Proxy-Based NAO Index Reconstructions?' *Geophysical Research Letters* 27:8 (2000): 1135–1138.

Schmidt, Gavin A., J. H. Jungclaus, C. M. Ammann, E. Bard, P. C. T. J. D. G. Braconnot, T. J. Crowley, G. Delaygue et al. 'Climate Forcing Reconstructions for Use in PMIP Simulations of the Last Millennium (v1.0)'. *Geoscientific Model Development* 4:1 (2011): 33–45.

Schneider, Lea, Jason E. Smerdon, Ulf Buntgen, Rob J. S. Wilson, Vladimir S. Myglan, Alexander V. Kirdyanov, and Jan Esper, 'Revising Midlatitude Summer Temperatures back to AD600 Based on a Wood Density Network'. *Geophysical Research Letters* 42 (2015): 4556–4562.

Schwartz, Stuart B. *Sea of Storms: A History of Hurricanes in the Greater Caribbean from Columbus to Katrina*. Princeton: Princeton University Press, 2015.

Scott, Hamish. *The Oxford Handbook of Early Modern European History, 1350–1750: Cultures and Power*. Oxford: Oxford University Press, 2015.

Shabalova, M. V. and A. F. V. van Engelen. 'Evaluation of a Reconstruction of Temperature in the Low Countries AD 764–1998'. *Climatic Change* (March 2000), 219–242.

Shorto, Russell. *Amsterdam: A History of the World's Most Liberal City*. New York: Doubleday, 2013.

Sicking, Louis. *Neptune and the Netherlands: State, Economy, and War at Sea in the Renaissance*. Leiden: Brill, 2004.

Sicre, Marie-Alexandrine, Jérémy Jacob, Ullah Ezat, Sonia Rousse, Catherine Kissel, Pascal Yiou, Jón Eiríksson, Karen Luise Knudsen, Eystein Jansen, and Jean-Louis Turon. 'Decadal Variability of Sea Surface Temperatures off North Iceland over the Last 2000 Years'. *Earth and Planetary Science Letters* 268: 1–2 (2008): 137–142.

Siegismund, Frank and Corinna Schrum. 'Decadal Changes in the Wind Forcing over the North Sea'. *Climate Research* 18:39–45 (2001): 39–45.

Sigl, Michael, Joseph R. McConnell, Lawrence Layman, Olivia Maselli, Ken McGqire, Daniel Pasteris, Dorthe Dahl-Jensen, Jørgen Peder Steffensen, Bo Vinther, Ross Edwards, Robert Mulvaney, and Sepp Kipfstuhl. 'A New Bipolar Ice Core Record of Volcanism from WAIS Divide and NEEM and Implications for Climate Forcing of the Last 2000 Years'. *Journal of Geophysical Research: Atmospheres* 118 (2013): 1151–1169.

Sigl, Michael, M. Winstrup, J. R. McConnell, K. C. Welten, G. Plunkett, F. Ludlow, U. Büntgen, M. Caffee, N. Chellman, D. Dahl-Jensen, H. Fischer, S. Kipfstuhl, C. Kostick, O. J. Maselli, F. Mekhaldi, R. Mulvaney, R. Muscheler, D. R. Pasteris, J. R. Pilcher, M. Salzer, S. Schüpbach, J. P. Steffensen, B. M. Vinther, and T. E. Woodruff, 'Timing and Climate Forcing of Volcanic Eruptions for the Past 2,500 Years'. *Nature* 523 (2015): 543–549.

Sluijter, Eric J. 'Didactic and Disguised Meanings? Several Seventeenth-Century Texts on Painting and the Iconological Approach to Dutch Paintings of this Period'. In *Looking at Seventeenth-Century Dutch Art: Realism Reconsidered*. Edited by Wayne Franits, 78–87. Cambridge: Cambridge University Press, 1997.

Smil, Vaclav. *Energy in World History*. Boulder: Westview, 1994.

Smith, Lacey Baldwin. *This Realm of England, 1399–1688*, 8th ed. Boston: Houghton Mifflin Company, 2001.

Snapper, Frits. *Oorlogsinvloeden op de Overzeese Handel van Holland, 1551–1719*. Amsterdam: Dukkerijen vh Ellerman Harms, 1959.

Soens, Tim. 'Explaining Deficiencies of Water Management in the Late Medieval Flemish Coastal Plain, 13th–16th Centuries'. In *Water Management, Communities, and Environment: The Low Countries in Comparative Perspective, C. 1000 – C. 1800*. Edited by Hilde Greefs, 35–62. Hilversum: Academia Press, 2006.

'Floods and Money: Funding Drainage and Flood Control in Coastal Flanders from the Thirteenth to the Sixteenth Centuries'. *Continuity and Change* 26:3 (2011): 333–365.

Solar, Peter M. 'Opening to the East: Shipping between Europe and Asia, 1770–1830'. *The Journal of Economic History* 73:3 (2013): 625–661.

Sonnino, Paul. *Louix XIV and the Origins of the Dutch War*. Cambridge: Cambridge University Press, 2003.

Sopers, P. J. V. M. and H. C. A. Kampen. *Schepen die verdwijnen*. Haarlem: Uitgeverij Hollandia, 2000.

Speck, W. A. 'Some Consequences of the Glorious Revolution'. In *The World of William and Mary: Anglo-Dutch Perspectives on the Revolution, of 1688–89*. Edited by Dale Hoak and Mordechai Feingold, 29–41. Stanford: Stanford University Press, 1996.

Spicer, Joaneath A. 'An Introduction to Painting in Utrecht, 1600–1650'. *In Masters of Light: Dutch Painters in Utrecht during the Golden Age*. Edited by Joaneath A. Spicer and Lynn Federle Orr, 13–48. New Haven: Yale University Press, 1998.

Spies, Marijke. *Arctic Routes to Fabled Lands: Olivier Brunel and the Passage to China and Cathay in the Sixteenth Century*. Amsterdam: Amsterdam University Press, 1997.

Bij noorden om. Olivier Brunel en de doorvaart naar China en Cathay in de zestiende eeuw. Amsterdam, 1994.

Staarman, A. 'De VOC en der Staten-Generaal in de Engelse Oorlogen: een ongemakkelijk bondgenootschap'. *Tijdschrift voor Zeegeschiedenis* 15 (1996): 3–24.

Stahle, David W. and Malcolm K. Cleaveland, 'Tree-ring Reconstructed Rainfall over the Southeastern U.S.A. during the Medieval Warm Period and Little Ice Age'. *Climatic Change* 26 (1994): 199–212.

Stahle, David W., Malcolm K. Cleaveland, Dennis B. Blanton, Matthew D. Therrell, and David A. Gay. 'The Lost Colony and Jamestown Droughts'. *Science* 280:5363 (1998): 564–567.

Starkey, David J. 'Voluntaries and Sea Robbers: A Review of the Academic Literature on Privateering, Corsairing, Buccaneering and Piracy'. *The Mariners Mirror* 97:1 (2001): 127–147.

Stearns, Peter. 'The Essence of Commodification: Caffeine Dependencies in the Early Modern World'. *Journal of Social History* 35 (2001): 269–294.

Stevens, Harm. *Dutch Enterprise and the VOC: 1602–1799*. Zutphen: Walburg Pers, 1998.

Stoffel, Markus, Myriam Khodri, Christophe Corona, Sébastien Guillet, Virginie Poulain, Slimane Bekki, Joël Guiot, Brian H. Luckman, Clive Oppenheimer, Nicolas Lebas, Martin Beniston, and Valérie Masson-Delmotte, 'Estimates of Volcanic-Induced Cooling in the Northern Hemisphere over the Past 1,500 Years'. *Nature Geoscience* 8 (2015): 784–790.

Stradling, R. A. *The Armada of Flanders: Spanish Maritime Policy and European War, 1568–1668*. Cambridge: Cambridge University Press, 1992.

Streeter, Richard and Andrew Dugmore. 'Late-Holocene Land Surface Change in a Coupled Social Ecological System, Southern Iceland: A Cross-Scale

Tephrochronology Approach'. *Quaternary Science Reviews* 86 (2014): 99–114.

Streeter, Richard, Andrew J. Dugmore, and Orri Vesteinsson, 'Plague and Landscape Resilience in Premodern Iceland'. *Proceedings of the National Academy of Sciences* 109:10 (2012): 3664–3669.

Struik, Dirk Jan. *The Land of Stevin and Huygens: A Sketch of Science and Technology in the Dutch Republic during the Golden Century*. Leiden: Springer, 1981.

Sundberg, Adam. 'Claiming the Past: History, Memory, and Innovation Following the Christmas Flood of 1717'. *Environmental History* 20:2 (2015): 238–261.

'Weathering the Little Ice Age - Wealth and Climate Adaptation during the Dutch Golden Age' with 'Floods, Worms, and Cattle Plague: Nature-induced Disaster at the Closing of the Dutch Golden Age 1672–1764'. PhD diss., University of Kansas, 2016.

Sutton, Peter C. *Jan Van Der Heyden (1637–1712)*. New Haven: Yale University Press, 2006.

Sutton, Roward T. and Daniel L. R. Hudson, 'Atlantic Ocean Forcing of North American and European Summer Climate'. *Science* 309 (2005): 115–118.

Swan, Claudia. *Art, Science, and Witchcraft in Early Modern Holland: Jacques de Gheyn II (1565–1629)*. Cambridge: Cambridge University Press, 2005.

't Hart, Marjolein. *The Dutch Wars of Independence: Warfare and Commerce in The Netherlands, 1570–1680*. London: Routledge, 2014.

'The Dutch Republic: The Urban Impact upon Politics'. In *A Miracle Mirrored, A Miracle Mirrored: The Dutch Republic in European Perspective*. Edited by C. A. Davids and Jan Lucassen. Cambridge: Cambridge University Press, 1996.

TeBrake, William. *Medieval Frontier: Culture and Ecology in Rijnland*. College Station: Texas A&M University Press, 1985.

Thomas, Chris D., Alison Cameron, Rhys Green, Michel Bakkenes, Linda J. Beaumont, Yvonne C. Collingham, Barend Frederik Erasmus, Marinez Ferreira De Siqueira, Alan Grainger, Lee Hannah, Lesley Hughes, Brian Huntley, Albert van Jaarsveld, Guy F. Midgley, Lera Miles, Miguel A. Ortega-Huerta, Andrew Townsend Peterson, Oliver Lawrence Phillips, and Stephen E. Williams, 'Extinction Risk from Climate Change'. *Nature* 427 (2004): 145–148.

Thomas, Werner. *De val van het Nieuwe Troje: Het beleg van Oostende 1601–1604*. Oostende: Davidsfonds/Leuven, 2004.

Thompson, David W.J. and John M. Wallace, 'The Arctic Oscillation Signature in the Wintertime Geopotential Height and Temperature Fields'. *Geophysical Research Letters* 25:9 (1998): 1297–1300.

Thomson, George Malcolm. *The North-West Passage*. London: Secker & Warburg, 1975.

Tiegs, Robert. 'Hidden Beneath the Waves: Commemorating and Forgetting the Military Inundations during the Siege of Leiden'. *Can. J. of Netherlandic Studies/Rev. can. d'études néerlandaises* 35 (2014): 1–27.

Ting, Mingfang, Yochanan Kushnir, Richard Seager, and Cuihua Li. 'Forced and Internal Twentieth-Century SST Trends in the North Atlantic'. *Journal of Climate* 22 (2009): 1469–1481.

Tol, Richard S. J. and Andreas Langen, 'A Concise History of Dutch River Floods'. *Climatic Change* 46 (2002): 357–369.

Tol, Richard S. J. and Sebastian Wager, 'Climate Change and Violent Conflict in Europe over the Last Millennium'. *Climatic Change* 99 (2010): 65–79.

Tooley, R. V. and C. Bricker. *A History of Cartography: 2500 Years of Maps and Mapmakers*. London: Thames and Hudson, 1969.

Totman, Conrad. *Early Modern Japan*. Berkeley: University of California Press, 1995.

Trouet, Valérie, Jan Esper, Nicholas E. Graham, Andy Baker, James D. Scourse, and David C. Frank. 'Persistent Positive North Atlantic Oscillation Mode Dominated the Medieval Climate Anomaly'. *Science* 324:5923 (2009): 78–80.

Trouet, Valérie, Grant L. Harleyb, and Marta Domínguez-Delmásc, 'Shipwreck Rates Reveal Caribbean Tropical Cyclone Response to Past Radiative Forcing'. *Proceedings of the National Academy of Sciences*, DOI: 10.1073/pnas.1519566113.

Trouet, Valérie, H. F. Diaz, E. R. Wahl, A. E. Viau, R. Graham, N. Graham, and E. R. Vook, 'A 1500-year Reconstruction of Annual Mean Temperature for Temperate North America on Decadal-to-Multidecadal Time Scales'. *Environmental Research Letters*, 8:2 (2013): 1–10.

Unger, Richard W. *Cogs, Caravels and Galleons: The Sailing Ship 1000–1650*. London: Conway Maritime Press, 1994.

Dutch Shipbuilding before 1800. Assen/Amsterdam: Van Gorcum, 1978.

'Energy Sources for the Dutch Golden Age; Peat, Wind and Coal'. *Research in Economic History* 9 (1984): 221–253.

Ships and Shipping in the North Sea and Atlantic, 1400–1800. Aldershot: Ashgate Publishing Limited, 1997.

'Ship Design and Energy Use, 1350–1875'. In *Shipping and Economic Growth, 1350–1850*. Edited by Jan Lucassen and Richard W. Unger, 249–267. Leiden: Brill, 2011.

Ships on Maps: Pictures of Power in Renaissance Europe. New York: Palgrave MacMillan, 2010.

Unwin, Rayner. *A Winter Away from Home: Willem Barents and the North-East Passage*. Seafarer Books: London, 1995.

Utterström, Gustaf. 'Climatic Fluctuations and Population Problems in Early Modern History'. *Scandinavian Economic History Review* 3:1 (1955): 3–47.

Van Aitzema, Lieuwe. *Saken van staet en oorlogh van Lieuwe van Aitzema*. The Hague: Johan Veekym Johan Tongerlos and Jasper Doll, 1669.

Van Aken, Hendrik M. *The Oceanic Thermohaline Circulation: An Introduction*. New York: Springer 2007.

Van Bavel, Bas. 'Manors and Markets. Economy and Society in the Low Countries (500–1600): A Synopsis'. *Tijdschrift voor Sociale en Economische Geschiedenis* 8:2 (2011): 62–65.

Van Berkel, Klaas. *Isaac Beckman on Matter and Motion: Mechanical Philosophy in the Making*. Washington, DC: Johns Hopkins University Press, 2013.

Van Berkel, Klaas, Albert van Helden, and Lodewijk Palm, ed. *A History of Science in the Netherlands: Survey, Themes, and Reference*. Leiden: E.J. Brill, 1999.

Van Dam, Petra J. E. M. 'Water, Steam, Ice: Environmental Perspectives on Historical Transitions of Water in Northwestern Europe'. *Nova Acta Leopoldina* 98:360 (2009): 29–43.

Van Dam, P. and L. Murre, 'Van Amsterdams Peil naar Europees niveauvlak'. Forthcoming.

Van Dam, Pieter. *Beschryvinge van de Oostindische Compagnie, Vol. 3*. Edited by F. W. Stapel. The Hague: Martinus Nijhoff, 1927; orig. 1701.

Van den Dool, H. M., H. J. Krijnen and C. J. E. Schuurmans. 'Average Winter Temperatures at De Bilt (the Netherlands) 1634–1977'. *Climatic Change* 1 (1978): 319–330.

Van den Heuvel, Charles. 'De verspreiding van de Italiaanse vestingbouwkunde in de Nederlanden in de tweede helft van de zestiende eeuw'. In *Vesting: Vier eeuwen vestingbouw in Nederland*. Edited by J. Sneep, H. A. Treu and M. Tydeman, 9–18. The Hague: Stichting Menno van Coehoorn, 1982.

Van der Krogt, Peter. *Joan Blaeu, Atlas Major of 1665*. Cologne: Taschen, 2010.

Van der Lem, Anton. *De Opstand in de Nederlanden, (1555–1609)*. Utrecht: Kosmos-Z&K Uitgevers, 1995.

Van der Moer, A. *Een zestiende-eeuwse Hollander in het verre oosten en het hoge noorden*. The Hague: Martinus Nijhoff, 1979.

Van Deursen, A. T. 'Holland's Experience of War during the Revolt of the Netherlands'. In *Britain and the Netherlands*. Edited by A. C. Duke, 19–53. Leiden: Springer Netherlands, 1977.

Van Duinkerken, Anton. *Het goud der gouden eeuw, bloemlezing uit de poëzie der zeventiende eeuw*. Utrecht: Het Spectrum, 1955.

Van Engelen, A. F. V., J. Buisman, and F. IJnsen. 'A Millennium of Weather, Winds and Water in the Low Countries'. In *History and Climate: Memories of the Future?* Edited by P. D. Jones, A. E. J. Ogilvie, T. D. Davies, and K. R. Briffa, 101–124. New York: Kluwer Academic/Plenum Publishers, 2001.

Van Eysinga, W. J. M. *De wording van het Twaalfjarig Bestand van 9 April 1609*. Amsterdam: Noord-Hollandsche Uitgevers, 1959.

Van Gelderen, Martin. *The Political Thought of the Dutch Revolt 1555–1590*. Cambridge: Cambridge University Press, 2002.

Van Holk, André Frederik Lambertus. 'Archeologie van de binnenvaart: wonen en werken aan boord van binnenvaartschepen (1600–1900)'. PhD diss., University of Groningen, 1997.

Van Hoof, J. P. C. M. 'Met een vijand als bondgenoot. De rol van het water bij de verdediging van het Nederlandse grondgebied tegen een aanval over land'. *BMGN* 103 (1985): 622–651.

Van Nierop, Henk. 'Alva's Throne – Making Sense of the Revolt of the Netherlands'. In *The Origins and Development of the Dutch Revolt*. Edited by Graham Darby, 29–47. London: Routledge, 2003.

The Nobility of Holland: From Knights to Regents, 1500–1650. Cambridge: Cambridge University Press, 1993.

Van Nimwegen, Olaf. *The Dutch Army and the Military Revolutions, 1588–1688*. Woodbridge: The Boydell Press, 2010.

Van Reine, Prud'homme. 'Michiel Adriaenszoon de Ruyter and his Biographer Gerard Brandt'. In *De Ruyter: Dutch Admiral*. Edited by Jaap R. Bruijn and Ronald Prud'homme van Reine, 37–56. Rotterdam: Karwansaray BV, 2011.

Van 't Zand, Laura. 'Gehannes met een admiraalsschip: de bouw van de 'Eendracht' (1652–1654)'. *Tijdschrift voor Zeegeschiedenis* 17:1 (1998): 135–144.

Van Tielhof, Milja and Petra J. E. M. van Dam. *Waterstaat in Stedenland: het Hoogheemraadschap van Rijnland voor 1857*. Utrecht: Matrijs, 2006.

Van Tielhof, Milja. 'Texel, kerstavond 1593. De ramp die Tesselschade haar naam gaf'. In *Bourgondië voorbij. De Nederlanden 1250–1650. Liber alumnorum Wim Blockmans*. Edited by M. Damen and L. Sicking, 311–324. Hilversum: Uitgeverij Verloren, 2010.

The Mother of All Trades: The Baltic Grain Trade in Amsterdam from the Late 16th to the Early 19th Century. Leiden: Brill, 2012.

Van Veen, Ernst. 'De Portugees-Nederlandse concurrentie op de vaart naar Indië (1596–1640)'. *Tijdschrift voor Zeegeschiedenis* 22:1 (2003): 3–16.

Van Vliet, A. P. 'Kapers op de kust: Maassluis en de Duinkerker kapers'. *Tijdschrift voor Zeegeschiedenis* 6:1 (1987): 3–12.

Van Zanden, Jan Luiten. *Arbeid tijdens het handelskapitalisme: Opkomst en neergang van de Hollandse economie 1350–1850*. Hilversum: Uitgeverij Verloren, 1991.

Vaquero, José M., M. C. Gallego, Ilya G. Usoskin, and Gennady A. Kovaltsov. 'Revisited Sunspot Data: A New Scenario for the Onset of the Maunder Minimum'. *The Astrophysical Journal Letters* 731:2 (2011): 1–4.

Veldhorst, N. and A. Blommensteijn, 'De overwintering op Nova Zembla in het negentiende-eeuwse kinderboek'. In *Behouden uit het Behouden Huys: catalogus van de voorwerpen van de Barentsexpeditie (1596), gevonden op Nova Zembla*. Edited by J. Braat, 62–74. Amsterdam: De Bataafsche Leeuw, 1998.

Vermeir, Koen. 'Mechanical Philosophy in an Enchanted World: Cartesian Empiricism in Balthasar Bekker's Radical Reformation'. In *Cartesian Empiricisms*. Edited by Mihnea Dobre and Tammy Nyden, 275–306. Dordrecht: Springer Netherlands, 2013.

Vinje, Torgny. 'Barents Sea Ice Edge Variation over the Past 400 Years'. *Extended Abstracts, Workshop on Sea-Ice Charts of the Arctic*. WMO/TD 949 (1999): 4–6.

Vonk, P. G. *De Victorieuze Zeeslag op Schoneveld: het hol van de Ruyter*. The Hague: Pieters, 1990.

Waalewijn, A. *Drie eeuwen Normaal Amsterdams Peil*. The Hague: Hoofddirectie van de Waterstaat, 1986.

Wagner, Sebastian and Eduardo Zorita. 'The Influence of Volcanic, Solar and CO2 Forcing on the Temperatures in the Dalton Minimum (1790–1830): A Model Study'. *Climate Dynamics* 25 (2005): 205–218.

Waite, Gary K. *Eradicating the Devil's Minions: Anabaptists and Witches in Reformation Europe, 1525–1600*. Toronto: University of Toronto Press, 2007.

Walsh Jr., John and Cynthia P. Schneider, *A Mirror of Nature: Dutch Paintings from the Collection of Mr. and Mrs. Edward William Carter*. New York: Los Angeles County Museum of Art, 1992.

Walter, Kathrin and H-F. Graf. 'The North Atlantic Variability Structure, Storm Tracks, and Precipitation depending on the Polar Vortex Strength'. *Atmospheric Chemistry and Physics* 5:1 (2005): 239–248.

Walton, Timothy R. *The Spanish Treasure Fleets*. Sarasota: Pineapple Press, 2002.

Wanamaker Jr, Alan D., Paul G. Butler, James D. Scourse, Jan Heinemeier, Jón Eiríksson, Karen Luise Knudsen, and Christopher A. Richardson. 'Surface Changes in the North Atlantic Meridional Overturning Circulation during the Last Millennium'. *Nature Communications* 3 (2012): 1–7.

Wanner, Heinz, Stefan Brönnimann, Carlo Casty, Dimitrios Gyalistras, Jürg Luterbacher, Christoph Schmutz, David B. Stephenson, and Eleni Xoplaki. 'North Atlantic Oscillation – Concepts and Studies'. *Surveys in Geophysics* 22:4 (2001): 321–381.

Weever, Thedoor. *The Poetry of the Netherlands in Its European Context 1170–1930*. London: Athlone Press, 1960.

Wegman, Anton. *De Waterlandse Melkschuit: varende boeren tussen Waterland en Amsterdam 1600–1900*. Amsterdam: Stichting de Waterlandse Melkschuit, 2011.

Welling, George M. 'De zin en onzin van schepen tellen'. *Tijdschrift voor Zeegeschiedenis* 28:1 (2009): 3–25.

Węsławski, J. M., Louwrens Hacquebord, Lech Stempniewicz, and Michal Malinga, 'Greenland Whales and Walruses in the Svalbard Food Web before and after Exploitation'. *Oceanologia* 42:1 (2000): 37–56.

Westermann, Mariët. *A Worldly Art: The Dutch Republic, 1585–1718*. New Haven: Yale University Press, 1996.

Whan, Kirien and Francis Zwiers. 'The Impact of ENSO and the NAO on Extreme Winter Precipitation in North America in Observations and Regional Climate Models'. *Climate Dynamics* (2016): 1–11.

Wheeler, Dennis. 'British Naval Logbooks from the Late Seventeenth Century: New Climatic Information from Old Sources'. *History of Meteorology* 2 (2005): 133–146.

'Understanding Seventeenth-Century Ships' Logbooks: An Exercise in Historical Climatology'. *Journal for Maritime Research* (2004): 21–36.

Wheeler, D., R. Garcia-Herrera, C. W. Wilkinson, and C. Ward. 'Atmospheric Circulation and Storminess Derived from Royal Navy Logbooks: 1685 to 1750'. *Climatic Change* 18 (2009): 257–280.

White, Sam. 'Animals, Climate Change, and History'. *Environmental History* 19 (2014): 319–328.

'Climate Change in Global Environmental History'. In *A Companion to Global Environmental History*. Edited by J. R. McNeill and Erin Stewart Mauldin, 394–410. Hoboken: Wiley-Blackwell, 2012.

The Climate of Rebellion in the Early Modern Ottoman Empire. Cambridge: Cambridge University Press, 2011.

'The Real Little Ice Age'. *The Journal of Interdisciplinary History* 44:3 (Winter, 2014): 327–352.

'Unpuzzling American Climate: New World Experience and the Foundations of a New Science'. *Isis* 106:3 (2015): 544–566.

White, Sam, Richard Tucker, and Ken Sylvester. 'Climate and American History: The State of the Field'. In *Cultural Dynamics of Climate Change and the Environment in Northern America*. Edited by Bernd Sommer. Leiden: Brill, 2015.

Wilkinson, Clive. 'British Logbooks in UK Archives, 17th–19th Centuries – A Survey of the Range, Selection and Suitability of British Logbooks and Related Documents for Climatic Research'. Norwich: Climatic Research Unit School of Environmental Sciences University of East Anglia, 2009.

Wilson, Derek. *Sweet Robin: A Biography of Robert Dudley, Earl of Leicester 1533–1588*. London: Allison & Busby LTD, 1981.

Wilson, Peter. *The Thirty Years War: Europe's Tragedy*. Cambridge: Harvard University Press, 2009.

World Meteorological Organization. *The Global Climate 2001–2010, A Decade of Climate Extremes – Summary Report*. Geneva: World Meteorological Organization, 2013.

Wrigley, E. A. *Continuity, Chance and Change: The character of the industrial revolution in England*. Cambridge: Cambridge University Press, 1988.

Wu, BingYi, JingZhi Su, and RenHe Zhang. 'Effects of Autumn-Winter Arctic Sea Ice on Winter Siberian High'. *Chinese Science Bulletin* 56:30 (2011): 3220–3228.

Zahedieh, Nuala. 'Regulation, Rent-Seeking, and the Glorious Revolution in the English Atlantic Economy'. *The Economic History Review* 63:4 (2010): 865–890.

Zandvliet, Kees. *Mapping for Money: Maps, Plans and Topographical Paintings and Their Role in Dutch Overseas Expansion during the 16th and 17th Centuries*. Amsterdam: Batavian Lion International, 2002.

Zeeberg, Jaap Jan. *Climate and Glacial History of the Novaya Zemlya Archipelago, Russian Arctic: With Notes on the Region's History of Exploration*. Amsterdam: Rozenberg Publishers, 2002.

Into the Ice Sea: Barents' Winter on Novaya Zemlya – A Renaissance Voyage of Discovery. Amsterdam: Rozenberg Publishers, 2005.

Terugkeer naar Nova Zembla: de laatste en tragische reis van Willem Barents. Zutphen: Walburg Pers, 2007.

Zhang, David D., Jane Zhang, Harry F. Lee, and Yuan-qing He, 'Climate Change and War Frequency in Eastern China over the Last Millennium'. *Human Ecology* 35 (2007): 403–414.

Zhang, Pingzhong, Hai Cheng, R. Lawrence Edwards, Fahu Chen, Yongjin Wang, Xunlin Yang, Jian Liu, Ming Tan, Xianfeng Wang, Jinghua Liu, Chunlei An, Zhibo Dai, Jing Zhou, Dezhong Zhang, Jihong Jia, Liya Jin, and Kathleen R. Johnson, 'A Test of Climate, Sun, and Culture Relationships from an 1810-Year Chinese Cave Record'. *Science* 322:5903 (2008): 940–942.

Zhong, Y., G. H. Miller, B. L. Otto-Bliesner, M. M. Holland, D. A. Bailey, D. P. Schneider, and A. Geirsdottir. 'Centennial-Scale Climate Change from Decadally-Paced Explosive Volcanism: A Coupled Sea Ice-Ocean Mechanism'. *Climate Dynamics* 37 (2011): 2373–2387.

Index